Financial Institutions

Financial Institutions

Robert W. Kolb
University of Miami

Ricardo J. Rodríguez
University of Miami

Copyright © Robert W. Kolb, Ricardo J. Rodríguez 1996

The right of Robert W. Kolb and Ricardo J. Rodríguez to be identified as authors of this work has been asserted in accordance with the Copyright, Designs and Patents Act 1988.

First published 1996

Blackwell Publishers, Inc.
238 Main Street
Cambridge, Massachusetts 02142
USA

Blackwell Publishers Ltd.
108 Cowley Road
Oxford OX4 1JF
UK

All right reserved. Except for the quotation of short passages for the purposes of criticism and review, no part may be reproduced, stored in a retrieval system, or transmitted, in any form or by any means, electronic, mechanical, photocopying, recording or otherwise, without the prior permission of the publisher.

Except in the United States of America, this book is sold subject to the condition that it shall not, by way of trade or otherwise, be lent, resold, hired out, or otherwise circulated without the publisher's prior consent in any form of binding or cover other than that in which it is published and without a similar condition including this condition being imposed on the subsequent purchaser.

Library of Congress Cataloging-in-Publication Data

Kolb, Robert W.
Financial institutions / Robert W. Kolb, Ricardo J. Rodríguez
p. cm.
Includes bibliographical references and index.
ISBN 1-55786-899-9 (pbk.)
1. Financial institutions--United States. 2. Finance--United States. 3. Banks and banking--United States. I. Title.
HG181.K649 1996
332.1'0973--dc20 95–39467
CIP

British Library Cataloguing in Publication Data

A CIP catalogue record for this book is available from the British Library.

Commissioning Editor: Rolf Janke
Production Manager: Jan Leahy
Text Design: Benchmark Productions
Typeset by Benchmark Productions

Typeset in 10 point Galliard by Benchmark Productions.
Printed in the United States of America

This book is printed on acid-free paper

Contents

Preface

Financial Institutions provides a thorough introduction to financial institutions in the United States and includes a substantial international focus as well. The text is equally suitable for a first course in finance or a course that follows an introductory corporate finance class. *Financial Institutions* has two special emphases that distinguish this text from its competitors. The text:

- Employs a more analytical approach
- Provides more comprehensive coverage

A More Analytical Approach

Many texts designed for courses on financial institutions remain merely descriptive and virtually ignore the analytical and conceptual tools that constitute the foundation of the finance discipline. *Financial Institutions* consciously breaks with this non-analytical tradition. For example, the text employs time value of money concepts throughout the text: in the discussion of bond pricing, stock valuation, and option pricing, for example. Almost all financial institutions texts discuss asset and liability management but offer only a purely descriptive treatment. By contrast, *Financial Institutions* explains duration, presents the formula and sample calculations, and illustrates the basic concepts with numerical examples of duration and its effect on bank balance sheets. In addition, the text utilizes the achievements of capital market theory to illuminate the behavior of financial institutions in many chapters.

While the text offers a full description of institutions and markets as well, this more analytical approach pervades the entire text: from duration, to equity valuation, to cash management, to the Black-Scholes option pricing model. Throughout, the analytics are presented, discussed, and illustrated numerically.

More Comprehensive Coverage

The economy relies on a financial system, but in many texts the idea of a financial system is lost, particularly because many texts omit important financial institutions. For example, many texts ignore finance companies, gloss over the role of pension funds, forget insurance companies, mention financial futures and options only in passing, and appear never to have heard of the swap market.

Financial Institutions stands in marked contrast to these texts with separate chapters on all of these topics. For example, Chapter 19, Pension Funds, discusses the Pension Benefit Guaranty Corporation and relates its financial troubles to those that have plagued depository institutions, discussed at length in Chapter 11, Regulation of Depository Institutions. Chapter 16, Financial Conglomerates and Subsidiaries, discusses the growing role of finance companies and shows how regulatory developments and the malaise affecting depository institutions have helped these firms to enter markets formerly dominated by banks and savings and loan associations. The chapter also provides detailed discussion of specific finance companies or subsidiaries, to show the wide variety of strategies and the different markets in which finance companies operate. I believe that *Financial Institutions* offers a more comprehensive and better integrated coverage of the financial system than any competing text.

Instructor's Materials

Financial Institutions provides extensive instructor support. The **Instructor's Manual** includes answers and solutions to all end-of-chapter questions and problems. The Instructor's Manual also includes a test bank for each chapter.

Acknowledgments

Creating F*inancial Institutions* required the sustained efforts of many people. We would like to begin by thanking those who worked on the previous edition of the text: Kateri Davis, Susan Lavery, Diane Rubler, Evelyn Gosnell, Debbie MacInnes, Brian Wilson, Andrea Coens, Sandy Schroeder, and Joe Rodríguez.

We would also like to thank those who contributed to this edition, including Andrea Coens, Paul Pieciak, Mary Beckwith, Mary Riso, Rolf Janke, and Jan Leahy, as well as Andrew Williams, Andrea Mulligan, Lissa Smith, Susan Gately, and Luminita Velicanu from Benchmark Productions.

Writing a text quickly teaches an author how much he or she must rely on others to complete a quality product. All of the people mentioned above contributed mightily to the project.

Robert W. Kolb
Miami, Florida

Part 1
Financial Institutions and the Economy

Part 1 of this book introduces some of the basic concepts that are necessary to understand the behavior of financial institutions and the markets in which they operate. This foundation is laid out in the first three chapters.

Chapter 1 presents an introduction showing the benefits that a society derives from a sophisticated financial system. Starting with a simple economy with no investment and no financial system, the chapter explains how investment and the possibility of borrowing and lending make individuals better off.

In the United States, the Federal Reserve, or simply the Fed, has the functions of a central bank. As such, it is responsible for controlling the money supply and overseeing the entire financial system. Chapter 2 describes the structure and functioning of the Federal Reserve system. It also gives a brief description of the main monetary policy instruments the Fed uses to control the stock of money in the economy: required reserves, open market operations, and the discount window.

While Chapter 1 introduces the concept of money in a simple "Robinson Crusoe" economy, Chapter 3 continues the study of money in a more realistic setting. For instance, concepts such as the velocity of money, the monetary base, and the money multiplier are discussed in detail. This chapter also provides a detailed explanation of how money is created by the actions of the Fed. It also shows how money is then multiplied by the actions of the entire banking system.

The Role of Financial Institutions

1

Overview

As we begin our study of financial institutions, this chapter explains why a financial system is important and how it benefits virtually all members of the economy. We begin by considering a financially primordial world – a world without money. Without money, there can be no financial assets, such as stocks or bonds, and there can be no financial investment. Investment choices are limited to real assets, such as tools and shelter, and to real investment, such as planting seed or making tools.

After examining such a primitive economy, we consider progressively more elaborate economies by allowing a richer structure of financial institutions and markets. Without question, the development of a financial system benefits society. For instance, the individual's opportunity to borrow funds against future income may improve the economic well-being of the borrower. Showing how the financial system enriches the lives of people in the economy is one of the main goals of this chapter.

If a healthy, robust, and well-developed financial system confers benefits on the members of an economy, it is certainly worth understanding. This text provides an overview of the financial system by focusing on the various financial markets and institutions and the ways they interact. This chapter concludes with a discussion of how the text is organized and the way in which it leads to an understanding of the role of the financial system in the broader economy.

An Economy with No Exchange

The most primitive economy imaginable is one in which there is no opportunity to exchange one good for another. In Daniel Defoe's famous novel, Robinson Crusoe was shipwrecked on an island alone, except for his man Friday. Considering Crusoe and Friday as one economic unit, there was no possibility of exchanging one good for another, simply because there were no other economic units in the island. In this simple economy, it is obvious that there is no financial system and no financial institutions.

Crusoe faces very few economic decisions. One of the most critical is the problem of consumption versus investment. Assume that Crusoe has some seed corn that was salvaged from the shipwreck. Crusoe and Friday may eat this corn now, store it for future consumption, or plant it to produce more corn for future consumption. Assuming that this corn is the only food Crusoe has and that it cannot be saved past next year, Crusoe must decide how much corn to consume this year and how much to save for the next period. Crusoe must consume some corn now to stay alive, so he cannot save or plant all of the corn.

Figure 1.1 shows Crusoe's consumption opportunities for this year (the current period) and for next year (the second period), assuming that Crusoe cannot plant the corn, perhaps because the island is made up of volcanic lava. Although this restriction on planting means that Crusoe's prospects for reaching old age are slim, his decision now becomes even easier. Crusoe's problem is to allocate the existing supply of corn to two periods. As Figure 1.1 shows, we assume that there are 100 pounds. of corn. On the horizontal axis, the graph shows Crusoe's maximum consumption opportunity in the current period. If Crusoe eats all of the corn this period, he can consume 100 pounds. This level of consumption will leave nothing for next year, so Crusoe will die next year. (We do not allow rescues!)

Theoretically, Crusoe could save all of the corn to eat next year and eat nothing this year. This is only a theoretical possibility, because Crusoe must eat some corn now to stay alive until next year. The extreme points on the diagonal line in Figure 1.1 depict the two consumption possibilities just discussed. Of course, other allocations are also possible. If Crusoe eats 60 pounds this year and saves 40 pounds for next year, he will be at point W on the diagonal. In fact, any point on the diagonal line is attainable by choosing a different allocation of corn for the two years, as long as the sum of the two allocations equals 100 pounds. The relationship between the consumption this period, C_0, and next year's consumption, C_1, depicted in the diagonal is given by:

$$C_1 = 100 - C_0$$

The maximum possible consumption of corn in the second period is the same as in the first – 100 pounds.

But wait. After wandering through the island a bit, Crusoe finds a plot of arable land. To his delight, Crusoe's initially meager choices are suddenly enriched. Assuming that the yield on planted corn is 20 percent, planting one pound of seed corn this year will produce 1.2 pounds

Figure 1.1
Crusoe's Consumption Opportunities with No Investment

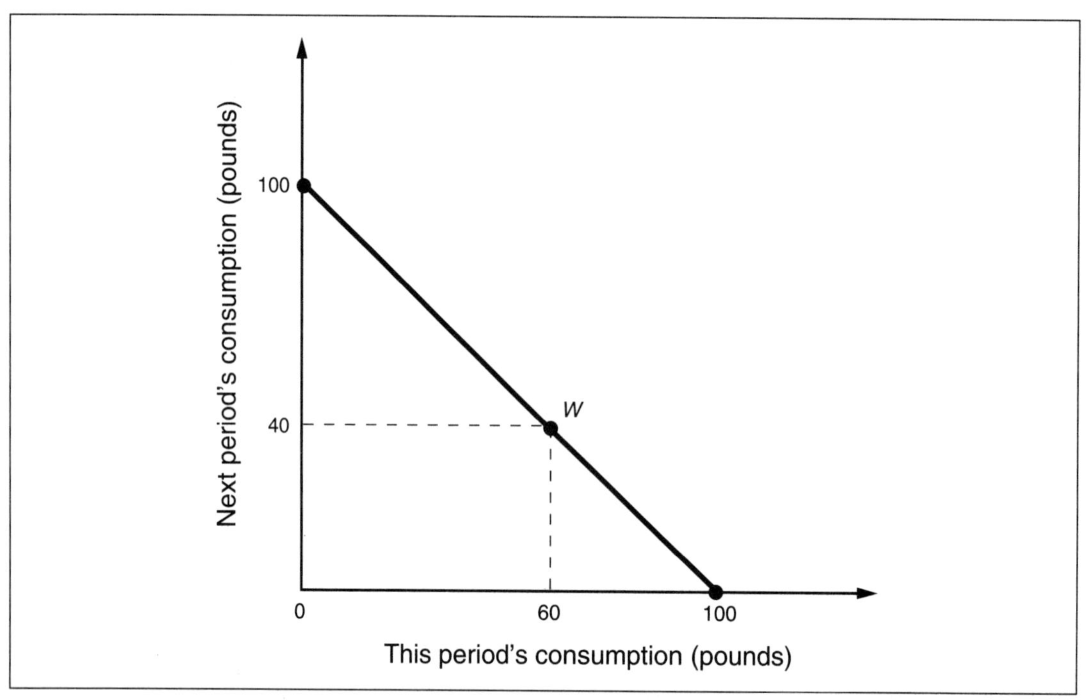

next year. We will assume throughout this chapter that the returns from this investment – corn planting – are certain. Figure 1.2 shows this new set of opportunities, along with the previous opportunities under the assumption of no opportunity to plant. With the possibility of planting, the relationship between consumption now and consumption later is given by:

$$C_1 = 120 - 1.2\ C_0$$

Thus, Figure 1.2 duplicates Figure 1.1, but it also shows the opportunities that are available to Crusoe from planting the corn. If Crusoe were to plant all 100 pounds, they would grow to 120 pounds for the next year. Therefore, with the opportunity to plant corn, the maximum possible consumption next year becomes 120 pounds, as shown by the dotted line in Figure 1.2. The arrow on the dotted line indicates that corn can only be planted now to produce corn in the next period. In other words, the process is not reversible.

Clearly, the opportunity to plant corn enriches Crusoe's consumption opportunities. In Figure 1.1, we noted that Crusoe could eat 60 pounds this year and 40 pounds next year. With the chance to plant corn, Crusoe can still eat 60 pounds this year and plant the remaining 40 pounds. With the growth rate of 20 percent, the planted 40 pounds will give a harvest of 48 pounds. Clearly, by planting corn, Crusoe can increase his consumption opportunities. Without planting, consuming 60 pounds this year left only 40 pounds to eat next year. If Crusoe plants 40 pounds this year, he can eat 60 pounds now and eat 48 pounds next year.

Figure 1.2
Crusoe's Consumption Opportunities with Real Investment

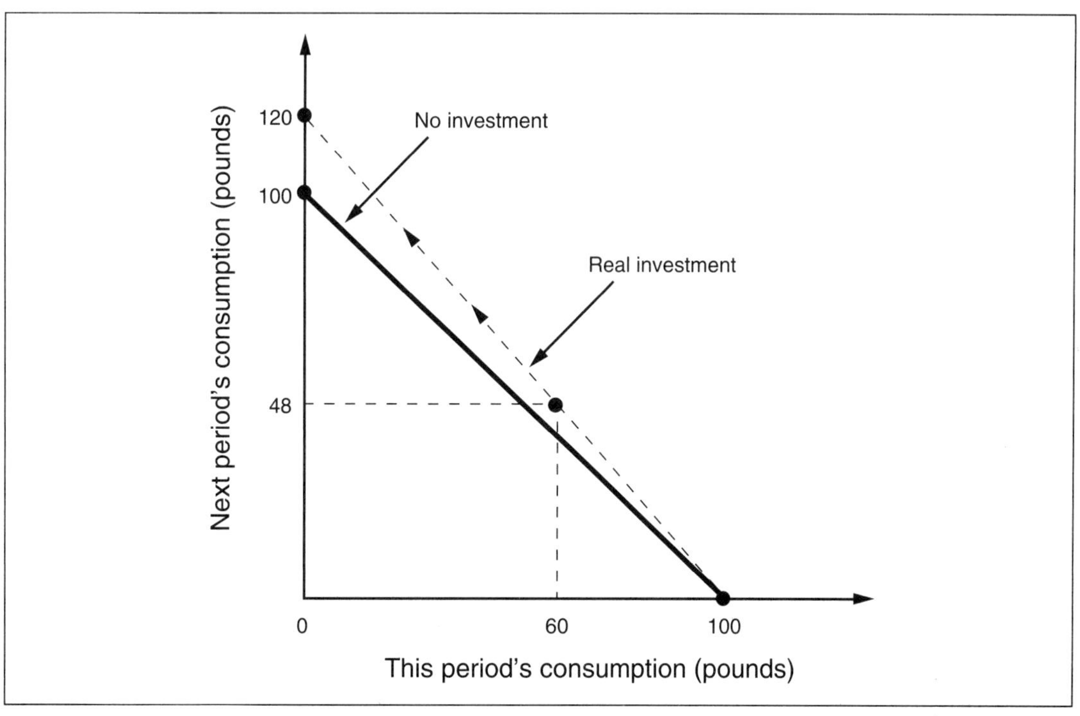

Notice that there is absolutely no financial system in the simple economy just described and that there is no exchange of one commodity for another. The next section considers a slightly richer economy, one allowing exchange.

An Exchange Economy Without Money

An economy without money is still very primitive, much like the island economy of Robinson Crusoe. However, in this slightly more complex economy, there are a number of economic units that can exchange goods with one another. With no money in the economy, two basic types of economic transactions are possible. First, one good may be exchanged for another. Second, investment of real capital is possible.

Without money, one good can be exchanged for another. The exchange of physical goods is **barter**, and an economy without money is a **barter economy**. Before the invention of money, all exchanges were made by barter.

Imagine a fisherman with a good catch of fish who needs a new sail for a boat. In a modern economy, the fisherman sells the fish for money and uses the money to buy the needed sail. In a barter economy, to secure the needed sail, the fisherman must find someone who needs fish and who is willing to exchange a sail for it. Imagine the ridiculous spectacle of the fisherman carrying fish around a village trying to exchange fish for a sail. This is extremely inefficient compared to an economy with money. While the fisherman merely wants to exchange one good for another, such a simple transaction is very difficult without money. From this fishy story, we can note a very important point. The introduction of money in an economy makes it much easier to exchange one good for another. Instead of a direct exchange of two physical goods, a physical good can be exchanged for money, which can then be exchanged for any other physical good. Thus, money serves as a **medium of exchange**, a good that can readily be exchanged for other goods.

Assume now that the fisherman's catch is really spectacular and after exchanging fish for the sail and other needed goods, the fisherman still has some of the catch left. Fishing is notoriously risky, and today's good catch may not be repeated for some time. To protect against those future fishless days, the fisherman wishes to save some of the catch for the future. This is not very easy, given the nature of fish. Unless the fish is dried, it cannot be stored, and this puts the fisherman in a predicament. Assuming that the fish cannot be dried, the fisherman can exchange all of the fish now for some other good, or he can let the unused fish spoil. Because of the nature of the commodity, the fisherman is worse off than Crusoe, who could store corn for future use. In this exchange economy, one item can be exchanged for another, but transactions are difficult and some commodities cannot be preserved easily. As a result, it is difficult to store value.

A Money Economy

Recall the fisherman's alternatives for the excess fish: consume the fish now, let the fish go to waste, or exchange it for some storable commodity. Of these alternatives, the fisherman would most like to exchange the excess fish for some storable commodity that can be used at a future date. The attempt to exchange the fish for a storable commodity gives the fisherman the old problem of needing to find someone who can use the fish and who is willing to exchange a storable commodity for them. Fish does not act as an effective store of value because it spoils so quickly. Also, fish does not provide an effective medium of exchange because it is difficult to exchange for other goods with reliability. Besides, fish is too smelly. The introduction of money into an economy is very useful because money acts as an excellent medium of exchange and as a **store of value**, a good that can be stored without losing its value.

Consider now the fisherman's situation in an economy with money. In a money economy, the fisherman can merely sell the fish and receive money. As a medium of exchange, the money received can be exchanged easily for other goods. If the fisherman has an excess supply of fish, the fish may be sold for money and the money will be available later to buy the needed goods. Money is an excellent store of value because it retains its value and is easily stored. Money under the mattress certainly keeps better than fish under the mattress. In this simple economy with money, the economic participants are better off because they now have money as a medium of exchange and as a store of value.

Money and Financial Investment

Thus far, we have considered very simple economies and have worked up to one with money. However, one notable feature of this money economy was that it did not allow for the investment of money. Money functioned as a medium of exchange and as a store of value, but there was no financial investment. Without financial investment, this economy is still primitive. In this section, we further enrich the economy by permitting investment in financial assets.

In the preceding section, the fisherman with an extra catch sold the excess for money. As we saw there, money functioned as a medium of exchange and as a store of value. However, without the opportunity for financial investment, the fisherman could only store the money under a mattress or in a cookie jar. With a more elaborate financial system, it is possible to invest money to increase its value. In this richer economy, the fisherman could deposit the money in a bank and earn interest. The innovation of financial investment makes the fisherman better off because he can increase future consumption.

With no financial investment, money serves as a store of value or a medium of exchange, but it cannot grow. Consistent with the fact that we now have an economy with money, we express the consumption opportunities in dollar terms. Let us assume that we have an initial amount of \$100. If money serves as a medium of exchange or as a store of value, but cannot be invested, then Figure 1.3 shows our consumption opportunities.

As Figure 1.3 shows, we can consume the entire \$100 now, or we can save the entire sum and consume \$100 in the next period. Alternatively, we could split our consumption between periods. One such alternative is shown as Q', a point at which we consume \$60 in this period and \$40 in the next period. In fact, we can consume any amount that we wish from \$0 to \$100 in the first period, and that consumption decision determines how much will be available for consumption in the next period. Notice, however, that there is no way to invest the money. For example, we may save \$40 for the next period, but it will be only \$40 after one year. The economy shown in Figure 1.3 does not allow for financial investment.

We now explicitly introduce the idea of financial investment to our economy. Let us assume that we now have the opportunity to invest money to earn a certain rate of interest of 10 percent. With our original \$100 available right now, Figure 1.4 shows our total consumption opportunities as the dotted line. The solid line repeats the information from Figure 1.3. The consumption opportunities without and with financial investment at 10 percent are shown on the following page:

Figure 1.3
Crusoe's Consumption Opportunities with an Initial Endowment

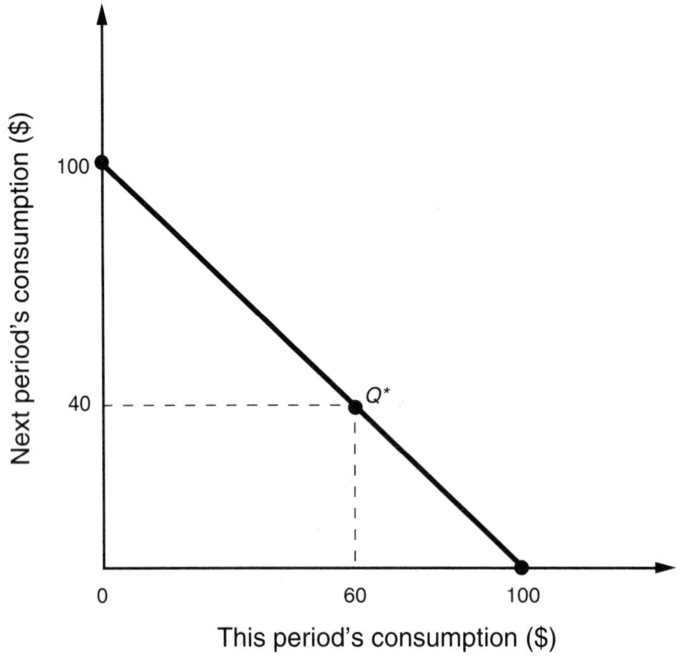

Period	Maximum Consumption without Financial Investment	Maximum Consumption with Financial Investment
0	$100	$100
1	$100	$110

Permitting financial investment allows a better choice of consumption opportunities. For example, if we consume $60 right now and invest the remaining $40 at the 10 percent rate of interest, we can consume $44 in the next period. If there were no financial investment and we consumed $60 now, we could consume only $40 in the next period. As this example emphasizes, the possibility of financial investment makes the members of an economy better off than they would be in a more primitive economy with no financial system. Figure 1.4 reflects this point as well.

Financial Markets and the Transformation of the Initial Endowment

The discussion of the previous section illustrates how financial markets improve the welfare of participants in the economy by allowing them to engage in financial investment. However, financial markets offer other important advantages. Let us continue to assume that the interest rate is 10 percent and consider ourselves as economic agents with a particular endowment. Specifically, we

Figure 1.4
Crusoe's Consumption Opportunities with Financial Investment

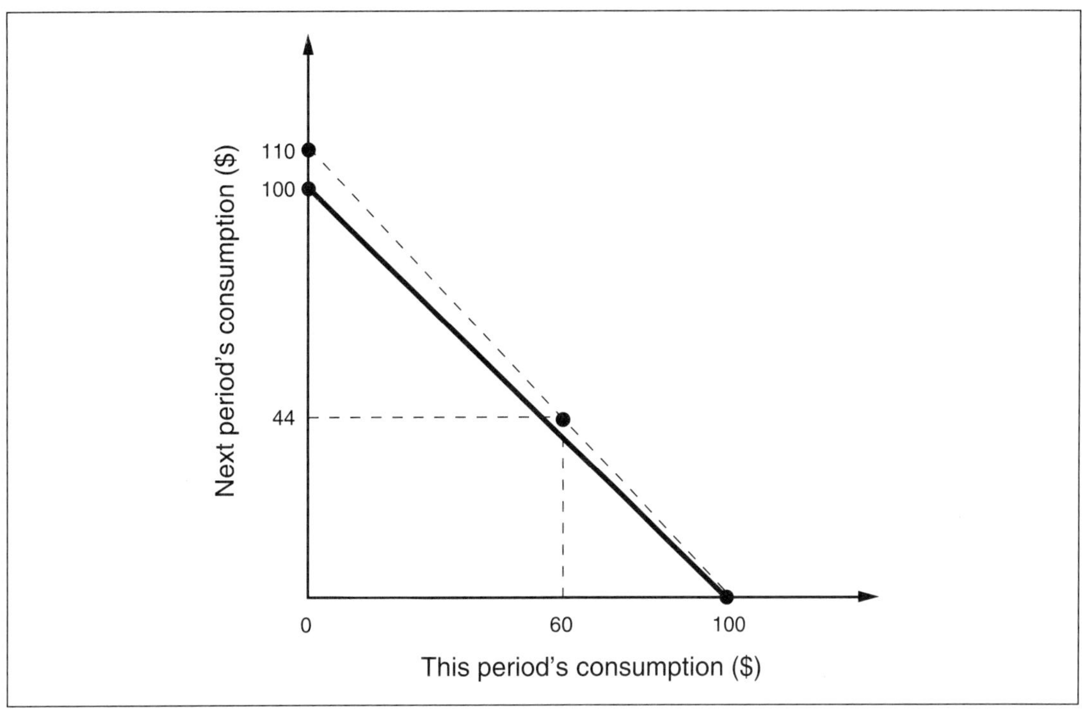

assume that we will receive \$100 now and \$100 in the next period. This is the **initial endowment** – the initial allocation of wealth to specific time periods.

With a financial system, we can change our initial endowment to one that suits us better. For example, we have our initial endowment of \$100 in each of two periods. If we wish to consume more than \$100 now, we can borrow. By contrast, if our initial endowment includes more than we want to consume in this period, we can save a portion of our current endowment to increase our consumption in the next period. This section shows how the initial endowment can be altered to make the person with the endowment better off. We have already considered the advantages that come from the chance to make financial investments, but other advantages can be obtained from a financial market that allows both investment and borrowing. In fact, we can preview the argument of this section in a single sentence: The richer the financial system, the better the choices for people in an economy and the better off they will be.

Table 1.1 shows the consumption opportunities available with the initial endowment of \$100 in this period and \$100 in the next period. With no financial market, money may be used as a store of value, but the value of money will not increase over time. This means that the maximum consumption next period is \$200. Table 1.1 shows this situation under the column "No Financial Markets."

If there is a financial market that allows only investment but no borrowing, it is possible to increase the amount of money available for consumption in the next period. With the specified initial endowment and a financial market that allows investment, the most the agent can consume

Table 1.1
Maximum Consumption Opportunities with and without a Financial Market (borrowing and lending at 10 percent)

Period	Initial Endowment	No Financial Markets	Investment Only	Both Borrow and Invest
0	$100	$100	$100	$190.91
1	$100	$200	$210	$210

in the current period remains $100. This would leave $100 to consume in the next period. As an alternative consumption pattern, the $100 could be saved until the next period, generating a total of $110. This $110, together with the next period's endowment of $100, would allow a maximum consumption of $210 in the next period. This economy is shown in Table 1.1 under the column "Investment Only."

Finally, with a financial market that allows borrowing and investment, opportunities are much richer. First, we could defer all consumption until next period. If we choose this strategy, the $100 will be invested at the prevailing interest rate of 10 percent, to yield $110 in the next period. This $110, combined with the initial endowment of $100 for the second period, means that the maximum consumption possible in the next period is $210. This is exactly the strategy that is available in a market that allows only financial investment and no borrowing. However, with a financial market allowing borrowing, we as economic agents can borrow against our future income. If we have an endowment of $100 in this period and $100 in the next period, we could promise to pay the entire $100 to be received in period 1 and borrow an amount now that would grow into that $100 next period, or $90.91:

$$\$90.91 \times 0.10 + \$90.91 = \$100$$

In other words, we could borrow the present value of the $100 that we will receive in the next period. If we borrow $90.91, we could consume in the current period the borrowed amount plus our initial endowment of $100, for a total of $190.91.

Figure 1.5 shows the consumption opportunities with these borrowing and investment opportunities. Point *I* shows the initial endowment of $100 in each period. As we have already seen, if only investment is allowed, the maximum that can be consumed in the current period is $100, as shown by the line from $100 to Point *I*. In a market with only financial investment, it is possible to reduce consumption now to permit greater consumption later. For example, if we consume only $50 in the current period, this allows us to invest $50, which will generate an additional $55 of consumption in the next period, for a total consumption then of $155.

If we can borrow, considering the same initial endowment of $100 per period, we can achieve consumption opportunities depicted by the line from $190.91 to Point *I*. For example, we have already seen that we could borrow against the entire $100 endowment from the next period (and consume it now along with our current endowment of $100) for a total of $190.91.

This ability to borrow makes an economic agent better off. Assume that we want to consume $130 in the current period. To do this, we would consume our initial endowment of $100

Figure 1.5
Crusoe's Consumption Opportunities with Financial Investment and Borrowing

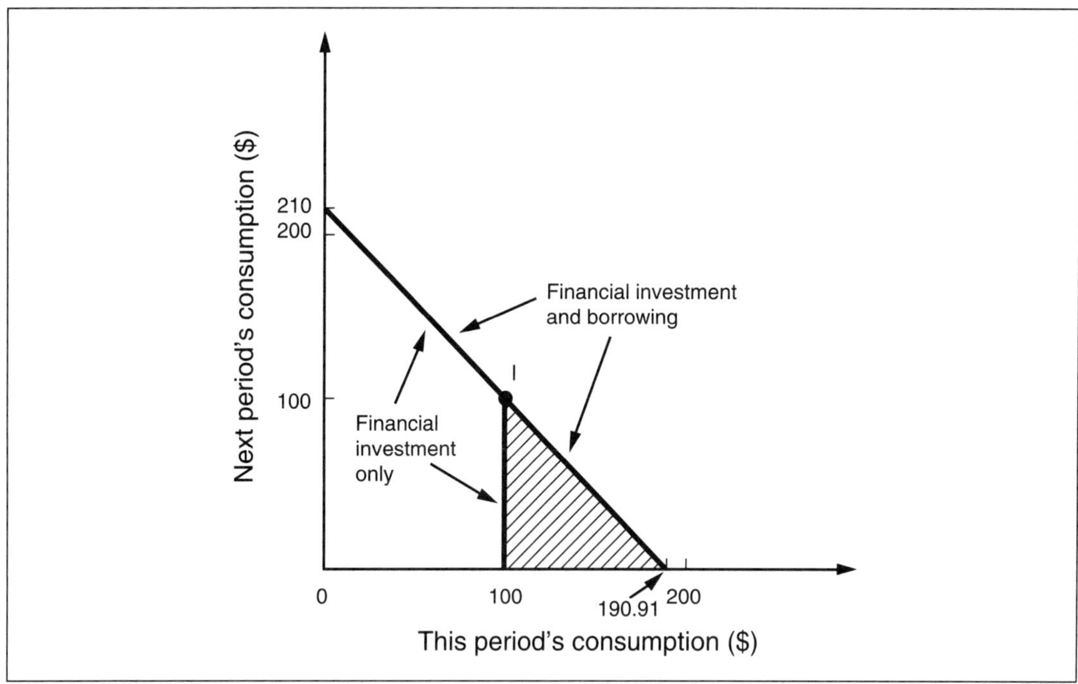

and borrow \$30 against our next period's endowment. In the next period, we would have to repay \$33, the \$30 that was borrowed plus the 10 percent interest, leaving us with a consumption level of \$67 in the next period. This pattern is possible only if borrowing is allowed. Given that some participants in the economy will want to borrow, a well-developed financial market allows a richer set of choices that can make people better off.

The general relationship between next period's consumption in dollars, C_1, and this period's consumption in dollars, C_0, given corresponding endowments of E_1 and E_0, and a certain rate of interest, r, is given by:

$$C_1 = E_1 + (E_0 - C_0)(1 + r) \tag{1.1}$$

This expression simply states that in period 1 we can consume our endowment of E_1, plus any amount we saved in period 0, $E_0 - C_0$, as well as the interest generated by the amount saved, $(E_0 - C_0)r$. In the example just discussed, if we consume nothing this period so that $C_0 = 0$, then next period we can consume a total of \$210:

$$\begin{aligned} C_1 &= 100 + (100 - 0)(1 + 0.10) \\ &= \$210 \end{aligned}$$

Similarly, if we wish to leave no consumption for next period, we can consume a total of \$190.91 this period:

$$0 = 100 + (100 - C_0)(1 + 0.10)$$
$$C_0 = 100 + 100/1.1$$
$$= \$190.91$$

Real Investment and Diminishing Profits

In developing our imaginary economies, we have considered one economy in which there is the opportunity to make real investment and another economy in which financial investment is possible. In a more robust economy, both real and financial investment are possible.

In our previous examples, we assumed that real investment earned a return of 20 percent and that financial investment earned a return of 10 percent. If an economy offers both kinds of investment, why wouldn't investors all make the same kind of investment – the one with the higher certain return? In fact, that is exactly what they would do. In the examples we have been considering, investors would all prefer to earn 20 percent on a real investment rather than 10 percent on a financial investment. To see why actual economies have both real and financial investment, we must add a bit more realism to our economy.

Consider a firm that makes real investment, like McDonald's of hamburger fame. In choosing locations for McDonald's restaurants, the firm would put the first restaurant in the location with the highest return. The second restaurant would go to the location with the second highest return, and so on. If the economy had only two kinds of investment, real investment in McDonald's earning 20 percent and financial investment earning 10 percent, then all investment would be directed toward McDonald's.

Consider, though, what must eventually happen to McDonald's as it saturates the market with hamburger restaurants. Eventually, the rate of return on the restaurants must fall. In the absurd case of four McDonald's at every crossroads, all cannot be earning the same original return of 20 percent. This tendency for incremental units of physical capital to earn lower returns is called the **decreasing marginal productivity of capital**. The unit of capital employed at the margin will earn a lower return than previously employed units of capital because investment will occur first in the uses with the highest return. This idea of a marginal return contrasts with the concept of the **average return** – the total return divided by the total investment. As the marginal productivity of capital falls, the average return on the entire investment must fall as well, because it is pulled down by the less productive units of capital that are being put into production.

Figure 1.6 graphs this decreasing marginal productivity of capital. To maintain continuity with our previous discussion, we assume that the total value available in the current period is \$190.91. The slope of the curved line in the figure shows the returns to real investment. The steeper the slope of the curve, the greater is the return. So, in the drawing, the return is highest at the bottom of the curve. The amount of investment is shown going from right to left.

To make this more concrete, consider an investment amount of \$40.91 and assume that the rate of return on this first amount of investment will be 120 percent. If this amount of investment is undertaken out of a total possible current consumption of \$190.91, this leaves \$150 to be

Figure 1.6
The Decreasing Marginal Productivity of Capital

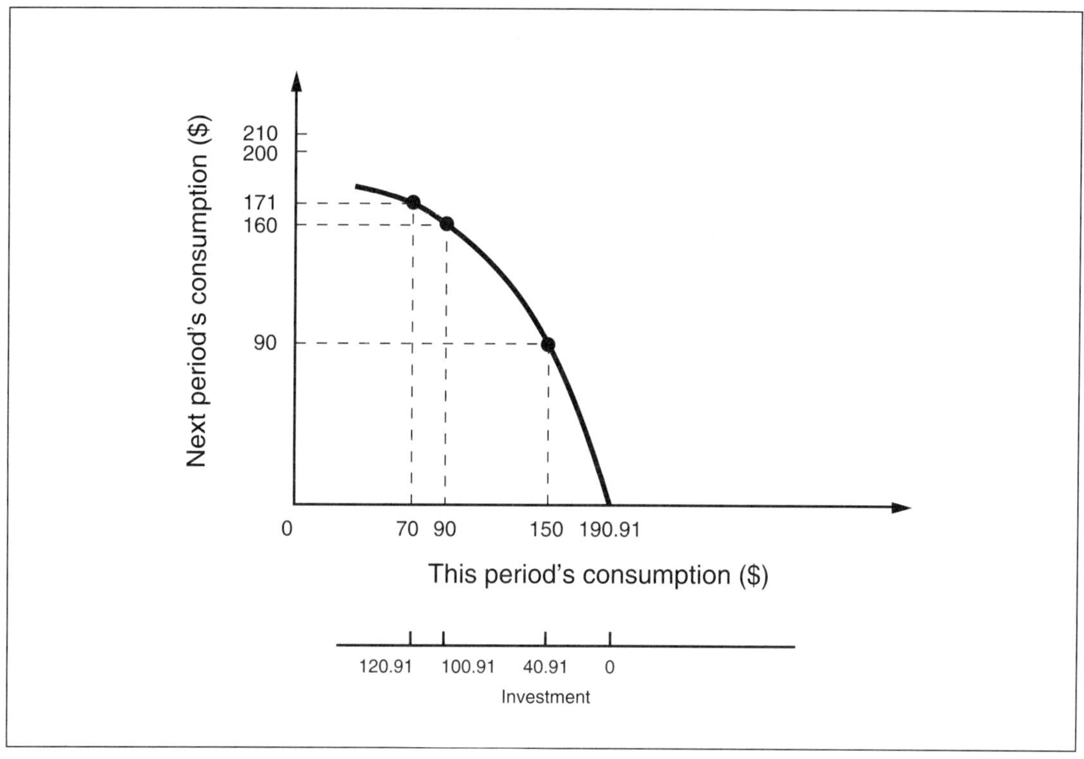

consumed in the current period, and next period's consumption will increase by the proceeds of this investment. In our example, shown in Figure 1.6, the $40.91 that is invested to earn a 120 percent return will grow to a total of $90.

$$\$40.91 + \$40.91 \times 1.20 = \$90.00$$

Consider now a higher level of investment. Let us assume that current consumption is restricted to $90, as Figure 1.6 shows. This leaves $100.91 available for investment, which provides for a consumption level in the next period of $160. The profit on the investment is $160 – $100.91, or $59.09. For this level of investment the average rate of return is $59.09/$100.91 = 0.59, or 59 percent. Notice that the falling rate of return is due to the diminishing marginal productivity of capital, meaning that less is earned on each additional unit of real investment.

What happens if we restrict current consumption to $70 in order to invest $20 more, bringing our total investment to $120.91? In that case, we have $70 of current consumption and $171 of consumption in the next period, as shown in Figure 1.6. This gives a profit on the entire investment of $50.09 and a rate of return on the entire investment of 41 percent.

Consider more closely what is happening as we expand the level of investment from $100.91 to $120.91. With investment of $100.91, we were able to consume $160 in the next period, but with an investment of $120.91, our consumption in the next period increased to only $171. We had to sacrifice $20 of consumption in this period to generate just $11 of consumption in the next period. That means that our total consumption actually fell as a result of investing that extra $20.

Another way of seeing the effect of the falling marginal productivity of capital is to examine the return on the $20 increase in our investment from $100.91 to $120.91. With investment of $100.91, consumption in the next period would be $160, and with investment of $120.91, it would be $171. So the extra consumption in the next period resulting from our extra $20 of investment is $11. Because we sacrificed $20 of consumption in the current period, we actually had a loss in total consumption of $9 ($11 increase in the next period minus $20 sacrificed consumption in this period). So the return on our $20 of additional investment was – $9/$20 or – 45 percent.

Table 1.2 presents the actual dollar return, plus the average and marginal returns for each level of investment. As the table shows, if we invest just $10.91, we will have a total of $28 next period, for an average return of 157 percent and a marginal return of 120 percent. Notice that the marginal return is less than the average return. This is always the case as long as the marginal return is falling, as in our example. In fact, for investment amounts above $70.91, the marginal return actually becomes negative. This means that an additional $10 of investment will produce less than $10 in the next period. Even with negative marginal returns, the average

Table 1.2
Average and Marginal Returns on Real Investment

Amount Invested ($)	Return ($)	Average Return (%)	Marginal Return[a] (%)
10.91	28	157	120
20.91	50	139	110
30.91	71	130	90
40.91	90	120	80
50.91	108	112	30
60.91	121	99	20
70.91	133	88	10
80.91	144	78	–20
90.91	152	67	–20
100.91	160	59	–40
110.91	166	50	–50
120.91	171	41	–60
130.91	175	34	

[a] *Percent return on next $10 of investment.*

return of the entire investment can still be positive, due to the profits earned on the previous investments.

If we examine Figure 1.6, can we decide how much should be invested? It is tempting to say that investment should stop as soon as the marginal return becomes negative, but this is not the case. Unfortunately, in the situation of Figure 1.6 we cannot say anything definite about how much investment should be undertaken. To answer this question, we must take the final step of considering real and financial investment together.

Real and Financial Investment

We now want to consider the interaction between real and financial investment. In the previous section, we noted that investors would always prefer an investment with higher returns in a situation of certainty. But we saw how the marginal returns on real investment change, depending on how much real investment is made. This leads to important interactions between real investment and the financial market. In this section, we merge the real investment analysis of the preceding section with a simple financial market in which the rate of interest is 10 percent. Figure 1.7 shows

Figure 1.7
Financial and Real Investment Opportunities

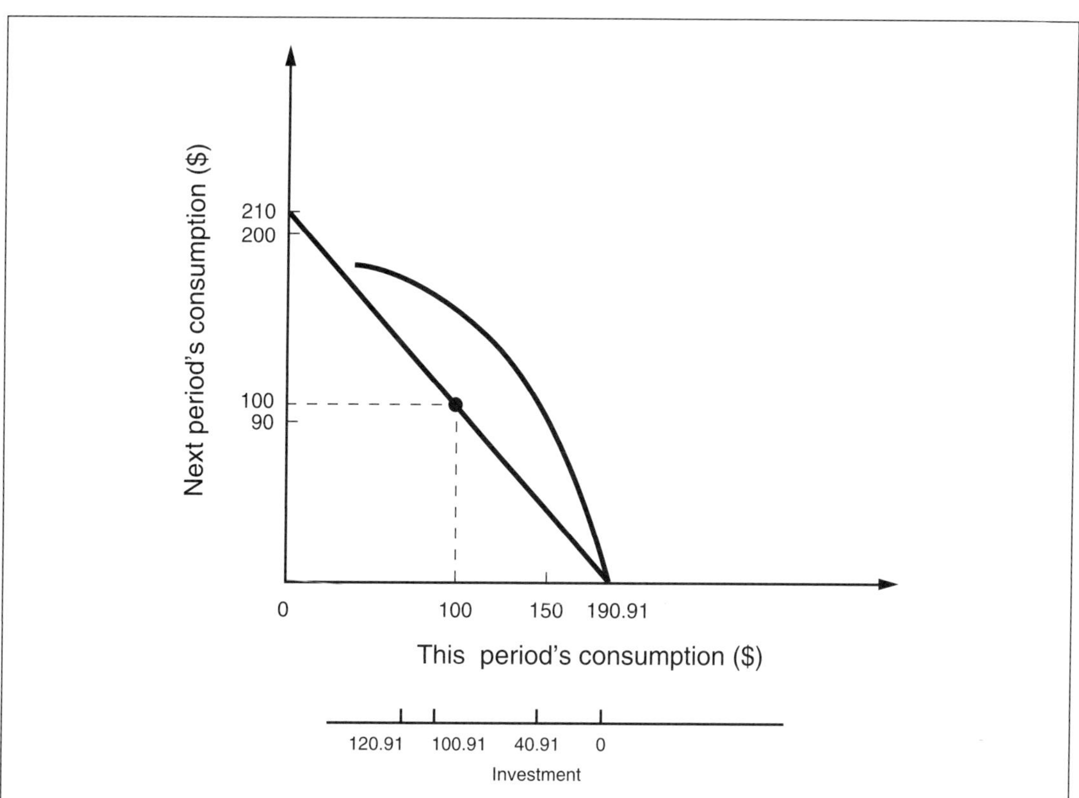

the real investment opportunities of Figure 1.6, but it also includes both the initial endowment of \$100 in each period and the straight line showing the different consumption opportunities that are available by transacting in the financial market.

By combining these real and financial investment opportunities, new and better consumption opportunities are available due to the high initial returns on real investment. For example, if we borrow against next period's endowment of \$100, we will obtain \$90.91 of investable funds right now. This means that immediate consumption could be left at \$100, in accordance with the initial endowment, and \$90.91 could be devoted to real investment. This \$90.91 of real investment would generate a 67 percent average return, as shown in Table 1.2, and a total consumption opportunity of \$152 in the next period. By making this real investment, next period's consumption increases by \$52.

How much real investment should be undertaken? Since we can invest money at 10 percent in the financial market, we will not make any real investment that returns less than 10 percent. Examining Table 1.2, we see that the marginal return on real investment hits 10 percent at an investment level of \$70.91. If we invest more than that, we earn a return less than 10 percent. Therefore, we should limit our real investment to \$70.91.

If we place \$70.91 in real investment, that leaves a maximum consumption opportunity of \$120 in the current period. But what if we wish to consume more than \$120 right now? Does that mean we should invest less than \$70.91? Recall that in addition to investing in the financial market at a rate of 10 percent, we can also borrow at 10 percent. This suggests the following strategy: Borrow at 10 percent to invest at a rate greater than 10 percent. If we look again at Table 1.2, we see that all investment up to \$70.91 has a marginal rate of return above 10 percent. This means that we should undertake all real investment with marginal returns above 10 percent, so we should place exactly \$70.91 in real investment.

Figure 1.8 shows the optimal amount of real investment as point Q^* on the opportunity curve for real investment. Notice how the real investment opportunities enrich the consumption opportunities. With real investment of \$70.91, a consumption of \$120 is attained in the current period, and a consumption of \$133 is allowed in the next period.

We can think of Q^* as representing our new initial endowment if we undertake our real investment opportunities. But what if we do not like this initial endowment? What if we do not want to consume \$120 now and \$133 in the next period? Perhaps we want to consume more now. Notice that Figure 1.8 has a straight line passing through Q^* with a slope that shows the opportunities in the financial market, represented by the ability to borrow and lend at 10 percent. We can use the financial market to alter our consumption patterns by borrowing and lending, but now, due to the real investment opportunities, we are at a higher level of consumption.

With our position at Q^* (\$120 of consumption now, and \$133 in the next period), we can change our consumption pattern. If we want to consume everything in the next period, we could invest our \$120 in the financial market at 10 percent, and this would give us \$132 (\$120 × 1.1) of additional consumption in the next period, for a total of \$265. If we wanted to consume everything now, we could borrow next period's available consumption of \$133 at a rate of 10 percent, which would yield an additional \$120.91 (\$133/1.1). Combined with our existing \$120, this

Figure 1.8
The Interaction of Real and Financial Investment Opportunities

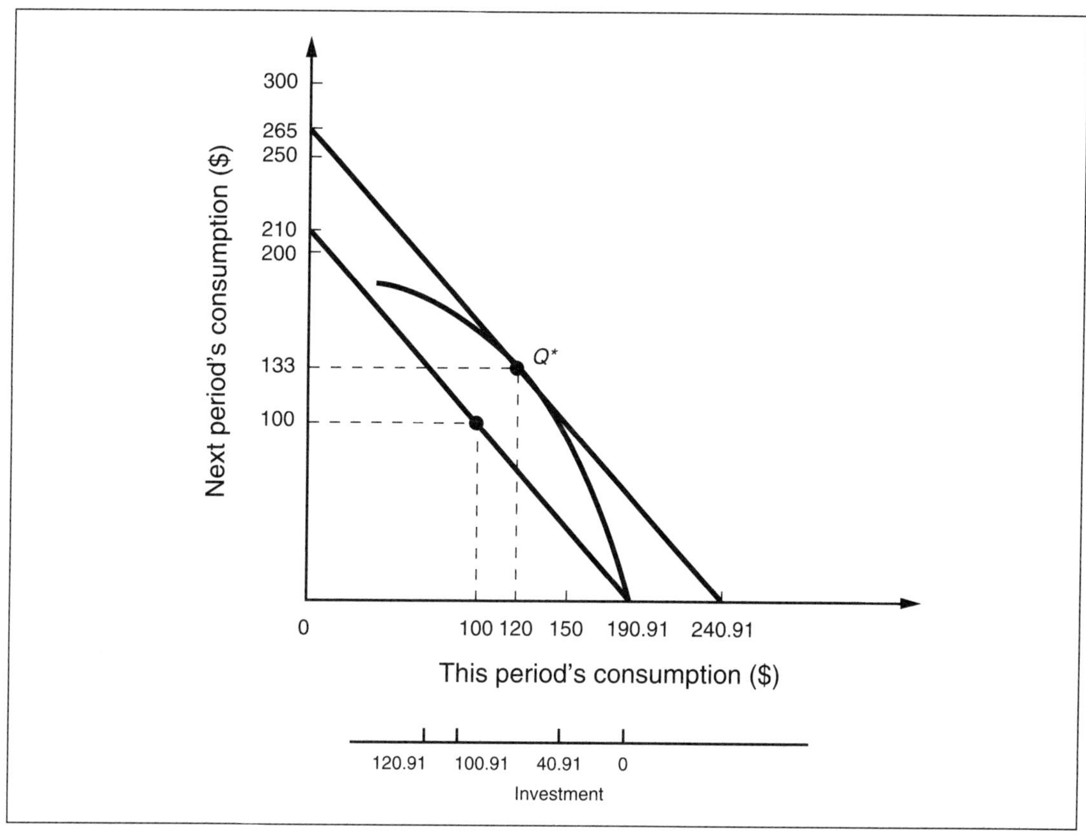

would give a maximum of current consumption equal to $240.91. In our example, the existence of a financial market working together with attractive real investment opportunities combines to make the economy better off.

Summary of Economies

To conclude, let us summarize the different economies that we have considered. In doing so, we assume that the interest rate is 10 percent and that our initial endowment is $100 in this period and $100 in the next.

No Financial Market/No Real Investment With no financial market and no real investment opportunities, we cannot consume more than $100 now, because there is no way to borrow against our future income. Also, if there is no financial market, we can merely store our $100 now and add it to our consumption for next period, making a total of $200 maximum consumption in the next period.

Financial Investment/No Borrowing/No Real Investment With the possibility of investing, we can improve our range of consumption choices, even with the same initial endowment. Because there is no borrowing, our maximum current consumption is still the \$100 of our initial endowment. But with investment, our \$100 current endowment can generate \$110 in the next period. This gives a maximum possible consumption in the next period of \$210.

Investment and Borrowing/No Real Investment If we borrow against our future income, we can consume a maximum of \$190.91 in the current period – our current period's endowment, plus the present value of our next period's endowment. On the other hand, if we invest everything until the next period, we can consume \$210 then – next period's endowment plus the future value of our endowment for the current year.

Lending and Borrowing/Real Investment In an economy with real investment and a financial market, we will undertake all real investment with a marginal return greater than the rate of return available in the financial market. In our example, this investment gave a consumption opportunity shown as Q^* in Figure 1.8. Using the financial market for borrowing and lending, we now have a maximum current consumption of \$240.91 and a maximum consumption in the next period of \$265. Of the three cases, we are best off with both a financial market and real investment opportunities.

Figure 1.9 summarizes all of these opportunities, indicating the initial endowment as I. People are better off the greater their consumption opportunities. As Figure 1.9 shows, the richer the economy, the better the consumption opportunities.

Financial Markets and Financial Institutions

Thus far, our discussion has referred to a limited range of financial markets and institutions. We have merely considered money and the chance to borrow and lend. As we will see, the existence of money in a modern economy presupposes an extremely rich set of financial institutions. Borrowing and lending may be conducted between the ultimate provider and ultimate user of funds directly, but in modern economies financial institutions play a powerfully important role in collecting funds from the ultimate providers and in making those funds available to the ultimate users. For example, a potential borrower in our economy is likely to go to a bank for a loan. The bank lends funds that it has collected from a large number of funds providers, so the bank is a financial institution that stands as an intermediary between the ultimate providers and users of funds. Understanding this sophisticated role of financial institutions and the specifics of how these institutions function is the main purpose of this book.

Organization of the Text

Financial Institutions is organized into four parts, each containing three to six chapters:

Part 1 The Financial System and the Economy
Part 2 Financial Markets and the Economy

Figure 1.9
Summary of Consumption Opportunities in Economies of Increasing Complexity

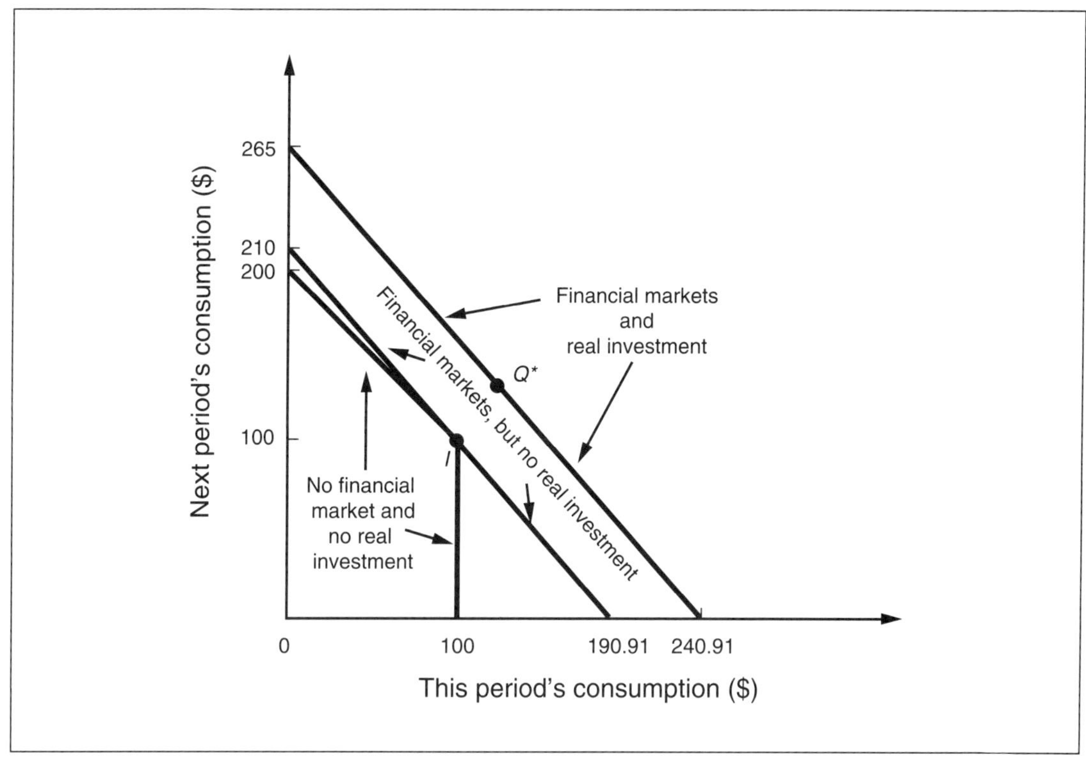

Part 3	Depository Institutions
Part 4	Non-Depository Financial Institutions

In the chapters that make up each of these parts, we consider more specialized topics. One of the special features of the book is the emphasis on the international dimension of financial institutions. Almost every chapter relates the chapter topic to the situation in countries outside the United States.

Each of the chapters that follow concludes with questions for you to consider. Most of these questions act to summarize the main ideas of the chapter, but some of them require more thought. Because understanding financial institutions and markets necessarily involves an analytical approach in planning and measuring results, many chapters conclude with problems and exercises to help you sharpen developing skills.

The Financial System and the Economy

The first part of the book sets the stage by considering the role of financial institutions and markets within the larger economy. Already in this chapter we have seen the benefits that a well-developed financial system can provide to individuals in the economy. In Chapters 2 and 3, we turn to a specific consideration of the U.S. economy. Chapter 2 focuses on the role of the Federal Reserve System, while Chapter 3 considers the money supply and its management.

Financial Markets and the Economy

Part 2 explores financial markets. As we will see, financial institutions act as intermediaries between the direct providers of funds and the ultimate users of those funds. To do so, financial institutions must interact with the financial markets where much of those funds become available. Consequently, Part 2 of the text provides an overview of the key markets and the conceptual underpinnings for understanding the instruments traded in financial markets.

Chapters 4, 5, and 6 focus on the debt market, the stock market, and the financial derivatives markets, respectively. As we will see, debt and equity (stocks) are the basic claims against governments and firms. Financial derivatives are instruments whose values and payoffs depend on more primitive securities. Examples of financial derivatives are forward contracts, futures, options, and swaps. A futures contract might have a value and payoff that depend on the performance of a debt obligation issued by the U.S. Treasury, for example.

The management techniques and goals of financial institutions, as well as the profitability and very survival of these institutions, depend on financial instruments such as bonds, stocks, and derivatives. Therefore, an understanding of financial institutions requires an understanding of the principles of operations of financial markets and the pricing of financial claims. Chapter 7 examines the level and structure of interest rates, which are key determinants of bond prices. Chapter 8 explores the world of investment banking because it is through the function of investment banks that securities are first brought into existence and first enter financial markets. To conclude Part 2 of the text, Chapter 9 considers the risk and return relationships that govern all finance and provide the central concepts of the entire finance discipline, as well as the basis for the operation of all financial institutions.

Depository Institutions

When thinking of financial institutions, it is natural to think of a commercial bank. For most of us, the bank that handles our checking account is probably the financial institution with which we have the most contact. A **depository institution** is a financial institution that accepts the deposit of funds from its customers. The prime example of the kinds of deposits that a financial institution might accept is the money in a checking account.

Part 3 considers the types, regulation, and management of depository financial institutions. The three basic types of depository institutions in the United States are commercial banks, savings institutions, and credit unions. Chapter 10 examines the different powers of the institutions and compares their size and importance in the exconomy. Because depository institutions are so important to economic well-being, they are subject to regulation. Chapter 11 considers the regulatory framework that governs these institutions. This topic is particularly important given the enormous losses and continuing scandals that afflict many savings institutions.

As we will see, commercial banks are the largest type of depository institution. Further, by understanding the functioning of commercial banks, the other types of depository institutions are easy to understand as well. Accordingly, Chapters 12-14 consider various aspects of commercial bank operations. Chapter 12 explores the overall operation of commercial banks. For example, it considers the types of lending in which commercial banks engage as well as their investment practices.

Chapter 13 explores the principles of commercial bank management in more detail. As we will see, a bank essentially raises funds by borrowing from its depositors. The bank must earn the interest promised to its depositors (plus a profit) by making loans to borrowers. Thus, a bank seeks to borrow at one rate and lend at a higher rate. Doing this successfully, while controlling risk, is a key attribute of commercial bank management that Chapter 13 addresses.

In simplest terms, a bank consists of a set of assets (principally the loans it has made) and liabilities (principally the deposits it has accepted). To prosper, or even survive, the bank must earn more from its assets than it pays for its liabilities. At the same time, one of the key problems the asset-liability manager must address is the financial riskiness of the liabilities compared to that of the assets. This highlights the importance of asset and liability management, which is the topic of Chapter 14.

Non-Depository Financial Institutions

In addition to depository institutions, non-depository institutions play an important role in the economy, and they are the subject of Part 4. Chapter 16 examines commercial finance companies and the financial subsidiaries of industrial corporations. Some of these firms are quite large. For example, General Motors Acceptance Corporation (GMAC) is a wholly owned subsidiary of General Motors. GMAC is principally in the business of financing the cars that General Motors makes. In addition to financial subsidiaries, commercial credit companies play an increasingly important role in the economy.

Investment companies accept funds from investors for the explicit purpose of investing those funds in securities. Chapter 17 examines the types of investment companies and explores their functions. The mutual fund is the dominant type of investment company. A **mutual fund** accepts funds from investors and uses those funds to buy a portfolio of securities. Each investor owns a fractional interest in the entire portfolio. Further, each investor can add new funds at will or can sell his or her interest at any time. Thus, a mutual fund provides a valuable service of providing access to well-diversified portfolios to small investors.

Almost all of us do business with insurance companies, whether for health, life, auto, or casualty insurance. Chapter 18 focuses on insurance companies. An insurance company promises to pay the insured if some unfortunate event occurs. In setting a rate for this coverage, the insurance company must correctly assess the probability that the insured event will occur. Further, the insurance company must collect funds from customers in advance and invest those funds to be sure that it will have enough cash to pay if the insured event occurs.

Pension funds have come to hold an increasing portion of the wealth of the nation. In Chapter 19, we examine the different types of pension funds, and we consider their investment policies. Like an insurance company, the pension fund accepts monies today and invests them to be able to pay a future obligation.

Summary

We assumed throughout this chapter that there was no risk in investment. We first considered an economy with no money or financial system and saw that the opportunities for investment and for altering consumption patterns were very limited. By introducing money and gradually making the economy more complex, we noted that the well-being of individuals in the economy is enhanced by the existence of a financial system.

With a well-developed financial system, it is possible to take better advantage of opportunities for real investment. As a consequence, the financial system and financial investment work together with real investment to improve the conditions of all participants in the economy.

Questions and Problems

1. Assume that an economy allows no exchange or investment. If your initial endowment is $1,000, what is the maximum lifetime consumption you can have? Explain.
2. In an economy without a financial system, what kinds of exchange are possible?
3. Contrast money and real goods as suitable stores of value.
4. Explain how money in an economy makes economic agents better off, even if there is no financial investment possible.
5. Explain how financial investment improves the condition of economic agents.
6. Why does real investment normally exhibit diminishing marginal returns?
7. In a world of certain returns on both real and financial investment, what will be the marginal return on real investment? Assume that the market rate of interest is 10 percent and that the economy is in equilibrium. Explain your reasoning.
8. What's the value of the slope of a line such as the one in Figure 1.5?
9. Explain the rationale underlying Equation 1.1.

Use this information to answer all of the following problems. Interest rates are 10 percent and you have an initial endowment of $1,000 in the current period and $1,000 in the next period.

10. What is your maximum immediate consumption opportunity?
11. What is your maximum consumption opportunity for the next period?
12. How would you invest or borrow to have a consumption level of $1,500 right now? What would be your consumption in the next period?

13. How would you invest or borrow to have a consumption level of $1,500 in the next period? What could you consume right now, in that case?

14. Draw a graph of your maximum consumption opportunities and show your consumption level for both periods if you consume $1,500 now.

15. If real investment pays 12 percent, what is your maximum possible consumption right now? Assume that borrowing is not possible.

16. If real investment pays 12 percent, what is your maximum possible consumption right now? Assume that borrowing is possible.

17. If real investment pays 12 percent, what is your maximum possible consumption in the next period? Assume that borrowing is not possible.

18. If real investment pays 12 percent, what is your maximum possible consumption in the next period? Assume that borrowing is possible.

The Federal Reserve in the U.S. Economy

2

Overview

The Federal Reserve System, or the Fed, performs the duties of the central bank of the United States. As such, it is responsible for formulating and implementing monetary policy, supervising banks, and providing financial services to depository institutions and the federal government. As an independent institution, it does not depend on either Congress or the executive branch of government. The Fed's structure differs from that of most other countries' central banks. For example, the decision-making functions are distributed among 12 regional members of the Fed.

This chapter discusses the basic structure of the Fed and the reasons underlying its peculiar organization. The Fed's pivotal role in the U.S. economy and the tools it uses to control monetary policy are also considered. For example, the Fed has the power to control the money supply, which determines the level of interest rates. Since the level of interest rates is a key variable in determining whether the economy will expand or contract in the future, the Fed has the power to affect our economic future. It is therefore important to understand how the Fed is organized and works. In Chapter 3 we will provide a detailed analysis of the process by which the Fed actually creates money.

History of the Federal Reserve System

Central to the political philosophy of the United States is the idea that distributing power among the various governmental institutions is essential to protect democracy. Checks and balances are good; centralized power is evil. Nevertheless, a few institutions have historically not been subjected to this essential principle. The Supreme Court and the Federal Reserve are the most prominent examples. The rationale is simple: By protecting their independence, society expects these institutions to be insulated from the short-term political fray. This allows them to act in ways that are in the best long-term interest of the nation. Unfortunately, this also means that independent institutions are subject to relatively little accountability. Given the advantages and disadvantages of independence, it is not surprising to find that the evolution of the Fed into its current form has been painful and controversial. In some ways the controversy continues to this day.

Prior to the creation of the modern Fed, two efforts were made to create a central bank in the United States. The first effort was initiated by Alexander Hamilton and resulted in the first Bank of the United States, which was chartered in 1791 and lasted until 1811. In 1816 another attempt at establishing a central bank resulted in the creation of the second Bank of the United States. This bank was chartered by Congress to help contain the runaway inflation that followed the War of 1812.

From the beginning, there was great opposition to the idea of a central bank that could potentially amass tremendous power. The forces against the Bank of the United States were led by President Andrew Jackson, who believed that the private bank had failed to provide a stable currency and was elitist and unconstitutional to boot. President Jackson's "Bank War" against the Bank of the United States was essentially won during 1833, when, in a bold move, Jackson withdrew all federal deposits from the bank. The bank was so weakened by this controversial action that when the bank's charter expired in 1836, so did the bank.[1]

The Federal Reserve System was chartered by Congress in December of 1913 through the Federal Reserve Act. Its main proponents were President Woodrow Wilson and Virginia Senator Carter Glass. The main purpose for its creation was to protect the banking system from the periodic crises it had been suffering. The panics of 1893 and 1895 and, worst of all, the deep crisis of 1907 had taken a heavy toll on the economy, and pressure had been mounting to create a centralized system that could stabilize the economy by controlling the money supply. In effect, the Fed's function was to act as the "bankers' bank" to assure the banking system's stability.

The ownership status of the Federal Reserve System is rather unique and has been questioned from time to time. In theory, the Fed is owned by all the private commercial banks that are members of the system, since all member banks are required to buy stock in the Federal Reserve Bank in their district. However, the Fed is also considered to be a government agency. This curious duality led to a legal challenge in the late 1930s by some congressmen. They charged that because the Fed had private owners, its building in Washington, D.C. should be subjected to local property taxes. After years of legal maneuvering, including an attempt to auction the Fed's building by the District of Columbia in 1941, the Fed was eventually officially declared an independent department of government. The Federal Reserve Banks are officially called "government instrumentalities," that is, corporations chartered by the federal government to act in the public interest.

Organization of the Federal Reserve System

The main elements of the Fed are the Board of Governors, the Federal Open Market Committee (FOMC), the 12 regional Federal Reserve banks, the Advisory Councils, and the member banks. Each of these entities plays a role in the decision-making process. Figure 2.1 depicts the basic structure of the Federal Reserve System. We now consider each of these elements.

The Board of Governors

The Board of Governors of the Federal Reserve System constitutes the highest authority in the Fed. Its function is similar to that of a Corporate Board of Directors, as it provides guidance and oversees the implementation of the Fed's directives and policies. The board has seven members appointed by the president of the United States and confirmed by the Senate. Originally, board members were appointed for ten years. The board members' terms were changed in the Banking Act of 1933 to 12 years, and again in the Banking Act of 1935 to the current single 14-year term.[2] The terms are staggered to provide continuity, with one of the seven terms expiring every even-numbered year.

---

[1] Not coincidentally, the disarray created by the turmoil surrounding Jackson's "Bank War" resulted in the panic of 1837.

[2] It is interesting to note the wide variety of terms for different high-level government jobs. For example, members of the House of Representatives must seek reelection every two years; the presidential cycle lasts four years; Senatorial terms last six years; Fed Governors are appointed to serve for 14 years; and Federal judges and Supreme court justices are appointed for life. This array of terms reflects the constant tension between accountability and independence of action that prevails in the U.S. political system.

Figure 2.1
Organization of the Federal Reserve System

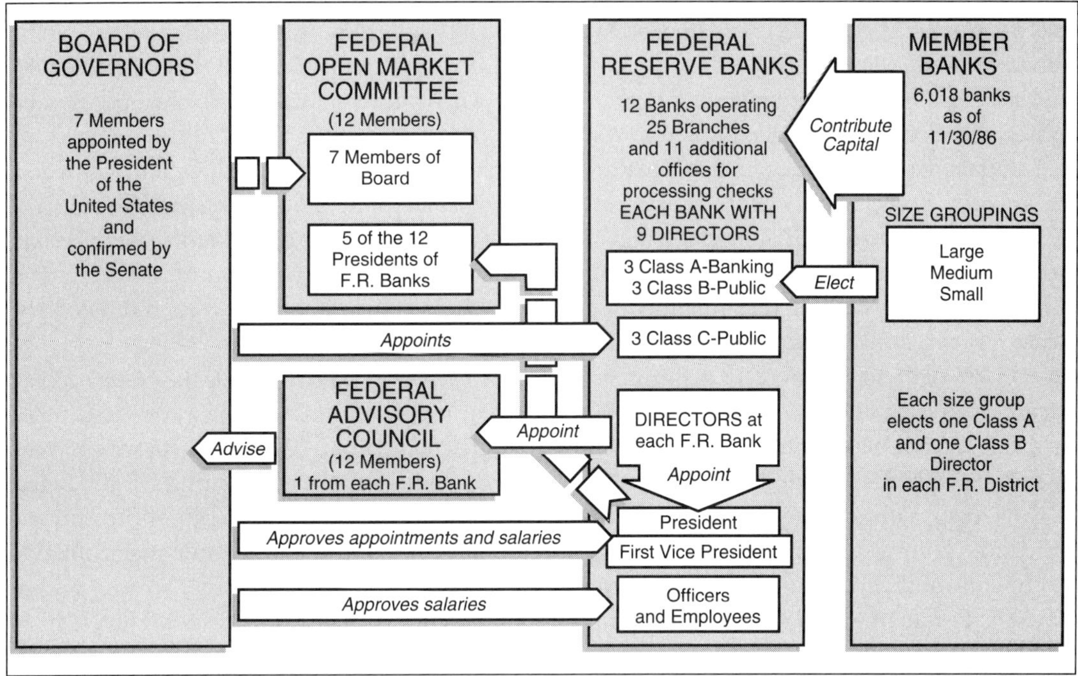

Source: *A Primer on the Fed*, Federal Reserve Bank of Richmond, p. 15.

The Board of Governors enjoys a mystical aura of authority. In particular, the chairman of the Board of Governors is generally viewed as a person of great economic insight by the public. To maintain this image, the chairman almost always votes with the majority, even if this means changing his vote after the fact.

The Chairman of the Board The Chairman of the Board of Governors reports to Congress twice a year, in February and July, on the Fed's monetary policies, the state of the economy, and other financial matters. Under the provisions of the Full Employment and Balanced Growth Act of 1978, also known as the Humphrey-Hawkins Act, the chairman must present a report to the Senate Committee on Banking, Housing, and Urban Affairs and to the House Committee on Banking, Finance, and Urban Affairs, on the Fed's monetary targets. He also meets regularly with the president of the United States and with the Secretary of the Treasury. The chairman of the Board of Governors is also a member of the National Advisory Council on International Monetary and Financial Problems of the U.S. government. Furthermore, the chairman is also the alternate U.S. representative to the International Monetary Fund.

One of the seven board members is chosen by the president of the United States to be chairman of the Board of Governors for a period of four years. Traditionally, a chairman that has not been reappointed has resigned from the Board of Governors, regardless of the time remaining in his 14-year appointment as a board member. This accounts for the historical fact that the actual terms served by the chairmen have varied widely.

The record for the longest period as chairman belongs to William McChesney Martin, who held that office from 1951 to 1970.[3] Martin thus served from the Truman to the Nixon administrations. Martin described the function of the Fed as that of "leaning against the wind," implying that the Fed should ease monetary policy when the economy was doing poorly and tighten the money supply when inflation was getting out of control.

Other recent chairmen include Arthur Burns, an Austrian-born economist who served in that capacity from 1970 to 1978. Burns was accused by some of helping the reelection campaign of President Nixon in 1972 by allowing money to grow excessively fast. Before the election, money grew at a rate of more than 10 percent and, as a result, the economy expanded. Unfortunately, to contain the inflation that ensued, the following year the Fed tightened the monetary reins and helped to precipitate the recession of 1974.

G. William Miller succeeded Burns in March 1978, but resigned in July 1979 to become Carter's Secretary of the Treasury. Miller's background was in business; he worked at Textron, Inc., since 1956, becoming its president in 1960 and its chairman in 1974.

Paul Volcker succeeded Miller in August 1979. When he was elected chairman of the Board of Governors, Volcker was the president of the New York Fed, the most powerful of the regional Fed banks. He was a highly respected economist with a towering presence, whose main function was to control the perilously high inflation rate that developed during 1979. Volcker was renominated by President Reagan in recognition of his achievements as an inflation fighter. He remained chairman until the end of his second term in 1987.

Volcker was succeeded by the current chairman, Alan Greenspan, who continued his predecessor's anti-inflationary policies. As a result, inflation in the United States declined to 2.9 percent in 1991. Although the economy sank into recession in 1990, Greenspan was renominated by President Bush in July 1991 to a second term as chairman.

Responsibilities of the Board of Governors One of the most important tasks of the Board of Governors is to set the monetary policy goals for the United States. In addition, the board determines the reserve requirements for banks and approves the discount rates set by the regional Fed banks. More generally, the board oversees the activities of the 12 Federal Reserve Banks. In addition, the Board of Governors supervises and regulates commercial banks that are members of the Fed, as well as bank holding companies. All members of the Board of Governors are also voting members of the important Federal Open Market Committee.

The board also commissions studies on the general financial health of the country. Many of these studies are conducted by the Fed's numerous in-house economists, who are constantly taking the economic pulse of the nation. In addition, the Board publishes the *Federal Reserve Bulletin*, a monthly magazine full of current economic and financial data, and the *Federal Reserve Regulatory Service*, in which the Board presents information relating to its regulatory tasks.

---

[3] Note that Martin's chairmanship lasted some 19 years, far exceeding the 14-year limit. While this was theoretically not possible, a technicality allowed a member who resigned prior to the expiration of the term to be available once again for the position.

The Federal Open Market Committee

The most important way in which the Federal Reserve controls the money supply is through the actions of the Federal Open Market Committee (FOMC). The law requires that the FOMC meet at least four times each year; in practice it meets about eight times each year. All seven members of the Board of Governors are members of the FOMC. In addition, five of the 12 regional Reserve Bank presidents are also members of the FOMC. Of these five members, the president of the Federal Reserve Bank of New York is a permanent member.[4] The other four positions are rotated annually among the other 11 Fed bank presidents. While only five regional bank presidents can vote in the FOMC, all 12 Fed presidents usually attend the deliberations and contribute to the discussion.[5]

In 1922, the FOMC was founded by the New York Fed Bank president to coordinate the open market transactions of the 12 Fed banks. In the first year, four, and then five, regional Fed bank presidents integrated the committee. By 1923, the importance of open market operations grew and the Board of Governors dissolved the original committee structure, simultaneously establishing the Open Market Investment Committee (OMIC) under its own control. In 1930, the OMIC was superseded by the Open Market Policy Conference, which included representatives from all 12 Fed banks but required approval of the Board of Governors for all its actions. In 1935 the committee was restructured as the Federal Open Market Committee. From that time, its structure has remained largely unchanged.

The law requires the Board of Governors to keep a detailed record of all actions taken by the FOMC on policy matters. To this end, a Record of Policy Actions is prepared after each meeting. However, the Record is not released until a few days after the next FOMC meeting. Another report, Minutes of Actions, gives an account of all actions, whether relating to policy or not.

The 12 Federal Reserve Banks

The Federal Reserve System is divided into 12 districts. Each district has a Federal Reserve Bank that oversees the operations of its member banks, sets the discount rate for the district (although in practice the Board of Governors effectively controls this rate through its veto power), and performs other banking duties. Each Fed bank may have branches in the major economic centers within its district. Additionally, it can also establish offices in other cities. For example, the Federal Reserve Bank of Cleveland serves the fourth district, which includes Ohio, western Pennsylvania, the northern panhandle of West Virginia, and eastern Kentucky, with branches in Cincinnati and Pittsburgh, and an office in Columbus, Ohio. Figure 2.2 shows a map with the Federal Reserve district boundaries.

---

[4] The special status of the New York Fed president as a permanent member of the FOMC is due to the fact that the committee's directives to buy or sell government securities are carried out at the open market desk of the New York Federal Reserve Bank.

[5] The terms begin on March 1 of each year. Rotation is conducted so that each of the four members is elected from the following groups of Reserve Banks: (1) Boston, Philadelphia, and Richmond; (2) Cleveland and Chicago; (3) Atlanta, St. Louis, and Dallas; and (4) Minneapolis, Kansas City, and San Francisco.

To give an idea of the financial structure of each of the 12 Federal Reserve Banks, Table 2.1 shows a typical percentage balance sheet for a Federal Reserve Bank. As the table shows, U.S. government securities are by far the greatest asset. Our illustrative Federal Reserve Bank shows no loans to depository institutions. When these loans are made, they help depository institutions meet their reserve requirements whenever the institutions have trouble meeting the requirement through their normal operations. On the liability side, Federal Reserve notes constitute the vast majority of the liabilities. Next are the reserves on deposit at Fed that all depository institutions in the district must have.

It is interesting to note how the politics of the day may have influenced the original choice of the 12 regions. For example, some say that Cleveland may have been chosen over Cincinnati and Pittsburgh because it was the hometown of President Wilson's secretary of war. Similarly, Richmond may have been picked over Baltimore because it was the capital of Senator Glass's home state. In any case, the overall choices provide a reasonable representation of the country's economic regions. The major exception to this is Missouri, which has two Federal Reserve Banks, one

Figure 2.2
Boundaries of the 12 Federal Reserve Districts

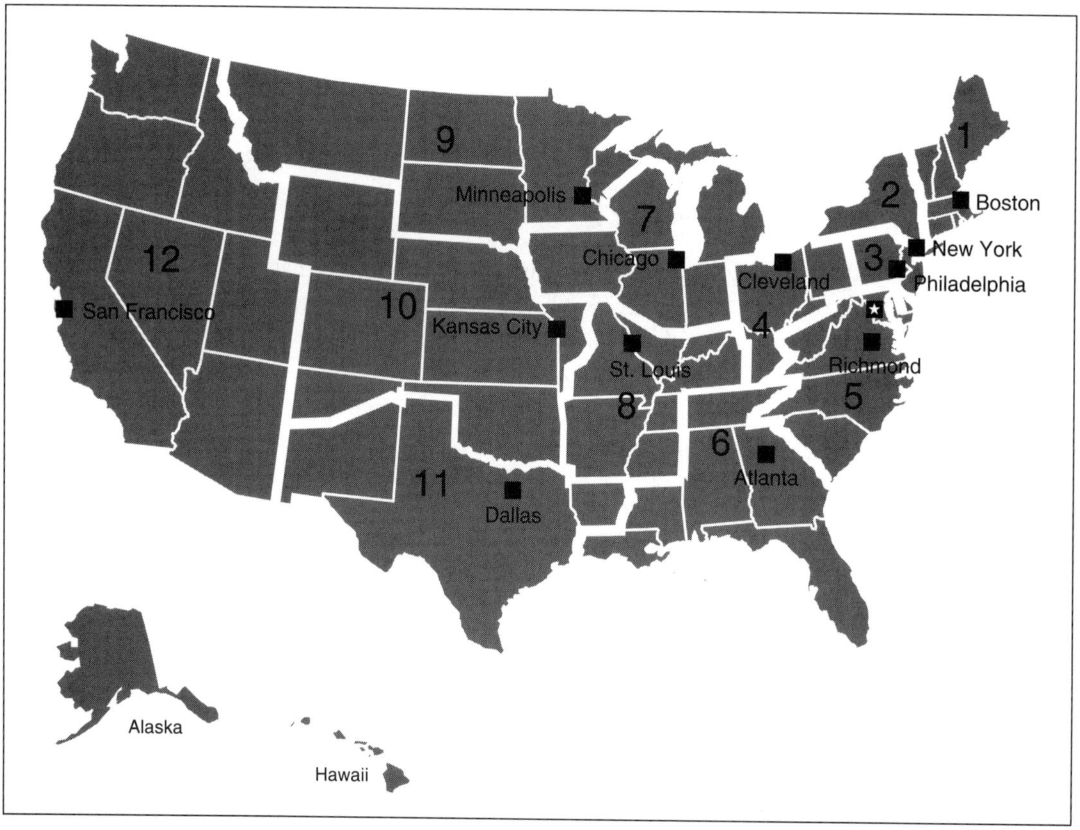

Source: *Federal Reserve Bulletin*, March 1995, p. A76.

Table 2.1
Percentage Balance Sheet of a Typical Reserve Bank
(millions of dollars)

ASSETS	
Gold certificate account	3.10%
Special drawing rights (SDR)	2.89
Coin	0.13
Loans to depository institutions	0.00
U.S. government securities	74.60
Other assets	19.28
TOTAL ASSETS	100.00%
LIABILITIES	
Federal Reserve notes	89.25%
Reserves on deposit	7.03
Other liabilities	2.28
TOTAL LIABILITIES	98.56
CAPITAL	
Capital paid in	0.72
Surplus	0.72
TOTAL CAPITAL	1.44
TOTAL LIABILITIES AND CAPITAL	100.00%

in St. Louis and the other in Kansas City. Likely reason: the speaker of the House of Representatives at the time of the Fed's creation was from Missouri.[6]

Every bank that has a national charter must be a member of the Federal Reserve System. One of the requirements of membership is to buy stock in the member bank's regional Fed bank. The amount of each member bank's stock subscription is equal to 6 percent of the bank's equity. However, only half of that amount must be paid-in capital, with the other half subject to a stock call by the Board of Governors. All members receive a statutory 6 percent dividend per year on the value of their paid-in capital. Unlike traditional common stock, the stock of member banks in the Fed cannot be traded, transferred, or used as collateral by the member banks to secure loans.

Stock ownership also entitles the member banks to elect six of the nine directors in the Fed Bank they own. Three of these directors are labeled class A and must be professional bankers. The other three are class B directors and must be chosen from businesses other than banking. The remaining three directors in each regional Fed Bank are labeled class C and are appointed by the Board of Governors. From the three class C directors, the Board of Governors designates a

[6] Source: William Greider, *Secrets of the Temple*, New York: Simon and Schuster, 1987.

chairman and deputy chairman of each regional Bank's board. This is yet another way in which the Board asserts its supremacy within the system.

The 12 Federal Reserve banks examine state chartered banks in their respective regions. They also clear checks, make loans to depository institutions, and issue paper currency, formally known as Federal Reserve notes. In addition, the regional Feds publish periodicals with academic articles on topics of current interest.

Advisory Councils

Over the years, several advisory councils have been created to advise the Board of Governors. Although the councils have little or no decision-making powers, they can potentially influence how the Board of Governors implements monetary policy. The main councils are the Federal Advisory Council, the Consumer Advisory Council, and the Thrift Institutions Advisory Council.

The Federal Advisory Council Created by the original Federal Reserve Act, this council consists of 12 members, usually influential bankers, from each of the Fed's districts. For example, the chairman of Citicorp, the nation's largest bank holding company, has been a member of the Council. Each of the 12 regional Fed Banks elects one member of the Federal Advisory Council. Since members are usually the CEOs of some of the largest banks in the United States, they are perceived by some as insiders that can potentially change the direction of the Fed's policies in their own interest. Furthermore, these insiders may be privy to the Fed's thinking in monetary matters before the general public becomes aware of that information.

On some occasions, the Federal Advisory Council has warned the Board of Governors to improve its performance. For example, it has in the past advised the Board of Governors to avoid large deviations from the target rate of growth of money. On other occasions, the Council has declared its conformity with the policies of the Board of Governors. In other words, the Advisory Council provides effective feedback from representatives of the financial marketplace to the Board of Governors.

The Consumer Advisory Council The Federal Reserve Board also considers input from the Consumer Advisory Council in making its policy decisions. Congress established this Council in 1976 to advise the Board in relation to its duties under the Consumer Credit Protection Act and other areas of consumer concern. It has 30 members that serve for three years. Members include representatives of the financial industry, consumers, academics, and legal experts in consumer matters. The Consumer Advisory Council meets three or four times each year with the Board of Governors.

The Thrift Institutions Advisory Council The Board of Governors established this council in 1980, as required under the Depository Institution Deregulation and Monetary Control Act (DIDMCA). The council consists of representatives from savings banks, credit unions, and savings and loans associations. This council advises the Board of Governors on issues of concern to thrift institutions.

The Member Banks

Any bank with a national charter must be a member of the Fed. In addition, any state bank may become a member of the Fed. All member banks must keep reserves at their district Federal Reserve Bank. These reserves do not earn interest.

Throughout the 1970s the number of member banks steadily decreased. By the end of the decade, the trend had reached alarming proportions. Banks left Fed membership because member banks had to keep funds idle in the form of reserves, while state banks faced lower reserve requirements and could earn interest on those reserves. As interest rates rose, the opportunity cost of the income lost from not investing the reserves became too high for an increasing number of member banks. As a result, many member banks threatened to leave the system.

In an effort to resolve the crisis, Congress passed the Depository Institutions Deregulation and Monetary Control Act (DIDMCA) in 1980.[7] This law effectively eliminated the distinctions between the various types of depository institutions. Among other changes, the legislation subjected all banks, members of the Fed or not, to the same reserve requirements. This new reserve requirement rule applied also to all other depository institutions, including savings and loans associations and credit unions. In exchange for this unsolicited regulation, nonmember institutions now may use Fed services, such as check clearing, on the same terms as member banks.

The DIDMCA had the intended result. In 1981, just after the legislation was enacted, about 5,500 (37 percent) of the 15,000 commercial banks in the United States were members of the Federal Reserve. By 1991, membership increased to more than 6,000 banks (43 percent) of the approximately 14,000 banks in the banking system. It is interesting to note that the majority of commercial banks are not members of the Fed.

Monetary Tools of the Fed

The main monetary control instruments of the Federal Reserve are reserve requirements, open market operations, and the discount rate. With each of these instruments, the Fed can affect the supply of money in the economy. In the early days, the discount window was the most important tool. In recent years, the Fed's open market purchases and sales of securities have been, by far, the most important monetary policy tool. Following is a discussion of each of the tools.

Reserve Requirements

In principle, whenever a depository institution receives new funds, a portion of those funds should be kept on deposit at the Fed or as vault cash. The proportion of the new funds that must remain with the Fed is called the **required reserve ratio**. This ratio varies according to the type and amount of funds held by the depository institution. Table 2.2 shows recent reserve requirements.

---

[7] The DIDMCA legislation had two separate titles, or parts. Title I is the Monetary Control Act (MCA), and title II is the Depository Institutions Deregulation Act (DIDA).

Table 2.2
Required Reserve Ratios for Depository Institutions
March 1995

Type of Deposit	Required Ratio (%)
Transaction accounts	
$0–$54 million	3
More than $54 million	10
Nonpersonal time deposits	0
Eurocurrency liabilities	0

Source: *Federal Reserve Bulletin*, March 1995.

The Depository Institutions Deregulation and Monetary Control Act of 1980 (DIDMCA) made reserve requirements the same for all depository institutions.[8] Under this law, depository institutions included commercial banks, savings and loan associations, credit unions, agencies and branches of foreign banks, and Edge Act corporations.[9]

The Board of Governors of the Fed has the authority to change reserve requirements within the range permitted by the DIDMCA. For example, the reserve ratio on transaction accounts over a certain size may vary between 8 and 14 percent. The current rate is 12 percent.[10] Note, however, that the Fed has no authority to impose reserve requirements on some types of deposits. For example, personal time deposits are exempt from reserve requirements, except in extraordinary circumstances.

A depository institution is required to hold a minimum amount of its reservable liabilities as **required reserves**. However, it usually holds more than the minimum in the form of **excess reserves**. By design, reserve requirements impose a smaller burden on smaller depository institutions. Table 2.2 illustrates that transaction accounts of up to $42.2 million are subject to only a 3 percent required reserve ratio, whereas a 12 percent ratio applies to any amount beyond $42.2 million.[11]

Reserves are provided as either **nonborrowed reserves** or **borrowed reserves**. Nonborrowed reserves are those that depository institutions can obtain from the Fed through open market operations. Borrowed reserves are obtained when the Fed lends to depository institutions through its discount window.

---

[8] Before 1980, only member banks were required to hold reserves at the Fed.

[9] The Edge Act of 1919 is an amendment to the Federal Reserve Act that allowed U.S. commercial banks to provide international banking services without being subject to all the regulations that U.S. banks must meet. The purpose was to make U.S. banks more competitive in the international banking arena.

[10] The Fed does not change the required reserve ratio very often. It does so only when it wants to make a strong statement to the financial community. For example, the ratio was changed three times during the recession of 1974.

[11] The cutoff amount between the low and high ratios changes annually. For transaction deposits, the initial amount subject to the 3 percent ratio was $25 million.

Open Market Operations

Open market operations involve the buying and selling of securities at the open market desk of the Federal Reserve Bank of New York. Every day, the Manager for Domestic Operations carries out these transactions in compliance with the FOMC's directives.[12]

Open market operations are the most powerful monetary weapon in the Fed's arsenal. In essence, they determine the amount of nonborrowed reserves available to depository institutions. If the Fed buys securities, reserves in the system increase; if it sells securities, reserves decrease. When a depository institution finds itself with excess reserves beyond the minimum required by the Fed, it will promptly expand its loan portfolio until it no longer has excess reserves. In this way, the Fed can directly affect the behavior of depository institutions and, through them, interest rates and the economy.

The Federal Reserve can affect the money supply by the mere act of buying or selling government securities because the Fed has the unique ability of issuing claims against itself. Furthermore, by definition, any claim held by a depository institution against the Fed is accounted as a reserve. Thus, when the Fed writes a check against itself, perhaps to pay for the purchase of a government security by an individual, the check will eventually be returned to the Fed by some depository institution to be "cleared." To clear the check, the Fed simply increases that institution's reserve account. This increase in reserves starts the process that eventually creates money.

To illustrate how the Fed's open market operations affect the amount of reserves in the system, assume it purchases a $1,000 bond from Amerilast Bank, for which it pays with a check drawn on the Fed. Amerilast then takes the check to the Fed, which promptly credits the $1,000 to Amerilast's reserve account at the Fed. In this way, Amerilast increases its total reserves and reduces its investment in bonds by $1,000. At this point, Amerilast would have excess reserves, assuming it had met its required reserves, and the bank can lend these excess reserves to its customers. This is in essence how the Fed controls the money supply. Chapter 3 presents a detailed explanation of the money-creation process.

The Discount Window

Since the passage of DIDMCA in 1980, all depository institutions have had access to the Fed's discount window. Individuals, partnerships, and corporations may also use the discount window to obtain loans "in unusual and exigent circumstances." Indeed, it is through the discount window that the Fed complies with its function of being the country's lender of last resort. Because of this, the discount window provides stability to the financial system, especially in times of crisis.

The Federal Reserve Act of 1913 requires that all discount loans be secured. In practice, U.S. Government securities are used as collateral. The rate charged on loans at the discount window is known as the **discount rate**. This rate is established by the Board of Directors of each Reserve Bank every 14 days, but the Board of Governors must approve it. Although in theory each district can have its own discount rate, in practice the discount rate is the same for all 12 districts in recognition of the fact that the U.S. economy is largely integrated.

---

[12] Another manager handles foreign market operations.

Changes in the discount rate occur infrequently. For the entire decade of the 1980s, for example, a total of 28 rate changes occurred, with the time period between rate changes fluctuating between 2 weeks and 20 months. Historically, the lowest discount rate of 0.5 percent was in effect from 1942 to 1946; the highest discount rate of 14 percent was in effect from May to November 1981. At year-end 1991, the discount rate stood at 3.5 percent, its lowest level in more than 15 years, while in early 1995, the discount rate was 5.25 percent.

Currently, the term "discount rate" is a misnomer. Today, loans made by the Fed accrue interest that is paid at the loan's maturity. However, prior to 1971, Fed loans to depository institutions were really made on a discount basis; that is, interest was deducted at the time the loan was made. Since in the early days, banks would borrow from the Fed by bringing securities as collateral to a teller's "window" and the loans were discounted, the term "discount window" arose.

Sometimes the Fed applies surcharges of 2 to 4 percent to the discount rate, especially to large depository institutions that are perceived to be using the discount window too frequently. The purpose of the surcharge is clearly to discourage abuses. Indeed, the discount window is viewed as an emergency outlet for institutions that cannot otherwise meet their obligations. In other words, use of the discount window is viewed by the Fed as a privilege rather than a right.

The loans made at the discount window are mostly in the form of adjustment credit; that is, credit given with the purpose of fixing a very short-term reserve deficiency. The Fed also provides seasonal loans to assist small depository institutions in meeting seasonal variations in loans or deposits. Seasonal credit is not available to institutions with more than $500 million in deposits because the Fed assumes that they can handle their needs through the money market. The two types of loans are independent in the sense that the use of seasonal credit does not impair an institution's ability to obtain adjustment credit.

Changes in the discount rate affect the cost to depository institutions of obtaining reserves to support deposit growth. Because changes in the discount rate affect the behavior of depository institutions, the discount window is an essential tool for implementing monetary policy.

The Fed's Balance Sheet

Table 2.3 presents the consolidated balance sheet for the Federal Reserve System as of December 31, 1994. As the table shows, most of the assets of the Fed are in the form of U.S. government securities. Indeed, over $370 billion of the $436 billion in total assets are securities. By contrast, loans to depository institutions are only $223 million. Since the former are used in the Fed's open market operations, and the latter are used in the Fed's discount window policy, it is apparent that open market operations are vastly more important than discount loans in implementing the Fed's monetary strategy.

On the liability side, the most important account is Federal Reserve notes. These represent most of the country's currency. As of December 31, 1994, there were more than $381 billion in Federal Reserve notes. Next in importance are the total deposits of over $39 billion.

Money and the Behavior of the Fed

Since it began operating in 1914, the Fed has periodically been attacked by some critics as a secretive institution that is not subject to much public scrutiny. Its critics cite, for instance, that even when the Fed publishes its decisions, it usually does so only after a significant delay. In particular,

Table 2.3
Balance Sheet of the Federal Reserve
for December 31, 1994
(millions of dollars)

ASSETS	
Gold certificate account	$11,051
Special drawing rights (SDR)	8,018
Coin	320
Loans to depository institutions	223
Federal agency obligations	4,662
Treasury securities	374,084
Items in collection	4,688
Bank premises	1,076
Other assets	32,364
TOTAL ASSETS	$436,486
LIABILITIES	
Federal Reserve notes	$381,505
Total deposits	39,075
Other liabilities	8,540
TOTAL LIABILITIES	$429,120
CAPITAL	
Capital paid in	$3,683
Surplus	3,683
TOTAL CAPITAL	$7,366
TOTAL LIABILITIES AND CAPITAL	$436,486

Source: *Federal Reserve Bulletin*, March 1995.

the deliberations of the Federal Open Market Committee are published in the *Federal Reserve Bulletin*, but become public only after the next FOMC meeting has taken place.

Before passage of the Humphrey-Hawkins Act in 1978, the Federal Reserve was not obligated to make public its target ranges for monetary growth. Since that time, though, the chairman of the Board of Governors must discuss and explain the Fed's monetary targets to Congress twice a year. Even so, the declarations may be perceived as too vague by some observers.

This apparent desire for secrecy by the Fed may be due to the fact that the acceptance of money by society requires a fundamental act of faith. In this context, the Fed acts as the keeper of the faith. After all, money may simply be a piece of paper or an electronic transaction in a computer, so its value is far from intrinsic; the value of money depends on the willingness of society to accept it as a medium of exchange.

Examples abound of societies that have lost faith in their money, resulting in disastrous consequences. The most infamous example in modern times is the case of Germany in the 1920s, when people would literally carry money around in wheelbarrows and prices often doubled overnight. The importance of that economic debacle cannot be overestimated, since it led to Hitler's rise to power and, eventually, to World War II.

It is interesting to note that monetary control in some societies has been associated with religion. For example, in ancient times Hebrews banked in temples. Coins were also minted in temples and sanctified by priests, an act that made the currency acceptable by society. Roman coins were made in the temple of the goddess Juno, also called *Moneta,* the Latin root for the word *money.* Even today, some central bank buildings have the appearance of temples.

Summary

The Federal Reserve System is responsible for formulating and implementing the monetary policy of the United States. The history and structure of the Federal Reserve System in the United States is unique. For example, even though its member banks own the Fed, it is legally a branch of the United States government. Similarly, contrary to central banks in many other countries, the Fed is fiercely independent.

The current system was created in 1913, after two unsuccessful attempts in the eighteenth and nineteenth century. Its main power resides in the seven members of the Board of Governors, who set monetary goals for the economy. Other important structural components of the Fed are the Federal Open Market Committee, the 12 regional Fed banks, the thousands of member banks, and the Federal Advisory Council.

The monetary tools available to the Fed are reserve requirements, open market operations, and the discount window. Reserve requirements act to restrict the capacity of banks to create money. They must be held as either deposits at the Fed or as vault cash at the depository institution. No other type of reserve is allowed. Open market operations are the most important monetary tool used by the Fed. The Fed buys and sells government securities in the open market, thereby increasing or decreasing the amount of reserves in the system. The discount window is used as the last resort when banks need funds, especially in times of crisis. It is also used for seasonal needs. Although the discount window was created with the intention of becoming the main monetary tool, it is much less important than open market operations.

We also presented the Fed's balance sheet. The Fed's main asset is U.S. government securities, consistent with the fact that open market purchases and sales of such securities are the main form in which the Fed controls monetary policy. The main liability is Federal Reserve notes, or currency, followed by deposits from depository institutions and the Treasury.

Finally, we discussed how the Fed has allegedly evolved into a secretive institution in the view of some observers. This may be due to the perception that the acceptance of money is essentially an act of faith on the part of society. Perhaps recognizing this, earlier societies conducted monetary policy through priests at religious temples.

Questions and Problems

1. Describe the attempts to create a central bank in the United States prior to the creation of the Federal Reserve System.
2. In what year was the Federal Reserve Act passed?

3. In what year did the Federal Reserve start its operations?
4. Describe the main circumstances that led to the creation of the Federal Reserve System.
5. Why was the Fed created as an independent institution?
6. Describe the main parts of the Fed's organizational structure.
7. Although the members of the Board of Governors are elected for a period of 14 years, in fact the actual terms vary widely. Why?
8. What are the main responsibilities of the Board of Governors?
9. Why is the president of the Federal Reserve Bank of New York a permanent member of the Federal Open Market Committee?
10. Why is Missouri the only state with two Fed districts?
11. Which banks must be members of the Federal Reserve System?
12. What are the three main advisory councils?
13. What is the function of the Federal Advisory Council?
14. What motivated the DIDMCA legislation?
15. Name the Fed's three main monetary tools.
16. What are the Fed's main assets?
17. What are the Fed's main liabilities?
18. What is the rationale for the Fed's alleged secretive behavior?

References

Bechter, D. M., "The Federal Reserve Today," Federal Reserve Bank of Richmond, 9th ed., 1990.

Board of Governors of the Federal Reserve System, "The Federal Reserve System: Purposes & Functions," Washington, 1985.

Broaddus, A., "A Primer on the Fed," Federal Reserve Bank of Richmond, 1988.

Bullard, J. B., "The FOMC in 1991: An Elusive Recovery," *Review*, The Federal Reserve Bank of St. Louis, March/April 1992, pp. 41–61.

Calomiris, Charles W., "Is the Discount Window Necessary? A Penn Central Perspective," *Review*, Federal Reserve Bank of St. Louis, May/June 1994, pp. 31–56.

Federal Reserve Bank of Boston, "Putting It Simply . . . The Federal Reserve," 1990.

Federal Reserve Bank of Cleveland, "Central Banking in the United States: A Fragile Commitment to Price Stability and Independence," 1991 Annual Report, pp. 4–17.

Greider, W., *Secrets of the Temple*, New York: Simon and Schuster, 1987.

Humpage, Owen F., "Central Bank Independence," *Economic Commentary*, Federal Reserve Bank of Cleveland, April 1, 1994, pp. 1–4.

Humphrey, T. M., "Lender of Last Resort: The Concept in History," *Economic Review*, Federal Reserve Bank of Richmond, July/August 1989, pp. 3–9.

Meek, P., "Open Market Operations," Federal Reserve Bank of New York, 1985.

Parthemos, J., "The Federal Reserve Act of 1913 in the Stream of U.S. Monetary History," *Economic Review*, Federal Reserve Bank of Richmond, July/August 1988, pp. 19–28.

Parthemos, J., "The Origins of the Fed," *Cross Sections*, Federal Reserve Bank of Richmond, Fall 1988, pp. 9–11.

Sellon, G. H., Jr., "The Instruments of Monetary Policy," *Economic Review*, Federal Reserve Bank of Kansas City, May 1984, pp. 3–20.

The Money Supply and Deposit Expansion

3

Overview

Chapter 1 introduced the concept of money in a simple "Robinson Crusoe" economy. In this chapter we continue our study of money in a more realistic setting. For instance, we discuss the various modern definitions of money. We also introduce concepts such as the velocity of money, the monetary base, and the money multiplier that are essential to understanding the role of money in today's economy.

Chapter 2 discussed the structure of the Fed, which acts as the central bank of the United States. We saw that one of the main functions of the Fed is to supply money to the economy. This chapter provides a detailed explanation of how the Fed creates money. We also show how money is then expanded, or multiplied, through the rational behavior of the entire banking system.

The Properties of Money

By definition, money is a medium of exchange, serves as the unit of account, and stores purchasing power. Gold, for example, has served as money in the past because it is a very stable metal, and many societies have accepted it as a medium of exchange. In this case, an ounce of gold might be set as the unit of account. Until 1973, for example, 35 U.S. dollar bills could be exchanged for one ounce of gold upon demand. The essential properties of money are also shared by silver, pearls, stones, and many other items such as green pieces of paper with engraved faces of presidents. Today's coins are remnants of the days when gold and silver served as money. In modern times, however, societies are more likely to use checks drawn against demand deposits and paper bills as money.

By contrast, it is easy to name items that would not serve well as money. We already saw in Chapter 1 that fish should not act as money because it is perishable. Similarly, apples, eggs, or even cars would not be very suitable, since they would not store their purchasing power for a long period of time. A good serves all three functions (medium of exchange, store of value, and unit of account) if it is to serve as money.

Money as a Medium of Exchange

As we all know, money can be used to pay for goods and services. It is the "medium of exchange" property of money that allowed societies to abandon the inefficient barter system discussed in Chapter 1. In a barter economy, two parties exchange one good or service for another good or service, without the intermediate step of exchanging money. For example, suppose Al is a mechanic and Dr. Quan is a physician living in Barterland. If Al is sick and Dr. Quan needs to repair her Lexus, then the two may agree as follows: Al will repair the Lexus in exchange for an immediate, complete physical checkup. In this case, both parties are happy.

A serious problem with the above arrangement arises if Al cannot take the checkup until a few weeks later, but the Lexus still needs to be repaired right away. After a moment's thought, Al decides he can repair the car in exchange for a document from Dr. Quan guaranteeing that the physical checkup will be performed whenever Al wishes. Judging from this example, Barterland must be a very inefficient country. Indeed, this type of arrangement can quickly get very messy and time-consuming in the absence of a medium of exchange accepted by all members of society. Rather than writing out a document each time the barter agreement cannot be performed simultaneously, as in the case of Al and Dr. Quan, it is much more efficient to agree to use a uniform "document," which we might call currency, to exchange for goods or services. One of the obvious advantages of currency is that simultaneity of transactions is no longer required. With money, goods and services are exchanged for money, which in turn is later exchanged for some other good or service, and so on.

Money as the Unit of Account

Money as a unit of account helps society by reducing the number of prices needed to conduct transactions. The price of all goods and services can be quoted in terms of a single unit of account, say dollars, rather than in terms of other goods and services. For example, we could state the price of a spear of broccoli as 2 lettuces or 3 oranges, and the price of 1 lemon as 1.5 oranges. Alternatively, we can say that broccoli is worth $6 per spear, lemons are $3 each, and oranges are $2 apiece. While the two systems are consistent, the latter is much more efficient when there are many goods and services to be exchanged. This system is depicted graphically in Figure 3.1, where we assume that there are only six products to be exchanged in the economy. In the barter system of Figure 3.1a, there are a total of 15 different prices needed for transacting. By contrast, an economy with money needs only six prices, as Figure 3.1b shows.

Money as a Store of Purchasing Power

In the previous example of Al the mechanic and Dr. Quan, there would be little sense in Al's accepting money in payment for repairing the doctor's Lexus if Al didn't have confidence that the money just received could retain its value for a reasonable amount of time. If Al decides to get a physical checkup three months after repairing the car, he wants to know that the car repair payment could be used to pay for the complete physical checkup, just as the two had agreed originally. If, instead, Al finds that the money from the car repair is now worth a blood pressure measurement but cannot pay for an electrocardiogram, he would quickly lose faith in money and would return to barter.[1]

---

[1] Actually, this scenario has happened many times throughout history when inflation has become rampant. Inflation erodes the purchasing power of money. When inflation is low, the problem is only a small nuisance. With hyperinflation, however, money does not store value for long and individuals will scramble to hold only real goods. Recent examples of hyperinflation have occurred in Argentina, Nicaragua, and some East European countries. As mentioned in the previous chapter, Germany's hyperinflation in the 1920s eventually resulted in disastrous consequences for the entire world.

Figure 3.1
Number of Prices in an Economy with Six Goods

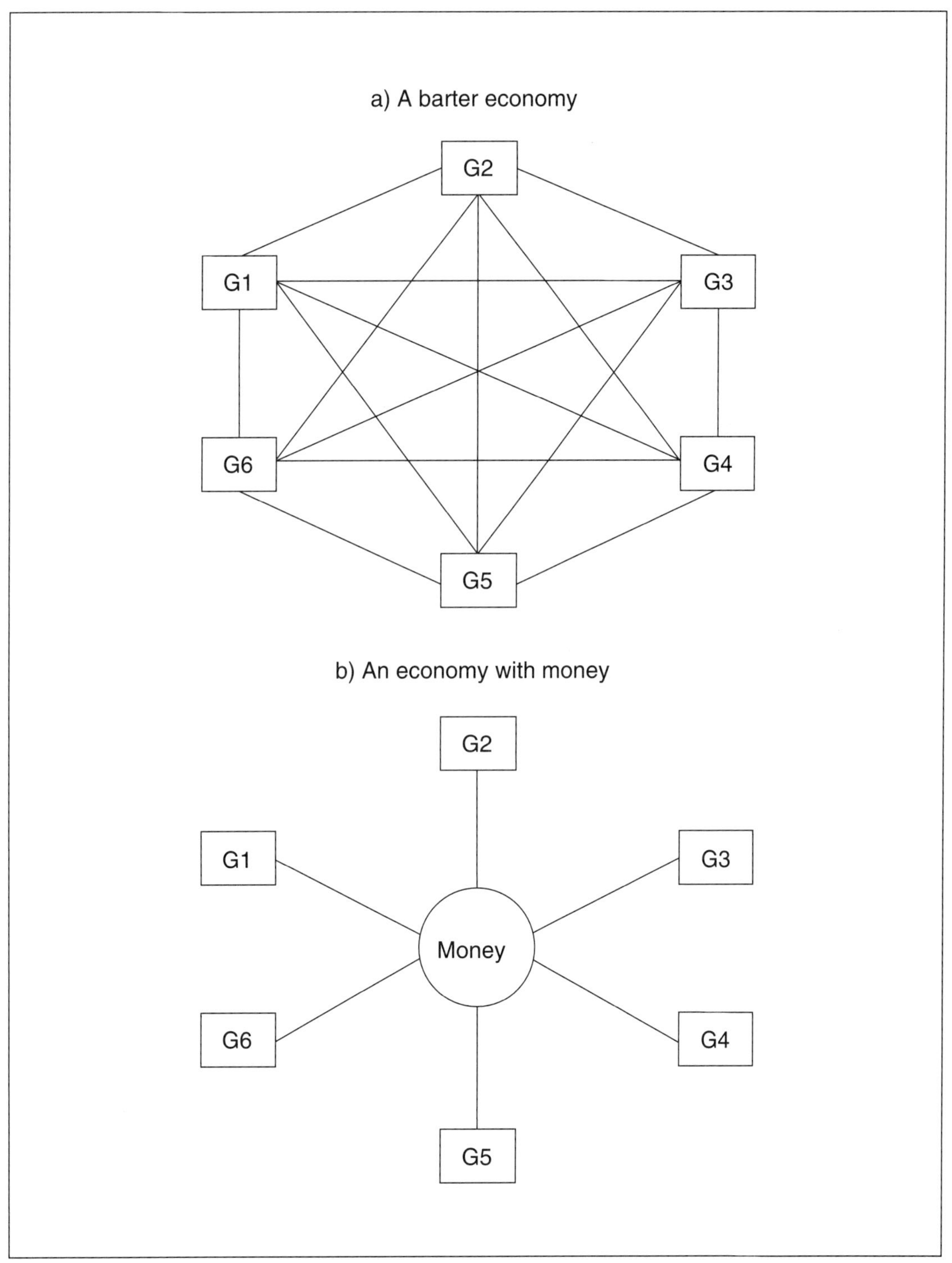

The Various Definitions of Money

We have seen that money is anything that is generally accepted as payment for goods and services. Obviously, coins and paper bills fit this definition and are, therefore, money. But the concept of money encompasses much more than just the currency we may have in our pockets or under the mattress at any given time. Indeed, a moment's thought reveals that the balance of our checking account is also money, since checks can be used to pay for many goods and services. Similarly, when traveling abroad, many tourists pay for hotel, food, and other amenities with traveler's checks or a credit card (after all, how can they leave home without it?). In a broad sense, these are also forms of money.

By now you can see that defining money is not as simple as it may appear at first. In fact, economists often debate about what exactly constitutes money. Perhaps as a compromise, several definitions of money are currently in use. We will discuss each one, from narrowest to broadest.

M1

M1 is the strictest definition of money because it only includes the most obvious items: currency in circulation, traveler's checks, demand deposits, and other checkable deposits. These are clearly money because they all serve as a medium of exchange. In the United States they are all denominated in dollars, and they can be used in the future without substantially losing their purchasing power.

Currency in circulation includes currency outside the U.S. Treasury, Federal Reserve Banks, and the vaults of depository institutions. Traveler's checks only include the outstanding checks issued by nonbank institutions. Traveler's checks issued by depository institutions are considered a component of demand deposits for the Fed's accounting purposes. Demand deposits include those at all commercial banks; they do not include those due to depository institutions, the U.S. government, and foreign banks. Other checkable deposits consist mostly of Negotiable Order of Withdrawal (NOW) and Automatic Transfer Service (ATS) accounts at depository institutions, credit union share draft accounts, and demand deposits at thrift institutions.

M2

The definition of M2 contains M1 as a subset. In addition, it also includes overnight repurchase agreements (repos) issued by all depository institutions and overnight Eurodollars issued to U.S. residents by foreign branches of U.S. banks worldwide. M2 also includes money market deposit accounts (MMDAs), savings deposits, small time deposits (less than $100,000), and money market funds. Excluded are individual retirement accounts (IRAs) and Keogh balances at depository institutions and money market funds.

M3

M3 contains both M2 and M1 as subsets. It also includes large time deposits issued by depository institutions and term Eurodollars held by U.S. residents at foreign branches of U.S. banks both worldwide and at all banking offices in the United Kingdom and Canada. Clearly, this is a less liquid definition of money than the previous two. For example, if you have funds in a one-year CD, you cannot use those funds before the CD matures without incurring a substantial penalty.

L

L is the least liquid measure of money in use. It adds to the previous definitions of money non-bank public holdings of assets such as U.S. savings bonds, commercial paper, bankers' acceptances and short-term Treasury securities. Table 3.1 presents the levels of the four measures of money for selected recent years.

Velocity and the Demand for Money

From time to time, economic policy makers reexamine the usefulness of the various measures of money.[2] In the mid-1980s, for example, the Federal Open Market Committee decided to abandon M1 as the primary monetary policy guide. Since that time, M2 has been used to target monetary growth. To understand why this change occurred, we must introduce the concept of **velocity**, which is simply the ratio of the country's Gross National Product (GNP) to the amount of money in the economy:

$$\text{Velocity} = \frac{\text{GNP}}{\text{Money}} \tag{3.1}$$

Clearly, there can be as many measures of velocity as there are measures of money. We focus on M1 and M2 velocity.

The velocity of M1 increased at a predictable and almost linear pace during the 1960s and 1970s. In the early 1980s the situation changed, as M1 velocity lost its long-term trend and started to drift and fluctuate erratically. The main reason given by economists for this dramatic change in behavior was the introduction of many financial innovations, along with sweeping deregulation of the banking industry. In contrast to the unexpected behavior of M1 velocity, M2 velocity seemed to be totally unaffected by the same events. M2 velocity has remained essentially constant for more than three decades. It is apparent that GNP has been slightly less than twice the

Table 3.1
The Money Stock in the United States
(billions of dollars)

Measure of Money	1990	1991	1992	1993	1994
M1	825	897	1,025	1,128	1,148
M2	3,327	3,426	3,509	3,568	3,600
M3	4,111	4,172	4,183	4,232	4,282
L	4,967	4,993	5,057	5,135	N/A

Source: *Federal Reserve Bulletin*, March 1995.

[2] This section is based on John B. Carlson and Susan M. Byrne, "Recent Behavior of Velocity: Alternative Measures of Money," *Economic Review*, Federal Reserve Bank of Cleveland, 1992 Quarter 1, 28:1.

level of M2 throughout the entire period, up to the early 1990s. In fact, since the founding of the Federal Reserve in 1913 to the early 1990s, M2 and gross national product have grown at about the same rate. Since M2 seems to be directly related to GNP, the Fed has found it more reliable as a policy guide in making decisions on the future course of the money supply.

This is no longer the case. Starting in about 1990, M2 grew much more slowly than it did historically. This sluggish growth has led some to question monetary aggregates as a guide to policy. In July 1993, Federal Reserve Chairman Alan Greenspan told Congress that monetary aggregates, including M2, were being de-emphasized as guides to monetary policy. Real interest rates and nominal income are two candidates to replace monetary aggregates as monetary policy guides. Some observers believe that monetary aggregates are no longer useful tools in monetary policy because the smorgasbord of investment opportunities has been so enriched that economic agents have many ways to hold funds.[3]

Money, Depository Institutions, and Social Welfare

When Willie Sutton was asked why he robbed banks, the famous crook supposedly responded: "Because that's where the money is." It is a fact that many people keep their money in depository institutions in the form of savings and checking accounts and certificates of deposits. An obvious reason for this is convenience and safety, Mr. Sutton notwithstanding. It certainly beats keeping money under the proverbial "mattress." A not so obvious reason for putting money in the banking system lies in the fact that depository institutions specialize in processing information on prospective borrowers, a task that would be too costly and time-consuming for individual savers. This specialization allows the bank, the saver, and the borrower to benefit. Consequently, social welfare improves with the existence of depository institutions.

The function of channeling money from savers to borrowers is known as **intermediation.** With intermediation, savers place excess funds in a depository institution, which lends those funds to borrowers. To see how society benefits from intermediation, consider the following simple scenario.

Suppose there are only two types of borrowers: those that pay all their debts as contracted ("good" borrowers), and those that default and pay nothing ("bad" borrowers). Assume that everyone knows that there are the same number of good and bad borrowers in society. However, it is very hard to discern to which category a given borrower belongs. When the lender does not know in what category the borrower belongs, but the borrower obviously does, we have a case of **asymmetric information**. A depository institution can reduce the information asymmetry by spending $100 on a credit evaluation of the borrower, thus identifying with 90 percent probability whether a given borrower is good. Individuals, on the other hand, do not have access to the resources required to obtain the credit information, such as mainframe computers and specialized personnel.

---

[3] For a discussion of the problems with monetary aggregates, see "Monetary Policy in the 1990s," Robert T. Parry, *Weekly Letter*, Federal Reserve Bank of San Francisco, March 4, 1994; "Policy Implications of Recent M2 Behavior," Byron Higgins, *Economic Review*, Federal Reserve Bank of Kansas City, 77:3, Third Quarter 1992, pp. 21–36; "Symposium on Mutual Funds and Monetary Aggregates," Federal Reserve Bank of St. Louis, *Economic Review*, 76:6, November/December 1994, pp. 3–78.

In a world without depository institutions, savers would lend to borrowers directly. Suppose a typical loan is for \$1,000, and that on average the lender wishes to neither win nor lose on a loan.[4] This means that the expected payoff from the loan should be equal to \$1,000. Since there is a 50 percent chance of giving the loan to either a good or a bad borrower, the nominal interest rate on the loan given directly by a saver must be set at $r_{LS} = 100$ percent. Analytically, we can find the nominal loan rate by solving the following equation for r_{LS}:

$$E(\text{Profit}) = 0 = [(1 + r_{LS}) \times \$1{,}000 \times 0.5 + \$0 \times 0.5] - \$1{,}000 \tag{3.2}$$

If we now allow for the existence of depository institutions specializing in credit risk evaluation, and if they are also happy to break even on the average loan, then the rate set on the loan can be reduced to $r_{LD} = 22.22$ percent, which is found by solving the equation:[5]

$$E(\text{Profit}) = 0 = [(1 + r_{LD}) \times \$1{,}000 \times 0.9 + \$0 \times 0.1] - \$1{,}000 - \$100 \tag{3.3}$$

We can see that the introduction of depository institutions has substantially lowered the borrowing cost, from 100 percent to 22.22 percent in the example, without affecting the saver's expected income.[6] Since borrowers are better off and savers are just as well off, society benefits from the intermediation provided by depository institutions. When none of the parties is hurt in a transaction and some of them benefit, the situation resulting from the transaction is said to be "Pareto superior."

Money Creation and Expansion: A Simple Model

In Chapter 2 we discussed the three main monetary policy tools of the Fed: setting reserve requirements, purchasing and selling securities in the open market, and providing loans to depository institutions through the Fed's discount window. In this section we describe in detail how these tools affect the supply of money to the economy. We begin with a simple model and then provide a more complete explanation of the process.

To simplify the model, we assume that the Fed's only assets are government securities and discount loans, and its only liabilities are reserve deposits. Similarly, the banking system's assets consist of reserves and loans, and its liabilities are demand deposits (which are subject to a 10 percent required reserve ratio) and the Fed's discount loans. For simplicity, the banking system's net worth is assumed to be zero. Table 3.2 shows the assumed initial amounts of each asset and liability for the Fed and the banking system.

---

[4] This is obviously not the case in the real world, but the conclusions will not change by making expected profits positive.

[5] In reality, we would have to subtract the rate of interest paid to the depositor. For consistency with our other simplifying assumptions, we assume the depositor gets no interest.

[6] In fact, the saver may be better off with a depository institution because the \$1,000 is certain to retain its value there. When lending directly to borrowers, the saver only expects to come out even, but there is some risk of losing money. Other things equal, savers prefer alternatives with lower risk, as Chapter 12 shows.

Table 3.2
Initial Balance Sheet for the Fed and the Banking System

(a) The Fed's Initial Balance Sheet

ASSETS		LIABILITIES	
Government securities	$10,000	Reserve deposits	$10,000
Discount loans	0	Net worth	0
Total	$10,000	Total	$10,000

(b) The Banking System's Initial Balance Sheet

ASSETS		LIABILITIES	
Required reserves	$10,000	Demand deposits	$100,000
Excess reserves	0	Fed discount loans	0
Loans	90,000	Net worth	0
Total	$100,000	Total	$100,000

The Fed, Total Reserves, and the Money Supply

The Fed can change the total reserves in the banking system in two ways: It can purchase or sell government securities through open market operations, or it can make discount loans to depository institutions. As discussed in Chapter 2, open market operations are by far the most important way in which the Fed controls reserves in the banking system.

The Money Supply and Open Market Operations Suppose the Fed has decided to increase the amount of reserves in the banking system by $1,000. To do this through an open market operation, the manager at the open market desk of the New York Federal Reserve purchases $1,000 in government securities, say from an individual. When the Fed buys the securities, it pays the seller by writing a check drawn against the Fed itself. The seller deposits this check at one of the depository institutions in the system. The depository institution, in turn, sends the check to the Fed to be cleared. The Fed clears the check by increasing (crediting) the depository institution's reserve account at the Fed with the $1,000. The Fed's objective of increasing the banking system's reserves is thus attained.

Soon after the purchase of government securities by the Fed, the banking system increases its reserves by $1,000. Demand deposits also increase by $1,000 because the seller of the government security deposits the Fed's check in the banking system. Note, however, that of the $1,000 in new reserves, $900 are in the form of excess reserves and $100 are required reserves, since 10 percent of all demand deposits must be set aside as required reserves. Table 3.3 shows the new balance sheets for the Fed and the banking system after the increase in reserves.[7]

---

[7] The numbers in parentheses in each table show the changes to the balance sheets relative to the previous table.

Table 3.3
Balance Sheets After the Fed's Purchase of a Government Security

(a) The Fed's Balance Sheet

ASSETS		LIABILITIES	
Government securities	$11,000 (+1,000)	Reserve deposits	$11,000 (+1,000)
Discount loans	0	Net worth	0
Total	$11,000 (+1,000)	Total	$11,000 (+1,000)

(b) The Banking System's Balance Sheet

ASSETS		LIABILITIES	
Required reserves	$10,100 (+100)	Demand deposits	$101,000 (+1,000)
Excess reserves	$900 (+900)	Fed discount loans	0
		Net worth	0
Loans	90,000		
Total	$101,000 (+1,000)	Total	$101,000 (+1,000)

Now that the Fed has generated $900 in excess reserves in the banking system, these reserves can be transformed by the banking system into new loans to individual and corporate borrowers. The $900 in excess reserves can support an additional $9,000 in deposits. This happens as follows. After the banking system receives the $900 increase in reserves, it lends $9,000 to borrowers by establishing $9,000 in checking accounts for them. This increases the total demand deposits and the outstanding loans in the system by $9,000. Since the new deposits require an additional $900 in reserves, there are no longer any excess reserves in the system. Table 3.4 shows the new situation.

This example shows how the Fed can increase the money supply (demand deposits in our example) by simply purchasing government securities in the open market. The Fed can exercise this magic because it has the unique ability of issuing claims against itself. A similar increase in the money supply can be obtained if a member of the banking system obtains a discount loan from the Fed, as the following section shows.

The Money Supply and Discount Loans Suppose that after the transactions described in the previous section, the Fed grants new discount loans for a total of $5,000 to the banking system. The Fed does not actually give money to the borrowing institutions; instead, it increases by $5,000 their reserve accounts, and at the same time it increases by $5,000 the Fed's discount loans asset account. The banking system registers the transaction as an increase of $5,000 in excess reserves and records the $5,000 discount loan as a liability in the system's balance sheet. The changes produced by the Fed's $5,000 discount loan to the balance sheets of the Fed and the banking system are shown in Table 3.5.

Table 3.4
Balance Sheets After the Banking System Eliminates the Excess Reserves Generated by the Purchase of Government Securities

(a) The Fed's Balance Sheet

ASSETS		LIABILITIES	
Government securities	$11,000	Reserve deposits	$11,000
Discount loans	0	Net worth	0
Total	$11,000	Total	$11,000

(b) The Banking System's Balance Sheet

ASSETS		LIABILITIES	
Required reserves	$11,000	Demand deposits	$110,000
	(+900)		(+9,000)
Excess reserves	0	Fed discount loans	0
	(−900)	Net worth	0
Loans	99,000		
	(+9,000)		
Total	$110,000	Total	$110,000
	(+9,000)		(+9,000)

As in the case of open market operations, the $5,000 excess reserves in the banking system can be used to support $50,000 additional loans on the banking system's assets and the same amount of new deposits on the liability side of the balance sheet, under the assumption of a 10 percent required reserve ratio. The new deposits require a 10 percent reserve, so there are no longer any excess reserves in the system. The final situation is shown in Table 3.6. Clearly, whether the Fed provides reserves through an open market operation or through discount loans, the money supply effect on the banking system is the same.

The Money Multiplier

The examples in the previous section make it clear that each additional dollar of reserves injected into the banking system can support ten dollars of additional demand deposits. More generally, the total amount of demand deposits in the system depends on both the total reserves supplied by the Fed and on the required reserve ratio. If we let D represent demand deposits, R represent total reserves in the banking system, and r represent the required reserve ratio, then the following relationship must hold:

$$D = \frac{1}{r} R \tag{3.4}$$

The term $1/r$ in Equation 3.4 is defined as the **money multiplier**, the ratio of demand deposits to required reserves when the system has no excess reserves. In our example, the money

Table 3.5
Balance Sheets After the Fed Grants a Discount Loan to the Banking System

(a) The Fed's Balance Sheet

ASSETS		LIABILITIES	
Government securities	$11,000	Reserve deposits	$16,000 (+5,000)
Discount loans	$5,000 (+5,000)	Net worth	0
Total	$16,000 (+5,000)	Total	$16,000 (+5,000)

(b) The Banking System's Balance Sheet

ASSETS		LIABILITIES	
Required reserves	$11,000	Demand deposits	$110,000
Excess reserves	$5,000 (+5,000)	Fed discount loans	$5,000 (+5,000)
Loans	$99,000	Net worth	0
Total	$115,000 (+5,000)	Total	$115,000 (+5,000)

multiplier is equal to $1/0.1 = 10$. Even though the example was presented for the case of deposit expansion, it works equally well in the opposite direction. If the Fed had sold government securities, it would have reduced the amount of reserves in the banking system, which would have resulted in the reduction of demand deposits and, thus, in a contraction of the money supply. Equation 3.4 also applies in the case of a monetary contraction.

A Closer Look at the Money Supply Process

Although the process by which an increase in reserves supports a much larger increase in demand deposits seems straightforward, in practice the process follows a lengthy path. This is needed because, in a banking system with many depository institutions, individual institutions should not create new loans in amounts greater than the amount of excess reserves they hold. This cardinal rule is based on the fact that borrowers do not normally leave the proceeds of loans idle for long. They use the funds to buy cars, to purchase new homes, and so on. In other words, the lending depository institution knows that the demand deposits created by the loans will disappear from the lending bank as soon as the borrower writes a check against those funds.[8] Once this happens, the excess reserves will also vanish because the Fed will clear the check by reducing that depository institution's reserve account.

How, then, does the banking system generate the multiplier effect, given that the excess reserves created by the Fed are short-lived? Table 3.7 illustrates this process. Suppose the Fed pur-

[8] We assume that the check cut by the borrower will be deposited at another depository institution. This is not a critical assumption, however.

Table 3.6
Balance Sheets After the Banking System Eliminates the Excess Reserves Generated by the Discount Loan

(a) The Fed's Balance Sheet

ASSETS		LIABILITIES	
Government securities	$11,000	Reserve deposits	$16,000
Discount loans	$5,000	Net worth	0
Total	$16,000	Total	$16,000

(b) The Banking System's Balance Sheet

ASSETS		LIABILITIES	
Required reserves	$16,000	Demand deposits	$160,000
	(+5,000)		(+50,000)
Excess reserves	0	Fed discount loans	5,000
	(–5,000)	Net worth	0
Loans	$149,000		
	(+50,000)		
Total	$165,000	Total	$165,000
	(50,000)		(+50,000)

chases $1,000 of government securities through an open market operation. When the seller of the securities deposits the Fed's check at Bank Uno and the check is cleared by the Fed, Bank Uno's reserves and demand deposits increase by $1,000. Bank Uno then decides to give a new loan of $900 to Julio, an amount equal to the excess reserves it holds after the $1,000 deposit is made. Bank Uno makes the $900 loan to Julio effective by increasing his demand deposit account at Bank Uno.

Being an avid audio buff, Julio decides to purchase a new stereo system that costs $900 at Wayne's Audio World, paying for it with a check against his demand deposit account at Bank Uno. Wayne deposits the $900 check in Bank Twain, which sends the check to be cleared by the Fed. Clearing the check means that the Fed adds $900 to Bank Twain's reserve account and subtracts the same $900 from Bank Uno's reserve account. Simultaneously, Julio's demand deposits at Bank Uno decrease by $900, and Wayne's demand deposit account at Bank Twain increases by the same amount, as Table 3.7 shows. To simplify, we assume that Bank Twain has zero reserves and zero demand deposits before this transaction. At this point, Bank Uno has reached equilibrium, with $100 in required reserves supporting the securities seller's $1,000 in demand deposits, and no excess reserves. Bank Twain, however, is not in an equilibrium situation, as it has $900 in total reserves, of which $90 are required and $810 are excess reserves.

Focusing on Bank Twain, it is clear that it should lend its excess reserves exactly as Bank Uno did. When Bank Twain lends the $810, its required reserves would increase to $171 ($90 + $81) and it would still have excess reserves of $729, but only as long as whoever borrows the $729 does not spend the loan funds. At this point the process repeats itself exactly as described previously, with the check for $729 being deposited at another bank, say, Bank Trois.

This process continues forever, in principle, with each successive loan and corresponding increase in demand deposits 10 percent smaller than the previous one. Thus, in equilibrium, an

Table 3.7
The Money Creation Process

(1) Bank Uno receives $1,000 in additional reserves from the Fed:

BANK UNO

Reserves		$1,000	Demand deposits		$1,000
Required	100		Securities' seller	1,000	
Excess	900				
Loans		0			

(2) Bank Uno generates a $900 loan to Julio, supported by its excess reserves:

BANK UNO

Reserves		$1,000	Demand deposits		$1,900
Required	190		Securities' seller	1,000	
Excess	810		Julio	900	
Loans		900			

(3) Julio buys a stereo for $900 from Wayne's Audio World. Wayne deposits the check at Bank Twain:

BANK UNO

Reserves		$1,000	Demand deposits		$1,000
Required	100		Securities' seller	1,000	
Excess	0		Julio	0	
Loans		900			

BANK TWAIN

Reserves		$900	Demand deposits		$900
Required	90		Wayne	900	
Excess	810				
Loans	0				

(4) Bank Twain makes a $810 loan to another borrower:

BANK TWAIN

Reserves		$900	Demand deposits		$1,710
Required	171		Wayne	900	
Excess	729		Borrower	810	
Loans		810			

initial injection of $1,000 in reserves into Bank Uno generates demand deposits of $1,000 in Bank Uno, $900 in Bank Twain ($1,000 × 0.9), $810 in Bank Trois ($900 × 0.9), $729 in Bank Quatro, and so on. To find the total effect on the money supply of the $1,000 in reserves added by the Fed to the banking system, it suffices to add all of the demand deposits generated in equilibrium by each of the banks in the system. The sum is:[9]

[9] The sum in parentheses is a well-known type of summation called a geometric series. In the limit, we have $1 + x + x^2 + x^3 + \ldots = 1/(1 - x)$. Thus, if $x = 0.9$, as in the example, the required summation is $\$1,000[1/(1 - 0.9)] = \$1,000 \times 10 = \$10,000$.

$$\begin{aligned} \text{Total Deposits} &= \$1{,}000 + \$900 + \$810 + 729 + \ldots \\ &= \$1{,}000(1 + 0.9 + 0.81 + 0.729 + \ldots) \\ &= \$1{,}000 \times 10 \\ &= \$10{,}000 \end{aligned}$$

Although the actual process needed to create money is rather involved, we confirm the simple fact that if the required reserve ratio is 10 percent, an injection of $1,000 additional reserves into the banking system will eventually translate into an additional money supply of $10,000. This is exactly the same result described by Equation 3.4.

Money Creation and Expansion: A Detailed Model

So far in our discussion, it seems as though the Fed has total control over the money supply. All that we need to determine the equilibrium amount of demand deposits in the economy is to know the required reserve ratio and the amount of reserves. In fact, the actual process of creating money is not so simple. For example, what if Julio, the audio aficionado, decides to keep $100 of the $900 loan he got from Bank Uno in the form of cash in his wallet. In that case, the process described by the simple model would no longer hold exactly, and the economy would not end up with $10,000 in additional demand deposits as a result of the Fed's action of increasing reserves by $1,000.

Furthermore, the simple model assumes that all of the excess reserves will be transformed into loans. In practice, depository institutions retain a small fraction of their excess reserves so that they don't have to scramble too often to meet required reserves when demand deposits increase unexpectedly.

These considerations clearly suggest that the money creation process involves more players than just the Fed. Specifically, the behavior of individuals and depository institutions also affects the ultimate amount of money in the economy. While the simple model considered in the previous section describes the essence of the money creation process, this section provides a richer model that better explains the actual behavior of money.

The Monetary Base

In the simple model of money creation, we saw that reserves were used to create money. In the more complete model to be developed, we will use the more general concept of the **monetary base** or **high-powered money**. The monetary base (B) is the sum of reserves (R) and total currency in circulation (C). Currency includes coins and Federal Reserve notes, or paper money. Thus:

$$B = R + C \tag{3.5}$$

Economists prefer to think in terms of the monetary base, rather than in terms of reserves alone, because open market operations or discount loans by the Fed affect the monetary base more directly than reserves. To see this, suppose that the Fed buys $1,000 worth of securities in the open market. As before, the seller receives a check for this amount against the Fed. In the simple model, the securities' seller had no alternative but to deposit the check in a checking account. In practice, however, the seller has another option: The Fed's check can be cashed for currency. In this case, the Fed's holdings of securities increase by $1,000 from the purchase of the securities, and there is an increase of $1,000 in the amount of currency in circulation. When the check is cashed for currency, reserves in the banking system do not change. Nevertheless, the effect of the Fed's open market purchase on the monetary base is certain: It will increase by exactly $1,000. It is now clear that the Fed has much better control of the monetary base than of total reserves.

Unfortunately, while the Fed can control open market operations, it cannot completely control the amount of discount loans the banking system will demand from the Fed's discount window. Of course, the Fed can exert some control over discount loans by varying the discount rate, but it can never predict with certainty how much depository institutions will decide to borrow.

The above considerations suggest distinguishing two components of the monetary base, one under complete control of the Fed and the other under partial control. The **nonborrowed monetary base** (N) is the component that results from the Fed's open market operations and is thus under much tighter control by the Fed. The other component of the monetary base is the discount loans (L) from the Fed. Thus:

$$B = N + L \tag{3.6}$$

We can now derive a model of the variables affecting the money multiplier. In the simple model, the required reserve ratio set by the Fed fully determined the money multiplier. In practice, the multiplier depends also on the public's desire to hold currency and on the depository institution's willingness to retain excess reserves. We develop the effect of these variables on the multiplier in the following section.

Variables Affecting the Money Multiplier

We have seen that individuals might want to hold currency in addition to demand deposits and that the banking system usually has some excess reserves. To model these variables as components of the money multiplier, we will make the assumption that currency in circulation and excess reserves in the banking system vary in direct proportion to the amount of total demand deposits. Let c be the ratio of currency in circulation (C) to demand deposits (D), and let e be the ratio of excess reserves (E) to demand deposits. Then, we have:

$$c = \frac{C}{D} \tag{3.7}$$

$$e = \frac{E}{D} \tag{3.8}$$

To begin, we note the identity that total reserves (R) in the system equal required reserves (Q) plus excess reserves (E):

$$R = Q + E \tag{3.9}$$

Since we will prefer to work with the monetary base, rather than reserves, in our derivation of the money multiplier we can add currency in circulation (C) to both sides of Equation 3.9. Recalling the definition of the monetary base as $B = R + C$, we obtain:

$$B = Q + E + C \tag{3.10}$$

We have seen previously that required reserves are calculated as a fixed percentage of demand deposits. If the required reserve ratio is r, then the level of required reserves is $R = r \times D$. Furthermore, we have also assumed that currency in circulation and excess reserves are directly tied to demand deposits, as shown in Equations 3.7 and 3.8. Therefore, Equation 3.10 can be rewritten as follows:

$$\begin{aligned} B &= r \times D + e \times D + c \times D \\ &= (r + e + c)\, D \end{aligned} \tag{3.11}$$

or, expressing demand deposits as a function of the monetary base, we have:

$$D = \frac{1}{(r + e + c)} B \tag{3.12}$$

If we now define money (M) as currency plus demand deposits, we have $M = C + D = (1 + c)D$. Using the demand deposit (D) equation given in Equation 3.12, we obtain the long-sought relationship that connects the monetary base and the money supply:

$$M = \frac{1 + c}{(r + e + c)} B \tag{3.13}$$

It is apparent from Equation 3.13 that the money multiplier (m) can be defined as:

$$m = \frac{1 + c}{(r + e + c)} \tag{3.14}$$

According to Equation 3.14, the money multiplier depends on three parameters: the required reserve ratio, the excess reserves ratio, and the currency ratio. Notice that this more complete version of the money multiplier is influenced by two parameters not considered in the simple version given in Equation 3.4, $m = 1/r$.

Example In the U.S. economy, the highest required reserve ratio on deposits is $r = 0.12$. Also, in recent years the excess reserves ratio has been about $e = 0.002$, and the currency ratio is about $c = 0.4$. Compute the maximum possible money multiplier for the U.S. economy, as well as the more realistic money multiplier.

Using Equation 3.4, we obtain the maximum possible value of the money multiplier:

$$m = \frac{1}{0.12} = 8.33$$

To obtain a number closer to the actual money multiplier, we use Equation 3.14:

$$m = \frac{1 + 0.4}{0.12 + 0.002 + 0.4} = 2.68$$

This example illustrates that the actual money multiplier is significantly lower than the upper bound for the money multiplier. Recall that the simple multiplier assumes that any action by the Fed will be completely and efficiently converted into deposit expansion. In reality, however, we know that some of the additional reserves created by the Fed will end up as currency and as excess reserves. In the example, these real-world "inefficiencies" cause the actual multiplier to be only about one-third of its maximum possible value. The value of 2.68 that we obtained is very close to the actual money multiplier. The actual money multiplier has fluctuated between 2.65 and 2.9 over recent years.

Changes in the Money Supply

Now that we have found the functional relationship between the money multiplier and the parameters that affect it, we can ask how the money supply will change as each of its component parameters changes. We can use calculus on Equation 3.13 to compute these effects.[10]

Changes in the Currency Ratio When individuals want to hold more currency relative to demand deposits, the currency ratio (c) increases and the money multiplier changes. The following expression shows how a change in the currency ratio, Δc, will affect the level of money in the economy.

$$\Delta M = -\frac{[1 - (r + e)]M}{(r + e + c)(1 + c)}(\Delta c) \tag{3.15}$$

Although Equation 3.15 seems menacing, we are mostly interested in focusing on the intuition it provides. First, the minus sign right after the equal sign indicates that an increase in the currency ratio ($\Delta c > 0$) will result in a negative effect on the money supply ($\Delta M < 0$). More generally, a change in the currency ratio produces an opposite change in the money supply. Second, the effect of any change in the currency ratio depends on the amount of money (M) prior to the change. The greater the original money supply, the greater the effect of a change in the currency ratio.

---

[10] The process required to obtain the formulas that follow is called **differentiation**. The formulas are valid only for infinitesimal changes in the parameter being considered. Therefore, when the formula is applied to a relatively large, or discrete, change, the formula will produce a slight error, which is usually negligible.

Example If individuals in the United States decide that they want to hold a greater amount of money in the form of currency, so that the currency ratio changes from $c = 0.4$ to $c' = 0.5$, what effect will this change have on the money supply? The other parameters for the U.S. economy are $r = 0.12$ and $e = 0.002$. Also, the money supply (M1) before the change is $952 billion.

Using Equation 3.15, we compute the estimated effect:

$$\Delta M = -\frac{[1 - (0.12 + 0.002)]\$952 \text{ billion}}{(0.12 + 0.002 + 0.4)(1 + 0.4)}(0.1)$$

$$= -\$114.38 \text{ billion}$$

The 0.10 increase in the currency ratio will result in a reduction of about $114 billion in the money supply.

Changes in the Required Reserves Ratio The Fed seldom changes the required reserves ratio (r). When it does, however, the effect is to change the money supply in the opposite direction. Thus, an increase in the required reserve ratio is a way for the Fed to contract the money supply. This is seen analytically in the following expression:

$$\Delta M = -\frac{M}{(r + e + c)}(\Delta r) \qquad (3.16)$$

Once again, the change is affected positively by the level of money (M) prior to the change. It is also affected negatively by the sum of the parameters of the model (r, e, c).

Example Let us use the same parameters as in the previous example. Assume now that the Fed decides to stimulate the economy by decreasing the required reserve ratio to $r' = 0.10$, so $\Delta r = -0.02$. What effect will this change have on the money supply?

To answer the question, we apply the data for the U.S. economy to Equation 3.16:

$$\Delta M = -\frac{\$952 \text{ billion}}{0.12 + 0.002 + 0.4}(-0.02)$$

$$= \$36.475 \text{ billion}$$

Thus, the Fed's action will increase the money supply by more than $36 billion.

Changes in the Excess Reserves Ratio Interestingly, the expression for a change in the excess reserves ratio has the same form as the effect of a change in the required reserves ratio:

$$\Delta M = -\frac{M}{(r + e + c)}(\Delta e) \qquad (3.17)$$

A decrease in the excess reserves ratio produces an increase in the money supply. This result is not surprising since, as the banking system utilizes more fully its available excess reserves to create loans, the money multiplier increases, and its effect on the money supply is greater.

Example Using the same parameters for the U.S. economy as in the previous two examples, let us calculate the effect of a change in the excess reserves ratio of $\Delta e = +0.0005$. Applying Equation 3.17, we get:

$$\Delta M = -\frac{\$952 \text{ billion}}{0.12 + 0.002 + 0.4}(0.0005)$$

$$= -\ \$0.91 \text{ billion}$$

Notice that although the assumed change represents a 25 percent increase over the current level of excess reserves, its effect on the money supply is less than \$1 billion. We conclude that the money supply is not very sensitive to changes in the excess reserves ratio.

Summary

This chapter has presented a detailed view of the process used by the Fed to create money. Many items have been used as money in the past: gold, silver, pearls, and even tobacco. Whatever is used as money, it must have the capability of being used as a medium of exchange and as a unit of account, and it must retain its purchasing power through time.

Surprisingly, even today there is still no consensus of what exactly constitutes money. Of course, currency is money, and so are checkable demand deposits as well as traveler's checks. In addition, some argue that other, less liquid assets are also money. Because of this, several definitions of money are in use. These are, from more to less liquid, M1, M2, M3, and L. Each of the definitions contains the previous one as a subset.

The chapter also presented a brief discussion of the concept of velocity – the ratio of gross national product to the amount of money in the economy. This concept is important because its behavior can serve to guide the Fed's money-creation policy. For instance, in the mid-1980s the Fed abandoned M1 as its main monetary policy guide in favor of M2 because the behavior of the latter's velocity is much more stable and predictable.

Since the creation of money requires that it be kept in depository institutions, we analyzed the advantages to society of doing so. We concluded that aside from the obvious benefit of safety, some individuals are better off and no one is worse off with the existence of depository institutions.

We analyzed the mechanics of the money creation and expansion process. Using a simple idealized model, we found that whenever the Fed creates new reserves, banks use them to generate new loans, which in turn generate new demand deposits. Thus, the Fed's initial action of creating reserves is transformed by the banking system into money. In the process, money is multiplied. For instance, if the required reserve ratio is 10 percent, one dollar of additional reserves may increase the money supply by \$10. For this to happen, the banking system must utilize all excess reserves and the public must not demand currency. However, in practice this is not usually the case. Therefore, an addition of one dollar of reserves usually leads to much less money creation than the idealized model indicates.

Finally, we derived an expression for the money multiplier in terms of the required reserve ratio, the currency ratio, and the excess reserves ratio. Using this expression, we investigated the effect that a change in each of the parameters of the money multiplier would have on the money supply.

Questions and Problems

1. What properties must any item used as money have?
2. Which of the following might serve well as money: bananas, finance textbooks, automobiles, personal computers? Explain.
3. Why is M1 the most liquid definition of money?
4. Why is L the least liquid definition of money?
5. Graphically, how could you characterize the essence of the relationship between M1, M2, M3, and L?
6. Define money velocity.
7. How many definitions of money velocity can you think of?
8. In principle, what would happen to velocity if all workers were paid every two weeks rather than every month?
9. Why does the Fed focus more on M2 than on M1 since the 1980s?
10. Why do most people and firms keep their money in depository institutions?
11. What is intermediation?
12. Why is asymmetric information in society important for the existence of banks?
13. Explain briefly how money is created when the Fed buys $1,000 in government securities in the open market.
14. Explain briefly how money is created when the Fed gives a depository institution a discount loan for $5,000.
15. How are the money multiplier and the required reserve ratio related in the simple model of money creation?
16. A depository institution should never create new loans in amounts greater than its excess reserves. Why?
17. Explain why the monetary base is a more general concept than reserves.
18. Why do economists prefer to use the monetary base rather than just reserves as a guide to monetary policy?

19. If the country of Lugo has a money velocity of 6 and its money supply is \$600 billion, what is Lugo's gross national product (GNP)?

20. If the GNP and the money supply in the tiny country of San Blas increase by 5 percent, by how much will its money velocity change?

21. If the GNP and the money supply in the tiny country of San Blas increase by \$5 billion, by how much will its money velocity change?

22. You are considering giving a \$1,000, one-year, 10 percent loan to someone who has a probability of full repayment of 80 percent. If the borrower defaults, you receive nothing. What are your expected profits? Should you grant the loan?

23. You are considering giving a \$1,000, one-year, 50 percent loan to someone who has a probability of full repayment of 80 percent. If the borrower defaults, you receive nothing. What are your expected profits? Should you grant the loan?

24. You are considering giving a \$1,000, one-year loan to someone who has a probability of full repayment of 60 percent. If the borrower defaults, you receive nothing. What interest rate should you charge if you want an expected profit of \$100 at the end of the year?

25. Using the simple money creation model, how much money in the form of demand deposits will \$1,000 support if the required reserve ratio is 3 percent?

26. Using the simple money creation model, how much money in the form of demand deposits will \$1,000 support if the required reserve ratio is 12 percent?

27. Modify the simple model and suppose that the required reserve ratio (r) is directly proportional to the amount of reserves in the banking system (R). What effect would the Fed's action of increasing reserves have on the money supply?

28. Modify the simple model and suppose that the required reserve ratio (r) is directly proportional to the square of the amount of reserves in the banking system (R). What effect would the Fed's action of increasing reserves have on the money supply?

29. What is the result of adding $1 + 0.5 + 0.25 + 0.125 + \ldots$? What does this have to do with the money supply, anyway?

30. If the banking system in the country of Mahagua has \$1 billion in reserves and has \$2 billion in currency in circulation, how much high-powered money is there in Mahagua?

31. In the detailed money creation model, suppose that the required reserve ratio is 0.12 and that the excess reserve ratio is 0.001. What is the currency ratio if the money multiplier is equal to 4?

32. Using the data of Problem 31, find the monetary base if the money supply is equal to \$100 billion.

33. Using the data of Problem 31, what would the money multiplier be in the detailed model if required reserves were 0 percent?

34. What would the money multiplier be in the simple model if required reserves were 0 percent?

For Problems 35 to 40 assume that $r = 0.10$, $e = 0.003$, $c = 0.5$, and $M = \$500$ billion. Use the detailed money creation model.

35. What is the effect on the money supply of a change of 0.0001 in the currency ratio?
36. Now suppose that a few months after the currency ratio increase of the previous problem, the currency ratio decreases by 0.0001. What is the new level of money supply? Is it the same as the initial value? What's going on?
37. What is the effect on the money supply of a change of 0.02 in the required reserves ratio?
38. Now suppose that, a few months after the required reserves ratio increase of the previous problem, the ratio increases again by an additional 0.01. What is the new level of money supply?
39. What is the effect on the money supply of a single change of 0.03 in the required reserves ratio (from its initial value of 0.1)?
40. Compare the results of the two previous problems. Why do the results differ?

Suggested REALDATA Exercises

The following *REALDATA* exercises explore the concepts developed in this chapter:
Exercises 1–4, 7–14

References

Altig, D., "An Ebbing Tide Lowers All Boats: Monetary Policy, Inflation, and Social Justice," *Economic Review*, Federal Reserve Bank of Cleveland, Second Quarter 1992, pp. 14–22.

Anderson, Richard G., "Symposium on Mutual Funds and Monetary Aggregates," *Economic Review*, Federal Reserve Bank of St. Louis, 76:6, November/December 1994, pp. 3–78.

Carlson, J. B. and S. M. Byrne, "Recent Behavior of Velocity: Alternative Measures of Money," *Economic Review*, Federal Reserve Bank of Cleveland, First Quarter 1992, pp. 2–10.

Duca, J. V., "The Case of the Missing M2," *Economic Review*, Federal Reserve Bank of Dallas, Second Quarter 1992, pp. 1–24.

Higgins, Byron, "Policy Implications of Recent M2 Behavior," *Economic Review*, Federal Reserve Bank of Kansas City, Third Quarter 1992, pp. 21–36.

Kretzmer, P. E., "Monetary vs. Fiscal Policy: New Evidence on an Old Debate," *Economic Review*, Federal Reserve Bank of Kansas City, Second Quarter 1992, pp. 21–30.

Leeper, E. M., "Facing Up to Our Ignorance about Measuring Monetary Policy Effects," *Economic Review*, Federal Reserve Bank of Atlanta, May/June 1992, pp. 1–16.

Meulendyke, A. M., "U.S. Monetary Policy and Financial Markets," Federal Reserve Bank of New York, 1989.

Parry, Robert T., "Monetary Policy in the 1990s," *Weekly Letter*, Federal Reserve Bank of San Francisco, March 4, 1994, pp. 1–3.

Roberds, W., "What Hath the Fed Wrought? Interest Rate Smoothing in Theory and Practice," *Economic Review*, Federal Reserve Bank of Atlanta, January/February 1992, pp. 12–24.

Smith, S. D. and L. D. Wall, "Financial Panics, Bank Failures, and the Role of Regulatory Policy," Federal Reserve Bank of Atlanta, January/February 1992, pp. 1–11.

Wheelock, D. C., "Monetary Policy in the Great Depression: What the Fed Did, and Why," *Review*, The Federal Reserve Bank of St. Louis, March/April 1992, pp. 3–28.

Part 2

Financial Markets and the Economy

Part 2 of this book explores the financial markets. These chapters acquaint the reader with the overall structure of securities markets and introduce some of the basic concepts necessary for a full understanding of our modern financial system. Chapter 4 focuses on the debt market, clearly distinguishing between the money and bond markets. Chapter 4 discusses firms, financial institutions, and the government, which are all major participants in the money market; the chapter also introduces the basic principles of bond valuation. As the chapter explains, the price of a bond is essentially the present value of the bond's promised payments.

Chapter 5 introduces the rights and obligations associated with common stock ownership and explores the institutional features of the stock market in the United States. The chapter focuses on the market for already existing shares, such as the most familiar stock market, the New York Stock Exchange. The organization of the U.S. stock market has changed radically in the last 15 years and gives every sign of further evolution. The market's recent history has been one of greater fragmentation in some respects, accompanied by greater integration in others. For example, major market movements have diminished the power of exchanges such as the New York Stock Exchange and have spread the trading of stocks across a broader spectrum of competing markets. The chapter also introduces the basic principles of stock valuation. Essentially, the value of a share of stock equals the present value of all cash flows to come from the share of stock.

A **financial derivative** is a financial instrument the value of which depends on the value of some more basic or primitive financial instrument. For example, an option on a share of stock is a financial derivative because the value of a stock option depends on the value of the underlying stock. Options and other financial derivatives are explored in Chapter 6. The principal financial drivatives are: forward contracts, futures contracts, options, and swap agreements. Financial derivatives have so many uses that the student of financial institutions must take them into account to fully understand the operations of depository and non-depository financial institutions and financial intermediaries generally. In addition to an overview of these markets, this chapter provides an introduction to the pricing of these instruments and the way that they can be used to manage financial risk.

In Chapter 7, we consider the factors that influence the level of interest rates, and we see why expected inflation is one of the most important of these. The chapter also considers the term structure of interest rates – the relationship between the maturity and yield of bonds that are similar in risk level. Finally, Chapter 7 considers the risk structure of interest rates, the yield differentials arising from differences in default risk for bonds that are similar in maturity and other respects.

Chapter 8 discusses the primary market – the market for the creation and original issuance of securities. The primary market is extremely important to firms because corporations raise the new capital necessary for the conduct of their businesses by issuing securities in the primary market. Only after a share or bond has been created in the primary market can it trade in the more familiar secondary market.

Chapter 9 considers what is perhaps the most fundamental concept in finance – the relationship between expected return and risk. As the chapter indicates, risk can be controlled by diversifying, and compensation for bearing risk is intimately tied to the management of diversified portfolios. The chapter also explores the Capital Asset Pricing Model, a theory that consistently relates the riskiness of a security to its price.

The Debt Market: An Overview

4

Overview

This chapter explores the institutional features of the debt market. The prices of all debt instruments depend on the payments that are promised by the issuer and the market conditions that determine the value of those promised payments. This chapter examines the valuation of debt instruments by introducing the bond pricing formula, a pricing relationship relating yields, prices, and promised payments on bonds. The relationships captured by the bond pricing formula hold for all debt instruments.

It is traditional to divide the debt market into two segments – the money market and the bond market. The money market is composed of those debt instruments that are issued with a maturity of one year or less. All debt instruments originally issued with maturities greater than one year are considered to be bonds. This chapter considers instruments in both the money and bond markets.

Our discussion of the money market considers some special methods for calculating yields and concludes with a survey of the more important types of money market instruments. In the money market, as in the bond market, different instruments have different levels of risk, and the expected returns offered by a given instrument reflect those risk differences. As we turn specifically to the bond market, we apply the principles of bond pricing to coupon bonds. The discussion then turns to the structure and composition of the bond market. We first focus on the bond market in the United States, which consists of the market for federal debt, the corporate bond market, and the municipal bond market. In discussing these different segments of the bond market, we examine the institutional features that distinguish each kind of bond from the other. Having surveyed the bond market, we also consider the mortgage market. As the discussion shows, we may profitably think of home mortgages as a special type of bond.

When a corporate issuer attempts to sell a bond to the public, there is always a bond contract. This contract specifies all of the promises that the issuer makes to induce the investor to lend money. As the discussion illustrates, the bond contract itself reveals much about the kind of bond that is being offered and the special provisions that the firm includes to make the bond attractive to the investing public.

Having considered the U.S. bond market in some detail, the chapter concludes with an overview of the international bond market. In general, the instruments used in the international market differ in important respects from the most common instruments in the U.S. market. For example, international bonds are issued in many different currencies, and international bonds typically make much broader use of floating rate debt instruments.

The Valuation of Debt Instruments

Chapter 1 introduced the basic concepts of borrowing and lending. This section elaborates the idea of return on investment in the context of the pricing of debt instruments. Debt instruments can be categorized as pure discount instruments or as coupon bonds. This section explores the algebra of bond pricing by examining the simpler case of pure discount instruments, which are quite common in the money market.

Pure Discount Instruments

To illustrate the idea of the pricing relationship, consider a straightforward type of debt security called a **pure discount bond**. This bond promises a certain single payment at a specified time in the future and is sold for less than this promised future payment. This type of security is simple in structure, yet it is important in the debt market. For example, many money market instruments, such as Treasury bills, are pure discount bonds. Normally, the promised future payment is the **par value** or **face value** of the bond – the final promised payment on a bond. The difference between the par value and the selling price is the **bond discount**. Such a security is a **pure discount bond**, because there is no payment between the original issue of the bond and the maturity of the bond when it pays its face value.

The price of a pure discount bond can be expressed as a function of the par value, the yield on the security, and the time until it matures:

$$P = \frac{C_m}{(1 + r)^t} \tag{4.1}$$

where:

P = the price of the instrument
C_m = the cash flow to be paid when the bond matures at time m
r = the annualized yield to maturity on the bond
t = the time in years until the bond matures

As an example, consider a pure discount bond that matures in five years and has a face value of \$1,000. If the bond has a yield to maturity of 12 percent,[1] its price must be \$567.43:

$$P = \frac{\$1{,}000}{(1.25)^5} = \$567.43$$

In this simplest kind of bond, the basic features of bond pricing are all present. The promised cash flow, the price, and the yield are all interrelated. The yield to maturity is the yield that will be realized if the promised payment is made. The riskier the promised payment, the higher the promised yield or expected return must be in order to induce investors to hold such bonds.

---

[1] The yield to maturity is the annualized return that would be earned over the life of the bond if all interim cash flows were reinvested at that same yield to maturity.

The Money Market

The **money market** is the market for debt instruments with a maturity of one year or less at the time of issuance. Some money market instruments are available only to certain kinds of financial institutions, but many are widely available to all types of investors. For the most part, instruments of the money market share many family resemblances. Their yields tend to move together and the method of price quotation is common to many of the instruments. After discussing yield quotations common to the money market, this chapter considers some of the most important money market instruments.

Money Market Yield Concepts

In the money market, **interest-bearing instruments** are issued with a given par value and a stated coupon rate. Interest is earned based on that par value and coupon rate. **Discount paper** is a money market instrument that is issued with a stated par value and no coupon rate. Discount paper is sold at a discount below its par value, and because these instruments have no coupons, they are short-term zero coupon bonds, in effect. Discount paper includes Treasury bills, bankers' acceptances, and commercial paper. Certificates of deposit and Eurodollar certificates of deposit are interest-bearing instruments. Conventions for yield quotations and pricing differ between the two types of instruments, so the distinction is quite important.

The Discount Yield Compared to the previous discussion of yields for debt instruments in general, the method of yield calculation and price quotation widely used in the money market is quite different. Many money market securities are quoted in terms of the **discount yield**. The price quotation is expressed in terms of this discount yield, but from this, we must calculate the actual dollar price of the instrument. The formula for the discount yield, *d*, is quite straightforward:

$$d = \left(\frac{360}{t}\right)\left(\frac{DISC}{FV}\right) \tag{4.2}$$

where:

$DISC$ = the dollar discount from the face value
FV = the face value of the instrument
t = the number of days until the instrument matures

The actual dollar price, *P*, depends on the face value and the amount of the dollar discount, *DISC*:

$$P = FV - DISC = FV\left(1 - \frac{(d)\,(t)}{360}\right) \tag{4.3}$$

As an example of the way this system works, consider a 90-day money market instrument with a face value of \$1,000,000 that has a discount yield of 11 percent. The dollar discount, *DISC*, for this instrument would be:

$$DISC = (\$1{,}000{,}000)\left(\frac{(.11)(90)}{360}\right) = \$27{,}500$$

and the actual dollar price would be:

$$P = FV - DISC = \$1{,}000{,}000 - \$27{,}500 = \$972{,}500$$

One feature of the discount yield is its assumption that the year has 360 days. Other yield measures use a year of 365 days. Even if the 360-day year assumption is acceptable, the discount yield still differs considerably from the yield given by the bond pricing formula. For this particular example, the difference is large and typical. Using the bond pricing formula of Equation 4.1, a 90-day pure discount instrument with a face value of \$1,000,000 and a price of \$972,500 would be yielding 11.31 percent:

$$\$972{,}500 = \frac{\$1{,}000{,}000}{(1 + .1131/4)}$$

The Bond Equivalent Yield To compare the yields on money market instruments with other kinds of bonds, it is necessary to get all of the instruments onto the same yield basis. To make discount instruments comparable to bonds, there is a **bond equivalent yield**. For the bond equivalent yield, the idea is to compute a yield that reflects the opportunity that bond market investors have to receive and reinvest semiannual coupon payments. For an instrument with a discount yield maturing in less than six months, the equivalent bond yield, *EBY*, can be given by the following formula:

$$EBY = \frac{(365)\,(d)}{360 - (d)\,(t)} \tag{4.4}$$

For the 90-day instrument used as an example above, the *EBY* would be:

$$EBY = \frac{(365)\,(d)}{360 - (11)\,(90)} = .11468$$

For maturities in excess of six months, the *EBY* is difficult to calculate, but Table 4.1 shows the way in which the discount yield and *EBY* differ. The differences between the discount yield and the bond equivalent yield are larger the higher the interest rate and the longer the time until maturity. In some cases, the difference between the two yields can approach 2 percent, as is the case for a discount yield of 14 percent and a 364-day maturity.

Table 4.1
Discount Yields versus Equivalent Bond Yields

Discount Yields	Equivalent Bond Yields (%)		
	30-day maturity	182-day maturity	364-day maturity
6	6.114	6.274	6.375
8	8.116	8.453	8.639
10	10.227	10.679	10.979
12	12.290	12.952	13.399
14	14.362	15.256	15.904

Source: Marcia Stigum, *The Money Market*, 3rd ed., Homewood, IL: Dow Jones Books, 1990, p. 49.

Major Money Market Instruments

Treasury Auctions Each week, the U.S. Treasury auctions Treasury bills in the money market. Some weeks the auction includes the sale of Treasury notes and bonds as well. Purchasers bid for the new securities by offering either competitive or noncompetitive bids through one of the 12 Federal Reserve Banks. In a competitive bid, the bidder specifies the amount of bills desired and the yield at which it is willing to accept them. Investors may also submit noncompetitive bids. In a noncompetitive bid, the securities are awarded at a yield that equals the average of the competitive bids. Large bond trading firms and bond dealers typically make competitive bids, while individual investors almost always specify noncompetitive bids.

The Federal Reserve transmits the collected bids to the Treasury Department, which takes account of the noncompetitive amount of securities desired. The Treasury then awards the securities to the competitive bidders offering the lowest yield (highest price). The noncompetitive bidders receive their securities at the average of the accepted competitive bids, and competitive bids are honored until the Treasury exhausts the amount it wishes to sell. Individuals can submit their own bids directly to a Federal Reserve Bank or through a regular securities broker. The largest amount that can be awarded to any single noncompetitive bidder is $1 million face value.

Treasury Bills One of the most important kinds of securities in the money market that is based on a discount yield is the **Treasury bill**. T-bills are obligations of the U.S. Treasury that are issued weekly with a maturity of 91 and 182 days. T-bills with a 52-week maturity are offered monthly. There are occasional additional offerings. Normally, auctions are held on Mondays, with bids being submitted before 1:30 p.m. Delivery normally takes place on the following Thursday. The bills have a minimum denomination of $10,000 and go up from that minimum in increments of $5,000.[2] Currently, there are more than $600 billion worth of T-bills outstanding, with daily trading volume exceeding $35 billion. As such, T-bills represent one of the most important instru-

[2] For more details on T-bills and the full range of money market securities, there are two excellent sources: Timothy Q. Cook and Bruce J. Summers, *Instruments of the Money Market*, 6th ed., Richmond, VA: Federal Reserve Bank of Richmond, 1986, and Marcia Stigum, *The Money Market*, 3rd ed., Homewood, IL: Dow Jones Books, 1990, p. 49.

ments of the money market. Further, since they are instruments issued by the U.S. Treasury, they also have the lowest yields, as Figure 4.1 indicates.

Figure 4.2 presents the quotations from *The Wall Street Journal*, which reports trading for the preceding business day. The bills are arranged in order of ascending maturity in the first column. The next two columns present the quotations, which are given as discount yields. Since these are yields, the bid quotation is greater than the asked quotation, but the bid price is naturally less than the asked price. One might read the bid quotation as an offer to pay an amount that will give a certain discount yield. In addition to the bid and asked yield quotations, the last column gives the bond equivalent yield. It is computed according to Equation 4.4, using the asked discount yield.

Commercial Paper Another important money market instrument is **commercial paper**, which also uses the discount yield method of quotation. Commercial paper consists of short-term debt obligations of industrial and financial firms. To escape the requirement of registering with the Securities and Exchange Commission (SEC), the maturity cannot exceed 270 days. The issuer of commercial paper promises to pay the holder a given fixed amount on a certain day in the future. The commercial paper is sold at a discount from that promised future payment. The issuer offers no collateral, except the firm's good faith and credit. By 1995, about $600 billion of commercial paper was outstanding. Most of the commercial paper continues to be issued by financial companies. Some of the particularly big issuers of commercial paper are the finance subsidiaries of American auto makers (e.g., General Motors Acceptance Corporation) and the major money center banks of New York (e.g., Citibank). One good source for yield quotations on commercial paper, as well as for other money market instruments, is the daily column in *The Wall Street*

Figure 4.1
Normal Yield Relationships in the Money Market

Very Short Maturity Instruments	
higher yields	Fed funds
lower yields	Repurchase aggreements
Longer Maturity Instruments	
higher yields	Eurodollar CDS Domestic CDs Bankers' acceptances Commercial paper
lower yields	Treasury bills

Figure 4.2
Quotations for Treasury Bills

TREASURY BILLS

Maturity	Days to Mat.	Bid	Asked	Chg.	Ask Yld.
Mar 30 '95	0	5.75	5.65	+0.19	0.00
Apr 06 '95	7	5.77	5.67	+0.10	5.76
Apr 13 '95	14	5.78	5.68	+0.14	5.77
Apr 20 '95	21	5.88	5.78	+0.19	5.88
Apr 27 '95	28	5.72	5.62	+0.08	5.72
May 04 '95	35	5.73	5.69	+0.06	5.80
May 11 '95	42	5.72	5.68	+0.06	5.80
May 18 '95	49	5.73	5.69	+0.09	5.81
May 25 '95	56	5.71	5.67	+0.06	5.80
Jun 01 '95	63	5.72	5.70	+0.06	5.84
Jun 08 '95	70	5.72	5.70	+0.06	5.84
Jun 15 '95	77	5.73	5.71	+0.08	5.86
Jun 22 '95	84	5.73	5.71	+0.07	5.87
Jun 29 '95	**91**	**5.71**	**5.69**	**+0.07**	**5.85**
Jul 06 '95	98	5.75	5.73	+0.07	5.90
Jul 13 '95	105	5.76	5.74	+0.07	5.92
Jul 20 '95	112	5.77	5.75	+0.07	5.94
Jul 27 '95	119	5.78	5.76	+0.07	5.95
Aug 03 '95	126	5.79	5.77	+0.07	5.97
Aug 10 '95	133	5.80	5.78	+0.06	5.99
Aug 17 '95	140	5.82	5.80	+0.05	6.02
Aug 24 '95	147	5.82	5.80	+0.05	6.02
Aug 31 '95	154	5.83	5.81	+0.05	6.06
Sep 07 '95	161	5.83	5.81	+0.05	6.06
Sep 14 '95	168	5.84	5.82	+0.05	6.08
Sep 21 '95	175	5.84	5.82	+0.06	6.07
Sep 28 '95	**182**	**5.83**	**5.81**	**+0.03**	**6.09**
Oct 19 '95	203	5.88	5.86	+0.05	6.13
Nov 16 '95	231	5.91	5.89	+0.06	6.17
Dec 14 '95	259	5.91	5.89	+0.06	6.18
Jan 11 '96	287	5.94	5.92	+0.08	6.23
Feb 08 '96	315	5.96	5.94	+0.08	6.27
Mar 07 '96	343	5.98	5.96	+0.10	6.33

Source: *The Wall Street Journal*, March 29, 1995.

Journal entitled "Money Rates" (see Figure 4.3). After the debacle of Penn Central's default on its commercial paper in the early 1970s, the market was receptive to only very good credit risks for quite a while. In recent years, less creditworthy issuers have gained access to the market, with these issues referred to as high-yield commercial paper.

Bankers' Acceptances The **bankers' acceptance** is a money market instrument priced on a discount yield basis and used almost exclusively to finance international trade. A bankers' acceptance is a draft against a bank ordering the bank to pay a specified amount at a future date. When the bank accepts that obligation and stamps the draft **accepted**, it creates a bankers' acceptance. The bank undertakes this obligation because the drawer of the draft (analogous to the writer of a check) has arranged for the bank to provide the service. Once the acceptance is created, it may be sold in a secondary market.

In international trade, few firms are willing to ship goods on open account, as is often done domestically. Since firms in two different countries may not know the other so well, and may not have strong measures of recourse against those who default on their obligations, it is useful to involve banks in the process. It is much easier for a foreign supplier to trust the name of a respected American bank than that of a small importing firm. The creation of a bankers' acceptance means that the bank is committed to making the specified payment even if the importing firm, for whom the acceptance was created, defaults. This gives the foreign supplier an added measure of safety. The original obligation of the American firm still remains, so bankers' acceptances

Figure 4.3
Money Market Rate Quotations

MONEY RATES

Tuesday, March 28, 1995

The key U.S. and foreign annual interest rates below are a guide to general levels but don't always represent actual transactions.

PRIME RATE: 9%. The base rate on corporate loans posted by at least 75% of the nation's 30 largest banks.

FEDERAL FUNDS: 6 3/16% high, 6% low, 6 1/16% near closing bid, 6 3/16% offered. Reserves traded among commercial banks for overnight use in amounts of $1 million or more. Source: Prebon Yamane (U.S.A.) Inc.

DISCOUNT RATE: 5¼%. The charge on loans to depository institutions by the Federal Reserve Banks.

CALL MONEY: 7¾%. The charge on loans to brokers on stock exchange collateral. Source: Dow Jones Telerate Inc.

COMMERCIAL PAPER placed directly by General Electric Capital Corp.: 5.95% 30 to 44 days; 5.96% 45 to 59 days; 5.99% 60 to 94 days; 6.02% 95 to 110 days; 6.07% 111 to 149 days; 6.08% 150 to 179 days; 6.10% 180 to 270 days.

COMMERCIAL PAPER: High-grade unsecured notes sold through dealers by major corporations: 6.07% 30 days; 6.09% 60 days; 6.12% 90 days.

CERTIFICATES OF DEPOSIT: 5.33% one month; 5.44% two months; 5.55% three months; 5.80% six months; 6.07% one year. Average of top rates paid by major New York banks on primary new issues of negotiable C.D.s, usually on amounts of $1 million and more. The minimum unit is $100,000. Typical rates in the secondary market: 6.10% one month; 6.21% three months; 6.40% six months.

BANKERS ACCEPTANCES: 5.99% 30 days; 6.02% 60 days; 6.05% 90 days; 6.08% 120 days; 6.11% 150 days; 6.14% 180 days. Offered rates of negotiable, bank-backed business credit instruments typically financing an import order.

LONDON LATE EURODOLLARS: 6⅛% - 6% one month; 6 3/16% - 6 1/16% two months; 6¼% - 6⅛% three months; 6 5/16% - 6 3/16% four months; 6⅜% - 6¼% five months; 6 7/16% - 6 5/16% six months.

LONDON INTERBANK OFFERED RATES (LIBOR): 6⅛% one month; 6¼% three months; 6 7/16% six months; 6 11/16% one year. The average of interbank offered rates for dollar deposits in the London market based on quotations at five major banks. Effective rate for contracts entered into two days from date appearing at top of this column.

FOREIGN PRIME RATES: Canada 9.75%; Germany 5.05%; Japan 3%; Switzerland 5.62%; Britain 6.75%. These rate indications aren't directly comparable; lending practices vary widely by location.

TREASURY BILLS: Results of the Monday, March 27, 1995, auction of short-term U.S. government bills, sold at a discount from face value in units of $10,000 to $1 million: 5.64%, 13 weeks; 5.80%, 26 weeks.

FEDERAL HOME LOAN MORTGAGE CORP. (Freddie Mac): Posted yields on 30-year mortgage commitments. Delivery within 30 days 8.55%, 60 days 8.59%, standard conventional fixed-rate mortgages; 6.375%, 2% rate capped o e-year adjustable rate mortgages. Source: Dow Jones Telerate Inc.

FEDERAL NATIONAL MORTGAGE ASSOCIATION (Fannie Mae): Posted yields on 30 year mortgage commitments (priced at par) for delivery within 30 days 8.55%, 60 days 8.61%, standard conventional fixed rate-mortgages; 7.450, 6/2 rate capped one-year adjustable rate mortgages. Source: Dow Jones Telerate Inc.

MERRILL LYNCH READY ASSETS TRUST: 5.51%. Annualized average rate of return after expenses for the past 30 days; not a forecast of future returns.

Source: *The Wall Street Journal*, March 29, 1995.

are normally **two-name paper** – the bank and the original firm for whom the acceptance was created are both obligated to make the payment.

Banks profit from these transactions by charging an interest rate on any funds advanced and by charging an acceptance fee of one-fourth to two full percentage points additional interest. Acceptances of differing maturities have different rates, as is the case with all debt instruments. In recent years, the bankers' acceptances market has been contracting, due to the growing popularity of other financing vehicles. By 1995, there was about $30 billion of bankers' acceptances outstanding, which is considerably less than in recent years.

Certificates of Deposit Banks acquire funds by accepting deposits and by borrowing money in other ways. One of the most important forms of bank borrowing is through **certificates of deposit**, or CDs. CDs may be either negotiable or non-negotiable. Small CDs are often held by individual investors, and these are typically non-negotiable. Large CDs, $100,000 or more, are negotiable and form an important part of the money market, exceeding even T-bills in market size.

Unlike the discount yield instruments discussed so far (T-bills, commercial paper, and bankers' acceptances), CDs are interest-bearing instruments, with the interest being added to a given principal amount. So, for example, the purchase price of a $1,000,000 three-month CD would be $1,000,000, with the issuing bank owing interest plus principal three months later.

Eurodollars A **Eurodollar** is a dollar-denominated bank deposit held in a bank outside the United States. A **Eurodollar CD** is a dollar-denominated CD issued by a bank outside the United States. In addition to Eurodollars, we sometimes hear mention of Asian dollars and Petro dollars. As defined here, these would be components of the Eurodollar market as well. Asian dollars are dollar-denominated deposits held in Asian-based banks, while Petro dollars are dollar-denominated deposits generated by oil-producing countries. The most important part of the Eurodollar market is the CD sector, which is about 50 to 60 percent as large as the domestic CD market. Many foreign banks issue Eurodollar CDs to attract dollar-denominated funds. Many investors prefer Eurodollar CDs to domestic CDs since, being somewhat riskier, Eurodollar CDs pay a somewhat higher rate.

The greater risk for Eurodollar CDs arises from the fact that the issuing banks are not as tightly regulated as U.S. banks. Accordingly, the issuing banks must pay more for their funds. Since they escape the cost of tighter regulation, they are also able to pay the higher rate the market demands. To a large extent, the Eurodollar market was created by United States banking regulation. Virtually all bank deposits in the United States are insured by the Federal Deposit Insurance Corporation (FDIC), an agency of the U.S. government. The charge for this insurance must be paid by the insured bank. For banks outside the United States, the insurance requirements are normally less stringent, so foreign banks can escape some of this cost.

Another feature of U.S. banking regulation that helps to keep the Eurodollar market in business is the imposition of reserve requirements. Banks in the United States must keep a certain percentage of their assets on deposit in the form of noninterest-earning assets, such as vault cash. If there were no reserve requirements, banks could create an infinite amount of loans from any deposit base. The higher the reserve requirement, as a percentage of deposits, the more restricted the bank is in the amount it can lend. Reserve requirements for U.S. banks tend to be far more stringent than those imposed on banks in other countries. Consequently, the cost of operating many foreign banks is lower than it would be for a U.S. bank.

These regulatory differences create important cost differences between U.S. banks and their foreign competitors, but they also create significant risk differences. Due to the differences in their risk levels and cost structures, banks taking Eurodollar deposits must pay, and are able to pay, a higher interest rate than would be paid by a domestic U.S. bank.

Repurchase Agreements A **repurchase agreement**, or **repo**, arises when one party sells a security to another party with an agreement to buy it back at a specified time and at a specified price. The difference between the sale and repurchase price defines the interest rate. In effect, a repurchase agreement involves the sale and purchase of the same security for different prices at different settlement dates.

Repos are useful mainly for short-term financing. In fact, the vast majority of repo agreements are for just one day. Because of this, they are often called **overnight repos**. Repurchase agreements for longer periods are called **term repos**. Many corporations find themselves with excess cash from time to time that can be invested for a very short period until it is needed. By buying a security with a commitment to resell it the next day at a slightly higher price, a corporation can put its excess cash to work. The desire for this kind of transaction has led to the creation of the repo market, with a current size exceeding $750 billion. Most of the securities used as collateral in the repo market are U.S. government securities.

Federal Funds Another example of a short-term market is the market for **Federal funds**, or **Fed funds**. As mentioned earlier, the Federal Reserve Board requires that commercial banks keep a certain amount of reserve balances on hand, such as vault cash. These reserve balances yield no return, so banks naturally try to minimize their excess reserves, which are reserves above the required limit. Because of this some banks find themselves temporarily needing additional reserves, while other banks find themselves with excess reserves to lend out.

This regulatory structure helped to give rise to a market in Fed funds. The vast majority of market participants for Fed funds are more than 10,000 commercial banks in the United States. Like repos, most Fed funds are loaned on an overnight basis, with average daily volume exceeding $130 billion. Participation in the market is limited, however. Since banks are prohibited from paying interest on overnight deposits received from nonbank institutions, the market is restricted in scope. For this reason, and because Fed funds are unsecured, their interest rate exceeds the rate on repurchase agreements.

Yield Relationships in the Money Market

Even though the money market is defined as consisting of those securities issued with original maturities of one year or less, there is a considerable difference in yields within the market. As we have seen, Figure 4.1 summarizes these relationships. For the very short (overnight) maturities, the repo rate typically lies below the Fed funds rate.

For those instruments with longer maturities, the T-bill offers the lowest rate. This is reasonable because it has the best backing of all instruments, the promise of the U.S. Treasury. Commercial paper and bankers' acceptances typically have rates that are very close, with commercial paper issued by top industrial corporations having a perhaps slightly lower yield. Both commercial paper and bankers' acceptances lie below the yield of CDs. The difference between the commercial paper and CD rates reflects the greater creditworthiness of the best industrial corporations in relation to the banks. A bankers' acceptance can offer a lower return than a CD because it is two-name paper, which gives the lender an added margin of security. Finally, Eurodollar CDs must pay a greater rate than domestic CDs because of their greater risk.

While the relationships shown in Figure 4.1 are the norm, we must recognize that there may exist occasional exceptions to these relationships. Also, within each of the categories of money market instruments, yield differentials reflect the varying creditworthiness of the particular issuers.

The remainder of the book will focus on longer-term investment media. Most investment managers direct their funds more toward longer-term instruments because they tend to have higher returns. This is not to say that the money market is not important for investment management. In fact, virtually every investment institution makes continual use of the money market. Every investment manager needs to be concerned about the liquidity of the investment portfolio, and every pool of money available for securities investment has funds that cannot be immediately put into longer-term securities. Participation in the money market is a way of putting to work excess funds or funds needed to maintain liquidity. It is in this sense that the money market is not the prime objective of securities investment for most participants. In spite of that fact, it is one of the most widely used of all markets.

The International Money Market

In our discussion of the international money market, we include a variety of short-term and medium-term forms of lending. In this section, we consider the different types of loans that dominate the short-term and medium-term international markets, and we consider the size and constitution of the market as well. Syndicated loans and other types of lending in the international market bend our rule that the money market is limited to original maturities of one year or less. While the one-year rule may hold for the U.S. market, many forms of international lending have original maturities longer than one year, yet these loans cannot be regarded as belonging to the bond market.

Syndicated Loans

One of the dominant forms of credit in the international market is a form of bank lending called a **syndicated loan** – a loan made by a consortium of banks to a single borrower. By far, syndicated loans dominate the short-term end of the international debt market. Annual syndicated lending now generally exceeds $100 billion. Syndicated loans are priced as a spread above **LIBOR – London Interbank Offered Rate**. LIBOR is the rate that banks participating in the international debt market charge each other for short-term loans. Thus, most syndicated loans are floating rate loans, with the interest rate being reset periodically to reflect the current LIBOR. In general, syndicated loans are not securitized; that is, the lender cannot sell the loan to another investor. Even though these loans are not securities, they merit our attention because of their crucial importance in international lending.

Average spreads for syndicated loans tend to be about 50 basis points above LIBOR. A **basis point** is 1/100 of 1 percent. Average maturities on new issues are about six years. In addition to the spread above LIBOR, the lenders typically charge a facilities fee. This fee compensates the lenders for processing the loan and for holding funds available to meet the terms of the financing commitment over the life of the loan.

For lenders, syndicated loans have important advantages because this form of lending allows them to participate in a loan without having to commit too large a portion of their capital. In effect, lenders achieve diversification through syndicated lending. For borrowers, syndicated lending allows a larger loan size than would be possible from a single lender. Corporations are major borrowers in the syndicated loan market, as are the governments of developing countries. Recently, Eastern European governments have become major borrowers via syndicated loans. Most syndicated loans are denominated in U.S. dollars.

Euro-Commercial Paper (ECP)

We have already explored the importance of commercial paper in the U.S. market, and we have observed the rapid growth of commercial paper in the United States. **Euro-commercial paper** is commercial paper traded in the international market, usually denominated in dollars. Each year about $50 billion of Euro-commercial paper is issued. To a large extent, Euro-commercial paper has been crowding out syndicated lending because industrial firms have credit ratings equaling or exceeding those of banks. Thus, these firms can float their own direct obligations on the market and save by circumventing bank lending.

Note-Issuance Facilities

A **note-issuance facility** (NIF) is a form of medium-term lending through a variety of instruments, usually floating rate notes. The borrower makes an arrangement with a syndicate of commercial banks that commits the banks to buy the borrower's notes or to lend funds to the borrower. Usually, the term of the facility is three to ten years. The banks charge an annual fee for providing the borrowing facility even if it is not used. Currently, borrowing through NIFs is about $5 billion annually, down substantially from the 1987-1988 range of $20 billion and the peak of $40 billion in 1985. The diminution of NIFs is largely due to the perceived increase in bank risk. Also, firms gaining direct access to capital markets place less reliance on NIFs guaranteed by banks.

Committed versus Back-Up Facilities

For the most part, NIFs represent a **committed facility** – the banks issuing the facility commit themselves to making the loans as promised to the borrower. In effect, an NIF is a committed back-up facility. It is also possible for a syndicate of lenders to offer an **uncommitted back-up facility** – an expressed intention, but no commitment, to lend under specified circumstances. These facilities are of dubious worth because the funds may not be available to meet the borrower's requirements. These uncommitted facilities are fairly unimportant in the international lending scene, with annual volume running about $20 billion.

The Valuation of Bonds

In the money market, many instruments have the structure of pure discount bonds, but that is not normally the case for longer maturity debt instruments. It is much more typical for there to be multiple payments associated with a bond. Most bonds issued today have a par value that is paid to the owner of the bond at a specified date in the future when the bond matures. Bonds typically make regularly scheduled payments between the original date of issue and the maturity date as well; these intervening payments are called **coupons**. In most cases, the coupon payments are made semiannually. For such bonds, the bond pricing formula becomes more complicated:

$$P = \sum_{t=1}^{m} \frac{C_t}{(1 + r)^t} \tag{4.5}$$

where:

C_t = the cash flow received by the bondholder at time t

Although more complex, this formula is very similar to Equation 4.1, but there are just more payments from the bond to consider. As a straightforward example, consider a coupon bond that has a face value of $1,000, a yield of 13 percent, pays a semiannual coupon of $60, and matures in one year. Normally, the last coupon payment is made at maturity, so on the maturity date, the bond will pay the face value amount plus the last coupon payment. With this information, the bond pricing formula can be applied to this bond in the following way:

$$P = \frac{\$60}{1 + .13/2} + \frac{\$1{,}060}{(1 + .13/2)^2}$$

$$= \$56.34 + \$934.56 = \$990.90$$

There are two important points to notice about this application of the bond pricing formula. First, the coupon rate is 12 percent applied to a $1,000 par value bond. Therefore, the total annual coupon is $120, but it is divided into the two semiannual coupon payments of $60 each. Second, because the cash flows occur semiannually, we must account for the semiannual compounding that this implies. Therefore, the stated yield of 13 percent is divided by 2, because there are two payments from the bond per year. In the computation, the present value of the bond, which equals its price, is based on a 6.5 percent semiannual rate of interest. Bond tables and bond price calculations are always based on this kind of computation.

Par, Premium, and Discount Bonds

In this example of the calculation of the yield to maturity, there is a slight difference between the market price and the face value. However, the market price of a bond often differs from its face value, and this difference can be quite large. When the market price exceeds the face value, the bond is a **premium bond**. If the market price equals the face value, the bond is a **par bond**. When the price is less than the face value, the bond is a **discount bond**. Notice that there is a difference, however, between a discount bond and a pure discount bond. Bonds with coupons can have prices less than their face values and are then discount bonds. Pure discount bonds will always have market prices less than the par values, except at the point of maturity. The unique feature of pure discount bonds is that they pay no coupons.

Accrued Interest

One peculiarity of the bond market that awaits the unwary investor is the unusual method used to quote bond prices. For most bonds, the bond price does not reflect the actual price that must be paid. Instead, we must pay the stated price plus the **accrued interest** – the portion of the next coupon payment that has been earned by the bondholder, but which the bondholder has not yet received. As an example, consider the five-year bond just discussed. At maturity the bond will pay $1,100, consisting of the final coupon payment plus the face value. Immediately prior to maturity, the bond must have a total value just slightly less than the promised payment of $1,100. However, its quoted price will be $1,000, but it will have $100 of accrued interest. The purchaser of a bond must pay the quoted price plus the accrued interest. The accrued interest is easily calculated using the following formula:

$$\text{Accrued Interest} = (\text{Coupon Payment})\left(\frac{\text{days since last coupon payment}}{\text{days between coupon payments}}\right) \tag{4.6}$$

The Bond Market in the United States

The U.S. bond market can be divided into three major categories by issuer – the U.S. government, corporations, and municipalities.[3] Each of these types of issuers has special characteristics that make its bonds different from those issued by a member of the other groups. These characteristics include maturity, tax status, and risk level. Consequently, it is easiest to focus, in turn, on each of the different segments of the market.

The Market for U.S. Government Bonds

The U.S. government is the world's single largest debtor, with new federal borrowing of about $-185 billion in 1994. The borrowing by the U.S. government can be divided between debt issued by the U.S. Treasury, such as Treasury bills (T-bills), notes (T-notes), and bonds (T-bonds), and debt issued by agencies of the U.S. Government, such as the Government National Mortgage Association (GNMA), the Federal Housing Administration (FHA), and the Tennessee Valley Authority (TVA). Together, they are responsible for a tremendous amount of outstanding debt, as shown in Figure 4.4. The total outstanding federal debt is now about $4.8 trillion, the consequence of a very rapid increase that began in 1975. Of this outstanding debt, the most important part is U.S. Treasury debt.

Treasury Debt The three principal kinds of U.S. Treasury obligations are Treasury bills, notes, and bonds. Treasury bills are debt instruments with an initial maturity of one year or less. While T-bills were considered earlier in this chapter, we now focus on longer maturity Treasury maturity issues – T-notes and T-bonds. Treasury notes and bonds have similar payment streams and differ only in their maturity. Officially, a Treasury note is an instrument having an original maturity lying in the range of 1 to 10 years, and a Treasury bond has a maturity when issued in excess of 10 years. In practice, Treasury bonds are issued for much longer maturities, usually for 30 years.

Table 4.2 shows the amount of outstanding Treasury obligations and the portion represented by bills, notes, and bonds. The current large portion of notes differs from the composition

---

[3] Mortgages are also considered in this chapter, but they are not normally regarded as bonds.

Figure 4.4
Net Federal Debt Outstanding

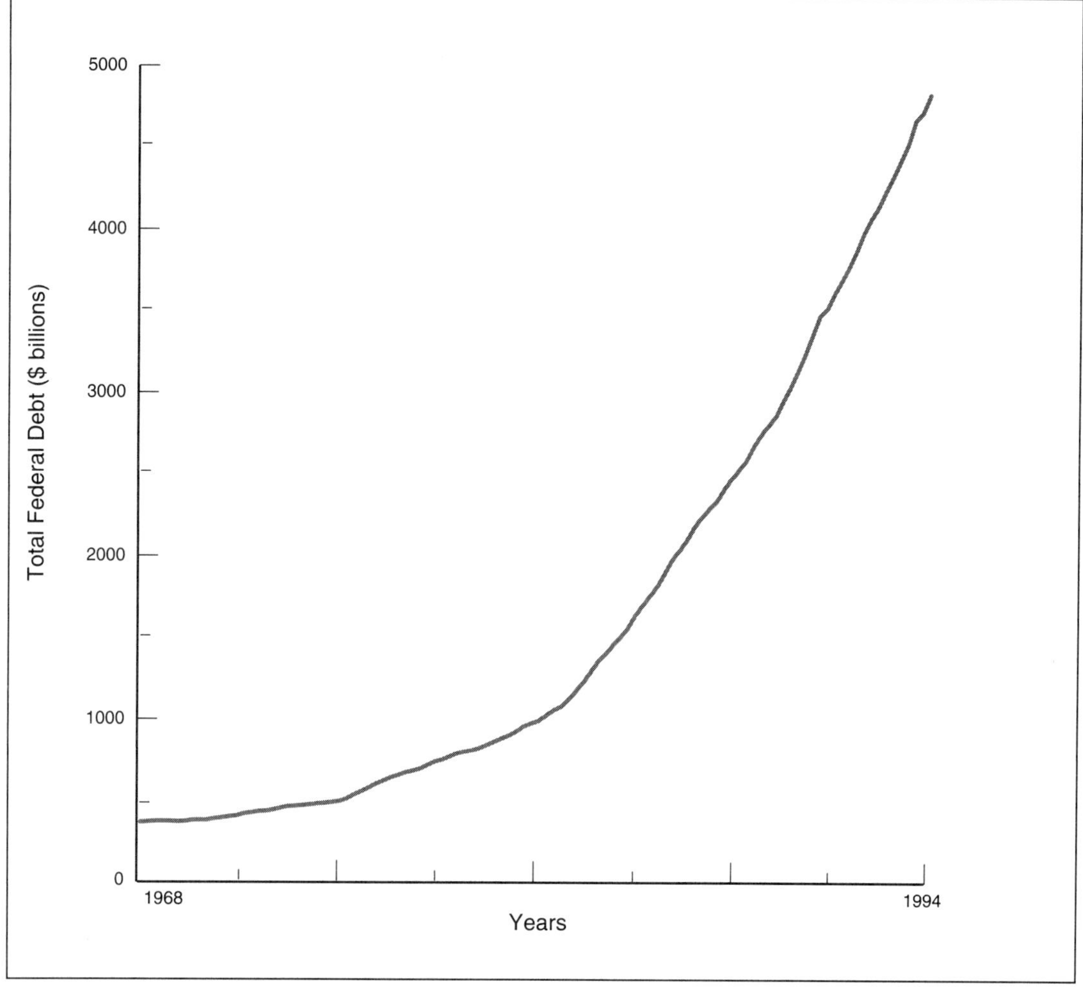

Source: *Federal Reserve Bulletin*, various issues.

of Treasury debt in earlier years, as a result of a shift from the longer-term bonds to the medium-maturity notes.

Quotations for various federal issues are carried daily in *The Wall Street Journal* and other major newspapers, as shown in Figure 4.5. The first three columns of the quotations identify the instrument. The first column indicates the annual coupon rate, as a percent of par. A rate of 10 percent on a bond with a par value of $10,000 means that the bond would pay annual interest payments of $1,000. Usually, this annual coupon amount will be paid in two equal semiannual installments. The next two columns indicate the year and month the bond matures. Since these instruments will always make the last semiannual coupon payment on the maturity date, one knows the cash flows that will come from the bonds from the first three columns. A particular

Table 4.2
Outstanding Treasury Bills, Notes, and Bonds

Treasury Issue	Amount Outstanding (billions)	Percentage (%)
Bills	733.8	23.59
Notes	1,867.0	60.01
Bonds	510.3	16.40

Source: *Federal Reserve Bulletin,* March 1995, Table 1.41.

bond, such as one identified as "10 1997 May," would be referred to as "the tens of ninety-seven." Since notes and bonds have the same structure, the quotations are mixed. Those securities originally issued as notes are identified by an "n" following the bond identifier.

Some of the bonds show two maturity dates. For example, if a bond shows a maturity such as 1997-2002, the second is the actual maturity date. The first indicates the first date at which the bond might be called. A bond is called when it is retired early at the discretion of the issuer. In the normal event, bonds will be called only when the prevailing interest rates lie below the coupon rate.[4]

As noted at the top of the listing, the prices shown are mid-afternoon quotations from the Federal Reserve Bank of New York, based on transactions of at least $1 million in size. These are not necessarily prices at which we could have actually traded, but, instead, they indicate the approximate market prices that prevailed at the time. The quotations themselves are expressed as a percentage of the par value of the bond. However, the use of the decimal point is likely to be very misleading. The portion to the right of the decimal indicates the number of 32nds of par. In other words, a price of 97.16 means that the bond is quoted at 97 and 16/32nds of par, or 97.50 percent of par. For a bond with a face value of $10,000, this would translate into a quoted price of $9,750. As in all markets, there is both a bid and an asked price, both of which are quoted here.[5] The "Bid Chg." column indicates the change in the bid price since the previous day's quotation.[6]

The "Ask Yld." column indicates the bond's yield to maturity. In spite of the fact that all of the bonds have the same issuer, and one of impeccable creditworthiness, there are important differences in yields among the different issues, even though they are of the same risk level.

In the past 69 years, investments in Treasury securities have been similar in their returns, but very different in their risk levels, as measured by the standard deviation or variance of returns. Over

---

[4] For a more detailed discussion of callable bonds, see the section on "The Bond Contract."

[5] The **bid price** is the price that prospective purchasers offer for the good, while the **asked price** is the price demanded by the owner of the instrument.

[6] Securities dealers make a market in a particular security by offering to buy it at one price (the bid price) and trying to sell it at a higher price (the asked price). The difference between the two prices is the **bid-asked spread**, and this difference constitutes the dealer's gross profit margin. We explore the concept of the bid-asked spread more fully for the stock market in Chapter 5.

Figure 4.5
Quotations for Treasury Notes and Bonds

TREASURY BONDS, NOTES & BILLS

Monday, November 20, 1995

Representative Over-the-Counter quotations based on transactions of $1 million or more.

Treasury bond, note and bill quotes are as of mid-afternoon. Colons in bid-and-asked quotes represent 32nds; 101:01 means 101 1/32. Net changes in 32nds. n-Treasury note. Treasury bill quotes in hundredths, quoted on terms of a rate of discount. Days to maturity calculated from settlement date. All yields are to maturity and based on the asked quote. Latest 13-week and 26-week bills are boldfaced. For bonds callable prior to maturity, yields are computed to the earliest call date for issues quoted above par and to the maturity date for issues below par. *-When issued.

Source: Federal Reserve Bank of New York.

U.S. Treasury strips as of 3 p.m. Eastern time, also based on transactions of $1 million or more. Colons in bid-and-asked quotes represent 32nds; 99:01 means 99 1/32. Net changes in 32nds. Yields calculated on the asked quotation. ci-stripped coupon interest. bp-Treasury bond, stripped principal. np-Treasury note, stripped principal. For bonds callable prior to maturity, yields are computed to the earliest call date for issues quoted above par and to the maturity date for issues below par.

Source: Bear, Stearns & Co. via Street Software Technology Inc.

GOVT. BONDS & NOTES

Rate	Maturity Mo/Yr	Bid	Asked	Chg.	Ask Yld.
4 1/4	Nov 95n	99:31	100:01	+ 1	2.76
4 1/4	Dec 95n	99:30	100:00	− 1	4.18
9 1/4	Jan 96n	100:16	100:18	− 1	5.22
4	Jan 96n	99:22	99:24	....	5.26
7 1/2	Jan 96n	100:11	100:13	− 1	5.22
4 5/8	Feb 96n	99:24	99:26	....	5.38
7 7/8	Feb 96n	100:16	100:18	− 1	5.30
8 7/8	Feb 96n	100:23	100:25	− 1	5.32
4 5/8	Feb 96n	99:24	99:26	....	5.27
7 1/2	Feb 96n	100:16	100:18	− 1	5.31
5 1/8	Mar 96n	99:27	99:29	....	5.35
7 3/4	Mar 96n	100:24	100:26	− 1	5.36
9 3/8	Apr 96n	101:15	101:17	− 2	5.38
5 1/2	Apr 96n	100:00	100:02	....	5.34
7 5/8	Apr 96n	100:28	100:30	− 1	5.42
4 1/4	May 96n	99:12	99:14	....	5.45
7 3/8	May 96n	100:27	100:29	− 1	5.43
5 7/8	May 96n	100:05	100:07	....	5.44
7 5/8	May 96n	101:02	101:04	....	5.41
6	Jun 96n	100:09	100:11	+ 1	5.42
7 7/8	Jun 96n	101:12	101:14	− 1	5.44
7 7/8	Jul 96n	101:15	101:17	....	5.44
6 1/8	Jul 96n	100:13	100:15	+ 1	5.43
7 7/8	Jul 96n	101:18	101:20	− 1	5.45
4 3/8	Aug 96n	99:06	99:08	....	5.43
6 1/4	Aug 96n	100:16	100:18	....	5.50
7 1/4	Aug 96n	101:08	101:10	....	5.49
6 1/2	Sep 96n	100:27	100:29	....	5.40
7	Sep 96n	101:08	101:10	....	5.41
8	Oct 96n	102:05	102:07	− 2	5.43
6 7/8	Oct 96n	101:09	101:11	....	5.39
4 3/8	Nov 96n	98:31	99:01	+ 1	5.40
7 1/4	Nov 96n	101:21	101:23	....	5.43
6 1/2	Nov 96n	101:00	101:02	....	5.42
7 1/4	Nov 96n	101:23	101:25	....	5.43
6 1/8	Dec 96n	100:25	100:27	+ 1	5.33
7 1/2	Dec 96n	102:05	102:07	....	5.41
8	Jan 97n	102:24	102:26	....	5.44
6 1/4	Jan 97n	100:28	100:30	....	5.43
7 1/2	Jan 97n	102:10	102:12	+ 1	5.42
4 3/4	Feb 97n	99:03	99:05	+ 1	5.47
8	Aug 96-01	101:19	101:23	....	5.57
13 3/8	Aug 01	137:00	137:04	+ 4	5.69
7 1/2	Nov 01n	108:27	108:29	....	5.72
15 3/4	Nov 01	150:07	150:11	+ 1	5.70
14 1/4	Feb 02	144:03	144:07	− 4	5.72
7 1/2	May 02n	109:11	109:13	....	5.74
6 3/8	Aug 02n	103:06	103:08	− 1	5.79
11 5/8	Nov 02	133:01	133:05	− 3	5.78
6 1/4	Feb 03n	102:14	102:16	− 1	5.82
10 3/4	Feb 03	128:19	128:23	− 2	5.83
10 3/4	May 03	129:10	129:14	− 2	5.84
5 3/4	Aug 03n	99:07	99:09	− 2	5.87
11 1/8	Aug 03	132:07	132:11	− 2	5.86
11 7/8	Nov 03	137:20	137:24	− 3	5.88
5 7/8	Feb 04n	99:28	99:30	− 2	5.88
7 1/4	May 04n	108:25	108:27	− 3	5.91
12 3/8	May 04	142:15	142:19	− 4	5.92
7 1/4	Aug 04n	108:28	108:30	− 3	5.92
13 3/4	Aug 04	152:19	152:23	− 4	5.93
7 7/8	Nov 04n	113:10	113:12	− 3	5.93
11 5/8	Nov 04	139:02	139:06	− 4	5.93
7 1/2	Feb 05n	110:29	110:31	− 3	5.94
6 1/2	May 05n	104:07	104:09	− 3	5.90
8 1/4	May 00-05	109:02	109:06	....	5.89
12	May 05	143:07	143:11	− 5	5.95
6 1/2	Aug 05n	104:08	104:10	− 2	5.91
10 3/4	Aug 05	134:24	134:28	− 3	5.97
9 3/8	Feb 06	125:27	125:31	− 3	5.95
7 5/8	Feb 02-07	108:08	108:12	− 2	5.99
7 7/8	Nov 02-07	110:28	111:00	− 2	5.93
8 3/8	Aug 03-08	114:26	114:30	− 2	5.94
8 3/4	Nov 03-08	116:29	117:01	− 1	6.03
9 1/8	May 04-09	120:03	120:07	− 2	6.04
10 3/8	Nov 04-09	129:17	129:21	− 3	6.05
11 3/4	Feb 05-10	140:04	140:08	− 3	6.01
10	May 05-10	127:30	128:02	− 2	6.06
12 3/4	Nov 05-10	149:16	149:20	− 3	6.05
13 7/8	May 06-11	159:25	159:29	− 3	6.07
14	Nov 06-11	162:23	162:27	− 4	6.07
10 3/8	Nov 07-12	135:00	135:04	− 5	6.18
12	Aug 08-13	150:18	150:22	− 5	6.19
13 1/4	May 09-14	163:20	163:24	− 8	6.20

Mat.	Type	Bid	Asked	Chg.	Ask Yld.
Aug 04	ci	59:17	59:22	− 2	6.00
Aug 04	np	59:22	59:27	− 3	5.97
Nov 04	ci	58:19	58:24	− 2	6.01
Nov 04	bp	58:16	58:21	− 2	6.03
Nov 04	np	58:24	58:28	− 2	5.98
Feb 05	ci	57:18	57:23	− 3	6.04
Feb 05	np	57:28	58:01	− 2	5.98
May 05	ci	56:21	56:26	− 3	6.05
May 05	bp	56:21	56:26	− 2	6.05
May 05	np	57:10	57:15	− 2	5.93
Aug 05	ci	55:25	55:30	− 3	6.06
Aug 05	bp	55:20	55:25	− 3	6.09
Aug 05	np	56:14	56:19	− 2	5.93
Nov 05	ci	54:29	55:02	− 3	6.07
Feb 06	ci	53:28	54:01	− 3	6.11
Feb 06	bp	54:10	54:15	− 4	6.03
May 06	ci	52:31	53:04	− 4	6.13
Aug 06	ci	52:03	52:08	− 4	6.14
Nov 06	ci	51:08	51:13	− 4	6.15
Feb 07	ci	50:12	50:17	− 4	6.17
May 07	ci	49:16	49:22	− 5	6.19
Aug 07	ci	48:22	48:27	− 5	6.20
Nov 07	ci	47:27	48:01	− 5	6.22
Feb 08	ci	47:01	47:07	− 3	6.23
May 08	ci	46:08	46:13	− 3	6.25
Aug 08	ci	45:15	45:21	− 3	6.26
Nov 08	ci	44:22	44:27	− 3	6.27
Feb 09	ci	43:28	44:01	− 3	6.30
May 09	ci	43:04	43:09	− 3	6.31
Aug 09	ci	42:13	42:18	− 3	6.32
Nov 09	ci	41:21	41:27	− 3	6.33
Nov 09	bp	41:03	41:09	− 4	6.43
Feb 10	ci	40:29	41:03	− 2	6.35
May 10	ci	40:06	40:12	− 2	6.36
Aug 10	ci	39:15	39:21	− 2	6.38
Nov 10	ci	38:25	38:30	− 2	6.39
Feb 11	ci	38:03	38:08	− 2	6.41
May 11	ci	37:14	37:19	− 2	6.42
Aug 11	ci	36:25	36:31	− 2	6.43
Nov 11	ci	36:05	36:10	− 2	6.44
Feb 12	ci	35:17	35:22	− 2	6.45
May 12	ci	34:28	35:02	− 2	6.46
Aug 12	ci	34:09	34:14	− 2	6.47
Nov 12	ci	33:22	33:27	− 2	6.48
Feb 13	ci	33:03	33:08	− 2	6.49
May 13	ci	32:16	32:21	− 2	6.50
Aug 13	ci	31:30	32:03	− 2	6.51
Nov 13	ci	31:12	31:18	− 2	6.52
Feb 14	ci	30:27	31:00	− 2	6.53
May 14	ci	30:10	30:15	− 2	6.53
Aug 14	ci	29:26	29:31	− 2	6.54
Nov 14	ci	29:09	29:15	− 2	6.54
Feb 15	ci	28:26	28:31	− 2	6.55
Feb 15	bp	29:13	29:18	− 4	6.44
May 15	ci	28:09	28:14	− 2	6.56
Aug 15	ci	27:25	27:30	− 2	6.57
Aug 15	bp	28:03	28:08	− 4	6.51
Nov 15	ci	27:09	27:14	− 2	6.58
Nov 15	bp	27:13	27:18	− 4	6.55
Feb 16	ci	26:25	26:30	− 3	6.59
Feb 16	bp	27:00	27:05	− 3	6.55
May 16	ci	26:10	26:15	− 3	6.59
May 16	bp	26:23	26:28	− 1	6.52
Aug 16	ci	25:28	26:01	− 3	6.60

Source: *The Wall Street Journal*, March 29, 1995.

the period from 1926-1994, Treasury bills have returned about 1 percent less than Treasury bonds, but T-bill returns have been much less risky. Figure 4.6 presents the year-by-year returns for both bills and bonds. The investor in Treasury bills has never had an actual loss in any given year because Treasury bills all mature in one year or less, and they have always been paid as promised. The investor in Treasury bonds has been stung on occasion, however. Even though all payments on Treasury bonds have been made as promised, an investor in Treasury bonds could

Figure 4.6
Annual Returns on Bonds and Bills, 1926–94

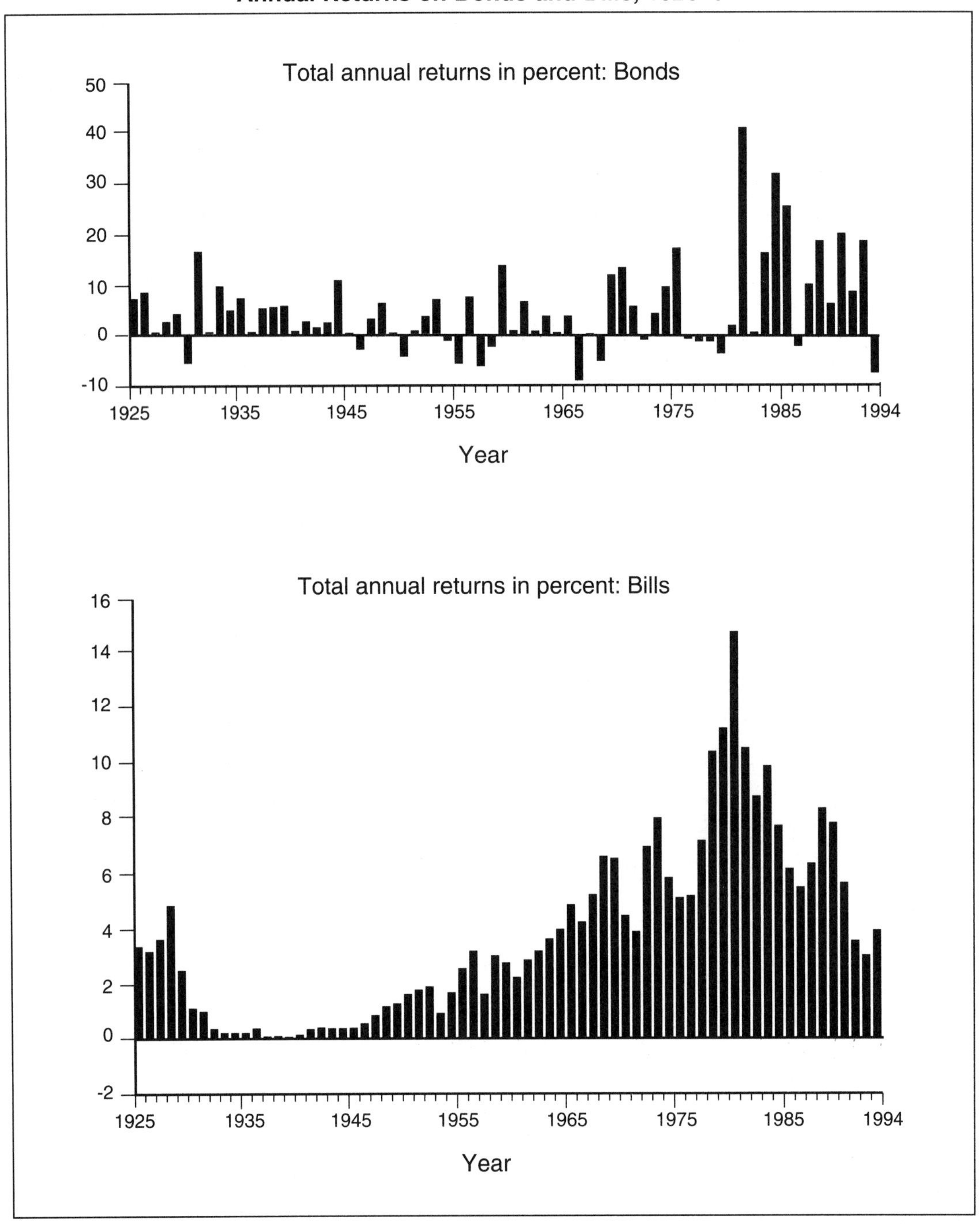

Source: Ibbotson Associates, *Stocks, Bonds, Bills, and Inflation: 1995 Yearbook*, Chicago: Ibbotson Associates, 1995.

still have a loss in a given year. The dollar return on holding a Treasury bond for a given year consists of the coupon payments received plus any price change in the bond itself. In the years of losses, the fall in the bond price exceeded the coupon income, giving a net loss on the holding of the Treasury bond.

Table 4.3 summarizes the returns for investment in both T-bills and T-bonds for the period from 1926 to 1994. On an inflation-adjusted basis, the real return (total return less the effect of inflation) is quite small. This is shown by the change in the purchasing power for an initial investment of $1,000. If we had invested $1,000 in T-bills and kept it in T-bills, we would have earned only a 0.55 percent increase in purchasing power over these years. The persistent Treasury bond investor would have had about a 1.65 percent increase in purchasing power. Clearly, over this period, the rate of return on Treasury securities was only slightly higher than the inflation rate.

Zero Coupons and STRIPS A Treasury note or bond consists of a stream of coupon payments and a final payment that returns the face value to the investor. **Coupon stripping** is the act of removing the individual interest coupons from the bond and treating each payment as a separate security. The resulting instruments are zero coupon bonds, because each represents a single payment due on a particular date. For example, a 20-year bond with a face value of $100,000 and a coupon rate of 10 percent could be stripped into 41 zero coupon instruments. One instrument has a face value of $100,000 and is due in 20 years. The other 40 instruments consist of the individual coupon payments of $5,000, and each would be due on the specified coupon payment date over then next 40 semiannual periods.

The market for stripped securities began in 1982 when Merrill Lynch stripped securities and marketed them under the name "TIGR," Treasury Investment Growth Certificates. Salomon Brothers, a competing firm, introduced a similar instrument called CATS, Certificates of Accrual on Treasury Securities. LIONS (by Lehman Brothers) soon followed CATS, making a total of three name-brand stripped Treasury-based products. In February 1985, the Treasury itself introduced its own version of a stripped bond and called it a STRIPS, Separate Trading of Registered

Table 4.3
Returns for Investment in Treasury Bills and Long-Term Bonds, 1926-94

	Bills	Bonds
Arithmetic Mean Return	3.7%	5.2%
Standard Deviation of Returns	3.3	8.8
Geometric Mean Return	3.7	4.8
Real Geometric Mean Return	0.55	1.65%
For a $1,000 Investment in 1926:		
Terminal Value	$12,186	$25,856
Terminal Purchasing Power	1,459	3,096

Source: Ibbotson Associates, *Stocks, Bonds, Bills, and Inflation: 1995 Yearbook,* Chicago: Ibbotson Associates, 1995

Interest and Principal of Securities. By 1995, the total value of STRIPS outstanding was about \$500 million, with the Treasury's STRIPS having largely crowded out the feline products.[7]

Federal Agency Debt In addition to the Treasury, many other federal agencies and federally sponsored agencies also issue debt. A **federal agency** is a direct arm of the U.S. government. These federal agencies do not issue debt on their own, but their financing needs are met through issues of the Federal Financing Bank. These federal agencies include the Defense Department, the Export-Import Bank, the Federal Housing Administration, and several other agencies. By contrast, a **federally sponsored agency** is a privately owned entity that raises funds in the market. Examples of these sponsored agencies include the Federal Home Loan Banks, Farm Credit Banks, Federal Home Loan Mortgage Corporation, and the Trust Funding Corporation (established in 1989 to deal with the Savings and Loan crisis). Collectively, their debt exceeded \$675 billion by late 1994.

With the exception of the Farm Credit Financial Assistance Corporation, there is no federal guarantee for these agency securities. Nonetheless, there is a perception that the federal government will not allow these securities to default. As a result, the yields on these agency issues are slightly higher than the yields on comparable Treasury issues, but slightly lower than the yields on comparable debt of corporations.

Figure 4.7 shows the quotations for federal agency debt issues. The system of quotation is very similar to that for Treasury issues. Note, however, that the coupon rates are expressed as decimals. Again, bid and asked prices are expressed as points and 32nds of par, just as they are for Treasury issues. Yields on Treasury issues are based on the actual number of days between coupon payments, but agency issue yields are based on the assumption that every month has 30 days.

Ownership of U.S. Government Securities and the Burden of Federal Debt

One of the developing public issues of the 1990s that promises to be of great importance is the continuing growth of the federal deficit and the burden that it creates. This section takes a brief look at the size of that burden and the owners of the securities that comprise the federal debt. By the end of 1994, this portion of the federal debt was more than \$2.7 trillion. In addition, there is a total of about \$1.6 trillion in nonmarketable debt, for a total of about \$4.3 trillion of debt on which the federal government pays interest. About \$1 trillion of this debt is held by the Federal Reserve and other arms of the government itself.

This still leaves about \$3.3 trillion in private hands. The major owners of federal securities are private nonbank financial and nonfinancial holders. The nonbank financial holders have grown very much in importance. This group includes pension funds, savings and loan associations, and various financial investment companies, such as money market mutual funds.[8] The private domestic nonfinancial holders consist mainly of various corporations and households.

---

[7] This account relies largely on the Federal Reserve Bank of New York's pamphlet, "Zero Coupons and STRIPS."

[8] **Mutual funds** are portfolios of securities that are owned in common by a group of investors. A money market mutual fund is one that invests in money market instruments.

Figure 4.7
Quotations for Agency Issues

GOVERNMENT AGENCY & SIMILAR ISSUES

Tuesday, March 28, 1995

Over-the-Counter mid-afternoon quotations based on large transactions, usually $1 million or more. Colons in bid-and-asked quotes represent 32nds; 101:01 means 101 1/32.

· All yields are calculated to maturity, and based on the asked quote. * – Callable issue, maturity date shown. For issues callable prior to maturity, yields are computed to the earliest call date for issues quoted above par, or 100, and to the maturity date for issues below par.

Source: Bear, Stearns & Co. via Street Software Technology Inc.

FNMA Issues

Rate	Mat.	Bid	Asked	Yld.
11.70	5-95	100:16	100:18	6.32
11.15	6-95	100:25	100:27	6.65
4.75	8-95	99:04	99:06	6.84
10.50	9-95	101:15	101:19	6.79
8.80	11-95	101:11	101:15	6.28
10.60	11-95	102:11	102:15	6.38
9.20	1-96	102:01	102:05	6.29
7.00	2-96	100:10	100:14	6.45
9.35	2-96	102:04	102:08	6.61
8.50	6-96	102:00	102:04	6.61
8.75	6-96	102:09	102:13	6.61
8.00	7-96	101:07	101:11	6.87
7.90	8-96	101:02	101:06	6.96
8.15	8-96	101:13	101:17	6.95
7.70	9-96	101:00	101:04	6.86
8.63	9-96	102:08	102:12	6.86
7.05	10-96	100:06	100:10	6.83
8.45	10-96	102:07	102:11	6.83
6.90	11-96*	99:26	99:30	6.93
7.70	12-96	101:09	101:13	6.80
8.20	12-96	102:01	102:05	6.85
6.20	1-97*	98:22	98:28	6.88
7.60	1-97	101:04	101:10	6.79
7.50	2-97*	100:28	101:02	6.21
7.05	3-97*	99:28	100:02	7.01
7.00	4-97*	99:25	99:31	7.01
6.75	4-97	99:18	99:24	6.88
9.20	6-97	104:18	104:24	6.82
8.95	7-97	103:28	104:02	6.98
8.80	7-97	103:23	103:29	6.94
9.55	9-97	105:15	105:21	6.99
5.70	9-97*	96:28	97:02	7.03
5.35	10-97*	95:26	96:00	7.11
6.05	10-97*	97:08	97:14	7.15
6.05	11-97	97:15	97:21	7.05
9.55	11-97	105:25	105:31	7.00
7.10	12-97*	100:01	100:07	7.00
9.55	12-97	105:30	106:04	7.01
6.30	12-97*	97:30	98:04	7.07
6.05	1-98	97:17	97:23	6.96
8.65	2-98	104:04	104:10	6.96
8.20	3-98	102:25	102:31	7.06
5.30	3-98*	95:02	95:08	7.11
5.25	3-98	94:28	95:02	7.11
9.15	4-98	104:30	105:04	7.23
8.38	4-98*	102:09	102:15	0.00
8.15	5-98	102:17	102:23	7.16
5.25	5-98*	94:13	94:19	7.21
5.40	5-98*	94:24	94:30	7.22
5.38	6-98	94:20	94:26	7.22
5.10	7-98*	93:28	94:02	7.14
8.20	8-98*	101:18	101:24	3.26
5.35	8-98*	94:17	94:23	7.14
9.80	5-00*	100:17	100:25	2.65
8.90	6-00	107:06	107:14	7.16
9.20	9-00	108:21	108:29	7.19
8.25	12-00	104:25	105:01	7.16
8.63	4-01*	103:08	103:16	5.08
8.70	6-01*	101:10	101:18	7.30
8.88	7-01*	103:13	103:21	5.85
7.80	12-01*	99:00	99:08	7.94
7.20	1-02*	96:03	96:11	7.90
7.50	2-02	99:09	99:17	7.59
7.90	4-02*	99:22	99:30	7.91
7.55	4-02	99:05	99:13	7.66
7.80	6-02*	99:23	99:31	7.80
7.30	7-02*	96:30	97:06	7.81
7.00	8-02*	96:01	96:09	7.67
6.93	8-02*	95:23	95:31	7.65
6.95	9-02*	95:25	96:01	7.66
7.30	10-02*	96:13	96:21	7.89
6.80	10-02*	94:30	95:06	7.65
7.05	11-02	95:28	96:04	7.73
6.80	1-03	95:14	95:22	7.54
6.40	3-03*	91:04	91:12	7.88
6.63	4-03*	92:15	92:23	7.86
6.45	6-03*	92:26	93:02	7.60
6.20	7-03*	91:10	91:18	7.59
6.25	8-03*	91:14	91:22	7.61
5.45	10-03	87:20	87:28	7.39
6.20	11-03*	91:07	91:15	7.56
5.80	12-03	89:20	89:28	7.40
6.40	1-04*	92:02	92:10	7.61
6.90	3-04*	94:17	94:25	7.72
6.85	4-04	96:08	96:16	7.39
7.60	4-04*	98:01	98:09	7.87
7.65	4-04*	98:11	98:19	7.87
7.55	6-04*	98:10	98:18	7.77
7.40	7-04	100:02	100:10	7.35
8.05	7-04*	100:10	100:18	7.77
7.70	8-04*	99:00	99:08	7.81
7.85	9-04*	100:08	100:16	7.71
8.25	10-04*	101:12	101:20	7.82
8.40	10-04*	102:08	102:16	7.74
8.63	11-04*	103:14	103:22	7.66
8.55	12-04*	102:22	102:30	7.32
8.50	2-05*	102:28	103:04	7.71
7.88	2-05	103:07	103:15	7.37
7.65	3-05	101:22	101:30	7.37
0.00	7-14	20:26	21:02	8.25
10.35	12-15	126:16	126:24	7.74
8.20	3-16	103:02	103:10	7.87
8.95	2-18	112:10	112:18	7.77
8.10	8-19	103:05	103:13	7.78
0.00	10-19	14:05	14:13	8.06
9.65	8-20*	109:22	109:30	0.91
9.50	11-20*	108:09	108:17	5.91

Federal Home Loan Bank

Rate	Mat.	Bid	Asked	Yld.
6.04	4-95	99:30	100:00	5.89
8.88	6-95	100:15	100:17	6.47
10.00	6-95	100:22	100:24	6.64
10.30	7-95	101:01	101:03	6.68
4.60	8-95	99:02	99:04	6.80
4.50	9-95	98:25	98:29	6.82
5.00	10-95	99:07	99:11	6.19
5.38	11-95	99:08	99:12	6.35
9.50	12-95	102:06	102:10	6.22
4.89	3-96	98:15	98:19	6.44
8.10	3-96	101:06	101:10	6.70
9.80	3-96	102:25	102:29	6.70
6.68	4-96	99:22	99:26	6.86
4.36	4-96*	97:17	97:21	6.66
7.75	4-96	100:29	101:01	6.73
8.25	5-96	101:11	101:15	6.89
8.25	6-96	101:13	101:17	6.92
6.13	7-96	99:00	99:04	6.85
4.41	7-96*	96:31	97:03	6.83
8.00	7-96	101:04	101:08	6.98
6.40	8-96*	99:06	99:10	6.94
6.13	8-96	98:30	99:02	6.86
7.70	8-96	100:30	101:02	6.89
6.36	9-96	99:07	99:11	6.84
8.25	9-96	101:27	101:31	6.83
7.10	10-96	100:08	100:12	6.84
8.25	11-96	102:00	102:04	6.86
6.85	2-97	99:28	100:02	6.81
7.65	3-97	101:11	101:17	6.81
9.15	3-97	104:02	104:08	6.82
6.99	4-97	100:01	100:07	6.87
6.34	6-97	98:14	98:20	7.03
9.20	8-97	104:20	104:26	6.98
6.86	10-97	99:17	99:23	6.98
7.25	10-97*	100:09	100:15	6.38
5.26	4-98*	94:16	94:22	7.22
9.25	11-98	106:08	106:14	7.21
9.30	1-99	106:19	106:25	7.23
5.43	2-99	94:09	94:15	7.07
8.60	6-99	105:00	105:06	7.15
7.05	7-99*	98:26	99:00	7.33
8.45	7-99	104:15	104:21	7.17
7.35	8-99*	99:25	99:31	7.36
8.60	8-99	105:05	105:11	7.16
7.12	9-99*	99:05	99:11	7.29
8.38	10-99	104:11	104:17	7.19
8.60	1-00	105:11	105:19	7.20
9.50	2-04	112:19	112:27	7.49

GNMA Mtge. Issues a-Bond

Rate	Mat.	Bid	Asked	Yld.
6.00	30Yr	87:11	87:19	7.76
6.50	30Yr	90:22	90:30	7.89
7.00	30Yr	93:28	94:04	7.96
7.50	30Yr	96:27	97:03	8.06
8.00	30Yr	99:12	99:20	8.19
8.50	30Yr	101:20	101:28	8.32
9.00	30Yr	103:13	103:21	8.46
9.50	30Yr	105:01	105:09	8.60
10.00	30Yr	107:10	107:18	8.60
10.50	30Yr	108:24	109:00	8.74
11.00	30Yr	110:02	110:10	8.89
11.50	30Yr	110:28	111:04	9.20
12.00	30Yr	111:28	112:04	8.95

Financing Corporation

Rate	Mat.	Bid	Asked	Yld.

Federal Farm Credit Bank

Rate	Mat.	Bid	Asked	Yld.
6.05	4-95	100:00	100:02	0.00
6.38	4-95	100:00	100:02	0.00
4.43	4-95	99:31	100:01	0.67
5.49	4-95	99:31	100:01	1.69
5.16	5-95	99:27	99:29	6.12
5.85	5-95	99:30	100:00	5.71
6.20	5-95	100:00	100:02	5.42
5.47	6-95	99:22	99:24	6.84
6.05	6-95	100:00	100:02	5.65
6.15	6-95	99:27	99:29	6.58
6.67	7-95	100:01	100:03	6.21
5.38	8-95	99:17	99:19	6.55
6.65	8-95	100:01	100:03	6.30
5.70	9-95	99:14	99:16	6.89
6.30	9-95	99:31	100:01	6.19
5.79	10-95	99:15	99:19	6.62
6.33	11-95	99:27	99:31	6.37
6.70	12-95	100:04	100:08	6.30
5.50	12-95	99:08	99:12	6.43
7.21	1-96	100:16	100:20	6.33
5.08	1-96	98:29	99:01	6.34
7.11	2-96	100:14	100:18	6.39
6.65	5-96	99:17	99:21	6.98
4.55	2-97*	95:25	95:31	6.91
5.12	3-97*	96:20	96:26	6.91
11.90	10-97	111:07	111:13	6.95
5.27	2-99*	92:30	93:04	7.36
5.79	3-99*	94:29	95:03	7.25
8.65	10-99	105:08	105:14	7.21
7.95	4-02*	99:30	100:06	7.91

Tennessee Valley Authority

Rate	Mat.	Bid	Asked	Yld.
4.38	3-96*	97:25	97:29	6.74
8.25	11-96	101:25	101:29	6.98
4.60	12-96*	96:02	96:06	7.00
6.00	1-97*	98:13	98:19	6.84
6.25	8-99*	95:29	96:03	7.31
7.63	9-99*	100:21	100:27	7.00
8.38	10-99	104:14	104:20	7.16
7.88	9-01*	101:08	101:16	7.20
7.45	10-01*	99:17	99:25	7.49
6.88	1-02*	96:18	96:26	7.48
6.88	8-02*	96:12	96:20	7.48
7.63	9-22*	95:08	95:16	8.03
7.75	12-22*	96:19	96:27	8.03
8.05	7-24*	99:28	100:04	8.04
8.63	11-29*	102:06	102:14	8.41
8.25	9-34*	99:07	99:15	8.30
8.25	4-42*	100:28	101:04	8.16
7.25	7-43	88:28	89:04	8.16
6.88	12-43*	84:22	84:30	8.13

Farm Credit Fin. Asst. Corp.

Rate	Mat.	Bid	Asked	Yld.
9.38	7-03	111:24	112:00	7.41
9.45	11-03*	107:25	108:01	6.91
8.80	6-05	109:06	109:14	7.46
9.20	9-05	106:11	106:19	8.25

Resolution Funding Corp.

Rate	Mat.	Bid	Asked	Yld.
8.13	10-19	103:00	103:08	7.82
8.88	7-20	112:25	113:01	7.70
9.38	10-20	117:16	117:24	7.77

Source: *The Wall Street Journal*, March 29, 1995.

Financing of the federal debt places a large burden on the taxpayer and consumes a significant portion of the annual budget of the federal government each year. By 1995, this annual interest cost had grown to exceed $200 billion. Today, many people are concerned that this mushrooming debt and the associated interest costs create a tremendous obligation that is being passed to future generations. Failure of current taxpayers to fund the current expenses of the government means that subsequent citizens must pay tomorrow for what we spend today.

The Corporate Bond Market

It is important to see corporate bonds in relationship to other nonfederal long-term debt. Figure 4.8 presents the major categories of long-term borrowings for issuers other than the Federal government. As the graph indicates, annual mortgage borrowing exceeds corporate bond issuances. The issues of state and local governments make up the municipal bond market and will be examined in the next section, followed by a discussion of the mortgage market.

Corporate Bond Quotations

One of the best, readily available sources for quotations on corporate bonds is *The Wall Street Journal*, where New York Exchange Bonds are quoted, as shown in Figure 4.9. In most respects, the quotations are similar to those of Treasury bonds, but there are some important differences. The identifier is essentially the same as in the Treasury bond market. The next column shows the **current yield**, which equals the annual dollar coupon amount divided by the current market price in dollars:

$$\text{Current Yield} = \frac{\text{Annual Coupon Payment}}{\text{Bond's Current Market Price}} \tag{4.7}$$

In some cases, the current yield column carries the designation "cv," which indicates that the bond is a **convertible bond**, a bond that may be converted into another security, usually common stock, at the option of the bond's owner. (Convertible securities are discussed in more detail later in this chapter.) In rare cases, the current yield column may show an "f," which indicates that the bond is traded **flat**. For a bond traded flat, the purchaser need not pay the accrued interest in addition to the bond price. This system of pricing is used when a bond is in default or when the next coupon payment is particularly uncertain.

The next column shows the day's trading volume expressed as the number of bonds. Since almost all corporate bonds have a face value of $1,000, the volume figure gives a quick guide to the face amount volume that was traded in a particular issue on a given day. The price quotations are expressed as a percentage of par. For example, on a bond with a $1,000 face value and a price quoted of 80 3/8, the actual dollar price would be 80.375 percent of the $1,000 par value, or $803.75. To actually acquire a bond with this quoted price, one would also have to pay the accrued interest as well. The final column shows the change in the price from the preceding day's close to the current day's close.

Although this page in *The Wall Street Journal* is the most readily available source of daily quotations, it is limited in many respects. Even though the dollar volume on the New York Stock Exchange (NYSE) often exceeds $30 million a day, relatively few bonds are traded over this

Figure 4.8
Annual Long-Term Nonfederal Borrowings

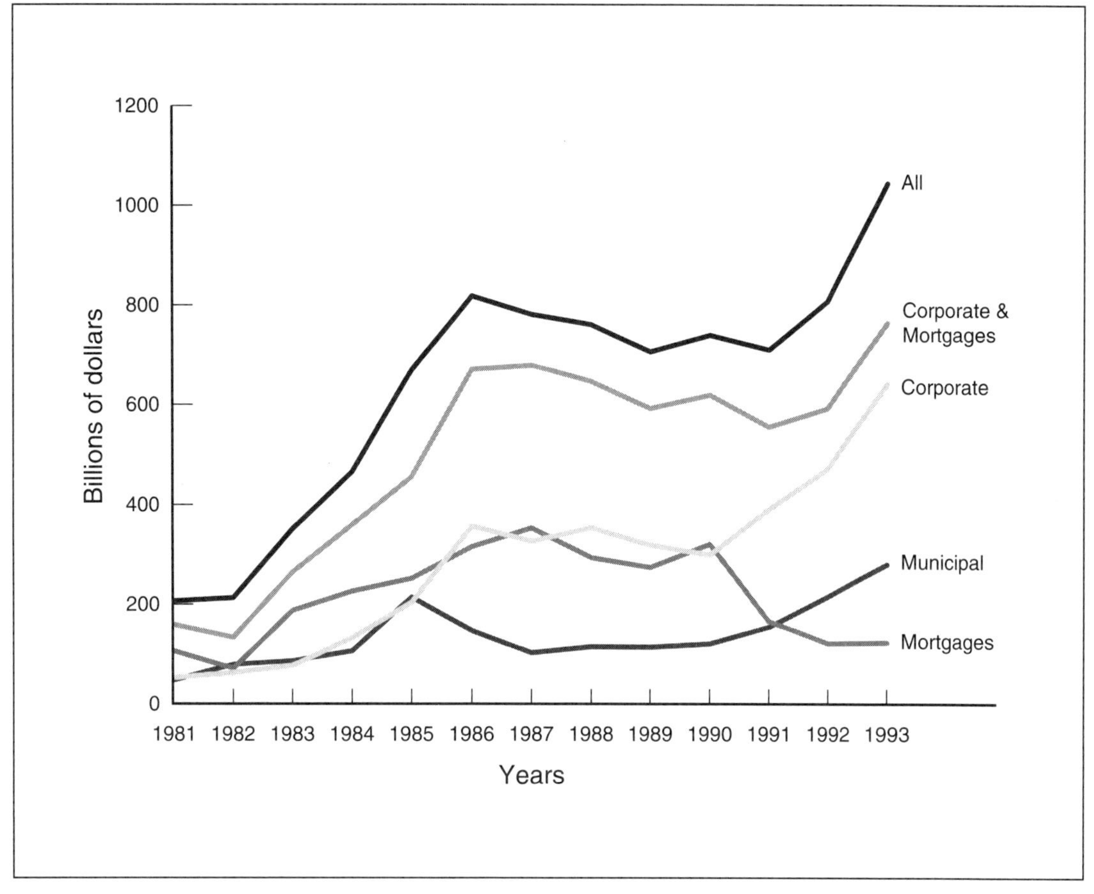

Source: *Federal Reserve Bulletin*, various issues.

exchange. This becomes clear if we examine the size of the day's trading for many of the issues. Seldom does the day's trading show more than 100 bonds of one type being traded.[9]

The Corporate Bond Over-the-Counter Market

The **over-the-counter market** (OTC) is a loose organization of traders without a centralized physical location. Rather, the OTC participants communicate with each other electronically from their own offices.[10] While there are few reliable statistics on the actual trading volume in the bond

---

[9] The American Stock Exchange also has a bond exchange associated with it. In both the bond market and the stock market, the New York Exchange dwarfs the American.

[10] The structure of the over–the–counter market is described in much more detail in Chapter 5.

Figure 4.9
Corporate Bond Quotations

NEW YORK EXCHANGE BONDS

Quotations as of 4 p.m. Eastern Time
Tuesday, March 28, 1995

Volume $34,544,000

	Domestic Tue.	Domestic Mon.	All Issues Tue.	All Issues Mon.
Issues traded	376	350	385	359
Advances	136	197	141	204
Declines	164	86	167	87
Unchanged	76	67	77	68
New highs	9	11	9	11
New lows	2	3	2	3

SALES SINCE JANUARY 1
(000 omitted)

1995	1994	1993
$1,794,277	$2,004,852	$2,792,001

Dow Jones Bond Averages

–1994– High	–1994– Low	–1995– High	–1995– Low		–1995– Close	–1995– Chg.	–1995– %Yld	–1994– Close	–1994– Chg.
105.61	93.56	98.06	93.63	20 Bonds	97.72	–0.34	7.57	101.19	– 0.37
103.43	88.99	93.88	89.08	10 Utilities	93.51	–0.37	8.02	99.11	– 0.42
107.93	97.93	102.25	98.08	10 Industrials	101.93	–0.32	7.11	103.28	– 0.32

CORPORATION BONDS
Volume, $32,702,000

Bonds	Cur Yld	Vol	Close	Net Chg.
AMR 9s16	9.1	30	98⅞	– ⅛
AMR 6⅛24	cv	11	94½	+ 2
ATT 7½06	7.5	405	99½	– ⅝
ATT 8.35s25	8.2	20	101½	+ ⅛
ATT 7¾07	7.7	340	100½	– 1
ATT 4¾98	5.1	14	93¾	– ⅛
ATT 4⅜96	4.5	5	98	+ 1½
ATT 6s00	6.4	38	94⅜	– ⅛
ATT 5⅛01	5.8	34	88½	+ ¼
ATT 8⅝31	8.4	71	102¾	...
ATT 7⅛02	7.2	402	98⅝	– ½
ATT 8⅛22	8.2	219	99⅝	– ¾
ATT 8⅛24	8.2	412	99½	– ⅛
ATT 6¾04	7.1	102	95⅛	– ⅜
Actava 9⅞97	9.8	15	100½	– ¼
Actava 9½98	10.1	100	94¼	...
AirbF 6¾01	cv	31	94½	+ 1
AlskAr 6⅞14	cv	19	78	– ¼
AlskAr zr06	...	52	44½	+ ¼
AlbnyInt 5¼02	cv	27	86¾	+ ¾
AlldC zr2000	...	13	67¾	+ ¼
AlldC zr99	...	95	72½	– ¼
AlldC zr09	...	80	32	– 1
AlegCp 6½14	cv	2	100	+ 2
AldSig 9⅞02	8.8	9	111⅞	– ⅝
AForP 5s30	8.3	10	60	+ 1
AmBrnd 9⅛16	8.8	10	103½	– 1½
AmBrnd 8⅝21	8.3	4	103¾	+ ¾
AMedia 11⅝04	11.0	10	106	+ 1
Amoco 8⅝16	8.3	10	103⅜	– ⅛
Ancp 13⅞02f	cv	32	99½	+ ½
Anhr 8⅝16	8.5	105	101	– ½
AnnTaylr 8¾00	8.8	125	100	+ ⅛
Arml 11⅜99	11.3	34	100¼	– ¾
Arrow 5¾02	cv	12	133½	+ 1½
Arvin 7½14	cv	2	94¾	+ ¾
Ashlnd 6¾14	cv	19	93¾	– ¼
Atchsn 4s95	4.1	5	98 9/16	– 1/16
AutDt zr12	...	15	44	+ ¼
Avnet 6s12	cv	5	104½	+ ½
Bally 10s06f	cv	11	83½	– ½
BkNY 7½01	cv	8	161	+ 2
BellPa 7⅛12	7.7	25	92	+ ⅛
BellPa 8⅛17	8.1	10	100	...
BellsoT 8¼32	8.3	121	99⅝	– ½
BellsoT 7⅞32	8.2	205	95⅝	+ ⅝
BellsoT 6½00	6.7	112	97	– ⅜
BellsoT 7s05	7.2	6	97	...
BellsoT 6¼03	6.7	15	92⅝	– ⅛
BellsoT 6¾33	8.1	10	83⅝	...
BstBuy 8⅝00	8.9	110	96½	+ ⅛
BethSt 9s00	9.0	50	100¼	– ⅛
BethSt 8.45s05	9.0	116	94¼	– 1
BethSt 8⅜01	8.7	27	96¾	+ ½

Bonds	Cur Yld	Vol	Close	Net Chg.
ClevEl 8⅜11	9.8	51	85½	– ⅝
ClevEl 8⅜12	9.8	6	85⅝	+ ⅛
Coastl 8⅛02	8.2	5	99	+ ½
Coeur 7s02	cv	20	115	– ¼
ColeWld zr13	...	176	30¾	+ 1½
v|ColuG 9s94f	...	9	129 9/32	– ⅝
v|ColuG 8¾s95f	...	6	127⅞	...
v|ColuG 9⅛s95f	...	38	129¾	+ ⅞
v|ColuG 7½970 f	...	5	121	+ ⅝
v|ColuG 9s93f	...	2	130⅝	– ⅜
v|ColuG 10½12f	...	10	135⅜	– ⅜
CmwE 7⅝03F	7.9	33	96⅛	+ ⅝
CmwE 7⅝03J	7.8	15	97¼	– ½
CmwE 8s03	8.1	80	99	– ¾
CmwE 8¼07	8.3	10	99½	+ 1
CompUSA 9½00	10.5	136	90⅜	+ ⅛
ConrPer 6½02	cv	44	77	– ¼
Consec 8⅛03	9.5	284	85⅞	– ⅛
CnNG 5⅞98	6.1	10	96⅛	+ ⅝
ConNG 7¼15	cv	68	100¼	– 1¼
CnPw 5⅞96	6.0	10	98	+ ⅜
CnPw 6⅞98	7.0	25	97⅞	+ ¾
Coopln 7.05s15	cv	414	100½	– ¼
Cornl 7¾98	7.7	50	100¼	...
CrayRs 6⅛11	cv	81	71	+ 1
CrossTmb 5¼03	cv	15	79½	+ ½
DataGn 01	cv	8	83	...
Datpnt 8⅞06	cv	6	25	– 1½
DeereCa 7.2s97	7.3	5	98⅜	– ⅛
DetEd 6.4s98	6.6	15	97	...
DevlDiv99	...	80	94	+ ¼
Dole 7s03	7.7	115	91½	– ¼
Dole 7⅞13	8.6	5	91½	– 1½
duPnt dc6s01	6.5	116	92½	...
EMC 4¼01	cv	1	106½	+ 2½
Eckerd 9¼04	9.2	277	101	...
ElPaso 8⅝12	8.2	2	105	...
EBP 6¾06	cv	15	71	– 1
Enron 10¾98	10.6	24	101¼	...
v|F&M 11½03f	...	203	17	...
FairCp 13⅛06	16.0	5	82	– ½
FedDS 10s01	9.5	40	105	...
Fldcst 6s12	cv	46	77½	+ 2¼
FFnMgt 5s99	cv	6	117	...
Florsh 12¾02	13.4	85	95¼	– ⅛
FreptM 10⅞01	10.4	5	104½	...
Frpt dc6.55s01	cv	14	91¾	+ ¼
FreptM zr06	...	1	36¾	+ ⅛
FremntGn zr13	...	125	34	...
GMA dc6s11	7.6	9	79	– ¼
GMA zr12	...	109	239	...
GMA zr15	...	87	192⅛	– ⅞
GMA 8¼16	8.4	139	98	– ¼
GMA 8⅜97	8.2	40	102¼	– ⅛
GPA Del 8¾98	11.0	110	79½	– ¼
GnCorp 8s02	8.1	16	98½	+ ½
GElCap 7⅞06	7.6	20	103	+ ⅝

Bonds	Cur Yld	Vol	Close	Net Chg.
ICN 12⅞98	12.6	19	101⅞	...
ITTF 8⅞03	8.3	5	107¼	+ 1⅜
IBM 9s98cld	...	105	100⅛	...
IBM 8⅜19	8.2	106	102½	+ ⅛
IBM 6⅜97	6.5	1340	98⅜	+ ⅛
IBM 7¼02	7.3	302	98¾	– ¼
IBM 6⅜00	6.7	196	95¾	– ¼
IBM 7½13	7.9	42	95⅛	– ½
IntShip 9s03	9.6	1	94	...
KaufB 9⅜03	10.4	163	90	+ ⅛
Kolmrg 8¾09	cv	5	91	...
Kroger 9s99	8.9	20	101½	+ ⅝
LaFrg 7s13	cv	22	100¼	+ ¼
LehmnBr 8¾02	8.7	686	100½	– 1
LehmnBr 10¾96	10.5	35	102½	– ¾
Leucadia 5¼03	...	5	95½	– 2¼
LibPrp 8s01	cv	129	100	...
Litton 12⅝cld	...	3	105⅛	...
LomasFn 9s03	cv	153	33¼	– ¼
LgIsLt 9⅝24	10.3	15	93½	...
LgIsLt 8½06	8.8	10	96½	...
LgIsLt 7.3s99	7.7	55	94¼	– ½
LgIsLt 8.9s19	10.7	538	83⅜	– ⅛
LsIsLt 9s22	10.6	135	85	+ ¼
LgIsLt 7½07	9.0	103	83¼	...
LgIsLt 8.2s23	10.4	367	78⅝	...
LgIsLt 8⅝04	8.8	25	97⅝	– 1⅜

Bonds	Cur Yld	Vol	Close	Net Chg.
NETelTel 4½02	5.5	5	82½	– ½
NETelTel 7⅜07	7.6	20	96½	+ ½
NETelTel 6¼03	6.8	25	92	– 1
NYEG 7⅝01	7.8	10	98¼	+ 1¼
NYTel 4⅞06	6.2	11	78½	+ ¼
NYTel 7¾06	7.9	25	98½	– ⅜
NYTel 7⅞17	8.1	20	96¾	+ ⅛
NYTel 7⅝23	8.3	8	92⅛	+ 1¾
NoPac 3s47	3.9	2	76	+ 3½
Novacr 5½2000	cv	63	81	– ⅞
OcciP 11¾11	10.8	77	108⅜	...
OcciP 10¾cld	...	50	100¼	– ⅛
OcciP 11⅛19	9.8	13	113½	+ ½
OcciP 9⅝99	9.4	75	102⅜	– ½
OcciP 10⅛09	8.9	5	113¼	– 1⅛
OcciP 10⅛01	9.0	65	112⅝	+ ⅝
OffDep zr08	...	25	56½	+ ⅜
OhBlT 7½11	7.9	10	95⅜	– 1⅛
OhBlT 7⅞13	8.0	120	98½	– ⅞
OldRep 5¾02	cv	6	103½	...
Olsten 4⅞03	4.4	2	110½	– ¼
Oryx 9¾98	9.7	85	100¼	– ¼
Oryx 10⅜18	10.1	30	102¾	+ ⅜
Oryx 7½14	cv	32	77½	+ ½
OwnIll 10¼99	10.1	85	101¼	– ⅝
OwIll 11s03	10.3	45	106⅞	– ¾
OwnIll 10s02	10.0	95	99¾	

Source: *The Wall Street Journal*, March 29, 1995.

market, it is possible to observe the annual issuance of bonds. By 1995, the total amount of corporate bonds issued annually was approaching $700 billion.[11]

[11] Chapter 8 considers the process by which firms issue new securities.

When it issues a bond, a corporation promises to make a series of payments of a certain amount on pre-specified dates. For the purchaser of the bond, the best thing that could happen is that the issuer keeps his promise. There is no question of hoping for payments above those that were promised. As a result, for many bond investors, the chance that the promise will be kept becomes extremely important. To aid bond investors in making their assessment about the future payment prospects of a particular bond, there are services that rate the quality of various bonds. Two of the most prominent bond ratings services are Standard & Poor's and Moody's. The ratings are designed to measure default risk – the chance that one or more payments on the bond will be deferred or missed altogether. Table 4.4 presents the categories of the two principal rating services. In general, these two rating systems follow each other very closely. Figure 4.10 shows the explanations of its ratings provided by Standard & Poor's. Moody's has a similar explanation for its rankings. Bond returns depend on other factors besides whether the promised payments are made. If we hold a bond until it matures and the issuer makes all payments as promised, we will earn the yield to maturity on the bond at the time of purchase. For shorter holding periods, bond returns are uncertain. Bond prices can change as a result of changes in interest rates and changes in the prospects of the issuing firm.

History of Corporate Bond Returns

Figure 4.11 presents the returns for a portfolio of high-quality long-term corporate bonds for 1926 to 1994. Over this period, these bonds returned an average annual rate of 5.4 percent. After subtracting inflation, the annualized real return was only 2.22 percent. As another guide to the returns, $1 invested in corporate bonds in 1926 would have grown to $38.01, and purchasing power would have increased from $1 in 1926 to $4.55 by year-end 1994.

These returns for top-quality bonds do not tell the entire story. There are many other types of bonds with different yields as well, with the differences in yields due largely to differences in risk. Figure 4.12 shows the yield relationship between top-quality and lower quality corporate bonds. The difference in yields between bonds of different quality rankings, or levels of default risk, appears to widen when interest rates are high and also when the economy is in recession. This

Table 4.4
Bond Rating Categories

	Moody's	Standard & Poor's
	Aaa	AAA
Investment	Aa	AA
Grade	A	A
	Baa	BBB
	Ba	BB
	B	B
Below		CCC–CC
Investment	Caa	C
Grade	Ca	
		DDD–D
	C	

Figure 4.10
Standard & Poor's Bond Ratings

DEBT

A Standard & Poor's corporate or municipal debt rating is a current assessment of the creditworthiness of an obligor with respect to a specific obligation. This assessment may take into consideration obligors such as guarantors, insurers, or lessees.

The debt rating is not a recommendation to purchase, sell or hold a security, inasmuch as it does not comment as to market price or suitability for a particular investor.

The ratings are based on current information furnished by the issuer or obtained by Standard & Poor's from other sources it considers reliable. Standard & Poor's does not perform any audit in connection with any rating and may, on occasion, rely on unaudited financial information. The ratings may be changed, suspended or withdrawn as a result of changes in, or unavailability of, such information, or for other circumstances.

The ratings are based, in varying degrees, on the following considerations:

I. Likelihood of default-capacity and willingness of the obligor as to the timely payment of interest and repayment of principal in accordance with the terms of the obligation;
II. Nature of and provisions of the obligation;
III. Protection afforded by, and relative position of, the obligation in the event of bankruptcy, reorganization or other arrangement under the laws of bankruptcy and other laws affecting creditor's rights.

AAA Debt rated 'AAA' has the highest rating assigned by Standard & Poor's Capacity to pay interest and repay principal is extremely strong.

AA Debt rated 'AA' has a very strong capacity to pay interest and repay principal and differs from the higher rated issues only in small degree.

A Debt rated 'A' has a strong capacity to pay interest and repay principal although it is somewhat more susceptible to the adverse effects of changes in circumstances and economic conditions than debt in higher rated categories.

BBB Debt rated 'BBB' is regarded as having an adequate capacity to pay interest and repay principal. Whereas it normally exhibits adequate protection parameters, adverse economic conditions or changing circumstances are more likely to lead to a weakened capacity to pay interest and repay principal for debt in this category than in higher rated categories.

BB, B, CCC, CC, C Debt rated 'BB', 'B', 'CCC', 'CC' and 'C' is regarded, on balance, as predominantly speculative with respect to capacity to pay interest and repay principal in accordance with the terms of the obligation. 'BB' indicates the lowest degree of speculation and 'C' the highest degree of speculation. While such debt will likely have some quality and protective characteristics, these are outweighed by large uncertainties or major risk exposures to adverse conditions.

BB Debt rated 'BB' has less near-term vulnerability to default than other speculative issues. However, it faces major ongoing uncertainties or exposure to adverse business, financial, or economic conditions which could lead to inadequate capacity to meet timely interest and principal payments. The 'BB' rating category is also used for debt subordinated to senior debt that is assigned an actual or implied 'BBB-' rating.

B Debt rated 'B' has a greater vulnerability to default but currently has the capacity to meet interest payments and principal repayments. Adverse business, financial, or economic conditions will likely impair capacity or willingness to pay interest and repay principal. The 'B' rating category is also used for debt subordinated to senior debt that is assigned an actual or implied 'BB' or 'BB-' rating.

CCC Debt rated 'CCC' has a currently identifiable vulnerability to default, and is dependent upon favorable business, financial, and economic conditions to meet timely payment of interest and repayment of principal. In the event of adverse business, financial, or economic conditions, it is not likely to have the capacity to pay interest and repay principal, The 'CCC' rating category is also used for debt subordinated to senior debt that is assigned an actual or implied 'B' or 'B-' rating.

CC The rating 'CC' is typically applied to debt subordinated to senior debt that is assigned an actual or implied 'CCC' rating.

C The rating 'C' is typically applied to debt subordinated to senior debt which is assigned an actual or implied 'CCC-' debt rating. The 'C' rating may be used to cover a situation where a bankruptcy petition has been filed, but debt service payments are continued.

Cl The rating 'Cl' is reserved for income bonds on which no interest is being paid.

D Debt rated 'D' is in payment default. The 'D' rating category is used when interest payments or principal payments are not made on the date due even if the applicable grace period has not expired, unless S&P believes that such payments will be made during such grace period. The 'D' rating also will be used upon the filing of a bankruptcy petition if debt service payments are jeopardized.

Plus (+) or Minus (-): The ratings from 'AA' to 'CCC' may be modified by the addition of a plus or minus sign to show relative standing within the major categories.

NR indicates that no public rating has been requested, that there is insufficient information on which to base a rating, or that S&P does not rate a particular type of obligation as a matter of policy.

Debt Obligations of issuers outside the United States and its territories are rated on the same basis as domestic corporate and municipal issues . The ratings measure the creditworthiness of the obligor but do not take into account currency exchange and related uncertainties.

Bond Investment Quality Standards: Under present commercial bank regulations issued by the Comptroller of the Currency bonds rated in the top four categories ('AAA,' 'AA,' 'A,' 'BBB,' commonly known as "Investment Grade" ratings) are generally regarded as eligible for bank investment. In addition, the Legal Investment Laws of various states may impose certain rating or other standards for obligations eligible for investment by savings banks, trust companies, insurance companies and fiduciaries generally.

Source: Standard & Poor's Corporation, *Bond Guide*, August 1991, p.10.

is likely to be the case because the probability of default for weaker bonds rises more rapidly in recessions than it does for top-rated bonds.[12]

High-Yield Corporate Bonds

The high-yield corporate bond market developed into special prominence in the 1980s. These bonds are lower rated or speculative grade bonds and are commonly referred to as **junk bonds** (S&P BB or lower, and Moody's Ba or lower). As Figure 4.10 shows, Standard & Poor's regards BB and lower grade bonds as "predominantly speculative with respect to capacity to pay interest and repay principal in accordance with the terms of the obligation." Before the late 1970s, virtually all publicly traded bonds were issued with an investment grade rating (S&P BBB or better or Moody's Baa or better). There were lower grade bonds trading in the market place, but these bonds had been issued as investment grade and had been subsequently downgraded as "fallen angels." About this time, some firms began to issue debt rated BB or Ba and lower under the leadership of the investment banking firm Drexel Burnham Lambert. Between 1977 and 1989, the

[12] For more on default risk and the yield differences it creates, see Chapter 7.

Figure 4.11
Returns on High-Quality Corporate Bonds, 1926–94

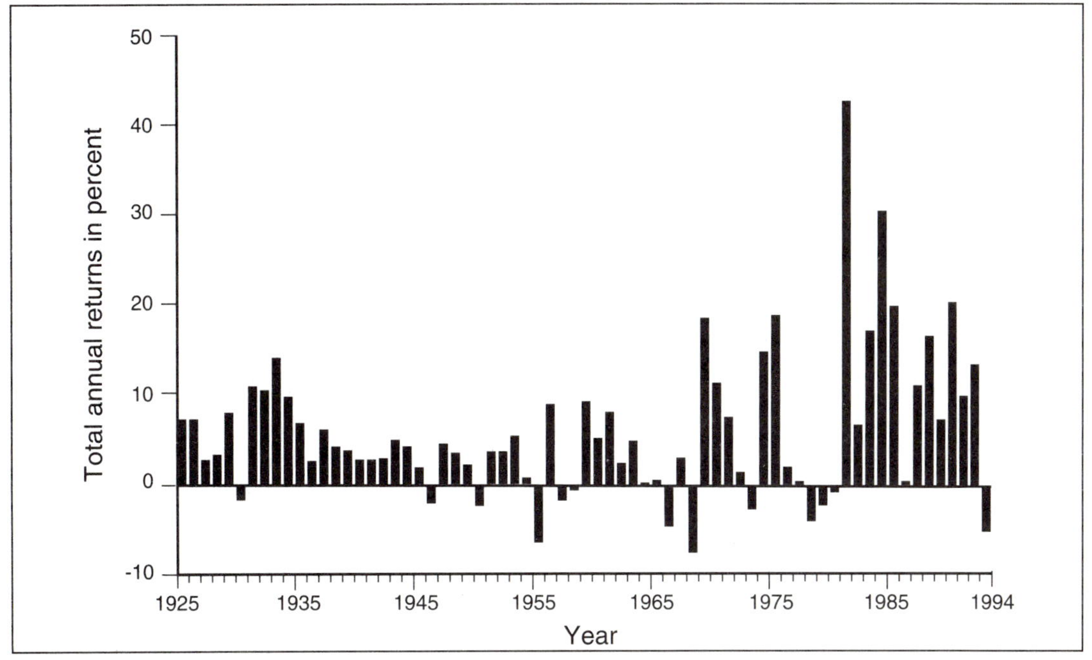

Source: Ibbotson Associates, *Stocks, Bonds, Bills, and Inflation: 1995 Yearbook*, Chicago: Ibbotson Associates, 1995, p.55.

amount of outstanding junk bonds increased from about $1.1 billion to $24.2 billion, and by 1989 about $205 billion in junk bonds were outstanding.[13] Much of this debt was issued in the waves of mergers and corporate restructurings that characterized the 1980s.[14]

The bond ratings of S&P and Moody's aim to measure **default risk**, the chance that one or more promised payments will not be made as promised. For an investor concerned with the risk/expected return trade-off, default risk is just one consideration. If junk bonds have a sufficiently high expected return, it might compensate for the greater chance that junk bonds would default. A variety of studies have sought to measure the default experience of corporate bonds, with the rough consensus being that bond portfolios might lose 1-2 percent of their value each year through default.[15] However, if yields are high enough to compensate for this loss through default, junk bonds could still be an attractive investment.

---

[13] For more on junk bonds, see M. E. Blume, D. B. Keim, and S. A. Patel, "Returns and Volatility of Low-Grade Bonds, 1977–1989," *Journal of Finance*, 46:1, March 1991, pp. 49–74. This account of junk bonds relies largely on this article.

[14] For example, a firm desiring to acquire a target company might issue junk bonds to obtain the necessary cash for the acquisition. Similarly, firms that were taken private by a management buyout of other shareholders (a leveraged buyout or LBO) would often obtain financing for the buyout by issuing junk bonds.

[15] See Howard S. Marks, "High Yield Bond Portfolios," in F. J. Fabozzi, T. D. Fabozzi, and I. M. Pollack, *The Handbook of Fixed Income Securities*, Homewood, IL: Business One Irwin, 1991, pp. 972–88 for a discussion of the issue of default losses.

Figure 4.12
Yield Differentials for Different Quality Corporate Bonds

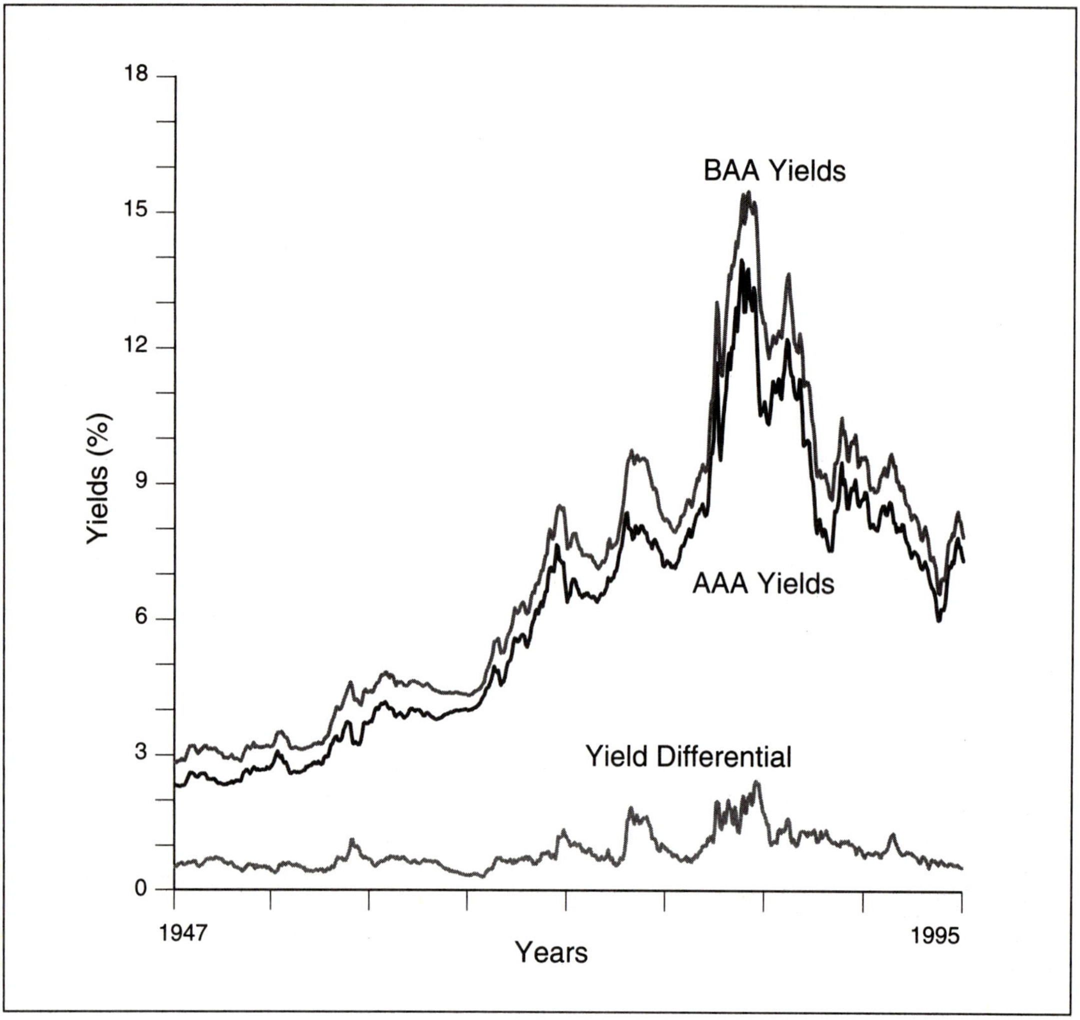

Source: *Federal Reserve Bulletin* , various issues.

The Municipal Bond Market

A **municipal bond** is a debt security issued by a government or a quasi-governmental agency, other than those associated with the federal government. Prime among these issuers are states, cities, and their political subdivisions. These securities form a distinct segment of the bond market due to the special character of their issuers and their tax status. Most municipal bonds are exempt from federal income taxation. This key feature distinguishes municipal bonds from the rest of the bond market.

Because of their tax exemption, municipal bonds are of greater relative value to investors with high marginal tax rates. Such investors can obtain the same after-tax return from a relatively low yielding municipal bond or a higher yielding taxable bond. As Equation 7.6 shows, the difference can be important.

$$\text{Equivalent Tax} - \text{Extempt Yield} = (1 - \text{Marginal Tax Rate})\,(\text{Taxable Yield}) \qquad (4.8)$$

For example, consider an investor with a 35 percent marginal tax rate, faced with a choice between a taxable bond yielding 10 percent and a tax-exempt bond yielding 7 percent. For bonds of like risk and maturity, the rational investor should prefer the bond that gives the higher after-tax return. The taxable bond yielding 10 percent has an equivalent after-tax yield equal to a tax-exempt yield of only 6.5 percent:

$$.065 = (1 - .35).10$$

Assuming that the bonds were equally risky and suitable in other respects, the investor should prefer the lower yielding tax-exempt bond, which will return an after-tax yield of 7 percent. Given the after-tax equivalences of municipal bonds, it is not surprising that market yields for tax-exempt securities are lower than those of risk-equivalent taxable securities. Figure 4.13 shows the historical yield relationships between AAA tax-exempt and AAA taxable securities. Although the rating systems for tax-exempt and taxable bonds are slightly different, AAA ratings are the highest for both categories, so they are approximately equal in risk. The yield spread between the two kinds of bonds reflects the eagerness of investors for opportunities to escape taxation.

In addition to exemption from federal taxation, some municipal bonds are also exempt from income taxation by the state and municipality in which they were issued. A bond exempt from federal, state, and municipal taxation is said to be **triple tax-exempt**. Such bonds are popular in states such as California and New York, which have locations that tax income at all three levels.

Although the municipal bond market is huge in total size, it is not a very liquid market.[16] Many municipal issues are not very large, and some investors want to hold on to issues once acquired. Consequently, it is somewhat difficult to acquire good information on the current prices of some issues. Two good sources are *The Wall Street Journal* and the Blue List of Standard & Poor's. Figure 4.14 presents a typical listing from *The Wall Street Journal*. Only the most closely followed issues are reported there, and the prices are given only in bid-asked form. The listing is not necessarily a listing of transaction prices.

Issues in the municipal bond market can be divided into **general obligation bonds** and **revenue bonds**. General obligation bonds are bonds backed by the issuer's taxing power, such as a state or local government. By contrast, revenue bonds are backed only by the revenue from some specific project. The administrators of port authorities, airports, turnpikes, and hospitals are typical issuers of revenue bonds. For revenue bonds, all bond payments must come from the revenue of the particular project. For example, a revenue bond issued by a hospital would have to be paid

---

[16] A **liquid market** is one in which an asset can be sold easily for a price that approximates its true value.

Figure 4.13
Yield Differentials for U.S. High Grade Corporate and Municipal Bonds

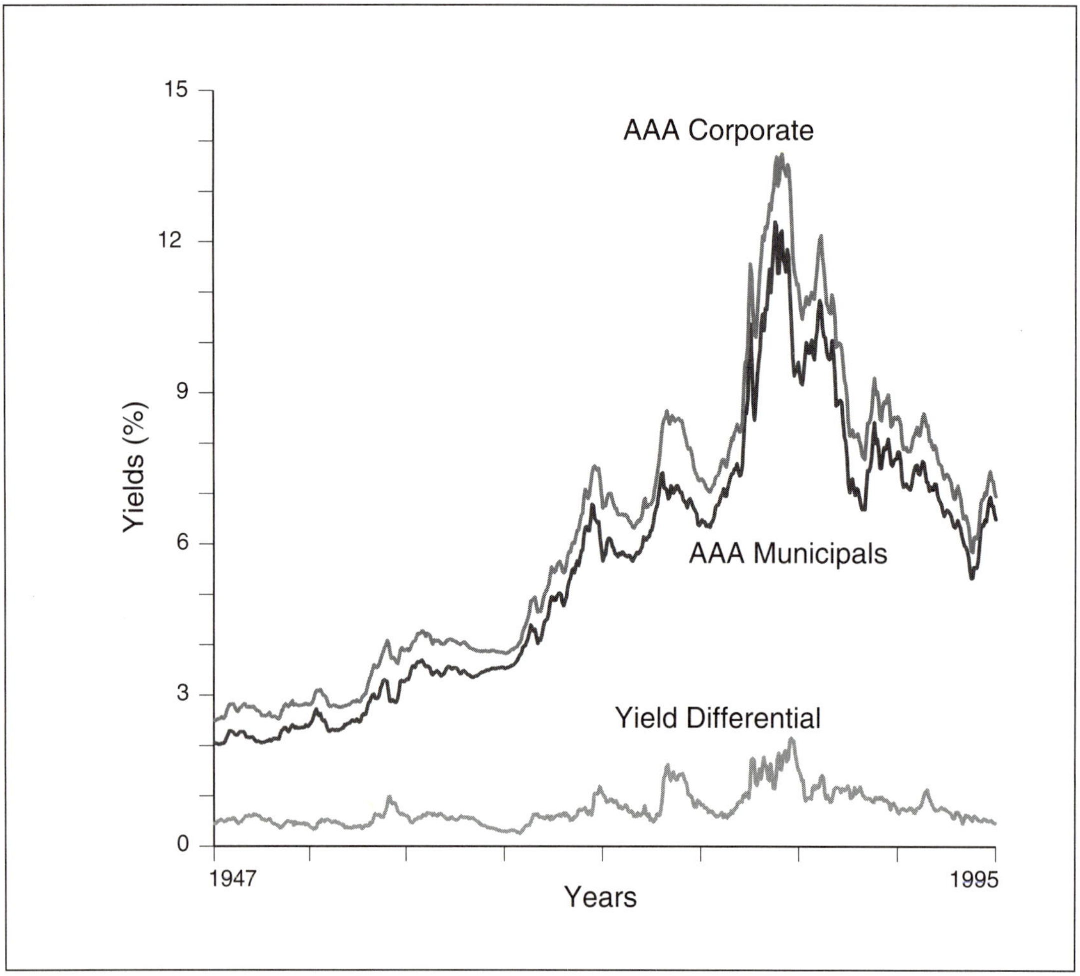

Source: *Federal Reserve Bulletin*, various issues.

for by the profits earned by the hospital. Without question, the revenue bonds have a certain risk element since the enterprise must be a success if the bondholders are to be repaid. For general obligation bonds, the issuer at least has taxing power to rely on to secure the necessary funds to repay the bondholders. Figure 4.15 shows the recent issuances of municipal bonds. By 1995, the annual issuance approached $300 billion.

The Mortgage Market

One of the largest components of debt is the **mortgage**, or the debt owed on real estate. In speaking of the mortgage market, it is important to distinguish between real estate mortgages and mortgages as a type of collateral for a debt obligation. In one sense, we mortgage a car to secure

Figure 4.14
Municipal Bond Quotations

TAX-EXEMPT BONDS

Representative prices for several active tax-exempt revenue and refunding bonds, based on institutional trades. Changes rounded to the nearest one-eighth. Yield is to maturity. n-New. Source: The Bond Buyer.

ISSUE	COUPON	MAT	PRICE	CHG	BID YLD	ISSUE	COUPON	MAT	PRICE	CHG	BID YLD
Anne Arundel Ser94	6.000	04-01-24	96⅞	– ¼	6.23	NYC Indus Devel Agcy	6.000	01-01-15	94¼	– ⅜	6.52
Calif Pub Wrks Bd	7.000	03-01-19	104¼	– ⅜	6.65	NYC Indus Devel Agcy	6.125	01-01-24	94⅛	– ⅜	6.58
Calif Pub Wrks Bd 94A	7.000	11-01-19	104¼	– ⅜	6.65	NYS Envrnmntl Ser 94D	6.900	11-15-15	107⅛	– ¼	6.29
Chgo Ill Gen Arpt	6.375	01-01-15	101⅝	– ⅛	6.23	NYS Med Care	6.200	02-15-28	98⅝	– ¼	6.30
Cleve Ohio Pub Pwr Sys	7.000	11-15-24	108⅜	– ¼	6.37	NYS Mortgage Agency	6.650	10-01-25	99½	– ¼	6.69
Douglas Co SD RE-1	6.500	12-15-16	104¼	– ¼	6.15	NYS Thruway	6.000	01-01-15	98½	– ¼	6.13
Florida St Bd Ed	5.800	06-01-24	96⅜	– ⅛	6.06	NYS Thruway Auth	6.000	01-01-25	97⅝	– ¼	6.18
Florida St Bd Ed	6.100	06-01-24	99⅝	– ⅛	6.13	Orange Co Fla	6.000	10-01-24	98½	– ⅛	6.11
Ga Muni Elec Auth	6.500	01-01-26	102¼	– ⅛	6.34	Pa Intergvt Coop Auth	6.750	06-15-21	104⅞	– ¼	6.37
Harris Co Hlth Tex	6.375	10-01-24	100⅜	– ⅛	6.35	PR Pub Imprvmt Ser94	6.500	07-01-23	101	– ⅛	6.43
Hawaii Hsng Fin & Dev	6.000	07-01-26	93½	– ⅜	6.49	Prtlnd Ore Swr 94 SerA	6.250	06-01-15	101¾	– ⅜	6.10
Ill Dev Fin Ser 94D	6.750	03-01-15	104⅜	– ⅛	6.36	Salem Co Poll Ctrl	6.250	06-01-31	99¾	– ⅜	6.26
Ill Regional TA	6.250	06-01-24	99¼	– ¼	6.31	Salem Co Poll Ctrl	6.550	10-01-29	102⅝	– ¼	6.36
KC Kan Util Sys	6.375	09-01-23	102½	– ⅛	6.19	San Fran Calif Sewer	5.375	10-01-22	90	– ¼	6.13
LA Harbor Dept Ser 95B	6.625	08-01-25	101½	– ¼	6.51	Santa Clara Calif	6.750	11-15-20	104⅞	– ¼	6.36
Lehigh Co Indus Dev	6.400	09-01-29	101⅛	– ¼	6.32	Santa Clara Valley Ca	6.000	02-01-24	97⅞	– ¼	6.16
Lower Neches Valley	6.400	03-01-30	98⅝	– ¼	6.50	SC Public Svc Auth	5.875	01-01-23	96⅝	– ⅛	6.12
MTA NY Series O	6.375	07-01-20	101¼	– ¼	6.28	TBTA NY	5.000	01-01-24	83¾	– ¼	6.21
NJ Economic Dev Auth	6.400	05-01-32	99½	– ⅛	6.43	Texas GOs Ser 94A	7.000	12-01-25	101¾	– ⅛	6.86
NYC GO Fiscal 95 Ser B	7.250	08-15-19	103⅛	– ⅜	6.98	Valdez Alaska Marine	5.650	12-01-28	90¼	+ ¼	6.35

Source: *The Wall Street Journal*, March 29, 1995.

a car loan. Anytime an asset is pledged to secure a loan, a mortgage is created. Because real estate loans are so typically secured by a pledge of real estate, such loans are themselves called mortgages. This section focuses on real estate mortgages, borrowing that is comparable in size to either corporate or municipal borrowing.

Most mortgages are for residential properties. The initial maturities for these mortgages range up to 30 years and often carry a fixed rate of interest for the entire period. Recently, so-called creative financing plans (including **variable-rate mortgages** and **balloon mortgages**) have become popular. A variable-rate mortgage allows the interest rate to vary with economic conditions. For example, the rate on the mortgage might be tied to the rate on Treasury bills and adjusted every six months. A balloon mortgage is structured so that the final payment, which might occur three to seven years after the mortgage is initiated, is much larger than the ordinary monthly payments.

The traditional 30-year fixed-rate mortgage is different from the typical bond with its coupon payments and return of principal upon maturity. The main difference in the structure of these instruments stems from the fact that a mortgage is typically an **amortized loan**. In an amortized loan, the payment remains the same over the life of the loan, with part of the payment going to pay interest and part going to pay the principal of the loan. Over time, the portion devoted to paying interest and the portion repaying principal change. As an example, consider a 30-year 10 percent mortgage with an initial principal amount of $100,000. For this mortgage, the monthly payment would be $877.57. Of this payment, $833.33, or 95 percent, would go toward paying the interest in the first month of the mortgage. Figure 4.16 shows how the proportion of the payment going to principal and interest changes over the life of the mortgage. For the illustration, we assume a 30-year mortgage at 10 percent. Of the first payment, 94.9 percent goes to repay inter-

Figure 4.15
Issuance of Municipal Bonds

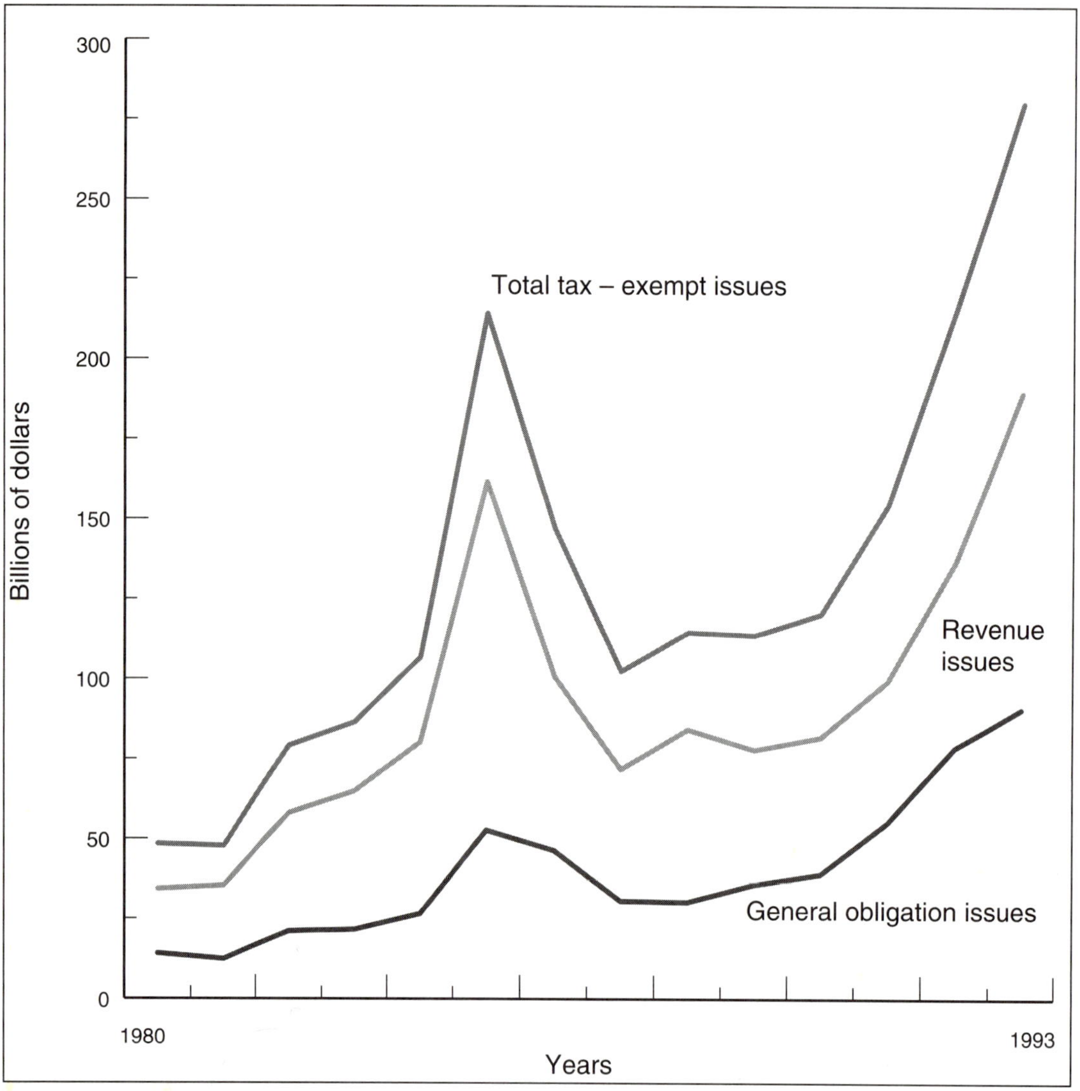

Source: *Federal Reserve Bulletin*, various issues.

est, leaving only 5.1 percent of the payment to reduce principal. By the end of the mortgage, that relationship has reversed, with almost all of the final payment paying off the last bit of principal.

Mortgage Pass-Through Securities

After a mortgage is granted by a financial institution, the institution may itself continue to own the mortgage, or it can sell the mortgage in the market for mortgage obligations. Currently, it has become very common to create a **mortgage pool** – a collection of individual mortgages that can

Figure 4.16
Monthly Mortgage Payments: Percentage Paying Principal and Interest

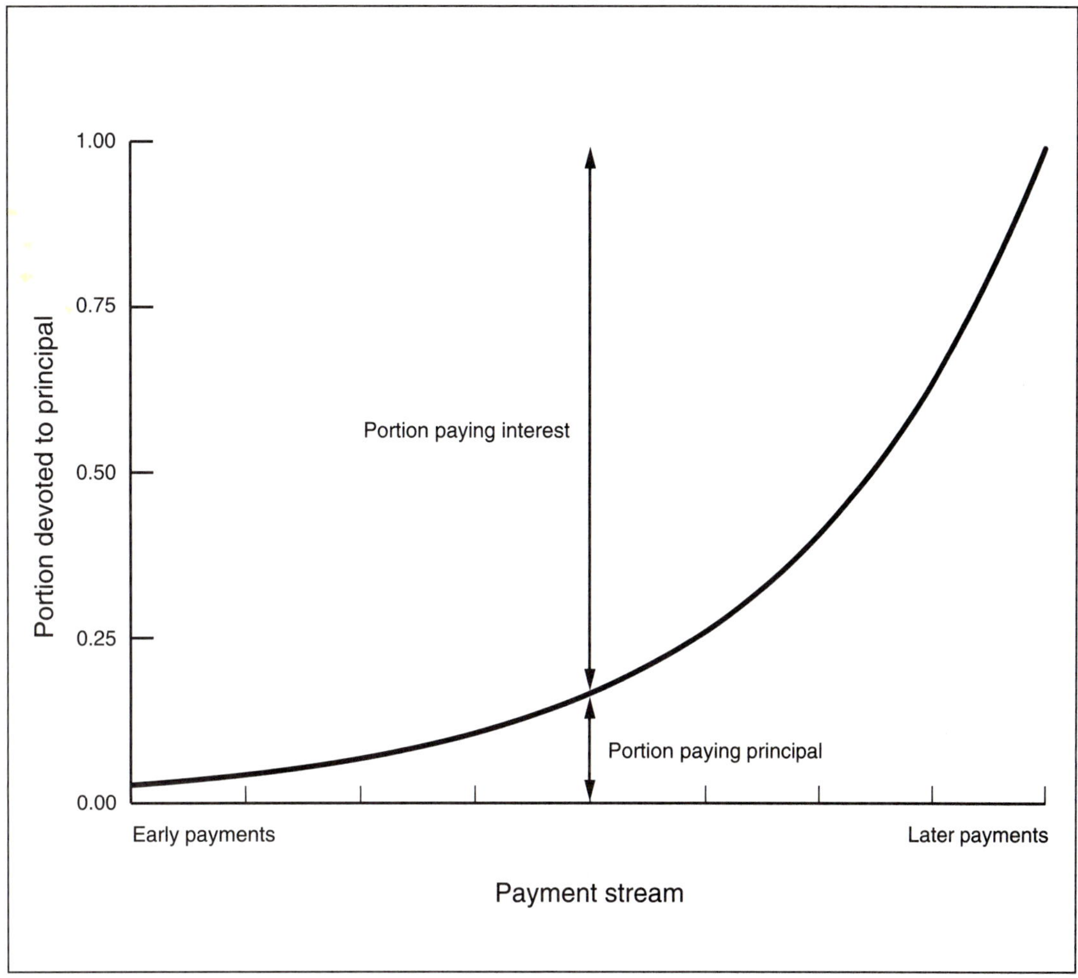

be treated as a unit. Once the pool is created, securities are created based on the mortgages in the pool. Thus, investors can buy a participation in the entire pool of mortgages, instead of investing in a single, particular mortgage.

These securities are a **mortgage pass-through security** because the original lender continues to collect payments from the borrower and passes them through to the investors in the mortgage pool. Each security holder receives a payment based on the investment made in the pool. The investors in the pool have a diversified mortgage investment, owning a portion of many mortgages. This provides diversification against default and the risk that the principal on an individual mortgage might be paid early.

Three federally sponsored agencies facilitate the development of mortgage pass-through securities in order to stimulate the mortgage market. They do this by issuing a guarantee that the payments will be made on the mortgages as promised. In effect, this substitutes the creditworthiness of the agency for the owner of the individual properties covered in the mortgage pool. These agencies are the Government National Mortgage Association (GNMA, pronounced "Ginnie Mae"), the Federal National Mortgage Association (FNMA, pronounced "Fannie Mae"), and the Federal Home Loan Mortgage Corporation (FHLMC, pronounced "Freddie Mac").

These agency-guaranteed mortgage pass-throughs provide an attractive means for individual investors or managers of bond portfolios to invest in residential mortgages. Because they are guaranteed by federally sponsored agencies, these mortgages tend to be quite safe from default risk, but they have a higher yield than Treasury issues. Nonetheless, these pass-throughs are subject to other risks that make them quite complicated. Principal among these risks is the chance that individual property owners will pay their mortgages early if interest rates fall. If this happens, the pass-through investor receives a return of principal that must face reinvestment at the new lower rates.

The Bond Contract

The **bond contract**, or **bond indenture**, is a legal document stating in precise terms the promises made by the issuer of a bond and the rights of the bondholders. For all corporate bonds issued in interstate commerce and having an issue size exceeding $5 million, the Trust Indentures Act requires that a trustee be established. The trustee for a bond issue is responsible for protecting the rights of the bondholders and monitoring the performance of the issuer to ensure that its promises are kept. The trustee will usually be a bank that is financially independent from the issuer. The bond indenture will be made out to the trustee, who acts as an agent for the bondholders in enforcing the terms of the bond contract.

In addition to specifying the amount and timing of payments to be made to the bondholders, the bond indenture also contains numerous covenants. Among the most important of these are the portions defining the security that the issuer is offering for the bond and the specification of how the bond is to be retired.

Bondholders naturally desire the greatest security possible for their investment, other things being equal. This leads some issuers to offer bonds backed by mortgages on specific corporate assets. For example, an issuer could offer a fleet of vehicles or a production plant as security for a bond issue. In the event of default, the trustee would be empowered to seize the specified assets in order to recoup the investment of the bondholders. Such a bond may be either a **first mortgage bond** or have some inferior status, such as a second or third mortgage. A first mortgage bond gives the bondholders first claim on the assets specified in the mortgage. In the event of a serious default or bankruptcy, those assets are earmarked to be used to repay the bondholders, so the first mortgage is the best kind of collateral available to bondholders.

In addition to mortgage bonds, some firms offer security under slightly different arrangements. For firms that do not have sufficient physical assets to offer as collateral, it is customary to pledge securities. Bonds secured by financial assets are known as **collateral trust bonds**. In the railroad industry, the railroad cars or rolling stock of the railroad have often been pledged as collateral. This type of security is called an **equipment trust certificate**. Under this form of security, the bond issuer does not actually own the equipment until the bond issue is paid off, which makes it easier for the bondholders to seize and dispose of the assets in the event of default. Although originated in the railroad industry, this type of collateral is used by a variety of transportation firms, such as airlines and shippers.

Most bonds issued by corporations have no security pledged to the bonds. This type of bond is known as a **debenture**. Debentures are often used by financially strong corporations that have no mortgage bonds outstanding. Sometimes, however, the debentures are issued after mortgage bonds are already outstanding. In such cases, the debentures have an inferior claim on the assets of the corporation. In addition to straight debentures, there are also **subordinated debentures**, which are unsecured bonds that have an inferior claim to other outstanding debentures. The subordinated debentures are said to be junior to the more senior, original debentures. Table 4.5 presents the priority of claims among the outstanding securities of corporations. First mortgage bondholders have the strongest position on the assets, while common stockholders have the weakest.

Without any specific security pledged to them, debentures may seem to be a very risky kind of investment. To offset that risk, bond contracts for debentures, as well as for mortgage bonds, often have certain restrictive covenants that protect the bondholders by restricting the behavior of the issuer. For example, a restrictive covenant might require a firm to maintain a certain level of current assets relative to its current liabilities, or the firm may be prohibited from issuing additional debt until the outstanding debt is retired. Still another type of restrictive covenant might constrain the amount of dividends that could be paid to common stockholders. All restrictions are designed to enhance the safety of the bond investment. The trustee is responsible for ensuring that the issuer complies with the restrictions.

The bond contract also specifies how the bond is to be retired, and there are many different ways of paying off a bond. Many corporate bonds, as well as many U.S. Treasury bonds, are callable bonds. For a **callable bond**, the issuer has the right to call the bonds in before maturity and pay them off at a certain price stipulated in the bond contract. Issuers have an incentive to call their existing bonds in if the prevailing interest rate is lower than the coupon rate being paid on the bond. Usually the issuer is not permitted to call the bond for a certain period of time after issue. Also, the price the issuer must pay to call the bond, the **call price**, usually gives a premium over the par value to the bondholder. This call price is usually above the par value of the bond and declines toward the par value as the bond approaches maturity. Often, only a portion of a bond

Table 4.5
Priority of Claims by Security Type

Highest Priority	First Mortgage Bonds Second Mortgage Bonds
	Debentures Subordinated Debentures
Lowest Priority	Preferred Stock Common Stock

issue is called, and the particular bonds to be called are selected at random, with the selected bonds being published by serial number in the financial press.

Callable bonds are often retired by the use of a **sinking fund**. The sinking fund provision of a bond contract provides for the orderly retirement of bonds prior to the maturity date. The sinking fund may operate in two basic ways. The trustee may use the resources of the sinking fund to purchase bonds in the open market, or the sinking fund may provide for retirement of a certain portion of the bonds on a redemption date. In such a case, specific bonds are called to be surrendered on a certain date.

Sometimes bonds are scheduled for retirement with a certain principal amount becoming due at predetermined dates. Such a bond is called a **serial bond**. This gives the investor an opportunity to select the maturity date that best suits the investment plan.

Another method of retiring bonds is through conversion. The bondholder of a **convertible bond** has the option of surrendering the bond and receiving in return a specified number of shares of common stock, thereby converting the bond into stock. The number of shares to be received for each bond is known as the **conversion ratio**. The **conversion price** is the price paid for each share of stock, assuming that the bond is converted, and equals the market price of the convertible bond divided by the conversion ratio. The **conversion premium** is the additional amount per share of stock that one pays to obtain the share by converting the bond rather than by buying the stock in the marketplace.

These terms may best be illustrated by an example. Consider a convertible bond with a par value of $1,000 and a market price of $940. The common stock of the issuing company is currently selling for $40. The bond contract allows the bondholder to convert the bond into 20 shares of common stock. In this case, the conversion ratio is 20. If the bond is converted, a bond worth $940 is surrendered for $800 worth of stock (20 shares, each worth $40). Since a $940 bond is being surrendered for 20 shares of stock, the conversion price of a share of stock equals $940/20 or $47. The price to acquire the stock through conversion exceeds the price of the stock by $7, the conversion price minus the market price of the stock. This $7 is known as the conversion premium.

The option to convert the bond into stock is a valuable right. The bondholder receives continuing interest payments but has the chance to convert the bond into stock if it becomes attractive. It is not always easy to say when the conversion should take place, but sometimes the right strategy is clear. In the previous example, assume that the market price of the bond stayed at $940, but the stock price went to $50. If this were ever to happen, the following strategy would guarantee a riskless profit without investment – an arbitrage opportunity.[17] We could buy the bond in the market for $940, convert it into 20 shares of stock with a total value of $1,000, sell the stock, and pocket $1,000. This would generate an immediate profit of $60, ignoring transaction costs.

For reasons to be explored in more detail later in this book, we cannot expect to find arbitrage opportunities. The example does illustrate one important point, however. The price of the convertible bond and the stock are interrelated. If the stock price is $50, the price of the convertible bond must be at least $1,000. Otherwise, there would be the arbitrage opportunity just

---

[17] **Arbitrage** is the opportunity to earn a return without risk or investment. As will become clear in later discussions, the existence of arbitrage opportunities violates the basic idea of the risk/return trade-off.

mentioned, and the existence of arbitrage opportunities is equivalent to money being left on the street without anyone bothering to pick it up. One cannot expect to find money lying on the street waiting to be picked up by a chance passerby – especially not on Wall Street.

The International Bond Market

An **international bond** is a bond available for sale outside the country of its issuer. For example, if a U.S. firm issued a bond that is available for sale both in the United States and abroad, it is an international bond. Similarly, if a U.S. firm issues a bond denominated in a foreign currency for sale exclusively in the country of the foreign currency, the bond is a **foreign bond**. An example of a foreign bond would be a bond issued by General Motors, denominated in Italian lira, and sold in Italy. An **external bond** is either an international bond or a foreign bond. In 1994, more than $426 billion of external bonds were issued. There are a number of different types of bonds issued on the international market including straight bonds, floating rate bonds, equity-related bonds, and Eurobonds. We consider each of the major types of international debt issues in turn.

Straight Bonds

A **straight bond** is a bond with a fixed payment schedule with no special features, such as convertibility into stock or a floating interest rate. In essence, a straight bond is similar to the corporate bonds we considered previously. By far, straight bonds constitute the largest component of the international debt market, with total issues of about $290 billion in 1994. Figure 4.17 shows the recent issues of straight international bonds. About 29 percent of the straight bonds issued in 1994 were denominated in U.S. dollars.

Figure 4.17
Issues of Straight International Bonds, 1994

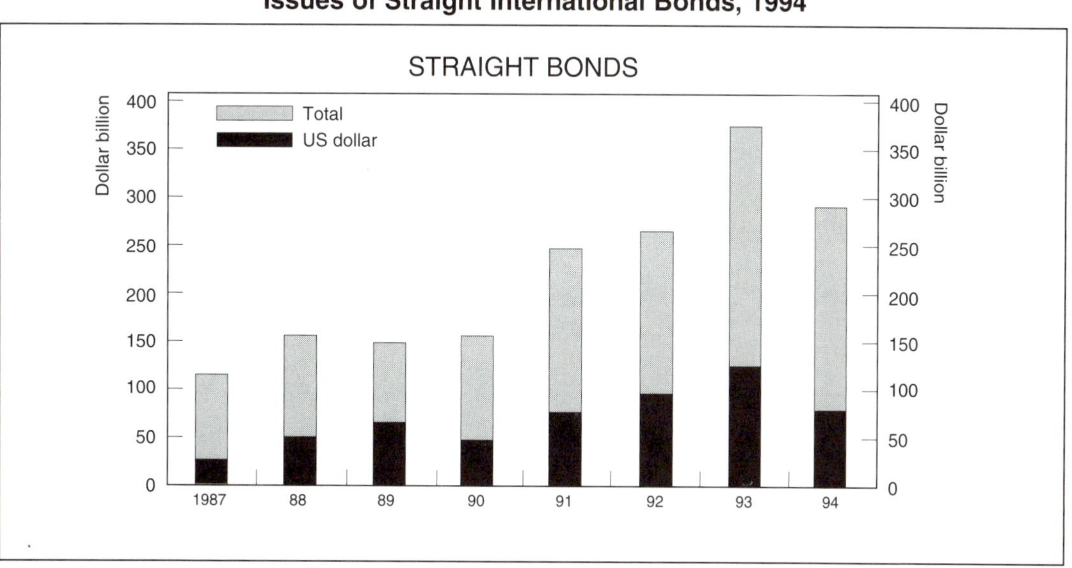

Source: Organization for Economic Cooperation and Development, *Financial Market Trends*, February 1995, p. 57.

Floating Rate Notes

A **floating rate note** (FRN) is a bond that pays a different coupon rate over time as the general level of interest rates fluctuates. Compared to the U.S. domestic bond market, floating rate notes are much more important in the international bond market. In 1994, there were about $96 billion of FRNs issued, with U.S. dollar denominated bonds accounting for about two thirds of that total.

Equity-Related Bonds

Equity-related bonds include both convertible bonds and bonds with equity warrants. We have considered convertible bonds earlier in this chapter. An **equity warrant** is a security that gives the holder the right to acquire a newly issued share of common stock from a company for the payment of a stated price. Equity warrants are often attached to bonds as a way of enticing prospective bond investors. For example, an equity warrant might be issued that gives the holder the right to buy a share for $100 within the next seven years. The value of this warrant depends on a number of factors, including the price of the share that can be bought and the length of time until the warrant expires. In most essential respects, warrants are similar to stock options that we discuss in Chapter 6. In 1994, $9.9 billion of bonds with equity warrants were issued, along with $21.7 billion of convertible bonds.

Eurodollar Bonds

A **Eurodollar bond** or a **Eurobond** is a bond issued by a borrower in one country, denominated in the borrower's currency, and sold outside the borrower's country. For example, a British steel company might issue a bond denominated in British pounds and sell it in the world market outside of Britain. A Eurobond can be a straight bond, an FRN, or an equity-related bond. In 1994, about $150 billion of Eurobonds issued, accounting for about 30 percent of all external bonds issued in 1994. About half of these Eurobonds were straight bonds.

Composition of the International Bond Market

We now consider the composition of the international bond market by the type of bond issued and by the currency in which the bond was denominated. Table 4.6 summarizes the composition of new external bond issues in 1994. Of these bonds, almost 70 percent were issued as straight

Table 4.6
New External Bond Issues, 1994

Instrument	Dollar Value (billions)	Percentage of Total (%)
Straight Bonds	288.8	68.4
Floating Rate Notes	96.3	22.8
Convertibles	21.7	5.1
With Equity Warrants	9.9	2.3
Zero Coupon Bonds	5.7	1.3

Source: Organization for Economic Cooperation and Development, *Financial Market Trends*, February 1995, p.44.

bonds. FRNs accounted for more than 20 percent, with other categories playing a minor role. Currently, about one-third of all issues are denominated in U.S. dollars, with about 15 percent being denominated in Japanese yen.

Summary

This chapter began by considering the basic principles of bond valuation. The price of any debt instrument equals the present value of all cash flows promised by the instrument when those cash flows are discounted at the instrument's yield to maturity. Because so many money market instruments are pure discount instruments, the discussion focused on applying bond valuation techniques to these zero coupon instruments. In the money market, different instruments have special conventions for computing their yields and in determining the price of the instrument. This chapter surveyed some of the major money market yield concepts, such as the discount yield and the equivalent bond yield.

The chapter then considered some of the major instruments of the money market, including T-bills, commercial paper, Eurodollar deposits, repurchase agreements, bankers' acceptances, and certificates of deposit. Slight differences in yield characterize these different instruments, and these normal yield relationships were shown to depend mainly on the default risk of the different instruments.

The discussion then turned to the international money market, an increasingly important market segment in this time of internationalization. Syndicated bank lending – the lending by a group of banks to a single borrower – remains a major source of funding in the short-term international debt market. Today syndicated loans are extended mainly to corporate borrowers. Much credit in the international money market is granted on a floating rate basis. Usually, these credits are tied to LIBOR, the London Interbank Offered Rate, the rate at which large international banks lend to each other. As LIBOR changes, the interest rates on many loans change to reflect the rise or fall in LIBOR. This chapter also focused on the bond market, beginning with an analysis of the institutional background of the debt market as it exists in the United States and abroad.

Questions and Problems

1. Why has the Eurodollar market flourished?
2. The money market reflects a relationship among yields on different types of instruments. What explains these yield differences?
3. Even within a given class of securities, such as certificates of deposit, there are well-established yield relationships. Assume that Bank A has traditionally had a yield on its CDs one-half of a percentage point lower than the yield on those of Bank B. If that difference became smaller, how would you interpret the change?
4. A bond is available with a price of $975 that promises to pay $1,000 one year from now with no intervening payments. What kind of a bond is this and what is its yield to maturity?
5. For a pure discount bond with a face value of $100, what will its price be if it matures in one year and has a yield to maturity of 16.5 percent?

6. A $10,000 T-bill matures in 47 days and is currently selling for $9,750. What is its discount yield? What is its bond-equivalent yield? What is its yield to maturity, based on the bond pricing formula?
7. What are the three principal classes of bond issuers?
8. What are the three principal kinds of U.S. Treasury debt?
9. Compared to the rest of the world, what is the relative size of the United States in the bond and equity markets?
10. In spite of the fact that T-bills and T-bonds have experienced virtually identical returns over the recent past, T-bonds seem to have had a greater variance of returns. Does this violate the basic idea of a trade-off between expected return and risk? Why or why not?
11. What do the bond ratings provided by firms such as Standard & Poor's and Moody's attempt to measure?
12. Why do municipal bonds tend to attract investors with high incomes? For an investor in Florida, which has no state income tax, would a municipal bond that is triple tax exempt in New York City be attractive? Why or why not?
13. The contract between a corporation and its bondholders often restricts the dividends that the firm can pay to stockholders. What is the purpose of this kind of provision?
14. Why do firms issue callable and convertible bonds? Other factors being equal, which kind of bond should have a higher yield? Why?
15. What is the difference between a foreign bond and a Eurobond?
16. A bond matures in two years, has a par value of $1,000, has a coupon rate of 11 percent paid semiannually, and yields 14 percent. What is its price? Is this a pure discount, par, discount, or premium bond? Why? Answer the preceding questions assuming that the same bond yields 8 percent.
17. Assume that a year has 360 days and that a bond with a coupon rate of 12 percent and a face value of $1,000 pays its coupon semiannually. If the bond last paid its coupon 60 days ago, what is the accrued interest on the bond? If the bond matures in 120 days, what is the full cash price that one must pay for the bond?
18. A bond has a coupon rate of 8.75 percent and is currently selling for $775 on a par value of $1,000. What is its current yield?

Suggested REALDATA Exercises

The following *REALDATA* exercises explore the concepts developed in this chapter:
Exercises 5, 6, 24, 55–61, 63

References

Fabozzi, F. J. and T. D. Fabozzi, "Treasury and Stripped Treasury Securities," *The Handbook of Fixed Income Securities*, 3rd ed., Homewood, IL: Business One Irwin, 1991.

Feldstein, S. G. and F. J. Fabozzi, "Municipal Bonds," *The Handbook of Fixed Income Securities*, 3rd ed., Homewood, IL: Business One Irwin, 1991.

Goodman, L. S., J. Jonson, and A. Silver, "Federally Sponsored Agency Securities," *The Handbook of Fixed Income Securities*, 3rd ed., Homewood, IL: Business One Irwin, 1991.

Hahn, Thomas K., "Commercial Paper," *Economic Quarterly*, Federal Reserve Bank of Richmond, 79:2, Spring 1993, pp. 45–67.

Ibbotson, R. G. and L. B. Siegel, "The World Bond Market: Market Values, Yields, and Returns," *The Journal of Fixed Income*, 1:1, June 1991, pp. 90–9.

LaRoche, Robert, K., "Bankers Acceptances," *Economic Quarterly*, Federal Reserve Bank of Richmond, 79:1, Winter 1993, pp. 75–85.

Long, R. D., "High-Yield Bonds," *The Handbook of Fixed Income Securities*, 3rd ed., Homewood, IL: Business One Irwin, 1991.

Lowell, L., "Mortgage Pass-Through Securities," *The Handbook of Fixed Income Securities*, 3rd ed., Homewood, IL: Business One Irwin, 1991.

Pavel, C. and J. N. McElravey, "Globalization in the Financial Services Industry," *Economic Perspectives*, Federal Reserve Bank of Chicago, 14:3, May/June 1990, pp. 3-18.

Stigum, M., *The Money Market*, Homewood, IL: Dow Jones Books, 1990.

Tran, H. Q., L. Anderson, and E. L. Drayss, "Eurocapital Markets," *The Handbook of Fixed Income Securities*, 3rd ed., Homewood, IL: Business One Irwin, 1991.

The Stock Market: An Overview

5

Overview

This chapter introduces the rights and obligations associated with common stock ownership and explores the institutional features of the stock market in the United States. In addition, the chapter explores the basic principles of equity valuation.

On the institutional side, the chapter focuses on the market for already existing shares, such as the most familiar stock market, the New York Stock Exchange. The chapter also introduces some of the most important stock market indexes. The organization of the U.S. stock market has changed radically in the last 15 years and gives every sign of further evolution. The market's recent history has been one of greater fragmentation in some respects, accompanied by greater integration in others. For example, strong leading movements beyond the major exchanges have diminished the power of leading institutions such as the New York Stock Exchange and have spread the trading of stocks across a broader spectrum of competing exchanges. Advances in electronic communication and computer technology have contributed to integration. As the technology has advanced, it has become increasingly easy to secure rapid and accurate communication, pulling the market toward more nearly complete integration. The development of foreign markets, particularly in Japan, now threatens to overshadow U.S. stock markets. These developments are also covered in this chapter, which begins with a discussion of the features of common stock itself.

As the second major theme of the chapter, we examine valuation principles for the second major segment of the capital market – preferred and common stock. As we will see, preferred stock is a hybrid security, sharing features of both bonds and common stock. As discussed earlier, common stock represents an ownership position in the firm. When a firm issues either preferred or common stock, it undertakes an obligation to pay a return on the investor's commitment of funds to the corporation. Because of this commitment, which is necessary for the firm to secure the funds it needs to operate, it is essential to understand the principles that determine the value of stock.

Common Stock Rights and Responsibilities

Common stock represents an ownership interest in a corporation. The management of the firm is charged with advancing the interests of the common stock owners, implying that management should maximize the price of a share of common stock. This outlook essentially identifies the interests of the shareholders with their wealth position in the stock. According to this view, the firm's managers act as agents of the shareholders, operating the firm as the shareholders would if they were the managers themselves. Problems arise in this relationship because the interests of the agent-managers are not always the same as those of the principal shareholders. For example, managers may overspend on fancy office furnishings – paid for out of the pockets of the shareholders – but the benefits are enjoyed only by the managers.[1]

As owners of the corporation, shareholders have privileges and responsibilities conferred upon them by owning the common stock. Because it represents ownership, common stock constitutes a **residual claim** on the assets and proceeds of the firm, that is, a claim on the value of the firm after other claimants have been satisfied. For example, owners of bonds issued by the corporation are entitled to receive their promised payments before the stockholders receive payments on their investments. In this sense, stockholders are the last in line to enforce their claims against the firm. By the same token, the residual claim is very important. The stockholders may be last in line to enforce their claims, but they can justifiably claim everything in the firm once the other claimants have been satisfied. The investor in common stock hopes that this residual amount will grow – that the excess over the claims due to others (bondholders, employees, suppliers, etc.) will be a growing amount.

In this sense, common stock is the riskiest claim against a firm. As will become increasingly clear, the hope of large returns normally goes with the acceptance of greater risk. In spite of the riskiness of common stock, stock has important risk-limiting features. In the United States, common stock ownership confers a limited liability to its owners. In a sole proprietorship, claims against a business can be pursued to capture the personal assets of the owner. For example, a shop owner without liability insurance conceivably could lose his house and personal automobile if a customer injured on the shop premises sues for damages. There is essentially no limitation on the liability of the owner in a sole proprietorship.

In a corporation, however, the owners cannot lose more than the value of their initial investment. The worst that could happen for a common stock investor would be for the stock to become worthless. In such an event, the entire purchase price of the common stock is lost, but the investor cannot lose more. For example, victims of a chemical spill for which a corporation was responsible might be able to acquire all of the assets of the firm. They could not, however, proceed against the stockholders to make them pay additional compensation out of their other resources.

Holders of common stock commit their funds and assume the last-place claim on the value of the firm in hopes of securing substantial profits. Payoffs to shareholders come in two forms. The price of the shares could increase, generating a capital gain. Alternatively, the firm could pay a cash dividend. Consequently, the wealth relative (WR) for an investor in common stock can be calculated as follows:

$$\text{WR} = \frac{\text{Current Stock Price} + \text{Cash Dividends Received}}{\text{Original Stock Price}} \tag{5.1}$$

While the stock is owned, the only cash flow from the shares is the cash dividend. Many firms, particularly new ones and those in financial distress, pay no dividends. Most firms that pay dividends do so on a quarterly basis, although that is not always the case.

---

[1] The conflict between principals and agents can be of much more momentous importance than the question of the budget for office furniture. See, for example, Michael Jensen and William Meckling, "Theory of the Firm: Managerial Behavior, Agency Costs and Ownership Structure," *Journal of Financial Economics*, 3, October 1976, pp. 305–60.

In addition to the right to receive cash dividends, owners of common stock have the right to vote on major matters pertaining to the operation of the firm. These voting rights are usually exercised at the time of the annual meeting. For the most part, this is not an important right, at least in major corporations with numerous shareholders. Typically, shareholders vote on issues that have been carefully defined by management with an eye toward securing the desired outcome. As an example, shareholders are often asked to vote on new directors for the corporation, with a slate of nominees having been picked by management. On occasion, however, the right to vote can be very important, perhaps on the issue of selecting new key management for the firm.

In the normal event, management directs the course of most corporate elections. One important tool for doing so is the use of the **proxy**. Since the votes are normally taken at the firm's annual meeting, it is impossible for most shareholders to actually appear at the meeting to cast their votes. Instead, they can empower some other party to vote for them by giving them a proxy. Management can solicit these proxies from indifferent shareholders or those shareholders who cannot attend the meeting. This situation enables management to acquire a great deal of voting power. In some firms, management has an even more effective means of amassing voting power. Shareholders who fail to return their proxy forms may be considered to have conferred their proxies to management. Given the normal inertia of many shareholders, this arrangement virtually guarantees effective control of the voting by the current management.

On occasion, real disputes arise that cause serious dissension and make the voting issue important. Dissident shareholders might try to unseat management or try to change fundamental managerial policies. To do so, the dissident shareholders need to acquire voting rights themselves by gaining proxies. This leads to a **proxy fight**, the struggle to gain voting rights from shareholders who will not be attending the annual meeting.

In some firms, common stock is classified, usually as either Class A or Class B. While this situation is unusual, it does exist. Usually the difference between the two classes of stock is simply the difference in voting rights. Normally, the Class A stock will have voting rights and the Class B stock will not. This difference in voting rights can generate a slight price differential between shares of the two classes, with the voting stock having a slightly higher price.[2]

Owners of common stock occasionally receive **stock dividends** or **stock splits**. These occurrences generate no cash flows for the owners of the stock, so they are substantially less important than cash dividends. A stock dividend occurs when additional shares are created by the firm and given to the current shareholders. A stock split is basically similar. This kind of distribution is called a **stock dividend** when the amount of increase in the number of shares is 25 percent or less. The distribution of shares is a **stock split** when the percentage increase is more than 25 percent. Stock splits occurred as early as 1682 when the East India Company declared a stock split of 2-for-1.[3]

To see how this works, assume that an investor owns 100 shares of a stock trading at $80, and the corporation decides on a 20 percent stock dividend. After the stock dividend, the stockholder would have 120 shares. The question then becomes how much those shares will be worth.

[2] American Maize Products, Inc., listed on the American Stock Exchange, has two classes of stock that fit this pattern, with a typical price difference between the two classes of shares of about 25 cents per share.

[3] J. Lakonishok and B. Lev, "Stock Splits and Stock Dividends: Why, Who, and When," *Journal of Finance*, 42:4, September 1987, pp. 913–32.

Other things being equal, this decision to have a stock dividend generates no cash flow for the firm. As such, it should have no impact on the value of the firm, which means that the shares should fall in value by an amount proportional to the stock dividend. The original market value of the 100 shares was $8,000. After the stock dividend, there are 120 shares. Since, by assumption, nothing has happened to make the firm's cash flows different, the wealth of the stockholder should be unchanged. This means that the 120 shares should have a total value of $8,000, or a price of $66.67 per share.

The decision to have a stock dividend or a stock split, by itself, cannot change the basic operations or the future cash flows of the firm, so it should not have any impact on the value of the firm.[4] Stock splits are usually spoken of as being a "2-for-1" split (the investor receives two shares to replace each original share held) or a "5-for-4" split and so on. Many firms have a practice of regular small stock dividends in the range of 2 to 5 percent.

Notice that a stock dividend or stock split with the cash dividend per share held constant implies an increased cash dividend. This is clear from the preceding example of a 5-for-4 stock dividend on a 100-share position with an initial share value of $80. Assume that the original cash dividend was 20 cents per share. This means that the annual dividend originally received was $20 per year. If that cash dividend is maintained at 20 cents per share, but the number of shares is increased to 120, then the annual cash dividend will be increased to $24 on the holding.

It is not clear why stock splits and stock dividends continue to be so popular, but several explanations are possible. First, some corporate managers either do not read or do not believe the research that has been conducted in this area. When a stock pays a dividend, the stock price must adjust in increments of 12½ cents. This may make it impossible for the share price to adjust exactly. Because of this and other market imperfections, it may be that share prices do not fully adjust to the stock dividend.[5] There is still a widespread tendency for firms to try to improve their stock prices by stock splits or dividends. Second, some proponents of stock distributions believe that investors perceive the additional stock as some kind of benefit. In fact, this may not be any benefit at all. Stock transaction costs are cheapest for a **round lot** – a block of stock of 100 shares or some multiple of 100. If a stock dividend or split leaves an investor with an **odd lot**, a holding not evenly divisible by 100, then the transaction costs can be higher on a percentage basis. In this situation, the stock dividend or split could cost the investor by raising transaction costs. Third, and

---

[4] The classic study of the impact of stock splits on share prices, "The Adjustment of Stock Prices to New Information," by E. Fama, L. Fisher, M. Jensen, and R. Roll, *International Economic Review*, 10, 1969, pp. 1–20, concludes that stock splits have no effect on the value of the underlying shares.

[5] For example, see J. Randall Woolridge, "Ex-Date Stock Price Adjustment to Stock Dividends: A Note," *Journal of Finance*, March 1983, pp. 247–55. In this paper, Woolridge finds that the stock price does not adjust completely for the stock dividend, particularly for very small dividends, such as those less than 6 percent. Other papers suggest that stock splits lead to increased price volatility, such as J. Ohlson and S. Penman, "Volatility Increases Subsequent to Stock Splits: An Empirical Aberration," *Journal of Financial Economics*, 14, 1985, pp. 251–66. D. A. Dubofsky, "Volatility Increases Subsequent to NYSE and AMEX Stock Splits," *Journal of Finance*, 46:1, March 1991, pp. 421–31, finds that the volatility increase is greater on the New York Stock Exchange than on the American Stock Exchange. Finally, C. G. Lamoureux and P. Poon, "The Market Reaction to Stock Splits," *Journal of Finance*, 42:5, December 1987, pp. 1347–70, argue that the increased volatility gives tax breaks to stock traders by allowing them to manage their tax-reported gains and losses and that this opportunity explains why stock prices increase after stock splits.

finally, stock splits may be a useful way of bringing the stock price into a popular trading range. Recent research indicates that this may be the most important motivation.[6] Some market observers believe that stock prices in the $20 to $40 range are most favored by investors. If a stock split moves the share price into this favored range, the increased popularity of the shares could make them more valuable. Unfortunately, there is no firm evidence in support of this view.[7]

General Organization of the Stock Market

This chapter deals with the **secondary market**, the market for already existing securities. There is also a **primary market**, a market for the sale of new securities, which is examined in Chapter 8. While this division is clear enough, some market developments have led to the existence of a third market and a fourth market. The secondary market consists of organized stock exchanges, such as the New York Stock Exchange (NYSE), the American Stock Exchange (AMEX), and a dealer market (the over-the-counter or OTC market). The third and fourth markets are informal trading arrangements used mainly by the very largest traders. Each division of the stock market will be discussed in turn.

Organized Exchanges

For many people, the stock market simply is the New York Stock Exchange, which dominates the market in certain respects. However, there are a number of organized stock exchanges in the United States and many foreign stock exchanges as well. An organized stock exchange is a stock market with a centralized trading floor, where all stock trading takes place under rules created by the exchange and the U.S. government. In the United States, the organized exchanges share many organizational features, largely because the smaller exchanges have patterned themselves after the NYSE. This makes it possible to discuss their common organizational features together. This section begins by examining those common principles of organization, and goes on to examine the two largest U.S. stock exchanges in greater detail. The section concludes by tracing the flow of an order from the public to the floor of the exchange and with a survey of the different types of orders that one might place.

General Organizational Features A **stock exchange** is a voluntary organization formed by a group of individuals to provide an institutional setting in which common stock, and other securities, can be bought and sold. Usually, the stock exchange is a non-profit corporation, which exists to further the financial interest of its members. Members of stock exchanges own memberships or **seats** on the exchange. The exchange formulates rules to govern trading activity on the exchange and enforces these rules on its membership. Only members of the exchange or their representatives are allowed to trade on the exchange. In that sense, the members have a monopoly position,

---

[6] See J. Lakonishok and B. Lev, "Stock Splits and Stock Dividends: Why, Who, and When," *Journal of Finance*, 42:4, September 1987, pp. 913–32.

[7] If the stock split lowers the price so that more investors can trade round lots, it might have the effect of reducing their transaction costs, thereby increasing the popularity of the shares and raising the price. Again, there is no persuasive evidence to support this hypothesis.

because all orders to buy or sell securities on a given exchange must flow through an exchange member.

One of the key regulations imposed by the exchange concerns restrictions on the place and time at which trading may occur. Each stock exchange allows trading only on the floor of the exchange and only during approved trading hours. The floor of an exchange is an actual physical location to which orders are transmitted for execution. The floor of the exchange is eletronically equipped to convey orders to the floor and to confirm execution of the order to the trader. Reports of trading activity are also communicated to the press and to financial news services, such as Reuters and Dow Jones.

People working on the floor of the exchange fall into several groups. First, the exchange employs workers to oversee the trading activity and report the outcomes of trades to the public on a continuous basis. Second, exchange members trade on the floor for their own account investing their own capital in the pursuit of profit. Brokers form a third group. A broker receives orders from the public outside the exchange and executes the order (to either buy or sell a given quantity of a specified security) and charges a commission for this service. As such, a broker does not trade for his own account, but executes the orders of others. Two of the largest brokerage firms are Merrill Lynch and PaineWebber.[8] A fourth group of floor participants consists of the specialists for each security. A specialist is assigned to each security traded on an exchange and stands ready to trade at least 100 shares of that stock. In addition, the specialist keeps a record of all orders awaiting execution in the stock. These key functions of the specialist require more examination.

The Specialist The **specialist**, who always holds a seat on the exchange, makes a market in an assigned security. This means that every share of stock traded on an exchange passes under the scrutiny of the specialist. As we will see, the specialist has a privileged position, and accompanying obligations. The specialist has two basic functions. First, the specialist acts as a broker on some transactions for other trading parties. In this brokerage function, the specialist facilitates transactions for others and charges a fee. Second, the specialist may act as a dealer, buying and selling for his or her own account. Exchange rules and laws regulate how the specialist may perform these two functions. We consider first the role of the specialist as a dealer and then turn to the specialist's brokerage function. We then review the rules that govern the specialist's behavior.

The Specialist as a Dealer The specialist stands ready to buy or sell securities on order from other members of the exchange or to the public. This requires considerable capital investment in the shares held in inventory, and it also involves taking a risk position in the stock. As compensation for the capital investment and the assumption of risk, the specialist attempts to make a profit on each share of stock traded. As a dealer, the specialist acts as a market maker and acts as either the buyer or the seller in the transaction. In today's market, the specialist acts as buyer or seller in about 15-20 percent of the share volume on the NYSE.

Acting as a dealer or **market maker**, the specialist maintains a **bid-asked spread** – the difference between the price at which she is willing to buy and to sell a share. The specialist offers to

[8] The operation of the brokerage industry is explained in a later section entitled "The Brokerage Industry."

buy shares at the lower bid price and to sell them at the asked price. For example, assume that the specialist believes that a share is worth exactly $100. The specialist can make money by buying shares for slightly less than the "true" price of $100 and by selling shares for slightly more than $100. For this example, the bid price might be $99.875 and the asked price might be $100.125. Thus, the bid-asked spread is $.25, and this difference represents the gross profit that the specialist tries to capture by trading.

As a pure market maker, the specialist might merely try to set bid and asked prices so that the number of buy orders exactly balanced the number of sell orders. This would leave the specialist's inventory at a constant level, and the specialist would make a gross profit equal to the bid-asked spread on the purchase and subsequent sale of each security.

However, the life of the specialist is not so easy. The specialist must constantly revise the bid and asked prices to reflect the new information that reaches the market. For example, if the news is favorable for a given stock, and the specialist does not adjust the bid and asked prices upward to reflect the new information, there will be more buy orders than sell orders. This order flow would soon deplete the inventory of the specialist, who would then be unable to fulfill the function of market-making. Further, the specialist would suffer a loss by selling shares out of the inventory for less than they are worth. For even the most conservative specialist, one merely seeking to make the bid-asked spread on each transaction, there is still a great deal of finesse required in order to create an even number of buy and sell orders in the face of changing market conditions.

The spread between the bid and asked prices represents the gross profit margin for the specialist; therefore, the wider the bid-asked spread, the greater the specialist's profits, other things being equal. The exchange, however, monitors the performance of the specialist to ensure that the bid-asked spread remains within a reasonably narrow range. Even so, the specialist has a certain degree of latitude in setting both the level of prices and the bid-asked spread. In times of great uncertainty in the stock market, due either to general market conditions or to developments affecting the specialist's particular security, the specialist may respond by widening the bid-asked spread.

At times, traders outside the exchange may know more about the future of the stock price for a given share than the specialist. Traders with this kind of special knowledge are called **informed traders**. They contrast with **liquidity traders** – traders who buy because they have funds to invest or who sell because they need cash. If the specialist confronts an informed trader, the specialist runs the risk of losing on trades due to a lack of information. Consequently, the specialist's first reaction to unusual trading activity will often be to widen the bid-asked spread. A wider spread provides a larger safety margin for the specialist because it increases the profit margin.

Compared to most traders for a particular stock, however, the specialist normally has a great deal of information. One of the richest sources of information comes from the fact that the specialist maintains the limit order book in which all limit orders awaiting execution are recorded. A **limit order** is an order to be executed only at a certain price, if that price becomes available. Maintaining this book provides the specialist with privileged access to information regarding supply and demand for the shares, and this information can become quite valuable. For example, imagine a situation in which a given share trades at $30 per share and the limit order book shows a large number of orders to sell shares at $30.50. The specialist then knows that the large contingent sell order will help to keep prices on the shares from going up very much. This tells the specialist not to increase inventory in hopes of a big price rise in the stock.

Another important decision facing the specialist concerns how large an inventory to hold. The specialist always needs to maintain at least some shares in inventory to meet immediate demand. However, if the specialist believes that share prices will rise in the near future, then he or she should increase the inventory. This could be accomplished by a slight adjustment in the level of prices quoted or by adjusting the bid-asked spread. The chance to make speculative profits, based on privileged information, is an important potential source of income for the specialist.

The Specialist as Broker Specialists do not trade for their own accounts in most stock transactions. Typically, specialists function as only brokers in about 80-85 percent of transactions. In these transactions, the specialists act as brokers to help execute transactions for other parties. In fact, exchange rules regulate the specialist's trading.

In the limit order book, the specialist holds a record of customers' willingness to buy and sell in a particular stock. Typically, there will be a number of orders to buy and a number of orders to sell, both at various prices. To make the analysis concrete, assume that the stock has just traded at $40 per share, and the specialist holds limit orders to sell at $40.25 and $41 and limit orders to buy at $39.75 and $39. The specialist herself is willing to trade for her own account with a bid-asked spread of $39.50 to buy and $40.50 to sell. Thus, the specialist does not offer the highest bid price nor the lowest asked price. For a potential customer, the specialist is obligated to reveal the highest bid price and the lowest asked price, which would be $40.25 asked and $39.75 bid. In this situation, a customer can buy at $40.25 or sell at $39.75, and the specialist would act only as a broker. Thus, to participate as a buyer or seller in the transaction, the specialist must bid more than any limit order to buy in the limit order book, or must ask less than any limit order to sell in the limit order book.

Another rule that often keeps the specialist from acting as a buyer or seller is the rule that gives public orders at the same price precedence over the specialist's desire to buy or sell. As an example of this rule, consider a limit order to buy a particular stock at $40. This order, as we have seen, would be reflected in the specialist's limit order book. While such an order is in the book, the specialist cannot buy at $40 for his own account. Instead, the specialist must give precedence to the outside order. In this situation, the specialist would allow the customer's limit order to be filled and would collect a brokerage commission for facilitating the transaction. (This brokerage fee for the specialist is typically about two cents per share.) A similar rule applies to customer limit orders to sell.

Obligations of the Specialist As we have seen, the specialist has significant trading advantages that are conferred upon her by the exchange. With these advantages come certain responsibilities. First, the specialist is obligated to make a market in the stock and to trade with the public in 100 share lots. The specialist cannot simply sit on the sidelines. If there are not complementary orders available from the public, the specialist must trade.

As a second obligation, the specialist must maintain price continuity. For example, if the last trade in a stock was at $50 and the current bid-asked spread from public orders is $45 bid/$55 asked, the exchange would expect the specialist to trade at a narrower bid-asked spread. For frequently traded stocks, the bid-asked spread is \$.125 to \$.25. A third obligation of the specialist is to stabilize prices. If orders from the public are running heavily on the sell side, the specialist is expected to act as a buyer to keep the prices from falling too much.

Summary In sum, the specialist occupies a unique position in a stock exchange. All transactions are funneled through the specialist, who acts as either a broker or as a principal in each transaction. Keeping the limit order book gives the specialist privileged information about the market, and this information has considerable value. By the same token, the specialist faces informed traders who have superior information, and the specialist can lose substantial sums by trading against those informed traders. In return for the monopoly position granted by the exchange, the specialist is required to make a market in the stock, to keep the bid-asked spread reasonably small, and to trade to stabilize prices.

The Floor Broker While all orders must eventually reach the specialist to be executed, the floor broker plays an important role as well. Typically, floor brokers facilitate the execution of larger orders. The floor broker may be an employee of a large brokerage firm, such as Merrill Lynch. Alternatively, the order may be handled by a free-lance floor broker, who makes a living by helping to execute orders that come to the floor of the exchange. In either case, the floor broker conveys the order to the specialist and has it executed.

The floor broker is much more than a messenger, however. Because floor brokers work larger orders, they generally have the discretion to **work an order** – to try to fill the order at the best price. If the order is a large buy order, for example, it may not be wise to try to execute the order all at once the moment it reaches the floor. The floor broker may be able to get a lower price per share by filling a portion of the order now and the rest in a few minutes. Because floor brokers are paid based on shares traded, they have an incentive to trade as quickly as possible. However, they know that the brokerage firm that gave them the order could have given the order to someone else, so the floor broker also has an incentive to do the best job in filling the order.

Order Flow We now consider how orders flow from the customer to the floor, how they are executed, and how the trade is reported to the customer. Customers must first open an account with a brokerage firm by completing a few forms. Once the account is opened, the customer may contact the brokerage frim and place an order, usually with the account representative assigned to the customer by the brokerage firm. Let us assume that the order is to buy 100 shares of IBM. The customer's account representative enters the order in the brokerage firm's communication system and the order is transmitted to the brokerage firm's representatives on the floor of the exchange.

Once an order reaches the exchange, it may be completed in one of two fundamentally different ways. First, if the order is large or requires special treatment, it will be given to a floor broker for execution, as described above. Second, if the order is small and requires no special treatment, it may be handled electronically through SuperDOT (Designated Order Turnaround). In this case, the order is electronically transmitted to the specialist, and the order is executed immediately without any effort by a floor broker. Our example of a 100-share order to buy IBM is a small order for a highly active stock, so it will almost certainly be handled through SuperDOT.

In both cases, the order arrives at the specialist's physical location, or **trading post**, on the exchange floor.

After the trade is executed, the transaction must be reported to the customer, the customer's brokerage firm, and the public at large. If the order was executed by a floor broker, the broker records the price and other relevant information on a card and returns this to the brokerage firm's booth on the floor of the exchange. If the order was handled through SuperDOT, the specialist confirms the trade to the brokerage firm's computer. In either case, the brokerage firm records all of the information for its own records and reports the trade to the account representative. The account representative reports the order to the customer. In our example, the account representative in Miami would receive confirmation of the purchase of IBM and would call the customer to report the price at which the shares were purchased. The transaction is also reported to the public by officials of the exchange. An exchange clerk enters the trade into the computer, which transmits an electronic ticker tape to subscribers all over the world. Within one minute of execution, the report of the trade has appeared on the tape, letting all interested parties know of the transaction. Figure 5.1 summarizes this order process, which typically takes one to two minutes. Final settlement for stock transactions occurs three business days after the transaction is made, and the customer is expected to have the necessary funds on deposit with the broker by that time, including the commission that must be paid to the brokerage firm for executing the transaction.

Figure 5.1
Order Flow for Stock Exchange Transaction

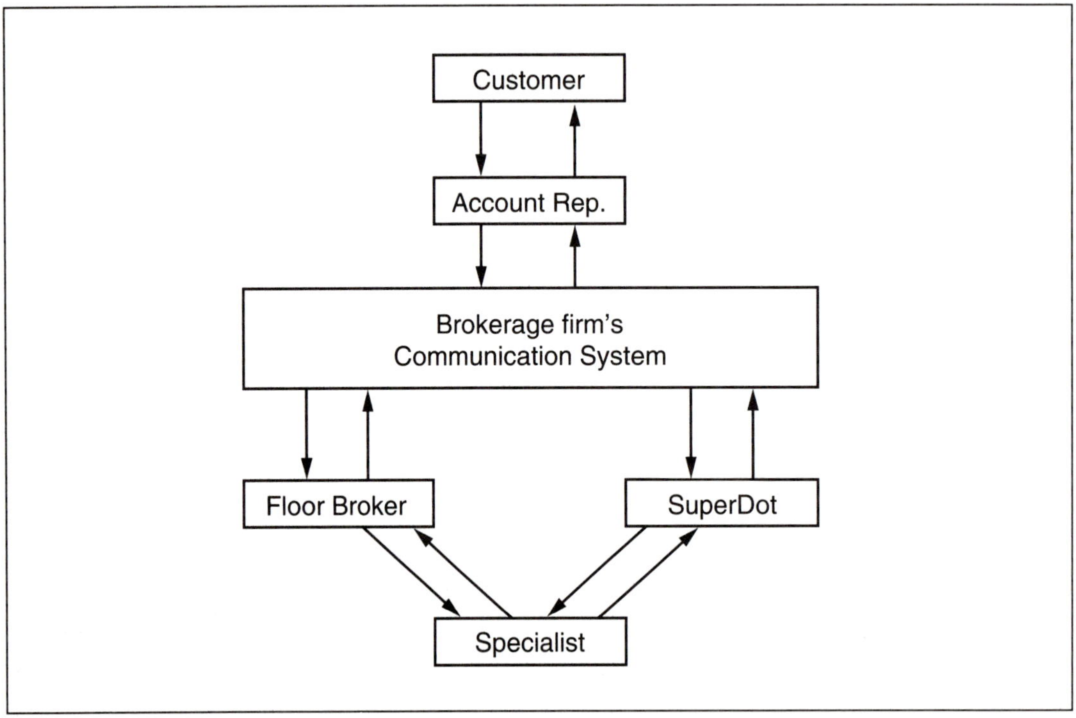

The New York Stock Exchange

By far, the New York Stock Exchange dominates the stock exchanges in the United States and matches any exchange in the world. Domestically, the NYSE accounts for about 50 percent of share volume and about 64 percent of dollar volume, due to the higher average price of NYSE shares. If we focus only on domestic organized exchanges and exclude the OTC market, the NYSE accounts for over 80 percent of share volume and 86 percent of dollar volume.

The NYSE traces its origins to May 17, 1792, when 24 brokers formed the first organized stock market in the United States. This meeting took place under a buttonwood tree at what is now 68 Wall Street. In 1817 the name "New York Stock and Exchange Board" was adopted, with the current name taking effect in 1863. From quite humble early beginnings, the NYSE has grown to mighty proportions, as the trading volume reflects. On March 16, 1830, the dullest day in the history of the exchange, 31 shares were traded. In spite of such times of lethargy, the NYSE has shown marked increases in volume. Currently, trading volume is typically 200-300 million shares per day, or about 6 billion shares monthly, as Figure 5.2 shows.[9]

Figure 5.2
Monthly Trading Volume of the New York Stock Exchange

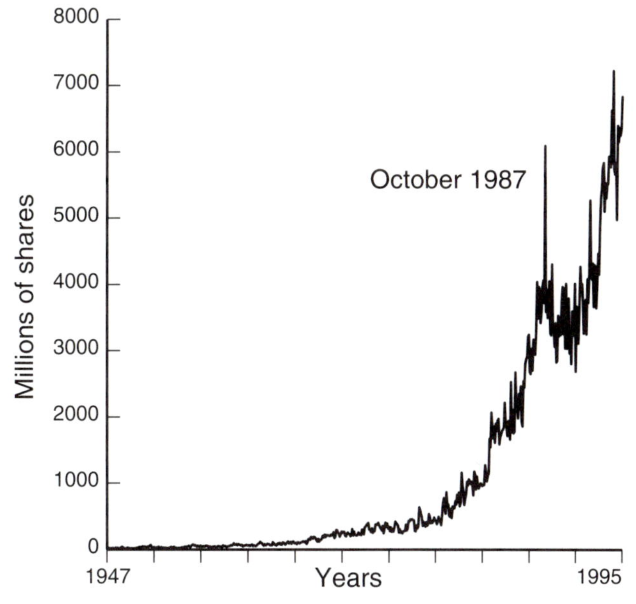

Source: *Federal Reserve Bulletin*, various issues.

[9] As Figure 5.2 shows, October 1987 was the month with the highest trade volume ever. On October 19, 1987, Black Monday, the market crashed, leading to a tremendous volume for that day and several succeeding days.

Not every firm can be listed on the NYSE; only those firms meeting certain minimum requirements are eligible. The exchange imposes requirements in the form of earning power, total value of outstanding stock, and number of shareholders. Table 5.1 presents the current minimum listing requirements for initial listing on the NYSE. Many shares listed on the NYSE are also listed on other exchanges. Transactions for all NYSE-listed securities are shown on one reporting system, called the **consolidated tape**, no matter where the transaction actually took place. Other organizations participating in the consolidated tape listing are the American, Pacific, Midwest, Philadelphia, Boston, and Cincinnati stock exchanges; the National Association of Securities Dealers; and Instinet. (The last two organizations are part of the over-the-counter market.) The NYSE consistently accounts for about 80-85 percent of the total consolidated tape volume, followed by the Midwest and Pacific Stock Exchanges. The American Stock Exchange (AMEX) has little role in the consolidated tape reporting system since very few firms are listed on both the NYSE and the AMEX.

The day's transactions for NYSE securities are reported widely in the financial press. *The Wall Street Journal* presents the consolidated tape quotations as the "NYSE-Composite Transactions" shown in Figure 5.3. Prices are quoted in dollars per share, with the smallest fraction of a dollar being 1/8, or 12½ cents. The first two columns of figures show the high and low share prices for a stock over the last year. The annual cash dividend is shown in dollars, based on the current dividend declaration of the firm. The column labeled "Yld %" is the dividend yield on the shares, which is given by the following equation:

$$\text{Divident Yield} = \frac{\text{Current Annual Divident}}{\text{Current Stock Price}} \tag{5.2}$$

The next column shows the P-E Ratio, or the **Price-Earnings Ratio**.

$$\text{P} - \text{E Ratio} = \frac{\text{Current Stock Price}}{\text{Current Annual Earnings}} \tag{5.3}$$

The next column shows the number of shares (in hundreds) traded on the day being reported. The next three columns, labeled "High," "Low," and "Close," show the respective prices for that day's trading. The final column, "Net Chg," shows the difference from the previous day's close to the close of the day being reported. As shown in Equation 5.1, the WR on a

Table 5.1
Initial Listing Requirements for the New York Stock Exchange

1. Current annual earnings (pre-tax) of $2.5 million.
2. Earnings in the preceding two years of $2 million.
3. Net tangible assets of $18 million.
4. Market value of outstanding shares of $18 million.
5. 1.1 million shares held publicly.
6. At least 2,000 shareholders owning 100 shares or more each, or 2,200 shareholders together with an average monthly trade of 100,000 shares.

Source: *New York Stock Exchange Fact Book*, April 1994, p. 26.

Figure 5.3
New York Stock Exchange Composite Transactions

NEW YORK STOCK EXCHANGE COMPOSITE TRANSACTIONS

Quotations as of 5 p.m. Eastern Time
Tuesday, March 28, 1995

52 Weeks Hi	52 Weeks Lo	Stock	Sym	Div	Yld %	PE	Vol 100s	Hi	Lo	Close	Net Chg
		-A-A-A-									
16½	11⅞	AAR	AIR	.48	3.8	21	158	13	12⅝	12⅝	– ⅜
24⅜	17⅝	ABM Indus	ABM	.60	2.6	13	129	22⅞	22⅝	22¾	...
11⅝	8⅛	ACM Gvt Fd	ACG	.90a	10.7	...	2063	8⅜	8 3/16	8⅜	+ ⅛
8¾	6⅜	ACM OppFd	AOF	.66	9.6	...	141	6⅞	6¾	6⅞	+ ⅛
10⅞	7⅜	ACM SecFd	GSF	.90	11.8	...	903	7⅝	7½	7⅝	+ ⅛
9⅜	5¾	ACM SpctmFd	SI	.75	12.2	...	1195	6¼	6	6⅛	– ⅛
13¾	7⅝	ACM MgmdInc	ADF	1.26	15.7	...	686	8¼	8	8	– ⅛
10	7⅜	ACM MgdIncFd	AMF	1.08a	13.9	...	157	7⅞	7¾	7¾	...
8⅝	7⅛	ACM MgdMultFd	MMF	.72	10.1	...	100	7¼	7⅛	7⅛	...
12¾	9⅛	ACM MuniSec	AMU	.90a	7.9	...	65	11⅜	11¼	11⅜	...
12	8½	ADT	ADT		...	16	3393	12⅛	11⅞	12⅛	+ ⅛
42¾	29	♣AFLAC	AFL	.46	1.1	14	1959	41⅞	41	41⅛	– ⅞
36¾	21½	AGCO Cp	AG	.04	.1	5	911	30¾	30⅜	30¾	+ ⅛
72¼	43	AGCO pf		1.64	2.7	...	62	60¾	60½	60¾	+ ¼
23⅛	12⅝	AL Pharma	ALO	.18	.8	dd	721	23	22⅛	23	+ ¾
22⅞	17	AMLI Resdntl	AML	1.68	9.5	...	7023	18⅛	17	17⅝	– ¾
39⅝	28¾	♣AMP	AMP	.92	2.5	21	3477	37⅛	36⅝	36⅞	– ⅛
65⅛	48⅛	AMR	AMR		...	29	8581	65⅝	64¾	65⅛	+ ¼
51	41¼	ARCO Chm	RCM	2.50	5.6	16	344	44¾	44½	44⅝	...
53¾	38⅝	ASA	ASA	2.00	4.3	...	1517	46⅛	45⅛	46⅛	+1
27¼	19¾	ATT Cap	TCC	.40	1.5	12	79	26¼	25⅞	26¼	+ ⅛
57⅛	47¼	AT&T Cp	T	1.32	2.5	17	14271	52¾	52	52½	+ ⅛
38⅜	25⅜	AbbotLab	ABT	.84f	2.2	20	8259	37¾	37⅜	37⅜	– ¼
8¼	5⅛	Abex	ABE		...	1	186	7⅝	7⅝	7⅝	– ⅛
s 14¾	7½	Aracruz	ARA	.51e	4.3	...	658	12⅛	11⅞	11⅞	– ⅛
9⅞	7¼	ArborProp	ABR	.70	8.1	dd	370	8¾	8½	8⅝	...
26¼	21¼	ArcadnPtnr	UAN	2.42	9.7	8	792	25⅛	24¾	24⅞	+ ⅛
s 21⅛	14⅛	ArcherDan	ADM	.10	.5	15	5529	19⅜	19	19⅛	– ¼
22⅝	14	Argentaria	AGR	.99e	6.8	...	31	14⅝	14¼	14½	+ ⅛
16¾	**7½**	**ArgntnaFd**	**AF**	**.73e**	**7.0**	**...**	**1061**	**11⅛**	**10½**	**10½**	**– ⅝**
23½	19⅜	ArizPubSvc pfW		1.81	8.0	...	33	22½	21⅞	22½	+ ⅝
n 26¾	24¾	ArizPubSvc un		.54e	2.0	...	115	26⅝	26⅜	26⅜	– ⅛
27¾	24⅝	ArkPower pf		2.40	9.1	...	8	26½	26¼	26¼	...
7⅜	4½	Armco	AS		...	12	1791	6⅞	6⅝	6¾	– ⅛
25	19¾	Armco pf		2.10	9.3	...	4	22⅞	22½	22½	– ⅜
54½	46	Armco pfB		3.63	6.9	...	10	52½	52½	52½	...
57¼	36	ArmstrngWld	ACK	1.28	2.8	9	2393	46⅞	45⅝	46½	+ ¾
44¼	33⅝	ArrowElec	ARW		...	17	1297	44¼	43⅞	44⅛	+ ⅛
7¼	**3½**	**ArtraGp**	**ATA**		**...**	**dd**	**45**	**3⅞**	**3⅞**	**3⅞**	**– ¼**
▼ 30	19⅞	♣ArvinInd	ARV	.76	3.8	dd	362	20⅛	19¾	20	– ⅛
34⅞	21⅜	Asarco	AR	.40	1.6	17	4159	25⅞	25⅜	25½	...
31¼	22½	AshlandCoal	ACI	.46	1.6	17	16	28¾	28⅝	28¾	– ⅛
43⅞	31¼	Ashland	ASH	1.10	3.2	14	1409	34⅞	34⅝	34¾	– ¼
72	53	Ashland pf		3.13	5.5	...	292	57	56⅝	56⅞	– ⅜
22½	12⅛	AsiaPacFd	APB	3.12e	21.0	...	761	15⅛	14¾	14⅞	+ ⅜
14⅜	8⅞	AsiaTigers	GRR	.21e	2.2	...	758	9¾	9½	9½	...
3½	1⅝	AssetInvest	AIC	.36e	15.2	8	244	2⅜	2¼	2⅜	...
▼ 23⅞	**18½**	**AssocEstate**	**AEC**	**1.60**	**8.6**	**16**	**8172**	**19⅝**	**17**	**18⅝**	**–1**
9	5¼	AtalantaSos	ATL	.15e	2.1	11	12	7	6¾	7	+ ⅜
36⅝	29⅛	AtlaGasLt	ATG	2.08	6.1	25	183	34½	34¼	34¼	– ⅜
26¼	21¾	AtlaGasLt pf		1.93	7.6	...	2	25¼	25¼	25¼	+ ¼
21½	16	AtlanEngy	ATE	1.54	8.6	13	494	18	17⅞	17⅞	– ¼
118	92½	AtlanRich	ARC	5.50	4.8	20	2876	115	113¾	114¼	– ⅝
25½	22	BankAmer pfL		2.04	8.2	...	235	25	24¾	24¾	– ⅛
25¼	21¼	BankAmer pfM		1.97	8.0	...	165	24¾	24½	24⅝	+ ⅛
26⅛	23	BankAmer pfN		2.13	8.4	...	183	25½	25¼	25⅜	...
50⅞	44½	BankAm pf1		3.75	7.6	...	312	49 19/64	49⅛	49 19/64	+ ⅛
25¾	16½	BkrsLife	BLH	.60	2.9	8	503	20¾	20⅝	20⅝	– ⅛
74	49¾	BkTrst	BT	4.00f	7.4	8	6367	54	53⅛	53¾	+ ⅜
n 25	22¾	BkTrst dep pfI			...	...	54	24⅛	23¾	24⅛	+ ⅛
n 25⅝	18¾	BkTrst dep pfQ		1.49e	7.5	...	5	20	19¾	19¾	– ¼
n 24⅜	19⅜	BkTrst dep pfR		.87e	4.4	...	71	20	19¾	20	+ ⅜
1	⅜	BanyanMtgInv	VMG		...	dd	3410	21/32	⅝	⅝	– 1/16
40¾	30	Barclays	BCS	2.17e	5.4	...	38	40⅜	39¾	40	– ¾
29⅜	25½	Barclays pfD		2.88	10.6	...	83	27½	27¼	27¼	– ⅛
24⅛	20½	Barclays prE		2.00	8.8	...	625	22⅝	22⅜	22⅝	+ ⅛
28⅝	25⅜	Barclays pfC		2.81	10.4	...	17	27	26⅞	27	+ ⅛
28¼	22¼	Bard CR	BCR	.60	2.2	19	1239	27¼	26¾	27¼	+ ¼
32¾	20	BarnesNoble	BKS		...	39	265	30¾	30	30⅝	+ ⅝
42⅜	29¾	BarnesGp	B	1.60	3.8	13	36	42⅜	42⅛	42⅜	...
48⅛	37¼	BarnettBks	BBI	1.64	3.6	9	1788	45⅜	44⅞	45	– ¼
92	73⅞	BarnettBks pfA		4.50	5.2	...	35	86	85⅞	86	...
67⅝	53	BarnettBks pfC		4.00	6.6	...	6	61¼	60¾	60¾	– ½
22¾	13¼	BarretRes	BRR		...	70	352	21⅛	20⅞	20⅞	– ¼
27⅜	19¾	BarckGld	ABX	.10	.4	30	15057	24	23¼	24	+ ⅛
18¼	15⅛	Bass	BAS	.81e	4.8	...	12	16⅞	16¾	16¾	+ ⅛
13	8⅞	BattleMtn	BMG	.05	.5	cc	6285	10¾	10½	10¾	...
69¾	51⅞	BattleMtn pf		3.25	5.7	...	63	58	56⅞	57½	– ¾
52	30⅝	BauschLomb	BOL	.98	2.8	cc	1809	35¾	35⅛	35¼	– ⅜
34⅞	21⅝	BaxterInt	BAX	1.05	3.1	16	25724	34¾	33⅝	34	– ⅝
22¾	17¾	BayApartmt	BYA	1.52	7.9	...	112	19⅛	19	19⅛	+ ⅛
26⅝	22¼	BayStGas	BGC	1.46	6.1	14	121	24	23	24	+ ⅝

Source: *The Wall Street Journal*, March 29, 1995.

share of common stock depends on the change in price on the share plus the payment of the cash dividend, if any.

The Secondary Market: The Over-the-Counter Market

Compared to the organized exchanges, particularly the NYSE, the over-the-counter (OTC) market receives relatively little attention. This is really an oversight. Trading on the OTC market has been growing faster than trading on organized exchanges, even the NYSE. Further, recent and future advances in computer technology will probably benefit the OTC market more than the organized exchanges because of the structural differences between the two types of markets.

General Organizational Features

The over-the-counter market differs from organized exchanges in a number of ways, but two important differences stand out. First, the OTC market does not rely on a central trading place. Instead, the market is made up of many people in diverse locations. Second, the OTC market does not use specialists. Instead, there are a number of **market makers**, firms and individuals making a market in particular stocks. In a sense, these differences are embodied metaphorically in the name over-the-counter. This nickname comes from the fact that participants in the market were originally thought to be like retailers who kept a supply of shares and sold them to buyers across the counter, just as one might buy a bolt of cloth in a general store. In important respects, this system continues in effect today, with a number of market makers for each security.

The privilege of trading in the OTC market is granted by the National Association of Securities Dealers (NASD), based on financial soundness and qualification examinations. This industry group plays a role analogous to the exchange as a regulator of market entry. In addition, the NASD plays an important self-regulatory role. The differences between the OTC market and the organized exchanges become clear when considering the flow of orders to buy or sell stock.

Flow of Orders

Only a member of the NASD is allowed to trade in the over-the-counter market. Buying or selling shares traded on the OTC market necessitates the use of a broker along with a brokerage account. Usually, opening a single account ensures that one can trade on both the organized exchanges and the OTC.

Having established an account, one may decide to place an order to buy 100 shares of Apple Computer, one of the leading securities traded on the OTC. The broker, trying to execute this order, does not have a centralized trading floor where these shares are traded. Instead, the broker needs to find a market maker who is willing to sell the Apple Computer shares out of inventory. Brokers and other traders in the OTC market use the National Association of Securities Dealers Automated Quotation (NASDAQ) system, which automatically shows the best available bid and asked prices.[10] The broker can normally complete the transaction within one or two minutes.

Stock Trading on the OTC Market

Firms traded OTC tend to be quite a bit smaller than their NYSE counterparts. Historically, smaller firms tend to have greater returns than larger firms, as well as more risk. This tendency of small firms to outperform large firms can be seen in several ways. First, within the NYSE itself, small firms tend to do better. Figure 5.4 shows how $1 invested at year-end 1925 would have grown by year-end 1994, depending on whether it was invested in typical NYSE securities or in the smallest 20 percent of NYSE securities. As shown in the figure, $1 invested in the typical larger firm would have grown to $810.54 by the end of 1994, while $1 put into the smaller firms would have grown to $2,842.77.[11]

The OTC market includes about 15,000 securities, yet many of these have only a local market, such as the stock of local banks. Only the larger, more important firms are carried on NASDAQ. NASDAQ has quotations for about 4,000 stocks, compared with about 1,800 listed on the NYSE. Also, following a mandate of Congress passed in 1975, the SEC has helped the NASD formulate a National Market System, in which prominent OTC stocks are reported. There are about 3,400 securities now quoted in the National Market System, a change that may stimulate the OTC market.

---

[10] NASDAQ is now upgrading broker workstations with a second generation system that can handle trading of up to 800 million shares per day.

[11] The large stocks were made up of the Standard & Poor's Composite Index. Until 1957, these were 90 of the largest stocks. After that time, it was made up of 500 of the largest firms.

Figure 5.4
Wealth Relatives for Large and Small Companies' Stock

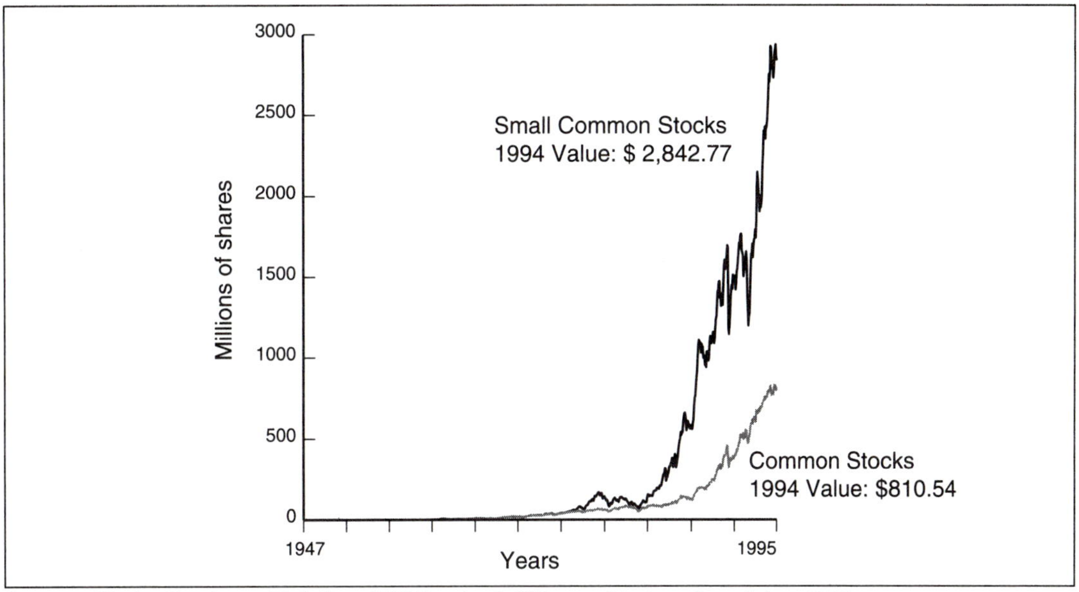

Source: *Stocks, Bonds, and Inflation: 1995 Yearbook*, Chicago: Ibbotson Associates, 1995

The National Market System

The purpose of the National Market System (NMS) is to provide more timely information on developments in the securities markets for the more important OTC stocks. For non-NMS NASDAQ securities, for example, a dealer only enters his bid and asked prices into the NASDAQ computer. For NMS securities, dealers must also report the price of any security traded within 90 seconds after the trade is made. For non-NMS securities, the dealers report the total transactions in each security at the end of the day. For NMS securities, dealers report the size of each trade along with the price report following each trade. This provides much better information to other traders and erodes the privileged position of the market maker. Table 5.2 shows the qualification standards for inclusion in the NMS. As the table indicates, the SEC requires some firms to be included, while others are eligible for voluntary inclusion.

Quotations for OTC securities appear each day in *The Wall Street Journal*, as shown in Figure 5.5. The quotations are similar in structure to those for the NYSE. Other quotations, aside from NMS securities, also appear in *The Wall Street Journal*. These typically show only a bid-asked price due to their small volume. For stocks of primarily local interest, quotations can often be found in the local newspaper but are unlikely to appear in *The Wall Street Journal*. Table 5.3 shows the ten most active NMS issues in 1994 and the annual share volume for each firm.

Contrasts with Organized Exchanges

There has been a long-standing debate over the best structure for a stock market. The system used by the organized exchanges gives the specialist a monopoly power, with a privileged trading

Table 5.2
Inclusion Criteria for the NASDAQ National Market System

Standard	Initial NASDAQ/NMS Inclusion: Alternative 1	Initial NASDAQ/NMS Inclusion: Alternative 2	Continued Inclusion
Registration under the Securities Exchange Act of 1934 or equivalent	Yes	Yes	Yes
Net Tangible Assets	$4 million	$12 million	$2-4 million
Net Income	$400,000	—	—
Pretax Income	$750,000	—	—
Public Float (Shares)	500,000	1 million	200,000
Operating History	—	3 years	—
Market Value of Float	$3 million	$15 million	$1 million
Minimum Bid	$5	—	—
Shareholders of Record	400-800	400	400
Number of Market Makers	2	2	2

* Domestic common stocks only.

Source: National Association of Securities Dealers, *Fact Book,* 1995, p. 44.

Figure 5.5
OTC-Traded Price Quotations

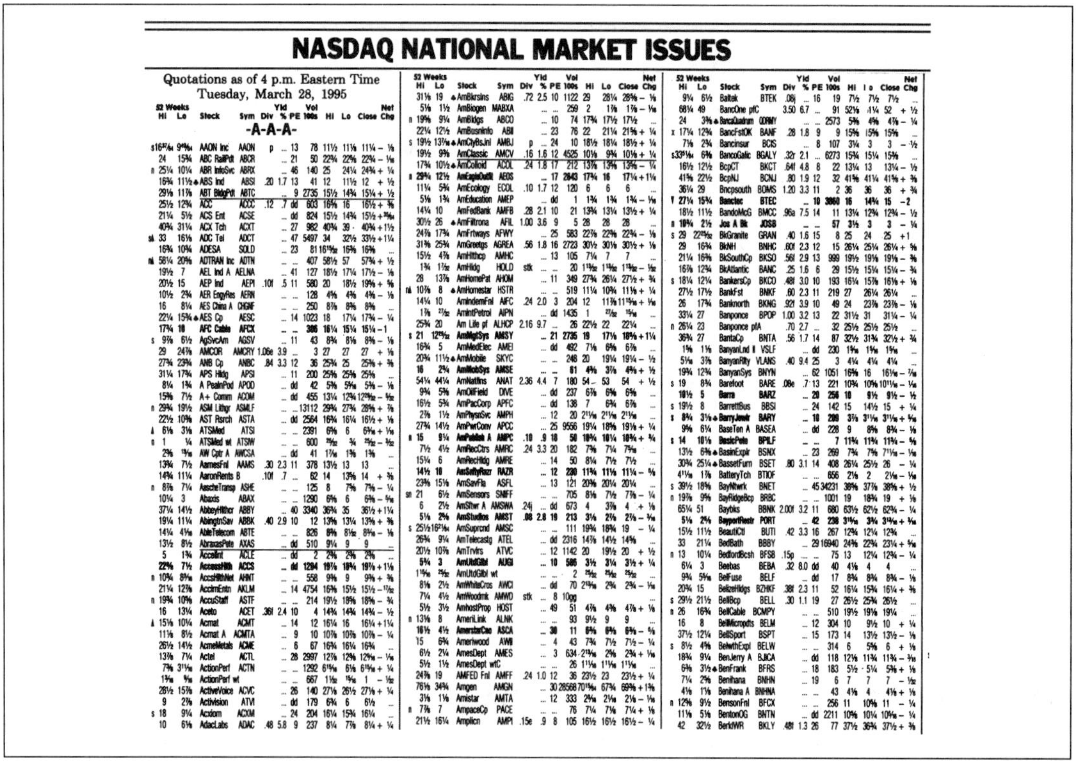

NASDAQ NATIONAL MARKET ISSUES

Quotations as of 4 p.m. Eastern Time
Tuesday, March 28, 1995

Source: *The Wall Street Journal*, March 29, 1995.

Table 5.3
Ten Most Active NMS Stocks, 1994

Company	1994 Share Volume (000s)
Intel Corporation	1,184,123
Cisco Systems, Inc.	1,007,533
Microsoft Corporation	841,594
Novell, Inc.	836,027
MCI Communications Corp.	772,992
Tele-Communications, Inc.	663,001
Oracle Systems Corporation	565,516
Apple Computer, Inc.	510,234
Lotus Development Corp.	434,852
DSC Communications Corporation	424,935

Source: National Association of Securities Dealers, *Fact Book,* 1995.

position and access to the limit order book. Presumably, the holder of a monopoly uses that power for profit. In a dealer market, there are a number of competing market makers. However, when markets are inactive and it is difficult to reach the various market makers for quotations, one can have a trade at an unfair price, due to lack of information. This criticism of the dealer market used in the OTC market is now much weaker than before NASDAQ and the NMS. In the major OTC stocks, the trader has information about current stock prices that is just as good as the information available to the trader on an organized exchange.

Sophisticated computer equipment allows instant access to the best prices available in the market. The requirement in NMS securities that transaction prices be reported virtually immediately helps market participants be sure they are receiving fair prices. Further developments in computer technology can be expected to extend the reporting requirements now in place for NMS securities to other smaller security issues.

Trading Procedures and Practices

In this section, we consider three basic types of trading procedures and practices. First, we consider the types of orders that traders can place. Second, we consider the rules that govern trading on margin. In margin trading, a trader pays for only part of the price of the stock and borrows funds from a broker to make up the difference. Third, we consider the basic rules that govern short selling – selling stock that one does not own.

Types of Orders

There are different ways to initiate an order when trading stocks. Whether one deals through an organized exchange or via the OTC market, the process is similar in most respects, so the following description assumes that trading is conducted over an organized exchange. Thus far, we have considered only a **market order**, an order to the broker to buy or sell a security at whatever price prevails on the market floor at that time the order is placed. A **limit order** is an order to transact only if certain conditions are met, rather than being an order for immediate execution. For example, a limit order to buy a stock at a share price of $70 means that the stock will be purchased if and only if it becomes available for a price of $70 or less. As a consequence, it is possible that limit orders might never be executed. A limit order to sell at $80 will be executed if the stock can be sold for $80 or more.

A **not held order** can be either a limit order or a market order. Marking an order as "not held" gives the floor broker the freedom to seek a better price. For example, a not held market order tells the broker to transact promptly, but instructs the broker to work the order to obtain the best price. This can be important if the order size is very large and attempting to transact the entire amount immediately might cause the price to move. In a not held limit order, the broker has the freedom to work the order for the best price, but the limit portion of the order instructs the broker not to exceed the limit. Thus, in a not held limit order to sell at $70, the broker is free to work the order to obtain the best price above $70, but the broker cannot sell for a price below $70.

A **percentage order** instructs the broker to make a transaction only as a certain percentage of the order flow in a given stock. For example, a 50 percent order to buy 1,000 shares at $40 instructs the broker to convert 100 shares of the percentage order into a limit order any time 100 shares of the stock trade below $40. A trader uses a percentage order to avoid initiating new, and perhaps unfavorable, trading prices. This can be important for large orders. If the order is very large, attempting to execute it all at once in its entirety may result in adverse price impacts.

A **stop order** is an order that becomes active when a certain price condition is met. It can be either a stop market order or a stop limit order. For example, let us assume that a share trades at $50. A trader might place a stop market order to buy at $48. If any transaction takes place at $48 with another trader, the stop market order becomes a market order to buy, and the order is executed at the current market price. This does not guarantee that the price obtained will be $48. For example, the stock might just have one trade at $48 that triggers the stop order, and the price might immediately bounce higher than $48. The stop market order would then be executed at that slightly higher price. The trader might have placed a similar order as a stop limit order to buy at $48, limit $48. This order is also activated when a trade occurs at $48, but the stop limit order now becomes a limit order to buy at $48. This specification ensures that the maximum price that the trader will pay is $48.

In addition to specifying the conditions under which orders will be executed, the trader can also control the time dimension of stop or limit orders or the portion of an order that can be filled. A **day order** is in effect just for the current trading day. If market conditions do not allow the order to be executed today, then the order is canceled. A **good until canceled order (GTC)** is an order that is left in effect until it is canceled, so it can stay in effect virtually forever. An **at the opening order** instructs that the order be executed only at the opening of the trading session. A **fill or kill order** instructs the broker to fill the entire order at a particular price immediately or cancel the order. An **immediate or cancel order** instructs the broker to fill the entire order, or any part, at a particular price immediately or cancel the order. An **all or none order** instructs the broker to fill the entire order or not to transact. A **market-on-close** order is an order to transact at the market price as close to the close of trading as possible. A **limit or market-on-close** order is a limit order left in effect during the trading day. If the order is not executed during the day, it becomes a market order at the close of trading.[12]

Margin Trading

As with almost every good in today's economy, it is also possible to purchase shares on credit. If one wishes to invest in stocks in an amount that exceeds the cash available to pay for them, one can buy the shares through **margin trading**. In this situation, one borrows some of the share price from the brokerage firm, which itself borrows money at the **broker's call rate**, the rate charged by banks for loans to brokerage houses on loans secured with securities. Combining the investor's own funds and the loan from the broker provides enough money to pay for the shares. The broker holds the shares as collateral for the loan. Since the Great Depression, the percentage that one can borrow has been regulated by the Federal Reserve Board Regulation T. The proportion of the share value that the investor must invest out of personal funds is called the **initial margin**. Currently, the maximum percentage of the shares' value that one may borrow is 50 percent. The advantage, and potential disadvantage, of margin trading is the greater leverage that it gives the investor. Assuming the investor borrows 50 percent of the invested funds from the broker, the investor realizes the full gain or loss on the shares, even though only one-half of the share value was invested.

In addition to the initial margin, stipulated by the Federal Reserve Board, the broker also imposes a **maintenance margin** requirement. When share prices fall, the value of the shares, which serve as the collateral for the broker, deteriorates. The broker can require additional cash funds from the investor in such a situation. This demand for more cash is known as a **margin call**. The investor must then pay the broker the new funds or the broker will sell the shares, retain the money owed to the brokerage firm, and return the excess to the investor.

In October of 1929, there were no restrictions on margins whatsoever, and it was customary for investors to borrow 100 percent of the share value from brokers. This allowed investors of very limited resources to assume enormous positions in the market. This practice was wonderful in a time of consistently rising prices, which existed in 1929. However, because of the extreme percentage of borrowed funds, any drop in prices would quickly cause margin calls from the broker. It was impossible for overextended investors to meet the margin calls. The broker would then sell the shares at whatever price the market would bear.

Under a fully leveraged system, as existed prior to 1929, a large drop in share prices could develop into a deadly spiral. The drop in share prices would generate margin calls, which many investors could not meet. Failure to meet the margin calls would bring many more shares on the market as brokers sold off shares to recoup their losses, which further depressed prices. The further drop in prices, of course, led to new margin calls. This spiral of falling stock prices and margin calls played an important role in the Great Crash of 1929 and was largely responsible for the onset of the Great Depression. In response to this danger, the Federal Reserve Board received authorization to regulate initial margin.

---

[12] This account of the types of orders relies on Robert A. Schwartz, *Equity Markets: Structure, Trading, and Performance*, New York: Harper & Row, 1988. Schwartz provides an extensive and insightful discussion of many aspects of stock trading.

Short Sales

Normally, we think of stock transactions as following a pattern of buying shares and eventually selling them, with the difference in purchase and sales price constituting the profit or loss on the transaction. It is also possible, however, to sell shares that one does not currently own, a practice known as **selling short** or **short selling**. In a **short sale**, the trader has the broker borrow shares from another investor and sell them in the market. Brokers have a ready supply of shares to borrow for most stocks, since they hold shares for many customers in **street name**. That is, customers simply leave their shares in the custody of their brokers. The broker is specifically authorized to loan these shares by the agreement which opens the brokerage account.

Figure 5.6 shows the flow of shares and funds in the short sale of 100 shares with an initial price of $30 per share. The figure assumes that the short seller receives 50 percent of the funds when the sale is initiated. The broker borrows shares for the short seller, and then sells them in the market for $3,000. After the purchaser pays for the shares, the broker retains 50 percent of the proceeds and passes the other half to the short seller, so the short seller receives $1,500 upon initiating the transaction. (This is consistent with a 50 percent margin requirement for short sales.) We assume that the price of the shares later drops to $20 per share and the short seller decides to cover the sale. The broker places a buy order and acquires the 100 shares, paying the seller $2,000. The $2,000 comes from the $1,500 that the broker retained when the short sale began, plus an additional $500

Figure 5.6
Flow of Shares and Funds in Short Selling

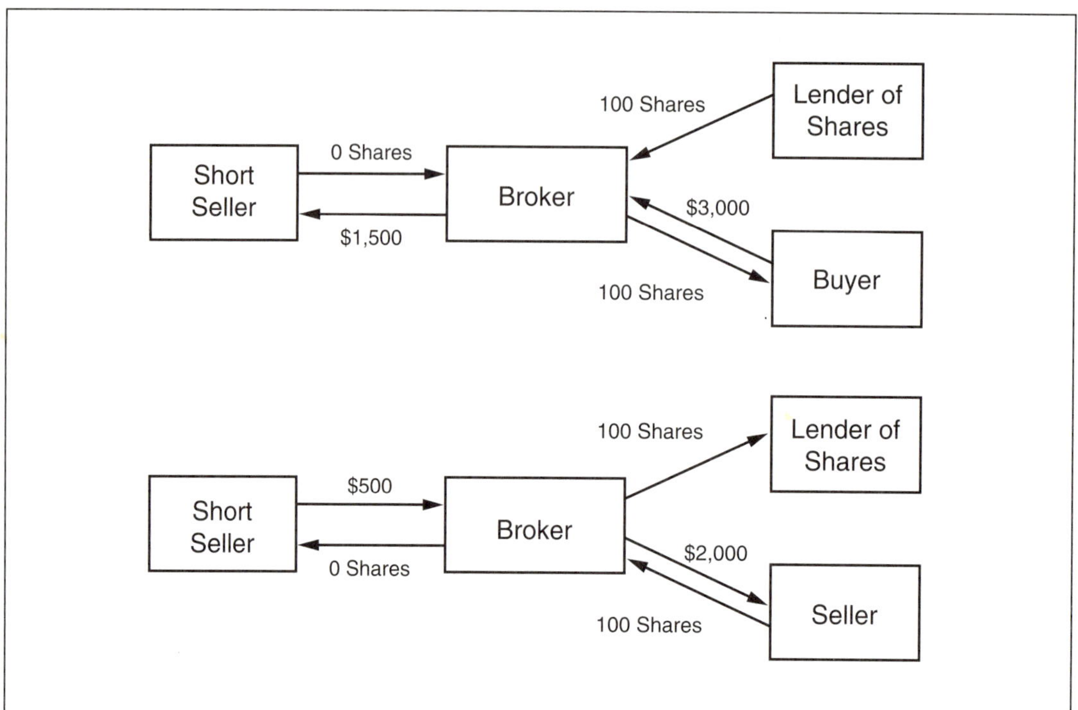

that the short seller must provide to the broker to close the transaction. The broker returns the shares to the original lender, and the short seller's total profit is $1,000 – the initial $3,000 sale price less the $2,000 purchase price to reacquire the shares and return them to the lender.

It should be recognized that short selling essentially involves trading on margin, since the short seller takes a position in the market without putting up the full value of the transaction. Also, the short seller must make any dividend payments to the lender of the shares. Finally, our example ignores the transaction costs involved in initiating and completing the short sale. These complications make it clear that one must have a thorough understanding of these intricacies and a clear agreement with one's broker before engaging in short sales.

The Third and Fourth Markets

Transactions for 10,000 or more shares of stock are called **block trades** and may involve billions of dollars. These trades and are executed on behalf of large institutional traders, such as pension funds, mutual funds, and charitable foundations. Block trading is an important activity for the organized exchanges, particularly for the NYSE. In today's market, about 55 percent of the entire share volume is through block trades. While block trading accounts for about half of the share volume on the NYSE, it is less important than it has been. The NYSE competes with the third and fourth markets for these large and lucrative block trades. The third and fourth markets are so named because they arose after the primary market (the market for new issues) and the secondary market (the organized exchanges and the OTC market).

The **third market** is a market for large blocks of shares that operates outside the confines of the organized exchanges and the OTC market. The major traders in the market are large institutions that have a frequent need to move large blocks of shares. In the third market, brokers assist the institutions by bringing buyers and sellers together. The third market arose to economize on brokerage commissions, that were fixed prior to 1975. A further refinement of this practice was the development of the **fourth market**. Like the third market, the fourth market consists mainly of institutional traders seeking to economize on transaction costs. The difference is that in the fourth market, the institutions trade among themselves without the intervention of any brokers.

Market Indexes

Market indexes provide a useful tool to summarize and to conceptualize the vast array of information generated by the continuous buying and selling of securities. At the same time, the use of market indexes presents new problems. First, many different indexes compete for attention. Second, indexes differ in construction and can differ widely in interpretation. There are indexes for almost all kinds of instruments. However, indexes for bonds, options, futures, and other instruments besides stocks are not well known or widely followed. The most widely quoted stock market indexes for the United States are the Dow Jones Industrial Average, the S&P 500, and the NYSE Composite Index. We briefly consider each in turn.

Dow Jones Industrial Average (DJIA)

The Dow Jones Industrial Average is the most widely quoted of all stock market indexes and reflects price movements of 30 of the very largest industrial firms on the NYSE. The firms included in the Dow Jones Industrial Average vary as the economy changes, but they are always 30 of the largest, most powerful, industrial firms, often called **blue chip stocks**.

The Dow is computed by adding the prices of the 30 stocks in the index and dividing by a special divisor to keep the index constant in the face of stock splits or the substitution of one stock for another. Because the prices are all added, the DJIA is a **price-weighted** index. Each stock contributes to the index value in proportion to its price. One of the most attractive features of the Dow Jones index is its availability. In addition to being widely quoted, *The Wall Street Journal* features it every day, as Figure 5.7 shows.The level of the index signifies nothing important by itself; only relative movements matter.

S&P 500

The Standard and Poor's (S&P) 500 Index is a broader market index than the Dow. As the name implies, the S&P index consists of 500 stocks drawn from various industries. The stocks included

Figure 5.7
The Dow Jones Averages

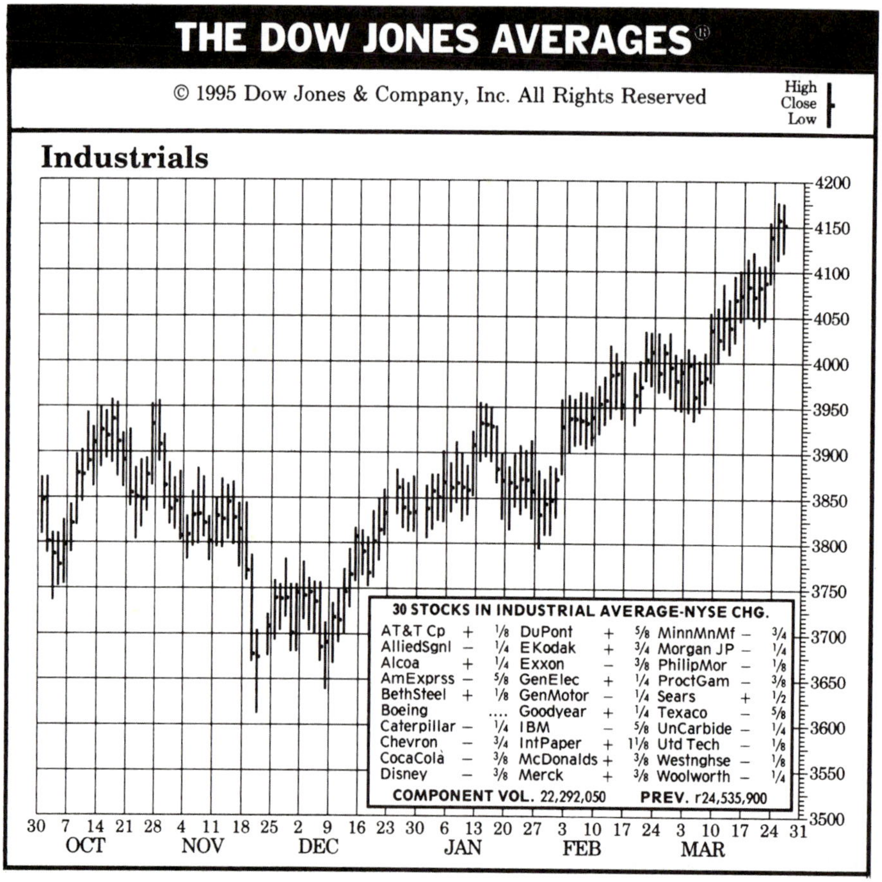

THE DOW JONES AVERAGES®

© 1995 Dow Jones & Company, Inc. All Rights Reserved

High / Close / Low

Industrials

4200, 4150, 4100, 4050, 4000, 3950, 3900, 3850, 3800, 3750, 3700, 3650, 3600, 3550, 3500

30 7 14 21 28 4 11 18 25 2 9 16 23 30 6 13 20 27 3 10 17 24 3 10 17 24 31

OCT NOV DEC JAN FEB MAR

30 STOCKS IN INDUSTRIAL AVERAGE-NYSE CHG.

AT&T Cp	+	1/8	DuPont	+	5/8	MinnMnMf	–	3/4
AlliedSgnl	–	1/4	EKodak	+	3/4	Morgan JP	–	1/4
Alcoa	+	1/4	Exxon	–	3/8	PhilipMor	–	1/8
AmExprss	–	5/8	GenElec	+	1/4	ProctGam	–	3/8
BethSteel	+	1/8	GenMotor	–	1/4	Sears	+	1/2
Boeing		....	Goodyear	+	1/4	Texaco	–	5/8
Caterpillar	–	1/4	IBM	–	5/8	UnCarbide	–	1/4
Chevron	–	3/4	IntPaper	+	1 1/8	Utd Tech	–	1/8
CocaColà	–	3/8	McDonalds	+	3/8	Westnghse	–	1/8
Disney	–	3/8	Merck	+	3/8	Woolworth	–	1/4

COMPONENT VOL. 22,292,050 **PREV.** r24,535,900

Source: *The Wall Street Journal*, March 29, 1995.

in the S&P 500 account for more than 80 percent of the market value of all stocks listed on the NYSE, although a few OTC-traded firms are included among the 500. Another feature of the S&P 500 is that each stock in the index is weighted according to the market value of its outstanding shares, so this index is a **value-weighted index**. For example, IBM receives a weight of almost 4 percent in the index, while General Cinema Corporation has a weight of about .05 percent. This reflects the fact that the market value of IBM's shares is about 80 times as large as those of General Cinema. The index is computed on a continuous basis during the trading day and reported to the public.

The New York Stock Exchange Composite

The New York Stock Exchange Composite Index is broader than the S&P 500, since it includes all stocks listed on the New York Stock Exchange. In today's market, about 2,400 issues trade on the NYSE and are, therefore, included in the index. The largest 50 companies account for about 40 percent of the value of the NYSE capitalization, with the others making up the remaining 60 percent.

The weight of each stock in the index is proportional to its value, so the NYSE index is a value-weighted index. The NYSE and S&P 500 indexes are calculated using a similar method.

Other Indexes

There are many other indexes for the stock market in addition to those discussed in this section. For example, the AMEX has its own index as does the NASDAQ. These are not as closely followed as those discussed here. All of the indexes mentioned in this section are reported on a daily basis in *The Wall Street Journal* in the "Stock Market Data Bank" column, as shown in Figure 5.8.

The Worldwide Stock Market

For many years after World War II, the U.S. stock market enjoyed a dominant position among world markets with a market value about as large as the rest of the world's through the 1970s. In the 1980s, this position changed dramatically. This section explores the growing importance of non-U.S. stock markets.

Alternative Trading Procedures

The U.S. stock market is a **continuous market**, a market in which a good is available for trading throughout the trading session. By contrast, some markets use an entirely different system. In a **call market**, each security is called for trading at a specific time and it can be traded only at that time. For example, Zurich and Frankfurt are call markets. A call market works as follows. An exchange employee calls a price for the share currently available for trading. Demand and supply of the shares are measured at the called price. Let us assume that the current price results in excess demand for the shares, with more shares wanted at the price than other participants are willing to supply. In this event, the exchange official will call a higher price and survey the supply and demand at the new price. This process continues until an equilibrium price is found. Then all transactions occur at that established price.

Figure 5.8
Stock Market Data Bank

STOCK MARKET DATA BANK 3/28/95

MAJOR INDEXES

HIGH	LOW (†365 DAY)		CLOSE	NET CHG	% CHG	†365 DAY CHG	% CHG	FROM 12/31	% CHG
DOW JONES AVERAGES									
4157.34	3593.35	**30 Industrials**	4151.81	− 5.53	− 0.13	+ 452.79	+ 12.24	+ 317.37	+ 8.28
1675.36	1371.89	**20 Transportation**	1631.79	+ 3.73	+ 0.23	− 43.57	− 2.60	+ 176.76	+ 12.15
201.23	173.94	**15 Utilities**	186.73	− 1.45	− 0.77	− 14.50	− 7.21	+ 5.21	+ 2.87
1386.80	1224.18	**65 Composite**	1385.40	− 1.40	− 0.10	+ 60.79	+ 4.59	+ 110.99	+ 8.71
474.80	416.31	**Equity Mkt. Index**	474.80	+ 0.64	+ 0.13	+ 45.57	+ 10.62	+ 41.73	+ 9.64
NEW YORK STOCK EXCHANGE									
271.92	243.14	**Composite**	271.92	+ 0.20	+ 0.07	+ 20.62	+ 8.21	+ 20.98	+ 8.36
345.05	298.30	**Industrials**	345.05	+ 0.41	+ 0.12	+ 35.24	+ 11.37	+ 26.95	+ 8.47
216.79	197.30	**Utilities**	206.63	− 0.48	− 0.23	− 5.26	− 2.48	+ 8.22	+ 4.14
257.00	212.94	**Transportation**	251.81	+ 0.65	+ 0.26	− 5.19	− 2.02	+ 29.35	+ 13.19
220.17	190.17	**Finance**	216.45	+ 0.16	+ 0.07	+ 8.79	+ 4.23	+ 20.65	+ 10.55
STANDARD & POOR'S INDEXES									
503.90	438.92	**500 Index**	503.90	+ 0.70	+ 0.14	+ 51.42	+ 11.36	+ 44.63	+ 9.72
182.71	162.44	**400 MidCap**	182.71	+ 0.20	+ 0.11	+ 7.96	+ 4.56	+ 13.27	+ 7.83
98.58	88.14	**600 SmallCap**	98.25	+ 0.22	+ 0.22	+ 1.00	+ 1.03	+ 4.08	+ 4.33
NASDAQ									
826.14	693.79	**Composite**	826.14	+ 3.51	+ 0.43	+ 70.85	+ 9.38	+ 74.18	+ 9.86
805.11	703.27	**Industrials**	805.11	+ 3.44	+ 0.43	+ 15.78	+ 2.00	+ 51.30	+ 6.81
1022.89	858.96	**Insurance**	1022.89	+ 2.74	+ 0.27	+ 129.20	+ 14.46	+ 97.02	+ 10.48
787.92	662.57	**Banks**	770.62	+ 1.73	+ 0.22	+ 86.63	+ 12.67	+ 73.55	+ 10.55
369.45	307.55	**Nat. Mkt. Comp.**	369.45	+ 1.62	+ 0.44	+ 34.75	+ 10.38	+ 34.21	+ 10.20
328.23	282.87	**Nat. Mkt. Indus.**	328.23	+ 1.46	+ 0.45	+ 10.98	+ 3.46	+ 22.19	+ 7.25
OTHERS									
461.52	420.23	**Amex**	461.52	+ 0.33	+ 0.07	+ 7.09	+ 1.56	+ 27.85	+ 6.42
267.80	235.50	**Russell 1000**	267.80	+ 0.32	+ 0.12	+ 24.94	+ 10.27	+ 23.16	+ 9.47
260.27	235.16	**Russell 2000**	260.27	+ 0.42	+ 0.16	+ 3.23	+ 1.26	+ 9.91	+ 3.96
286.89	254.01	**Russell 3000**	286.89	+ 0.36	+ 0.13	+ 24.57	+ 9.37	+ 23.45	+ 8.90
294.48	266.56	**Value-Line**(geom.)	290.72	+ 0.38	+ 0.13	− 0.39	− 0.13	+ 13.20	+ 4.76
4940.44	4373.58	**Wilshire 5000**	4940.44	+ 7.30	+ 0.15	+ 404.82	+ 8.93	+ 399.82	+ 8.81

†-Based on comparable trading day in preceding year.

Source: *The Wall Street Journal*, March 29, 1995.

Markets may use several calls per day for each stock. By trading only one stock at a time, as some markets do, all attention focuses on a particular stock. This process concentrates the market's available liquidity on the stock being called and may lead to more efficient pricing. This can be important in a market with low liquidity. Trading procedures are radically different at exchanges around the world with many exchanges using some variant of the call system.

Computerized trading is also surging in popularity. In the United States, the OTC market is essentially a computerized trading environment. Some exchanges have developed the computerization more fully. For example, the Toronto Exchange developed the Computer

Assisted Trading System (CATS) and this system has been adopted by other exchanges in other countries.[13]

World Equity Market Capitalization

This section briefly considers the comparative capitalization of stock markets around the world. We begin by considering the largest stock markets in the world, those of Japan, the United States, Britain, Germany, and France. We then consider the smaller European exchanges, and we conclude by discussing some markets in emerging nations. As we will see, the market value of the top few major markets far exceeds the combined value of all other markets.

The World's Largest Stock Markets For decades, the United States stock market has had the greatest value of any market. That is no longer true. Table 5.4 presents the market capitalization of the five largest markets and shows their annual growth rate over the 1984–93 period. The United States has the largest market capitalization by far. However, this has not been true for the entire period. In 1989, for example, the market capitalization of Japan was the largest in the world. In the early 1990s, Japan lost almost half of its market value. Other countries in Table 5.4 have a higher growth rate than the United States, so the relative dominance of the United States equity markets is likely to decrease over time.

Smaller European Stock Markets Virtually every European country has its own stock market. Table 5.5 shows the market capitalization of selected European stock exchanges, along with the rate of growth and the number of firms listed in these markets.

Stock Markets in Emerging Nations Table 5.6 shows data on selected stock markets in emerging nations, presenting information on market capitalization, growth in market capitalization, and the number of shares listed. Some of these markets have recorded very rapid growth within the last decade. Nonetheless, market capitalization remains small, as does the volume of shares traded.

Table 5.4
Market Capitalization of the World's Largest Markets

Country	Market Capitalization ($ billions)	Annualized Growth 1984–93	Number of Domestic Firms Listed
United States	$5,223.8	12.14%	7,607
Japan	3,000.0	18.18	2,155
Britain	1,151.6	18.89	1,646
Germany	463.5	21.83	426
France	456.1	30.66	472

Source: International Finance Corporation, *Emerging Stock Markets Fact Book,* 1994.

[13] Bruno Solnik, *International Investments,* 2e, Reading, MA: Addison–Wesley, 1991, pp. 110–11.

Table 5.5
Market Capitalization of the World's Smaller European Stock Markets

Country	Market Capitalization ($ billions)	Annualized Growth 1984–93	Number of Domestic Firms Listed
Holland	181.9	21.68%	245
Italy	136.2	20.35	210
Spain	119.3	27.71	376
Sweden	107.4	17.22	*
Belgium	78.1	22.90	165
Denmark	41.8	20.85	257
Austria	28.4	38.67	*
Luxembourg	19.3	12.60	*

Source: International Finance Corporation, *Emerging Stock Markets Fact Book 1994.* (*) indicates fewer than 124 firms listed.

In the coming years, it is likely that the fledgling Chinese market will develop rapidly. Currently, the newly formed nations that constituted the Soviet Union are developing their economic plans and struggling to create viable financial markets. Considered from a global point of view, most of the growth in equity markets will come from smaller developed markets and these emerging markets. Consequently, the markets of the developed world will become less dominant over time. This change is likely to be slow. Using the classification of the International Finance Corporation of developed and emerging markets, the developed markets held 97.5 percent of all equity market capitalization in the world in 1983. In 1994, the developed markets still held 88 of the world's

Table 5.6
Market Capitalization of Selected Emerging Stock Markets

Country	Market Capitalization ($ billions)	Annualized Growth 1984–93	Number of Domestic Firms Listed
Mexico	$200.7	65.14	190
Korea	139.4	41.27	693
Taiwan	195.2	39.29	285
Malaysia	220.3	30.99	410
India	98.0	35.48	6,800
Thailand	130.5	61.77	347
Brazil	99.4	14.67	550
Chile	44.6	40.39	263
China	40.6	N/A	183

Source: International Finance Corporation, *Emerging Stock Markets Fact Book,* 1994.

equity capital. For investors in countries with developed markets, investment in smaller and emerging markets can be a valuable tool in diversification.

Dual Listing and American Depositary Receipts

Some stocks are listed on several exchanges in different countries. For example, multinational pharmaceutical and oil firms may be traded on many different exchanges around the world. As we have seen for the NYSE, exchanges impose listing requirements before they accept a firm's shares for trading. Rules for listing differ markedly in different countries, with U.S. requirements being among the most restrictive. For example, a foreign firm wanting to list on a U.S. exchange must register with the Securities Exchange Commission and provide detailed financial reports that conform with U.S. accounting practices. In addition, the firm must disclose relevant information in conformity with U.S. laws. Many countries require far less disclosure than the United States, so these firms may be quite unwilling to reveal so much proprietary information merely to have their shares listed on U.S. exchanges.

To avoid these restrictions on trading in the United States, the American Depositary Receipt was created. An **American Depositary Receipt (ADR)** is a document showing that shares of stock have been deposited with a bank that acts as a depositary for the shares. The bank holds the foreign shares and trades ADRs that represent title to those shares it holds on deposit. In effect, the bank owns the shares and trades claims against those shares. The purchaser of an ADR holds a claim for a certain number of shares deposited with the bank. The company whose stocks are held by the depositary pays dividends to the bank, and these dividends are paid in the currency of the issuing firm. The depositary exchanges the foreign funds into U.S. dollars and pays the American investor a dollar dividend.

Today more than 800 foreign stocks trade as ADRs in the United States. Some of these are listed on the NYSE and through NASDAQ. NYSE ADR volume was 3.647 billion shares (worth about $142 billion), while NASDAQ volume was 4.4 billion shares (worth about $73 billion). For the U.S. investor, ADRs provide an important vehicle for gaining investment access to foreign shares.

Foreign Stock Market Indexes

Virtually every stock market has some stock market index designed to summarize trading results. For the United States, we have already seen that the major indexes are the S&P 500, the Dow Jones Industrial Average, and the NYSE Composite. Table 5.7 describes the indexes on major non-U.S. exchanges. These have received increasing attention in recent years and are likely to become more important. The Financial Times Stock Exchange (FTSE) from London and the Nikkei from Tokyo are reported daily in *The Wall Street Journal.* With the Dow having values of about 3,000, a jump of 50 points still attracts considerable attention. By contrast, the Nikkei index has values in the 25,000 range. Accordingly, jumps of 200-400 points are not so unusual for the Nikkei.

The Europe, Australia, Far East Index (EAFE) is compiled and reported by Morgan Stanley Capital International (MSCI). This index summarizes stock activity from 22 countries and is widely reported. A similar index, the FT-Actuaries, is published by the *Financial Times*, the British

Table 5.7
Market Indexes for Major Non-U.S. Exchanges

Country	Principal Exchange	Market Index
Great Britain	London Stock Exchange	FTSE 100 (Financial Times Stock Exchange) – 100 stocks
Japan	Tokyo Stock Exchange	Nikkei Stock Average – 225 stocks
France	Paris	CAC (Compagnie des Agents de Change) – 249 stocks
Germany	Frankfurt	DAX
Hong Kong	Hong Kong	Hang Seng Index – 33 stocks
Canada	Toronto	TSE 300 Composite Index (Toronto Stock Exchange) – 300 stocks

counterpart of *The Wall Street Journal.* There are different versions of the FT-Actuaries, some focusing on particular regions. Together, the FT-Actuaries cover about 2,500 stocks.

Basic Principles of Equity Valuation

In this section, we consider the valuation of two types of stock, preferred stock and common stock. As with all assets, we can analyze the value of a share of stock as the present value of all future cash flows from the security. The value of a share of preferred or common stock equals the present value of the dividends the stock will pay over the indefinite future.

Preferred Stock

Preferred stock is usually issued with a stated par value, such as $100. Payments made on preferred stock are called dividends and are usually expressed as a percentage of the par value. With a $100 par value and a 6 percent dividend, the annual dividend on a share of preferred stock would be $6. In many respects, the dividend on a preferred stock is similar to the coupon payments made on a corporate bond. There are, however, important differences between preferred stock and corporate bonds. First, preferred stock never matures. Second, as a consequence of the fact that preferred stock never matures, the purchaser never receives a return of the par value. Third, unlike the case of corporate bonds, the firm does not default if it misses a scheduled payment on preferred stock, and the preferred stockholder has no immediate legal remedy against the corporation.

Most preferred stock is cumulative. With **cumulative preferred stock**, any dividend payments that the firm misses must be paid later, as soon as the firm is able. In fact, the agreement between the firm and the cumulative preferred stockholders typically requires that dividends not be paid to the common stockholders until all late payments to the preferred stockholders have been made.

This cumulative feature offers partial protection for missed payments to the preferred stockholders. If a firm must temporarily suspend dividend payments to the holder of cumulative preferred stock, there is still a chance that the payments will be made up later. These features of no maturity, no return of principal, and no default when a payment is missed combine to make preferred stock riskier than a corporate bond issued by the same corporation.

Like many bonds, some preferred stock is callable. The issuing firm can require the preferred stockholders to surrender their shares in exchange for a cash payment. The amount of this cash payment, known as the call price, is specified in the agreement between the preferred stockholders and the firm. Usually, preferred stockholders (like bondholders) are not allowed to vote on matters of concern to the firm.

The Valuation of Preferred Stock

Preferred stock may be analyzed as a **perpetuity** – a bond that makes interest payments of a fixed amount forever and never returns its principal. However, the holder of preferred stock has a weaker position among the firm's capital contributors than the bondholder does. The claims of bondholders must be satisfied before those of preferred stock investors. Also, payments from preferred stock are dividends, not interest payments, for purposes of federal taxation. Because 80 percent of dividends received by corporations are exempt from federal taxation, preferred stock may be more attractive to corporations than to private investors. The value or price of a share of preferred stock equals the present value of all cash flows that will come from the stock

$$P = \frac{D_p}{k_p} \tag{5.4}$$

where:

P = the price of the preferred share
D_p = the dividend payment from the preferred share
k_p = the discount rate appropriate to the preferred share

In this valuation formula, the obligated payments are known, because the dividend is given by the par value and the dividend rate on the shares. The rate of discount, k_p, is the rate of return required by the preferred stockholders and depends on the risk that the firm will go bankrupt or that it will delay some payments on the preferred stock.

As an example, consider a share of preferred stock with a par value of $100 that pays an 8 percent annual dividend. If the discount rate for this share should be 12 percent, the preferred stock would be worth:

$$P = \frac{\$8}{.12} = \$66.67$$

Common Stock Valuation

Holders of common stock commit their funds and assume the last-place claim on the value of the firm in hopes of securing substantial profits. While a firm exists, the only cash flows that come from a share of common stock are cash dividends. These cash flows are risky. For example, some firms pay no dividends but hope to pay dividends at an unspecified time in the future. Each year, some firms that have paid dividends for a long period of time fall on hard times and either reduce or eliminate their dividends. Since dividends are not contractually obligated payments, their timing becomes much more a matter of prediction and speculation than is the case with bond coupon payments. This speculative element in the amount and timing of dividend payments arouses great concern over risk assessment for equity securities. The perceived riskiness of shares is reflected in the rate of return required by stockholders, which is the discount rate applied to the firm's dividend stream.

The Dividend Valuation Model

The value of a common share can be expressed by the **dividend valuation model**:

$$P_0 = \sum_{t=1}^{\infty} \frac{D_t}{(1+k)^t} \tag{5.5}$$

Equation 5.5 states that the price of a share of stock equals the present value of all future dividends to be paid by the share. Equation 5.6 gives an alternative expression of Equation 5.5.

$$P_0 = \frac{D_1}{(1+k)} + \frac{D_2}{(1+k)^2} + \frac{D_3}{(1+k)^3} + \frac{D_4}{(1+k)^4} + \ldots \tag{5.6}$$

where:

P_t = the price of the share at time t
D_t = the expected dividend to be paid at time t
k = the discount rate appropriate to the riskiness of the expected dividends

Equation 5.5 states that the current stock price (P_0) equals the sum of the present values of all future expected dividends (D_t) when those dividends are discounted at the stockholder's required rate of return (k). This implies that the value of a share is determined solely by the present value of the cash dividends to come from owning the stock.

The Dividend Valuation Model and Capital Gains

According to the dividend valuation model, the only cash flows that matter to an investor in common stock are the dividends that are expected to be paid to the shareholder. Yet, many investors buy stocks for the expected **capital gain**, an increase in the price of an asset. Many investors buy stocks that pay no dividends, planning to sell them later for a profit. This behavior is quite rational. In the last 20 years, dividends have contributed an average return of about 4 percent of invested capital each year, ranging from about 3-5 percent. By contrast, capital gains have ranged from about −30 percent to +30 percent. Thus, while dividends are an important component of investment return, the total return is largely determined by the capital gain or loss the investor receives.

The dividend valuation model does not ignore capital gains, but it treats them indirectly, through their relationship to dividends. To see how the dividend valuation model takes account of capital gains, consider a stock that pays a dividend annually. An investor might buy such a stock, with a plan to hold it for three years. In this situation, the cash flows that would come to the investor would consist of the three annual dividends that are to be paid during the time the stock is held plus the value of the share when it is sold. In terms of the dividend valuation model, the value of such a share would be:

$$P_0 = \frac{D_1}{(1 + k)} + \frac{D_2}{(1 + k)^2} + \frac{D_3}{(1 + k)^3} + \frac{P_3}{(1 + k)^3} \quad (5.7)$$

In this case, P_3 is the value of the share when it is sold three years after purchase, right after the third dividend is paid. An investor with the planned three-year holding period would be looking forward to receiving three dividends and would be hoping for a capital gain equal to the increase in the price of the stock over the three-year period, which would be equal to $P_3 - P_0$.

At first glance, Equation 5.7 appears to contradict the dividend valuation model of Equation 5.5, because it contains the term for the price at the end of the third year, P_3. This is only an apparent discrepancy, however. The value of the share in three years depends on the future dividends expected to be paid to shareholders from that time forward. In other words, the value of the share in the third year (P_3) depends on the dividends to be paid in subsequent years, D_4, D_5, and so on:

$$P_3 = \frac{D_4}{(1 + k)} + \frac{D_5}{(1 + k)^2} + \frac{D_6}{(1 + k)^3} + \frac{D_7}{(1 + k)^4} + \ldots \quad (5.7)$$

Equation 5.8 is just like Equation 5.5 or 5.6 except that the subscripts denoting the timing of the dividends are changed to reflect the fact that the value of the share is being measured at the end of the third year instead of at time 0. If Equation 5.8 is substituted into Equation 5.7, the result is exactly the same as the original version of the dividend valuation model, namely Equation 5.6.

This discussion shows that the anticipated capital gain over the three years that the stock is to be held is due to the changing valuation of the future dividends. So even if capital gains are not explicitly shown in the dividend valuation model of Equation 5.5, they are reflected *implicitly*. One other way of seeing that the value of a share depends on the expected future dividends is to reflect upon the following question: How much is a share of stock worth, assuming that everyone knows it will absolutely never pay a dividend? In this case, investing in such shares would be investing in something that will never generate any cash flows. If the investment will generate no cash flows, it has no value and the price of such a share should be zero.

The Indefinite Future of Dividends

Another apparent problem with the dividend valuation model of Equation 5.5 is the possibly infinite number of dividends populating the right side of the equation. If one wishes to apply the model in actual practice, how is it possible to sum the present value of all of those dividends? We have already seen in the case of preferred stock that the solution is very straightforward if the dividends are constant. As shown in Equation 5.4, the price is merely equal to a payment divided by the discount rate. However, if the dividends change over time, as is likely with common stock, no such easy solution is possible.

The Constant Growth Model

Even if dividends are not constant, there is still a way to apply the model and to avoid the pitfall of trying to add a potentially infinite number of dividends. Most successful firms hope to be able to pay increasingly larger dividends as time progresses, so there may be some growth in dividends. If the dividends grow at a regular rate, g, then the dividend valuation model can be greatly simplified. In such a case, the dividend in the second year equals the dividend in the first year plus the growth in dividends, or:

$$D_2 = D_1(1 + g)$$

Likewise, the dividend in the third year is given by:

$$D_3 = D_2(1 + g) = D_1(1 + g)(1 + g) = D_1(1 + g)^2$$

In this case, knowing the value of D_1 provides enough information to calculate the value of all subsequent dividends. For this special case of a constant growth rate in dividends, the dividend valuation model is mathematically equal to:

$$P_0 = \frac{D_1}{k - g} \tag{5.9}$$

This model is known as the **constant growth model**. The mathematics required to prove this result lie beyond the scope of this text. However, the essential technique employed to reach this result is to calculate the value of an infinite sum. There are several assumptions behind this simplification of the model:

1. The dividends grow each year at the constant growth rate g.
2. The dividends grow at the rate g forever.
3. The growth rate g is less than the discount rate k. (Otherwise, the denominator of Equation 5.7 would be zero or negative, and the resulting price would be meaningless.)

No firm is able to pay dividends at a constant rate of growth forever, so Equation 5.9 is a simplification of reality. Nevertheless, it is useful because it provides a way of dealing with the intractable problem of a potentially infinite series of dividends. To see how this simplified version of the dividend valuation model can be applied, consider a stock that you expect will pay $1.20 in dividends at the end of the year. Based on your assessment of the riskiness of the security, you believe that such an investment should pay a return of 17 percent, and you expect that the long-term growth rate for the dividends of the company should be 3 percent. According to Equation 5.9, the share should be worth $8.57, as shown below.

$$P_0 = \frac{D_1}{k - g} = \frac{\$1.20}{.17 - .03} = \$8.57$$

The value of a share of stock is highly sensitive to the discount rate or cost of capital, k, and the expected long-term growth rate in dividends, g. This sensitivity is reflected in Table 5.8, which shows the value of a share as given by Equation 5.9, assuming an initial level of dividends of $1 per share. For example, Table 5.8 shows that the share might be worth as much as $50.00, with a cost of capital of 12 percent and a growth rate in dividends of 10 percent. Alternatively, it could be worth as little as $5.00, if the cost of capital is 20 percent and dividends are not expected to grow.

The Dividend Valuation Model and Irregular Dividend Patterns

Thus far, it might appear that the dividend valuation model still has an insurmountable difficulty. On the one hand, Equation 5.5 has an infinite number of dividend payments to consider. On the other hand, the workable version of the model, presented in Equation 5.9, seems to hold only for the extremely improbable case of a dividend that grows at a constant rate forever. The model is really much more flexible than that, as this section will demonstrate.

Historically, many of the best buys in the stock market have been for shares that paid no dividends. In fact, many of the super growth firms are likely to pay no dividends early in their lives. This has been true of Coca-Cola, IBM, Xerox, and many other companies. One challenge for the dividend valuation model is its applicability to such stocks. Actually, the dividend valuation model can be applied quite directly to such shares. For a stock paying no current dividends, the dividend valuation model simply says that the future dividends are the cash flows that are worth worrying about, and the model can handle that quite well.

This can be illustrated by an example. Imagine a small new firm that is launching successful new products in the computer industry. All of its profits are being put back into new investment, so there is no money available to pay the shareholders a dividend. Currently, there are many such firms operating in the microcomputer industry, and without doubt, some of them will emerge as successful, well-established firms. In 1996, an imaginary firm, Prune Computer, traded in the range of $23 to $30 and paid no current dividend. According to the dividend valuation model, that price of $23 to $30 must be based on the expected dividends that will come later from Prune. After serious investigation, you expect that Prune will not pay any dividends for the next three years, due to the need to reinvest all profits in new product development and the marketing of existing products. In the fourth year, however, you expect that Prune will be able to pay a dividend of $1.50 per share, and that it will be able to pay a dividend that grows at a long-term rate of 10 percent. On an investment as risky as Prune, you feel that you must demand a rate of return of 18 percent. The question is, how much is Prune worth, given these assumptions?

Consistent with these assumptions, here is the expected dividend stream for Prune for the next ten years:

D_1	$0
D_2	0
D_3	0
D_4	1.50
D_5	1.65
D_6	1.82
D_7	2.00

D_8	2.20
D_9	2.42
D_{10}	2.66

Remember that the dividends are presumed to go on growing at a rate of 10 percent forever. The main point to observe is the way in which the dividend valuation model can be applied to a case similar to the Prune example, even where the dividend flows have not yet started.

To apply the dividend valuation model, a two-step procedure is necessary. First, there is a period, beginning with the fourth year, in which the imagined dividend pattern of Prune Computer matches the requirements of the dividend valuation model. From the vantage point of the end of the third year, the next year's dividend for Prune Computer is estimated to be \$1.50, to grow at a growth rate, g, of 10 percent, and to warrant a cost of capital, k, or required rate of return, of 18 percent. According to the dividend valuation model, the value of the shares at year 3 must be given by the following expression:

$$P_3 = \frac{D_4}{k - g} = \frac{\$1.50}{0.18 - 0.10} = \$18.57$$

If the time were three years from now, and the dividend stream from Prune were expected to start next year, then the price of a share of Prune computer should be \$18.75.

However, what is really of interest is what the price of Prune should be now, at time $t = 0$, according to the dividend valuation model, not what the price should be three years from now. To convert the price at year 3 into the current price according to the model, the value of Prune Computer at year 3 must be discounted back to the present at Prune's appropriate discount rate:

$$P_0 = \frac{D_1}{(1 + k)} + \frac{D_2}{(1 + k)^2} + \frac{D_3}{(1 + k)^3} + \frac{P_3}{(1 + k)^3}$$

$$P_0 = \frac{\$0}{(1.18)} + \frac{\$0}{(1.18)^2} + \frac{\$0}{(1.18)^3} + \frac{\$18.75}{(1.18)^3}$$

$$= \$11.41$$

Notice that this example is really just like Equation 5.7, except that there are no dividends to consider in the first three years for Prune.

Another kind of situation is one in which there are irregular dividend payments in the near term. Industries, and the firms in them, often go through a cycle of growth. Normally, the growth is more rapid at the beginning and then settles down to a lower long-term growth rate.

As an example of such a firm, consider the imaginary mobile-phone company, Cellular Technodynamics. At the end of 1996, you forecast the following dividend stream. For 1997, you expect a dividend of \$1.40, for 1998, \$1.95, for 1999, \$2.80, and then a long period of growth at 10 percent. These dividends are listed in the following table and are depicted graphically in Figure 5.9.

1997	$1.40
1998	1.95
1999	2.80
Then 10% growth thereafter:	
2000	3.08
2001	3.39, etc.

Even for such an irregular flow of dividends, the dividend valuation model applies. The dividend stream from Cellular Technodynamics can be broken into two parts, the part with the regular growth rate of 10 percent and the earlier period of rapid growth. Clearly, the dividend discount model can handle the period of regular growth. At year-end 1999, the dividend expected for the next year is $3.08, followed by dividends that grow at a rate of 10 percent. Assuming a stockholder's required return of 16 percent, the price of a share of Cellular Technodynamics at the end of 1999 is given by:

$$P_3 = \frac{D_{1998}}{k - g} = \frac{\$3.08}{.16 - .10} = \$51.33$$

Figure 5.9
The Dividend Stream for Cellular Technodynamics

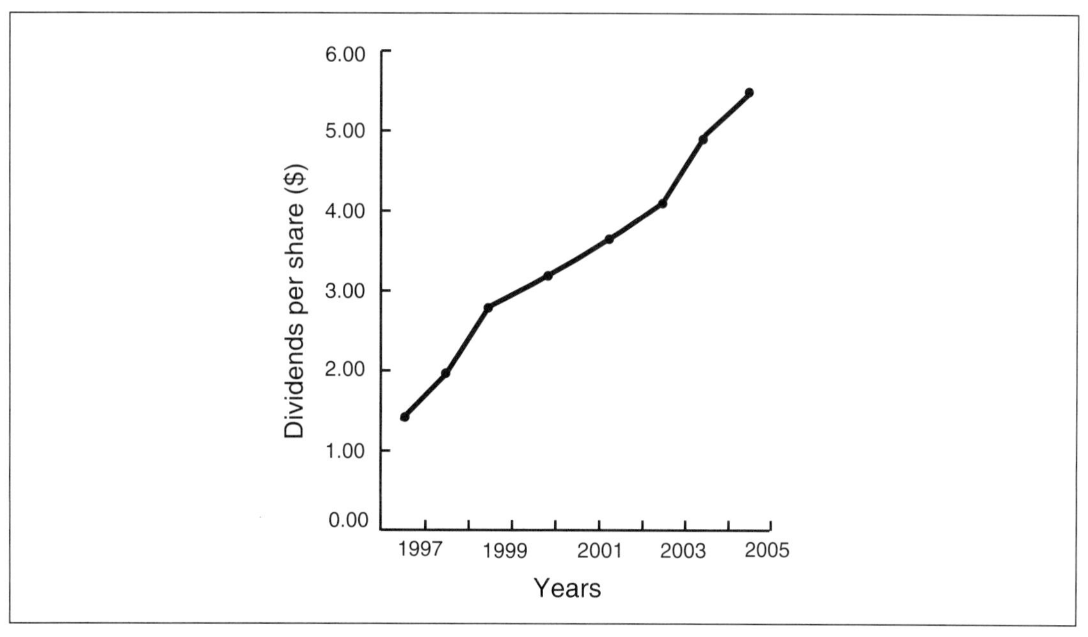

According to the dividend valuation model, the share price at year-end of 1999 is expected to be \$51.33. It remains only to take account of the value of the earlier dividend payments and the fact that a price must be calculated for the present, which is the end of 1996. The value of Cellular Technodynamics depends on the dividends received in the years before the dividend becomes smooth, plus the value of the shares at the time the dividend growth rate becomes constant, 1999.

$$P_{1994} = \frac{D_{1995}}{(1+k)} + \frac{D_{1996}}{(1+k)^2} + \frac{D_{1997}}{(1+k)^3} + \frac{P_{1997}}{(1+k)^3}$$

$$= \frac{\$1.40}{(1.16)} + \frac{1.95}{(1.16)^2} + \frac{2.80}{(1.16)^3} + \frac{51.33}{(1.16)^3}$$

$$= 1.21 + 1.45 + 1.79 + 32.88 = 37.33$$

Notice that the price expected for the end of 1999 must also be discounted back to the present. Also, it should be noted that the dividend to be paid at year-end 1999 and the value of the shares in 1999 are both discounted back for three years. The assumption here is that the \$51.33 expected value of the shares at the end of 1999 is the value immediately after the 1999 dividend has been paid.

These examples illustrate the flexibility of the dividend valuation model. With minor adjustments, it can handle more realistic situations, such as those for firms with initially irregular dividend streams, or even for those firms paying no current dividends. The model is not applicable, however, to firms that will never have any regular growth in dividends, but in practice this is a minor problem.

Summary

This chapter considered the rights and responsibilities of the stockholder and examined the organization of the stock market. It also presented the principles for valuing preferred and common stock.

The owner of a share of stock owns a fraction of the issuing corporation. As an owner, the shareholder has the right to participate in making key decisions and to share in the profits that the firm earns. As an owner, the shareholder has a claim on the value of the firm after the firm's obligations have been met. If the firm loses money continually and goes bankrupt, the law protects shareholders from losing more than their original investment.

The stock market consists of a number of organized stock exchanges and an active dealer market called the over-the-counter market. The stock exchanges have a central physical location for trading. By contrast, the over-the-counter market matches buyers and sellers through the use of electronic communications. In the third market, large institutions work through brokers to consummate large block trades. In the fourth market, large institutions make block trades of stock without the assistance of intermediating brokers.

The value of both preferred and common stock follows the basic rule that the value of any investment equals the present value of all of the cash flows expected from the investment. In the case of preferred stock, the flows are stated as a percentage of the face value. This practice implies a fixed dollar dividend, so preferred stock may be valued as a perpetuity. In the case of common stock, the matter is more complicated. The dividends may not exist at the present, or, if they do exist, they may grow yet larger. For those periods when dividends are growing at a constant rate, they may be valued with the constant growth model. This valuation technique is also useful under even more restrictive circumstances.

Questions and Problems

1. The chemical spill in Bhopal, India, at a Union Carbide plant raised fears that the settlement cost could exceed the value of the entire firm and throw Union Carbide into bankruptcy. If Union Carbide's share price had gone to zero, might investors have to contribute additional funds to cover the settlement? Why or why not?

2. Sometimes the interest of the shareholders and the managers of the firm might not agree. Is this ever a problem in practice? Can you give examples of ways in which their interests might disagree?

3. Why is stock ownership a residual claim on the firm?

4. What are the differences in liability for the owners of a corporation and a sole proprietorship?

5. Can a securities market function without a specialist?

6. What are the main differences between the OTC market and an organized securities exchange?

7. If you were a specialist for XYZ Corp. and saw that there were a large number of limit orders to buy at $12, how would adjust your inventory if current trading was at 12 1/4? Why?

8. In a well-functioning securities market, what would happen to a specialist or broker that consistently had the largest bid-asked spread? Why?

9. What informational advantages and disadvantages does the specialist have?

10. You had a limit order to sell Fly-by-Night Airlines at $12. *The Wall Street Journal* quotations show that the high for FBN was $12. Can you be sure that your shares sold? Why? What if the reported high price were 12 1/4?

11. Assume that you place an order to buy 10,000 shares of a thinly traded stock. What might be the effects of this on the share price? What does this suggest about the optimal size of portfolio management firms?

12. Assume that you manage a large portfolio dedicated to investments in the very largest industrial firms in the U.S. Which of the stock market indexes would be most relevant to your task? Which would be the second most suitable?

13. The discussion of foreign stock markets gives information on the risk level and level of returns experienced in these markets. Are these results consistent with the basic idea that higher expected returns tend to be accompanied by higher risk?

14. An investor buys a share of stock for $73 and holds it for three years, at which time the share is sold for $97. During the three years, dividends were received in the amount of $2.80,

$2.80, and $3.15. What was the wealth relative for this investment, ignoring any proceeds from re-investing dividends? What was the annualized wealth relative?

15. Assume that you own 130 shares of a stock trading at $14. If the firm has a 4 percent stock dividend, what would you expect to own from the firm after the dividend? How has your wealth changed?

16. For Fly-by-Night Airlines, the current stock price is $12 and the current quarterly dividend is $.10. The most recently reported quarter of earnings was $.23. What is Fly-by-Night's dividend yield and P-E ratio? How does the P-E ratio respond to an increase in the stock price?

17. With FBN Airlines selling at $11, you buy 1,000 shares using the maximum margin of 50 percent. You are able to borrow funds from your broker at 14 percent and you sell FBN at $14 after holding it for one year. What is your wealth relative for this investment? What would it have been if no funds had been borrowed? Answer the same questions assuming that FBN was sold at $12.

18. A new firm makes a 100 percent believable commitment never to pay dividends. What should the price of the shares in that firm be worth? Why?

19. Respond to the following claim: "The dividend valuation model is worthless as a guide to stock prices because it completely neglects capital gains."

20. Why do many new firms pay no dividends? Does this imply that their share prices should be zero? Why or why not?

21. React to the following criticism: "The dividend valuation model is not very useful because it can only be applied to firms having smoothly growing dividends. For example, it cannot be applied to firms that might experience a period of rapidly and erratically growing dividends."

22. How would you respond to the following attack on the dividend valuation model? "The dividend valuation model assumes that dividends grow at a rate g forever. This is obviously unrealistic, so the model cannot be applied in practice."

23. In terms of the dividend valuation model, why does a firm with a higher growth rate of dividends have a higher discount rate?

24. If a firm cuts its dividend, should its price fall according to the dividend valuation model?

25. Consider a firm that announces a very attractive new investment opportunity and also announces that it is eliminating its dividend in order to finance the new investment. What should happen to the stock price according to the dividend valuation model?

26. Consider a firm that pays a dividend in the next period of $.70 and that has a growth rate of 11 percent for the next four years. What are the dividends for these periods? Assume that the firm will never pay any dividends beyond the fifth year. According to the dividend valuation model, what should be the price of this share, if the discount rate is 12 percent?

27. For a share paying a dividend in the coming period of $1.20, with a long-term growth rate of 4 percent and a cost of equity capital of 10 percent, what is the share price according to the dividend valuation model?

28. What happens, for the previous share, as the growth rate accelerates and other factors are held constant? Graph the share price as a function of the difference between the cost of equity capital 10 percent and the growth rate, as the growth rate increases.

29. You estimate that a firm will have the following dividends for the next three periods: $1.17, $1.44, $1.88. After these dividends you expect dividends to grow at their long-term growth rate of 3 percent. What is the share price according to the dividend valuation model? What would it be if the long-term growth rate were 5 percent rather than 3 percent? Assume k = 10 percent.

Suggested REALDATA Exercises

The following *REALDATA* exercises explore the concepts developed in this chapter:
Exercises 24, 30, 33, 35–39

References

Ang, J. S., "Do Dividends Matter? A Review of Corporate Dividend Theories and Evidence," *Monograph Series in Finance and Economics*, Vol. 2, 1987.

Baer, H. L. and D. D. Evanoff, "Payments System Issues in Financial Markets That Never Sleep," *Economic Perspectives*, Federal Reserve Bank of Chicago, 14:6, November/December 1990, pp. 2–15.

Campbell, J. Y. and R. J. Shiller, "Stock Prices, Earnings, and Expected Dividends," *Journal of Finance*, 43:3, July 1988, pp. 661–76.

DeGennaro, R. P., "Settlement Delays and Stock Prices," *Economic Review*, Federal Reserve Bank of Cleveland, 25:4, 1989 Quarter 4, pp. 19–28.

Electronic Bulls and Bears: U.S. Securities Markets and Information Technology, Washington, DC: U.S. Government Printing Office, September 1990.

Fortin, R. D., R. Grube, and O. Joy, "Bid-Ask Spreads for OTC NASDAQ Firms," *Financial Analysts Journal*, 46:3, May/June 1990, pp. 76–9.

Solnik, B., "The Distribution of Daily Stock Returns and Settlement Procedures: The Paris Bourse," *Journal of Finance*, 45:5, December 1990, pp. 1601–9.

Treynor, J. L., "The Economics of the Dealer Function," *Financial Analysts Journal*, 43:6, November/December 1987, pp. 27–34.

Wagner, W. H., "Broker to Floor," *The Complete Guide to Securities Transactions*, New York: Wiley, 1989, pp. 79–90.

The Financial Derivatives Market: An Overview

6

Overview

A **financial derivative** is a financial instrument the value of which depends on the value of some more basic or primitive financial instrument. For example, an option on a share of stock is a financial derivative because the value of a stock option depends on the value of the underlying stock. Similarly, a futures contract on foreign currency is a financial derivative because its value depends on the value of the underlying currency. There are three basic types of financial derivatives, forwards and futures, options, and swaps. This chapter provides a brief overview of these instruments and their markets.

A **forward contract** is an agreement reached at one point in time calling for the delivery of some commodity at a specified later date at a price established at the time of contracting. For example, an agreement made today to deliver one ton of sugar a year from today at a price of $.59 per lb., with the payment to be made upon delivery, is a typical kind of forward contract. A **futures contract** is a type of forward contract that is traded on an organized futures exchange. A futures contract has less flexible and much more specific terms that a forward contract, but futures have certain advantages that make them very attractive to many traders.

As the name implies, an **option** is the right to buy or sell, for a limited time, a particular good at a specified price. Such options have obvious value. For example, if IBM is selling at $120 and an investor has the option to buy a share at $100, this option must be worth at least $20, the difference between the price at which you can buy IBM ($100) and the price at which you could sell it in the open market ($120). A **swap** is an agreement between two or more parties to exchange sets of cash flows over a period in the future. For example, Party A might agree to pay a fixed rate of interest on $1 million each year for five years to Party B. In return, Party B might pay a floating rate of interest on $1 million each year for five years. The parties that agree to the swap are known as **counterparties**. The cash flows that the counterparties make are generally tied to the value of debt instruments or to the value of foreign currencies. Therefore, the two basic kinds of swaps are **interest rate swaps** and **currency swaps**.

This chapter provides a basic introduction to all of these types of financial derivatives. As we will see, these markets have grown tremendously during recent years. Financial derivatives have so many uses that the student of financial institutions must take them into account to fully understand the operations of depository and non-depository financial institutions and financial intermediaries generally. In addition to an overview of these markets, this chapter provides an introduction to the pricing of these instruments and the way that they can be used to manage financial risk.

Forward Contracts

In a typical forward contract, calling for the delivery of a commodity at a future time for a payment to be made upon delivery, two parties come together and agree to terms that they believe to be mutually beneficial. The interbank foreign exchange market is the pre-eminent example of a forward market. In this market, banks enter forward contracts for the future delivery of foreign currency at a price that is established today. For example, a U.S. bank might agree to buy DM5,000,000 for delivery in 90 days at a price of $.70 per Deutschemark, for a total price of $3.5 million to be paid at the time of delivery. In a forward market, the contracting and establishment of a transaction price occurs at one date, and the delivery of the good and payment for the good occur at a mutually agreed future date. These contracts are quite flexible with respect to the quantity, timing, an d method of delivery. The forward market for foreign exchange is a multi-trillion dollar market and plays a major role in foreign commerce.

While forward contracts work quite well for the interbank market, in which large institutions make repeated transactions with each other and reputations are well-known and carefully protected, forward contracts have some inherent disadvantages as well. First, both contracting parties must trust each other to perform as promised. Second, in some circumstances, it may be difficult to find a trading partner. Third, it may be difficult to fulfill the contractual obligation without actually completing delivery.

Because of these kinds of difficulties – establishing the contract terms, finding a trading partner, and lacking a flexible means of settling the contract – forward markets have always been restricted in size and scope.[1] Futures markets have emerged to provide an institutional framework that copes with these deficiencies of forward contracts. The organized futures exchange standardizes contract terms and guarantees performance on the contracts to both trading partners. It also provides a simple mechanism that allows any trader to complete his or her obligation at any time. In the process, however, the futures market has developed its own peculiarities that also need to be understood.

Futures

In this section, we consider futures markets. As we see initially, futures are a type of specialized forward contract that trade on futures exchanges with fixed contract terms. We analyze the principles for pricing futures, and we explore how futures can be used to manage financial risk.

The Futures Exchange

A futures exchange is a nonprofit organization composed of members holding seats on the exchange. These seats are traded on an open market, so an individual wishing to become a member of the exchange can do so by buying an existing seat from a member and by meeting other exchange-imposed criteria for financial soundness and ethical reputation. The exchange provides

---

[1] The forward market for foreign currencies escapes these limitations because the parties must maintain their reputations for repeated transactions, because the international banking community is in constant communication, and because the liquidity of this market makes it easy for one bank to offset its trading commitments by entering into further forward contracts.

a setting in which futures contracts can be traded by its members and other parties who trade through an exchange member. The exchange members participate in committees that govern the exchange and also employ professional managers to execute the directives of the members. The futures market in the United States is regulated by the Commodity Futures Trading Commission (CFTC), an agency of the U.S. government. Table 6.1 lists the major world futures exchanges and the types of contracts traded by each.

Futures Contracts and Futures Trading

Each exchange provides a trading floor where all of its contracts are traded. The rules of an exchange require all of its futures contracts to be traded only on the floor of the exchange during its official hours. By specializing in a limited range of commodities, and by standardizing contract terms, the futures contract overcomes some of the difficulties noted earlier in the case of forward contracts. For example, the Chicago Mercantile Exchange trades futures on the S&P 500 stock market index. These contracts expire on a certain day in March, June, September, and December of each year. Each contract has a value equal to 500 times the S&P index level. The exchange also standardizes the way in which fulfillment of contract obligations occurs.

A futures contract is created when an order is executed on the floor of the exchange. The order can originate with a member of the exchange trading in pursuit of profit, or it can originate with a trader outside the exchange who enters an order through a broker. These outside orders are transmitted electronically to the floor of the exchange, where actual trading takes place in an area called a **pit**-a particular area of the exchange floor designated for the trading of a particular commodity. The rules of the exchange require that any offer to buy or sell must be made by **open-outcry** to all other traders in the pit. This form of trading gives rise to the appearance of chaos on the trading floor, because each trader is struggling to gain the attention of other traders. Once a trade is executed, the information is communicated to the exchange officials who report the transaction over a worldwide electronic communication system. Also, the trader whose order was executed will receive confirmation of the trade.

The trade from an outside party must be executed through a broker, and the broker must, in turn, trade through a member of the exchange. Normally, the two parties to a transaction will be located far apart and will not even know each other. This raises the issue of trust and the question of whether the traders will perform as they have promised. We have already seen that this can be a problem with forward contracts. To resolve this uncertainty about performance in accordance with the contract terms, each futures exchange has a **clearinghouse** – a well-capitalized financial institution that guarantees contract performance to both parties. As soon as the trade is consummated, the clearinghouse interposes itself between the buyer and seller. The clearinghouse acts as a seller to the buyer and as the buyer to the seller. At this point, the original buyer and seller have obligations to the clearinghouse and no obligations to each other. This arrangement is shown in Figure 6.1. In the top portion of the figure, the relationship between the buyer and seller is shown when there is no clearinghouse. The seller is obligated to deliver goods to the buyer, who is obligated to deliver funds to the seller. This arrangement raises the familiar problems of trust between the two parties to the trade. In the lower portion, the role of the clearinghouse is demonstrated. The clearinghouse guarantees that goods will be delivered to the buyer and that funds will be delivered to the seller.

Table 6.1
Futures Exchanges and the Contracts They Trade

	Principal Types of Contracts				
Standard	Date Founded	Physical	Currencies	Interest Rates	Indexes
Futures Markets in the United States					
Chicago Board of Trade (CBOT)	1848	♦		♦	♦
Chicago Mercantile Exchange (CME)	1919	♦	♦	♦	♦
Coffee, Sugar and cocoa Exchange (New York)	1882	♦			♦
Commodity Exchange, Inc. (COMEX) (New York)	1933	♦			
Kansas City Board of Trade (KCBT)	1856	♦			♦
Mid-American Commodity Exchange (Chicago)	1880	♦	♦	♦	
Minneapolis Grain Exchange	1881	♦			
New York Cotton Exchange, Inc.	1870	♦	♦		♦
Citrus Associates of the New York Cotton Exchange	1966	♦			
Petroleum Associates of the New York Cotton Exchange	1971	♦			
New York Futures Exchange (NYFE)	1979				♦
New York Mercantile Exchange	1872	♦			
Chicago Rice and Cotton Exchange	1976	♦			
Principal Foreign Futures Markets					
International Futures Exchange (INTEX) (Bermuda)	1984	♦			♦
Bolsa de Mercadorios de Sao Paulo	1917	♦			
London International Financial Futures Exchange (LIFFE)	1982		♦	♦	♦
Baltic International Freight Futures Exchange (BIFFEX) (London)	1985				♦
Tokyo Financial Futures Exchange	1985		♦	♦	♦
Singapore International Monetary Exchange (SIMEX) (Singapore)	1984		♦	♦	♦
Hong Kong Futures Exchange	1977	♦			♦
New Zealand Futures Exchange	1985	♦	♦	♦	
Sydney Futures Exchange	1960	♦	♦	♦	♦
Toronto Futures Exchange	1984		♦	♦	♦
Kuala Lumpur Commodity Exchange	*1985	♦			

*Reorganized after default.

Source: *The Wall Street Journal, Futures Magazine, Intermarket Magazine,* various issues, and Chicago Mercantile Exchange, *1985 Annual Report.*

Figure 6.1
The Function of the Clearinghouse in Futures Markets

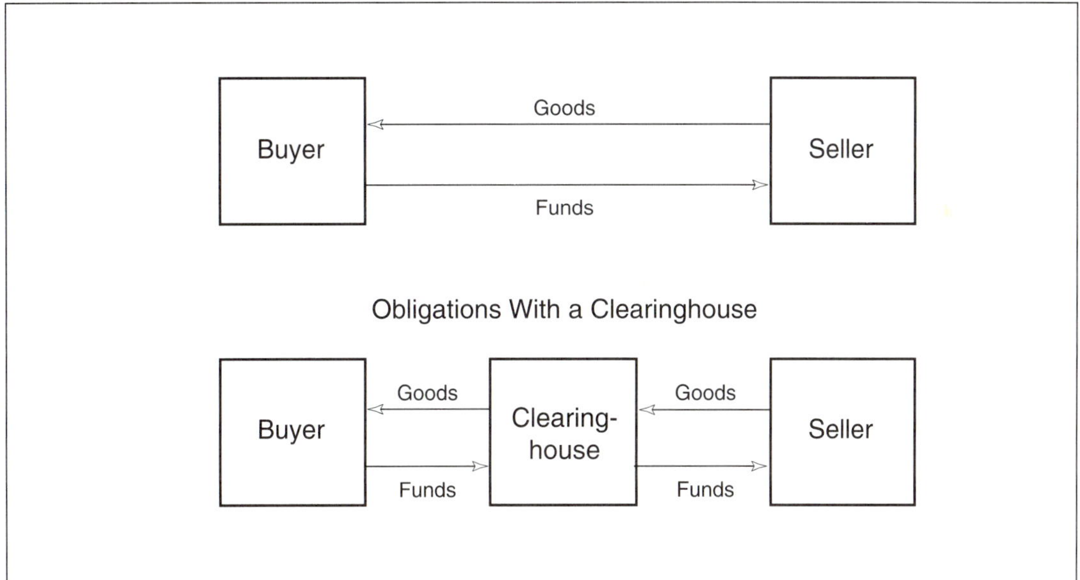

At this point, the traders only need to trust the clearinghouse, instead of each other. Because the clearinghouse has a large supply of capital, there is little need for concern. Also, as the bottom portion of Figure 6.1 shows, the clearinghouse has no net commitment in the futures market. After all the transactions are completed, the clearinghouse will have neither funds nor goods. It only acts to guarantee performance to both parties.

The Clearinghouse and the Trader While the clearinghouse guarantees performance on all futures contracts, it now has its own risk exposure, because the clearinghouse will suffer if traders default on their obligations. To protect the clearinghouse and the exchange, traders must deposit funds with their brokers in order to trade futures contracts. This deposit, known as **margin**, must be in the form of cash or short-term U.S. Treasury securities. This margin acts as a good-faith deposit with the broker. If the trader defaults on his or her obligations, the broker may seize the margin deposit to cover the trading losses. This provides a measure of safety to the broker, the clearinghouse, and the exchange.

This margin deposit, however, is normally quite small relative to the value of the goods being traded. The margin deposit might normally have a value equal to only 5 to 10 percent of the goods represented by the futures contract. Because potential losses on the futures contract could be much larger than this margin deposit, the clearinghouse needs other protection from potential default by the trader. To give this protection, futures exchanges have adopted a system known as **daily settlement** or **marking-to-market**. The policy of daily settlement means that futures traders realize their paper gains and losses in cash on the results of each day's trading. The trader may withdraw the day's gains and must pay the day's losses.

The margin deposit remains with the broker. If the trader fails to settle the day's losses, the broker may seize the margin deposit and liquidate the trader's position, paying the losses out of the margin deposit. This practice limits the exchange's exposure to loss from a trader's default. Essentially, the exchange will lose on the default only if the loss on one day exceeds the amount of the margin. This is unlikely to happen and even if it does, the amount lost would probably be very small.

After executing a futures contract, both the buyer and seller have undertaken specific obligations to the clearinghouse. Fulfillment of those obligations can be accomplished in two basic ways. First, the trader may actually make or take delivery as contemplated in the original contract. Second, if a trader does not wish to make or take delivery, the trader can fulfill all obligations by entering a reversing or offsetting trade.

Before delivery, buyers and sellers are not associated with each other because the clearinghouse has interposed itself between all the pairs of traders. This allows any trader a means to end his or her commitment in the futures market without actually making delivery. To enter a **reversing trade** a trader trades to bring his or her net position to zero, thereby ending any further obligation in the futures market. For example, if a trader previously bought a September S&P futures contract, he or she would sell a September S&P futures contract. This trade would reverse, or offset, the previous obligation and would release the trader from any future obligation.

Futures Price Quotations Futures price quotations are available daily in *The Wall Street Journal* and other newspapers. Figure 6.2 presents a sample of futures price quotations as they appear in *The Wall Street Journal*. Financial futures include: interest rate futures, foreign exchange futures, and stock index futures. Interest rate futures contracts exist for several kinds of U.S. government obligations, including Treasury bills, notes, and bonds. Foreign exchange futures are traded on the German mark, British pound, Japanese yen, Swiss franc, and Canadian dollar. Stock index futures are traded on several different indexes, including the S&P 500, the Value Line Composite Index, the NYSE Composite Index, and the Major Market Index, which closely tracks the Dow Jones Industrial Average. As Figure 6.2 indicates, contracts for several different delivery months trade for most commodities. The figure shows the opening, high, low, and settlement price for each day of trading. The **open interest** is the number of contracts currently obligated for delivery, which will equal the number of contracts initiated since the contract was listed for trading, less those contracts that were closed by a reversing trade. The **volume** is the number of contracts traded in a particular day.

Futures Pricing

The **basis** is a key concept in understanding futures prices and is defined as:

$$\text{Basis} = \text{Cash Price} - \text{Futures Price} \qquad 6.1$$

Traders in the futures markets watch the basis very closely because its behavior is governed by certain rules. Also, the various pricing theories can be stated in terms of rules about how the basis will behave. First, the basis must equal zero at the delivery date for the futures contract to exclude arbitrage possibilities. For example, if the cash price were lower than the futures price at delivery,

Figure 6.2
Futures Price Quotations in *The Wall Street Journal*

FUTURES PRICES

Tuesday, March 28, 1995

Open Interest Reflects Previous Trading Day.

	Open	High	Low	Settle	Change	Lifetime High	Lifetime Low	Open Interest
GRAINS AND OILSEEDS								
CORN (CBT) 5,000 bu.; cents per bu.								
May	247¾	250	247¼	249¼	+ 1	285½	228	106,340
July	254	256¼	253¼	255½	+ 1	285½	232½	110,387
Sept	257½	259½	257	259	+ ½	270½	238	21,181
Dec	261	262½	260¼	262¼	+ ¾	263½	235½	93,118
Mr96	267	268¾	266¼	268¾	+ 1	269¾	249½	8,749
May	271½	272¾	270½	272¾	+ ¾	273	259½	513
July	273¼	274¾	273	274¾	+ ½	275¼	254	4,631
Dec	255	256¼	254½	256	+ ¼	258½	239	3,093
Est vol 33,000; vol Mon 28,986; open int 348,012, +372.								
OATS (CBT) 5,000 bu.; cents per bu.								
May	131½	133¾	131	133¾	+ 1½	151	122¼	7,150
July	136¾	139¼	136½	139	+ 1¾	142½	127½	4,379
Sept	141	143¼	140½	143	+ 2	143¼	132	298
Dec	146¼	148½	146¼	148½	+ 1¾	148½	136	1,317
Est vol 1,000; vol Mon 1,012; open int 13,205, −71.								
SOYBEANS (CBT) 5,000 bu.; cents per bu.								
May	577	59¼	574½	577½	+ ¾	705½	553¼	43,301
July	586½	590	584¾	588¼	+ ¾	706½	559¼	50,186
Aug	591½	594	589½	592½	+ ¾	612	562¾	6,486
Sept	593½	597	592	594½	+ 1	615	564¾	3,823
Nov	601	603½	598¼	602¼	+ 1¾	645	573¼	28,493
Ja96	608	611	607	609½	+ 1¼	621	582¾	1,974
Mar	616½	618	614½	618	+ 1½	629	590½	498
May	....	....	....	620½	+ ½	633	602	103
July	625	627½	625	626¼	+ ½	636¼	599½	764
Nov	608	609	605½	608¼	− ¾	615½	585	1,420
Est vol 33,000; vol Mon 35,068; open int 137,051, −2,732.								
SOYBEAN MEAL (CBT) 100 tons; $ per ton.								
May	165.50	166.70	164.10	165.90	+ .40	207.00	155.30	34,020
July	170.10	171.40	168.60	170.40	+ .60	206.00	159.80	29,911
Aug	171.80	173.00	170.60	172.40	+ .80	182.60	162.10	7,760
Sept	173.80	175.00	172.50	174.30	+ .70	182.70	164.00	5,300
Oct	175.10	176.10	174.10	175.60	+ 1.00	181.80	166.00	8,990
Dec	177.70	179.10	177.00	178.40	+ .60	185.20	169.30	12,367
Ja96	179.00	179.20	178.00	178.70	+ .50	185.20	171.00	723
Est vol 12,000; vol Mon 13,374; open int 99,071, −1,283.								
Dec	75.90	76.10	74.70	74.70	− 1.28	79.95	66.25	26,166
Mr96	76.95	76.95	75.80	75.85	− 1.10	80.75	68.80	5,999
May	77.55	77.55	76.65	76.65	− .90	81.30	72.70	1,271
Jly	77.60	77.60	76.90	76.90	− .70	81.50	76.00	199
Est vol 15,000; vol Mon 11,810; open int 78,927, −1,150.								
ORANGE JUICE (CTN)–15,000 lbs.; cents per lb.								
May	106.00	108.25	105.75	107.35	+ 2.20	126.60	96.65	11,782
July	110.50	112.25	109.75	111.20	+ 2.15	129.00	100.50	5,576
Sept	114.00	115.50	113.75	114.75	+ 2.55	132.00	102.50	4,454
Nov	na	112.50	111.10	112.50	+ 2.35	129.00	105.00	2,316
Ja96	113.50	114.25	112.50	114.20	+ 1.95	129.20	125.50	1,643
Mar	113.25	116.20	113.25	116.20	+ 2.95	130.20	110.00	193
Est vol 4,000; vol Mon 1,016; open int 25,986, +158.								
METALS AND PETROLEUM								
COPPER-HIGH (Cmx.Div.NYM) – 25,000 lbs.; cents per lb.								
Mar	143.00	143.00	140.80	141.65	− .75	143.15	76.30	1,740
Apr	141.10	141.10	139.40	139.70	− 1.05	141.70	90.10	1,777
May	138.75	139.40	136.80	137.80	− .95	139.40	76.85	28,601
June	134.70	135.50	134.50	135.00	− 1.05	136.20	106.30	639
July	134.40	134.50	132.30	132.90	− 1.05	134.50	78.00	6,851
Aug	130.60	130.60	130.60	130.65	− 1.10	131.70	111.40	375
Sept	130.00	130.00	128.20	128.45	− 1.10	130.50	79.10	3,428
Oct		....	....	127.00	− 1.20	126.90	113.00	423
Nov		....	....	125.50	− 1.35	126.00	113.95	291
Dec	125.70	125.70	125.00	124.15	− 1.35	126.10	88.00	3,053
Ja96		....	....	122.85	− 1.35	123.50	88.50	224
Mar		....	....	120.35	− 1.35	122.00	99.20	1,159
May		....	....	117.80	− 1.40	118.50	107.00	369
July		....	....	115.80	− 1.40	117.00	105.50	196
Sept		....	....	114.60	− 1.40	116.00	105.25	153
Dec		....	....	114.10	− 1.40	116.80	112.00	94
Est vol 9,000; vol Mon 7,172; open int 49,377, +121.								
GOLD (Cmx.Div.NYM)–100 troy oz.; $ per troy oz.								
Mar		....	....	383.10	+ .90	385.70	375.20	0
Apr	383.00	383.50	382.00	383.20	+ .90	425.00	374.50	36,192
June	384.50	385.80	384.30	385.50	+ .80	430.00	351.00	46,489
Aug	388.20	389.20	387.80	388.70	+ .80	414.50	380.50	16,560
Oct		....	....	392.10	+ .90	419.20	387.20	5,212
Dec	395.00	395.80	394.80	395.60	+ .90	439.50	358.00	13,462
Fb96		....	....	399.20	+ 1.00	424.50	393.60	10,283
Apr		....	....	402.90	+ 1.10	430.20	398.70	5,576

Source: *The Wall Street Journal*, March 29, 1995.

a trader could buy the good in the cash market, sell a futures contract, and deliver the good. This would give a riskless profit without investment equal to the difference between the futures and cash price of the same good.

The Cost-of-Carry Relationship for Futures Prices

While the cash and futures price must be equal at the contract's delivery date and the basis must be zero, we still need to understand how futures prices are formed prior to delivery. The **cost-of-carry model** provides our basic understanding of futures prices. The cost-of-carry is the cost of carrying a physical good forward in time from the present to the delivery of a futures contract. For physical goods, the cost-of-carry includes storage, transportation, insurance, and the financing cost of holding the good. For financial futures, transportation, insurance, and storage are negligible, so the cost-of-carry for financial goods is essentially the interest cost of the funds used to acquire the stocks, bonds, or foreign currency that underlie the futures contract.

First, the cost-of-carry model asserts that the futures price must be less than or equal to the cash market cost of the deliverable good, plus the cost of carrying the good forward to the delivery date:

$$F \leq S(1+r) \tag{6.2}$$

where: F = the futures price
S = the spot price
r = the interest rate to cover the period between the present and the delivery date.

If this relationship did not hold, we could guarantee a risk-free profit without investment by selling the futures, buying the spot good and carrying it to delivery against the futures contract. To make this more concrete, assume that a futures contract expires in one year and has a price of $115. The price of the spot good is $100, and the interest rate is 10 percent. A trader could sell the futures contract now for a contract price of $115, buy the good for $100, and finance it for the next year. The purchase price plus the financing cost of carrying to good forward for a year would be a total of $110. This good could be delivered against the futures contract at a price of $115, guaranteeing a $5 profit. Thus violations of Inequality 6.2 lead to arbitrage.

The cost-of-carry model also asserts that the futures price must equal or exceed the spot price of the good plus the cost of carrying it forward to delivery:

$$F \geq S(1+r) \tag{6.3}$$

If the relationship in Equality 6.3 did not hold, a trader could sell the spot good short and invest the proceeds to earn interest between the present and the delivery date. The trader would also buy the futures contract. At the delivery date, the trader would receive delivery and pay on the futures contract with the proceeds from the invested funds. The trader would then complete the transaction by returning the good that was sold short. As an example, assume that a financial good trades for $100, that the interest rate is 10 percent, but that the futures price for this good is only $105, a violation of Inequality 6.3. The trader would buy the futures contract, and would sell the good short for $100, and would invest the proceeds for one year at 10 percent. At the delivery date, the investment proceeds would be $110, and the trader would pay $105 in fulfillment of the futures delivery. The trader would now have the physical good and $5. To complete the short sale, the trader would return the physical good and would pocket an arbitrage profit of $5.

Notice that the two Inequalities, 6.2 and 6.3, together imply that the futures price must equal the spot price plus the cost of carrying it forward to delivery:

$$F = S(1+r) \tag{6.4}$$

This is the basic relationship of the cost-of-carry model. It is important to note that this relationship holds as described in perfect markets and assumes that a trader can earn interest on the full proceeds of a short sale. Market imperfections such as transaction costs and restrictions on short selling will prevent Equation 6.4 from holding exactly. Financial futures markets are nearly perfect, however, and Equation 6.4 provides a nearly complete description of financial futures pricing.[2]

Interest Rate Futures

In the futures markets today, a wide variety of goods is traded, ranging from pork bellies to financial instruments. These goods are also very diverse with respect to their economic features, such as their storage characteristics and the quality of the markets for their short sale. Because of this tremendous diversity, it is impossible to cover all of the important features of these markets here.[3] Consequently, this section focuses on some key issues of financial futures. This approach illustrates how certain issues in financial futures are related to some of the other problems discussed in this book.

Interest Rate Futures and the Yield Curve

As discussed in Chapter 7, the yield curve is extremely important for bond investing and bond portfolio management. The different maturities of bonds and their commensurate yields allows investors to commit their money for different periods of time in order to take advantage of a particular shape that the yield curve might possess at any given moment. We have also seen how forward rates of interest play an important role in two theories of the term structure – the pure expectations theory and the liquidity premium theory.

In the interest rate futures markets, the exchanges have made a conscious effort to offer interest-rate futures that cover the yield curve. For example, the International Monetary Market (IMM) of the Chicago Mercantile Exchange (CME) has specialized in the shorter maturity instruments. The IMM currently offers interest rate futures contracts on Treasury bills, bank CDS, and Eurodollar deposits, all with maturities of about three months. By contrast, the Chicago Board of Trade (CBOT) has focused on the longer maturities. The CBOT trades a contract on long-term T-bonds, the most successful futures contract ever introduced. It also offers contracts on two-, five-, and ten-year Treasury notes.

To illustrate the connection between the yield curve and interest rate futures, we will focus on the IMM's T-bill contract. This contract calls for the delivery of T-bills with a face value of $1 million having 90 days to maturity at the time of delivery. Prices for the T-bill futures are quoted according to a system known as the IMM Index. The IMM Index is simply the discount yield on the T-bill futures subtracted from 100. So, for example, a quoted settlement value of 94.00 means that the futures yield would be 6 percent. To contract for delivery of a 90-day T-bill with a futures price of 94.00, for example, a trader would have to agree to pay a price that was commensurate with a discount yield of 6 percent.

---

[2] For a more thorough treatment of the cost-of-carry model and a description of the effect of market imperfections, see R. W. Kolb, *Futures, Options, and Swaps*, Miami: Kolb Publishing Company, 1994.

[3] For a treatment of futures markets in the United States, see R. Kolb, *Understanding Futures Markets*, 4th ed., Miami: Kolb Publishing, 1994.

There is an important relationship between yields implied by futures prices and the yields on spot market instruments. Essentially, interest rate futures yields may be interpreted as forward rates of interest. For example, the yield of the March 1998 T-bill futures contract is the forward rate of interest for a 90-day T-bill to run from March to June 1998. In other words, if we calculated from the spot market the forward rate for the same period as that covered by the March 1998 T-bill futures contract, we should find a result that almost exactly matches the yield on the T-bill futures.

If that were not the case, and markets were perfect, it would be possible to generate arbitrage profits. This would be accomplished by buying and selling spot market T-bills and T-bill futures to take advantage of the yield discrepancy. In fact, if markets were perfect, and included in this is the opportunity for unrestricted short selling, the forward rates of interest and the yield on the futures contract would have to be exactly equal. Actual markets, however, are not perfect, so the relationship would not have to hold exactly. If we take into account transaction costs, though, the difference between the forward rate of interest calculated from the spot market and the rate of interest implied by the futures contract would still have to be very close.

This issue has been examined in great detail by a number of authors, but the definitive study was conducted by Rendleman and Carabini.[4] They attempted to determine if there were arbitrage opportunities between spot and futures market T-bills, given the fact that traders would have to pay transaction costs. One of these costs is the fact that short selling is constrained. In their study, they found that it cost about one-half of a percentage point, or 50 basis points, to sell a T-bill short.[5] This meant that futures yields and forward rates of interest could differ by this amount without giving rise to any arbitrage opportunities.

Using daily data for two years from 1976 to 1978, which gave a total of 1,606 observations, Rendleman and Carabini tested for the presence of arbitrage opportunities, given the 50 basis point cost of short selling in the T-bill futures markets. Figure 6.3 depicts their results graphically. For all 1,606 observations, a random sample of which are shown in Figure 6.3, they found that the difference in yields between the forward rate and the futures rate fell within 50 basis points from perfect equality. In other words, there were no arbitrage opportunities, given the existence of transaction costs and the 50 basis point cost of short selling. This is reflected by the fact that all of the plotted points fall within a distance of 50 basis points from perfect equality. Also, as the figure shows, most of their observations fell exactly on the line of perfect equality between the forward rate and the futures rate. For these cases, this would mean that there were no arbitrage opportunities even if there were no cost to short selling.

Rendleman and Carabini's results tie in very closely with the other themes that we have been developing regarding the yield curve and the interpretation of futures prices. First, it is appropriate to treat yields on interest rate futures as forward rates, because the two are virtually identical. Second, we can be sure that they are virtually identical, because if they were not, there would be arbitrage opportunities. Finally, the results of Rendleman and Carabini are consistent with the

---

[4] See R. Rendleman and C. Carabini, "The Efficiency of the Treasury Bill Futures Market," *Journal of Finance*, September 1979. Rendleman and Carabini also review much of the previous research on this topic.

[5] Remember that short selling involves borrowing the good that is to be sold short. In this case, the 50 basis points is the charge imposed by the owner for lending the security.

Figure 6.3
Observed Yield Diferentials Between Forward and Futures Yields in the T-Bill Market

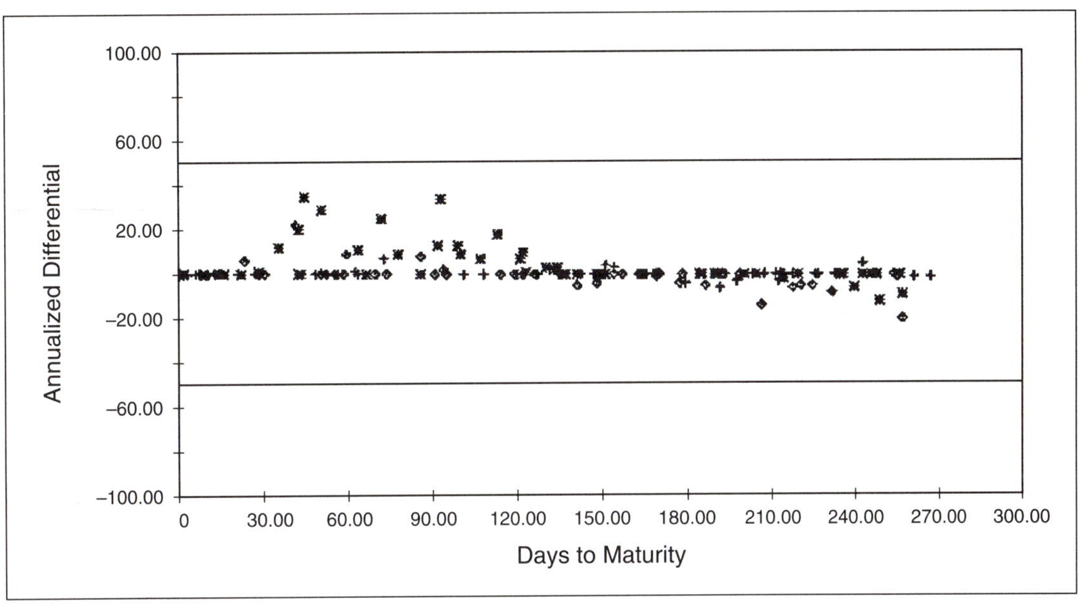

Source: R. Rendleman and C. Carabini, "The Efficiency of the Treasury Bill futures Market," *Journal of Finance*, 34, 1979, pp. 907. Reprinted with permission from the *Journal of Finance.*

cost-of-carry framework, because it is only in the presence of costs for short selling that there are divergences between the forward rate and the futures rate of interest.

Stock Index Futures

In recent years, stock index futures trading has flourished and received a great deal of attention from a concerned public. The most important stock index futures contracts are based on the S&P 500 stock index and on the Major Market Index (MMI). The MMI is an index of 20 stocks designed to mimic the Dow Jones Industrial Average. For both of these futures contracts, the futures price represents the current value of the stocks adjusted for the cost-of-carry. The cost-of-carry is essentially the financing cost of holding the stocks, adjusted for the dividends the stocks are expected to pay between the current date and the expiration of the futures. Because of the high liquidity and ease of trading financial assets, such as stocks, stock index futures obey the cost-of-carry model.

Stock Index Arbitrage From time to time, slight discrepancies arise between the futures price and the value of the stocks comprising the index. For example, it may sometimes be the case that a trader could sell a futures contract for a price that exceeded the cost of buying the stocks in the index and carrying them forward to delivery. As we have seen for other commodities, such a discrepancy can lead to arbitrage activity. Efforts to exploit discrepancies between stock index futures prices and the prices of the underlying stocks are known as **stock index arbitrage**.

Traders use computers to monitor futures prices and stock prices constantly, always searching for arbitrage opportunities. When such an opportunity arises, the trader will either buy or sell the futures contract and simultaneously sell or buy the stocks that constitute the index. For the S&P 500 contract, this means selling or buying 500 different stocks. Exploiting any arbitrage opportunity depends critically on speed in responding to a momentary opportunity. The trader must execute orders for the stocks very quickly, being sure to trade the right number of each share. This is the perfect job for a computer.

Program trading is the use of computer programs to initiate orders to buy or sell stocks, and program trading plays a key role in stock index arbitrage. When an arbitrage opportunity develops, the trader can use a program trading strategy to immediately initiate orders to buy or sell the stocks that underlie the index.

Program Trading and Stock Market Volatility Program trading strategies can lead to massive orders to buy or sell stocks, and some observers have maintained that program trading may have led to increasing stock market volatility and may even have played a role in market disruptions, such as the crash of October 1987. These issues are highly controversial and the subject of continuing investigation. Therefore, the following summary of current thinking must be regarded as provisional.

General Stock Market Volatility There has been a general impression of increased volatility in the stock market. This view has been strengthened by occurrences such as the October 1987 crash and the frequency of days with 50-point swings in the Dow. However, most studies conclude that stock market volatility in the 1980s (the period of stock index futures trading) has not been noticeably larger than during other periods. Thus, there does not seem to be a general increase in the overall volatility in the stock market.

Episodic Volatility While overall volatility may not have increased, some scholars have been concerned that short-term volatility may be higher due to stock index futures trading. For example, the massive orders associated with program trading might lead to temporary episodes of extremely high volatility, even though the month-to-month volatility shows no real change. This concern focuses on the volatility for a period of a day or even an hour and these bursts of volatility have become known as **episodic volatility** or **jump volatility**. The bulk of evidence suggests a connection between stock index futures trading and jump volatility. However, the evidence does not suggest that the temporary increase in volatility associated with futures trading impairs the functioning of the stock market.[6] As we noted at the beginning of this discussion, these issues of stock market volatility and the role of futures markets in contributing to volatility remain very controversial.

The Social Function of Futures Markets

Futures markets have often come under attack from different interest groups in society and from legislative bodies. The U.S. Congress actually forbade trading in onion futures and came very close, at one point, to banning futures trading. Currently, futures markets are thriving, partially in

---

[6] For a discussion of stock index futures and stock market volatility with references to many specific studies, see R. Kolb, *Understanding Futures Markets*, 4th ed., Miami: Kolb Publishing, 1994, pp. 431–45.

recognition of the useful social function that they serve. There are two principal social functions of futures markets. The first is the role of price discovery, and the second is assisting in the transference of risk in society.

Price discovery refers to the information that the futures market may impart about future commodity prices. Futures prices constitute very good forecasts of future prices, at least relative to most alternative forecasts, because they aggregate the opinions of many different traders in the marketplace. In fact, there have been a number of studies testing the performance of the futures price as a predictor of subsequently observed spot prices. While the forecast embodied in the futures price often has large errors, it does seem to perform very well on average. Further, there is considerable evidence that futures prices perform better than professional forecasting services.

The second major social function of the futures market is the opportunity that it provides for **risk transference**. As we have seen in our discussion of the CAPM, the bearing of risk can be a very important function in the capital markets, a function that can be richly rewarded. However, as we have also seen, different investors will have different degrees of risk tolerance. Therefore, a market that allows investors to modify the amount of risk that they bear can be very useful. The futures market allows great latitude in the transference of risk from one trader unwilling to bear it to others who will accept the bearing of risk in the hope of profit.

Options

There are two major classes of options, call options and put options. Ownership of a **call option** gives the owner the right to buy a particular good at a certain price, with that right lasting until a particular date. Ownership of a **put option** gives the owner the right to sell a particular good at a specified price, with that right lasting until a particular date. For every option, there is both a buyer and a seller. In the case of a call option, the seller receives a payment from the buyer and gives the buyer the option of buying a particular good from the seller at a certain price, with that right lasting until a particular date. Similarly, the seller of a put option receives a payment from the buyer. The buyer then has the right to sell a particular good to the seller at a certain price for a specified period of time.

In all cases, ownership of an option involves the right, but not the obligation, to make a certain transaction. The owner of a call option may, for example, buy the good at the contracted price during the life of the option, but there is no obligation to do so. Likewise, the owner of a put option may sell the good under the terms of the option contract, but there is no obligation to do so. Selling an option does commit the seller to specific obligations. The seller of a call option receives a payment from the buyer, and in exchange for this payment, the seller of the call option (or simply, the call) must be ready to sell the given good to the owner of the call, if the owner of the call wishes. The discretion to engage in further transactions always lies with the owner or buyer of an option. Option sellers have no such discretion. They have obligated themselves to perform in certain ways if the owners of the options so desire. Later in this chapter we will see the conditions under which buyers and sellers find it reasonable to act in different ways.

Option Terminology

There is a great deal of special terminology associated with the options market. The seller of an option is also known as the **writer** of an option, and the act of selling an option is called **writing**

an option. If the owner of the call takes advantage of the option, he or she is said to **exercise the option**. An owner would exercise a call option by buying a good under the terms of an option contract. Each option contract stipulates a price that will be paid if the option is exercised, and this price is known as the **exercise price, strike price, or striking price**. In our first example of the call option to buy IBM at $100, when it is selling at $120, the exercise price would be $100 because this is the amount that must be paid at exercise. An **American** option can be exercised at any time, while a **European** option can be exercised only at expiration.

Every option involves a payment from the buyer to the seller. This payment is simply the price of the option, but it is also called the **option premium**. Also, every option traded on an exchange is valid for only a limited period of time. For example, an option on IBM might be valid only through August of the present year. The option has no validity after its **expiration date** or **maturity**. This special terminology is used widely in the options market and throughout the rest of this chapter.

Option Exchanges

As shown in Table 6.2, there are quite a few options exchanges in the United States trading a variety of goods. This list can be expected to expand in the future. The present is a time of expansion and experimentation in the options market, and there will be a continuing process of maturation.

Table 6.2
U.S. Options Exchanges and Goods Traded

Exchange	Goods Traded
Chicago Board Options Exchange	
	Individual Stocks
	Long–Term Options on Individual Stocks
	Stock Indexes
	Interest Rates
American Exchange	
	Individual Stocks
	Long–Term Options on Individual Stocks
	Stock Indexes
Philadelphia Exchange	
	Individual Stocks
	Long–Term Options on Individual Stocks
	Stock Indexes
	Foreign Currency
	Precious Metals Index
Pacific Exchange	
	Individual Stocks
	Long–Term Options on Individual Stocks
	Stock Indexes
New York Stock Exchange	
	Individual Stocks
	Long–Term Options on Individual Stocks
	Stock Indexes

Note: This listing does not include options on futures contracts.

In many respects, options exchanges and futures exchanges are organized similarly. In the options market, as in the futures market, there is a seller for every buyer, and both markets allow offsetting trades. To buy an option, a trader simply needs to have an account with a brokerage firm holding a membership on the options exchange. The trade can be executed through the broker with the same ease as executing a trade to buy a stock. The buyer of an option will pay for the option at the time of the trade, so there is no more worry about cash flows associated with the purchase. For the seller of an option, the matter is somewhat more complicated. In selling a call option, the seller is agreeing to deliver the stock for a set price if the owner of the call so chooses. This means that the seller may need large financial resources to fulfill his or her obligations. The broker is representing the trader to the exchange and is, therefore, obligated to be sure that the trader has the necessary financial resources to fulfill all obligations. For the seller, the full extent of these obligations is not known when the option is sold. Accordingly, the broker needs financial guarantees from option writers. In the case of a call, the writer of an option may already own the shares of stock and deposit these with the broker. Writing call options against stock that the writer owns is called writing a **covered call**. This gives the broker complete protection because the shares that are obligated for delivery are in the possession of the broker. If the writer of the call does not own the underlying stocks, he or she has written a **naked option**, in this case a naked call. In such cases, the broker may require substantial deposits of cash or securities to ensure that the trader has the financial resources necessary to fulfill all obligations.

The Option Clearing Corporation (OCC) oversees the conduct of the market and assists in making an orderly market. As in the futures market, the buyer and seller of an option have no obligations to a specific individual, but they are obligated to the OCC. Later, if an option is exercised, the OCC matches buyers and sellers and oversees the completion of the exercise process, including the delivery of funds and securities. This management of the exercise process and the standardization of contract terms are the largest contributions of the OCC. Standardized contract terms have made it possible for traders to focus on their trading strategies without having to learn the intricacies of many different option contracts. The benefits of the OCC in the marketplace are perhaps clearest in considering option quotations.

Option Quotations

No matter what the exchange or the good underlying the option, the quotations are similar. Because the market for individual stocks is the oldest and has the most overall trading activity, we will use the quotations for IBM to illustrate the basic features of the prices. Figure 6.4 shows the quotations for call and put options on individual stocks from *The Wall Street Journal*, and Figure 6.5 focuses on the quotations for options on IBM in particular. Options on IBM trade on the Chicago Board Options Exchange (CBOE) and the quotations pertain to the close of trading on the previous trading day.

Beneath the identifier "IBM," the quotations list the closing price of IBM stock for the day, while the second column lists the various striking prices or exercise prices that are available for IBM. The striking prices are kept fairly near the prevailing price of the stock. As the stock price fluctuates, new striking prices are opened for trading, at intervals of $5. As a consequence, volatile stocks are likely to have a greater range of striking prices available for trading at any one time. Each contract is written on 100 shares, but the prices quoted are on a per-share basis. Upon payment,

Figure 6.4
Quotations for Options on Individual Stocks

LISTED OPTIONS QUOTATIONS

Tuesday, March 28, 1995

Composite volume and close for actively traded equity and LEAPS, or long-term options, with results for the corresponding put or call contract. Volume figures are unofficial. Open interest is total outstanding for all exchanges and reflects previous trading day. Close when possible is shown for the underlying stock on primary market. CB-Chicago Board Options Exchange. AM-American Stock Exchange. PB-Philadelphia Stock Exchange. PC-Pacific Stock Exchange. NY-New York Stock Exchange. XC-Composite. p-Put.

MOST ACTIVE CONTRACTS

Option/Strike			Vol	Exch	Last		Net Chg	a-Close	Open Int
Olicom	Apr	10	p 18,187	CB	5/16		...	11 1/8	277
MicrTc	Apr	70	5,741	XC	15	+	4	84 1/2	9,226
MicrTc	Apr	75	5,658	XC	11	+	3 1/2	84 1/2	6,568
MicrTc	Apr	85	5,104	XC	4	+	1 7/8	84 1/2	2,287
MicrTc	Apr	80	4,696	XC	7 1/4	+	3 1/8	84 1/2	5,449
Dig Eq	Apr	35	4,381	XC	3 3/8	+	1	38	8,042
TelMex	Apr	30	3,911	XC	13/16	−	5/16	28 5/8	36,397
Dig Eq	Jul	35	3,412	XC	5 1/4	+	1 1/4	38	3,205
Biogen	Apr	40	3,306	XC	3	+	2	42	2,391
LDDS	Sep	30	3,135	PC	1 3/16	−	1/4	25 3/8	7,705
Compaq	Apr	35	2,873	PC	1 5/16	+	1/16	35	21,284
Intel	Apr	85	2,787	AM	4 7/8	+	3/4	88 1/2	11,106
Intel	Apr	90	2,781	AM	2	+	3/8	88 1/2	3,348
Intel	Apr	85	p 2,555	AM	1 1/16	−	5/16	88 1/2	2,783
Cisco	Apr	40	2,545	XC	3/4	+	5/16	39 1/8	6,442
TelMex	Apr	35	2,478	XC	1/8		...	28 5/8	8,230
Ph Mor	Apr	65	p 2,420	AM	5/16		...	67 1/2	1,644
MicrTc	Apr	80	p 2,382	XC	2 1/4	−	1 3/8	84 1/2	935
IntrDig	Apr	12 1/2	2,346	PC	2 1/8	+	1/2	12 5/8	13,860
MicrTc	Jul	80	2,324	XC	11 1/8	+	2 1/8	84 1/2	1,209

Option/Strike			Vol	Exch	Last		Net Chg	a-Close	Open Int
Intel	Apr	80	2,268	AM	9	+	7/8	88 1/2	9,628
I B M	Apr	85	2,179	CB	1 7/16	−	1/4	84 1/2	15,065
Intel	Apr	80	p 2,097	AM	1/4	−	3/16	88 1/2	6,366
D S C	Apr	30	2,052	AM	4 7/8	+	1/2	34 1/2	2,189
LDDS	Sep	25	2,025	PC	3 1/8	−	5/8	25 3/8	3,019
Carmrk	May	15	2,010	XC	5	+	7/8	19 3/4	440
IntrDig	Apr	15	1,992	PC	1 1/4	+	3/8	12 5/8	9,286
Teldyn	May	25	1,911	CB	2 1/2		...	26 5/8	...
Motrla	Apr	55	1,867	AM	3	+	1/8	56 5/8	17,383
TelMex	Apr	30	p 1,861	XC	2 1/16	+	7/16	28 5/8	6,997
Intel	Apr	75	1,844	AM	14	+	7/8	88 1/2	10,735
Motrla	Apr	60	1,793	AM	5/8		...	56 5/8	20,806
WelptH	Apr	35	1,766	XC	1 1/4	+	1/4	34 5/8	1,391
CalGlf	Apr	15	p 1,653	XC	1 1/8	−	1/4	14 1/4	4,122
Intel	May	80	1,627	AM	9 3/4	+	3/4	88 1/2	2,080
Limitd	May	17 1/2	1,601	CB	4 1/2	+	2 1/8	22 1/8	3,019
Amgen	Apr	70	1,572	AM	1 13/16	+	5/8	69 5/8	10,947
GTelev	Apr	15	1,554	XC	1 13/16		...	16 5/8	9,831
QuakrO	May	45	1,455	PB	7/16	−	3/16	34	989
Chryslr	Apr	40	1,446	CB	7/8	+	3/16	39 1/8	8,552

Option/Strike		Exp.	Call Vol.	Call Last	Put Vol.	Put Last
ADC Tel	35	May	88	2 1/2	...	...
ADT	10	Jun	130	2 3/8	...	...
AGCO	30	May	35	2	...	...
ALC Cm	30	Jun	57	5	5	1 1/4
34	35	Apr	...	...	481	1 15/16
34	35	May	757	1 5/8	...	...
A M R	60	May	46	6 1/2	20	9/16
65 1/4	65	Apr	72	1 3/4	...	...
65 1/4	65	May	1066	2 3/4	...	...
65 1/4	65	Aug	66	4 5/8	16	2 7/8
A S A	45	Apr	178	1 3/4	251	3/8
46 1/8	45	May	60	2 1/16	...	...
46 1/8	50	Apr	10	1/4	100	3 7/8
46 1/8	50	May	218	5/8	...	...
46 1/8	50	Aug	89	1 9/16	1	4 5/8
46 1/8	55	May	100	1/8	1	8 3/4
AST Rs	15	Apr	62	1 1/2	10	1/8
16 1/2	15	May	68	1 5/8	5	1/2
AT&T	50	Apr	76	2 3/4	30	3/16
52 5/8	50	May	43	3 1/8	212	3/8
52 5/8	50	Jul	45	3 3/4	30	13/16
52 5/8	50	Oct	...	...	152	1 1/8
52 5/8	55	Apr	119	3/16	5	2 3/4
52 5/8	55	Jul	74	1	65	3 1/4
52 5/8	55	Oct	114	1 3/4	...	...
Abbt L	30	May	100	7 1/2	...	...
37 3/8	35	Apr	355	2 1/2	...	...
37 3/8	35	Aug	6	3 5/8	1025	3/4
37 3/8	40	May	77	1/4	...	...
37 3/8	40	Aug	1046	1	...	...
37 3/8	40	Nov	14	1 1/2	30	3 1/4

Option/Strike		Exp.	Call Vol.	Call Last	Put Vol.	Put Last
53 5/8	50	Jul	...	...	52	1 7/8
53 5/8	55	Apr	213	1/2	15	2 9/16
53 5/8	55	May	109	1 1/4	12	3 5/8
53 5/8	55	Jul	40	1 7/8	10	4 5/8
BanySy	17 1/2	Nov	50	2	...	...
Barnet	40	Apr	203	5 1/4	...	...
45	40	May	200	5 1/2	...	...
45	45	Apr	5	1 3/16	30	13/16
BarickG	20	Apr	93	4	50	1/16
24	20	Oct	...	...	31	1/2
24	22 1/2	Apr	377	1 11/16	270	1/4
24	22 1/2	May	46	2 1/16	...	...
24	25	Apr	1303	3/8	9	1 1/2
24	25	May	45	3/4	...	...
24	25	Jul	102	1 5/16	14	2 1/4
24	25	Oct	165	2 1/8	...	...
BattlM	10	Apr	116	7/8	20	3/16
10 3/4	10	Jul	31	1 1/2	...	...
10 3/4	12 1/2	May	30	3/16	...	...
10 3/4	12 1/2	Jul	30	3/8	...	...
BausLm	35	Apr	18	1 1/16	90	7/8
35 1/4	35	Jul	...	...	120	1 1/2
35 1/4	40	Jul	118	7/8	2	4 3/4
Baxter	30	May	50	4 3/4	...	...
BayNtw	25	Jun	5	13 3/4	66	1/8
38 5/8	30	Apr	143	8 1/4	30	1/8
38 5/8	35	Apr	240	3 3/4	1	3/8
38 5/8	35	May	101	4 3/8	27	1/2
38 5/8	35	Jun	52	5 1/8	40	1 3/16
38 5/8	40	Apr	144	5/8	...	...
38 5/8	40	May	283	1 1/2	66	2 11/16

Option/Strike		Exp.	Call Vol.	Call Last	Put Vol.	Put Last
39 1/8	40	May	488	1 3/8	69	2
39 1/8	40	Jul	386	2 1/4	77	2 7/8
39 1/8	45	Apr	32	1/8	3	6
39 1/8	45	May	104	5/16	4	6 1/2
39 1/8	45	Jul	127	11/16	...	...
39 1/8	50	Apr	...	...	30	11 1/8
39 1/8	50	Jul	1031	1/4	10	11 3/8
CinBel	22 1/2	Apr	50	1/8	...	...
21 3/4	22 1/2	May	50	5/16	...	...
CircaPh	20	May	70	5/8	10	2
18 1/8	20	Oct	98	1 13/16	...	...
CirCty	22 1/2	Apr	50	3	...	...
Circus	22 1/2	Jun	...	...	30	1/16
32 1/4	25	Jun	46	7 5/8	4	1/8
32 1/4	30	Apr	238	2 9/16	20	3/8
32 1/4	30	May	222	3	...	...
32 1/4	30	Jun	208	3 1/2	35	7/8
32 1/4	30	Sep	50	4 1/2	...	...
32 1/4	35	Apr	92	3/8	...	...
32 1/4	35	May	48	13/16	10	3 1/2
32 1/4	35	Jun	101	1 1/4	50	3 3/4
32 1/4	35	Sep	86	2 1/4	...	...
Cirrus	40	Apr	80	3/4	5	2 3/8
Cisco	25	Apr	50	13 5/8	...	...
39 1/8	30	Apr	93	9	5	1/16
39 1/8	35	Apr	1349	4 1/4	1256	3/16
39 1/8	35	May	284	4 7/8	235	7/16
39 1/8	35	Jul	618	5 5/8	184	1 1/8
39 1/8	35	Oct	43	7	11	1 7/8
39 1/8	40	Apr	2545	3/4	208	1 9/16
39 1/8	40	May	1215	1 5/8	474	2 3/8

Source: *The Wall Street Journal*, March 29, 1995.

the owner of the call would have the right to purchase 100 shares of IBM for the exercise price of, we assume, $100 per share, and this right would last until the expiration date. For the purchaser of the option, the total price to acquire a share of IBM would be the option premium plus the exercise price. The option writer would receive the premium as soon as the contract is initiated; this amount belongs to the option writer no matter what develops. However, the option writer is obligated to sell 100 shares of IBM to the call purchaser for $100 per share, if the option

Figure 6.5
Quotations for Options on IBM Stock

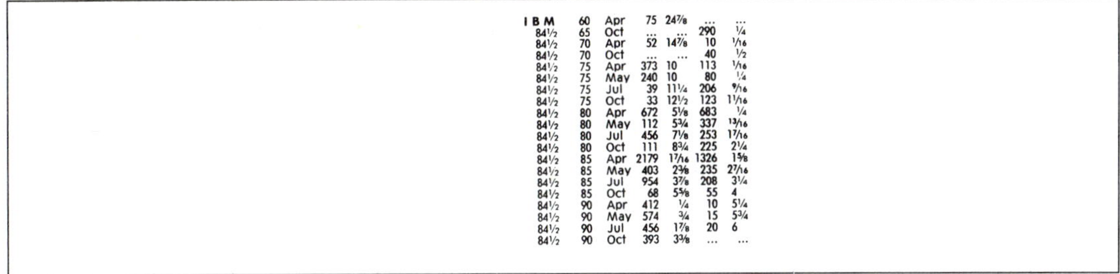

IBM	60	Apr	75	24 7/8	...	...
84 1/2	65	Oct	...	...	290	1/4
84 1/2	70	Apr	52	14 7/8	10	1/16
84 1/2	70	Oct	...	...	40	1/2
84 1/2	75	Apr	373	10	113	1/16
84 1/2	75	May	240	10	80	1/4
84 1/2	75	Jul	39	11 1/4	206	9/16
84 1/2	75	Oct	33	12 1/2	123	1 1/16
84 1/2	80	Apr	672	5 1/8	683	1/4
84 1/2	80	May	112	5 3/4	337	13/16
84 1/2	80	Jul	456	7 1/8	253	1 7/16
84 1/2	80	Oct	111	8 3/4	225	2 1/4
84 1/2	85	Apr	2179	1 7/16	1326	1 5/8
84 1/2	85	May	403	2 3/8	235	2 7/16
84 1/2	85	Jul	954	3 7/8	208	3 1/4
84 1/2	85	Oct	68	5 5/8	55	4
84 1/2	90	Apr	412	1/4	10	5 1/4
84 1/2	90	May	574	3/4	15	5 3/4
84 1/2	90	Jul	456	1 7/8	20	6
84 1/2	90	Oct	393	3 3/8	...	...

Source: *The Wall Street Journal*, March 29, 1995.

purchaser chooses to exercise the option. However, the purchaser must exercise the option before it expires.

Obviously, the right to buy IBM at $100 per share, when the market price of IBM is above $100, is very valuable. By contrast, there is also a put option traded on IBM, which allows the owner to sell a share of IBM for, we assume, $100. Investors are not willing to pay very much for the right to sell IBM at $100 via an options contract if it could be sold for more than $100 in the marketplace.[7]

There are a number of important features about options that can be illustrated from the price quotations, such as those shown in Figure 6.4. First, for any given expiration, the lower the striking price for a call, the greater will be the price. Similarly, the longer the time to expiration, the higher will be the price of an option. The same relationship holds true for put options. As we will see in the section on option pricing, there are very clear reasons why these kinds of pricing relationships must obtain in the marketplace.

Option Pricing

Option pricing affords one of the showcase results of research in modern finance. The pricing models that have been developed for options perform very well, and a study of these models is very useful for the trader. In fact, traders on the options exchanges have immediate access to the information provided by option pricing models through machines located on the floors of the exchanges. Prices of options on stocks without cash dividends depend upon five factors:

Stock Price	S
Exercise Price	E
Time until Expiration	T
Volatility of the Underlying Stock	σ
Risk-Free Interest Rate	R_f

[7] In the place of some prices, the letters "r" and "s" appear. An *r* indicates that a particular option was not traded on the day being reported. An *s* indicates that no option with those characteristics is being made available for trading by the exchange.

The Pricing of Call Options at Expiration The term **at expiration** refers to the moment just prior to expiration. If the option is not exercised at this time, it will expire immediately and have no value. The value of options at expiration is an important topic because many of the complications that ordinarily affect option prices disappear when the option is about to expire. With this terminology in mind, let us consider the value of a call option at expiration, where $T = 0$. In this case, only two possibilities may arise regarding the relationship between the exercise price (E) and the stock price (S). Either $S > E$ or $S \leq E$. If the stock price is less than or equal to the exercise price ($S \leq E$), the call option will have no value. To see why this is the case, consider a call option with an exercise price of $80 on a stock trading at $70. Since the option is about to expire, the owner of the option has only two alternatives. The option may be exercised, or it may be allowed to expire.[8] If the option is exercised in this situation, the holder of the option must pay the exercise price of $80 and receive a stock trading in the market for only $70. In this situation, it does not pay to exercise the option and the owner will allow it to expire worthless. Accordingly, this option has no value and its market price will be zero. Therefore, a call option must have a value that is equal to zero or to the difference between the stock price and the exercise price, whichever is greater. This condition must hold, otherwise there will be arbitrage opportunities awaiting exploitation.[9]

$$\text{At expiration: } C = \text{MAX}\{0, S - E\} \tag{6.5}$$

Similar arguments indicate that the value of put at expiration must equal the maximum of zero of the exercise price minus the stock price:

$$\text{At expiration: } P = \text{MAX}\{0, E - S\} \tag{6.6}$$

The Pricing of a Call Option with a Zero Exercise Price and Infinite Time until Expiration It may appear unimportant to consider an option with a zero exercise price and an infinite time until expiration because such options are not traded in the options market. However, this kind of option represents an extreme situation, and, as such, it can be used to set boundaries on possible option prices. An option on a stock that has a zero exercise price and an infinite time to maturity can be surrendered at any time, without any cost, for the stock itself. Since such an option can be transformed into the stock without cost, it must have a value as great as the stock itself. Similarly, an option on a good can never be worth more than the good itself. This allows us to state another principle of option pricing.

$$C(S, 0, \infty) = S \tag{6.7}$$

---

[8] We are assuming that it is too late to sell the option because expiration is imminent.

[9] Most of the principles indicated here were originally proven rigorously by Robert C. Merton, "Theory of Rational Option Pricing," *Bell Journal of Economics and Management Science*, 1973, pp. 141–83.

A call option with a zero exercise price and an infinite time to maturity must sell for the same price as the stock. Together, these first two principles allow us to specify the upper and lower possible bounds for the price of a call option as a function of the stock price, the exercise price, and the time to expiration. These boundaries are shown in Figure 6.6. If the call has a zero exercise price and an infinite maturity, the call price must equal the stock price, and this situation is shown as the 45 degree line from the origin. This represents the upper bound for an option's price. Alternatively, if the option is at expiration, the price of the option must lie along the horizontal axis from the origin to the point at which the stock price equals the exercise price ($S = E$), and then upward at a 45 degree angle. If the stock price is less than or equal to the exercise price, the call price must be zero, as shown in the graph. If the stock price exceeds the exercise price, the option must trade for a price that is equal to the difference between the stock price and the exercise price. Other options such as those with some time remaining until expiration and with positive exercise prices would have to lie in the interior region between these two extremes. The Black-Scholes option pricing model gives the exact value of options before expiration with positive exercise prices.

The Option Pricing Model

As mentioned earlier, there are five variables that affect the value of a call option. In the following list, a plus sign (+) by a variable indicates that the price of a call option is larger the larger the value of the associated variable.

Increase in Factor:		Influence on Call Price	Influence on Put Price
Stock Price	S	Positive	Negative
Exercise Price	E	Negative	Positive
Time to Expiration	T	Positive	May be positive or negative
Risk-Free Interest Rate	R_f	Positive	Negative
Variability of the Stock's Returns	σ	Positive	Positive

These relationships hold for European style call and put options on non-dividend paying stocks.

The Option Pricing Model (OPM), developed by Fischer Black and Myron Scholes, draws on a branch of mathematics known as stochastic calculus. While the details of this derivation lie beyond the scope of this text, we may note that Black and Scholes were able to derive their model by assuming that stock prices follow a certain kind of path through time called a stochastic process. A **stochastic process** is simply a mathematical description of the change in the value of some variable through time. The particular stochastic process used by Black and Scholes is known as a **Wiener process.** The key features of the Wiener process are that the variable changes continuously through time and that the changes that it might make over any given time interval are distributed normally. Figure 6.7 shows a graph of the path that stock prices might follow if they followed a Wiener process. The price of a call option according to the Black-Scholes OPM is:

$$C = SN(d_1) - Ee^{-R_f T}N(d_2) \tag{6.2}$$

Figure 6.7
One Possible Realization of a Wiener Process

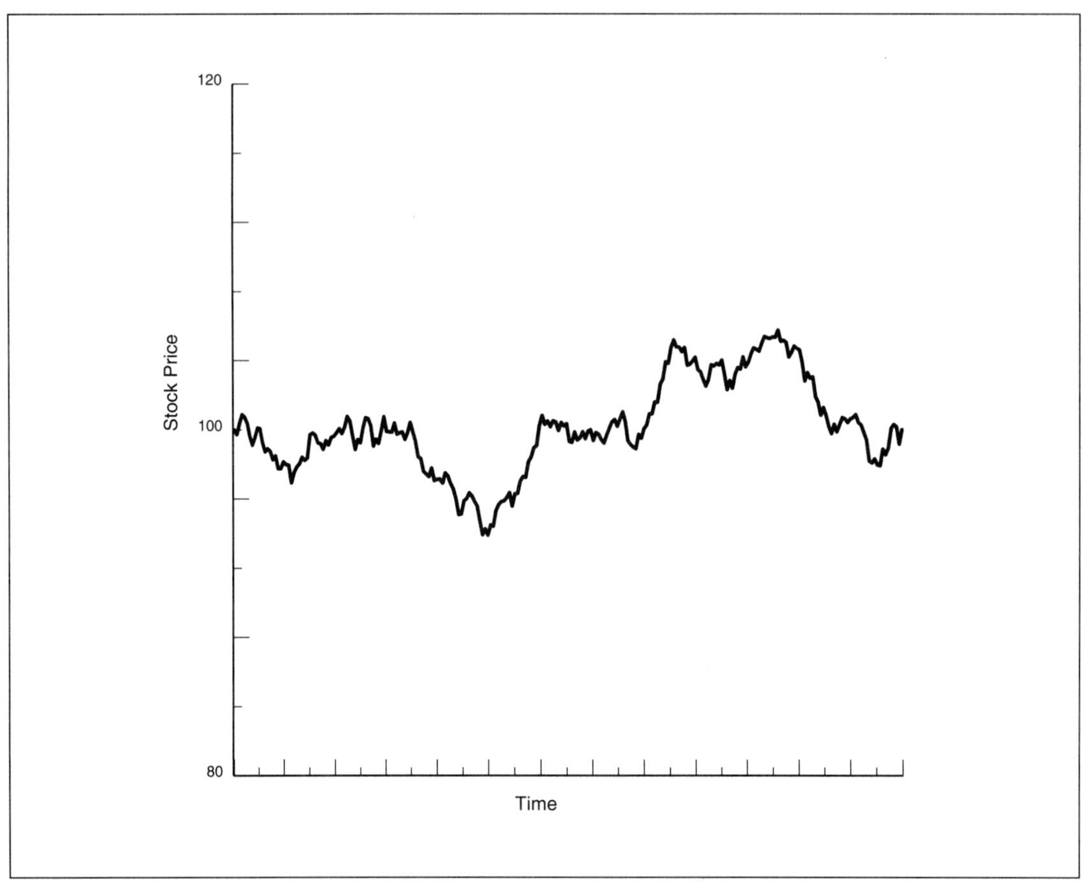

The most difficult part of this formula to understand is the use of the normal cumulative probability function, $N(.)$. However, this is exactly the part of the OPM that takes account of the risk and allows the model to give such good results for option prices. The best way to understand the application of the model is with an example. Let us assume values for the five parameters and calculate the Black-Scholes value for an option. For purposes of the example, assume the following:

S	=	\$100
E	=	\$100
T	=	1 year
R_f	=	12%
σ	=	10%

These values make it possible to calculate the Black-Scholes theoretical option value, and the first task is to calculate values for d_1 and d_2.

$$d_1 = \frac{\ln(S/E) + [R_f + (1/2)\sigma^2]T}{\sigma\sqrt{T}}$$

$$= \frac{\ln(100/100) + [.12 + 1/2(.01)]1}{(.1)(1)} = \frac{0 + .1250}{.1}$$

$$= 1.25$$

$$d_2 = d_1 - \sigma\sqrt{T}$$

$$= 1.25 - (.1)(1) = 1.15$$

Having calculated the values of d_1 and d_2, the next step is to calculate the cumulative normal probability values of these two results. Essentially, these two values are simply z-scores from the normal probability function, such as the one shown in Figure 6.8. In this graph the two values of interest, 1.15 and 1.25, are shown. In calculating the cumulative normal probability values of $d_1 = 1.25$ and $d_2 = 1.15$, we simply need to determine the proportion of the area under the curve that lies to the left of the value in question. For example, if we were interested in a z-score of 0.00, we would know that 50 percent of the area under the curve lies to the left of a z-score of 0.00. This is because the normal probability distribution is symmetrical about its mean, and we know that the z-scores are standardized so that they have a mean of 0.00.

Because the standardized normal probability distribution is so important and so widely used, tables of its values are included in virtually every statistics textbook. Table 6.3 shows a typical table. As we can see, the probability of drawing a value from this distribution that is less than or equal to $d_1 = 1.25$ is .8944. So, the two values we seek are:

$$N(d_1) = N(1.25) = .8944$$
$$N(d_2) = N(1.15) = .8749$$

Returning to the OPM, we can now make the final calculation:

$$C = S\,N(d_1) - E\,e^{-R_f T}\,N(d_2)$$

$$C = \$100(.8944) - \$100e^{-(.12)(1)}(.8749)$$

$$= \$89.44 - \$100(.8869)(.8749)$$

$$= \$89.44 - \$77.60$$

$$= \$11.84$$

In this calculation, the term $e^{-R_f T} = .8869$ is simply the discounting factor for continuous time with an interest rate of 12 percent and a period of one year. So, according to the OPM, the call option should be worth \$11.84.

Figure 6.8
The Normal Probability Function

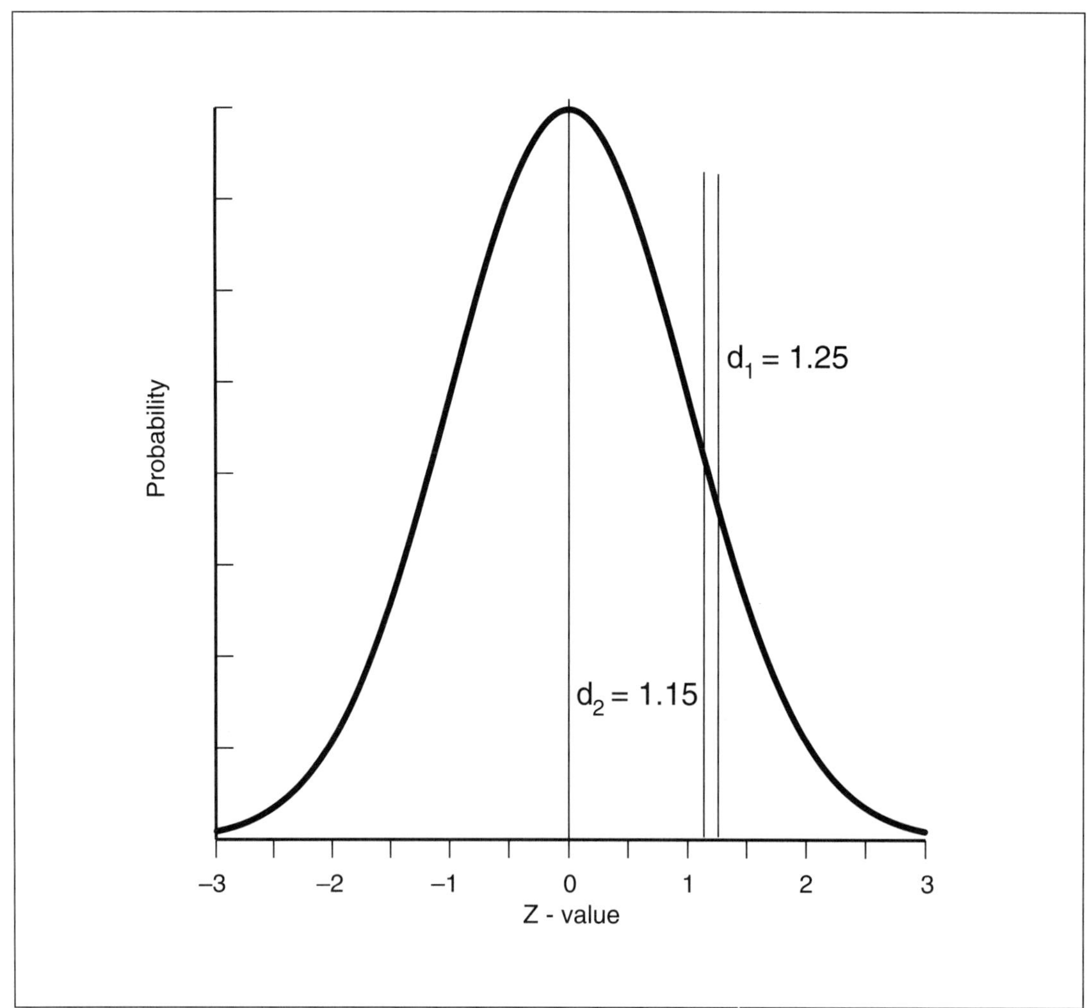

Upon first acquaintance with the OPM, many people think that it is too complicated to be useful. Nothing could be further from the truth. Of all of the models in finance, the OPM is among those receiving the widest acceptance by actual investors. For example, there are machines on the floor of the CBOE that give traders OPM prices for all options using instantaneously updated information on all of the parameters in the model. Further, most investment banking houses have staffs that specialize in options and that use the OPM on a daily basis. Finally, the OPM has achieved such widespread acceptance that some calculator manufacturers have even made special modules to allow their calculators to calculate OPM values automatically.

This widespread acceptance is due in large part to the very good results of the OPM. The Black-Scholes theoretical model price is usually very close to the market price of the option. Without doubt, the OPM has contributed greatly to our understanding of option pricing and many traders use it as a key tool in their trading strategies.

Table 6.3
Cumulative Distribution Function for the Standard Normal Random Variable

	.00	.01	.02	.03	.04	.05	.06	.07	.08	.09
0.0	.5000	.5040	.5080	.5120	.5160	.5199	.5239	.5279	.5319	.5359
0.1	.5398	.5438	.5478	.5517	.5557	.5596	.5636	.5675	.5714	.5753
0.2	.5793	.5832	.5871	.5910	.5948	.5987	.6026	.6064	.6103	.6141
0.3	.6179	.6217	.6255	.6293	.6331	.6368	.6406	.6443	.6480	.6517
0.4	.6554	.6591	.6628	.6664	.6700	.6736	.6772	.6808	.6844	.6879
0.5	.6915	.6950	.6985	.7019	.7054	.7088	.7123	.7157	.7190	.7224
0.6	.7257	.7291	.7324	.7357	.7389	.7422	.7454	.7486	.7517	.7549
0.7	.7580	.7611	.7642	.7673	.7704	.7734	.7764	.7794	.7823	.7852
0.8	.7881	.7910	.7939	.7967	.7995	.8023	.8051	.8078	.8106	.8133
0.9	.8159	.8186	.8212	.8238	.8264	.8289	.8315	.8340	.8365	.8389
1.0	.8413	.8438	.8461	.8485	.8508	.8531	.8554	.8577	.8599	.8621
1.1	8643	.8665	.8686	.8708	.8729	.8749	.8770	.8790	.8810	.8830
1.2	.8849	.8869	.8888	.8907	.8925	.8944	.8962	.8980	.8997	.9015
1.3	.9032	.9049	.9066	.9082	.9099	.9115	.9131	.9147	.9162	.9177
1.4	.9192	.9207	.9222	.9236	.9251	.9265	.9279	.9292	.9306	.9319
1.5	.9332	.9345	.9357	.9370	.9382	.9394	.9406	.9418	.9429	.9441
1.6	.9452	.9463	.9474	.9484	.9495	.9505	.9515	.9525	.9535	.9545
1.7	.9554	.9564	.9573	.9582	.9591	.9599	.9608	.9616	.9625	.9633
1.8	.9641	.9649	.9656	.9664	.9671	.9678	.9686	.9693	.9699	.9706
1.9	.9713	.9719	.9726	.9732	.9738	.9744	.9750	.9756	.9761	.9767
2.0	.9772	.9778	.9783	.9788	.9793	.9798	.9803	.9808	.9812	.9817
2.1	.9821	.9826	.9830	.9834	.9838	.9842	.9846	.9850	.9854	.9857
2.2	.9861	.9864	.9868	.9871	.9875	.9878	.9881	.9884	.9887	.9890
2.3	.9893	.9896	.9898	.9901	.9904	.9906	.9909	.9911	.9913	.9916
2.4	.9918	.9920	.9922	.9925	.9927	.9929	.9931	.9932	.9934	.9936
2.5	.9938	.9940	.9941	.9943	.9945	.9946	.9948	.9949	.9951	.9952
2.6	.9953	.9955	.9956	.9957	.9959	.9960	.9961	.9962	.9963	.9964
2.7	.9965	.9966	.9967	.9968	.9969	.9970	.9971	.9972	.9973	.9974
2.8	.9974	.9975	.9976	.9977	.9977	.9978	.9979	.9979	.9980	.9981
2.9	.9981	.9982	.9982	.9983	.9984	.9984	.9985	.9985	.9986	.9986
3.0	.9987	.9987	.9987	.9988	.9988	.9989	.9989	.9989	.9990	.9990
3.1	.9990	.9991	.9991	.9991	.9992	.9992	.9992	.9992	.9993	.9993
3.2	.9993	.9993	.9994	.9994	.9994	.9994	.9994	.9995	.9995	.9995
3.3	.9995	.9995	.9995	.9996	.9996	.9996	.9996	.9996	.9996	.9997
3.4	.9997	.9997	.9997	.9997	.9997	.9997	.9997	.9997	.9997	.9998

The Valuation of Put Options

Although the OPM pertains specifically to call options, it can also be used to price put options, through the principle of **put-call parity.**[10] Assume that an investor makes the following transactions:

Buy one share of stock $S = \$100$
Buy one put option with price $P = ?$, $E = \$100$, and $T = 1$ year
Sell one call option with price $C = \$11.84$, $E = \$100$, and $T = 1$ year

Assume also that the put and call options are on the same stock.

At expiration, the stock price could have many different values, some of which are shown in Table 6.4. The interesting feature about this portfolio is that its value will be the same, $\$100 = E$, no matter what the stock price is at expiration. Consistent with Table 6.4, no matter what the stock price at expiration might be, the value of the entire portfolio will be $\$100 = E$. Holding these three instruments in the way indicated gives a risk-free investment that will pay $\$100 = E$ at expiration, so the value of the whole portfolio must equal the present value of the riskless payoff at expiration. This means that we can write:

$$S - C + P = \frac{E}{(1 + R_f)^T} \tag{6.11}$$

The value of the put-call portfolio equals the present value of the exercise price discounted at the risk-free rate.

Since it is possible to know all of the other values, except for the price of the put P, we can use this put-call parity relationship to calculate P. To see how this is done, let us assume, as before, that $R_f = 12$ percent and that the call value is \$11.84, as was calculated according to the OPM. Rearranging the put-call parity formula gives a put value of \$1.13.

$$P = \frac{E}{(1 + R)^T} - S + C$$

$$P = \frac{\$100}{(1.12)} - \$100 + \$11.84 = \$1.13$$

Table 6.4
Possible Outcomes for Put–Call Parity Portfolio

Stock Price	Call Value	Put Value	Portfolio Value
\$ 80	\$0	\$20	\$100
90	0	10	100
100	0	0	100
110	–10	0	100
120	–20	0	100

[10] The put-call parity relationship was first derived by Hans Stoll, “The Relationship Between Put and Call Option Prices,” *The Journal of Finance*, December 1969, pp. 802–24.

Hedging with Options

As we have seen with futures, very risky financial instruments can be used to control risk. One of the most important applications of options is their use as a hedging vehicle. Once again, the OPM gives important insights into this process.

To illustrate the idea of hedging with options, let us use our original example of a stock selling at $100 and having a standard deviation of 10 percent. Recall that a call option with an exercise price of $100 and a time to expiration of one year would sell for $11.84. Recall, too, that a sudden 1 percent price rise in the stock from $100 to $101 would drive the option price to $12.73. If the stock price and the option price are so intimately related, it should be possible to use options to offset risk inherent in the stock. This possibility is shown in Table 6.5.

Consider an original portfolio comprised of 8,944 shares of stock selling at $100 per share and assume that a trader sells 100 call option contracts, or options on 10,000 shares, at $11.84. In the table, this short position in the option is indicated by a minus sign. That entire portfolio would have a value of $776,000. Now consider the effect of a 1 percent change in the price of the stock. If the stock price increases by 1 percent to $101, the shares will be worth $903,344. The option price will increase from $11.84 to $12.73. But this portfolio involves a short position in 10,000 options, so this creates a loss of $8,900. After these two effects are taken into account, the value of the whole portfolio will be $776,044. This is virtually identical to the original value.

On the other hand, if the stock price falls by 1 percent, there will be a loss on the stock of $8,944. The price of the option will fall from $11.84 to $10.95, and this means that the entire drop in price for the 10,000 options will be $8,900. Taking both of these effects into account, the portfolio will then be worth $775,956. As this example indicates, the overall value of the portfolio will not change no matter what happens to the stock price. If the stock price increases, there is an offsetting loss on the option. Likewise, if the stock price falls, there will be an offsetting gain on the option.

Table 6.5
A Hedged Portfolio

Original Portfolio	S = $100	C = $11.84	
8,944 shares of stock			$894,400
A short position for options on 10,000 shares (100 contracts)			–$118,400
		Total Value	$776,000
Stock Price Rises by 1%	S = $101	C = $12.73	
8,944 shares of stock			$903,344
A short position for options on 10,000 shares (100 contracts)			–$127,300
		Total Value	$776,044
Stock Price Falls by 1%	S = $99	C = $10.95	
8,944 shares of stock			$885,456
A short position for options on 10,000 shares (100 contracts)			–$109,500
		Total Value	$775,956

In this example, holding .8944 shares of stock for each option sold short will give a perfect hedge. The value of the entire portfolio will be insensitive to any change in the stock price. How can we know exactly the right number of options to trade to give this result? The careful reader might recall the number .8944. When the value of this call option was calculated, we saw that $N(d_1) = .8944$. This value gives the appropriate hedge ratio to construct a perfect hedge, and the principle can be summarized by the following rule.

A portfolio composed of a short position of one option and a long position of $N(d_1)$ shares of the stock will have a total value that will not fluctuate as the share price fluctuates.

Alternatively, to hedge a long position of one share in a stock, sell a number of options equal to $1/N(d_1)$. This hedge will hold for infinitesimal changes in the stock price. In the preceding example, the hedge was not quite perfect because the change in the stock price was discrete. Actually, the value of the portfolio fluctuates by only .00057. Also, a change in the stock price will change the value of $N(d_1)$, because the value of d_1 will change. This means that the hedge must be adjusted periodically as the stock price changes if it is to be kept perfect. Of course, we may not always want to implement a perfect hedge of the type we have been considering. Different risk exposures can be obtained by changing the ratio between the number of options and the number of shares. This approach can be used to obtain any risk level that a trader may desire.

The Swap Market

In this section, we consider the special features of the swap market. In large part, the swap market has emerged because swaps escape many of the limitations inherent in futures and exchange-traded options markets. Swaps, of course, have some limitations of their own. Swaps are custom tailored to the needs of the counterparties. If they wish, the potential counter parties can start with a blank sheet of paper and develop a contract that is completely dedicated to meeting their particular needs. Thus, swap agreements are more likely to meet the specific needs of the counterparties than exchange-traded instruments. The counterparties can select the dollar amount that they wish to swap, without regard to some fixed contract terms, such as those that prevail in exchange-traded instruments. Similarly, the swap counterparties choose the exact maturity that they need, rather than having to fit their needs to the offerings available on an exchange. This is very important in the swap market because this flexibility allows the counterparties to deal with much longer horizons than can be addressed through exchange-traded instruments. On futures and options exchanges, major financial institutions are readily identifiable. For example, in a futures pit, traders will be able to discern the activity of particular firms because traders know who represents which firm. Therefore, exchange trading necessarily involves a certain loss of privacy. In the swap market, by contrast, only the counterparties know that the swap takes place. Thus, the swap market affords a privacy that cannot be obtained in exchange trading.[11]

---

[11] This does not mean to imply that exchange trading sacrifices all anonymity. However, traders watch the activities of major institutions. When these institutions initiate major transactions, it is not possible to maintain complete privacy. It is somewhat ironic that individual traders can trade on futures and options markets with a discretion that is not available to multi-billion dollar financial institutions.

The swap market also has some inherent limitations. First, to consummate a swap transaction, one potential counterparty must find a counterparty that is willing to take the opposite side of a transaction. If one party needs a specific maturity, or a certain pattern of cash flows, it can be very difficult to find a willing counterparty. Second, because a swap agreement is a contract between two counterparties, the swap cannot be altered or terminated early without the agreement of both parties. Third, for futures and exchange-traded options, the exchanges effectively guarantee performance on the contracts for all parties. By its very nature, the swap market has no such guarantor. As a consequence, parties to the swap must be certain of the creditworthiness of their counterparties.

As we will see later in this chapter, the swap market has developed mechanisms to deal with these three limitations. The problem of potential default is perhaps the most important. Assessing the financial credibility of a counterparty is difficult and expensive. Therefore, participation in the swap market is effectively limited to firms and institutions that either engage in frequent swap transactions or have access to major swap facilitators that can advise on creditworthiness. In effect, the swap market is virtually limited to firms and financial institutions, and there are few or no individual transactors in the market.

The Emergence of the Swap Market

The origins of the swap market can be traced to the late 1970s, when currency traders developed currency swaps as a technique to evade British controls on the movement of foreign currency. The first interest rate swap occurred in 1981 in an agreement between IBM and the World Bank. Since that time, the market has grown rapidly. Table 6.6 shows the amount of swaps outstanding at year-end for 1987–93. By the end of 1993, interest rate and currency swaps with $6.2 trillion in underlying value were outstanding. About 80 percent of the swaps are interest rate swaps, and the remaining 20 percent are currency swaps. Of these swaps, about 50 percent involved the U.S. dollar. Table 6.7 details the initiation of interest rate and currency swaps during semi-annual periods from 1987 to 1994. The numbers in Table 6.7 reveal truly astonishing growth. The issuance of interest rate swaps has grown at an annual rate of 51 percent, while currency swap issuances have grown at a rate of 23 percent per year.

Table 6.6
Value of Outstanding Interest Rate and Currency Swaps
($ Billions of Notional Principal)

Year	Total Swaps Outstanding
1987	$ 682.9
1988	1,010.2
1989	1,539.2
1990	2,311.5
1991	3,065.1
1992	3,851.0
1993	6,177.0

Source: International Swaps and Derivatives Association.

Table 6.7
Swaps Initiated by Semi-Annual Periods
($ Billions of Principal)

Semi annual Period	Total Interest Rate Swaps	Total Currency Swaps
1987:1	$181.5	$43.5
1987:2	206.3	42.3
1988:1	250.5	60.3
1988:2	317.6	62.3
1989:1	389.2	77.6
1989:2	444.4	92.0
1990:1	561.5	94.6
1990:2	667.8	118.1
1991:1	762.1	161.3
1991:2	859.7	167.1
1992:1	1,318.3	156.1
1992:2	1,504.3	145.8
1993:1	1,938.4	156.8
1993:2	2,166.2	138.4
1994:1	3,182.9	181.0

Source: International Swaps and Derivatives Association.

Plain Vanilla Swaps

In this section, we analyze the different kinds of swaps that are available, and we show how swaps can help corporations manage various types of risk exposure. We begin by considering the mechanics of the simplest kinds of swaps. A **plain vanilla swap**, the simplest kind, can be an interest rate swap or a foreign currency swap.

Interest Rate Swaps In a plain vanilla interest rate swap, one counterparty has an initial position in a fixed rate debt instrument, while the other counterparty has an initial position in a floating rate obligation. In this initial position, the party with the floating rate obligation is exposed to changes in interest rates. By swapping this floating rate obligation, this counterparty eliminates exposure to changing interest rates. For the party with a fixed rate obligation, the interest rate swap increases the interest rate sensitivity. (Later, we explore the motivation that these counterparties might have for taking their respective positions. First, however, we need to understand the transactions.)

To see the nature of the plain vanilla interest rate swap most clearly, we use an example. We assume that the swap covers a five-year period and involves annual payments on a $1 million principal amount. Let us assume that Party A agrees to pay a fixed rate of 12 percent to Party B. In return, Party B agrees to pay a floating rate of LIBOR + 3 percent to Party A. LIBOR stands for "London Interbank Offered Rate," and it is a base rate at which large international banks lend funds to each other. Floating rates in the swap market are most often set as equaling LIBOR plus some additional amount. Figure 6.9 shows the basic features of this transaction. Party A pays 12

Figure 6.9
A Plain Vanilla Interest Rate Swap

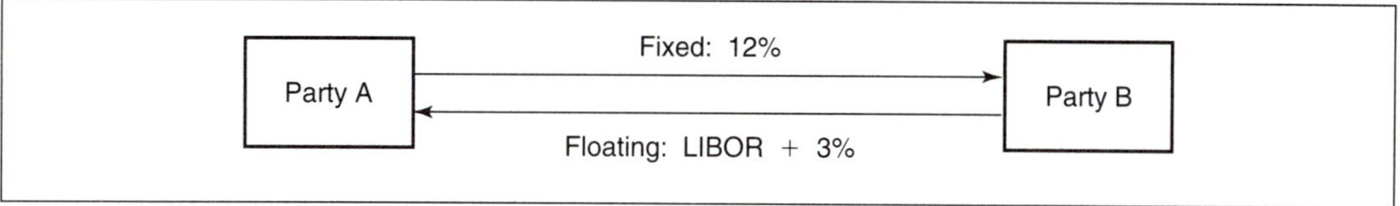

percent of $1 million, or$120,000 each year to Party B. Party B makes a payment to Party A in return, but the actual amount of the payments depends on movement in LIBOR.

Conceptually, the two parties also exchange the principal amount of $1 million. However, actually making the transaction of sending each other $1 million would not make practical sense. As a consequence, principal amounts are generally not exchanged. Instead, the principal plays a conceptual role in determining the amount of the interest payments. Because the principal is not actually exchanged, it is called a **notional principal**, an amount used as a base for computations, but not an amount that is actually transferred from one party to another. In our example, the notional principal is $1 million, and knowing that amount lets us compute the actual dollar amount of the cash flows that the two parties make to each other each year.

Let us assume that the LIBOR is 10 percent at the time of the first payment. This means that Party A will be obligated to pay $120,000 to Party B. Party B will owe $130,000 to Party A. Offsetting the two mutual obligations, Party B owes $10,000 to Party A. Generally, only the **net payment**, the difference between the two obligations, actually takes place. Again, this practice avoids unnecessary payments.[12]

Foreign Currency Swaps In a currency swap, one party holds one currency and desires a different currency. The swap arises when one party provides a certain principal in one currency to its counterparty in exchange for an equivalent amount of a different currency. For example, Party C may have German marks and be anxious to swap those marks for U.S. dollars. Similarly, Party D may hold U.S. dollars and be willing to exchange those dollars for German marks. With these needs, Parties C and D may be able to engage in a currency swap.

A plain vanilla currency swap involves three different sets of cash flows. First, at the initiation of the swap, the two parties actually do exchange cash. The entire motivation for the currency swap is the actual need for funds denominated in a different currency. This differs from the interest rate swap in which both parties deal in dollars and can pay the net amount. Second, the parties make periodic interest payments to each other during the life of the swap agreement. Third, at the termination of the swap, the parties again exchange the principal.

As an example, let us assume that the current spot exchange rate between German marks and U.S. dollars is 2.5 marks per dollar. Thus, the mark is worth $.40. We assume that the U.S. interest rate is 10 percent and the German interest rate is 8 percent. Party C holds 25 million marks

---

[12] The practice of net payments and not actually exchanging principal also protects each counterparty from default by the other. For example, it would be very unpleasant for Party A if it paid the principal amount of $1 million in our example and Party B failed to make its payment to Party A. Making only net payments greatly reduces the potential impact of default.

and wishes to exchange those marks for dollars. In return for the marks, Party D would pay $10 million to Party C at the initiation of the swap. We also assume that the term of the swap is seven years and the parties will make annual interest payments. With the interest rates in our example, Party D will pay 8 percent interest on the 25 million marks it received, so the annual payment from Party D to Party C will be 2 million marks. Party C received $10 million dollars and will pay interest at 10 percent, so Party C will pay $1 million each year to Party D.

In actual practice, the parties will make only net payments. For example, assume that at year 1 the spot exchange rate between the dollar and mark is 2.2222 marks per dollar, so the mark is worth $.45. Valuing the obligations in dollars at this exchange rate, Party C owes $1 million and Party D owes $900,000 (2 million marks times $.45). Thus, Party C would pay the $100,000 difference. At other times, the exchange rate could be different, and the net payment would reflect that different exchange rate.

At the end of seven years, the two parties again exchange principal. In our example, Party C would pay $10 million and Party D would pay 25 million marks. This final payment terminates the currency swap. Figure 6.10 shows the first element of the swap, which is the initial exchange of principal. Figure 6.11 represents the payment of interest, and in our example there would be seven of these payments, one for each year of the swap. Finally, Figure 6.12 shows the second exchange of principal that completes the swap.

Figure 6.10
A Plain Vanilla Currency Swap (Initial Cash Flow)

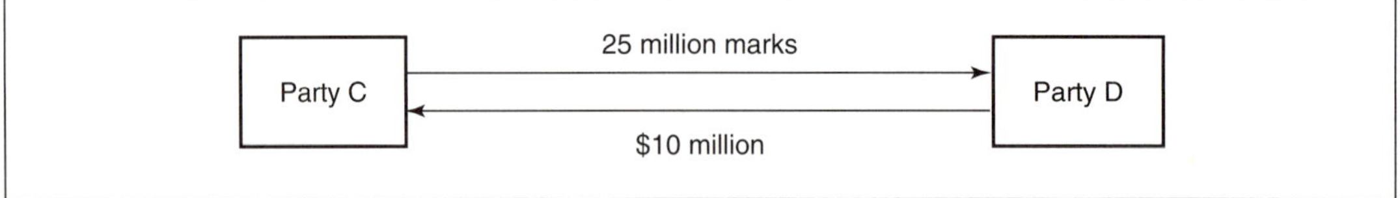

Figure 6.11
A Plain Vanilla Currency Swap (Annual Interest Payment)

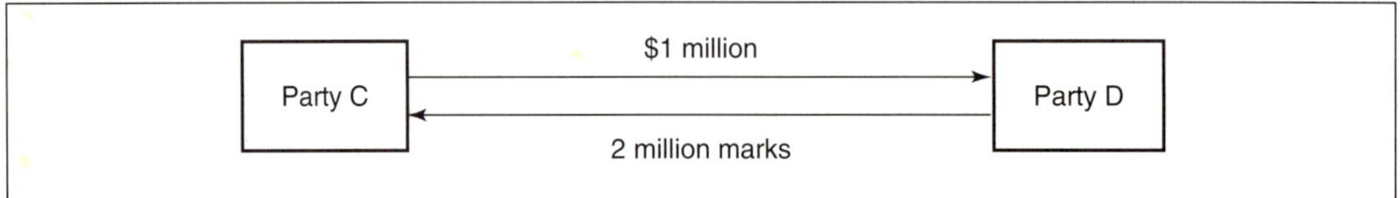

Figure 6.12
A Plain Vanilla Currency Swap (Repayment of Principal)

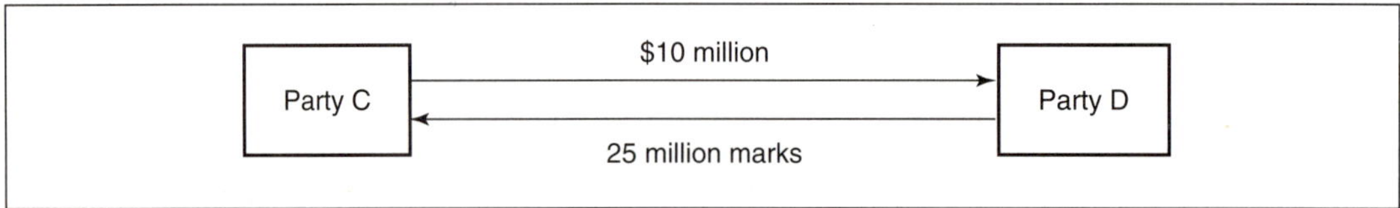

Summary In this section we considered the transactions involved in plain vanilla interest rate and currency swaps. As we saw for an interest rate swap, the essential feature is the transformation of a fixed rate obligation to a floating rate obligation for one party, and a complementary transformation of a floating rate obligation to a fixed rate obligation for the other party. In a currency swap, the two parties exchange currencies to obtain access to a foreign currency that better meets their business needs. To this point, we have only focused on the elementary transactions involved in simple swaps, but we have not considered the motivation that leads to swap agreements.

Motivations for Swaps

In our example of a plain vanilla swap, we saw that one party begins with a fixed rate obligation and seeks a floating rate obligation. The second party exchanges a floating rate for a fixed rate obligation. For this swap to occur, the two parties have to be seeking exactly the opposite goals. Two basic motivations could lead firms to engage in a swap. First, the normal commercial operations of some firms naturally lead to interest rate and currency risk positions of a certain type. Second, some firms may have certain advantages in acquiring specific types of financing. Firms can borrow in the form that is cheapest and use swaps to change the characteristics of the borrowing to one that meets the firm's specific needs. In this section, we consider several simple examples of motivations for swaps.

Commercial Needs As an example of a prime candidate for an interest rate swap, consider a typical savings and loan association. Savings and loan associations accept deposits and lend those funds for long-term mortgages. Because depositors can withdraw their funds on short notice, deposit rates must adjust to changing interest rate conditions. Most mortgagors wish to borrow at a fixed rate for a long time. As a result, the savings and loan association can be left with floating rate liabilities and fixed rate assets. This means that the savings and loan is vulnerable to rising rates. If rates rise, the savings and loan will be forced to increase the rate it pays on deposits, but it cannot increase the interest rate it charges on the mortgages that have already been issued.

To escape this interest rate risk, the savings and loan might use the swap market to transform its fixed rate assets into floating rate assets or transform its floating rate liabilities into fixed rate liabilities. Let us assume that the savings and loan wishes to transform a fixed rate mortgage into an asset that pays a floating rate of interest. In terms of our interest rate swap example, the savings and loan association is like Party A – in exchange for the fixed rate mortgage that it holds, it wants to pay a fixed rate of interest and receive a floating rate of interest. Engaging in a swap as Party A did will help the association to resolve its interest rate risk.

To make the discussion more concrete, we extend our example of the plain vanilla interest rate swap. We assume that the savings and loan association has just loaned \$1 million for five years at 12 percent with annual payments, and we assume that the savings and loan pays a deposit rate that equals LIBOR plus 1 percent. With these rates, the association will lose money if LIBOR exceeds 11 percent, and it is this danger that prompts the association to consider an interest rate swap.

Figure 6.13 shows our original plain vanilla interest rate swap with the additional information about the savings and loan that we have just elaborated. In the figure, Party A is the savings and loan association, and it receives payments at a fixed rate of 12 percent on the mortgage. After it enters the swap, the association also pays 12 percent on a notional principal of \$1 million. In

Figure 6.13
Motivation for the Plain Vanilla Interest Rate Swap

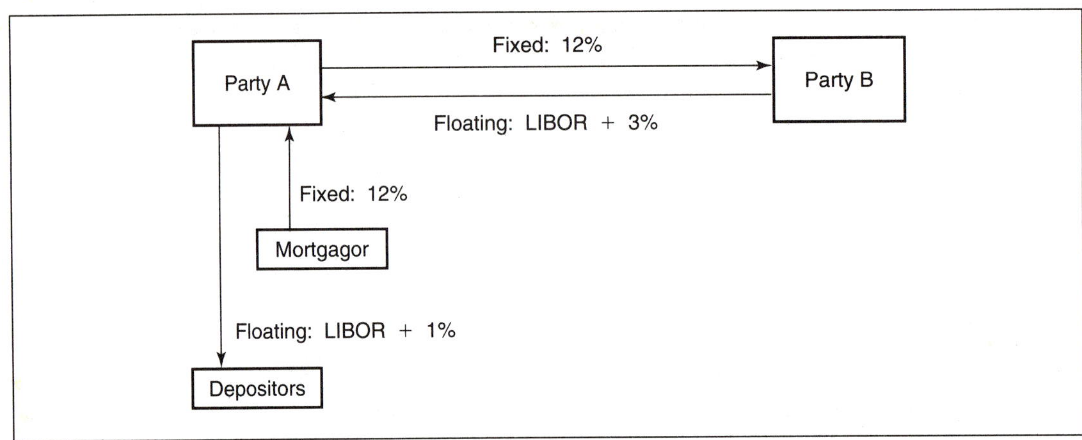

effect, it receives mortgage payments and passes them through to Party B under the swap agreement. Under the swap agreement, Party A receives a floating rate of LIBOR plus 3 percent. From this cash inflow, the association pays its depositors LIBOR plus 1 percent. This leaves a periodic inflow to the association of 2 percent, which is the spread that it makes on the loan.

In our example, the association now has a fixed rate inflow of 2 percent, and it has succeeded in avoiding its exposure to interest rate risk. No matter what happens to the level of interest rates, the association will enjoy a net cash inflow of 2 percent on $1 million. This example clarifies how the savings association has a strong motivation to enter the swap market. From the very nature of the savings and loan industry, the association finds itself with a risk exposure to rising interest rates. However, by engaging in an interest rate swap, the association can secure a fixed rate position.

Comparative Advantage In many situations, one firm may have better access to the capital market than another firm.[13] For example, a U.S. firm may be able to borrow easily in the United States, but it might not have such favorable access to the capital market in Germany. Similarly, a German firm may have good borrowing opportunities domestically but poor opportunities in the United States.

Table 6.8 presents borrowing rates for Parties C and D, the firms of our plain vanilla currency swap example. In the plain vanilla example, we assumed that, for each currency, both parties faced the same rate. We now assume that Party C is a German firm with access to marks at a rate of 7 percent, while the U.S. firm, Party D, must pay 8 percent to borrow marks. On the other hand, Party D can borrow dollars at 9 percent, while the German Party C must pay 10 percent for its dollar borrowings. As the table shows, Party C enjoys a comparative advantage in borrowing marks, and Party D has a comparative advantage in borrowing dollars. These rates raise the possibility that each firm can exploit its comparative advantage and share the gains by reducing overall borrowing costs. This possibility is shown in Figures 6.14-6.16, which parallel Figures 6.10-6.12.

---

[13] This discussion of comparative advantage draws on the excellent analysis by K. Kapner and J. Marshall in *The Swaps Handbook*, New York: New York Institute of Finance, 1990.

Table 6.8
Borrowing Rates for Two Firms in Two Currencies

Firm	U.S. Dollar Rate	German Mark Rate
Party C	10%	7%
Party D	9%	8%

Figure 6.14 resembles Figure 6.10, but it provides more information. In Figure 6.14, Party C borrows 25 million marks from a third party lender at its borrowing rate of 7 percent, while Party D borrows $10 million from a fourth party at 9 percent. After these borrowings, both parties have the funds to engage in the plain vanilla currency swap that we have already analyzed. To initiate the swap, Party C forwards the 25 million marks it has just borrowed to Party D, which reciprocates with the $10 million it has borrowed. In effect, the two parties have made independent borrowings and then exchanged the proceeds. For this reason, currency swaps are also known as an **exchange of borrowings**.

Figure 6.15 shows the same swap terms we have already analyzed. Party C pays interest payments at a rate of 10 percent on the $10 million it received from Party D, and Party D pays 2 million marks interest per year on the 25 million marks it received from Party C. Notice that these rates are the same ones that the two firms could obtain from other sources. However, Figure 6.15 also shows the interest payments that Parties C and D must make on their borrowings. Party C pays 1.75 million marks interest annually, but it receives 2 million marks from Party D. For its part, Party D receives $1 million from Party C, from which it pays interest of $900,000.

Now we can clearly see how the swap benefits both parties. Party C gets the use of $10 million and pays out 1.75 million marks. Had it borrowed dollars on its own, it would have paid a full 10 percent, or $1 million per year. At current exchange rates of 2.5 marks per dollar, Party C is effectively paying $700,000 annual interest on the use of $10 million. This is an effective rate of 7 percent. Party D pays $900,000 interest each year and receives the use of 25 million marks. This is equivalent to paying 2,250,000 marks annual interest ($900,000 times 2.5 marks per dollar) for the use of 25 million marks, or a rate of 9 percent. By using the swap, both parties achieve

Figure 6.14
A Plain Vanilla Currency Swap (Initial Cash Flow with Lenders)

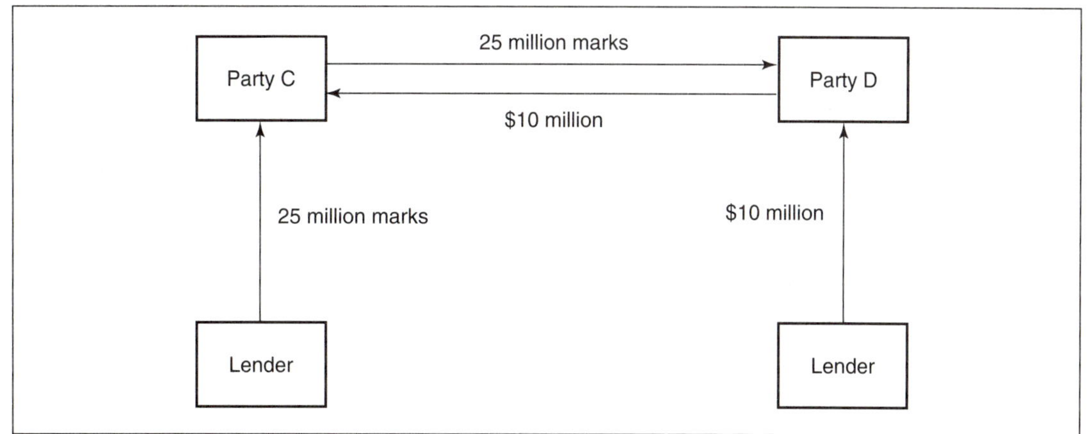

Figure 6.15
A Plain Vanilla Currency Swap (Interest Payments with Lenders)

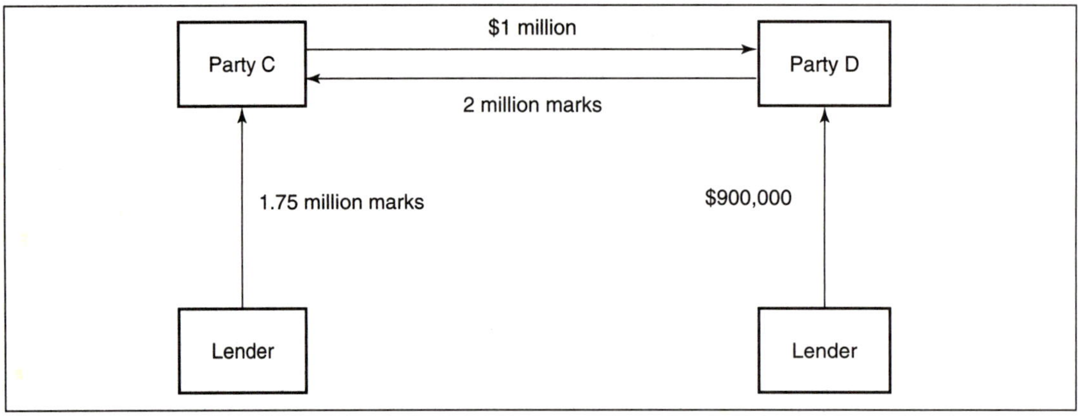

an effective borrowing rate that is much lower than they could have obtained by borrowing the currency they needed directly. By engaging in the swap, both firms can use the comparative advantage of the other to reduce their borrowing costs. Figure 6.16 shows the termination cash flows for the swap, when both parties repay the principal.

Summary In this section, we have explored two motivations for engaging in swaps – commercial needs and comparative borrowing advantages. The first led to an interest rate swap, while the second motivated a currency swap. Both swaps that we have analyzed are plain vanilla swaps. While swaps can become much more complex, they are generally motivated by the considerations that we have explored in this section.

Swap Facilitators

As we mentioned earlier, a swap facilitator is a third party who assists in the completion of a swap. When a swap facilitator acts strictly as an agent, without taking any financial position in the swap

Figure 6.16
A Plain Vanilla Currency Swap (Repayment of Principal with Lenders)

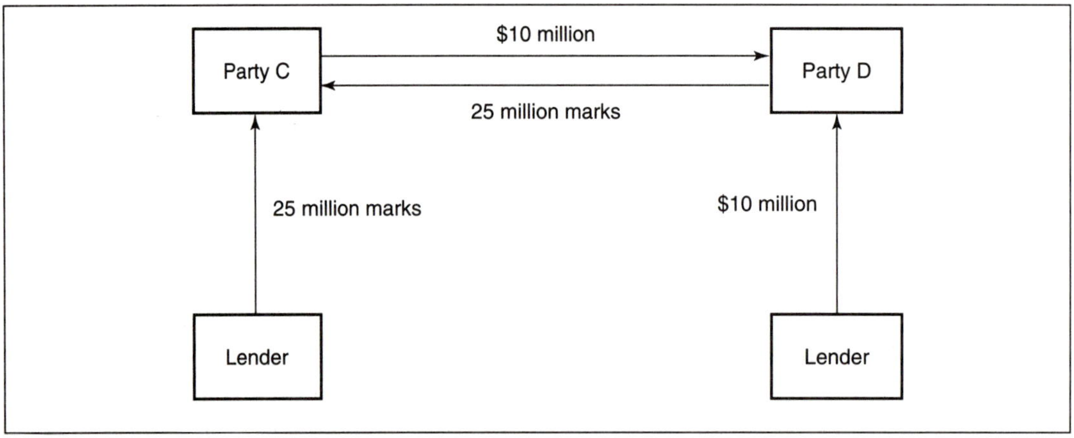

transaction, the facilitator acts as a **swap broker**. In some instances, a swap facilitator may actually transact for its own account to help complete the swap. In this case, the swap facilitator acts as a **swap dealer**. Both swap brokers and swap dealers are known as **swap banks**, so a swap bank is equivalent to a swap facilitator. This section explores the role of swap brokers and dealers.

Swap Brokers For a swap transaction to occur, two counterparties with matching needs must find each other. As we have seen, a firm with a short-term and fairly standard risk exposure might use futures or exchange-traded options to manage that risk. Special risk exposures often lead firms to look beyond futures and exchange-traded options to the swap market for the management of that special exposure. For example, even with the plain vanilla interest rate and currency swaps examples that we considered, the risks faced by the parties could not be managed completely with futures or exchange-traded options. As the risk exposure goes beyond the plain vanilla variety, futures and exchange-traded options are even less adequate for managing these more complex risks.

For a potential swap participant with a specific need, finding a counterparty can be very difficult. The difficulty of finding counterparties creates an opportunity for a swap broker. A swap broker has a number of firms in her client base and stands ready to search for swap counterparties upon demand. Having a swap broker conduct a search for a counterparty also preserves the privacy of the firm's intentions to enter the swap market. After finding a suitable swap counterparty, the broker helps to negotiate and complete the swap contract. For her services, the swap broker receives a fee from each of the counterparties.

In summary, the swap broker serves as an information intermediary. The broker uses her superior knowledge of potential swap participants to find the right counterparty. The broker exercises discretion by protecting the identity of the potential counterparties until the swap partners are found. Notice that the swap broker is not a party to the swap contract. As a broker, the swap facilitator does not bear financial risk, but merely assists the two counterparties in completing the swap transaction.

Swap Dealers A swap dealer fulfills all of the functions of a swap broker. In addition, a swap dealer also takes a risk position in the swap transaction by becoming an actual party to the transaction. Just because the swap dealer may take a risk position to complete a swap transaction does not mean that the swap dealer is a speculator. Instead, the swap dealer accepts a risk position to complete the transaction for the initial counterparty. The swap transaction may leave the swap dealer with a risk position, but the swap dealer will then try to offset that risk. The swap dealer functions as a financial intermediary, earning profits by helping to complete swap transactions. If completing a swap results in a risk position for the swap dealer, the dealer will then try to minimize that risk by its own further transactions.

To explore the functions served by the swap dealer, we assume that the dealer begins with its optimal set of investments. In other words, the swap dealer has financial assets, but they are invested in a way that the swap dealer finds optimal. Therefore, if the swap dealer takes part in a swap transaction and has his financial position altered as a result of that transaction, we assume that the change in the swap dealer's position represents an unwanted risk that the dealer accepted only to help complete the swap transaction and to earn profits thereby. Against this background, we return to our example of a plain vanilla interest rate swap to explore the additional role performed by the swap dealer.

In the plain vanilla interest rate swap example, we noted that Party A was a savings and loan association that paid a floating rate of LIBOR + 1 percent to its depositors and made a five-year fixed rate mortgage loan at 12 percent. This initial business position left Party A exposed to rising interest rates, and Party A wanted to avoid this risk by converting the fixed rate it received on its mortgage loan to a floating rate. Party A's ability to complete this swap depended on finding a suitable counterparty with a matching need, such as Party B in our example.

If a firm like Party B cannot be found, Party A is left unable to complete the swap. Often a swap broker will be unable to find a suitable counterparty, or the swap broker can find only a partial match. In many instances, the swap broker may be able to find a potential counterparty that will take only a portion of the swap that the initial counterparty wants to complete, or the potential counterparty does not want to transact at the time the initial counterparty desires. To complete the swap transaction for Party A, the swap dealer may act as a counterparty. Figure 6.17 shows the plain vanilla interest rate swap example as before, except the swap dealer acts as the c-ounterparty to Party A. As a result, we see that the swap gives the swap dealer the same cash flows that Party B had in Figure 6.9.

As a result of this transaction, the swap dealer now has an undesired risk position. Over the next five years the dealer is obligated to pay a floating rate of LIBOR + 3 percent and to receive a fixed rate of 12 percent on a notional amount of $10 million. The swap dealer must believe that he can make money by acting as a counterparty to Party A. To do so, the swap dealer wants to offset the risk that he has undertaken, but he needs to offset that risk on better terms than he undertook as a counterparty to Party A.

Let us assume that the dealer knew of a potential party in the swap market, Party E, that was willing to pay a floating rate of LIBOR + 3.1 percent in exchange for a fixed rate of 12 percent on a notional amount of $10 million. However, Party E is willing to accept a term of only three years, not the five years that Party A desires. Given a knowledge of this client, the swap dealer

Figure 6.17
A Plain Vanilla Interest Rate Swap with a Swap Dealer

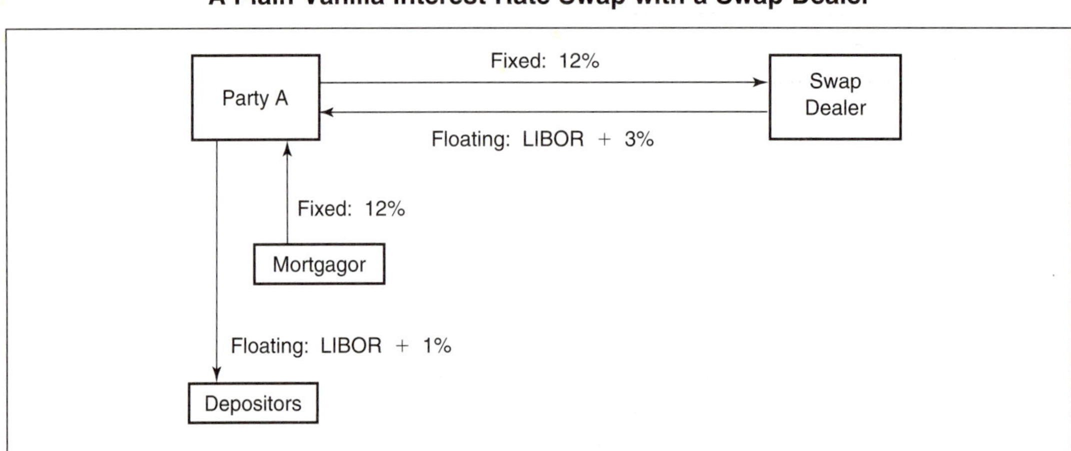

decides to act as a counterparty to Party A. By also transacting with Party E, the swap dealer is able to offset a substantial portion of the risk he accepts by transacting with Party A. Figure 6.18 shows the transactions involving Parties A and E, along with the swap dealer. After completing these transactions, we see that the swap dealer has some profits to show for his efforts. Specifically, the dealer is making 10 basis points on the floating rate side of the transaction because he receives LIBOR + 3.1 percent and pays LIBOR + 3 percent. However, the swap dealer still has considerable risk as a result of the transaction.

Table 6.9 shows the swap dealer's cash flows resulting from the swap. The first two columns of Table 6.9 show the cash flows that result from the swap dealer's transactions with Party A. To serve the needs of Party A, the swap dealer has agreed to receive a 12 percent fixed rate payment in exchange for paying LIBOR + 3 percent on a $10 million notional amount. Based on the portion of the transaction with Party A, the swap dealer will receive $1.2 million each year and pay LIBOR + 3 percent on $10 million each year. Which set of cash flows is better is uncertain because the future course of interest rates is not known. For example, if LIBOR stays constant at 8 percent over the five years, the swap dealer will profit handsomely, making 1 percent per year for five years on $10 million. However, if LIBOR jumps to 11 percent and remains constant, the swap dealer will be paying 14 percent on $10 million each year. As a result, the swap dealer will receive $1.2 million but must pay $1.4 million each year, for an annual net loss of $200,000. Thus, the riskiness of acting as a counterparty to Party A is clear.

Figure 6.18
The Swap Dealer as Intermediary in a Plain Vanilla Interest Rate Swap

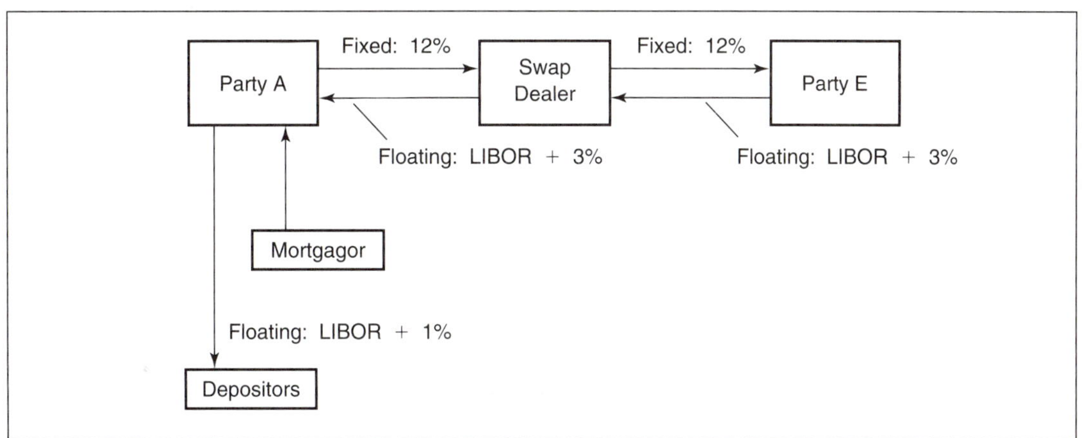

Table 6.9
The Swap Dealer's Cash Flows

Year	From Party A	To Party A	From Party E	To Party E	Dealers Net Cash Flow
1	$1,200,000	LIBOR +3%	LIBOR +3.1%	$1,200,000	$10,000
2	1,200,000	LIBOR +3%	LIBOR +3.1%	1,200,000	10,000
3	1,200,000	LIBOR +3%	LIBOR +3.1%	1,200,000	10,000
4	1,200,000	LIBOR +3%	0	0	$1,200,000 – LIBOR +3%
5	1,200,000	LIBOR +3%	0	0	$1,200,000 – LIBOR +3%

Table 6.9 also shows the swap dealer's cash flows that result from transacting with Party E. For each of the first three years, the dealer will pay a fixed interest rate of 12 percent on $10,000,000, which is $1,200,000. In addition, the dealer will receive a rate of LIBOR + 3.1 percent on a notional amount of $10,000,000.

The final column of the table shows the swap dealer's net cash flows. For the first three years, the swap dealer has achieved a perfect match in cash flows, receiving $1.2 million from Party A and paying it to Party E. The dealer has a net zero cash flow on this part of the transaction. During the first three years, the dealer also receives LIBOR + 3.1 percent from Party E and pays LIBOR + 3 percent to Party A, both on notional amounts of $10 million. On this portion of the transaction, the dealer receives a net spread of 10 basis points on a $10 million notional amount. Taking all of the dealer's cash flows during the first three years into account, we see that the dealer has a net cash inflow of $10,000 per year.

Even after transacting with both Parties A and E, the swap dealer has a residual risk that is evident in Table 6.9. In years 4 and 5, the dealer will receive $1.2 million from Party A, but he must pay LIBOR + 3 percent. Whether this will create a profit or loss for the dealer depends on future interest rates. However, in Table 6.9 we can see that the dealer has substantially reduced his risk position by trading with Party E.

Swap Dealers as Financial Intermediaries Table 6.9 also shows that the swap dealer is making a profit as a financial intermediary. Because of his superior knowledge of the market, the dealer was able to find Party E. By transacting with Party E, instead of just transacting with Party A, the swap dealer secures a 10 basis point spread on the notional amount for three years. In addition to earning a profit on the spread, the dealer's transaction with Party E offsets a substantial portion of the risk inherent in acting as a counterparty to Party A in the initial swap transaction.

In our example of the swap dealer's transactions, we assumed that the swap dealer had an initial portfolio of assets that met his needs in terms of risk and diversification. By acting as a counterparty to Party A, the swap dealer assumed a risk in pursuit of profit. The dealer could have taken this position as a speculation on interest rates. However, the swap dealer prefers to act as a financial intermediary, making a profit by providing informational services. In our example, the swap dealer is able to capture a spread of 10 basis points and reduce risk by transacting with Party E. Ideally, the swap dealer acting as a financial intermediary would also like to avoid the remaining risk exposure in years 4 and 5. Being able to do so requires that the dealer find another swap partner. We explore the ways in which swap dealers manage the risks associated with acting as counterparties later in this chapter.

Summary In this section, we have seen that swap facilitators or swap banks may act as either brokers or dealers. A swap broker facilitates swap transactions by bringing potential counterparties together, but the broker does not take a risk position in the swap. By contrast, a swap dealer acts as a counterparty in the swap, in addition to providing the informational assistance provided by a broker. Notice that the same firm can act as a swap broker in some transactions and as a swap dealer in others. Calling a firm a swap broker or swap dealer refers to the function that the firm fulfills in a particular transaction.

By taking a position in a swap transaction, a swap dealer accepts a risk position. The firm that accepts this risk position could approach the transaction as a speculator or as a swap dealer. Functioning as a swap dealer, the firm accepts the position with the idea of avoiding as much of the risk exposure as possible. Specifically, the firm acting as a financial intermediary will attempt to offset the initial risk and will be satisfied to make a profit by acting as a conduit between other swap parties. When the swap dealer acts as a counterparty, the dealer intends to be only a temporary substitute for an unavailable counterparty.

Pricing of Swaps

In this section, we explore the principles that underlie swap pricing. To simplify the discussion, we focus on plain vanilla interest rate swaps, and we assume that the swap dealer wishes to act as a pure financial intermediary. That is, the swap dealer does not want to assume a risk position with respect to interest rates. The principles apply, however, to swaps of all types. The swap dealer must price swaps to reflect a number of factors. These include the creditworthiness of the potential swap partner, the availability of other swap opportunities that will allow the swap dealer to offset the risk of an initial swap, and the term structure of interest rates.[14] We discuss each of these in turn.

Creditworthiness The swap dealer must appraise the creditworthiness of the swap partner. As we have seen earlier in this chapter, there is no clearinghouse in the swap market to guarantee performance on a contract if one of the counterparties defaults. If the swap dealer suffers a default by one of its counterparties, the dealer must either absorb the loss or institute a lawsuit to seek recovery on the defaulted obligation.

Because of the potential costs associated with default, the swap dealer will adjust the pricing on swaps to reflect the risk of default. Parties that have a high risk of default are likely to be excluded from the market. For example, airlines under bankruptcy protection probably have very limited access to the swap market. As we noted earlier, the swap market is mainly a market for financial institutions and corporations due to the importance of default considerations and the need for one party to be able to confirm the creditworthiness of a prospective counterparty.

Availability of Additional Counterparties Because we are assuming that the swap dealer wishes to act only as a financial intermediary, the swap dealer will be very concerned about how the risk involved in a prospective swap can be offset by participating in other swaps. The swap dealer will want to avoid a position that cannot be eliminated through further transactions. If a prospective swap agreement is likely to leave the dealer in such a position, the swap dealer will only enter the agreement at a price that compensates for the necessity of bearing the additional risk. Similarly, if the risk for the swap dealer of a prospective swap agreement can be easily offset, the swap dealer may be willing to provide her services for a small cost. In sum, the swap dealer will be very pleased to create a structure of swaps that leaves no interest rate risk and still provides a decent profit.

---

[14] The swap dealer will also consider some other issues in setting final pricing terms. If the swap is very complicated, the swap dealer may charge a higher price than otherwise. Similarly, if the swap is to involve cross-border currency flows, the dealer may be concerned with regulatory constraints that might impede the flow of funds.

The Term Structure of Interest Rates As we will see in more detail in the next chapter, the term structure of interest rates is an important feature in bond pricing. Not surprisingly, the market for interest rate swaps must reflect the term structure that prevails in the bond market. If the swap market did not reflect the term structure, traders would find ready arbitrage opportunities, and they could quickly discipline swap traders to pay attention to the term structure. For example, if the term structure is rising, the swap dealer must charge a higher yield on swaps of longer maturity. The next section illustrates these considerations from the term structure.

Summary

This chapter has given a general introduction to financial derivatives markets. It distinguished futures and forward contracts by noting the differences in their cash flow commitments. We then examined the institutional features of futures markets, including the flow of orders, the role of the clearinghouse, and the fulfillment of commitments in the futures market. The chapter also examined the principles of futures pricing, particularly the cost-of-carry model. We noted that futures can be useful for managing risk, and we considered examples of using interest rate and stock index futures.

The chapter then turned to an overview of the options market in the United States. Options can be classified as put or call options, each of which may be bought or sold. Ownership of a call option confers the right to buy a given good at a specified price for a specified period of time. Selling a call option confers those same rights to the owner of a call option in exchange for a payment from the call option purchaser. Ownership of a put option permits the sale of a good at a specified price for a specified period of time. Selling a put option gives those rights to the buyer in exchange for a payment from the buyer.

We saw that the price of options depends on the price of the underlying stock, the exercise price, the riskiness of the underlying stock, the time until expiration, and the risk-free rate of interest. We considered the Option Pricing Model developed by Black and Scholes, which gives an exact price for a call option as a function of the same five variables. While their model is a theoretical model, it has been shown to accord very well with option prices that are actually observed in the market. By put-call parity, it is also possible to value put options. We saw that options can be used to hedge risk or to tailor the risk exposure of a particular position.

The chapter also introduced the swap market. From origins in the late 1970s and early 1980s, the swap market has grown to enormous proportions, with notionals exceeding $6 trillion. In contrast with futures and exchange-traded options, we noted that swap agreements are extremely flexible in amount, maturity, and other contract terms. As further points of difference between futures and exchange-traded options versus swaps, the swap market does not utilize an exchange and is virtually free of governmental regulation.

The chapter analyzed plain vanilla interest rate and currency swaps. We saw that an interest rate swap essentially involves a commitment by two parties to exchange cash flows tied to some principal, or notional, amount. One party pays a fixed rate, while the second party pays a floating rate. In a foreign currency swap, both parties acquire funds in different currencies and exchange those principal amounts. Each party pays interest to the other in the currency that was acquired, with these interest payments taking place over the term of the swap agreement. To terminate the agreement, the parties again exchange foreign currency. Motivations for swaps arise from a desire to avoid financial risk or a chance to exploit some borrowing advantage.

Swap brokers and dealers are two kinds of swap facilitators. A swap broker helps counterparties complete swaps by providing introduction and guidance in the negotiation of the swap, but the swap broker does not take a risk position in the swap. By contrast, a swap dealer provides the services of the swap broker, but also will act as a counterparty in a swap. For the swap dealer, we considered the factors that influence pricing, and we discussed the techniques that swap dealers use to manage the risk associated with their portfolios of swaps.

Questions and Problems

1. What problems with forward contracts are resolved by futures contracts?
2. What are the two most important functions of the clearinghouse of a futures exchange?
3. What is the investment for a trader who buys a futures contract? Justify your answer.
4. What are the two ways to fulfill a futures contract commitment? Which is used more frequently? Why?
5. What is the difference between "open interest" and "trading volume"?
6. What is the "basis" and why is it important?
7. Assume that you are a bond portfolio manager and that you anticipate an infusion of investable funds in three months. How could you use the futures market to hedge against unexpected changes in interest rates?
8. Assume that the spot corn price is $3.50, that it costs $.017 cents to store a bushel of corn for one month, and that the relevant cost of financing is 1 percent per month. If a corn futures contract matures in six months and the current futures price for this contract is $3.65 per bushel, explain how you would respond. Explain your transactions for one contract, assuming 5,000 bushels per contract, all storage costs must be paid at the outset of the transaction, and borrowing and lending rates are equal.
9. Respond to the following claim: "Buying a call option is very dangerous because it commits the owner to purchasing a stock at a later date. At that time the stock may be undesirable. Therefore, owning a call option is a risky position."
10. "I bought a call option with an exercise price of $110 on IBM when IBM was at $108 and I paid $6 per share for the option. Now the option is about to expire and IBM is trading at $112. There's no point in exercising the option, because I will wind up paying a total of $116 for the shares – $6 I already spent for the option plus the $110 exercise price." Is this line of reasoning correct? Explain.
11. What is the value of a call option on a share of stock if the exercise price of the call is $0 and its expiration date is infinite? Explain.

12. Why is the value of a call option at expiration equal to the maximum of zero or the stock price minus the exercise price?

13. Two call options are identical except that they are written on two different stocks with different risk levels. Which will be worth more? Why?

14. Assume the following: a stock is selling for $100, a call option with an exercise price of $90 is trading for $6 and matures in one month, and that the interest rate is 1 percent per month. What should you do? Explain your transactions.

15. Explain the differences between a plain vanilla interest rate swap and a plain vanilla currency swap.

16. What are the two major kinds of swap facilitators? What is the key difference between the roles they play?

17. Assume that you are a financial manager for a large commercial bank and that you expect short-term interest rates to rise more than the yield curve would suggest. Would you rather pay a fixed long-term rate and receive a floating short rate, or the other way around? Explain your reasoning.

18. Explain the role that the notional principal plays in understanding swap transactions. Why is this principal amount regarded as only notional? (Hint: What is the dictionary definition of "notional"?)

19. Consider a plain vanilla interest rate swap. Explain how the practice of net payments works.

20. Explain why a currency swap is also called an "exchange of borrowings."

21. Assume a swap dealer attempts to function as a pure financial intermediary avoiding all interest rate risk. Explain how such a dealer may yet come to bear interest rate risk.

References

Abken, P. A., "Beyond Plain Vanilla: A Taxonomy of Swaps," *Economic Review*, Federal Reserve Bank of Atlanta, 76:2, March/April 1991, pp. 12–29.

Abken, P. A., "Interest-Rate Caps, Collars, and Floors," *Economic Review*, Federal Reserve Bank of Atlanta, November/December 1989, pp. 2–23.

Bhattacharya, A. K. and J. Breit, "Customized Interest-Rate Agreements and Their Applications," *The Handbook of Fixed Income Securities*, 3e, Homewood, IL: Business One Irwin, 1991.

Black, F., "Fact and Fantasy in the Use of Options," *Financial Analysts Journal*, 31:4, July/August 1975, pp. 36–72.

Black, F., "How to Use the Holes in Black-Scholes," *Journal of Applied Corporate Finance*, 1:4, Winter 1989, pp. 67–73.

Black, F. and M. Scholes., "The Pricing of Options and Corporate Liabilities," *Journal of Political Economy*, 1973, pp. 637–54.

Dattatreya, R. E., "Asset Allocation Using Futures and Options," *The Handbook of Fixed Income Securities*, 3e, Homewood, IL: Business One Irwin, 1991.

Edwards, F. R., "Does Futures Trading Increase Stock Market Volatility?" *Financial Analysts Journal*, 44:1, January/February 1988, pp. 63–9.

Einzig, R. and B. Lange, "Swaps at Transamerica Analysis and Applications," *Journal of Applied Corporate Finance*, 2:4, Winter 1990, pp. 48–58.

Gastineau, G. L., "Arbitrage, Program Trading, and the Tail of the Dog," *The Institutional Investor Focus on Investment Management*, Cambridge, MA: Ballinger, 1989, pp. 101–13.

Giddy, I., "Foreign Exchange Options," *Journal of Futures Markets*, 3:2, 1983, pp. 143–66.

Goodman, L. S., "The Use of Interest Rate Swaps in Managing Corporate Liabilities," *Journal of Applied Corporate Finance*, 2:4, Winter 1990, pp. 35-47.

Kapner, K. R. and J. F. Marshall, *The Swaps Handbook: Swaps and Related Risk Management Instruments*, New York: New York Institute of Finance Corp., 1990.

Kolb, R., *The Financial Derivatives Reader*, Miami: Kolb Publishing, 1992.

Kolb, R., *Futures, Options, and Swaps*, Miami: Kolb Publishing, 1994.

Kolb, R., *Options: An Introduction*, 2nd ed., Miami: Kolb Publishing, 1994.

Kolb, R., *Understanding Futures Markets*, 4th ed., Miami: Kolb Publishing, 1994.

Kritzman, M., "What's Wrong with Portfolio Insurance?" *The Institutional Investor Focus on Investment Management*, Cambridge, MA: Ballinger Publishing, 1989, pp. 755–61.

Rendleman, R., and C. Carabini, "The Efficiency of the Treasury Bill Futures Market," *Journal of Finance*, 34:4, September 1979, pp. 895–914.

Rubinstein, M., "Portfolio Insurance and the Market Crash," *Financial Analysts Journal*, 44:1, January/February 1988, pp. 38–47.

Tompkins, R. G., "International Portfolio Diversification with Stock Index Derivatives," *Quantitative International Investing: A Handbook of Analytical and Modeling Techniques and Strategies*, Chicago: Probus Publishing, 1990, pp. 35–54.

Smith, C. W. Jr., C. W. Smithson, and L. M. Wakeman, "The Market for Interest Rate Swaps," *The Handbook of Financial Engineering*, New York: Harper Business, 1990, pp. 212–29.

Venkatesh, R. E. S., V. Venkatesh, and R. E. Dattatreya, "Introduction to Interest Rate Swaps," *The Handbook of Derivative Instruments*, Chicago: Probus Publishing, 1991, pp. 129–59.

Zurack, M., "Establishing an Arbitrage Program: Stock Index Arbitrage," *The Institutional Investor Focus on Investment Management*, Cambridge, MA: Ballinger Publishing Company, 1989, pp. 115–32.

The Level and Structure of Interest Rates 7

Overview

In Chapter 4, we introduced bond pricing and discussed the general structure of the bond market. This chapter builds on that foundation, giving particular emphasis to the issues that confront bond portfolio managers. Because many financial institutions hold large investments in bonds, bond portfolio management is a key skill for a successful financial institution. This chapter begins by focusing on bonds that are free of default risk, but we consider risky bonds later in this chapter.

One of the most basic questions facing a bond manager concerns the proper maturity characteristics of the bonds to hold in a portfolio. We have already observed that yields on bonds can be graphed as a **yield curve**, a graph that shows the relationship between the maturity of a bond and its yield to maturity. Even for a bond portfolio of U.S. Treasury bonds, bond yields vary simply because of differences in maturity.

Longer maturity bonds tend to be more sensitive to interest rate changes and are riskier than short maturity bonds in the sense that their prices may fluctuate more. However, longer maturity bonds often pay a higher yield than short maturity bonds, making them enticing for a bond portfolio manager.

To structure a successful bond portfolio, the manager must understand the relationship between maturity and yield in order to determine the appropriate maturity structure of the bond portfolio. By adjusting the maturity of a bond portfolio, the bond manager determines the sensitivity of the portfolio to changes in interest rates. Making the correct adjustments can have a dramatic influence on the portfolio's returns. As a consequence, the analysis of the yield curve, or the term structure of interest rates, is important for bond portfolio management.

Thus far, we have focused almost exclusively on bonds that are free of default risk. **Default risk** is the risk that one or more of the payments on a bond will not be paid as promised. However, much of the bond market is composed of corporate issues and municipal bonds, all of which have default risk. Differences in default risk give rise to the risk structure of interest rates. The **risk structure of interest rates** is the relationship between the yields of different securities as a function of their level of default risk. Risk levels of various bonds change over time, and the yield differences of bonds from different classes change over time as well. The bond portfolio manager must comprehend those differences and the reasons for their occurrence. In fact, choosing the correct level of default risk is one of the most important decisions the bond portfolio manager must face. By accepting more default risk in the portfolio, the manager secures a greater promised return but increases the danger of missed payments on the bonds.

In practice, choosing the correct maturity composition of the portfolio and selecting the appropriate risk level are two of the prime functions of the bond portfolio manager. However, neither issue would be very important if the manager could forecast interest rates accurately. In fact, if portfolio managers could forecast interest rates with a greater degree of accuracy than the market as a whole, they could reap enormous returns. This chapter also examines the success that can be expected in forecasting interest rates. As the discussion indicates, there is little hope of consistently successful forecasting.

The Level of Interest Rates

We have seen that the sensitivity of a bond's price depends on the three key variables of maturity, coupon rate, and the level of interest rates. Because so much of bond investing depends on changes in interest rates, the bond investor needs to understand the basic factors that influence the level of interest rates and the changes from one level of rates to another.

In discussing interest rates, it is customary to speak of the overall level of rates, the term structure of interest rates, and the risk structure of interest rates. The term and risk structures of interest rates are important for the choice of individual bonds, but they are even more crucial for managing bond portfolios. Accordingly, Chapter 8 focuses on the term and the risk structures of interest rates and their relationship to bond portfolio management. As a preliminary to considering the full range of issues associated with bond portfolio management, this section focuses strictly on the level of interest rates for bonds that are free of default risk. In practice, this means that the discussion is limited to the determinants of the level of interest rates on U.S. Treasury obligations.

The Nominal Rate of Interest

Yields on debt securities are almost always quoted as a nominal rate of interest. The **nominal rate of interest** reflects only the promised dollar payments without reference to the purchasing power of the payments. For example, a one-year loan of \$100 at a rate of 12 percent will return \$112. In this case, the nominal rate of interest is 12 percent. When the loan matures and the investor receives the \$12 interest payment, the \$12 may have a purchasing power that differs from that which was expected. To better understand the determinants of nominal rates of interest, which are, in fact, the market rates of interest, it is customary to identify two components of the nominal rate of interest. Following the work of the great economist Irving Fisher, we express the nominal rate of interest on a default-free security as being composed of the real rate of interest and the expected rate of inflation.[1] For any single period, this relationship can be expressed as follows.

For a bond with no default risk:

$$(1 + r) = (1 + r^*)\,[1 + E(I)] \qquad (7.1)$$

where:

r = the nominal rate of interest
r^* = the real rate of interest
$E(I)$ = the expected rate of inflation over the period

For the multiperiod case, the same relationship can be expressed as:

---

[1] See his classic work, Irving Fisher, *The Theory of Interest*, New York: A. M. Kelley, Publishers, 1965. The book was originally published in 1930.

$$(1 + r)^t = (1 + r^*)^t [1 + E(I)]^t \tag{7.2}$$

assuming that the rates for the different components are constant over the t periods.

The Real Rate of Interest and the Expected Inflation Rate

The **real rate of interest** has many other names, such as the **pure price of time** and the **marginal productivity of capital**. All three names point to the same idea. When an investor buys a bond, the inflation rate over the period of the bond's life is uncertain. However, the investor will demand some increase in the purchasing power of funds committed for the bond's life. This leads to a definition of the **real rate of interest** – the expected change in purchasing power necessary to induce investors to postpone consumption.

To continue the previous example of a one-year bond investment with a nominal rate of 12 percent, investors will not be pleased if the inflation rate during that period is 14 percent. The investor who invests \$100 in these circumstances will lose purchasing power over the year. The \$100 initial investment will increase in value by \$12. With an inflation rate of 14 percent, however, what \$100 would buy at the outset of the investment will require \$114 at year's end. The investor's purchasing power will have fallen over the year from \$100 to \$98.25, measured in constant dollars. The relative purchasing power of an investment can be found by using Equations 7.1 or 7.2, assuming the rate of inflation and the rate of return for the period are known.

$$\text{Relative Purchasing Power} = \frac{C(1 + r)}{C(1 + I)} = \frac{1 + r}{1 + I} \tag{7.3}$$

where:

C = the initial investment
I = the actual inflation rate over the investment period

In our example,

$$\text{Relative Purchasing Power} = \frac{\$100(1.12)}{\$100(1.14)} = \frac{\$112}{\$114} = .9825$$

The investors' purchasing power after making the investment was only 98.25 percent of the original purchasing power and resulted in a negative real rate of return. This also explains why the real rate is also known as the pure price of time. The **pure price of time** is the change in purchasing power investors demand for postponing their consumption. The price is a pure price because it assumes that no risk is involved in the investment. It is simply a price for postponing consumption, not for bearing default risk.

Having defined the real rate as the expected change in purchasing power necessary to induce investment, the next question becomes: What level of real rate is possible and what do investors demand? As noted, the real rate of return is also called the marginal productivity of capital. If investors demand and receive some real rate of interest, it can only be because some other parties are willing to pay that rate. Rational economic agents will pay a given rate only if the funds obtained at that rate can be employed to generate a higher rate of return.

The **marginal productivity of capital** is the rate of return that can be earned by the next unit of capital to be invested. This is also a real rate, and we can interpret it as the rate at which physical capital can reproduce itself. Additional funds for capital investment will be available only when the capital investment pays a rate of return equal to or greater than the cost of those funds. Because expected inflation affects bond rates and capital investment returns alike, the problem becomes one of balancing the marginal productivity of capital against the real rate of interest. As long as the marginal productivity of capital exceeds the real rate of interest, more funds will be demanded for investment. An equilibrium will be reached when the real rate of interest equals the marginal productivity of capital.

Figure 7.1 presents this situation graphically. It depicts a situation in which the real rate of interest is 3 percent per year. On the horizontal axis, $1 at time = 0 can be transformed into $1.03 of purchasing power at time = 1. The slope of the line running from $1 at time = 0 to $1.03 at time = 1 represents the real rate of interest. A steeper slope would indicate a higher real rate of return. Figure 7.1 also shows the returns for investment in physical capital. The horizontal axis represents the units of physical capital being employed. Notice that the numbers get larger reading right to left. The vertical axis shows the number of units of physical capital produced by the employment of a given number of units of capital on the horizontal axis.

The curved line in Figure 7.1 shows the changing productivity of investment. When no capital is being utilized, the first unit put to work is extremely productive. This happens because the capital will be employed first where it has the greatest return, and the graph reflects this high productivity by the very steep slope near the zero level of capital employment. As more and more capital is employed, successive units are less and less valuable, as reflected by the changing slope

Figure 7.1
The Real Rate of Interest and the Marginal Productivity of Capital

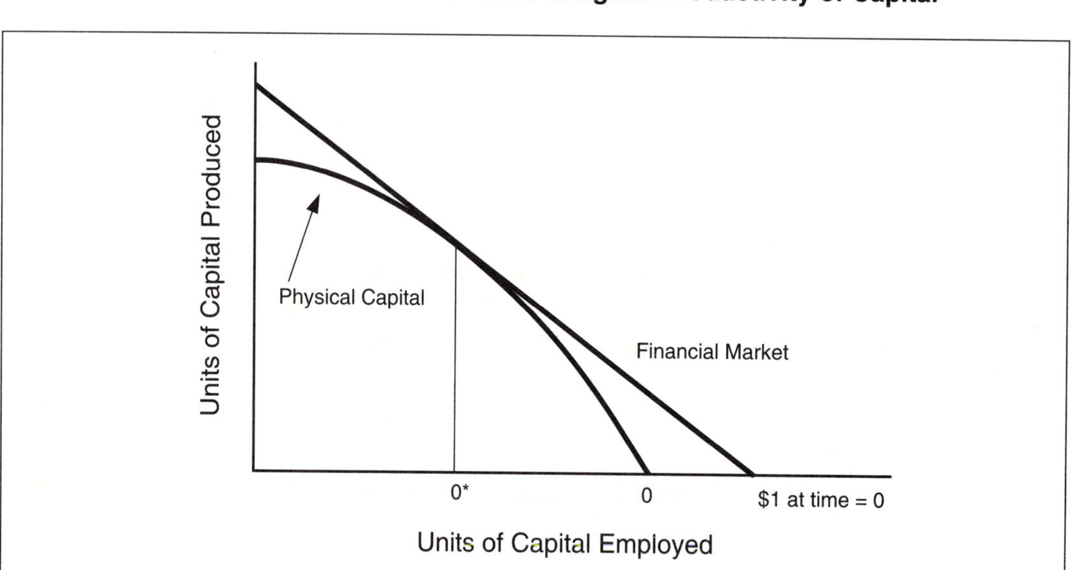

of the curved line in Figure 7.1. At any point, the slope of the curved line represents the rate of return on the last unit of capital employed.

How much capital will be employed ultimately? The curved line (showing the productivity of capital) is tangent to the straight line (showing the 3 percent real rate of interest) at a single point. Starting with zero capital investment, investment continues so long as the rate of return on capital exceeds the real rate of interest. When the return is less than the real rate, further investment in capital goods is a losing proposition.

Following this line of reasoning, there will be investment in capital along the curved line of Figure 7.1 up to the point where the slope of the curved line equals the slope of the line showing the rate of return in the capital market. At this point, Q^*, the marginal rate of return on capital – the marginal productivity of capital – equals the real rate of interest. Any further investment in capital goods earns a rate of return below the real rate of interest and will be counterproductive because a higher real rate of return could be earned in the bond market.

Strictly speaking, this graphical analysis assumes a world where the real rate of return and the returns to capital investment are both certain.[2] Further complications present themselves when the more complicated situation of uncertainty is considered.

In the securities markets, the investor always faces uncertain future prospects. Given a stated nominal rate on some investment, the investor remains uncertain as to which portion of that nominal rate should be attributed to expected real returns or to expected inflation. Presumably, the expected real return is never negative. If that is a reasonable assumption, investors are often disappointed. There have been numerous cases where the realized real rate of return has been negative. Figure 7.2 presents the returns for the period from 1970 through 1994 for investment in Treasury bills. As the graph shows, this period includes periods of volatile interest rates and high inflation. During this time, real returns were sometimes negative. Assuming that investors make investments only where the expected real return is positive, some investors' expectations were clearly wrong during this period.

It should be noted that this period was very unusual, covering the period of the oil crisis and the subsequent economic adjustments. Also, investors in the early 1980s enjoyed very high real returns, as shown in the bottom panel of Figure 7.2. For a more accurate view, it is useful to consider a long period of time. For the years 1926–94, the real rate of return on investment in U.S. Treasury securities was about 0.5 percent in Treasury bills and about 1.7 percent in Treasury bonds.[3] While experts disagree about the best estimate of the real rate of return, it must be put somewhere in the range from 0 to 2 percent. Given that contemporary interest rates frequently have been above 10 percent, it must be acknowledged that the real rate is not very important in determining interest rates. Instead, the nominal interest rate is mainly composed of the expected inflation rate. This is shown also in Figure 7.2, in which the nominal rate has exceeded the inflation rate for Treasury bills in recent years.

---

[2] In fact, this analysis follows the introductory portion of an influential analysis of these issues presented in J. Hirschleifer, "Investment Decision Under Uncertainty: Choice–Theoretic Approaches," *The Quarterly Journal of Economics*, 79:4, November 1964, pp. 509–36.

[3] See Ibbotson Associates, *Stocks, Bonds, Bills and Inflation: 1995 Yearbook*, Chicago: Ibbotson Associates, Inc., 1995.

Figure 7.2
Nominal and Real T-Bill Returns, 1970–94

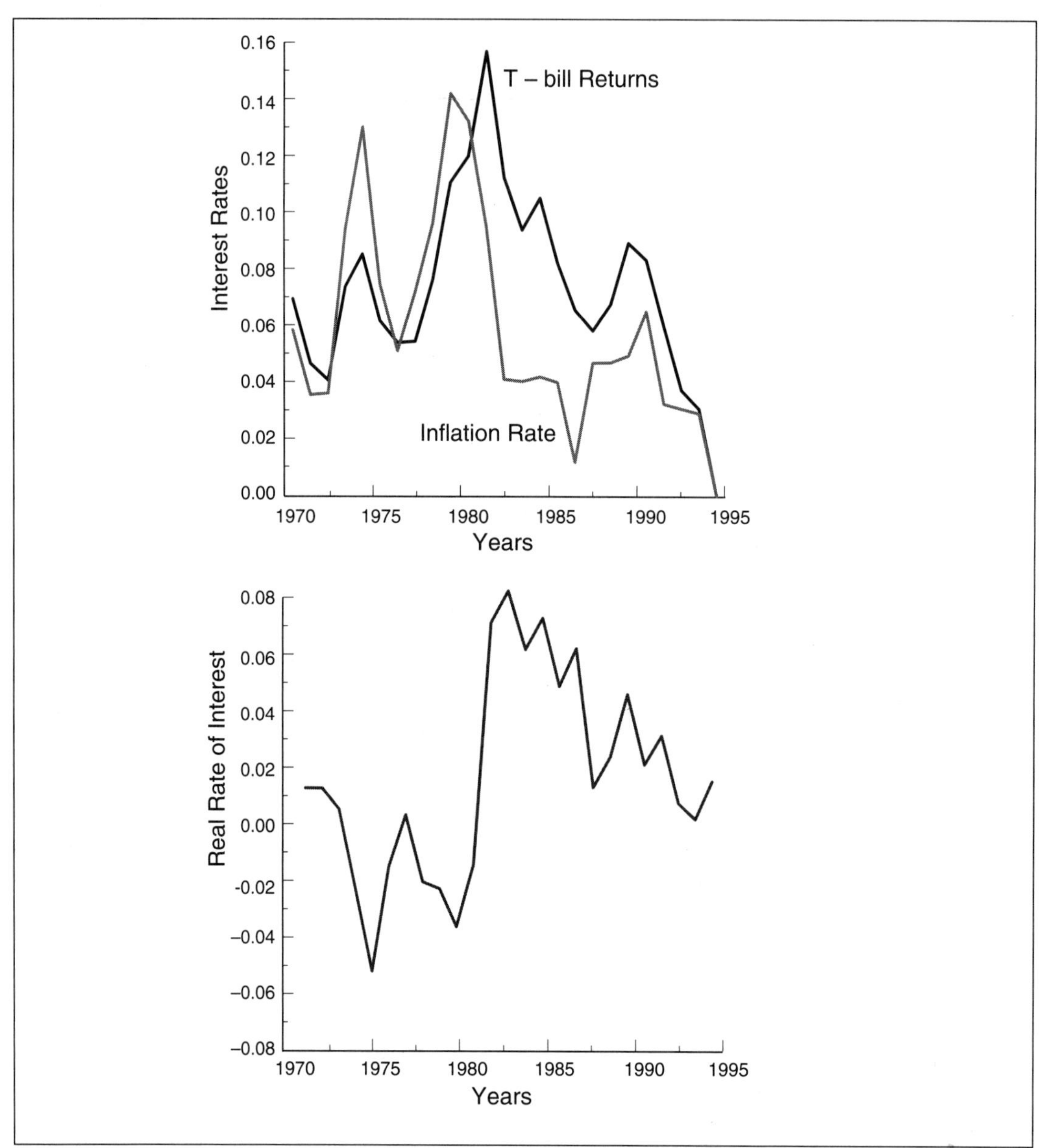

Source: Ibbotson Associates, *Stocks, Bonds, Bills, and Inflation: 1995 Yearbook*, Chicago: Ibbotson Associates,

However, this experience is clearly from the past and reflects actually achieved returns and experienced inflation rates. We must emphasize that the nominal rate of interest depends on the expected rate of inflation, not the actual rate. Quoted interest rates pertain to investment over some future time period. As such, they cannot depend on the actual inflation rate to be sustained during the investment period, since that is not known. Instead, *expected* inflation is the key component.

The Term Structure of Interest Rates

In 1995, short-term Treasury bills had yields as low as 5.0 percent, while long-term Treasury bonds had yields as high as 8 percent. At first glance, this is very strange. Both have equal backing by the U.S. Treasury, so they have the same level of default risk. In fact, the only essential difference between these two issues is the length of maturity. This difference in yields, due solely to differences in maturities, is described by the yield curve or the term structure of interest rates. Naturally, this gap of 5 percent in yield is of prime importance to the bond portfolio manager. It appears that the portfolio manager should accept the higher yields of the long-term bonds. However, this simple solution is not necessarily correct since it leaves out the important considerations associated with the term structure of interest rates.

The **term structure of interest rates** is the relationship between the term to maturity, or time left until maturity, and the yield to maturity for bonds similar in all respects except their maturities. Since the purpose of yield curve or term structure analysis is to understand the differences in bond yields that arise strictly from differences in maturity, the bonds used in the analysis must be as similar as possible in all other respects. For example, all of the bonds used in a yield curve should be similar in their risk level and should have the same call provisions, sinking-fund characteristics, and tax status.

These requirements for similarities among bonds used in the yield curve analysis are cumbersome because it is difficult to find a pool of bonds that meets all of those conditions. For this reason, it is customary to focus on the term structure of Treasury securities. Treasury securities all have the same level of default risk and tend to be alike in their tax status and other features as well. Also, because Treasury securities are lowest in risk, the Treasury yield curve provides the basic yield curve to which the yields of other securities can be related. For these reasons, this section focuses on the Treasury yield curve, shown in Figure 7.3.

In Figure 7.3, the yield curve has a gentle upward slope; that is, the longer maturity instruments have a somewhat higher yield than short maturity instruments. At other times, the yield curve may take on different shapes. For example, Figure 7.4 shows yield curves for high-grade corporate bonds during this century. Notice the dramatically different shapes. Even within a very short period, violent swings in the shape of the yield curve and in the level of rates can occur. The shape of the yield curve is important because it contains information about the future course of interest rates. Since the future of interest rates is the single most valuable piece of information a bond investor would like to have, understanding the yield curve is extremely important. Developing this understanding of yield curves first requires a knowledge of forward rates.

Forward Rates

Forward rates of interest cover future time periods implied by currently available spot rates. A **spot rate** is a yield prevailing on a bond for immediate purchase. Given a set of spot rates, it is possible to calculate forward rates for any intervening time period.

Figure 7.3
The Treasury Yield Curve

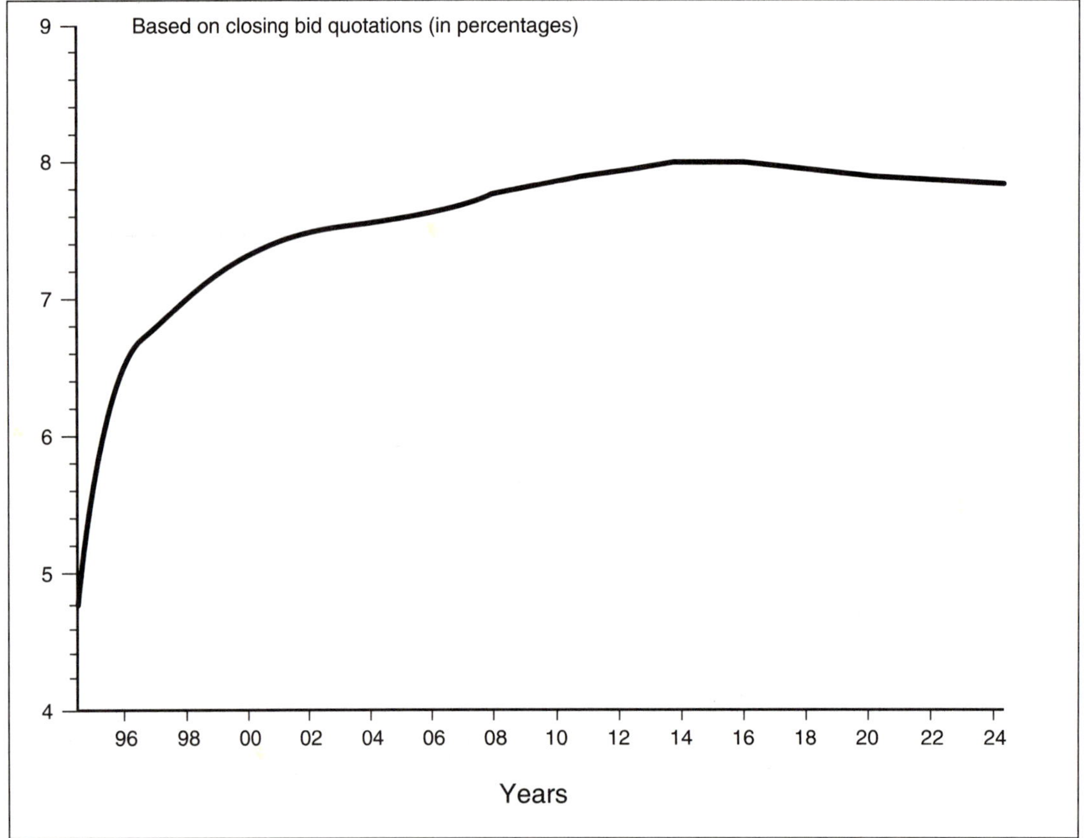

Source: *Treasury Bulletin*, December 1994, p. 66.

For convenience, let us introduce the notation that a bond yield expressed as $r_{x,y}$ is the rate to prevail on a bond for the period beginning at time x and maturing at time y. The present is always time 0, so a bond yield covering any time span beginning at time 0 is a spot rate. For example, $r_{0,5}$ would be the spot rate for an instrument maturing in five years. If the time covered by a particular rate begins after time 0, it is a forward rate. The forward rate to cover a period beginning two years from now and extending three years to time 5 would be expressed as $r_{2,5}$ in our notation. Using this notation, we can now introduce a principle that can be used for the calculation of forward rates.

Principle of Calculation for Forward Rates

Forward rates are calculated on the assumption that returns over a given period of time are all equal, no matter which maturities of bonds are held over that span of time.

Figure 7.4
Historical Yield Curves

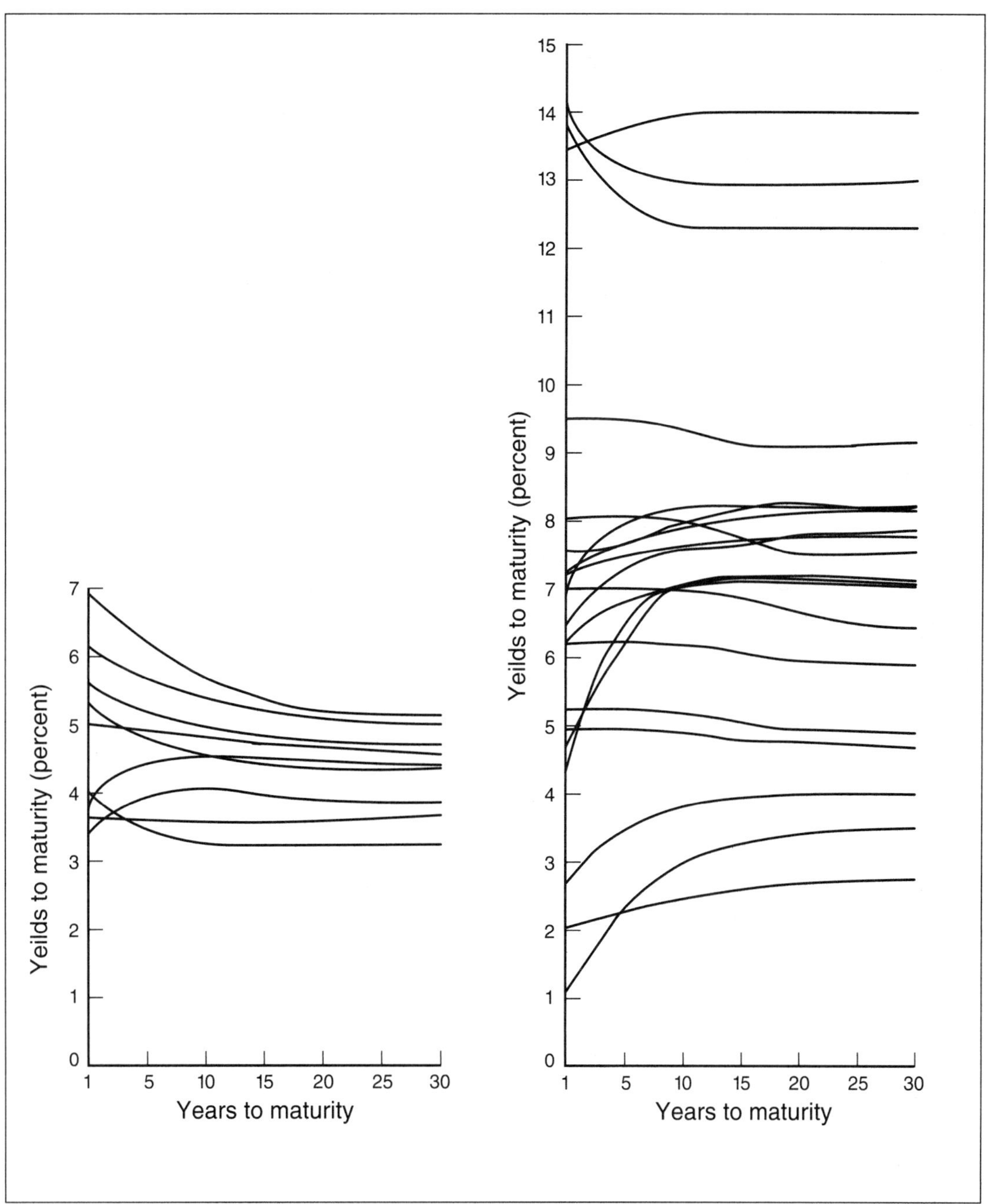

Source: John Wood, "Do Yield Curves Normally Slope Up? The Term Structure of Interest Rates, 1862–1982," *Economic Perspectives*, Federal Reserve Bank of Chicago, July/August 1983, p. 18.

Taking a five-year period as an example, this principle implies that forward rates can be calculated over the five years on the assumption that all of the following strategies would earn the same returns over the five-year period:

1. Buy the five-year bond and hold it to maturity.
2. Buy a one-year bond and when it matures, buy another one-year bond, following this procedure for the entire five years.
3. Buy a two-year bond and when it matures, buy a three-year bond and hold it to maturity.

According to the Principle of Calculation, holding bonds of any maturity over this five-year period would give the same return. Notice that this is not a prediction of returns, but it is an assumption used to calculate forward rates.

In terms of the notation being used in this chapter, we can express these three strategies as follows:

1. Hold one five-year bond for five years
   Total Return = $(1 + r_{0,5})^5$
2. Hold a sequence of one-year bonds
   Total Return = $(1 + r_{0,1})(1 + r_{1,2})(1 + r_{2,3})(1 + r_{3,4})(1 + r_{4,5})$
3. Hold a two-year bond followed by a three-year bond
   Total Return = $(1 + r_{0,2})^2 (1 + r_{2,5})^3$

We can calculate the forward rates appearing in these strategies by applying the Principle of Calculation, which says that those total returns should all be equal:

$$(1 + r_{0,5})^5 = (1 + r_{0,1})(1 + r_{1,2})(1 + r_{2,3})(1 + r_{3,4})(1 + r_{4,5})$$
$$= (1 + r_{0,2})^2 (1 + r_{2,5})^3$$

To apply the Principle of Calculation, consider a situation in which the following yields obtain for Treasury securities of various maturities.

Spot Rate	Yield	Maturity
$r_{0,1}$	.08	1 year
$r_{0,2}$	.088	2 years
$r_{0,3}$	.09	3 years
$r_{0,4}$	.093	4 years
$r_{0,5}$	.095	5 years

These yields are all spot yields and describe an upward-sloping yield curve because the yield increases with the maturity of the bond. These spot rates also imply a set of forward rates to cover periods ranging from time 1 to time 5. An investor with a five-year horizon might hold a five-year bond, with a yield of 9.5 percent. However, there are numerous alternative ways of holding a bond investment over the same time period. As an example of how to calculate forward rates, consider the third strategy in which the investor might hold a two-year bond followed by holding a three-year bond. Right now, at time 0, it is impossible to know what the yield will be on the three-year bond to cover the time period from time 2 to time 5. This rate cannot be known with certainty until time 2 actually arrives. At time 0, however, it is possible to calculate a forward rate to cover the time span from time 2 to time 5. As shown earlier, the Principle of Calculation implies:

$$(1 + r_{0,5})^5 = (1 + r_{0,2})^2 (1 + r_{2,5})^3$$

Using the spot rates given above:

$$1.095^5 = 1.088^2 (1 + r_{2,5})^3$$

Now the only unknown is the forward rate, so the equation can be solved for its value:

$$1.5742 = 1.1837 (1 + r_{2,5})^3$$

$$1.5742/1.1837 = (1 + r_{2,5})^3$$

$$(1 + r_{2,5}) = \sqrt[3]{\frac{1.5742}{1.1837}} = 1.0997$$

$$r_{2,5} = .0997 = 9.97\%$$

The forward rate, implied by this set of spot rates, to cover the period from year 2 to year 5, is 9.97 percent. Given the relevant spot rates, it is possible to calculate any forward rate. For the five years of this example, all intervening forward rates can be calculated with the data supplied. Notice that nothing has been said so far about how the forward rates are to be interpreted. Different theories of the term structure interpret forward rates in somewhat different ways. However, all of the theories that use forward rates to understand the term structure agree that forward rates give important information about the future course of interest rates.

Theories of the Term Structure

Three theories of the term structure have received the greatest attention. They are the pure expectations theory, the liquidity premium theory, and the market segmentation theory. This section considers these theories in detail. The pure expectations theory and the liquidity premium theory both use forward rates as a key element, and both theories can be stated by their interpretation of forward rates.

The Pure Expectations Theory

The **pure expectations theory** states that:

> Forward rates are unbiased estimators of future interest rates.
> *or*
> Forward Rates = Expected Future Spot Rates

An unbiased estimator is one whose expected value equals the true value of the parameter being estimated. In somewhat more straightforward language, the pure expectations theory claims that today's forward rate equals the expected future spot rate for the period corresponding to the forward rate. In terms of the previous example, where it was calculated that the forward rate for a three-period bond to cover from time 2 to time 5 was 9.97 percent, the pure expectations theory would say that 9.97 percent is a good estimate of the spot rate that will prevail on a three-year bond beginning two years from now. The actual rate that occurs may be higher or lower than 9.97 percent, but on average, the forward rate will equal the subsequently observed spot rate.

This theory has strong practical implications. If it is true, the observable term structure contains predictions of future interest rates. Why should anyone believe this theory? Its defenders explain it this way. The bond market is well developed and populated with many participants having different wealth levels and different preferences. There are many people in the bond market who do not have any particular preference about the maturity of instruments that they hold. In the absence of any strong maturity preference, these investors seek the best rate of return. So, assume for the moment that the expected total return for a five-year investment in Treasury securities is greater if we held a 5-year bond for five years, rather than hold a two-year bond followed by a three-year bond. These investors, without strong maturity preferences, would prefer the five-year bond. Anyone holding the two-year bond would sell it in order to invest the funds in the better-performing five-year bond.

As the two-year bonds were sold in order to buy five-year bonds, there would be strong price effects on both bonds. The price of the two-year bond would fall, and the price of the five-year bond would rise. These investors would stop switching from the two-year to the five-year bond only when the expected returns from the two strategies were equal, eliminating any incentive to switch from one to the other. According to the pure expectations theory, there are many bond investors who will switch their funds to any maturity with a higher yield. However, the willingness of these investors to hold whichever maturity has higher expected returns means that all maturity strategies must have the same expected return in equilibrium. In other words, after all of the maturity switching has stopped and an equilibrium has been achieved, there must be an equal expected return for any investment period, no matter what maturities of instruments are held over that period.

Now we can see how the pure expectations theory ties together forward rates and expected future spot rates. In the previous example, the investor in the five-year bond yielding 9.5 percent is expecting to earn 9.5 percent per year over the five-year period. According to the pure expectations theory, an investor with a five-year horizon holding a two-year bond and planning to follow that by holding a three-year bond must expect to earn the same 9.5 percent annual return over the entire period. However, the yield to maturity on the two-year bond is only 7.8 percent. The investor who earns 7.8 percent for the first two years of a five-year holding period must earn much more in the last three years to have a 9.5 percent rate of return over the whole period.

One dollar invested for five years at 9.5 percent will be worth $1.57 at the end of the period. If the investor planning to hold the two-year bond at 7.8 percent followed by a three-year bond wants to earn the same rate of return, he or she must experience a higher yield on the three-year bond. In fact, the expected rate of return on the three-year bond must be sufficient so that the returns from the two maturity strategies give the same final wealth for equal investments. It must be that:

$$1.095^5 = 1.088^2\,(1 + x)^3$$

where x equals the expected yield on the three-year bond to cover the period from time 2 to time 5. What then is the value of x? Solving this equation for x gives:

$$1.5742 = 1.1837(1 + x)^3$$
$$(1 + x)^3 = 1.5742/1.1837$$
$$(1 + x) = \sqrt[3]{\frac{1.5742}{1.1837}}$$
$$x = 9.97\%$$

Notice that this expected interest rate for the three-year bond exactly equals the forward rate for the same bond previously calculated. This is the crux of the argument for the pure expectations theory. If expected returns from all maturity strategies are equal, forward rates must necessarily equal expected future spot rates. The equality of forward rates and expected future spot rates follows logically from the view that all maturity strategies have the same expected return over any given holding period. If there are enough investors who do not care about the maturity of the instruments they hold and merely seek the highest expected return, they will ensure that all different maturity strategies have the same expected return, and they will force the major conclusion of the pure expectations theory to be true, namely, that forward rates equal expected future spot rates. Ultimately, the truth of the pure expectations theory depends upon the presence of bond investors who are indifferent to the maturities of the bonds they hold and who seek the greatest expected returns.

The Liquidity Premium Theory

In many ways, the liquidity premium theory resembles the pure expectations theory. At least, both theories see the problem in very similar terms. The **liquidity premium theory** can also be stated by reference to forward rates:

Forward rates are upwardly biased estimators of expected future spot rates; that is, the estimates are too high.

or

Forward Rates > Expected Future Spot Rates

The liquidity premium theorists acknowledge the pure expectations theory claim that if enough bond investors care only about returns, they will trade to ensure that all maturity strategies over a given time span have the same expected return. However, they reject the claim that there are numerous investors who are indifferent about the maturities of the bonds they hold.

The defenders of the liquidity premium theory assert that bondholders greatly prefer to hold short-term bonds rather than long-term bonds. The short-term bonds have less interest rate risk. As explained in Chapter 14, the shorter the maturity, the less interest rate risk there will be. The fact that prices of short-term bonds will not change dramatically when interest rates change makes them more attractive than long-term bonds to many investors. According to the liquidity premium theory, short-term bonds are so much more attractive than long-term bonds that investors are willing to pay more for short-term bonds than for long-term bonds. This extra amount they are willing to pay is the **liquidity premium**.

The willingness of investors to pay a liquidity premium for the short-term bonds also implies that yields on short-term bonds will be lower than the yields on long-term bonds, other things being equal. Another way of saying the same thing is to notice that long-term bonds must pay a greater return than short-term bonds to induce investors to commit their funds to the long-term instruments.

If yields on short-term instruments are normally lower than those on long-term bonds, total returns from investing in short maturities will be less than the total return from investing in long maturities, even when the two strategies cover the identical time interval. For example, assume that a five-year bond must pay 1/10 of 1 percent greater yield than a one-year bond because of investor preferences for short-term securities. Using the values of our continuing example, the five-year bond returns 9.5 percent over its life. With a 1/10 of 1 percent higher yield per annum for the five-year over the one-year instrument, the strategy of holding five one-year bonds in succession must return only 9.4 percent over the five-year period. The one-year spot instrument has a yield of 8 percent. So the yield on the four following one-year bonds must be such that the average annual yield on the strategy of holding the one-year bonds turns out to be 9.4 percent:

$$(1.094)^5 = (1.08)(1 + x)^4$$
$$x = 9.753\%$$

If the total realized return over the five-year period is to be 9.4 percent per year from the strategy of holding one-year bonds, the expected average return per year for years two through five must be 9.753 percent.[4] The forward rate $r_{1,5}$ can be calculated as well:

$$(1 + r_{0,5})^5 = (1 + r_{0,1})(1 + r_{1,5})^4$$
$$(1.095)^5 = (1.08)(1 + r_{1,5})^4$$
$$(1 + r_{1,5}) = \sqrt[4]{\frac{1.5742}{1.08}}$$
$$r_{1,5} = 9.88\%$$

---

[4] Here it is not possible to say what the expected rate for each of the one-year bonds would be. But the geometric average of these returns must be 9.753 percent. Fortunately, that is enough for the present purpose.

According to the key claim of the liquidity premium theory, the expected rate of return on a succession of one-year bonds must be less than the expected rate of return on a long-term bond when the two maturity strategies are pursued over the same time. The returns would differ by the amount of the liquidity premium, other things being equal. In this example, the assumed yield differential between the five-year and the one-year bonds, caused by the liquidity premium, was 1/10 of 1 percent. This implied that the expected rate of return on the one-year bonds covering the last four of the five years was 9.753 percent. However, the forward rate for the same 4-year period was 9.88 percent.

Notice that this result is exactly consistent with the claims of the liquidity premium theory. The forward rate (9.88 percent) is greater than the expected rate (9.753 percent) over this four-year period. If the liquidity premium theory is correct, using forward rates to estimate future spot rates of interest gives estimates that are too high due to the presence of the liquidity premium.

Both the pure expectations and liquidity premium theories are rigorous and follow logically from their respective beliefs about the preferences and behavior of bond market participants. The basic disagreement between the two theories turns on whether bondholders prefer short-term instruments to long-term instruments.

The Market Segmentation Theory

Unlike the pure expectations theory and the liquidity premium theory, the market segmentation theory is not expressly stated in terms of forward rates. Rather, the **market segmentation theory** takes a more institutional approach. According to this theory, the yield curve reflects the actions and preferences of certain major participants in the bond market. To a large extent, the bond market is dominated by large financial institutions, with each kind of institution having strong maturity preferences stemming from the kind of business it pursues. Commercial banks, for example, have relatively short-term liabilities in the form of demand deposits and certificates of deposit (CDs). As a consequence, they prefer to invest in relatively short-term bonds.[5] Life insurance companies, by contrast, have their liabilities falling due far in the future upon the death of policyholders. Correspondingly, life insurance companies prefer long-term bonds. Casualty insurers, such as those writing auto and home insurance, have liabilities that fall due in the medium term and, therefore, favor medium-maturity bonds for their investments.

These preferences of different types of financial institutions stem from the nature of their businesses and a desire to match the maturity of their assets and liabilities in order to control risk. Because of these preferences, the institutions tend to trade bonds only in their respective maturity ranges. For example, to induce a bank to invest in long-term bonds, the bonds must pay an attractively higher yield in comparison to the short-term bonds that banks prefer for business reasons. The desire of these different institutions to participate only in certain maturity segments of the bond market leads directly to the segmented markets hypothesis:

> *The yield curve is determined by the interplay of supply and demand factors in different segments of the maturity spectrum of the bond market. Financial institutions with strong matu-*

---

[5] The reasons for these kinds of preferences are explained in Chapter 17.

rity preferences occupy those different segments and effectively cause the bond market to splinter into separate market segments based on maturity.

These preferences for certain maturity ranges, it must be stressed, are not absolute. If the institutions dominated the bond market and never left their preferred maturity habitats, it might even be possible to observe a discontinuous yield curve, such as that shown in Figure 7.5. However, according to the market segmentation theory (also known as the preferred habitat theory), the institutions have preferred maturity ranges, but the preference is not absolute. In a situation such as that in Figure 7.5, the casualty insurers could make themselves much better off by taking a slightly shorter maturity than their current shortest maturity and taking a slightly longer maturity than their current longest maturity. In both cases, the yields on those bonds would increase. In fact, this is clearly what bond market participants would do in such a case. As a consequence, a discontinuous yield curve is not found in the actual market.

How the Three Theories Explain Different Observed Yield Curves

To understand these three theories of the term structure, it is important to realize that each theory is capable of explaining any observed market yield curve. For example, if the yield curve slopes upward, the forward rates increase as they go further into the future. According to the pure expectations theory, this means that short-term interest rates are expected to rise. With a flat yield curve, all forward rates equal the current short-term spot rate, so the pure expectations theory interprets this as the market's belief that interest rates will remain constant. For a downward-sloping yield curve, the pure expectations theory stresses the fact that forward rates will be smaller the farther they are in the future and interprets this as the market's belief that short-term interest rates are expected to fall.

Figure 7.5
An Extreme Case of a Segmented Bond Market

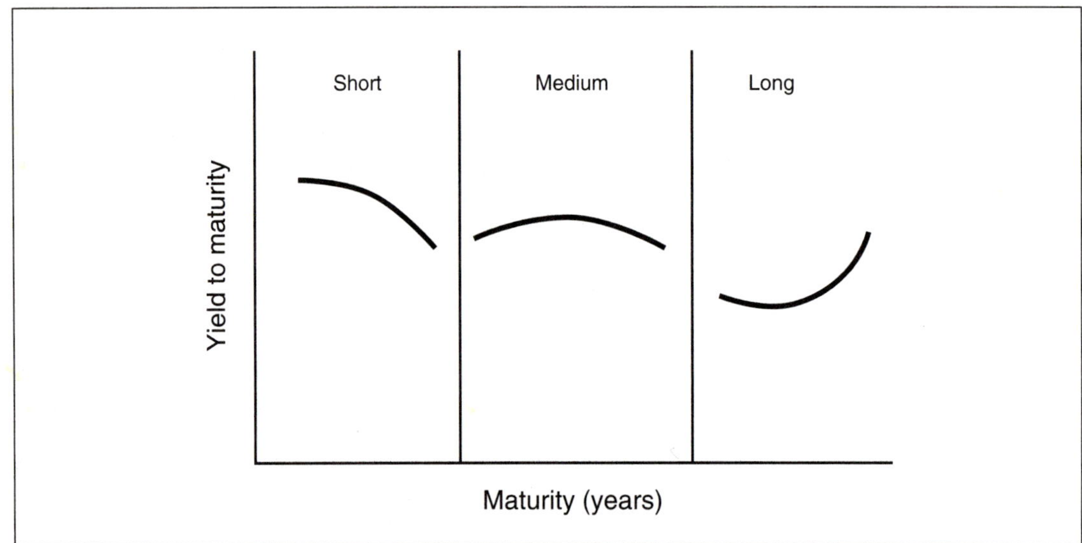

The liquidity premium theory can explain any observed yield curve with equal facility, but the liquidity premium makes the explanation more complicated. To see the effect of the liquidity premium, assume the market expects short-term interest rates to be constant forever. The liquidity premium would then force a long-term bond to pay a higher yield. According to the liquidity premium theory, this means that the yield curve will be sloping slightly upward even when short-term rates are expected to remain constant. The tendency for the yield curve to slope upward would be due strictly to the impact of the liquidity premium. This situation is shown in Figure 7.6. The dotted line in the figure is at the level of the constant expected short-term interest rates. Nonetheless, the yield curve slopes upward because of the liquidity premium. For this reason, many people believe that an upward sloping yield curve, such as that shown in Figure 7.6, is the normal shape of the yield curve.

The liquidity premium theory cites two factors favoring a strongly upward-sloping yield curve: the impact of the liquidity premium and the market's expectation of higher interest rates (see Figure 7.7). The dotted line indicates where the yield curve would be with just a liquidity premium and no expectation of higher rates in the future. The liquidity premium always makes the observed yield curve more strongly upward-sloping than it would be otherwise. The actual yield curve lies above the dotted line because interest rates are also expected to rise in this example.

For a downward-sloping yield curve, the liquidity premium theory argues that interest rates are expected to fall by an amount greater than the effect of the liquidity premium. The liquidity premium always has the effect of making the yield curve slope upward more than it otherwise would. An observed downward slope indicates that the market must be expecting a drop in interest rates sufficiently large to offset the effect of the liquidity premium.

The market segmentation hypothesis explains all observed yield curve shapes as resulting from the supply and demand factors in each segment of the bond market. According to this view,

Figure 7.6
The Yield Curve with Equal Expected Future Short-Term Rates According to the Liquidity Premium Theory

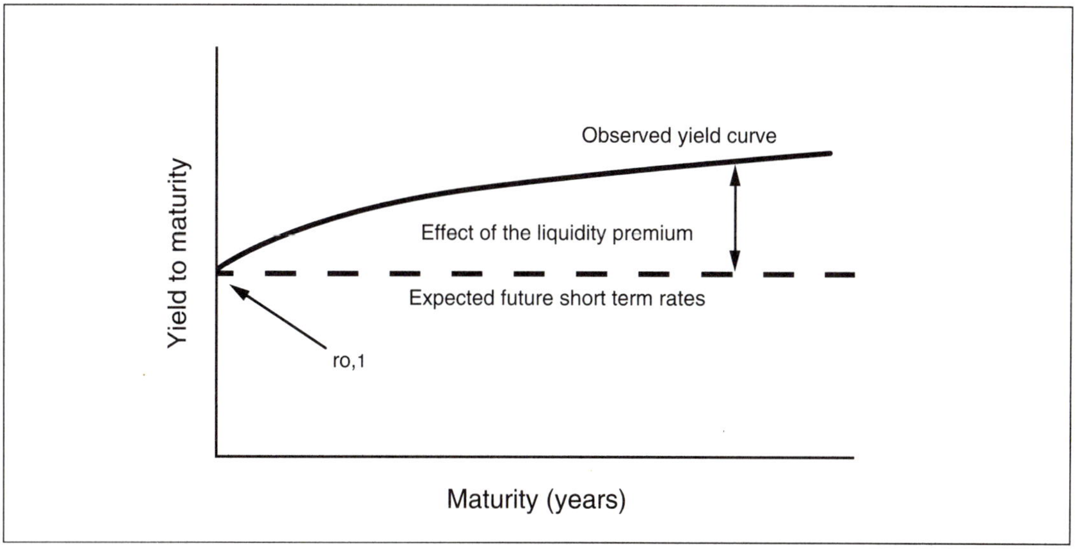

Figure 7.7
The Liquidity Premium Theory's Explanation of a Yield Curve with a Strong Upward Slope

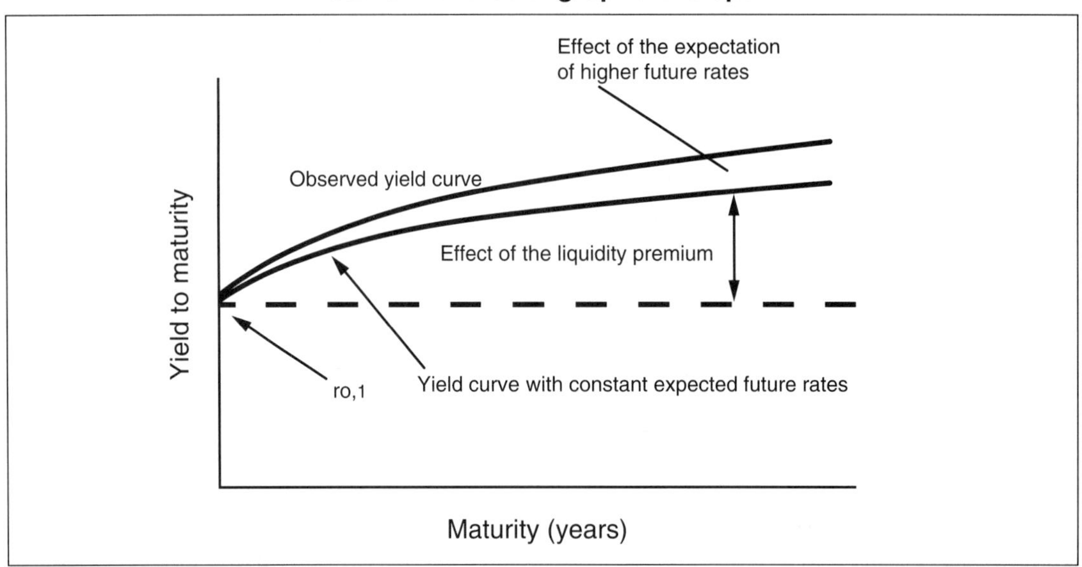

expectations are also important, but the emphasis is on the interest and maturity preferences of the different institutional participants.

Evidence on the Three Theories

The competing theories of the term structure have given rise to many attempts to determine which theory is correct. Not surprisingly, the issue is still not fully determined. In spite of some evidence in support of the market segmentation theory, there does seem to be a consensus that it alone cannot explain the yield curve.[6] As a consequence, the real struggle is between the pure expectations theory and the liquidity premium theory.

Meiselman and Santomero both find empirical evidence supporting the pure expectations hypothesis.[7] Opposed to these results is research by Nelson and McCulloch.[8] McCulloch finds a

---

[6] The market segmentation theory was first advanced by Franco Modigliani and Richard Sutch, "Innovations in Interest Rate Policy," *American Economic Review*, May 1966. Empirical support for the theory can be found in Edward J. Kane and Burton G. Malkiel, "The Term Structure of Interest Rates: An Analysis of a Survey of Interest Rate Expectations," *Review of Economics and Statistics*, August 1967; Wayne Lee, Terry Maness, and Donald Tuttle, "Nonspeculative Behavior and the Term Structure," *Journal of Financial and Quantitative Analysis*, March 1980; and J. W. Elliot and M. E. Echols, "Market Segmentation, Speculative Behavior, and the Term Structure of Interest Rates," *Review of Economics and Statistics*, February 1976.

[7] David Meiselman, *The Term Structure of Interest Rates*, Englewood Cliffs, NJ: Prentice Hall, 1962; Anthony M. Santomero, "The Error Learning Hypothesis and the Term Structure of Interest Rates in Eurodollars," *Journal of Finance*, June 1975.

[8] Charles Nelson, "Estimation of Term Premiums from Average Yield Differentials in the Term Structure of Interest Rates," *Econometrica*, March 1972; J. Huston McCulloch, "An Estimate of the Liquidity Premium," *Journal of Political Economy*, February 1975.

definite, but small, liquidity premium and also finds that virtually all of this premium is confined to very short maturities of about one year or less. Froot finds that the expectations hypothesis has little merit for short-term rates, but that it works well for long-term rates.[9] Cook and Hahn find limited support for the expectations hypothesis as well, although they regard the expectations contained in the term structure to be not very accurate forecasts of future interest rates.[10]

While the different theories of the term structure are sure to survive and to attract more research, it is important not to be misled by minor differences of opinion when there is major agreement. Most theorists would agree on the fundamental proposition that the shape of the yield curve expresses the market's opinion about future interest rates. In general, an upward-sloping yield curve implies that rates are expected to rise; a downward-sloping yield curve implies that rates are expected to fall. Further, if a liquidity premium does exist, it is not very large, so forward rates still provide a very good guide to the market's expectation of future interest rates. In fact, the forward rates of interest often provide better forecasts of future interest rates than professional forecasting services.

The Risk Structure of Interest Rates

Just as there is a term structure, there is also a risk structure of interest rates. The risk structure of interest rates analyzes the differences in risk among different classes of bonds. Since it focuses only on risk differences, the risk structure holds constant other factors affecting yield, such as maturity, callability, mortgage features, sinking funds, and the other important institutional features of bonds.

For two classes of bonds differing only in their risk level, the yield difference that results from a difference in risk is called a **yield differential**, **yield spread**, or **risk differential**. The yield spread can be observed between any two classes of bonds that differ in their risk level. Figure 7.8 presents a graph of the risk structure of interest rates over the recent past for different classes of long-term bonds. In Figure 7.8, it is possible to examine the risk structure of interest rates using U.S. government bonds and Moody's Aaa and Baa Corporate Bond indexes. These different classes of bonds are similar in tax status, maturity, and other features, but differ in their risk levels. Treasury bonds have the lowest risk and pay the lowest rate of return.

In comparing risk-free Treasury bonds and risky corporate bonds, the yield differential is also known as the **risk premium**. While the rate of return on Treasury bonds is always less than that for corporate bonds, the size of the yield differential varies dramatically over time. In the early 1930s, for example, the risk premium suddenly became very large. In other periods, such as the late 1950s, the risk premium for Aaa bonds was almost zero. For an investor, an understanding of these risk premiums and the way in which they fluctuate can be very important. For an aggressive investor, the greater risk premium that is sometimes available might be a good reason to hold riskier bonds.

---

[9] K. A. Froot, "New Hope for the Expectations Hypothesis of the Term Structure of Interest Rates," *Journal of Finance*, 44:2, June 1989, pp. 283–305.

[10] T. Cook and T. Hahn, "Interest Rate Expectations and the Slope of the Money Market Yield Curve," *Economic Review*, Federal Reserve Bank of Richmond, 76:5, September/October 1990, pp. 3–26.

Figure 7.8
The Risk Structure of Interest Rates

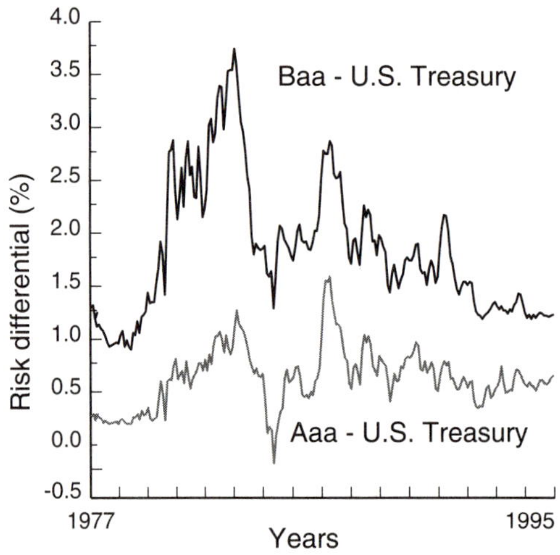

Source: *Federal Reserve Bulletin* various issues.

Determinants of the Risk Premium

Certain relationships between the risk premium and other economic variables are important in understanding why the risk premium behaves as it does. One of the largest risk premiums in U.S. history occurred in the early 1930s when the Great Depression was at its worst. In times of economic prosperity, the risk premium tends to be much smaller. For example, in the boom year of 1984, the risk premium for Aaa corporate bonds almost vanished, as Figure 7.8 shows. Clearly, the risk premium varies inversely with the business cycle. Yield spreads are large in recessions and small in booms, other things being equal.[11] In times of economic hardship, weaker companies move much closer, relatively speaking, to the brink of disaster than do the firms issuing high-quality bonds. In times of prosperity, even the weaker companies can survive with relative ease. Accordingly, the risk premium should be larger the worse the general economic conditions.

Other factors seem to be of potential importance in explaining the risk structure of interest rates, but there is little conclusive evidence on the significance of the other factors. The level of interest rates appears to have some importance. In general, when interest rates are high, risk premiums tend to be large. The maturity of the instruments seems to have some bearing on the yield spread as well. The evidence on the importance of the maturity of particular bonds on the yield

---

[11] This observation has been formally substantiated by a number of studies. See, for example: Calvin M. Boardman and Richard W. McEnally, "Factors Affecting Seasoned Corporate Bond Prices," *Journal of Financial and Quantitative Analysis*, 16:2, 1981, pp. 207–26; Dwight M. Jaffee, "Cyclical Variation in the Risk Structure of Interest Rates," *Journal of Monetary Economics*, 1, 1975, pp. 309–25; and David S. Kidwell and Timothy W. Koch, "The Behavior of the Interest Rate Differential Between Tax-Exempt Revenue and General Obligation Bonds: A Test of Risk Preferences and Market Segmentation," *Journal of Finance*, March 1982, pp. 73–85.

spread is somewhat mixed, but it tends to support the view that the longer the maturity of the bond, the greater the yield spread.[12] Also, there is evidence that the marketability of the particular bond issue affects the size of the risk premium.[13] While the risk premium seems to be sensitive to all of these factors – business conditions, maturity, marketability, and the level of interest rates – the size of the risk premium is itself a gauge of another more important factor. The risk premium essentially measures the risk of default.

The Risk Premium as a Measure of Default Risk

The greater the chance of default, the larger is the risk premium that a bond must pay to attract investors. The main reason that the risk premium seems to be so closely related to the business cycle is that the chance of default is much greater in periods of economic distress. If the marketability of a bond issue helps to keep a bond's risk premium smaller, it is because a risky (but highly marketable) bond can be sold more easily before default in comparison with a less marketable bond.

The bond rating services, such as Moody's and Standard & Poor's, attempt to summarize all factors that affect default risk and determine the risk premium in their bond ratings. As Figure 7.8 shows, low-rated bonds tend to have greater risk premiums than high-rated bonds. In fact, historical default experience matches the ratings very closely. Table 7.1 summarizes some results of

Table 7.1
Default Experience for Corporate Bonds

Rating Category	Comparable S&P Rating	Percent Defaulting
I	AAA	6
II	AAA	6
III	AAA	13
IV	BBB	19
V—IX	below BBB	42

Source: W. B. Hickman, *Corporate Bond Quality and Investor Experience*, Princeton University Press, 1985, as cited in Robert C. Radcliffe, *Investment: Concepts, Analysis, and Strategy*, Glenview, IL: Scott, Foresman, 1987, p. 234.

---

[12] The impact of the maturity has been assessed by a number of authors who have reached different conclusions. Lawrence Fisher, "Determinants of Risk Premiums on Corporate Bonds," *The Journal of Political Economy*, June 1959, pp. 217–37; Ramon E. Johnson, "Term Structure of Corporate Bond Yields as a Function of Risk of Default," *Journal of Finance*, May 1967, pp. 313–45; Thomas H. McInish, "Behavior of Municipal Bond Default-Risk Premiums by Maturity," *Journal of Business Research*, 8, 1980, pp. 413–18; Roland T. Robinson, *Postwar Market for State and Local Government Securities*, National Bureau of Economic Research, New York, 1960, pp. 184–8; and James C. Van Horne, "Behavior of Default-Risk Premiums for Corporate Bonds and Commercial Paper," *Journal of Business Research*, 7, December 1979, pp. 310–13.

[13] Lawrence Fisher, "Determinants of Risk Premiums on Corporate Bonds," *The Journal of Political Economy*, June 1959, pp. 217–37 and Calvin M. Boardman and Richard W. McEnally, "Factors Affecting Seasoned Corporate Bond Prices," *Journal of Financial and Quantitative Analysis*, 16:2, 1981, pp. 207–26.

a study by W. B. Hickman, who examined the default experience of all corporate bonds issued between 1900 and 1943, grouping the bonds by their ratings.[14] Figure 7.9 provides more recent evidence on default rates, covering the period 1970–90. It shows the percentage of speculative grade bonds defaulting for each year. Specifically, for bonds with a speculative rating at the beginning of a year, it shows the proportion that defaulted within that year. (A speculative grade bond has a Moody's rating of Ba or lower.) As the graph shows, 1970 and 1990 were the worst years, with default rates around 9–11 percent.

When a bond is issued it receives an initial rating. Later, Moody's or Standard & Poor's might change their rating. Figure 7.10 shows the default experience for bonds within one year of their issuance, with the defaults being categorized by the original rating. Thus, as the figure shows, there were no defaults among Aaa rated bonds in the first year, while 7.08 percent of B rated bonds defaulted in the first year. Figure 7.11 shows the default experience for bonds within their first ten years of life. Of bonds that received an initial rate of Aaa, only 0.37 percent had defaulted within ten years. By contrast, 24.17 percent of bonds with an initial rating of B had defaulted within ten years.

Earlier we noted that yields tend to match the ratings very closely. This fact, along with Hickman's evidence, shows very clearly that the risk premium is a good indicator of default risk. This is only appropriate, because as an investor accepts riskier bonds to capture greater expected returns, he or she also must accept a greater chance of default risk. Choosing the appropriate level of default risk is one of the chief decisions that a bond investor must make. The decision turns on

Figure 7.9
One-Year Speculative Grade Default Rates

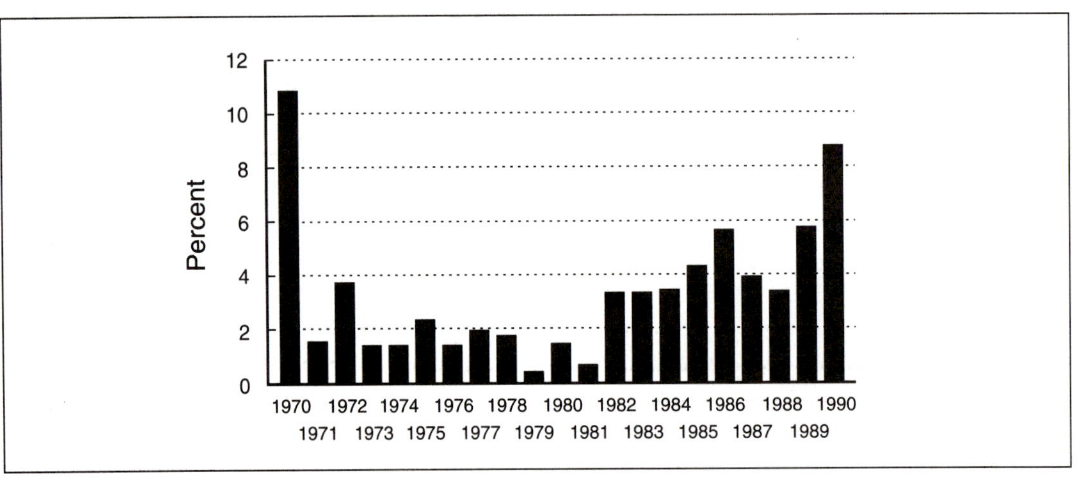

Source: Fons, J. S. and A. E. Kimball, "Corporate Bond Defaults and Default Rates 1970–1990," *The Journal of Fixed Income*, 1:1, June 1991, pp. 36–47.

---

[14] See W. B. Hickman, *Corporate Bond Quality and Investor Experience*, Princeton, NJ: Princeton University Press, 1958.

Figure 7.10
One-Year Default Rates for Various Grades of Bonds

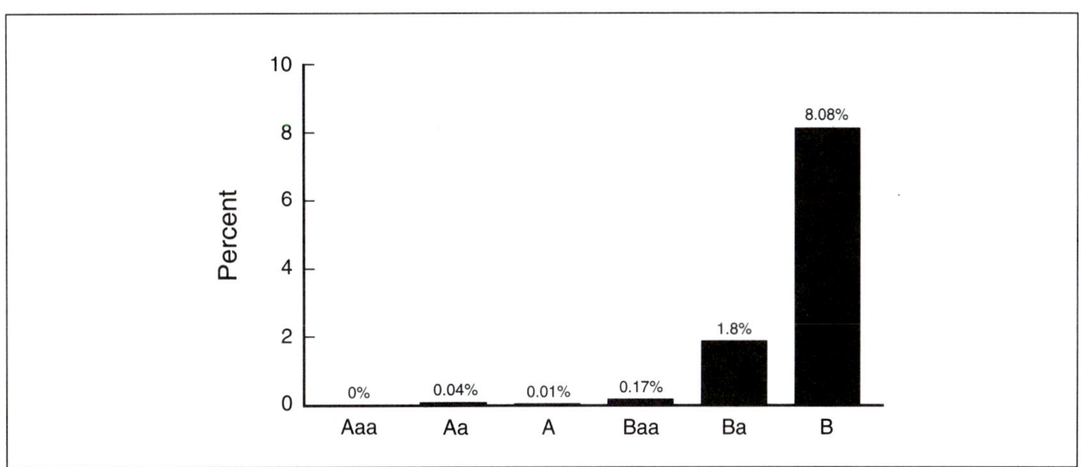

Source: Fons, J. S. and A. E. Kimball, "Corporate Bond Defaults and Default Rates 1970–1990," *The Journal of Fixed Income*, 1:1, June 1991, pp. 36–47.

the investor's tolerance of risk. While it is not possible to specify a general rule for how much default risk should be undertaken, it is clear that the promised return will increase with greater default risk.

Bond Portfolio Maturity Strategies

In discussing the term structure, we saw that the choice of maturities is a very important issue for any bondholder. When numerous bonds are held in a portfolio, there will be some average maturity of the portfolio. Even after the average maturity for the portfolio is chosen, there is still another important investment decision that concerns the maturity structure of the bond portfolio.[15] The maturity structure of the portfolio concerns the way in which funds are allocated to bonds of differing maturities. Depending on the technique chosen, the bond portfolio manager can make the portfolio easy to administer, or the manager can choose maturities to allow dramatic changes in the interest rate sensitivity of the portfolio.

There are two basic approaches, one called the **laddered strategy** and the other the **dumbbell strategy** or **barbell strategy**. Each has its own advantages and disadvantages. In the laddered strategy, funds in the bond portfolio are distributed approximately evenly over the range of maturities. This approach is shown graphically in Figure 7.12. (The name of the laddered strategy comes from the fact that funds are evenly distributed across the maturity range, just as the rungs of a ladder are evenly spaced.) The main advantage of the laddered strategy is ease of management. Each year, the short-term bonds mature, and the funds provided from this source are committed

---

[15] The ideas of this section may be stated with respect to both maturity and duration. Because duration is discussed in Chapter 17, the focus here is on maturity.

Figure 7.11
Ten-Year Default Rates for Various Grades of Bonds

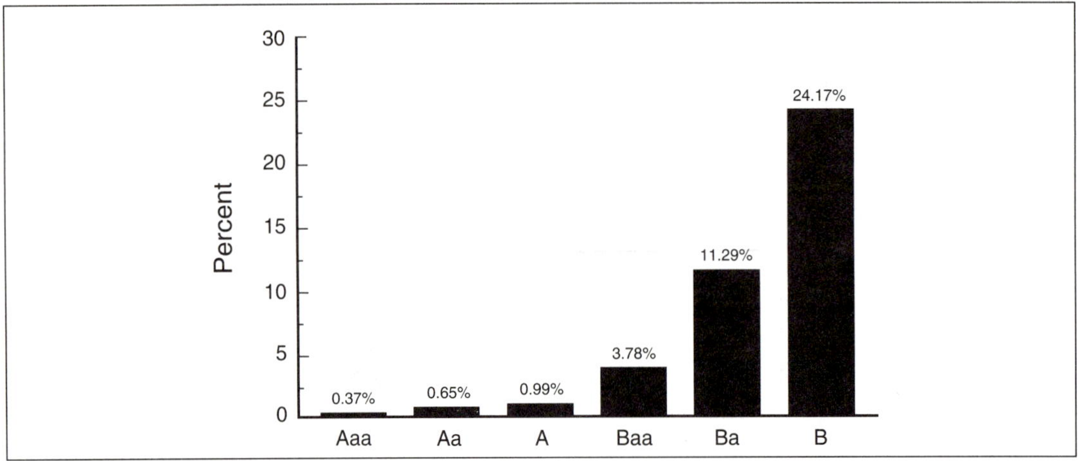

Source: Fons, J. S. and A. E. Kimball, "Corporate Bond Defaults and Default Rates 1970–1990," *The Journal of Fixed Income*, 1:1, June 1991, pp. 36–47.

to long-term bonds. Thus, it is very easy to maintain the same kind of maturity distribution with very low transaction costs.

The disadvantage of the laddered approach is the difficulty in changing the maturity composition of the portfolio. Aggressive bond portfolio managers sometimes wish to change the maturity structure of a bond portfolio to take advantage of anticipated shifts in yields. (Recall the bond pricing principles from Chapter 4, which noted that a drop in yields would cause an increase in bond prices and that the effect of a given drop in yields would be greater the longer the maturity of a particular bond, other factors being equal.) With that principle in mind, if a bond manager believes interest rates will soon drop by a large amount, he or she might wish to lengthen the average maturity of the portfolio to get a bigger effect when the drop in yields causes an increase in the price of bonds. With the laddered strategy, it is difficult to have a major effect on the portfolio's maturity without trading many bonds. To lengthen the average maturity of the portfolio, the manager would sell bonds with the shortest maturities and invest the funds in the bonds with the longest maturities. However, with all of the maturities receiving roughly equal investment, there will be too few short-term bonds to sell to have a major effect on the average maturity of the portfolio. After the short-maturity bonds are exhausted, the manager would sell medium-maturity bonds and use the proceeds to buy long-maturity bonds. But shifting funds from medium- to long-maturity bonds has relatively little effect on the average maturity of the portfolio. As a consequence, the laddered portfolio strategy makes it more difficult to shift the portfolio's maturity structure by large amounts.

With the dumbbell approach, the funds in the bond portfolio are divided between short-maturity and very long-maturity bonds. This distribution of maturities is shown graphically in Figure 7.13. As the graph shows, the shape of the maturities looks like a dumbbell, with the bells being the bulges of funds in the short and long maturities and the bar being formed by the virtu-

Figure 7.12
The Laddered Maturity Strategy for a Bond Portfolio

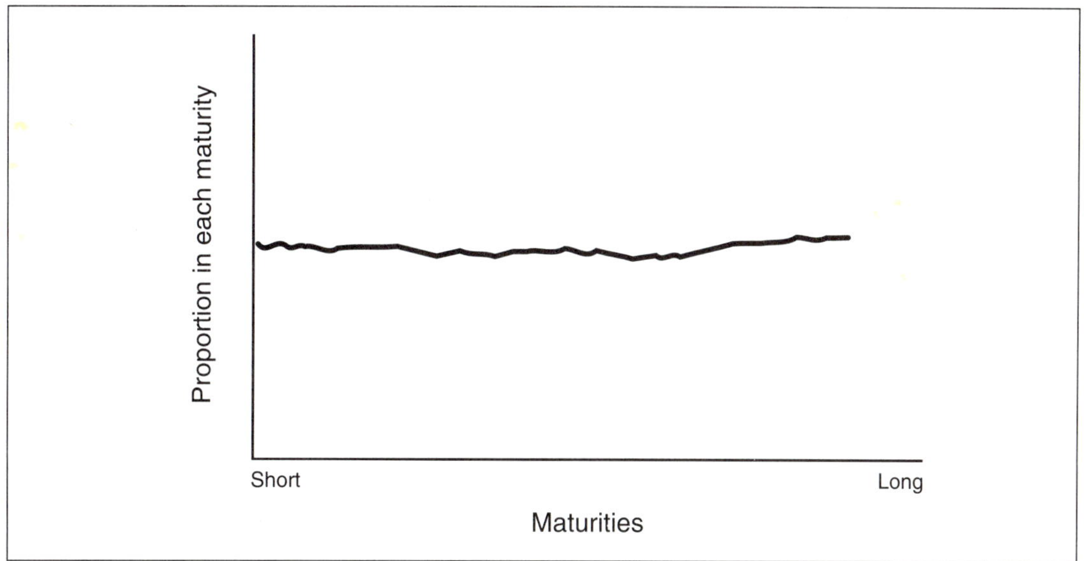

ally vacant middle-maturity range. The active bond manager using the dumbbell strategy can easily shorten or lengthen the maturity structure of the portfolio because funds can be shifted between very short and very long maturities, respectively.

The dumbbell approach has its disadvantages, however. In many ways, the dumbbell strategy is like having two portfolios – one with very long maturities and one with very short maturities,

Figure 7.13
The Dumbbell Maturity Strategy for a Bond Portfolio

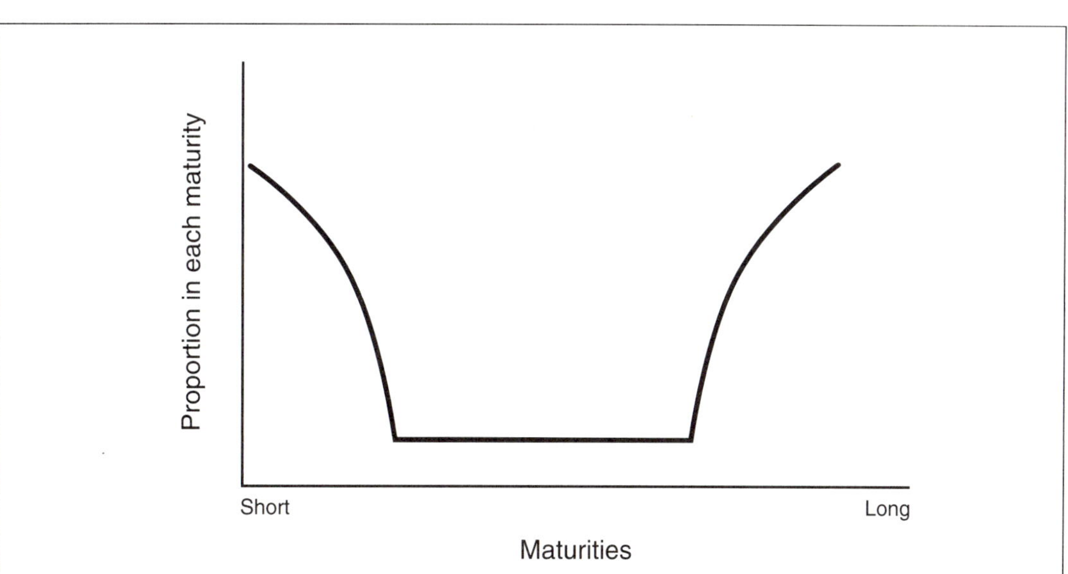

each requiring separate management. For the short-maturity portion of the portfolio, the manager must keep reinvesting proceeds from maturing bonds. This need to roll over the maturing funds requires considerable management attention. For the long-maturity portion of the portfolio, the problems are even more acute. Over time, the long-maturity bonds become middle-maturity bonds. To maintain the dumbbell shape, middle-maturity bonds must be sold and the proceeds reinvested in long-maturity bonds. This requires active management as well. Selling these bonds and purchasing new long-term bonds produces higher transaction costs. In general, the dumbbell strategy has the disadvantages of requiring considerably greater management effort and higher transaction costs.

The choice of strategy depends on whether we wish to engage in active management of the bond portfolio. Active management consists essentially of attempting to alter the maturity structure of the bond portfolio in order to take advantage of forecasted changes in interest rates. For the active manager, the dumbbell strategy is clearly preferred. The advisability of active bond management depends on the ability to forecast interest rates. Some portfolio managers believe that it is impossible to forecast interest rates with sufficient accuracy to make active bond portfolio management practical. These managers engage in a passive management strategy. For them, the key is to avoid unnecessary management expense and to control transaction costs, leading naturally to a preference for the laddered portfolio strategy. The decision to follow an active or passive management strategy depends on the manager's beliefs about his or her interest rate forecasts.

Summary

The importance of changes in interest rates on bond prices demands that investors understand the basic factors that influence interest rates. Following the analysis of Irving Fisher, we saw that the nominal or market rate of interest for a risk-free bond equals the real rate of interest plus the expected rate of inflation. In a riskless world, the real rate of interest equals the rate of return earned by newly employed physical capital.

This chapter analyzed the yield curve, or the term structure of interest rates, which expresses the relationship between yield to maturity and term to maturity for bonds of the same risk level. Because bond yields differ by maturity, an understanding of these relationships is important to the bond manager. The bond manager needs to understand the opportunities and risks inherent in pursuing higher yields, which lead to an exploration of theories of the term structure. These theories generally concur in assigning a very important role to expectations of future interest rates in the explanation of the term structure.

Bond yields differ not only by maturity but also by the level of default risk, as expressed by the risk structure of interest rates. The bond portfolio manager must seek higher yields for the portfolio, while striving to avoid risk. Consequently, it is important to understand the factors contributing to the riskiness of bonds.

Even after the bond manager chooses the appropriate average maturity and the correct risk level, the choice of a bond maturity strategy is still an open question. The dumbbell strategy places the bonds in the very short and very long maturities, which makes it easy to shift the average maturity of the portfolio by trading relatively few bonds. Alternatively, the laddered portfolio strategy spreads the bonds out across the entire maturity range, which makes it quite easy to maintain the chosen maturity distribution of bonds.

Questions and Problems

1. What is the relationship between the nominal and market rates of interest?

2. Evaluate the following argument: "Over the past year, inflation has been quite high. Because interest rates depend upon the real rate of interest and the inflation rate, interest rates now should be quite high."

3. What market forces exist to make the real rate of interest equal to the marginal productivity of physical capital in a riskless environment?

4. How would you form an estimate of the market's expectations of future inflation?

5. Why should the nominal rate of interest exceed the expected rate of inflation?

6. Five years ago you invested $100,000 in a portfolio of Treasury bills and kept all proceeds fully invested in the portfolio. Today your portfolio is worth $146,932. What nominal rate of interest have you earned over this period? At the time of purchase, the Consumer's Price Index (CPI) stood at 133, and today it is at 189. What was the average inflation rate over the period? (Question: Is this a geometric or arithmetic mean?) How much did your purchasing power increase over this entire period? What was your real return on an annual basis?

7. What are the three major theories of the term structure?

8. In examining the yield curve, why should you use bonds of the same risk level?

9. How could differences in tax status among bonds used in yield curve analysis affect the analysis?

10. Liquidity premium theorists would maintain that it is normal for the yield curve to slope upward. Are there instances in history of flat or downward-sloping yield curves?

11. How would the premium expectations theory and the liquidity premium theory explain a downward-sloping yield curve?

12. Consider holding five successive one-year T-bills vs. holding a five-year Treasury bond for five years. According to the liquidity premium theory of the term structure, which should have the greater expected return? Why? How would the pure expectations theory differ?

13. In order for the liquidity premium theory to be true, investors must have preferences for short-term bonds. How does the market segmentation theory make use of the idea that investors have different maturity preferences? Are these theories really the same?

14. Long maturity bonds have considerable "price risk" because their prices can move a great deal in response to a change in interest rates. How does this price risk differ from "default risk"? Which is analyzed by the risk structure of interest rates?

15. What is the "risk premium" and what factors are important in determining the size of the risk premium?

16. What are the advantages and disadvantages of the two major portfolio maturity strategies we have considered?

17. A two-year bond is yielding 15 percent and a one-year bond is yielding 11 percent. What is the forward rate for a bond to cover the second year? Does the yield curve slope upward in this case?

18. Consider the following rates for bonds of differing maturities:

Maturity (years)	Yield %
5	14
4	13
3	12
2	11
1	10

Compute all possible forward rates. (Note: There are a total of ten forward rates to calculate, four one-year rates, three two-year rates, two three-year rates, and one four-year rate.)

19. Using the data of the preceding problem, what would be the interest rate forecast of a pure expectations theorist for one-year rates three years from now? How would the forecast of the liquidity premium theorist differ?

Suggested REALDATA Exercises

The following *REALDATA* exercises explore the concepts developed in this chapter:
Exercises 59, 62, 64, 65

References

Abken, P. A., "Innovations in Modeling the Term Structure of Interest Rates," *Economic Review*, Federal Reserve Bank of Atlanta, 75:4, July/August 1990, pp. 2–27.

Altman, E. I., "The Anatomy of the High-Yield Bond Market," *Financial Analysts Journal*, 43:4, July/August 1987, pp. 12–25.

Altman, E. I. and M. L. Heine, "How 1989 Changed the Hierarchy of Fixed Income Security Performance," *Financial Analysts Journal*, 46:3, May/June 1990, pp. 9–12.

Becketti, S., "The Truth about Junk Bonds," *Economic Review*, Federal Reserve Bank of Kansas City, July/August 1990, pp. 45–54.

Bernanke, B. S., "On the Predictive Power of Interest Rates and Interest Rate Spreads," *New England Economic Review*, Federal Reserve Bank of Boston, November/December 1990, pp. 51–68.

Blume, M. E. and D. B. Keim, "Lower-Grade Bonds: Their Risks and Returns," *Financial Analysts Journal*, 43:4, July/August 1987, pp. 26–33.

Blume, M. E., D. B. Keim, and S. A. Patel, "Returns and Volatility of Low-Grade Bonds, 1977-1989," *Journal of Finance*, 46:1, March 1991, pp. 49–74.

Cook, T. and T. Hahn, "Interest Rate Expectations and the Slope of the Money Market Yield Curve," *Economic Review*, Federal Reserve Bank of Richmond, 76:5, September/October 1990, pp. 3–26.

Cornell, B. and K. Green, "The Investment Performance of Low-Grade Bond Funds," *Journal of Finance*, 46:1, March 1991, pp. 29–48.

Douglas, L. G., *Bond Risk Analysis*, New York: New York Institute of Finance, 1990.

Fabozzi, F. J., *Fixed Income Mathematics*, Chicago: Probus Publishing Company, 1988.

Fisher, I., *The Theory of Interest*, New York: A. M. Kelley, Publishers, 1965.

Fons, J. S., "The Default Premium and Corporate Bond Experience," *Journal of Finance*, 42:1, March 1987, pp. 81–97.

Froot, K. A., "New Hope for the Expectations Hypothesis of the Term Structure of Interest Rates," *Journal of Finance*, 44:2, June 1989, pp. 283–305.

Hickman, W. B., *Corporate Bond Quality and Investor Experience*, Princeton, NJ: Princeton University Press, 1958.

Hirschleifer, J., "Investment Decision Under Uncertainty: Choice-Theoretic Approaches," *The Quarterly Journal of Economics*, 79:4, November 1964, pp. 509–36.

Ho, T. S. Y., *Strategic Fixed-Income Investment*, Homewood, IL: Dow Jones Books, 1990.

Hradsky, G. T. and R. D. Long, "High-Yield Default Losses and the Return Performance of Bankrupt Debt," *Financial Analysts Journal*, 45:4, July/August 1989, pp. 38–49.

Ibbotson, R. and R. Sinquefield, *Stocks, Bonds, Bills and Inflation: The Past and the Future*, Charlottesville, VA: The Financial Analysts Research Foundation, 1982.

Jones, F. J. and B. Wolkowitz, "The Determinants of Interest Rates on Fixed Income Securities," *The Handbook of Fixed Income Securities*, 3rd ed., Homewood, IL: Business One Irwin, 1991.

Litterman, R. and J. Scheinkman, "Common Factors Affecting Bond Returns," *The Journal of Fixed Income*, 1:1, June 1991, pp. 54–61.

Litterman, R., J. Scheinkman, and L. Weiss, "Volatility and the Yield Curve," *The Journal of Fixed Income*, 1:1, June 1991, pp. 49–53.

Malkiel, Burton G., "Expectations, Bond Prices, and the Term Structure of Interest Rates," *Quarterly Journal of Economics*, May 1962, pp. 197–218.

McCulloch, J. H., "An Estimate of the Liquidity Premium," *Journal of Political Economy*, February 1975.

McEnally, R. W. and J. V. Jordan, "The Term Structure of Interest Rates," *The Handbook of Fixed Income Securities*, 3rd ed., Homewood, IL: Business One Irwin, 1991.

Meiselman, D., *The Term Structure of Interest Rates*, Englewood Cliffs, NJ: Prentice Hall, 1962.

Nelson, C., "Estimation of Term Premiums from Average Yield Differentials in the Term Structure of Interest Rates," *Econometrica*, March 1972.

Rose, A. K., "Is the Real Interest Rate Stable?" *Journal of Finance*, 43:5, December 1988, pp. 1095–112.

Rosenberg, M. R., "International Fixed Income Investing: Theory and Practice," *The Handbook of Fixed Income Securities*, 3rd ed., Homewood, IL: Business One Irwin, 1991.

Santomero, A., "The Error Learning Hypothesis and the Term Structure of Interest Rates in Eurodollars," *Journal of Finance*, June 1975.

Sarig, O. and A. Warga, "Some Empirical Estimates of the Risk Structure of Interest Rates," *Journal of Finance*, 44:5, December 1989, pp. 1351–60.

Woolford, W. D., "Forecasting Interest Rates," *The Handbook of Fixed Income Securities*, 3rd ed., Homewood, IL: Business One Irwin, 1991.

The Primary Market and Investment Banking

8

Overview

When most people think of buying or selling securities, they naturally think first of the large stock exchanges, such as the New York Stock Exchange. These are clearly the most visible institutions in the securities business. However, the securities traded on the New York Stock Exchange are being traded on a **secondary market** – a market for already existing securities.

Before securities reach the secondary market, they must be issued by corporations or governments. This initial offering of securities takes place in the **primary market**, the market for the issuance of new securities. The primary market is much less visible than the secondary market, but it is crucial to the world of investments.

This chapter explores the primary market and the important role played in it by the investment banker. In the United States, investment banking has been kept almost totally distinct from the more familiar commercial banking by a law known as the Glass-Steagall Act. Instead of accepting deposits, as does a commercial bank, the investment banking firm aids corporations and governments in the initial distribution of securities. In doing so, the investment banker typically acts as a consultant to the institution offering the securities, aids in distributing securities, and often bears considerable risk in the process of the initial distribution.

The Primary Market: Size and Scope

New issues in the primary market can be distinguished by the type of issuer and the type of security being issued. The basic issuers of securities are governments and corporations. The securities offered may be either bonds, common stock, or preferred stock. **Preferred stock** is a cross between a bond and common stock. It normally pays a fixed dividend, but the firm is obligated to make the payments only if enough funds are available. Also, the firm need not retire the preferred stock as it normally does a bond by returning the principal. A security is retired when all promised payments have been made.

Of the three types of securities mentioned – common stock, bonds, and preferred stock – only corporations issue common stock and preferred stock. Since stock, particularly common stock, represents an ownership claim on the issuing entity, it is clear that governments cannot issue stock. Therefore, it is necessary to separate the two kinds of issuers. Table 8.1 presents the recent record of new securities issued by U.S. corporations, with the issues being broken down by broad industrial classifications. For all issues combined – common stock, bonds, and preferred stock – the total has grown steadily over the recent years. Figure 8.1 shows this growth and the changing mix of common stock, preferred stock, and bonds. In 1983, for the first time, the total of the new issues exceeded $100 billion, and it has generally continued to grow since then. As the table shows, corporations issued about $765 billion of securities in 1993.

Table 8.1
New Security Issues of Corporations

1.46 NEW SECURITY ISSUES U.S. Corporations

Millions of dollars

Type of issue, offering, or issuer	1991	1992	1993	1994							
				Apr.	May	June	July	Aug.	Sept.	Oct.[r]	Nov.
1 **All issues**[1]	**465,246**	**559,827**	**764,509**	**35,110**	**44,263**	**49,457**	**29,153**[r]	**38,437**[r]	**29,406**[r]	**32,161**	**33,566**
2 **Bonds**[2]	**389,822**	**471,502**	**641,498**	**29,645**	**40,589**	**43,126**	**25,489**[r]	**35,061**[r]	**25,973**[r]	**28,600**	**28,100**
By type of offering											
3 Public, domestic	286,930	378,058	486,879	26,436	33,414	38,387	21,772[r]	30,655[r]	22,726[r]	24,000	23,300
4 Private placement, domestic[3]	74,930	65,853	116,240	n.a.	n.a.	n.a.	n.a.	n.a.	n.a.	n.a.	n.a.
5 Sold abroad	27,962	27,591	38,379	3,209	7,175	4,738	3,718	4,406	3,248	4,600	4,800
By industry group											
6 Manufacturing	86,628	82,058	88,002	2,229	3,266	2,093	1,857[r]	2,251	2,165	2,500	2,600
7 Commercial and miscellaneous	36,666	43,111	60,443	990	2,496	3,177	1,413	3,604[r]	2,052[r]	2,039	2,302
8 Transportation	13,598	9,979	10,756	97	150	1,082	248	315	229	327	339
9 Public utility	23,944	48,055	56,272	546	1,071	681	472	520[r]	707	1,601	1,649
10 Communication	9,431	15,394	31,950	1,298	944	618	429	345	526	379	421
11 Real estate and financial	219,555	272,904	394,076	24,484	32,662	35,475	21,070[r]	28,027[r]	20,294[r]	21,754	20,789
12 **Stocks**[2]	**75,424**	**88,325**	**113,472**	**5,465**	**3,674**	**6,331**	**3,664**	**3,376**[r]	**3,433**[r]	**3,561**	**5,466**
By type of offering											
13 Public preferred	17,085	21,339	18,897	2,248	695	1,366	599	710	555	1,191	279
14 Common	48,230	57,118	82,657	3,218	2,979	4,965	3,065	2,666[r]	2,877[r]	2,370	5,187
15 Private placement[3]	10,109	9,867	11,917	n.a.	n.a.	n.a.	n.a.	n.a.	n.a.	n.a.	n.a.
By industry group											
16 Manufacturing	24,111	22,723	22,271	2,696	956	1,056	489	569	904[r]	745	1,970
17 Commercial and miscellaneous	19,418	20,231	25,761	773	850	1,853	708	838	821[r]	1,105	1,717
18 Transportation	2,439	2,595	2,237	106	105	449	75	50	223	79	76
19 Public utility	3,474	6,532	7,050	75	239	297	0	180	78	4	333
20 Communication	475	2,366	3,439	0	32	28	0	0	0	0	0
21 Real estate and financial	25,507	33,879	49,889	1,815	1,492	2,647	2,386	1,734[r]	1,407[r]	1,628	1,350

1. Figures represent gross proceeds of issues maturing in more than one year; they are the principal amount or number of units calculated by multiplying by the offering price. Figures exclude secondary offerings, employee stock plans, investment companies other than closed-end, intracorporate transactions, equities sold abroad, and Yankee bonds. Stock data include ownership securities issued by limited partnerships.

2. Monthly data cover only public offerings.

3. Monthly data are not available.

SOURCES. Beginning July 1993, Securities Data Company and the Board of Governors of the Federal Reserve System.

Source: *Federal Reserve Bulletin*, March 1995, Table 1.46.

Private Placements and Public Offerings

As Table 8.1 shows, there are two types of offerings – public offerings and private placements. In a **public offering**, the issuer offers the security to the public at large, giving any investor the right to purchase the new issue. In a public offering, the entire process of issuance is governed by regulations of the Securities and Exchange Commission (SEC). As an alternative to making a public offering, many companies prefer to make a private placement. In a **private placement**, an entire bond issue is sold to a single buyer, or small consortium of buyers, without the issue ever being made available to the public.

There are several advantages to private placements. If a corporation makes a private placement, the process of issuing the security escapes SEC governance. Because the SEC imposes fairly rigorous and costly rules on the process of publicly issuing securities, it can be cheaper for the firm to engage in a private placement. Another advantage for the issuing firm is the chance to avoid too much public disclosure of its business plans. This disclosure is required by the SEC in any public offering. For a firm engaged in an industry where secrecy is important, particularly for high-technology firms in the computing or defense industries, making a public disclosure can be very undesirable.

Figure 8.1
Corporate Security Issues

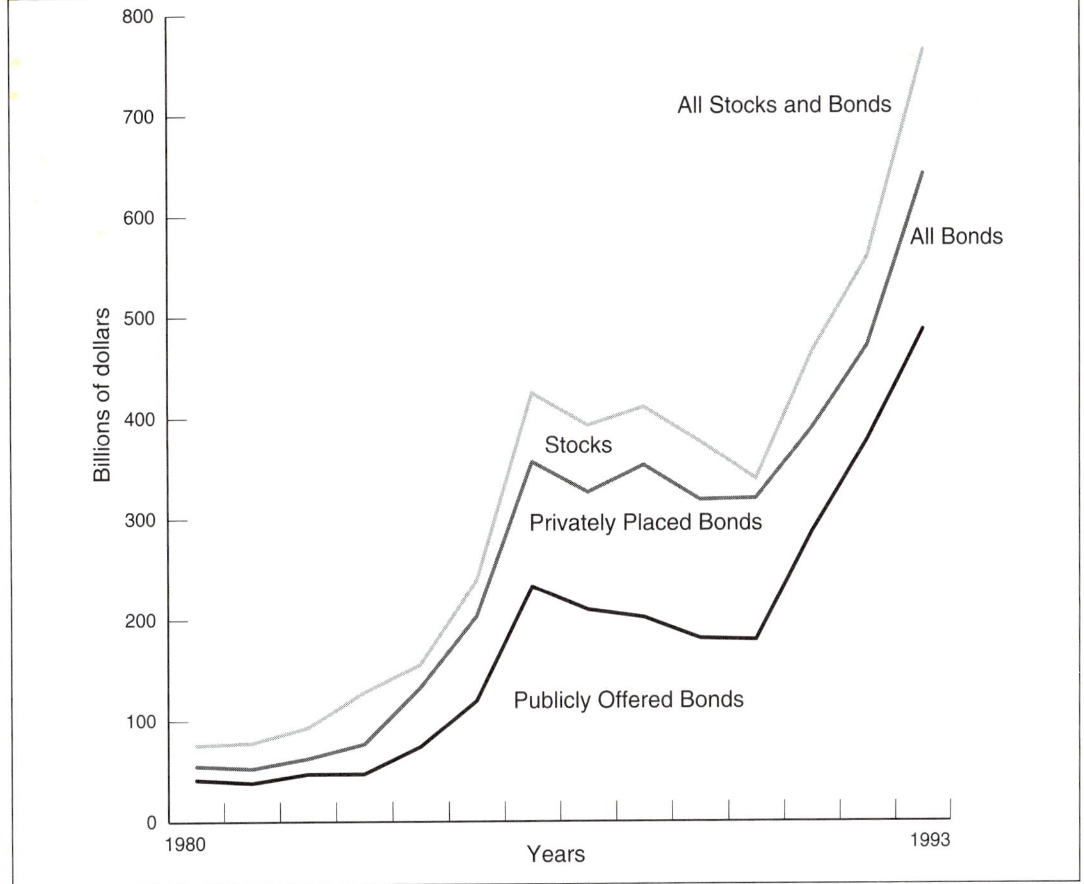

Source: *Federal Reserve Bulletin*, various issues.

In private placements, the buyers of the securities tend to be large cash-rich institutions, such as insurance companies. For these buyers, there are certain advantages to participating in a private placement. Usually bonds that are privately placed pay an interest rate slightly higher than that available in a public offering. For large investors, even a small interest rate differential can be important. For the buyer of a privately placed issue there is also an important disadvantage. The holder of a privately placed security cannot sell the bond because it has never been scrutinized as required for a public offering. This means that the buyer of a privately placed issue sacrifices liquidity in order to obtain the higher rate of interest paid on private placements. **Liquidity** is a measure of how easily an asset may be converted into cash without loss of value.

As Table 8.1 shows, about 35 percent of the new bond issues are privately placed, with the rest being offered publicly. It is also apparent, particularly from Figure 8.1, that the importance of private placements has been growing in recent years. Some common and preferred stock is also privately placed, but only very small amounts.

Relative Size of Issuers

The vast majority of stock issues are for common stock. In recent years, preferred stock has fallen out of favor as a financing vehicle, in part because corporations must pay preferred stock dividends from after-tax income. This contrasts with bonds, because the interest payments are paid from before-tax income, providing an important tax advantage to corporations that issue bonds rather than preferred stock.[1] Considering the dollar volumes reported in Table 8.1, it is striking to notice that bonds dwarf stocks by a ratio of about 5-to-1. As Figure 8.1 shows, this has been true since 1980. In spite of the fact that common stocks generally attract more investor attention than the bond market, the stock market is really quite small compared to the bond market, at least with the primary market. In the secondary market, stocks are traded much more frequently than bonds, so the degree of activity in stock trading is really higher than its size in the primary market would indicate.

The largest issuer of securities in the world is the U.S. government, as shown in Table 8.2, which presents the recent public debt offerings by the U.S. government.[2] The federal govern-

Table 8.2
Public Borrowing of the U.S. Government

Year	Amount ($ millions)
1976	82,913
1977	53,516
1978	59,106
1979	33,641
1980	70,515
1981	79,329
1982	134,912
1983	212,425
1984	170,817
1985	197,269
1986	236,187
1987	150,070
1988	166,139
1989	141,806
1990	264,453
1991	276,802
1992	310,918
1993	248,619
1994	184,998

Source: *Federal Reserve Bulletin*, various issues, Table 1.38.

[1] This view would be disputed by some, however. See Merton H. Miller, "Debt and Taxes," *Journal of Finance*, May 1977, pp. 261–76.

[2] In a certain sense, Table 8.2 understates the magnitude of the U.S. government's role. The figures in Table 8.2 show only the change in the level of the government debt. Each year some debt is repaid and replaced with new debt, however. So the amount of securities issued by the government is really larger than it appears. For example, if we consider Treasury bills (securities issued with original maturities of one year or less) alone, over $300 billion per year is being issued.

Table 8.3
Securities Issued by State and Local Governments

1.45 NEW SECURITY ISSUES Tax-Exempt State and Local Governments

Millions of dollars

Type of issue or issuer, or use	1991	1992	1993	1994							
				May	June	July	Aug.	Sept.	Oct.	Nov.	Dec.
1 **All issues, new and refunding**[1]	**154,402**	**226,818**	**279,945**	**13,563**	**15,076**	**13,400**	**12,175**	**7,810**	**10,537**	**11,685**	**9,502**
By type of issue											
2 General obligation	55,100	78,611	90,599	4,029	5,556	7,110	4,177	2,309	2,891	5,592	2,261
3 Revenue	99,302	136,580	189,346	8,359	9,223	5,340	8,133	5,325	6,899	6,093	7,241
By type of issuer											
4 State	24,939	24,874	27,999	1,158	1,733	4,686	1,675	1,009	952	1,528	151
5 Special district or statutory authority[2]	80,614	138,327	178,714	8,085	9,335	4,931	7,963	4,962	6,511	6,148	7,270
6 Municipality, county, or township	48,849	63,617	73,232	3,145	3,711	2,833	2,672	1,663	2,327	4,009	2,081
7 **Issues for new capital**	**116,953**	**101,865**	**91,434**	**9,465**	**9,913**	**10,843**	**10,479**	**6,155**	**8,893**	**10,137**	**8,486**
By use of proceeds											
8 Education	21,121	18,852	16,831	1,933	1,945	1,147	2,075	883	1,596	1,716	1,725
9 Transportation	13,395	14,357	9,167	1,037	2,033	290	1,088	334	1,135	799	299
10 Utilities and conservation	21,039	12,164	12,014	423	856	694	784	433	1,887	644	1,244
11 Social welfare	25,648	16,744	13,837	2,136	1,312	1,698	2,117	1,897	1,887	1,535	2,172
12 Industrial aid	8,376	6,188	6,862	657	935	959	1,128	403	420	688	1,007
13 Other purposes	30,275	33,560	32,723	2,939	2,645	5,560	3,401	2,011	2,396	4,750	2,039

1. Par amounts of long-term issues based on date of sale.
2. Includes school districts.

SOURCES. Securities Data Company beginning January 1993; *Investment Dealer's Digest* before then.

Source: *Federal Reserve Bulletin*, March 1995, Table 1.45.

ment, together with state, county, and municipal governments and agencies, constitutes another vast segment of the primary market.

In addition to the U.S. government, state and local governments issue vast quantities of securities, called **municipals**, or **municipal bonds**. These securities, discussed in Chapter 4, are often exempt from federal and state income taxation. As shown in Table 8.3, this market is also very large, as measured by the dollar volume of new security issues, and has been growing in size relative to the market for corporate securities. When we consider the tendency of corporations to issue bonds in preference to stocks, and add the billions of dollars in bonds issued by governments, it becomes even more apparent how large the bond market is in relation to the stock market.

The Process of Issuing Securities

This section describes the process by which a corporate issuer brings a new security to market. Developing a good relationship with an investment banker is very important to the financial management of a corporation. Most firms attempt to maintain a close working relationship with one or two investment bankers to whom they can turn when the need arises. Assuming that such a relationship has been established, the corporation and the investment banker would be in regular contact as the financing needs of the firm evolve over time.

The investment banker normally fulfills three functions for the corporation in the process of issuing a new security:

1. Consulting
2. Forming a distribution network
3. Bearing risk involved in the issuance of the new security

As the firm prepares to issue the new security, it must resolve questions such as the timing of the issuance and the pricing of the security. In a public offering, the issuer must meet many regulations of the SEC as well. The investment banker plays a critical role in helping the issuer with all of these matters.

The Investment Banker as Consultant

In the role of consultant to the issuing firm, the investment banker works in three main areas:

1. Preparing the necessary registration and informational materials
2. Timing the issuance
3. Setting the price at which the security will be issued

One of the important SEC requirements for the public offering of new securities is the formal disclosure of the firm's financial condition and future plans. This is done in a **prospectus**, which is a legal document required by the SEC. The investment banker often plays an important advisory role in creating the prospectus.

The prospectus includes a report of the firm's financial condition, the names of the principal officers in the corporation, and an accounting of their holdings in the firm. The document also gives information about the firm's line of business and its plans for future expansion. This information must be detailed and highly accurate. Since the firm offers the securities for sale through the prospectus, any error in the prospectus could make the firm liable for losses sustained by investors. Consequently, the prospectus is usually written by the legal staff in legal prose. The authors of the prospectus usually include top management from the issuing firm, the legal staff of the issuing firm, and legal specialists in prospectus writing. Some of the expertise for the prospectus usually comes from the investment banker.

All firms prefer to issue their securities when they can sell them for a high price. For stocks, the ideal would be to issue securities when the (secondary) stock market peaks. The ideal time to issue bonds occurs when interest rates are very low, helping to ensure a high price for the bonds.[3] Investment bankers often give firms advice on this issue of timing. Another crucial aspect of timing concerns the commercial policy of the firm. Firms, particularly small or relatively new ones, often issue securities after introducing a new product that is expected to be quite successful.

Pricing of the securities is very important as well. Since investment bankers are constantly engaged in the primary market, they should be in a good position to advise on the proper pricing of the new security. The goal of the pricing strategy is to set the highest price that will allow all of the issue to be sold in a fairly short period of time. (An issue that sells out rapidly is said to go **out the window**.) If the price is set too low, the issue will sell out virtually immediately, but it

---

[3] As explained in Chapter 4, bond prices and interest rates are inversely related. Other things being equal, this means that bond prices are at their highest when interest rates are at their lowest.

will not bring the firm as much cash as it could have obtained had it been priced properly. On the other hand, an issue that is priced too high will not be sold out promptly. (Such securities are said to be **sticky issues**.)

The Distribution Network

Figure 8.2 shows the typical structure of the distribution network. The issuing corporation creates the security and passes it to the lead bank and the syndicate members. The **lead bank** is the investment bank with primary responsibility for issuing a particular security. The **syndicate members** are other investment banking firms that have committed themselves to assisting in the flotation of a given security. The **flotation** is the initial sale of the security. From the numerous members of the syndicate, the securities are distributed to members of the **selling group**, those investment houses that participate to a smaller degree in the distribution process. Only when the securities reach the brokers is the point of contact with the public achieved. The brokers are in direct contact with their customers, who are the final investors in the securities.

Officially, only the prospectus offers securities for sale. For that matter, only investors who have received a copy of the prospectus are allowed to buy the security anyway. Securities are often announced, however, in *The Wall Street Journal* with advertisements such as those shown in Figure 8.3. This kind of advertisement is known as a **tombstone**, due to its size, shape, and color. The tombstone announces the firm making the issue, the price, and the number of securities. It also lists the members of the syndicate. Notice the disclaimer, "This announcement is neither an

Figure 8.2
Organization of the Distribution Network

Issuing firm
↓
Lead investment banker
Various syndicate members
↓
Selling group
↓
Brokers
↓
Investing public

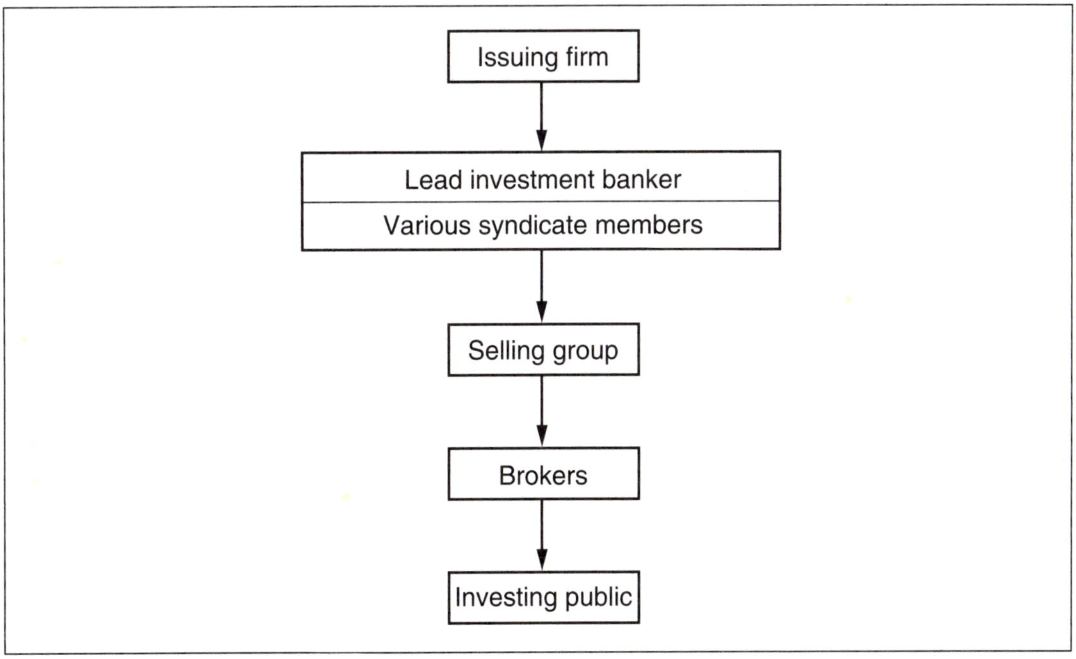

Figure 8.3
A Typical Tombstone

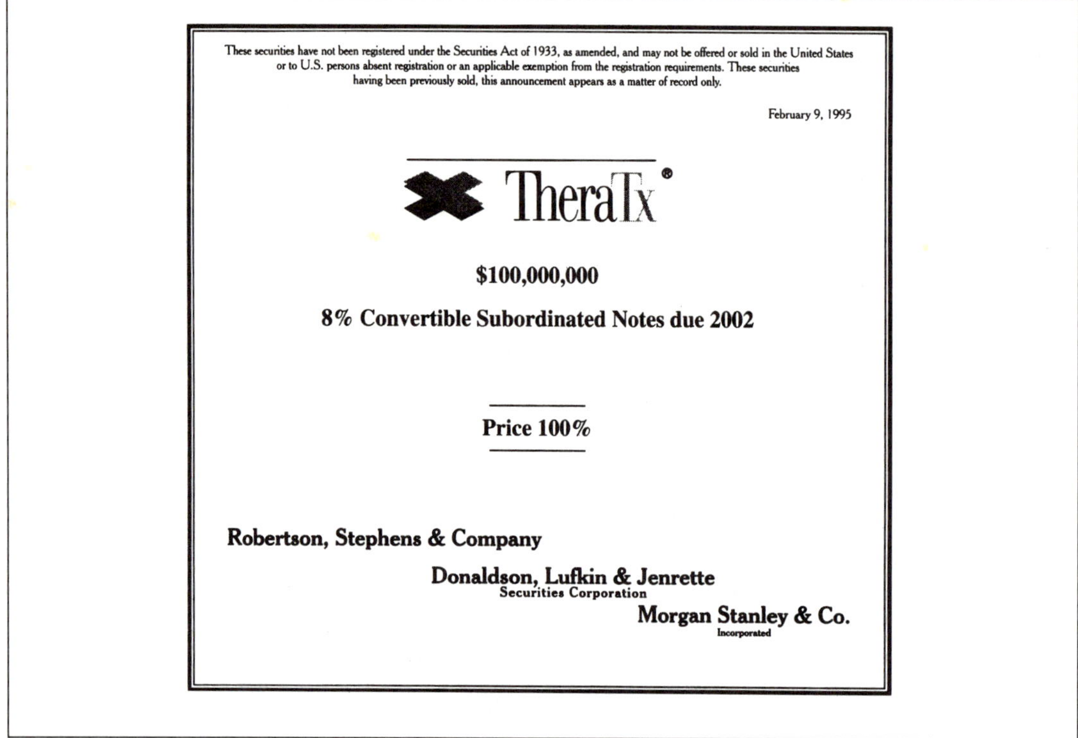

These securities have not been registered under the Securities Act of 1933, as amended, and may not be offered or sold in the United States or to U.S. persons absent registration or an applicable exemption from the registration requirements. These securities having been previously sold, this announcement appears as a matter of record only.

February 9, 1995

TheraTx®

$100,000,000

8% Convertible Subordinated Notes due 2002

Price 100%

Robertson, Stephens & Company

Donaldson, Lufkin & Jenrette
Securities Corporation

Morgan Stanley & Co.
Incorporated

Source: *The Wall Street Journal*, March 29, 1995.

offer to sell nor a solicitation of an offer to buy any of these securities. The offer is made only by the Prospectus." Because of the strict regulations on security issuance, an obvious advertisement to sell securities has to say that it is not offering securities for sale.

To illustrate this process of issuing a security, consider a firm making a fairly large size issue ($20 million to $50 million), with the corporation receiving $100 per share of common stock, as shown in Table 8.4. As the security flows through the network of intermediaries, each layer tacks on its profit margin. By the time the security reaches the members of the public, its final price may well be 6 percent or more above the amount received by the corporation. The prices shown in Table 8.4 assume that the security flows through the entire chain, but this will not be true of all of the shares of stock in the issue. For example, the lead bank also markets the shares through its own internal distribution network. The total price difference between the price paid by the final investor and the amount the issuing firm receives is known as the **spread**; the lead bank keeps a much greater percentage of the spread on securities it sells itself.

The Service and Cost of Risk-Bearing

The forming of the distribution network and the marketing of securities are parts of the retailing function. But the compensation that the investment banker receives is not only for acting as a

Table 8.4
Typical Spreads in a Common Stock Issuance

Price per Share	Received by
$100.00	Corporation
101.25	Lead investment bank
103.00	Other syndicate members
104.50	Selling group members
106.00	Brokers making sales directly to the public

retailer. The investment banker has two basic ways of distributing securities for the issuer; he may act as an underwriter for the issue, or he may undertake to sell the issue on a best efforts basis. If the investment banker acts as an **underwriter**, the bank actually buys the securities from the issuing firm and then tries to sell them to the public at a profit. In this case, the investment bank bears a great deal of risk, and the spread constitutes the compensation for the investment banker's risk-bearing service as well as the distribution cost. If the investment bank distributes the issue on a **best efforts basis**, it promises to sell the securities at the best price it can obtain. However, the issuing firm continues to own the securities during the distribution process, and the issuer bears the risk associated with price fluctuations.

The services of investment bankers do not come cheaply. The talents of the firm's employees and the risk-bearing service that the firm provides demand a high level of compensation. This section examines the compensation paid, either directly or indirectly, to the investment banker. These costs of issuing securities – known as **flotation costs** – have a strong impact on the cost of acquiring funds and also on the investment desirability of new issues.

Corporations pay their investment bankers in two ways.[4] First, they typically pay out-of-pocket expenses for consulting services, legal fees, and document preparation. Second, the issuer offers securities at a price that allows the investment bankers, and other members of the distribution network, to make a profit. Of these two classes of expense, the second is generally the larger.

When an investment banking syndicate acts as an underwriter, the price the corporation receives must be low enough to allow the syndicate to distribute the securities to the public at a profit. The spread constitutes the gross margin for the distribution network, but in an issue that is underwritten, a large portion of the spread is compensation for bearing risk.

While the prices of Table 8.4 are fairly representative, it should be recognized that the spread depends on the size of the issue and the kind of security that is under consideration. As Table 8.5 shows, spreads are typically lower for debt issues than for issues of common stock. Further, the spread, as a percentage of the proceeds, is smaller the larger the issue size. For very small issues, flotation costs become prohibitively expensive. In addition to the spread, the issuing firm also pays certain out-of-pocket expenses mentioned earlier. While smaller than the spread, they can add significantly to total flotation costs, as shown in Table 8.6. For small issues, total flotation costs

[4] This section focuses only on the process for corporations. Governments and their agencies operate somewhat differently. Many are required by law to offer securities under a process of competitive bidding, rather than through an underwriting system. The U.S. government issues securities through its own special media, including Federal Reserve Banks and U.S. government security dealers.

Table 8.5
Spread Size by Size Type of Issue

	Spread	
Size of Issue ($ millions)	Common Stock	Bonds
Under .5	11.3%	7.4%
.5 – .9	9.7	7.2
1.0 – 1.9	8.6	7.0
2.0 – 4.9	7.4	4.2
5.0 – 9.9	6.7	1.5
10.0 – 19.9	6.2	1.0
20.0 – 49.9	4.9	1.0
50.0 and over	2.3	0.8

Source: Block and Hirt, *Foundations of Financial Management*, Homewood, IL: Richard D. Irwin, 1985, p. 324.

Table 8.6
Spread Size by Size Type of Issue

Size of Issue ($ millions)	Common Stock	Out-of-Pocket	Total
Under .5	11.3%	7.3%	18.6%
.5 – .9	9.7	4.9	14.6
1.0 – 1.9	8.6	3.0	11.6
2.0 – 4.9	7.4	1.7	9.1
5.0 – 9.9	6.7	1.0	7.7
10.0 – 19.9	6.2	.6	6.8
20.0 – 49.9	4.9	.8	5.7
50.0 and over	2.3	.3	2.6

Source: Block and Hirt, *Foundations of Financial Management*, Homewood, IL: Richard D. Irwin, 1985, p. 324.

approach 20 percent. For the largest issues, they can be less than 3 percent. The issuing firm must make at least the total flotation cost on the investment being financed by the security issuance in order to break even. This is a sobering fact for the securities investor because it indicates just how much profit the firm must make before the investor can expect a positive return to be generated on the security.

The Green Shoe Option

For underwritten new issues, the investment banker often has a Green Shoe option. The **Green Shoe option** is the right of the investment banking firm to buy an additional number of securities from the issuer at the original price. The option gets its name because it was first used in an offering by the Green Shoe Company. Usually, the number of securities is limited to some fraction of the total issuance size. The chance to buy additional securities from the issuer at the issue price is a valuable right. So, in effect, the Green Shoe option is a form of compensation that the issuing corporation offers to the investment banker.

As an example of the Green Shoe option, assume that the issue price for a share is $100 and that the issue goes out the window and quickly moves up in price to $110 in the **aftermarket** – the market for the security shortly after its issuance. If the investment bank has a Green Shoe option, it can buy additional shares at $100 and sell them in the open market for $110. The rationale for the Green Shoe option is that it allows the investment banker to meet customer demand if an offer is over-subscribed by interested investors. The option typically remains available to the investment bank for about 30 days following the initial issuance. The value of an option depends on the interest rate and the riskiness of the good on which the option exists.

Generally, the Green Shoe option has considerable value. Table 8.7 presents the typical costs for granting the Green Shoe option in stock issuances. The table categorizes the cost depending on the level of interest rates, the volatility of the stock being issued, and the percentage the stock is underpriced. These estimates indicate that the Green Shoe option costs the issuer from 4.67 percent to 9.15 percent of the entire value of the stock. This is a very substantial portion of the total cost of issuance.

For example, assume that interest rates are 10 percent, the security is correctly priced (0 percent underpricing in Table 8.7), the stock is of normal volatility, and the Green Shoe option allows the investment bank to purchase up to 15 percent of an initial issuance of $35 million. In Table 8.7 the cost of the option in this case is 6.33 percent. For our example, the investment bank can

Table 8.7
Value of the Green Shoe Option as a Percentage of the Security's Value

	Percentage of Underpricing		
Interest Rate (%)	0	1	2
		Low-Volatility Security	
8	4.67	5.23	5.83
10	4.75	5.32	5.93
12	4.84	5.41	6.03
		Average-Volatility Security	
8	6.25	6.81	7.40
10	6.33	6.90	7.49
12	6.41	6.98	7.58
		High-Volatility Security	
8	7.83	8.39	8.98
10	7.91	8.48	9.07
12	7.99	8.56	9.15

Source: Robert Hansen, "Evaluating the Costs of a New Equity Issue," *Midland Corporate Finance Journal*, 4:1, Spring 1986, pp. 42–55.

purchase \$5,250,000 (\$35,000,000 times .15) in shares at the issue price. With the 6.33 percent value of this option, the issuer effectively pays the investment bank \$332,325 (\$5,250,000 times .0633) in the form of the Green Shoe option.

Investment Bankers and Investing in New Issues

In spite of the high flotation costs just discussed, many new issues do quite well for investors. Pricing of new issues is really an art, rather than a science. A price set too low means that the issuer does not receive full value, while a price set too high means that security purchasers are likely to have low returns. Whether a new issue should have high returns immediately upon issuance depends largely on whether one is an issuer or an investor.

It might appear that investors should seek investment bankers who issue securities that generate large profits. Similarly, firms might choose investment bankers who price securities very aggressively, so that they get the maximum price for their securities. In fact, it seems that an equilibrium can be achieved only when the new issues offer a return comparable with investment opportunities available elsewhere. Otherwise, either investors or the issuing corporations will be displeased and will learn to avoid particular investment bankers. That, of course, would be disastrous for investment bankers, since their role as an intermediary between the corporation and the investors is based on having good relations with both.

Initial Public Offerings

A firm engages in an **initial public offering** (IPO) when it offers securities to the public for the first time. An established firm, such as Exxon, might issue new securities in the primary market, but these issuances would not be an IPO because Exxon has already issued securities before. As an example of an IPO, a partnership might incorporate and sell stock to the public.

Figure 8.4 presents the number of IPOs by month from 1960 to 1987, and it clearly shows that IPOs occur in waves. A period of intense IPO issuance is called a **hot issue market**. The figure shows that the mid-1980s were very hot, as was the 1968–69 period. By contrast, 1974–78 was virtually dead, coinciding with and following the recession of the mid-1970s. For example, there were 780 IPOs in 1969 and only 9 in 1974. Recession struck in 1990, there were few IPOs, and the top 15 investment banking firms only launched \$10 billion of new issues. Through 1994, there has been no dramatic comeback in the primary market.

Figure 8.5 shows the initial return and the returns in the first month of issuance on these IPOs for the same period, 1960–87. These returns also followed a definite pattern, with the largest initial returns preceding the hot issues market by about six months.

Asymmetric Information and the Pricing of IPOs

The returns in Figure 8.5 appear to be extremely high, and numerous researchers have concluded that the returns on IPOs are so high that they violate the normal relationship between risk and return. Thus, other scholars have attempted to explain the high returns. One attractive thesis was advanced by Kevin Rock.[5] Rock points out that potential investors in the security possess

[5] See Kevin F. Rock, "Why New Issues Are Underpriced," *Journal of Financial Economics*, 15, 1986, pp. 187–212.

Figure 8.4
Number of Offerings by Month for SEC Registered IPOs

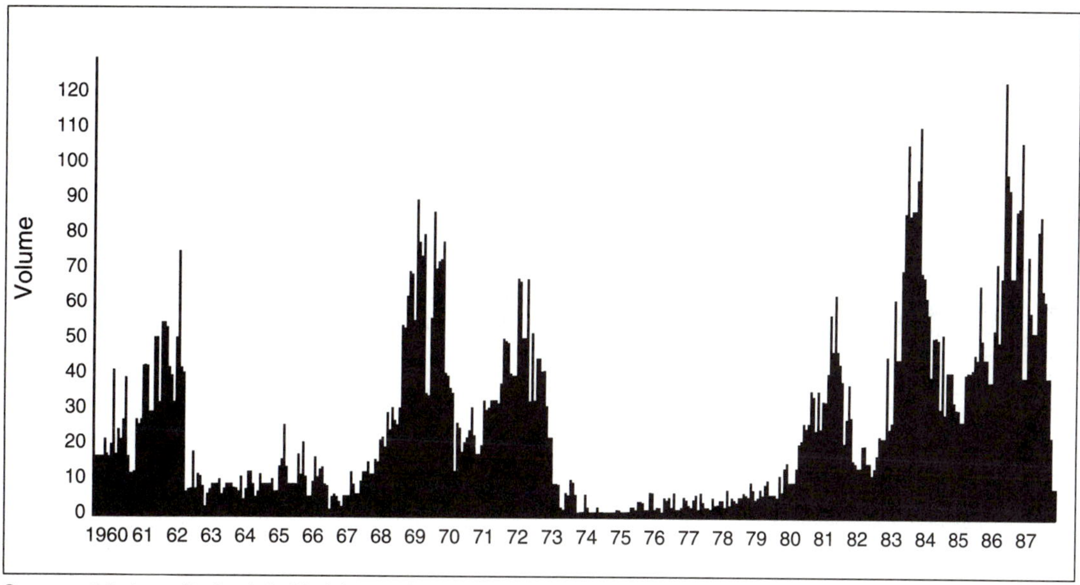

Source: Ibbotson, R. G., J. L. Sindelar, and J. R. Ritter, "Initial Public Offerings," *Journal of Applied Corporate Finance*, 1:2, Summer 1988, p. 40.

asymmetric information, a condition that arises when one party has information that is superior to another's. In the case of new issues, some potential investors may better assess the true value of the securities than do other investors. The investors with the good information are said to be **informed investors**. Rock's argument assumes that underwriters sometimes price the securities too high, sometimes too low. When the underwriter offers an underpriced security, the informed investors will flock to buy as much of the security as possible. Similarly, the informed investors will avoid overpriced issues. This means that the uninformed investors buy little of the underpriced issues, and they buy a great proportion of the overpriced securities.

Underwriters, according to Rock, must price securities in a way that gets them sold. The underwriter must attract both the informed and the uninformed investor. This leads to a systematic underpricing of IPOs in order to sweeten the deal and attract the uninformed investor. In short, IPO underpricing compensates uninformed investors for the risk of trading against superior information.

Are IPOs Underpriced?

It has become widely accepted that IPOs are underpriced, as the very high returns in Figure 8.5 appear to indicate.[6] If we consider the price movement of newly issued shares from the offering date to a time shortly thereafter, it appears that IPOs are offered at a price significantly below the price that is expected to prevail in the aftermarket. In fact, the estimated underpricing ranges from

[6] For a review of this literature, see C. W. Smith, "Investment Banking and the Capital Acquisition Process," *Journal of Financial Economics*, 15, 1986, pp. 3–29.

Figure 8.5
Average Initial Returns by Month for SEC Registered IPOs

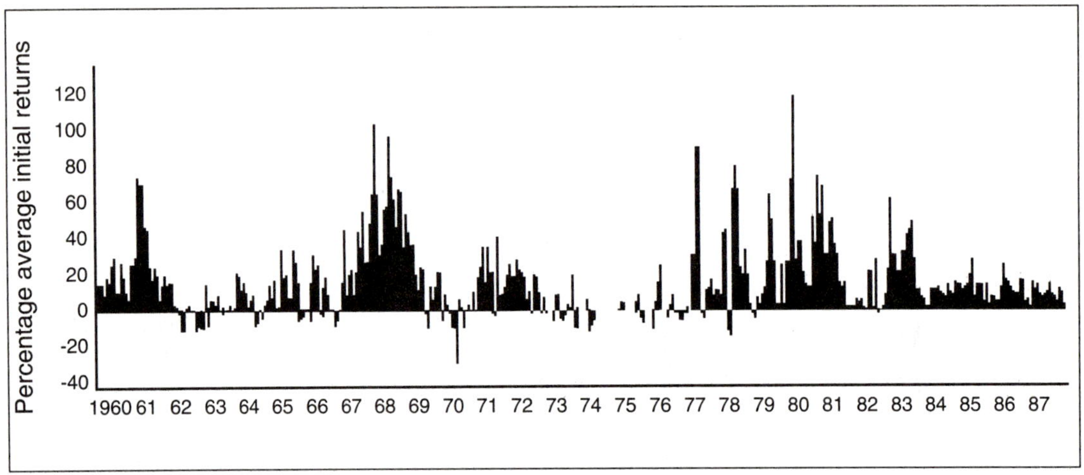

Source: Ibbotson, R. G., J. L. Sindelar, and J. R. Ritter, "Initial Public Offerings," *Journal of Applied Corporate Finance*, 1:2, Summer 1988, p. 40.

11 percent to 48 percent for initial public equity offerings.[7] Evidence indicates that new issues of shares and bonds for existing firms are also underpriced, but only by a relatively small amount. A very dramatic example was the 1986 IPO of Microsoft, the personal computer software firm. The preliminary prospectus indicated a price in the range of $16 to $19. The actual issue price was $21. On its first day of trading, the shares closed at $27.75. However, this type of underpricing appears to fluctuate, with the greatest underpricing occurring at the outset of a hot issues market. Later in the hot issues market, when new issues become very frequent, the magnitude of the underpricing appears to fall or disappear altogether.

Evidence also suggests that prestigious underwriters sponsor issues in which the underpricing is less severe. For the largest potential underpricing, investors might seek issues underwritten by less prestigious firms. The securities underwritten by these less prestigious firms also seem to have a greater variability in their degree of underpricing.[8]

The underpricing appears to be quite short-lived, lasting only a few days or a few weeks. Jay Ritter examined the long-run investment performance and concluded that IPOs underperformed comparable stocks over their first three years.[9] Compared to similar stocks, these IPOs return only 83 cents on the dollar after three years. Firms that issued at the height of a hot issues market

---

[7] See Clifford W. Smith, Jr., "Raising Capital: Theory and Evidence," *Midland Corporate Finance Journal*, 4:1, 1986, pp. 6–22.

[8] See R. Carter and S. Manaster, "Initial Public Offerings and Underwriter Reputation," *Journal of Finance*, 45:4, September 1990, pp. 1045–67.

[9] See J. R. Ritter, "The Long-Run Performance of Initial Public Offerings," *Journal of Finance*, 46:1, March 1991, pp. 3–27.

appeared to do the worst. It seems that these firms were attracted to issuing new securities by the high concentration of issues shown in Figure 8.4. Also, Ritter concludes that some firms seem to go public to take advantage of industry-specific fads.

The entire issue of the pricing of IPOs continues to receive scrutiny. Investors can expect that new research will cause a tempering of some of the conclusions discussed in this section.

Shelf Registration

One of the most significant developments in the primary security markets in recent years has been the advent of shelf registration. As we discussed earlier, the process of issuing securities can be quite expensive. These high costs have been deemed necessary by regulators, notably the SEC, to protect the investing public and to maintain a smoothly functioning primary market. Requiring issuers of securities to go through lengthy procedures to guarantee full disclosure and to seek representation by investment bankers for every issue is, undoubtedly, very expensive.

As an experiment to determine whether such costs could be reduced, the SEC, under its Rule 415, first permitted shelf registrations on a temporary basis, and since January 1, 1984, as a permanent technique for issuing a security. **Shelf registration** allows firms to register with the SEC once and then to offer securities for sale through agents and through the secondary markets for a period of two years following the registration. The rule applies to both stocks and bonds.[10]

There appear to be two chief advantages of this rule for corporations. First, a corporation can reduce its expense of offering securities by registering several securities at one time. Also, shelf registration allows firms to avoid the fixed-commission system of the investment bankers discussed earlier. Not surprisingly, the investment banking community lobbied very hard against the adoption of Rule 415.

The second advantage to corporations arises from the greater flexibility the firm achieves in timing an offering. Before shelf registration, the final "go/no-go" decision on a security issuance had to be made about three to six weeks before the actual offering was to occur. With security markets exhibiting radical fluctuations, the issuing firm can now take advantage of favorable market conditions by issuing quickly under the provisions of shelf registration.

There are also two potential disadvantages to shelf registration. First, the short period required to issue a new security may not provide enough time for the investment banker handling the shelf registration to ensure that no misstatements or omissions appear in the registration statement. This requirement for the investment banker to verify the claims made in the registration statement is known as a **due diligence obligation**. Rapid issuing of securities may impair investment bankers' abilities to perform their due diligence obligation.

A second potential problem with shelf registration is that it may lead to higher concentration in the investment banking industry. With rapid issuance of securities under shelf registration, smaller regional investment banking firms may not be able to participate in the syndicate. Also, under time pressure, the larger firms that lead a syndicate might be less willing to include the regional firms. Both factors could lead to higher concentration in investment banking.

---

[10] For more on the exact terms of Rule 415, see John Paul Ketels, "SEC Rule 415—The New Experimental Procedures for Shelf Registration," *Securities Regulation Law Journal*, 10, 1983, pp. 318–38.

In general, the evidence on shelf registration supports the view that shelf registration has led to lower issuing costs for firms that have used it. However, the debate continues with some observers finding little or no benefits to shelf registration.[11]

The Condition of the Investment Banking Industry

In spite of the popularity of shelf registration, the investment banking community has not collapsed. However, recent years have seen a change in the source of investment banking industry profits. This section considers the concentration in the industry and the sources of industry profits.

Firm Size and Concentration in Investment Banking

Table 8.8 shows size rankings according to *Investment Dealers' Digest*. It is interesting to note the extent of concentration in the investment banking industry. Focusing on the top 15 firms, which basically constitute the entire industry in size, Table 8.9 shows the percentage of the industry rep-

Table 8.8
Size Rankings of Major Corporate Underwriters

	Firm	$ Volume (millions)	No. of Issues
1	Merrill Lynch & Co.	$173,783.7	1,007
2	Goldman, Sachs	127,265.4	634
3	Lehman Brothers	115,976.5	681
4	Kidder, Peabody	94,441.1	306
5	Salomon Brothers	91,178.5	504
6	CS First Boston	90,373.8	454
7	Morgan Stanley	67,717.0	413
8	Bear Stearns	56,236.6	288
9	Donaldson, Lufkin & Jenrette	36,911.1	235
10	PaineWebber	29,889.9	179
11	Prudential Securities	28,336.2	161
12	J.P. Morgan and Co., Inc.	22,614.1	149
13	Smith Barney Shearson	14,284.4	171
14	Citicorp Securities	14,139.0	126
15	Nomura Securities Co. Ltd.	13,857.9	40
Total		$1,061,752.3	7,209

Source: *Investment Dealers' Digest*, January 10, 1994, p. 26. Figures show all domestic issues based on full credit to lead manager.

[11] For two recent studies, see F. D. Foster, "Syndicate Size, Spreads, and Market Power During the Introduction of Shelf Registration," *Journal of Finance*, 44:1, March 1989, pp. 195–204, and D. S. Allen, R. E. Lamy, and G. R. Thompson, "The Shelf Registration of Debt and Self Selection Bias," *Journal of Finance*, 45:1, March 1990, pp. 275–87.

Table 8.9
Concentration in the Investment Banking Industry

Largest 3 firms	39.28%
Largest 5 firms	56.76
Remaining Top 12 Firms	60.72
Remaining Top 10 Firms	43.24

Source: *Investment Dealers' Digest*, January 10, 1994, p. 26.

resented by the largest three and the largest five firms. These proportions are known as **industry concentration ratios**.[12] By almost any standard, the investment banking industry is extremely concentrated, with the largest three firms having almost 40 percent of the market, and the largest five garnering 56.8 percent.

The International Primary Market

In this section, we briefly consider the major investment banking firms that are active in the international bond and equity markets. We then turn to a consideration of the investment banking industry in Great Britain and Japan.

Major Investment Banking Firms in the International Market

Major investment banking firms in the international market come mostly from five countries: Japan, the United States, Great Britain, Switzerland, and Germany. Table 8.10 shows the five leading investment banking firms for international bonds and international equities. Three U.S. investment banks are among the top five for both bonds and equities. (SG Warburg is British; CS First Boston is Swiss; Deutsche Bank is German; Goldman Sachs, Morgan Stanley, and Merrill Lynch are from the United States.)

Table 8.10
Leading International Investment Banking Firms

Rank	International Bonds	International Equities
1	Goldman Sachs	Goldman Sachs
2	Deutsche Bank	Merrill Lynch
3	Morgan Stanley	SG Warburg Securities
4	CS First Boston	CS First Boston
5	Merrill Lynch	Morgan Stanley

Source: *Euromoney*, April 1994.

[12] The use of industry concentration ratios is a common technique in the exploration of industrial structure. For an application of this technique to commercial banking, see A. A. Heggestad and J. J. Mingo, "Prices, Nonprices, and Concentration in Commercial Banking," *Journal of Money, Credit, and Banking*, 8, 1976, pp. 107–17.

Table 8.11
Leading Investment Banking Firms in the British Market

	Bond Issues	Equity Issues
1	GSFB	Samuel Montagu
2	S.G. Warburg	Goldman Sachs
3	Baring Brothers	N.M. Rothschild
4	Salomon Brothers	Scroder Wagg
5	Morgan Grenfell	Lazard Brothers

Source: S. Hayes and P. Hubbard, *Investment Banking*, Boston: Harvard Business School Press, 1990. Data are for 1988.

Investment Banking in Great Britain and Japan

In 1986, Great Britain experienced the **Big Bang** – a major liberalization of regulations governing securities dealing. As part of the deregulation, foreign competition was allowed much more fully than ever before, leading to the merger of many domestic firms and the inclusion of foreign, especially American, firms. Thus, Table 8.11 includes some well-known American firms in its listing of major investment houses in the British market. During the first half of the 1990s, American firms continued to be extremely competitive with native British firms.

In Japan, investment banking has been dominated traditionally by the **Big Four** securities firms: Nomura, Daiwa, Nikko, and Yamaichi. There are other firms, but these four account for a very large percentage of the Japanese market, and they are most active internationally. In the market for new corporate debt and equity, the lead investment bank is almost always a member of the Big Four. In the Japanese financial system, the Ministry of Finance plays a lead role and consults with the investment banks to establish the terms of the offering. Lead manager status rotates among the Big Four, with the other three being named as co-managers. In the 1990s, the reputation of these firms has suffered severely with the revelation of various kickback schemes and questionable connections with members of the Japanese government. These problems, in conjunction with the poor performance of the Japanese economy, have driven these firms from the international prominence they formerly enjoyed. Traditionally, the four firms have ranked from largest to smallest as follows: Nomura, Yamaichi, Nikko, and Daiwa. Among international equity investment banking firms in 1994, only Daiwa made the list of the top 55 investment banking firms.[13]

Summary

This chapter introduced the primary market and explained the function of the investment banker in that market. The United States is the most active country in the world in the flotation of new securities, accounting for approximately one-half of all new securities.

In the process of issuing securities, the investment banker acts as a distribution network for most issues by corporations and municipalities. This is essentially a retailing function. In many cases, the investment banker also underwrites the new issue of security. In an underwriting, an

[13] See *Euromoney*, April 1994.

investment banking syndicate buys the issue of securities from the issuer and tries to sell them at a profit. The difference between the amount the issuer receives and the amount the final investor pays is known as the spread. This spread constitutes the gross profit margin; the investment banking syndicate takes this spread as compensation for its retailing and risk-bearing services. In many cases, the risk accepted by the investment banking syndicate is very large.

Questions and Problems

1. Which entity is the largest issuer of securities in the world?
2. What information is found in a prospectus?
3. Consider the relationship between risk and expected return. How might the fees charged by investment bankers for risk bearing be related to the creditworthiness of the issuer, the issuer's general reputation, and the current stability of financial markets?
4. For some popular new issues, a broker might not have enough of the security to satisfy all of the demand among his or her customers. How might the broker allocate the available securities? What does that imply for the choice of a "full-service" broker vs. a discount broker that does not participate in any syndicates?
5. Why does the federal government issue only debt and no equity?
6. How much cash does IBM receive if an investor buys a share of IBM on the secondary market?
7. Will a small or a large issue of securities have higher percentage flotation costs? Why?
8. In the United States, which is larger, the bond or the stock market?
9. If you were the president of a software firm trying to raise funds for the introduction of a revolutionary product for personal computers, what considerations would be important to you when choosing between a public offering and a private placement? Why?

Suggested REALDATA Exercises

The following *REALDATA* exercise explores the concepts developed in this chapter:
Exercise 24, 31, 32, 36

References

Foster, F. D., "Syndicate Size, Spreads, and Market Power During the Introduction of Shelf Registration," *Journal of Finance,* 44:1, March 1989, pp. 195–204

Hayes III, S. L. and P. M. Hubbard, *Investment Banking: A Tale of Three Cities,* Boston: Harvard Business School Press, 1990

Ibbotson, R. G., J. L. Sindelar, and J. R. Ritter, "Initial Public Offerings," *Journal of Applied Corporate Finance,* 1:2, Summer 1988, pp. 37–45

Jog, V. M. and A. L. Riding, "Underpricing in Canadian IPOs," *Financial Analysts Journal,* 43:6, November/December 1987, pp. 48–55

Kuhn, R. L., *Investment Banking: The Art and Science of High-Stakes Dealmaking,* New York: Harper & Row, Ballinger Division, 1990

Ritter, J. R., "The Long-Run Performance of Initial Public Offerings," *Journal of Finance,* 46:1, March 1991, pp. 3–27

Ruud, J. S., "Another View of the Underpricing of Initial Public Offerings," Federal Reserve Bank of New York *Quarterly Review,* 16:1, Spring 1991, pp. 83–5

Tinic, S. M., "Anatomy of Initial Public Offerings of Common Stock," *Journal of Finance,* 43:4, September 1988, pp. 789–822

Tucker, J. F., *Buying Treasury Securities at Federal Reserve Banks,* Richmond: Federal Reserve Bank of Richmond, 1983

Risk and Return in Securities Markets

9

Overview

In this chapter we introduce the concepts of risk and return. High risk almost always accompanies high expected returns. The investor must know how to measure both return and risk, and how to choose the investment with the most favorable combination.

Armed with these techniques for measuring risk and expected return, we can study how to combine securities to form portfolios. A **portfolio** is a collection of securities held by a single investor. As this chapter explains in detail, one of the main incentives for forming portfolios is diversification. **Diversification** is the allocation of investable funds to a variety of securities in order to reduce risk.

We continue the development of the model by introducing a risk-free asset. The risk-free asset is used to develop a market standard for risk and return against which we can compare the performance of any investment. We also examine the **separation theorem**, which states that all investors should hold the same portfolio of risky assets, no matter how risk tolerant or risk averse they may be. The chapter leads to the Capital Asset Pricing Model (CAPM), which provides a general model that expresses the expected rate of return for an asset as a function of its risk.

Principles of Risk and Return

This section introduces the basic concepts of risk and return. These concepts constitute the foundation of all of portfolio theory.

Expected Return

Suppose you have the opportunity to invest \$1 in Bernoulli Research Corporation. This risky investment has two possible outcomes. If the outcome is favorable (F), you receive \$4. If the outcome is unfavorable (U), the project generates no cash and you lose your entire \$1 investment. Thus, the net payoff, or simply payoff, is either \$3 or −\$1. Assume the outcome occurs almost immediately, so you can disregard the time value of money. Suppose the probability of each outcome is 50 percent. You want to know the expected payoff and the risk of the investment.

With the information given, we can obtain a probability distribution of the possible payoffs. A **probability distribution** is a list of all possible payoffs from the investment, along with their respective probabilities. For this investment the probability distribution is given in Table 9.1.

How much can you expect to earn or lose on average if you make a similar investment repeatedly? In this example, you expect to win \$3 half the time and to lose \$1 the other half. This suggests that the expected payoff can be found as follows:

$$E(\text{Payoff}) = (\$3) \times 0.5 + (-\$1) \times 0.5 = \$1$$

Table 9.1
Probability Distribution of Payoffs for Bernoulli Research Corporation

Outcome	Probability	Payoff
F	0.50	+$3
U	0.50	–$1

In general, if a random variable r can have n possible outcomes r_i, where $I = 1, 2, \ldots, n$, and each outcome has probability p_i, then the expected value of r is given by the summation:

$$E(r) = \sum_{i=1}^{n} r_i p_i \tag{9.1}$$

We also note the basic fact that the sum of all the probabilities must add to 1.0. This is true because we know with certainty that some outcome will be observed.

Variance and Standard Deviation

Risk may be casually defined as the possibility that the actual outcome will differ from the expected outcome. Thus, the notion of risk is associated with the dispersion of possible outcomes. A common way to measure the dispersion of any random variable, r, around its mean is to calculate its variance, σ^2, as follows:

$$\sigma^2 = \sum_{i=1}^{n} [r_i - E(r)]^2 p_i \tag{9.2}$$

For Bernoulli Research, the variance of the payoffs is equal to:

$$\sigma^2 = [3-1]^2 \times 0.5 + [-1-1]^2 \times 0.5 = 4$$

Notice that if the unit for the random variable is dollars, the unit for the variance is dollars squared, making the variance hard to interpret. Because of this difficulty, the standard deviation is often used as an alternative measure of risk. The **standard deviation** of a random variable is the square root of its variance and is denoted by σ. The standard deviation measures the dispersion of a random variable around its mean. For the $1 investment in Bernoulli, the standard deviation of the random payoffs is $2. Since Bernoulli has an expected payoff of $1, the standard deviation of $2 indicates that we can expect most payoffs to be between −$1 ($1 − $2) and $3 ($1 + $2). In fact, in this example the standard deviation gives the entire range of possible payoffs: −$1 and $3.[1]

To continue our example, now suppose that you have found another firm, Binomial Software, which offers the same payoff distribution as Bernoulli Research. You wonder if there is

[1] This is not generally the case. For example, if the payoffs obeyed the rules of a normal distribution, then the payoffs would fall within one standard deviation of the mean payoff about two-thirds of the time.

any benefit in investing \$0.50 in Bernoulli and the other \$0.50 in Binomial. After all, they look exactly alike in terms of their payoff probability distributions. Because you invest half as much as before in each firm, you will receive a payoff of \$1.50 from one of the firms if the outcome of that firm is favorable, and you will lose \$0.50 for each firm with an unfavorable outcome.

Let us assume that Bernoulli and Binomial are **independent investments**. This means that the outcome of Bernoulli will not have any influence on the outcome of Binomial. Because the payoffs of the two firms are independent, the probability distribution of the combined investment consists of four equally likely outcomes, as shown in Table 9.2.

Knowing the probability distribution of this two-investment strategy, we can compute its expected payoff of \$1 from Equation 9.1. We conclude that dividing money into two identical independent investments provides the same expected payoff as putting all the money into one of the investments. However, consider what happens to the risk of the combined investment. Using Equation 9.2, we compute a variance of 2.00 for the combined investment. Thus, the variance from investing equally in Bernoulli and Binomial is half the variance of investing the entire \$1 in Bernoulli alone. Most importantly, there is no cost associated with this risk reduction because the expected payoff is unchanged.

This simple example with two independent identical investments illustrates the following general result. By investing in equal proportions in n identical independent projects, the expected payoff will be the same as the expected payoff of investing all the money in only one of the projects. However, the overall standard deviation from the n project investment is lower than the standard deviation from the single project investment. If σ_1 is the standard deviation of the single project investment and σ_n is the standard deviation of the n project investment, then:

$$\sigma_n = \frac{\sigma_1}{\sqrt{n}} \tag{9.3}$$

In the case of Bernoulli and Binomial, there is no need to calculate the standard deviation of the two-project investment directly from the definition. Rather, since we already know that the standard deviation of each of the two identical independent projects is \$2, we can use Equation 9.3 directly to find σ_2 = \$1.41, or $\sigma_2^2 = 2.00$, the same result as before.

Table 9.2
Probability Distribution of Payoffs from Combining Bernoulli and Binomial

Bernoulli Outcome	Binomial Outcome	Probability	Bernoulli Payoff	Binomial Payoff	Total Payoff
F	*F*	0.25	\$1.50	\$1.50	\$3.00
F	*U*	0.25	\$1.50	–\$0.50	\$1.00
U	*F*	0.25	–\$0.50	\$1.50	\$1.00
U	*U*	0.25	–\$0.50	–\$0.50	–\$1.00

Covariance

The covariance measures the tendency of any pair of random variables to move together. Intuitively, the covariance measures the "connection" between two random variables. For example, because tall people tend to weigh more than short people, we can say that height and weight have a positive covariance. In finance, when interest rates increase unexpectedly, the stock market index tends to decrease. This is an example of two variables with a negative covariance. A further example is that of tossing two coins. Since the outcome of tossing one coin does not affect the outcome of the other coin toss, the two outcomes are independent. For pairs of independent random variables, the covariance is zero, since these variables are not connected.

To formalize these ideas, suppose two random variables, x and y, have n possible combined outcomes. When combined outcome I occurs, the value of x is x_i and the value of y is y_i. Assume that the probability that outcome I occurs is p_i. Let the expected values of x and y be $E(x)$ and $E(y)$, respectively. Then, the covariance between these two random variables is defined as follows:

$$\mathrm{COV}(x, y) = \sum_{i=1}^{n} [x_i - E(x)][y_i - E(y)]\, p_i \tag{9.4}$$

With this definition, we can compute the covariance between the payoffs of Bernoulli Research and the payoffs of Binomial Software, using the data in Table 9.2:[2]

$$\begin{aligned}\mathrm{COV}(x, y) &= [1.50\ -0.5][1.50-0.5]\ 0.25\\ &\quad + [1.50\ -0.5][1.50-0.5]\ 0.25\\ &\quad + [1.50\ -0.5][1.50-0.5]\ 0.25\\ &\quad + [1.50\ -0.5][-1.50-0.5]\ 0.25\\ &= (1 - 1 - 1 + 1)\ 0.25\\ &= 0.00\end{aligned}$$

This computation tells us that there is no covariance between the two identical firms. This should not be surprising, since we already know that the two investments are independent of each other and, therefore, do not covary.

It is useful to note that the variance is just a special case of the covariance of an asset with itself. For example, the covariance of asset x with itself is, according to Equation 9.4:

$$\begin{aligned}\mathrm{COV}(x, y) &= \sum_{i=1}^{n} [x_i - E(x)][x_i - E(x)]\, p_i = \sum_{i=1}^{n} [x_i - E(x)]^2\, p_i \\ &= \sigma_x^2\end{aligned} \tag{9.5}$$

Another useful property of the covariance is that the order of the variables is irrelevant in its computation. Thus, $\mathrm{COV}(x, y) = \mathrm{COV}(y, x)$. These properties will be useful when we discuss multiple-asset portfolios.

---

[2] Notice that while the expected payoff of the combined investment is \$1, the expected payoff of each investment considered separately is \$0.50.

Correlation Coefficient

The covariance has two major disadvantages. First, the covariance may turn out to be any number, however large or small. Second, the numerical value of the covariance depends on the units used to measure the random variables. These problems make comparisons of different covariances difficult.

Fortunately, the problem of comparing the degree of connection between different pairs of random variables can be solved through the ingenious trick of dividing the covariance between two random variables by the product of their standard deviations. It is a remarkable fact that by performing this operation on the covariance, the resulting number will always be between −1 and +1. This number is called the correlation coefficient between the two random variables. The **correlation coefficient** between two random variables x and y is given by the following formula:[3]

$$\rho\,(x, y) = \frac{\mathrm{COV}(x, y)}{\sigma_x\,\sigma_y} \tag{9.6}$$

For the example of Bernoulli and Binomial, we found that the covariance between the two firms' payoffs is zero. It follows from Equation 9.6 that their correlation coefficient is also zero, confirming that there is no connection between the two investment payoffs.

Risk and Return in the New York Stock Exchange

We now apply the concepts of risk and return to the recent history of the New York Stock Exchange. Figure 9.1 shows the yearly rate of return on large common stocks for the period 1926–94. The largest return occurred in 1933 and was 53.99 percent, with the smallest, −43.44 percent, coming two years earlier in 1931. It is also clear from the figure that years of gains occurred more often than years of losses. But perhaps most striking is the great tendency for radical swings from one year to the next.

For these stocks, the mean rate of return over the entire period was 10.2 percent, and the standard deviation of the returns was 20.3 percent. These statistics provide a convenient way of summarizing a great deal of information.

Two-Asset Risky Portfolios

We use a two-asset risky portfolio to illustrate diversification and the building of portfolios. The expected return of a two-asset portfolio depends on the expected returns of the individual assets and the relative percentage of funds invested in each.

The Expected Return of a Two-Asset Risky Portfolio

The expected return of a portfolio consisting of Assets A and B is:

$$E(r_P) = w_a\,E(r_a) + w_b\,E(r_b) \tag{9.7}$$

---

[3] When there is no possible confusion, we will simply write ρ instead of $\rho\,(x, y)$.

Figure 9.1
Yearly Rates of Return on Common Stocks

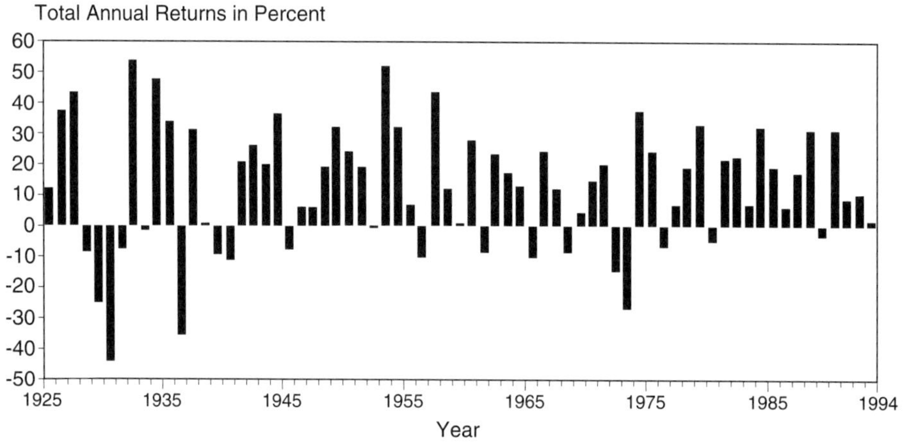

Total Annual Returns in Percent

Year

Source: *Stocks, Bonds, Bills, and Inflation: 1995 Yearbook,* Chicago: Ibbotson Associates, 1995.

where:

w_i = percentage of funds, or weight, committed to Asset $I = a, b$

$E(r_i)$ = the expected return on Asset I, where $I = a, b,$ or P

Notice also that, because all of the funds under consideration are committed to one asset or another to form the portfolio, we must have:

$$w_a + w_b = 1 \tag{9.8}$$

Equation 9.8 implies that we can express one of the weights in terms of the other. Notice also that the expected return of a two-asset portfolio is a simple weighted average of the expected returns of the individual assets.

The Risk of a Two-Asset Portfolio

The risk of a portfolio, like that of any asset, is measured by its variance and standard deviation. If we already have the expected return and the variance of each of the portfolio Assets A and B, as well as the covariance between them and the weight of each asset in the portfolio, then Equation 9.2 can be transformed into the following expression:

$$\sigma_P^2 = w_a^2\sigma_a^2 + w_b^2\sigma_b^2 + 2w_a w_b\, COV(r_a, r_b) \tag{9.9}$$

We can also express the variance of a two-asset portfolio using the correlation coefficient, ρ, instead of the covariance. The formula is:[4]

$$\sigma_P^2 = w_a^2\,\sigma_a^2 + w_b^2\sigma_b^2 + 2w_a\;w_b\;\sigma_a\;\sigma_b\,\rho \tag{9.10}$$

Risk, Covariance, and Correlation

The risk of a portfolio depends mainly upon the covariance or correlation among the assets in the portfolio. We can illustrate this fact for a two-asset risky portfolio. Consider two Securities *A* and *B* and assume they have the following risk/return characteristics.

	A	*B*
$E(r)$	0.10	0.18
σ	0.08	0.22
w	0.40	0.60

Notice that although the correlation between two assets affects the risk of a portfolio, it has no effect on the portfolio's return. This is clear from Equation 9.7, the formula for the expected return of a portfolio. In the case of our portfolio made up of *A* and *B*, the expected return is:

$$E\,(r_P) = 0.4 \times 0.10 + 0.6 \times 0.18 = 0.148$$

To see how the correlation of returns determines the risk of a portfolio, we consider two special cases and examine the effect on the portfolio's risk. The first special case arises when the correlation between the assets equals 1. This is the case of perfect positive correlation. A second special case arises when the correlation equals -1. This is the case of perfect negative correlation.

Correlation = +1 If the correlation coefficient between the two assets equals +1, the last term in Equation 9.10 becomes $2w_aw_b\,\sigma_a\,\sigma_b$. In this special case, the expression for the variance is a perfect square:[5]

$$\sigma_P^2 = w_a^2\,\sigma_a^2 + w_b^2\,\sigma_b^2 + 2\,(w_a\,\sigma_a)\,(w_b\,\sigma_b)$$

$$= (w_a\,\sigma_a + w_b\,\sigma_b)^2$$

Taking the square root on both sides of this expression gives:

$$\sigma_P = w_a\sigma_a + w_b\sigma_b \tag{9.11}$$

---

[4] To obtain this version of the formula, note that from Equation 9.6 we have COV(A, B) = $\rho\,\sigma_a\,\sigma_b$.

[5] Recall from your high school math that $(a + b)^2 = a^2 + b^2 + 2\,ab$.

When the correlation coefficient equals +1, the risk of the portfolio depends only on the risk of the individual assets and on the proportion of each asset in the portfolio. If Assets A and B have perfect positive correlation, the standard deviation is:

$$\sigma_P = 0.4 \times 0.08 + 0.6 \times 0.22 = 0.164$$

Other portfolio weights would give portfolios of different risk levels. In fact, if we construct different portfolios of A and B by just choosing different weights, we can find the locus of all possible portfolios of A and B in risk/return space. Figure 9.2 shows the position of A and B in risk/return space. Notice that when the correlation between A and B is $\rho = +1$, all possible portfolios lie on the straight line determined by A and B.

Correlation = –1.0 The second special case arises when the correlation coefficient between the two assets equals -1. In this case, the last term in Equation 9.10 becomes $-2w_a w_b \sigma_a \sigma_b$. Once again, the expression for the variance is a perfect square:

$$\sigma_P^2 = w_a^2 \sigma_a^2 + w_b^2 \sigma_b^2 - 2(w_a \sigma_a)(w_b \sigma_b)$$

$$= (w_a \sigma_a - w_b \sigma_b)^2$$

Figure 9.2
Possible Risk/Return Combinations of *A* and *B* When ρ = 1

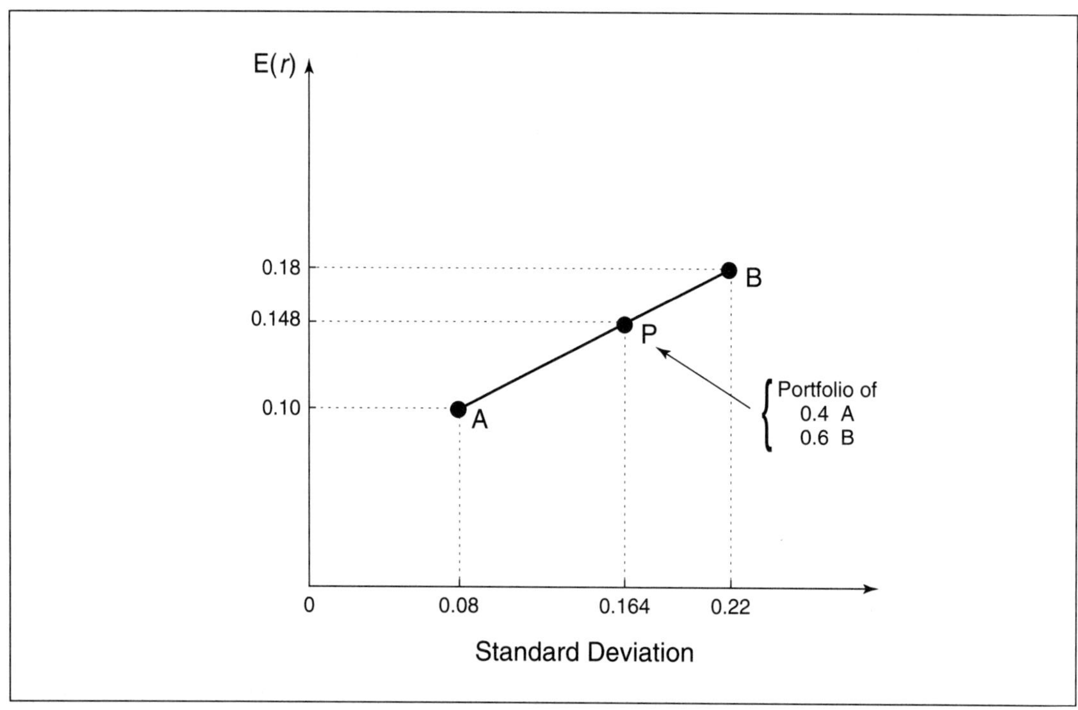

Taking the square root on both sides of this expression gives:

$$\sigma_P = w_a \sigma_a - w_b \sigma_b \tag{9.12}$$

For our portfolio of *A* and *B*, the standard deviation is:

$$\sigma_P = 0.6 \times 0.22 - 0.4 \times 0.08 = 0.10$$

Notice that when two assets are perfectly negatively correlated we can form a risk-free portfolio. By making an appropriate choice of the proportions of each asset in the portfolio, the two terms will cancel. To find the proportions of each asset that lead to a risk-free portfolio, recall that $w_b = 1 - w_a$. Using this expression in Equation 9.12 and solving for w_a we get:

$$w_a = \frac{\sigma_b}{\sigma_a + \sigma_b} \tag{9.13}$$

In our example, the proportion of Asset *A* required to form a risk-free portfolio is:

$$w_a = \frac{0.22}{0.08 + 0.22} = 0.73$$

Since we require 73 percent of the investment in Asset *A*, the other 27 percent should be allocated to Asset *B*. In our example, these are the only weights that result in a risk-free portfolio of Assets *A* and *B*.

Figure 9.3 shows the possible portfolio combinations we can construct from Assets *A* and *B* when $\rho = -1$. The line from *B* to the vertical axis and from there to *A* defines the risk/return possibilities, which include a risk-free portfolio, *F*.

Figure 9.3 also illustrates the idea of **dominance**. By combining *A* and *B* in the correct amounts, we can form a portfolio at point *G* on the line between *B* and *F*. Portfolio *G* is said to dominate Asset *A* because *G* has the same level of risk as *A* but offers greater expected return. In fact, some portfolio on the line from *F* to *B* will dominate any portfolio on the line from *A* to *F*. Because *A* is dominated, no investor should hold *A* alone.

The concept of dominance leads to that of the efficient set. The **efficient set** is the set of all assets and portfolios that are not dominated. Similarly, the **efficient frontier** is the graphical representation of the elements of the efficient set. For example, in Figure 9.3 the efficient frontier is given by the line *FB*.

Correlation Between –1 and +1 Because the correlation coefficient must lie within $\rho = +1$ and $\rho = -1$, these two extremes define the entire realm of risk/return possibilities we can form using Securities *A* and *B*. However, for most security pairs, the correlation of returns between them lies at neither extreme.

Most securities pairs are positively correlated. Figure 9.4 shows the portfolio possibilities between *A* and *B* for a correlation of 0.7. This value is typical of the correlations between stocks in the marketplace.

Figure 9.3
Possible Risk/Return Combinations of *A* and *B* When $\rho = -1$

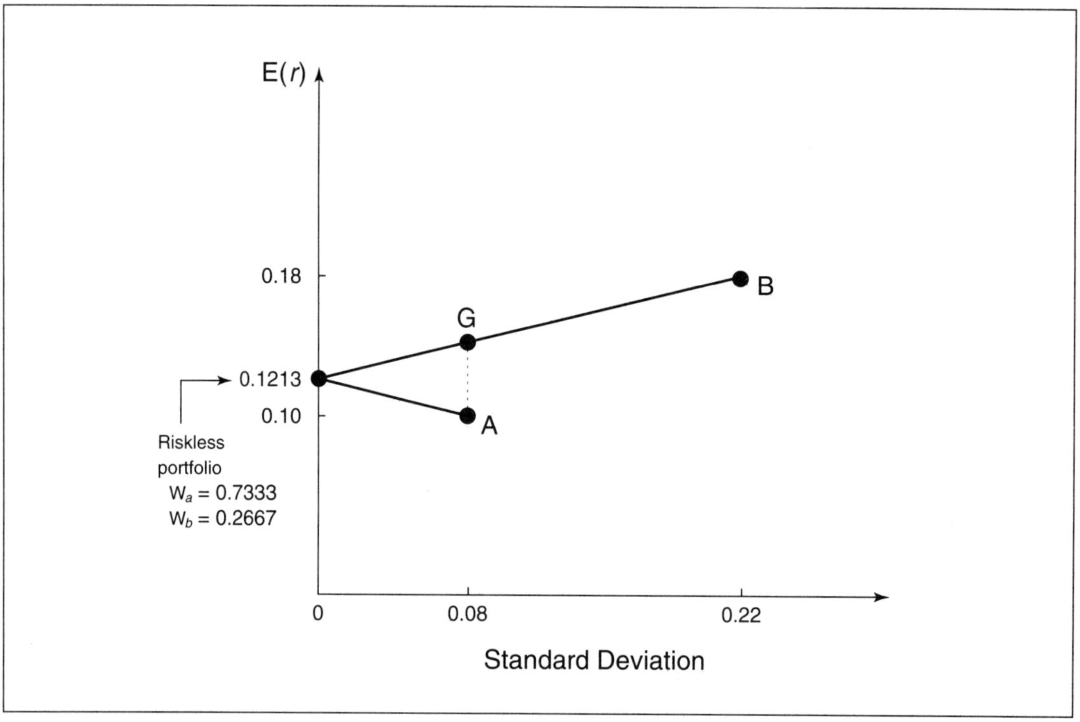

Multiple-Asset Portfolios

All of the basic ideas introduced in the context of two-asset portfolios still hold when we allow investors to construct portfolios of many assets. The formulas for the expected return and risk of a portfolio with many assets are essentially the same as they were for the two-asset case, only somewhat lengthier. For example, the expected return for an n-asset risky portfolio is:

$$E\,(r_P) = \sum_{i=1}^{n} w_i\, E(r_i) \qquad (9.14)$$

and the variance of an n-asset portfolio is given by:

$$\sigma_P^2 = \sum_{i=1}^{n} \sum_{j=1}^{n} w_i\, w_j\, COV(i, j) \qquad (9.15)$$

Although the expression for the variance of a multiple-asset portfolio seems menacing, do not despair because there is a simple way to make it operational, using the so-called covariance matrix method. The **covariance matrix method** for finding the variance of an n-asset portfolio consists of forming an $n \times n$ matrix containing a total of n^2 cells.[6] Each cell in the matrix is filled

Figure 9.4
Possible Risk/Return Combinations of *A* and *B* When ρ = 0.7

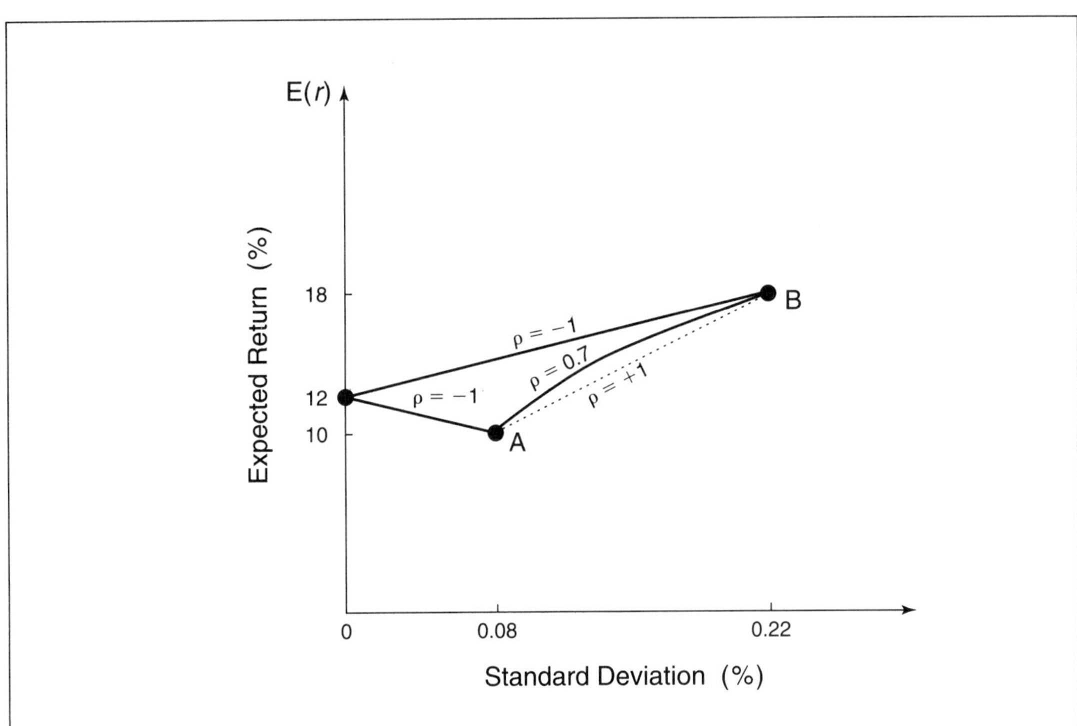

using the same simple general expression. Once the matrix is full, we can compute the variance of the portfolio by simply adding the values of all the cells in the matrix.

To illustrate the covariance matrix method, consider the two-asset portfolio discussed earlier. From Equation 9.9, we know that the formula for the variance of a portfolio of Assets *A* and *B* is:

$$\sigma_P^2 = w_a^2 \sigma_a^2 + w_b^2 \sigma_b^2 + 2 w_a w_b \, \mathrm{COV}(r_a, r_b)$$

We can express the right-hand side of this expression differently using the covariance matrix method. The key is to realize that the last term of the above formula is really the sum of two equal terms (hence the 2 in that term); there are really four terms in the variance formula. These four terms can be arranged in a 2 × 2 matrix, as follows:

	Column *j*	
Row *I*	**1**	**2**
1	$(w_a \sigma_a)^2$	$w_a w_b \, \mathrm{COV}(a, b)$
2	$w_b w_a \, \mathrm{COV}(b, a)$	$(w_b \sigma_b)^2$

[6] In general, a matrix is nothing but an array of numbers, organized into rows and columns.

Each cell in the covariance matrix may be denoted by $c(I, j)$, where the index I indicates the row and the index j indicates the column in the matrix. In this two-asset example we have $c(2, 1) = w_b w_a \text{COV}(b, a)$, and $c(1, 2) = w_a w_b \text{ COV}(a, b)$. Since $\text{COV}(a, b) = \text{COV}(b, a)$, it follows that $c(2, 1) = c(1, 2)$. Whenever $c(I, j) = c(j, I)$, a matrix is said to be symmetric. A useful property to note is that any covariance matrix is symmetric.

Following the example of a 2×2 covariance matrix, we can now generalize these ideas to a matrix of arbitrary size. In the general case of an n-asset portfolio, each cell of the $n \times n$ covariance matrix can be filled using the following simple formula:

$$c(i, j) = w_i \, w_j \, \text{COV}(i, j) \tag{9.16}$$

It is important to note that Equation 9.16 is also valid for the cells along the main diagonal. This is true because the covariance of any asset with itself is equal to the variance of that asset.

Introduction of the Risk-Free Asset

The risk-free asset is an asset with no default risk, so we have $E(r_f) = r_f$, and the expected return for a portfolio involving the risk-free asset is:

$$E(r_p) = w_f \, r_f + w_j \, E(r_j) \tag{9.17}$$

Also, for the risk-free asset, $\sigma_f^2 = 0$ and $\text{COV}(f, j) = 0$. Consequently, the variance of a two-asset portfolio which includes the risk-free asset will be:

$$\sigma_P^2 = w_j^2 \sigma_j^2 \tag{9.18}$$

From this, the standard deviation of the portfolio is:

$$\sigma_P = w_j \, \sigma_j \tag{9.19}$$

We can combine any risky Portfolio j with the risk-free asset, f, as in Figure 9.5. However, investors may prefer to combine other risky portfolios with f. In fact, no matter what an investor's risk preferences might be, investing in risky Portfolio j is never optimal. To see why, consider risky Portfolios j and k in Figure 9.5. Just as we could combine f and j to achieve portfolios on the line fj, we can combine f and k to achieve portfolios on the line fk. However, every portfolio on the line fj is dominated by a portfolio on the line fk. This means that every investor would prefer to hold risky Portfolio k rather than risky Portfolio j.

From this comparison between j and k, we see that one should move up the curve beyond k to find yet better risky portfolios. This process ceases when the line from f to the risky portfolio is just tangent to the efficient frontier. Figure 9.5 shows this portfolio of risky assets M. When we combine portfolio M with f, we can reach any portfolio on the line fMZ. Introducing the risk-free asset changes the efficient frontier. The new efficient frontier runs along the line fMZ. Notice that we here are explicitly assuming that there is no possibility of borrowing or using leverage. The next section considers how investors can use leverage to increase their expected return and risk.

Figure 9.5
Borrowing and Lending on the Capital Market Line

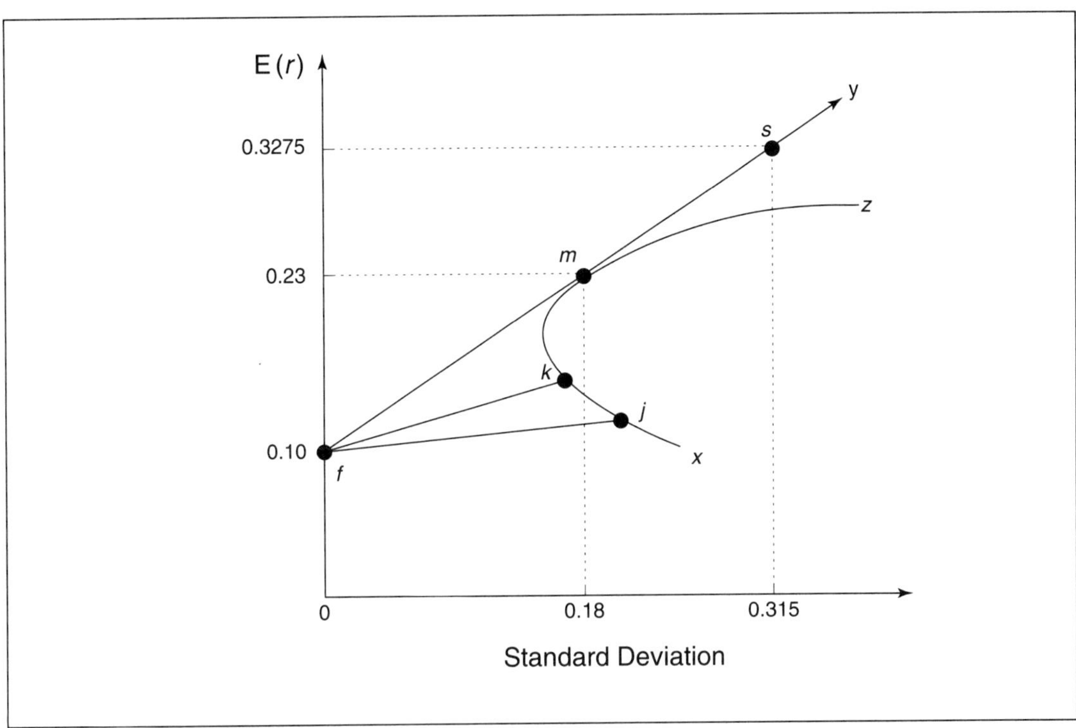

Borrowing and Lending

Thus far, we have determined that investors seek portfolios on the line *fMZ*. How can we trade to create such portfolios? To build portfolios that lie on the line from *f* to *M*, the investor must hold the risky Portfolio *M* and also invest some money in the risk-free asset. We can think of this risk-free asset as a Treasury bill. Investing in Treasury bills is equivalent to lending to the government. The investor can also achieve portfolios on the curve from *M* to *Z* by selecting the risky portfolio represented by the point on that line segment.

In addition to lending portfolios, there are also borrowing portfolios. We can construct borrowing portfolios by borrowing funds and investing the borrowed funds, in addition to the original capital, in a risky portfolio. Because we assume perfect markets, we can borrow and lend at the risk-free rate r_f. The chance to borrow at a rate r_f improves the investor's opportunity set. To illustrate this improvement, consider the following example, using the data given below.

Asset	r_f	M
$E(R)$	0.10	0.23
σ	0.00	0.18

Assume an initial wealth of $1,000. To create a borrowing portfolio, consider a situation in which the investor borrows $750 at a rate r_f = 10 percent. The borrowed funds plus the original capital of $1,000 are invested in the risky Portfolio *M*. Table 9.3 shows the different portfolios, with their expected returns and standard deviations.

To understand the borrowing portfolio more fully, assume that the risky Portfolio *M* actually earns the expected return in the period under analysis. Then the value of the portfolio at the end of the period will be $1,750 × 1.23 = $2,152.50. At the end of the period, the investor must repay the $750 loan with 10 percent interest, or $825. After the risky portfolio earns the 23 percent return and the investor repays $825, $1,327.50 remains. The investor has then earned $327.50 on the original capital of $1,000. This implies a 32.75 percent annual rate of return. As this example shows, borrowing increases the expected return on the original capital.

Not only does borrowing at r_f to invest in a risky portfolio increase the expected return, it also increases the risk. To see how the risk increases, assume the risky Portfolio *M* earns a return one standard deviation above or below its expected return. Under these assumptions we compute the returns on the borrowing portfolio. If the risky portfolio earns one standard deviation less than its expected return, it earns 0.23 − 0.18 = 0.05, or 5 percent. In this situation, the borrowing portfolio will be worth 1.05 × $1,750 = $1,837.50. From this amount, the investor pays the debt of $825, leaving $1,012.50. This gives a return of 1.25 percent on the original capital. If the return on the risky portfolio is one standard deviation above the expected return, the risky portfolio will earn 0.23 + 0.18 = 0.41, or 41 percent. The portfolio will be worth 1.41 × $1,750 = $2,467.50 at the end of the period. From these proceeds, the investor repays $825, leaving $1,642.50. On the initial capital of $1,000, the investor earns a return of 64.25 percent.

An alternative way of obtaining the same results is through the use of Equations 9.17 and 9.19, as follows:

$$E(r_P) = -0.75 \times 10\% + 1.75 \times 23\% = 32.75\%$$

$$\sigma_P = 1.75 \times 18\% = 31.5\%$$

Figure 9.5 shows the leveraged portfolio, S, of this example. Clearly, by borrowing at the risk-free rate and using the funds to invest in risky Portfolio *M*, the investor increases both the expected return and the risk of the investment. Notice now that the risky portfolios between points *M* and *Z* are dominated by portfolios lying beyond *M* on the line *fMS*.

In fact, with the ability to both borrow and lend, there is only one risky portfolio that is not dominated, and that is Portfolio *M*. Therefore, all investors will hold *M* as their risky portfolio, although they may differ in the proportion of funds they choose to invest in *M*. Some will invest a portion of their funds in *M* and some in *f*. Bolder investors might borrow funds at a rate r_f and

Table 9.3
Portfolios Constructed from the Risk-Free Asset *f* and Risky Portfolio *M*

w_f	w_M	$E(r_p)$	σ_p
0.5	0.5	0.165	0.09
0.0	1.0	0.23	0.18
–0.75	1.75	0.3275	0.3150

invest the proceeds in *M* along with their original capital. However, all investors who hold any of their funds in risky assets will put those funds in Portfolio *M*.

The Market Portfolio and the Separation Theorem

So far, we have seen that all investors who commit any funds to risky securities will do so by investing in Portfolio *M*, shown in Figure 9.5. Therefore, we need to understand the characteristics of this special Portfolio *M*.

We now show that Portfolio *M* is the market portfolio. The **market portfolio** is the portfolio of risky assets that includes every risky security in the marketplace, with each security having a weight proportional to its market value. For example, if the total market value of IBM's shares is $4 billion, and the combined market value of all securities is $100 billion, then IBM would have a weight of 4 percent in the market portfolio. Accordingly, the market portfolio is a value-weighted portfolio.

We know that Portfolio *M* must be the market portfolio from reflecting on the following two facts. First, we know all investors hold *M* as their risky portfolio. Second, we know that someone owns each security. There are simply no securities floating around without owners. It follows that all securities can have an owner and all investors can have the same risky portfolio only if each investor holds all possible securities. This is the same as saying that all investors hold the market portfolio.

Because all investors who hold any risky assets hold Portfolio *M*, the choice of a risky portfolio is independent of the choice of a particular portfolio on the line *fMS*. This is the **separation theorem** – the investment decision is separate from the financing decision. Every investor who holds risky assets holds Portfolio *M*. The financing decision – whether to borrow or lend, and how much – is separate from the choice of investing in a portfolio of risky assets.

The Capital Market Line

Since investors can only move along the line *fMS* in Figure 9.5, that line represents the trade-off between risk and return available in the capital market. As such, it is the **Capital Market Line** (CML). Because the CML slopes upward, it reveals graphically that the acquisition of greater expected return requires that the investor accept more risk.

We can express the CML as an equation. Consider any portfolio *j* on the CML with an expected return of $E(r_j)$ and a risk of σ_j. Applying the equation of a straight line to portfolio *j*, we have, after some rearranging:[7]

$$E(r_j) = r_f + \frac{\sigma_j}{\sigma_m}[E(r_m) - r_f] \qquad (9.20)$$

Risk and Expected Return for Individual Securities

The CML is important because it expresses the relationship between the risk and expected return of a portfolio consisting of a mix of the market portfolio and the risk-free asset. The slope of the CML reveals how much extra return investors obtain for each extra unit of risk they bear.

---

[7] Recall that a straight line has the form $y = b + m\,x$, where *m* is the slope of the line ("rise over run") and *b* is its intercept with the vertical, or *y*, axis.

Therefore, the slope of the CML gives the market price of risk for fully diversified portfolios. It is important to note that the CML pertains only to well-diversified portfolios.

Another important relationship, the Security Market Line (SML), expresses the expected return of an individual security as a function of its level of relevant risk. What is the relevant risk for each security in the market portfolio? We know it cannot be the variance of the security, since part of that variance can be diversified away when the security is part of a portfolio. We also know all investors hold the market portfolio of risky assets. Therefore, the only relevant risk of an individual security is the risk it contributes to the overall risk of the market portfolio. It is also clear that the market portfolio risk arises from some aggregation of the relevant risk of its component securities. We measure this relevant risk of individual securities by their **beta**.

Beta

We have already examined the behavior of multiple-asset risky portfolios using the covariance matrix method to compute the portfolio variance. Using the same technique, we can also compute the variance of the market portfolio in terms of each of its component securities. This computation will reveal the contribution of each security to the overall risk of the market portfolio.

If there are n risky assets in the market, and the proportion of the value of asset I relative to the value of the market is w_i, then the variance of the market portfolio, σ_m^2, is the sum of all the entries in the following covariance matrix:

	1	2	. . .	n
1	$(w_1\sigma_1)^2$	$w_1 w_2 \text{COV}(1, 2)$	. . .	$w_1 w_n \text{COV}(1, n)$
2	$w_2 w_1 \text{COV}(2, 1)$	$(w_2 \sigma_2)^2$	. . .	$w_2 w_n \text{COV}(2, n)$
3	$w_3 w_1 \text{COV}(3, 1)$	$w_3 w_2 \text{COV}(3, 2)$	. . .	$w_3 w_n \text{COV}(3, n)$
. . .	. . .	...	. . .	. . .
n	$w_n w_1 \text{COV}(n, 1)$	$w_n w_2 \text{COV}(n, 2)$	. . .	$(w_n \sigma_n)^2$

We will sketch only the intermediate steps, which can be completed as a challenging exercise. If we sum across each row of the matrix, recall that $\text{COV}(I, I) = \sigma_I^2$, and note that for any random variables y, x_1, and x_2, and arbitrary numbers a_1 and a_2, the covariance can be expressed as:

$$\text{COV}(y, a_1 x_1 + a_2 x_2) = a_1 \, \text{COV}(y, x_1) + a_2 \, \text{COV}(y, x_2)$$

we eventually arrive at the following expression

$$\sigma_m^2 = w_1 \text{COV}(1, m) + w_2 \text{COV}(2, m) + \ldots + w_n \text{COV}(n, m)$$

Finally, we multiply and divide the right-hand side of this expression by the variance of the market, σ_m^2, to get:

$$\sigma_m^2 = \sigma_m^2 \left(w_1 \frac{\text{COV}(1, m)}{\sigma_m^2} + w_2 \frac{\text{COV}(2, m)}{\sigma_m^2} + \ldots + \frac{\text{COV}(n, m)}{\sigma_m^2} \right) \qquad (9.21)$$

We now define the beta of asset I as the ratio of the covariance of that asset with the market, over the variance of the market:

$$\beta_i = \frac{\text{COV}(i,m)}{\sigma_m^2} \tag{9.22}$$

With this definition of beta, we can rewrite Equation 9.21 as follows:

$$\sigma_m^2 = \sigma_m^2 [w_1 \beta_1 + w_2 \beta_2 + \ldots w_n \beta_n] \tag{9.23}$$

This is the expression we were seeking. It shows that the overall risk of the market portfolio, σ_m^2, is the weighted average of the betas of the individual component securities. It follows that beta measures the risk of an individual security, when that security is part of a well-diversified portfolio.

It is sometimes useful to express the beta of an asset in an alternative form, based on the identity $\text{COV}(I, m) \equiv \sigma_i \sigma_m \rho_{(i,m)}$:

$$\beta_i = \frac{\sigma_i}{\sigma_m} \rho(i\ m) \tag{9.24}$$

A direct consequence of Equation 9.23 is that the weighted average of all the betas in the market portfolio is equal to 1. Equivalently, the beta of the market portfolio is $\beta_m = 1$. A security or portfolio with a beta greater than 1 is **aggressive** because it has more risk than the market portfolio. A security or portfolio with a beta less than 1 is **defensive** because it has less risk than the market portfolio.

Figure 9.6 presents the actual distribution of betas for firms in the stock market for the period 1926–85. The figure contains several interesting features. First, it shows that the distribution of betas is skewed to the right, indicating that most firms tend to be defensive. Second, almost all firms have positive betas. Third, the figure confirms that the average risk of all firms in the market is 1.

The Security Market Line

The Security Market Line (SML) expresses the central idea of the Capital Asset Pricing Model (CAPM): The expected return of a security increases linearly with risk, as measured by beta. This relationship is shown in Figure 9.7.

We can construct the SML using the knowledge we have already acquired. By definition, the risk-free asset has zero risk, and a return of r_f. We also know that the market portfolio has a beta of 1 and its expected return is $E(r_m)$. It is also clear from our previous discussion that $E(r_m) > r_f$, since bearing risk is compensated by the market. This means that the SML will be upward sloping and will pass through the points for the risk-free asset and the market portfolio.

In equilibrium, each security lies on the SML and receives compensation for its level of beta risk. We can express the expected return for a security by the equation for the SML. To find the equation for the SML, we use the basic equation for a straight line, $y = b + mx$, noting that for the

Figure 9.6
The Distribution of Betas in the Stock Market

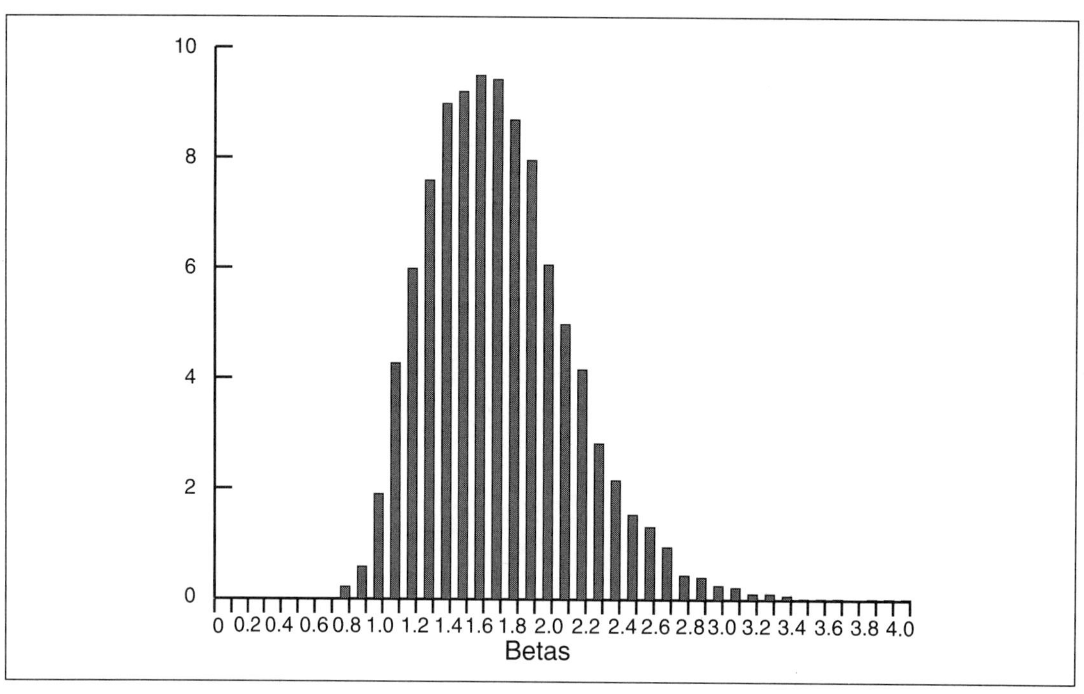

SML the intercept is the risk-free rate and the slope of the line is found by comparing the coordinates of points M and r_f. We can then see that the basic equation of the Capital Asset Pricing Model is:

$$E(r_i) = r_f + [E(r_m) - r_f]\beta_i \tag{9.25}$$

In Equation 9.25, the market risk premium is $E(r_m) - r_f$. The market risk premium is the additional return the investor expects to earn by holding the market portfolio rather than the risk-free asset. It is also equal to the slope of the SML.

Summary

This chapter has adopted the viewpoint that investors are concerned with achieving return and avoiding risk. Assuming that investors desire portfolios with high expected return and low risk, we saw the important benefits of diversification that arise from combining individual securities into portfolios.

When returns are less than perfectly positively correlated, forming portfolios will reduce risk, but not completely. In a market with many risky assets, there will be many investment opportunities that are not dominated. The non-dominated investment opportunities constitute the efficient set and may be graphed in risk/return space as the efficient frontier. Individual investors may choose different risky portfolios according to their different attitudes toward risk. Risk-tolerant

Figure 9.7
The Security Market Line

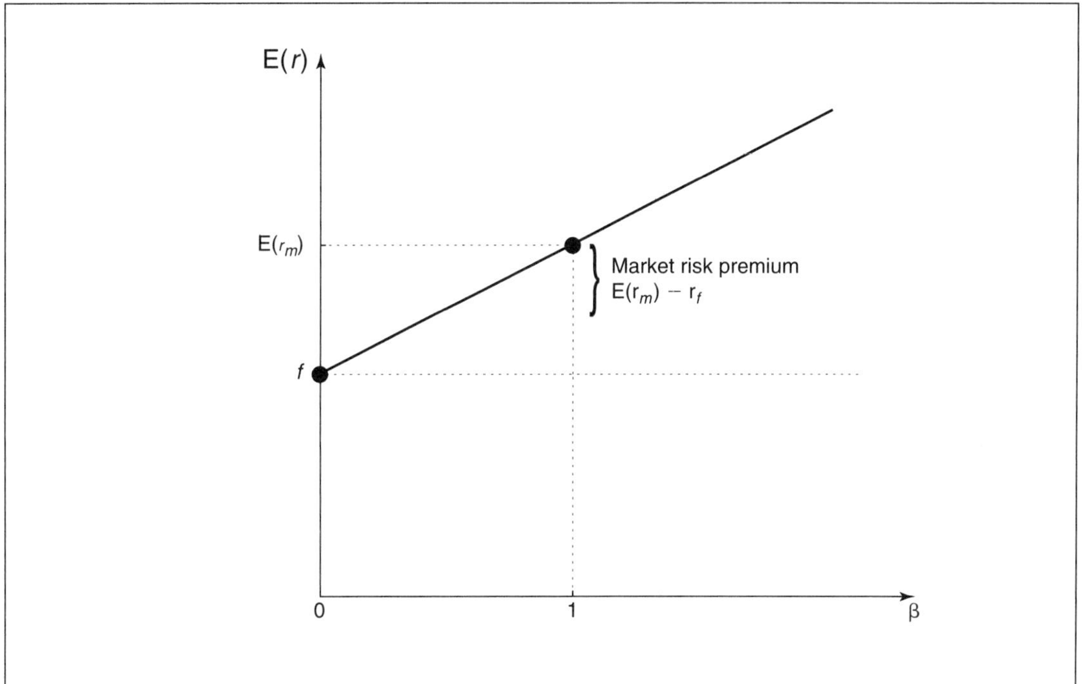

investors choose portfolios that offer high expected returns and high risk, while conservative investors choose portfolios with lower expected returns and lower risks.

We also traced the main outlines of Capital Market Theory. After discussing that beta is the relevant measure of risk, we derived the main result of the Capital Asset Pricing Model. This result states that the expected return of any security or portfolio increases linearly with its beta risk. This relationship is described graphically by the security market line, SML.

Questions and Problems

1. In this book, we generally assume that investors dislike risk. If a particular investor liked both risk and high expected returns, what kinds of opportunities would that investor find in the financial marketplace?

2. The standard deviation and variance consider outcomes that are both above and below the mean return. Someone might argue that this makes them poor measures of investment risk, because the only risk of concern to an investor is the chance that the result might be **below** the mean. How could you respond to this criticism?

3. Why do investors diversify?

4. Which is important to the investor's decision as we have defined it, return or expected return?

5. Security A has an expected return of 14 percent, while Security B has an expected return of 12 percent. Is this enough information to determine whether A dominates B?

6. If Security A has an expected return of 14 percent and a standard deviation of returns of 20 percent, while Security B has an expected return of 12 percent and a standard deviation of returns of 19 percent, does A dominate B? Why or why not?

7. Your broker tells you that it is important to diversify because doing so will increase your expected returns, even if you diversify by randomly selecting stocks. What should you do?

8. Your broker tells you that the standard deviation of returns for a portfolio depends only on the standard deviations of the individual securities and the amount of funds invested in each. What should be your response? Why?

9. What is the relationship between the covariance of returns and the correlation of returns?

10. You already have a one-stock portfolio and, after reading this chapter, you are urgently considering adding a second. Your broker recommends against the one you are considering because it has a high covariance with the stock you already own. However, he does not know the standard deviation of either stock's returns. What should you do? Why?

11. Securities C and D have returns with a correlation of –0.9. Can you combine them to form a risk-free portfolio?

12. Your new broker is helping you form a new portfolio and recommends that you select from 30 stocks that the research department says lie on the efficient frontier. What should you do? Why?

13. Your second new broker says that no individual stock could ever lie on the efficient frontier. Is this correct? Why or why not?

14. In the case of many risky assets, why does the efficient frontier stop at the minimum risk investment opportunity?

15. Why is the covariance between Assets A and B the same as the covariance between Assets B and A?

16. Why is the covariance a more general concept than the variance?

17. Can the variance of a random variable be computed without knowledge of the expected value of that random variable?

18. Why do the weights committed to different securities in a portfolio have to sum to 1?

19. Why should the firm consider risk from the point of view of the shareholder?

20. If we put $1,000 in an investment with a standard deviation of 0.2 and $1,000 in an investment with a standard deviation of 0.1, what is the standard deviation of the resulting portfolio? Can the question be answered with the information provided? Explain.

21. On what factors does the risk of a two-asset portfolio depend?

22. Of all investment opportunities, assume that one has the highest expected return. Can it ever be dominated? Explain.

23. What is the difference between the efficient set and the efficient frontier?

24. Evaluate the following claim: "Diversification reduces risk, but only at the expense of reducing expected return."

25. What interpretation does beta have for a stock with a beta equal to 1?

26. Why do some industries tend to have high betas or low betas?

27. For what factors do investors demand compensation?

28. What is the market risk premium?

29. If the risk of Asset *A* is twice the risk of Asset *B*, does it follow that the expected return of *A* is twice the expected return of *B*? Explain.

30. You know that the standard deviation of Specialized Motors is lower than the standard deviation of the market, and that SM has a positive correlation with the market. Can the stock of SM be aggressive? Explain.

31. If the risk-free rate increases 2 percent, and the market risk premium remains the same, what happens to the expected return of defensive and aggressive stocks?

32. If the risk-free rate increases by 3 percent, and the expected return on the market remains the same, what happens to the expected return of defensive and aggressive stocks?

33. For a five-year period, a stock portfolio had the following rates of return: −15 percent, 23 percent, 11 percent, −3 percent, and 37 percent. What was the mean rate of return and the variance of the returns?

34. Mr. Diversey held a portfolio with three stocks. He invested 20 percent of his funds in stock *A*, 45 percent in Stock *B*, and 35 percent in Stock *C*. The rate of return for Stock *A* was 13 percent; for Stock *B*, −5 percent; and for Stock *C*, 9 percent. What was the rate of return for the entire portfolio?

35. Over three years, Security *Q* had returns of 10 percent, 14 percent, and −3 percent. For the same three years, Security *R* had returns of 12 percent, 10 percent, and 5 percent. What is the variance and standard deviation of returns for these two securities? What is the covariance of returns between these securities? What is the correlation of returns?

36. Consider a portfolio with 40 percent of the funds invested in Security *Q* from the preceding question and with 60 percent invested in Security *R*. What is the variance of returns for this two-asset portfolio?

37. Show that the correlation coefficient of an asset with itself is always 1.

38. You combine Assets *A* and *B*, and the resulting portfolio is risk-free. The variance of Asset *B* is four times larger than the variance of Asset *A*. Also, the expected returns on *A* and *B* are 10 percent and 18 percent, respectively. Find the expected return on the portfolio.

39. You are considering investing \$6 in two identical and independent projects with a probability p of a favorable outcome. Only one other outcome – unfavorable – is possible. If you invest all your money in one of the projects and the outcome is favorable, the payoff is \$10. If it is unfavorable, the payoff is −\$6. On average, you expect the payoff from each project to be zero. What is the probability of a favorable outcome?

40. You combine two risky assets in equal proportions. If both assets have the same variance, and the resulting portfolio has a variance equal to one-fourth the variance of each asset, what is the correlation between the assets?

41. Assets A, B, and C form a portfolio. The proportions in each are 25 percent, 25 percent, and 50 percent, respectively. The correlation is $\rho = 0.5$ for the three possible pairs of assets. The variances are equal to 100 for all three assets. Find the standard deviation of this portfolio.

42. Security X has an expected return of 0.25 and a standard deviation of returns of 0.20. Security Y has an expected return of 0.18 and a standard deviation of returns of 0.18. Plot the two securities in risk/return space. Does one dominate the other?

43. Find the expected return of a portfolio with 30 percent invested in Security X of the preceding problem, and 70 percent invested in Security Y.

44. For the portfolio created in Problem 43, what would be the expected return if we put 50 percent of our funds in that portfolio and 50 percent in Security Z, which has an expected return of 12 percent?

45. Security V has expected returns of 13 percent and a standard deviation of 20 percent, and Security W has expected returns of 5 percent and a standard deviation of 13 percent. If the two securities are perfectly negatively correlated, how much money would you put in each to have a zero risk portfolio? What would be the expected return of the portfolio?

Security A has an expected return of 0.15 and a standard deviation of 0.2. Security B has an expected return of 0.1 and a standard deviation of 0.15. Use this information to solve Problems 46–50.

46. If the correlation between Securities A and B is 0.8, what is the expected return of a portfolio with half of the funds invested in each security?

47. What is the standard deviation of the portfolio in the previous problem?

48. If 30 percent of the funds are put in Security A, what is the expected return of the portfolio made up of A and B?

49. What is the standard deviation of the portfolio in the previous problem?

50. The correlation between Security C and the market is 0.8. If the standard deviation of Security C is 0.2 and the standard deviation of the market is 0.17, what is the beta of Security C?

51. Solve the previous problem, except assume that the standard deviation of security *C* is 0.14.

52. Solve the previous problem, except assume that the standard deviation of security *C* is 0.17.

53. The current risk-free rate is 12 percent, the expected return on the market is 0.18, and Security *D* has a beta of 1.2. According to the CAPM, what is the expected return on Security *D*?

54. Security *E* has a beta of 1. If the risk-free rate of interest is 0.10 and the market risk premium is 8 percent, what is the required rate of return on Security *E*, according to the SML equation?

55. A reputable firm, Muskrat Manor, is considering expanding its food franchising operation by opening another store to sell its smash hit food product, Muskrat Nuggets. Already operating 157 stores nationwide, the firm knows that the beta of these previous projects is 1.2. With risk-free interest rates at 12 percent, and assuming the standard market risk premium of 8.9 percent, what required rate of return should be applied to the new store project?

56. If Muskrat Manor goes ahead with the new store, it expects sales of $1 million per year, with total costs of $800,000 per year, all stated on an after-tax basis. The project should last 20 years. Investment for the new store would be $800,000. Should they open the new store?

57. Muskrat Manor is considering an addition to the menu at its stores–hamburgers. In spite of the fact that this is a new product for them, the firm believes that it is relatively low risk and assigns a beta of 0.9 to the project. With the standard market risk premium of 8.9 percent and a risk-free rate of 11 percent, what should be the required rate of return for the hamburger project?

58. For Muskrat's hamburger project, considerable investment costs are involved, including market testing, promotion, and outfitting stores with necessary equipment. All of this investment should cost about $15 million. However, the firm believes that the hamburger might catch on. It estimates nationwide sales at $30 million per year, with total costs of $24 million, all after tax. Should Muskrat sell hamburgers?

Use these data in solving Problems 59–61. Current risk-free interest rates are 11 percent. The market risk premium is 8.9 percent.

59. A firm is considering a project that will generate after-tax annual cash flows of $300,000 for five years. The beta of the project is 0.8. The investment cost for the project is $900,000. Should the firm undertake the project?

60. A firm is considering a project that will generate after-tax cash flows of $300,000 for five years. The beta of the project is 1.3. The investment cost for the project is $850,000. Should the firm undertake the project?

61. Draw a graph of the SML and locate the projects of Problems 59 and 61 on the graph.

62. If IBM has the same variance as the market, and the correlation between the two is 0.7, what is IBM's beta?

63. Asset *A* has a beta of 0.7, while Asset *B* has a beta of 1.3. The expected rates of return are 10 percent and 14 percent, respectively. Find the risk-free rate of return.

64. Frisky Foods, Inc., has a beta of 0.8 and an expected return of 13 percent. If Double Whammy Mfg. has a beta of 1.6 and the risk-free rate is 9 percent, what is the expected return on Double Whammy? Under what circumstance would the answer be 26 percent? Is this a realistic circumstance?

Suggested REALDATA Exercises

The following *REALDATA* exercises explore the concepts developed in this chapter:

Exercises 25–27, 40–43, 46–51, 53

Part 3

Depository Institutions

Part 3 of this book begins with a consideration of the main financial intermediaries. A financial intermediary is a financial institution that acquires funds from one group of investors and makes them available to another economic unit.

Chapter 10 provides an overview of the main depository financial institutions in the U.S. economy: commercial banks, thrift institutions (savings banks and savings and loan associations), and credit unions. The chapter analyzes the different powers of each type of depository institution.

All depository institutions in the United States must operate under a regulatory framework. Describing the regulatory structure is the main purpose of Chapter 11. The current regulatory environment is the result of an evolutionary process. This chapter traces the process from the Great Depression to the present day. It also discusses the thrift crisis—the failure of hundreds of savings and loan associations during the 1980s. Understanding the regulatory environment helps to explain why some states have many banking offices and a robust banking industry, while other states have highly restricted banking operations.

Chapter 12 discusses some of the main operational areas of commercial banks. Concepts such as bank liquidity and the optimal amount of vault cash are discussed. We also describe the credit-granting decision at commercial banks. Since granting loans eventually leads to loan losses, we discuss this topic and its importance in recent years. The chapter ends with a discussion of bank capital and explains why the banking sector of the economy has substantially lower capital ratios than most other industries. As we will see, commercial banks can use so much leverage because they have the ability to diversify much more than most other types of businesses.

The management of commercial banks is the subject of Chapter 13. The chapter reviews a commercial bank's financial statements and discusses financial ratio analysis at length. The chapter also discusses how a commercial bank's liabilities can affect risk and return. It is shown that a bank's expected profitability can increase only at the expense of taking greater risks. The chapter ends by presenting a plausible explanation for the collapse of the S&L industry in the 1980s.

Chapter 14 deals with the management of a commercial bank's assets and liabilities. This area of bank management has increased in importance as the volatility of interest rates has increased in recent years. A key concept introduced in this chapter is duration, which is instrumental in many of the strategies a bank can use to immunize its assets and liabilities against unexpected changes in the level of interest rates.

Chapter 15 concentrates on international banking operations. The last decade has seen a tremendous growth of international financing, paralleling the growth in global trade. While a global financial market presents banks with new opportunities, it also presents them with risks. The bank manager must be aware of these opportunities and risks to survive in the emerging global marketplace.

Banks, Thrift Institutions, and Credit Unions 10

Overview

This chapter begins by considering the theory of financial intermediation. A **financial intermediary** is a financial institution that acquires funds from one group of investors and makes them available to another economic unit. The financial intermediary plays a vital role in the economy by channeling funds from surplus to deficit spending units. The intermediary repackages the funds it obtains from surplus units to make the funds more useful to the deficit spending units it serves. For providing this service, the intermediary charges a fee in the hope of making a profit.

The chapter then provides a broad overview of the different depository financial institutions prominent in the U.S. economy. A **depository institution** is a financial institution empowered to accept and hold monies from the public. As the title of this chapter implies, these depository institutions are commercial banks, thrift institutions (savings banks and savings and loan associations), and credit unions. The chapter analyzes the different powers of each type of depository institution. As we will see in some detail, commercial banks hold the greatest share of deposits by far.

The Role of Financial Intermediaries

In Chapter 1, we considered a desert island economy populated only by Robinson Crusoe and his man Friday. We then engaged in a thought experiment and allowed that economy to become successively richer by introducing financial refinements. We noted that the introduction of money allowed Crusoe to escape from the world of barter because money served as a medium of exchange. Additionally, money served Crusoe as a store of value. We also allowed the possibility that Crusoe could lend money this year to earn interest for next year and thereby enhance his consumption opportunities. Finally, we considered the benefits of borrowing, which would allow Crusoe to borrow the resources that would be available to him next year in order to increase his consumption opportunities today. This rudimentary example of Crusoe's economic opportunities showed how his life was enriched by the existence of a financial system. In this section, we consider how depository institutions specifically serve society.

Chapter 3 explained the vital role that commercial banks play in regulating the money supply. Although money creation is among the most important functions of commercial banks, it has been covered in detail. Accordingly, this section focuses on other social benefits created by depository institutions, benefits that arise through the role of depository institutions as financial intermediaries.

Types of Intermediation

To understand the role of intermediation, consider first an economy with only manufacturing firms and individual savers, but no financial intermediaries. The manufacturing firm needs large amounts of funds to be available for protracted periods to invest in risky real goods. Individual savers have small amounts of money that they may need on short notice, and they may be unwilling to accept the level of risk involved in a manufacturing venture. Table 10.1 summarizes the mismatch between the needs of the firm and the needs of individual savers. Given the very different situations of firms and investors, it may be inefficient for firms to acquire funds directly from individuals. Figure 10.1 highlights this inefficiency in Panel (a), in which a large borrower attempts to acquire funds directly from many small savers.

Table 10.1
Mismatch in Needs Between Firms and Savers

Firms	Savers
Need large amounts of funds	Need to invest small amounts
Need long-term commitments	Need ready access to funds
Projects involve high risk	Prefer low-risk investments
Superior knowledge of project's payoffs and risk	Less knowledge of firm's investment opportunities

Figure 10.1
Size Intermediation

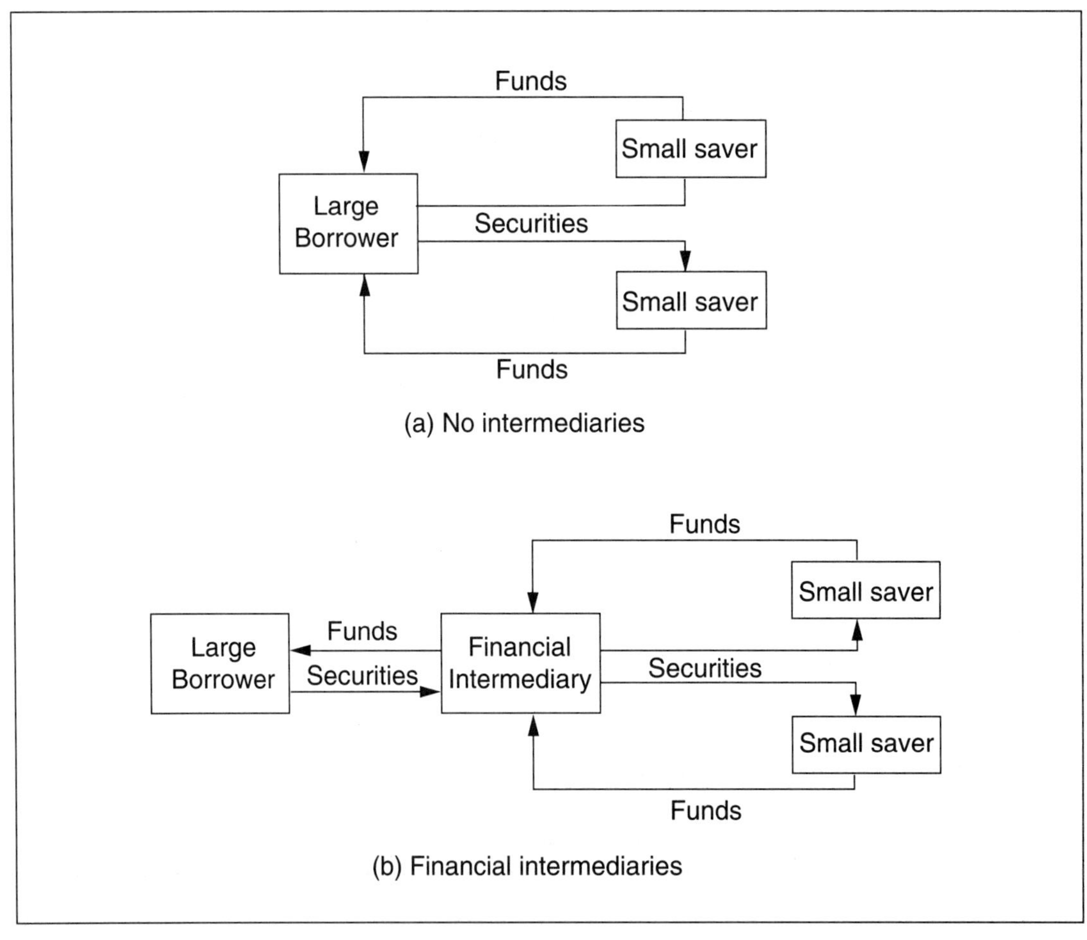

To highlight just one of the mismatches, consider the firm's need for a long-term commitment of funds and the saver's desire for ready access to funds. A firm may seek funds to build a chemical plant with a construction time of 5 years, and the firm may want to repay those funds over the next 30 years. By contrast, small savers may wish to earn a return on their savings but may also wish to have quick access to those funds for unexpected medical expenses, educational needs, and so on. This kind of mismatch between the needs of firms and individual savers creates a very useful role for financial intermediaries.

Panel (b) of Figure 10.1 shows how a financial intermediary, such as a commercial bank, can play a useful role in the economy by stepping between the firm and the individual savers. In the process, the bank eliminates the mismatches between the firm and savers, shown in Table 10.1, by performing four types of intermediation:

1. Size intermediation
2. Maturity intermediation
3. Risk intermediation
4. Information intermediation

Our preceding example contained elements of several different kinds of intermediation; we now discuss each of the four types of intermediation separately.

Size Intermediation In our economy, households tend to be surplus-spending units while firms tend to be deficit-spending units. Economic efficiency requires that funds flow from surplus to deficit units and that the deficit units pay a return to the surplus units providing the funds. Large firms have a large appetite for funds. Households, as the major surplus spending units, are small individually. This creates a size mismatch between the surplus and deficit spending units and provides an opportunity for a financial intermediary. The intermediary can gather funds from households efficiently and combine these small amounts into larger packages that are attractive to deficit-spending units, such as firms.

In the process of providing this service, the intermediary strives to make a profit by borrowing from the surplus-spending units at a lower rate and providing funds to deficit-spending units at a higher rate. The difference between the rate at which funds are acquired and the rate at which they are invested is the **spread**. For a financial intermediary, this spread is the gross profit margin. From this spread, the intermediary must pay the cost of gathering and disbursing funds and must pay its own investors a return for providing funds to the intermediary.

Maturity/Liquidity Intermediation Not only are there mismatches in the size of surplus and deficit-spending units, but the time horizons and liquidity needs of providers and users of funds often do not match as well. In our earlier example, we considered a firm planning to build a chemical plant with a horizon of 30 years between the acquisition and final repayment of funds. Very few households can commit funds for such a long time. The need to bridge the time preferences of surplus-and deficit-spending units provides an opportunity for the financial intermediary.

By developing a pool of many small savers, the intermediary amasses the funds desired by the chemical firm and solves the problem of size intermediation. However, because the intermediary creates the pool of funds by attracting many small contributors, the intermediary can also resolve the time mismatch. Some contributors of funds at the outset of the project may withdraw their funds before the project is completed, but the intermediary can provide continuous financing to the chemical firm over the entire time horizon by attracting new contributors of funds to replace the earlier contributors that withdraw their money.

Without an intermediary, the chemical firm would not only have to acquire funds from many small contributors, it would need to continue to find new contributors to replace those that withdraw their money over time. If the financial intermediary can step between the ultimate surplus spending units and the chemical firm to manage this time mismatch more efficiently, it can make a profit. Because they specialize, intermediaries are often more efficient than other types of firms in acquiring funds from small surplus units and making a large package available to a deficit–spending unit for extended periods.

Risk Intermediation/Risk Pooling Intermediaries also act to resolve mismatches in the risk preferences of surplus- and deficit-spending units. In our example of the chemical plant, the level of risk of the project may be too high for many surplus-spending units. As a consequence, the surplus units will not invest directly in the chemical firm. By acquiring funds at one risk level and lending them at a higher risk level, the financial intermediary has an opportunity to make a profit by intermediating this risk mismatch between the suppliers and users of funds.

Banks accept deposits from individuals and guarantee to repay those deposits with interest. In fact, the federal government backs the bank's promise in many cases, as we will explore in Chapter 11. Therefore, we may regard most commercial bank deposits as free of default risk. The bank can then lend these funds to firms desiring to invest in a risky project.

In our example, if the chemical firm attempted to raise funds directly from the risk-averse surplus spending units, it would have difficulties in guaranteeing the level of safety that the surplus units demand. By being organized for intermediation, financial institutions can provide the risk intermediation service much more efficiently than other non-specializing firms.

The difference between the risk of its deposits and its loans is a major contributing factor to the size of the spread the bank is able to earn. The risk level of deposits is fixed effectively because of the government guarantees. In this environment, banks have an incentive to adopt a risky posture by making riskier loans with higher rates of interest.

Information Intermediation If the spread that the bank earns varies directly with the risk difference between its deposits and its loans, why don't depositors make the risky loans themselves and capture the higher rate of interest? There are two basic reasons, one of which we have already seen by noting that many depositors are risk averse and prefer the safety of government guaranteed bank deposits. The second reason is that making risky loans requires information about the actual extent of the risks and about the borrower's willingness and ability to pay as promised. Gathering the relevant information about borrowers requires capital, effort, and expertise. From one perspective, we may view financial institutions as information intermediaries.

For example, assessing the risk of a chemical plant is very difficult. A good job of risk assessment requires knowing the financial position of the firm in detail, knowing the structure of the chemical industry, and projecting future demand and supply for the chemical being produced.

Because of their limited resources, individuals are in a poor position to gather the relevant information, a situation that provides an opportunity for a specialist in information processing.

In many cases, financial institutions can assess information more efficiently than individuals, due to their larger scale, their corresponding ability to amortize fixed costs associated with the information gathering process, and their specialization in financial matters. For an individual investor with just $10,000 to invest, a thorough investigation of the chemical firm's prospects is not feasible. By contrast, a financial institution may be prepared to lend $10 million to the chemical firm. Accordingly, it can afford to devote, say, $10,000 to determining the wisdom of making the loan. In many instances, the bank has a continuing relationship with a large borrower, so it will already have a high level of knowledge about the borrowing firm. In summary, financial institutions are better information processors than individuals for three major reasons:

1. Financial institutions deal with larger sums, so they can commit more resources to information collection and evaluation.
2. Because of continuing relationships with prospective borrowers, financial institutions already have much of the information.
3. Financial institutions specialize in risk evaluation and processing financial information beyond the capacity of individuals.

Diversification

Financial institutions offer another service in addition to intermediation. **Diversification** is the allocation of investable funds to a variety of investment opportunities in order to reduce risk. As we have seen in detail in Chapter 9, by dividing investable funds among a variety of different investment opportunities, investors can reduce risk dramatically. For a small investor, it is not easy to achieve the risk-reduction benefits of diversification. For example, an investor with $1,000 to invest would find it difficult to invest $100 in ten different investment projects.

Financial intermediaries, however, help small investors diversify. They collect funds from a number of investors and pool those funds. Because the pool is large, it can be invested in a variety of investment opportunities. Then each of the contributors of funds has, in effect, a share of the diversified investment portfolio.

Another popular kind of financial intermediary that provides diversification is the **investment company**. An investment company, such as a mutual fund, collects funds from many investors and uses the proceeds to buy securities such as stocks and bonds. Each of the contributors to the investment company owns a fraction of the entire portfolio that is created with the pool of funds. This provides very efficient diversification for even the smallest investor. For example, with an investment of only $1,000, an investor can own a fraction of an investment company's portfolio that may include hundreds of securities.

We note that the diversification service provided by an investment company or other financial intermediary is not the same service as risk intermediation discussed earlier. In risk intermediation, the financial intermediary bears a higher level of risk and issues claims to its depositors, for example, at a lower level of risk. In providing a diversification service, an investment company merely collects funds from individuals and invests them more efficiently. In the investment company, the contributors of funds still bear the entire risk. However, the amount of risk is reduced due to diversification.

The Intermediary as a Business

We have seen how the financial intermediary performs five important services: size intermediation, maturity and liquidity intermediation, risk intermediation, information intermediation, and diversification services. Figure 10.2 summarizes these basic services. Funds flow from surplus-spending units to the financial intermediary. In return, the surplus-spending units hold direct claims against the intermediary. Usually, these claims are for small amounts, are highly liquid, and are low risk. In addition, the claims are on the intermediary as a whole, so they are indirect claims on a diversified portfolio of investments undertaken by the intermediary.

For its part, the intermediary raises its own capital by selling stock and by issuing bonds. The intermediary then accepts funds from surplus-spending units. The intermediary alters the characteristics of the funds received from the surplus-spending units. The intermediary, after transforming the funds it receives from the surplus-spending units, makes the funds available to deficit–spending units, usually business firms that need long-term commitments of funds in large amounts. The ultimate providers of funds, the surplus-spending units, hold a direct claim against the financial intermediary, but they also hold an indirect claim against the deficit-spending units, through the financial intermediary.

From Figure 10.2, we can see the business role played by the financial intermediary. In short, the financial intermediary pays surplus-spending units one rate of return, transforms the funds it collects, and charges the deficit-spending units a higher rate for using the funds. This difference between the rate paid to acquire funds and the rate charged for the use of funds constitutes the intermediary's spread. Part of this spread is earned by bundling the funds and changing their liq-

Figure 10.2
The Role of the Intermediary in the Flow of Funds

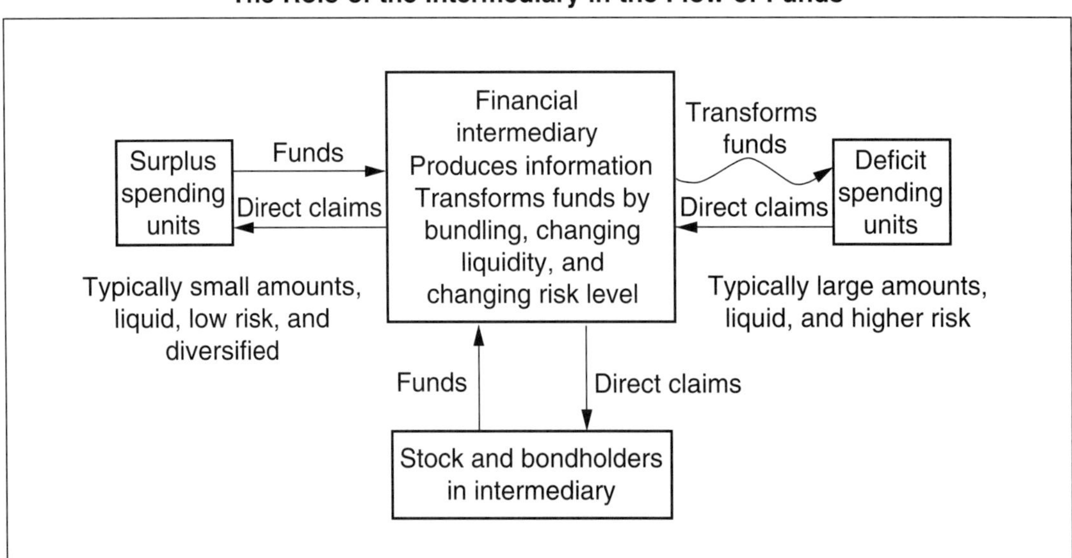

uidity; part of it is compensation for greater risk of the project the deficit-spending unit will undertake.

Disintermediation

We have already observed that financial intermediaries earn the spread between the rate they pay to the surplus-spending units and the rate they charge the deficit-spending units because of the intermediation services they provide. Nonetheless, it would be tempting for the surplus- and deficit-spending units to get together to eliminate the intermediary. By providing funds without an intermediary, the surplus units might receive a higher rate for their funds. Similarly, by raising funds directly from surplus units, the deficit units might acquire their needed funds at a lower rate. This process of direct contact between surplus- and deficit-spending units is known as **disintermediation**. For example, many large industrial firms raise short-term funds directly from small surplus-spending units. Similarly, many industrial firms own financing companies. As a typical example, General Motors owns the General Motors Acceptance Corporation (GMAC), specializing in automobile financing. A buyer that purchases a General Motors automobile can acquire financing from a bank or directly from GMAC. Today, there is an increasing tendency to leave the bank out of the process entirely.

Powers of Depository Institutions

In this section, we consider the different powers that are allowed to commercial banks, thrift institutions, and credit unions. As we will explore in more detail in Chapter 14, each of these types of institutions is subject to a web of governmental regulation specifying the permissible activities of each institution. The regulations that govern these institutions have developed over decades, so the particular powers allowed to each type of institution often have a complex history. In this chapter, we focus on the powers that are currently allowed to each type of institution.

As depository institutions, the defining power of these institutions is their ability to accept deposits from the public. In return, the institution must stand ready to return those funds to depositors upon demand for certain types of accounts, or after a specified period for other types of accounts.

Commercial Banks

Like all financial intermediaries, the commercial bank acquires funds from one group of surplus-spending units and makes these funds available to other deficit units. In this section, we consider the powers available to commercial banks by seeing the sources and uses of funds available to the typical bank. In essence, banks raise funds by accepting deposits, borrowing funds, and issuing equity in the banking firm. The bank uses these funds to buy securities and to make loans.

Deposits Commercial banks accept deposits from individuals, business firms, and governmental entities. These deposits go into accounts that may be classified as transaction accounts, savings accounts, or time deposits. A **transaction account** is an account used for holding funds on a short-term basis in anticipation of spending those funds. In essence, we may think of a transaction account as a checking account. Funds in transaction accounts are generally available to the depositor on an immediate basis, and transaction accounts are also known as **demand deposits**.

A **savings account** is an account designed to hold funds for a longer term. The bank may impose certain restrictions on the availability of funds in savings accounts. Years ago, savings accounts were generally accompanied by a "passbook" in which each transaction was recorded. Withdrawing funds typically required the depositor to present the passbook in person at the bank. Further, the federal government imposed restrictions on the rate of interest the bank could pay on these funds.

Today, banks are free to set interest rates on savings accounts to compete with market forces, but they can still require the depositor to give notice of an intention to withdraw funds. In practice, however, funds in savings accounts are generally available on demand.

One popular type of savings account is the **Money Market Deposit Account (MMDA)**. The bank can set the interest rate for its MMDAs as it chooses, and it may stipulate requirements for minimum balances as well. However, federal law limits depositors to six third-party transfers per month. MMDAs have grown tremendously. Consistent with the general movement toward deregulating financial services (the topic of Chapter 11), the distinction between transaction accounts and savings accounts has been substantially reduced.

A **time deposit** is the deposit of funds in a depository institution for a specific period. Typically, the depositor commits funds for a certain number of months or years at a stated rate of interest. Generally, the rate is higher the longer the period of commitment. The most important form of time deposits is the **certificate of deposit (CD)**. These are available in different forms to both small savers and large depositors. Generally, small CDs (less than $100,000) carry a higher rate of interest than MMDAs, but the funds are committed for a specific period. (Actually, one can obtain these funds in an emergency, but they carry a "substantial penalty for early withdrawal.")

Large CDs (deposits of $100,000 or more) are an important source of funds for commercial banks. In many cases, these large CDs are negotiable and are traded in an active secondary market. In this sense, negotiable CDs are like bonds. They are obligations of the bank in which the deposit was made, and the right to receive repayment from the bank can be traded in the secondary market.

Borrowed Funds Upon accepting deposits, a bank borrows from the depositor. Nonetheless, it is customary to distinguish bank deposit taking from bank borrowing. Banks have a variety of short-term sources of funds available to them. The important short-term sources of borrowed funds for commercial banks are repurchase agreements, federal funds, federal reserve bank loans, and Eurodollar transactions.

Repurchase Agreements In a **repurchase agreement**, the owner of a security borrows funds from a lender and surrenders the security to the lender as collateral. In addition, the borrower promises to repurchase the security at a specific time for a higher price. The difference between the funds borrowed and the promised repurchase price defines the interest that the borrower pays. Most repurchase agreements (also called **repos**) are for a single day and are called **overnight repos**. More extended periods of borrowing are also possible, and these longer-term repurchase agreements are called **term repos**. By entering a repurchase agreement, a bank acquires immediate access to cash by surrendering a security as collateral. Because it also agrees to repurchase the security at a later date, the bank's investment in the security is unaffected by the borrowing.

Federal Funds As discussed in Chapters 2 and 3, commercial banks are required to keep deposits of reserves at Federal Reserve Banks, and these deposits are subject to minimum requirements. Often, however, banks have excess funds on deposit. Other banks may wish to acquire additional reserves to meet their own minimum requirements or to increase their reserves to permit greater lending. In the market for Federal funds (or Fed funds), a bank with excess reserves can lend the excess to another bank that wishes to increase its reserves.

Like the repo market, the Fed funds market tends to specialize in loans that mature in one day. Also, the typical amounts are quite large, usually in multiples of $1 million. While the typical maturity of a Fed funds loan might be one day, it is generally possible for a bank to renew the loan each day.

Federal Reserve Bank Loans In addition to borrowing reserves from each other through the Fed funds market, banks may also borrow reserves directly from their Federal Reserve Bank. This borrowing from the **discount window** is for short periods, usually about 15 days. With permission, the banks may renew their loans. However, the Fed discourages over-reliance on this type of borrowing to meet reserve requirements.

Eurodollars A **Eurodollar** is a U.S. dollar-denominated deposit held in a bank outside the United States; it may be a demand deposit or time deposit. Banks borrow and lend these funds among themselves, so access to the Eurodollar market provides another source of funds for a bank. Large transactions in the **interbank market** are usually conducted at the **London Interbank Offered Rate (LIBOR)** – the rate at which banks in the interbank market offer to lend to other banks.

Long-Term Borrowing In addition to the sources of short-term borrowing just discussed, banks have access to a range of longer-term sources of borrowed funds. Like any corporation, banks may issue notes and bonds in the capital market to raise funds for their long-term financing needs.

Bank Equity Like all corporations, banks require equity capital financing. Banks attain this financing by issuing stock in the corporation.

Cash Holdings Compared to many corporations, banks hold large amounts of cash. First, we have seen in Chapter 3 that banks must hold substantial amounts of cash as reserves to back their lending. In addition, banks must hold sufficient amounts of **vault cash**, cash at their banking locations, to meet the transaction demands of their customers.

Bank Investment in Securities Because banks may face large demands for liquidity, they generally hold substantial investments in liquid debt instruments, with an emphasis on short-term money market instruments. These include Treasury securities – Treasury bills, notes, and bonds – generally with an emphasis on T-bills. In addition, banks invest in government agency securities such as GNMAs and FHLMC mortgages instruments. Bank security portfolios also include municipal securities.

We have seen that bank sources of funds include borrowing Fed Funds, entering repurchase agreements, and borrowing in the Eurodollar market. In these borrowings, other banks are often lenders. Thus, by owning these securities, banks also invest in securities. The provider of funds in a repurchase agreement is said to have entered a **reverse repurchase agreement (reverse repo)**. Similarly, in providing Federal Funds, the bank records its position as **Federal Funds sold**.

Bank Lending As a business firm, the commercial bank must acquire funds from surplus economic units at lower rates, repackage these funds, and provide them to deficit economic units at higher rates to earn a profit. While investment in securities is important for bank liquidity and provides some return, banks derive the principal share of their revenues from lending.

The bread and butter of bank lending is in lending to commercial firms. Banks lend principally to business firms in retailing, manufacturing, service industries, and agriculture. In addition, banks are large lenders to individual consumers, and banks have become major suppliers of loans for real estate.

Commercial and Industrial Loans Before the deregulation of the financial system, commercial and industrial (C&I) loans were the special province of commercial banks. Today, many other institutions are permitted to make C&I loans, but banks continue to dominate the market. These loans vary widely by size and by type of customer. Banks lend to small businesses in their own localities, but they also can make enormous loans to large industrial corporations.

In many instances, the bank's borrowing customers will establish a line of credit with the bank. A **line of credit** is a guarantee from a lender to a borrower to provide a certain level of financing for a certain period. Banks often charge a fee for providing a line of credit, even if the borrower does not call on the bank for an actual loan. Under a line of credit, many firms will borrow for seasonal financing needs. For example, retailers build their inventory in late summer and fall in anticipation of the Christmas selling season. After they collect on the Christmas sales, the retailer will often repay the bank and clear its line of credit.

In C&I lending, banks also make **term loans** – a loan of a specified amount for a given period, usually one year or longer. These loans may often have a term of five to seven years and may be amortized or paid in full upon maturity.

Consumer Loans Commercial banks are major sources of consumer loans. These include, as examples, home repair, educational, and automobile loans. In the last 20 years, credit card lending has become an extremely important part of consumer lending for banks.

Real Estate Loans Real estate loans consist almost entirely of mortgage loans secured by either residential or commercial real estate. Before financial deregulation, banks had little presence in the market for residential real estate loans. (Thrift institutions traditionally have been the primary lenders for residential real estate.) Today, commercial banks dominate commercial real estate lending, and they are a major force in residential real estate lending. For many small banks, residential real estate loans are the major loan category.

Assets and Liabilities of Commercial Banks Figure 10.3 presents the assets and liabilities of all FDIC-insured depository institutions in the United States as of December 31, 1993. Total assets exceeded \$4.7 trillion, with \$3.7 trillion, or 79 percent of those assets being held in commercial banks. The remaining \$1 trillion was held in savings institutions. Among commercial banks, those with national charters hold 57 percent of all assets, with a total of \$2.1 trillion. For banks, the major class of liability is deposits, representing 79 percent of all liabilities. Equity capital stood at \$297 billion, or about 8 percent of assets.

Income and Expenses of Commercial Banks The consolidated 1993 income statement for all FDIC-insured banks appears in Figure 10.4. In 1993, commercial banks had total interest and fee income of \$245 billion. Of this amount, national banks earned \$145 billion, or 59 percent. This statistic emphasizes that national banks tend to be larger than state-chartered institutions. The major expense of banks is the interest that they must pay on deposits. For national banks, this totaled \$65 billion in 1993, down from \$204 billion in 1990, due mainly to falling interest rates

Figure 10.3
Assets and Liabilities of Commercial Banks (millions of dollars)

TABLE RC ASSETS AND LIABILITIES OF FDIC–INSURED DEPOSITORY INSTITUTIONS
Institutions Grouped by Charter Class
(Amounts in Millions of Dollars)

DECEMBER 31, 1993	Total FDIC Insured[1]	COMMERCIAL BANKS & TRUST COMPANIES				SAVINGS INSTITUTIONS			
		TOTAL	National Charter	State Charter Fed Member	State Charter Fed Nonmember	TOTAL[1]	Federal Charter[1]	State Charter[1]	RTC Conservatorships (SAIF Member)
Number of institutions	**13,221**	**10,957**	**3,304**	**971**	**6,682**	**2,264**	**1,228**	**1,036**	**63**
Total assets	**4,707,235**	**3,705,947**	**2,100,530**	**727,550**	**877,867**	**1,001,288**	**690,884**	**310,404**	**21,901**
Cash and due from depository institutions	304,230	272,967	163,628	57,122	52,216	31,264	20,362	10,902	1,669
Noninterest–bearing	204,512	188,813	117,995	33,875	36,944	15,698	10,457	5,241	466
Interest–bearing	99,719	84,153	45,633	23,248	15,272	15,565	9,905	5,661	1,203
Investment securities	1,112,239	836,562	436,679	157,323	242,560	275,677	185,255	90,421	5,448
Federal funds sold and securities purchased under agreements to resell	160,390	150,292	87,606	29,431	33,255	10,098	4,580	5,519	390
Loans and leases, net	2,723,895	2,097,184	1,238,176	348,849	510,158	626,712	438,257	188,454	9,876
Plus: allowance for losses and allocated transfer risk reserve	61,276	52,631	31,399	10,741	10,491	8,645	5,890	2,755	715
Loans and leases, total	2,785,171	2,149,815	1,269,576	359,590	520,649	635,357	444,148	191,209	10,591
Assets held in trading accounts	124,722	122,399	44,998	76,062	1,340	2,323	1,663	661	0
Bank premises and fixed assets	66,664	55,525	32,209	10,226	13,090	11,140	7,548	3,591	336
Other real estate owned	25,281	16,826	10,527	2,193	4,105	8,455	5,633	2,822	846
Intangible assets	24,057	18,023	13,104	2,049	2,870	6,034	5,114	920	203
All other assets	165,756	136,170	73,602	44,296	18,273	29,585	22,472	7,114	3,133
Total liabilities, limited–life preferred stock, and equity capital	**4,707,235**	**3,705,947**	**2,100,530**	**727,550**	**877,867**	**1,001,288**	**690,884**	**310,404**	**21,901**
Total liabilities[2]	4,331,798	3,409,126	1,935,628	674,712	798,786	922,672	639,415	283,257	27,304
Deposits, total	3,528,347	2,753,929	1,576,519	476,703	700,707	774,418	518,624	255,794	17,913
Federal funds purchased and securities sold under agreements to repurchase	308,460	274,686	161,957	64,425	48,304	33,774	26,482	7,291	0
Demand notes issued to the U.S. Treasury[3]	34,986	34,951	20,477	11,392	3,082	35	NA	35	NA
Other borrowed money (includes mortgage indebtedness)	288,343	188,134	90,282	65,167	32,685	100,210	83,387	16,823	8,058
Subordinated notes and debentures	39,905	37,372	24,393	10,233	2,746	2,533	2,499	34	0
All other liabilities[2]	131,757	120,054	62,000	46,793	11,261	11,702	8,422	3,280	1,333
Total equity capital	**375,437**	**296,822**	**164,902**	**52,838**	**79,081**	**78,616**	**51,469**	**27,147**	**(5,403)**
Perpetual preferred stock	3,103	1,524	165	417	942	1,579	986	593	0
Common stock	34,522	32,836	16,700	6,760	9,376	1,686	860	826	0
Surplus	158,410	126,440	72,482	19,675	34,283	31,970	22,077	9,893	1
Undivided profits	180,490	137,109	76,351	26,274	34,483	43,381	27,546	15,834	(5,404)
Cumulative foreign currency translation adjustments	(1,088)	(1,088)	(796)	(288)	(3)	0	NA	0	NA
Net worth certificates	0	NA	NA	NA	NA	0	NA	0	NA

[1]Excludes savings institutions in Resolution Trust Corporation conservatorship.
[2]Includes limited–life preferred stock and related surplus.
[3]Not reported by institutions filing a Thrift Financial Report.
NA – Not available

Source: *FDIC, Statistics on Banking, 1993, Table RC.*

Figure 10.4
Income Statement for Commercial Banks
(millions of dollars)

TABLE RI INCOME AND EXPENSE OF FDIC–INSURED DEPOSITORY INSTITUTIONS
Institutions Grouped by Charter Class
(Amounts in Millions of Dollars)

CALENDAR YEAR 1993	Total FDIC Insured[1]	COMMERCIAL BANKS AND TRUST COMPANIES				SAVINGS INSTITUTIONS			
		TOTAL	National Charter	State Charter Fed Member	State Charter Fed Nonmember	TOTAL[1]	Federal Charter[1]	State Charter[1]	RTC Conservatorships (SAIF Member)
Number of institutions	**13,221**	**10,957**	**3,304**	**971**	**6,682**	**2,264**	**1,228**	**1,036**	**63**
Total interest and fee income	**311,361**	**245,158**	**144,764**	**41,409**	**58,985**	**66,202**	**44,973**	**21,230**	**1,173**
Domestic office loans	200,160	150,284	85,107	22,062	43,114	49,876	34,147	15,730	800
Foreign office loans[2]	24,942	24,942	20,311	4,348	283	0	NA	0	NA
Lease financing receivables[2]	3,432	3,397	2,547	394	456	35	NA	35	NA
Balances due from depository institutions[2]	6,263	6,178	4,364	1,211	603	85	NA	85	NA
Investment securities	64,687	48,922	26,198	9,266	13,458	15,764	10,547	5,217	373
Assets held in trading accounts	6,993	6,694	3,408	3,210	76	299	279	21	0
Federal funds sold and securities purchased under agreements to resell[2]	4,883	4,741	2,829	917	996	142	NA	142	NA
Total interest expense	**140,369**	**105,780**	**64,616**	**18,851**	**22,314**	**34,589**	**24,428**	**10,161**	**1,104**
Domestic office deposits	87,720	59,209	31,718	8,522	18,969	28,512	19,318	9,193	824
Foreign office deposits[2]	20,423	20,423	15,457	4,293	674	0	NA	0	NA
Federal funds purchased and securities sold under agreements to repurchase[2]	8,624	8,487	5,021	2,179	1,287	138	NA	138	NA
Demand notes issued to the U.S. Treasury and other borrowed money	21,005	15,345	10,923	3,214	1,209	5,660	4,840	820	279
Mortgage indebtedness and obligations under capitalized leases[2]	156	153	96	33	24	4	NA	4	NA
Subordinated notes and debentures	2,440	2,164	1,401	611	152	276	269	7	0
Net interest income	**170,992**	**139,378**	**80,148**	**22,559**	**36,671**	**31,613**	**20,545**	**11,069**	**70**
Provisions for loan and lease losses and allocated transfer risk	**20,820**	**16,589**	**9,018**	**2,858**	**4,713**	**4,231**	**3,267**	**964**	**432**
Total noninterest income	**82,899**	**74,962**	**45,335**	**16,778**	**12,850**	**7,936**	**5,739**	**2,197**	**(586)**
Service charges on deposit accounts[2]	15,231	14,920	9,358	2,164	3,398	311	NA	311	NA
Total noninterest expense	**164,470**	**139,585**	**82,102**	**26,171**	**31,312**	**24,885**	**16,623**	**8,262**	**1,325**
Salaries and employee benefits	68,173	58,204	33,011	12,035	13,157	9,969	6,532	3,437	319
Premises and equipment	22,549	18,471	10,784	3,718	3,970	4,078	3,009	1,069	184
All other noninterest expense	73,749	62,910	38,307	10,418	14,185	10,838	7,082	3,756	822
Pre–tax net operating income	**68,600**	**58,167**	**34,364**	**10,307**	**13,496**	**10,433**	**6,394**	**4,040**	**(2,274)**
Gains (losses) on securities not held in trading accounts	**3,470**	**3,064**	**1,578**	**886**	**600**	**406**	**127**	**279**	**1**
Applicable income taxes	23,787	19,892	11,784	3,445	4,663	3,895	2,313	1,583	(3)
Income before extraordinary items	48,283	41,339	24,158	7,748	9,434	6,944	4,208	2,736	(2,270)
Extraordinary items, net	2,152	2,090	1,629	244	217	61	(125)	186	(16)
Net income	**50,435**	**43,430**	**25,787**	**7,991**	**9,651**	**7,006**	**4,083**	**2,923**	**(2,285)**

[1]Excludes savings institutions in Resolution Trust Corporation conservatorship.
[2]Not reported by institutions filing a Thrift Financial Report.

NA – Not available

Source: *FDIC, Statistics on Banking, 1993, Table RI.*

in the early 1990s. In addition, banks earned another $83 billion in non-interest income, coming largely from various fees that banks impose for services. Just for service charges on deposit accounts, banks charged almost $15 billion. As a group, Figure 10.4 shows that commercial banks incurred a tax liability of almost $20 billion and had a net income after taxes of $43 billion, up markedly from industry profits of $16 billion in 1990.

Thrift Institutions

In the United States, there are two principal types of thrift institutions: savings banks and savings and loan associations. Savings banks originated principally in the northeastern United States in the early years of the 1800s, and they originally provided a means for small depositors to save and earn a return on their deposits.

Savings and loan associations (S&Ls) began as building societies in the first half of the nineteenth century, organized for the purpose of financing home ownership. In their early years, individual members pooled their personal funds to finance home construction. After each member eventually had a home, the association might dissolve.

After many thrifts failed in the Great Depression, federal guarantees were extended to depositors. Because of their different origins, savings banks and S&Ls eventually fell under different regulatory bodies. Savings banks were insured and regulated by the FDIC, while S&Ls fell under the jurisdiction of the Federal Home Loan Bank Board and were insured by the Federal Savings and Loan Insurance Corporation.

Early Practices and a Changing Industry

True to their origins, these thrift institutions continued to draw deposits from small savers and to focus primarily on home mortgage lending into the 1970s. Compared to savings banks, S&Ls grew much more rapidly, largely due to governmental policies. Specifically, in the years of regulated rates on deposits, S&Ls were allowed to offer an interest rate 25 basis points higher than that permitted for commercial banks. By 1980, 90 percent of all thrift associations were S&Ls.

With the wave of financial deregulation in the early 1980s, the differential in deposit rates between S&Ls and commercial banks was phased out. With rising interest rates in the late 1970s and early 1980s, many S&Ls fell upon hard times and were consolidated into larger S&Ls. In addition, thrift institutions were granted new powers under financial deregulation. In many instances, thrifts used these new powers to expand aggressively into new higher-risk lines of business, often with disastrous results.

Deposits

Thrift institutions garner most of their deposits from individuals. Today, these include both demand and time deposits. Before financial deregulation, thrift institutions were not permitted to accept demand deposits. As deregulation began, thrifts were allowed to accept deposits that could be immediately withdrawn by a **negotiable order of withdrawal (NOW)**. Although the name is different, these so-called NOW accounts functioned as checking accounts. Today there is virtually no difference between thrift institutions and commercial banks in their handling of checkable deposits. Like commercial banks, thrift institutions also offer a wide range of time deposits, and MMDA accounts and certificates of deposit are widely available at thrift institutions.

In spite of now having virtually the same deposit-accepting powers as commercial banks, thrift institution deposits continue to be concentrated in savings and time deposits, rather than demand deposits. This is part of the continuing legacy of the regulatory system that was dismantled in the 1980s.

Brokered deposits are deposits that an institution attracts through the services of a third party that acts as a broker. The broker arranges for a depositor to commit funds to a particular institution, and the broker receives a fee for this service from the institution. In addition to paying a brokerage fee, the institution must offer terms that are attractive to the depositor. This usually means that brokered deposits are secured by offering a higher rate of interest. Thus, brokered deposits cost the institution the higher rate paid on the deposit, plus the fee paid to the broker.

Brokered deposits have been particularly attractive to S&Ls that were unable to attract sufficient deposits to fuel their desired growth. Some observers blame brokered deposits for contributing to the S&L crisis. The typical S&L raising funds through brokered deposits incurs a relatively high cost of funds. To make a profit, the S&L must then find investments that pay enough to offset the high cost of funds. Thus, a reliance on brokered deposits gives the S&L an incentive to make risky loans. Because of potential problems associated with brokered deposits, regulations now place restrictions on their use by troubled institutions.

Other Sources of Funds

In addition to deposits, thrifts acquire funds by borrowing. For thrifts as a whole, the overwhelming portion of these funds, about 88 percent, are borrowed from Federal Home Loan Banks, a part of the U.S. government that acts to provide liquidity to the thrift industry. In addition to borrowing from Federal Home Loan Banks, some thrifts borrow from banks, and a few issue their own bonds. In total, these non-deposit resources are about 10 percent of the thrift industry's total liabilities. Thus, thrift institutions raise almost all of their funds from deposits of one form or another.

Loans As we have seen, thrifts began with a strong emphasis on lending for homes. To some extent, this emphasis continues today, although thrifts have the authority to make consumer and commercial loans as well. At year-end 1994, savings institutions held $587 billion in mortgages, $38 billion in consumer loans, and $10 billion in commercial loans.

Mortgages The bread-and-butter lending business of thrift institutions has been, and continues to be, lending for residential real estate. As we have just noted, for the thrift industry as a whole, 93 percent of all their lending is for mortgages of all types. The classic home mortgage is a 30-year amortized, fixed-rate loan. In the last decade, there has been a strong movement toward home mortgages with different terms. These include mortgages shorter than 30 years and mortgages with adjustable interest rates.

While home mortgages continue to dominate thrift loan portfolios, thrift institutions make a variety of mortgage loans. In addition to loans for single-family housing, thrifts lend for multifamily housing and farms, and they also offer commercial mortgages. Of all their mortgages, thrifts still have 79 percent concentrated in lending for single-family housing. Multifamily and commercial mortgages are each about 10 percent of thrift loan portfolios. With 93 percent of their loans in mortgages and 79 percent of mortgages in single-family loans, lending for single-family housing continues to constitute about 75 percent of the thrift industry's loan portfolio.

Consumer and Commercial Lending Savings banks have long had the authority to make consumer loans, but until 1980 the ability of S&Ls to lend to consumers was greatly restricted. (Basically, S&Ls could lend to consumers for home improvement loans, education loans, or loans secured by the borrower's deposits.) With financial deregulation, all thrifts can make consumer loans of virtually all types. Today, thrifts can lend for cars, vacations, boats, and travel. As we have seen, however, loans to consumers are still not a large portion of thrift lending. Financial deregulation has also given thrifts the power to make commercial loans, but this area of lending has remained small.

Security Holdings Thrift institutions also invest heavily in securities, particularly government agency instruments, such as GNMAs and FHLMCs. As we have seen for banks, all depository institutions require substantial liquid funds. Thrifts meet this need largely by holding Treasury bills, notes, and bonds and by investing in government agency instruments. Government agency instruments are relatively much larger than holdings of Treasury issues. At year-end 1994, S&Ls held $160 billion in agency issues, but only $28 billion in Treasury instruments.

Service Companies A **service company** is a firm owned by a financial institution, usually an S&L, that provides services to the parent firm. For example, it is fairly common for an S&L to own a firm that services mortgages by managing collections, titles, deeds, and other paperwork associated with mortgage lending. Other typical industries in which S&L service companies operate include insurance agencies, property appraisal and development, and data processing. Some service companies operate in industries quite far afield from the core business of a depository institution, such as restaurants and funeral homes. By law, S&Ls are permitted to invest 3 percent or less of total assets in service companies, although the portion of assets actually invested in service corporations remains less than 2 percent.

Credit Unions

A **credit union** is a depository financial institution composed of members who have a common bond. This federally imposed **requirement of a common bond** may be based on a similarity of occupation, religious affiliation, or geography. For example, a credit union might be open to all employees of a particular company. Credit unions also operate under a rule that allows membership to someone forever, even if the common bond is broken, say by a change in employment. Credit unions are owned by their members, and the credit union's board of directors appoints managers to operate the credit union.

Credit unions based on an occupational common bond account for about 75 percent of the approximately 17,000 credit unions in the United States. At year-end 1994, these credit unions held assets of $300 billion and had about 63 million members.

Deposits Like banks and thrift institutions, credit unions accept demand deposits and time deposits. Most credit union deposits (about 80 percent) are time deposits, with about 20 percent of all deposits being held in demand accounts. A time deposit at a credit union is known as a **share account**, a designation reflecting the ownership role of each member. The interest each holder of a share account receives is called a **dividend**. A demand deposit account at a credit union is known as a **draft account**. Members can write drafts that provide for the immediate payment of funds. To have a draft account, a member must also have a share account. These distinctions have primarily a technical interest, because share accounts function in the same way as a time deposit, and draft accounts are the same as a checking account at a commercial bank or thrift institution. Virtually all of a credit union's funds derive from these deposits; non-deposit sources of funds are virtually non-existent for credit unions.

Loans Credit unions hold the overwhelming bulk of their assets as loans to members. Almost half of all credit union assets are held in the form of consumer loans to members. Another 25 percent consist of mortgage loans to members. (The remaining 25 percent of assets is mostly held in liquid form, such as investment in Treasury instruments.) Thus, credit unions are institutions that draw almost all of their funds from members' deposits and commit all of their lending to the service of their members.

Comparison of Activities: Banks, Thrifts, and Credit Unions

In comparing banks, thrifts, and credit unions, banks are much larger than all other types of institutions and are the dominant depository institution. Table 10.2 presents key financial statistics for each type of institution, focusing on assets, deposits, and loans. As Table 10.2 shows, commercial banks hold about three times as many assets as S&Ls, savings banks, and credit unions combined. The same is true for deposits and loans outstanding.

Deposit and Loan Structure

Comparing commercial banks with other types of depository institutions reveals a marked difference in deposit and loan structure. Table 10.3 presents the percentage of deposit and loan categories for each type of institution. Focusing first on deposits, we see that all institutions hold most of their deposits as small time and savings deposits. For thrifts and credit unions, this category of deposits accounts for about 80 percent of all deposits. Even for commercial banks, however, small time and savings deposits account for almost 60 percent of total bank deposits. As Table 10.2 shows, banks hold the vast majority of all checking balances. Banks clearly dominate the market for large time deposits, but even banks hold only about 30 percent of their deposits as large time deposits. In summary, banks are relatively more involved with checking accounts than the other types of institutions. By contrast, thrifts and credit unions are more devoted to providing small time and savings accounts.

Table 10.2
Comparison of Depository Institutions
(billions of dollars)

	U.S. Chartered Commercial Banks	Savings Institutions[1]	Credit Unions
Financial Assets	4058.9	1,013.2	294.6
Deposits			
Total	2,434.3	744.0	266.6
Checkable	734.7	82.5	27.4
Small Time and Savings	1,376.7	589.5	232.1
Large Time	322.9	72.0	7.1
Loans Outstanding			
Total	2,231.8	635.5	175.5
Commercial	803.5	10.2	0.0
Mortgages	989.0	587.4	60.5
Consumer	439.3	37.9	115.0

Source: Board of Governors of the Federal Reserve System, Flow of Funds Accounts, Financial Assets and Liabilities, December 7, 1994.

[1] This category includes savings and loan associations and savings banks.

Table 10.3
Deposit and Loan Structure of Depository Institutions
(percentage of each category)

	U.S. Chartered Commercial Banks	Savings Banks	Credit Unions
Deposits	100.0	100.0	100.0
Checkable	30.2	11.1	10.3
Small Time and Savings	56.5	79.2	87.1
Large Time	32.3	9.7	2.6
Loans Outstanding	100.0	100.0	100.0
Commercial	36.0	1.6	0.0
Mortgages	44.3	92.4	34.5
Consumer	19.7	6.0	65.5

Source: Board of Governors of the Federal Reserve System, Flow of Funds Accounts, Financial Assets and Liabilities, December 7, 1994.

Differences in loan categories highlight the different lines of business pursued by banks, thrifts, and credit unions. As Table 10.3 shows, only commercial banks have a large business in commercial lending, with about one-third of all bank loans going for commercial purposes. Banks, thrifts, and credit unions all have active mortgage lending businesses, but thrifts commit over 90 percent of their lending to mortgage financing. While banks are active in consumer lending, these loans account for only 20 percent of their total loans. This compares with 65 percent of loans in the consumer area for credit unions. By contrast, thrift institutions play only a minor role in consumer lending.

We can summarize these differences in the lines of business followed by these institutions. Commercial banks lead in accepting checkable deposits and totally dominate commercial lending. Thrift institutions' deposits are overwhelmingly concentrated in small time and savings deposits, and thrifts lend almost exclusively for home mortgages. Credit unions accept mainly time deposits and focus most strongly on consumer lending with virtually no commercial lending. Of the different types of institutions, commercial banks are the largest and offer the broadest range of services, both in accepting deposits and in making loans. Further, as Table 10.2 shows, commercial banks as a group dominate the dollar volume of all types of deposits and loans.

Summary

This chapter began by considering the role played by a financial intermediary in the U.S. economy. As we noted, a financial intermediary gathers funds from surplus economic units, transforms those funds, and provides them to deficit economic units. The intermediary transforms funds with respect to size, maturity, and risk level. In addition, the financial intermediary also performs the role of information intermediation. In performing these functions, the financial intermediary is essentially a business enterprise, seeking to make a profit by acquiring funds from surplus economic units at a lower rate and making them available to deficit economic units at a higher rate. In addition, the financial intermediary often provides diversification services.

Depository institutions, such as commercial banks, thrift institutions, and credit unions, are a prominent type of financial intermediary. This chapter surveyed the powers of these different depository institutions by considering the sources of funds upon which they draw and the use they make of these funds. In the present environment of financial deregulation, there is relatively little difference in the powers permitted to each institution by law. However, the institutions remain quite different in their sources and uses of funds. Commercial banks, for instance, draw funds in a fairly balanced way from checkable deposits, small time and savings deposits, and large deposits. Banks provide these funds to a broad range of consumers, commercial interests, and those in need of mortgage financing. By contrast, thrift institutions draw principally small time and savings deposits and commit most of these funds to mortgages. Credit unions also attract mainly small time and savings deposits but make mostly consumer loans.

Questions and Problems

1. What are the four principal types of intermediation services provided by financial intermediaries?
2. Explain the transformation provided in size intermediation.
3. How is risk intermediation possible? Isn't risk a feature of the provider of funds that cannot be changed by a financial institution? Explain.
4. What is the "spread," and how is it important for financial intermediation?
5. Explain the value and importance of information intermediation. How do financial intermediaries provide this service?
6. Explain the concept of "disintermediation" and explain why it has become increasingly important in the world of finance.
7. Compare and contrast risk intermediation with the diversification services that financial intermediaries often provide.
8. Explain the difference between a savings bank and a savings and loan association.
9. From an historical point of view, why do commercial banks, as compared to thrift institutions, concentrate more in commercial lending than do thrift institutions?
10. What are brokered deposits?
11. Explain the distinction between a demand and time deposit.
12. For a credit union, explain the difference between a draft account and a share account.
13. Explain the differences among a NOW account, a checking account, and a draft account.
14. Why do all depository institutions hold a significant portion of their assets in highly liquid form?
15. Explain the basic function of the Fed funds market.

References

Benston, G. J. and C. W. Smith, Jr., "A Transactions Cost Approach to the Theory of Financial Intermediation," *Journal of Finance*, 31, May 1976, pp. 215–31.

Erdevig, E. H., "New Directions for Economic Development – The Banking Industry," *Economic Perspectives*, Federal Reserve Bank of Chicago, 12:5, September/October 1988, pp. 17–24.

Felgran, S. D., "Bank Participation in Real Estate: Conduct, Risk, and Regulation," *New England Economic Review*, Federal Reserve Bank of Boston, November/December 1988, pp. 57–73.

Lown, C. S., "Banking and the Economy: What Are the Facts?" *Economic Review*, Federal Reserve Bank of Dallas, September 1990, pp. 1–14.

Nakamura, L. I., "Lessons on Lending and Borrowing in Hard Times," *Business Review*, Federal Reserve Bank of Philadelphia, July/August 1991, pp. 13–21.

Williamson, S. D., "Recent Developments in Modeling Financial Intermediation," *Quarterly Review*, Federal Reserve Bank of Minneapolis, 11, Summer 1987, pp. 19–29.

Regulation of Depository Institutions 11

Overview

This chapter begins by discussing the regulation of depository institutions in the United States. The current regulatory environment is the result of an evolutionary process that we will trace from the Great Depression to the present day. As we will also see, depository institution regulation is currently in crisis and is undergoing a fundamental change.

Regulation of depository institutions has been very broad historically. Regulations cover critically important matters, such as the adequacy of bank capital and the guarantees given to depositors. However, regulations also extend to minor issues such as the number of branches or bank offices a particular bank may have and where they can be located.

Against the background of regulation, this chapter also discusses the thrift crisis – the failure of hundreds of savings and loan associations in a brief period concentrated in the late 1980s. The failure of so many institutions, and the resulting loss of billions of dollars, has shaken the entire regulatory system and led to the passage of important new laws.

The industrial organization of the banking industry is a direct outgrowth of the regulatory environment in which it operates. Understanding the regulatory environment helps to explain why some states have many banking offices and a robust banking industry, while other states have highly restricted banking operations.

The Pre-Depression Framework of Banking Regulation

Banking is a form of commerce that has existed for hundreds, if not thousands of years. While banking's fascinating history extends beyond the money changers that Jesus evicted from the temple to the great Florentine bankers of the Renaissance, this section briefly reviews the banking scene in the United States in the nineteenth and early twentieth centuries, while the next section focuses primarily on the United States in the post-depression era.

Prior to the Great Depression, banking in the United States was subject to regulation, largely stemming from the National Bank Act of 1863. As we will see, the act helped to create a unique system of bank regulation in the United States. Other major acts in the pre-depression period included the Federal Reserve Act of 1913 and the Pepper-McFadden Act of 1927.

National Bank Act of 1863

The National Bank Act established the Office of the Comptroller of the Currency (OCC) and charged it with the general supervision of all national banks. Commercial banks are permitted to operate in the business of banking by holding a bank charter. The OCC can grant federal charters, while state banking agencies permit banks to operate under state charters. Every commercial bank must hold either a federal or state charter. If a bank operates under a federal charter, it is a **national bank**. Only a national bank may use the word "national" in its name. Each state has an office of bank regulation that grants charters to state chartered banks.

The National Bank Act pertained only to national banks, those holding a national charter and regulated by the OCC. The act imposed new requirements designed to make banks safer, to avoid bankruptcies, and to increase public confidence in the banking system. First, the act imposed new capital requirements on national banks. To operate, national banks were required to have more investment by the owners of the bank than had been demanded previously. Second, the act demanded greater reserves. As explained in Chapter 3, higher reserves reduce the amount of loans a bank can make. Other things being equal, higher reserves tend to increase the safety of a bank because there is more capital available to meet the demands of depositors. Third, the act restricted the amount and types of loans that commercial banks could make. Under this law, national banks were prohibited from lending on real estate and forbidden to lend more than 10 percent of the bank's capital stock to any single borrower. While these requirements may not appear onerous by modern standards, they constituted a marked strengthening of the previously existing regulatory system.

Dual Regulation

Because the provisions of the National Bank Act of 1863 applied only to national banks, banks with state charters were not affected by this new law. While state banking regulators generally have powers similar to those of the OCC, many state laws remained lax after the passage of the Act. State banks continued to issue their own paper money and to operate in a freer environment than nationally chartered banks. While some lawmakers hoped that state chartered banks would convert to national charters, state banking persists today, although state chartered banks today are not necessarily any less responsible than banks holding a national charter.

Because the United States banking industry has two fundamentally different chartering bodies (state and federal governments), the banking industry has historically been subject to **dual regulation** – the regulation of national banks by the OCC and the regulation of state-chartered banks by state governments. The system of dual regulation, initiated in the National Bank Act of 1863, remains in place today, although the system has been altered repeatedly during the last 130 years.

Under dual regulation, all banks operating in a given state are subject to the regulations of that state. With every state having different banking laws, banks operating in one state may be permitted many more activities than a similar bank operating in another state. Both nationally and state chartered banks operating in a single state can also be subject to different regulations. While both the state-chartered and nationally chartered banks are subject to the regulations of the state banking office, national banks are subject to regulation by the OCC as well. If the regulations of the OCC are more restrictive than the laws of a given state, national banks operating in that state are potentially at a disadvantage. In sum, the behavior of national banks must conform not only to the laws of the state in which they are operating but must follow the regulations of the OCC as well.

Federal Reserve Act of 1913

The Federal Reserve Act of 1913 established the Federal Reserve System. As discussed more fully in Chapters 2 and 3, the Federal Reserve serves as a banker to banks, in addition to playing an important role in regulating the supply of money in the economy. Further, the Federal Reserve controls the level of bank capital demanded of banks by its imposition of capital requirements. Reserve requirements affect the amount of lending that commercial banks may undertake, and thus the requirements affect the money supply.

The new reserve requirements imposed by the Federal Reserve Act of 1913 applied to all banks, whether operating under a national or a state charter. For the first time, the conduct of state banks was brought under the purview of federal regulation. Even after the passage of the Federal Reserve Act, other aspects of state bank behavior were free of federal regulation. By imposing reserve requirements on all banks, the law was largely designed to avoid **banking panics** – the sudden loss of confidence in the banking system, usually accompanied by massive withdrawals of deposits and the failure of affected banks. Banking panics had been a serious problem through the nineteenth and early twentieth centuries, with significant panics occurring every decade or so. The panics of 1873 and 1907 were particularly strong, with the panic of 1907 leading directly to enactment of the Federal Reserve Act.

The Pepper-McFadden Act of 1927

The creation of the Federal Reserve and the imposition of reserve requirements still left a strongly dualistic banking system. In many states, state chartered banks had a much freer rein to make loans and to operate without adequate capital. In this environment, national banks operated at a strong competitive disadvantage. The Pepper-McFadden Act of 1927 (more popularly known simply as the McFadden Act) sought to level the playing field between national and state-chartered banks.

At the time of the McFadden Act (which was amended in 1933) national banks were not permitted to open **bank branches** – banking offices additional to the principal banking office. In many states, laxer regulation permitted state-chartered banks considerably greater freedom to open branches. Because accessible branches offer considerable convenience to the banking public, restrictions on branches constituted a significant competitive disadvantage for national banks. The Pepper-McFadden Act gave national banks in each state the same right to open branches as state law permitted to state-chartered banks. For example, some states have traditionally permitted only **unit banking** – a system in which each bank can have only a single office. In such unit-banking states, the McFadden Act implied that national banks too could have only one office. (In such states, national and state-chartered banks were on an even footing even before the passage of the Pepper-McFadden Act because national banks were not permitted to open branches.) In states with more liberal bank branching laws, national banks could follow state restrictions on opening bank branches. As we will see later in this chapter, restrictions on bank branching within a single state and across state lines have provided a strong impetus to reform of banking regulation.

Summary

Before the Great Depression, the banking system in the United States was characterized by a strongly dualistic system under the National Bank Act of 1863. Banks operated under state charters or national charters. State-chartered banks were subject only to the often lax banking regulations of the state in which they operated. By contrast, nationally-chartered banks were subject to state regulations and the regulations of the Office of the Comptroller of the Currency. The passage of the Federal Reserve Act of 1913 provided a central bank for the United States and imposed similar reserve requirements on national and state banks. Finally, the Pepper-McFadden Act of 1927 recognized the competitive disadvantage of national banks and sought to place national and state banks on an even footing in the opening of bank branches. However, the dual banking structure was still extremely important, with state banks continuing to have other competitive advantages over national banks; these advantages stemmed from less aggressive state banking regulation.

Erecting the Edifice: Post-Depression Bank Regulation

The Great Depression was initiated by the Great Crash of 1929 and persisted through the 1930s, although it was most intense in the early 1930s. The Depression was a watershed experience for many Americans. The hardships of stock market collapse, vast unemployment, the failure of many banks, the loss of savings in bankrupt financial institutions, and the impossibility of securing credit for worthwhile businesses all led to the demand for profound change in the financial system to ensure that such a catastrophe would not strike again.

From this period of disaster, there emerged a wave of financial regulation designed to stabilize the financial sector. Much of the new regulation focused on depository institutions. The laws passed in the 1930s substantially altered the previous regulatory structure, and these post-depression laws remain the essential ingredients in the regulatory structure under which depository institutions continue to operate.

Banking Act of 1933 (Glass-Steagall)

The Banking Act of 1933, sponsored by Senator Glass and Representative Steagall, was a direct response to the collapse of banking during the Great Depression. It sought to place the banking system on a sound footing and to restore the faith of the public. The faith of the public in banks had been virtually destroyed by bank failures, as many people lost their life savings when banks closed. The act followed a two-pronged strategy. First, it contained provisions designed to make banks sounder by restricting their activities and by controlling their borrowing from depositors. Second, the act included guarantees to depositors that they would not lose their deposits.

The act prohibited commercial banks from acting as investment banks or acting as a broker or dealer in securities transactions. As discussed in Chapter 8, an investment bank assists firms in issuing securities and earns a fee for this service. Brokers and dealers act as middlemen in securities transactions. This provision of the Glass-Steagall Act effectively barred commercial banks from any meaningful participation in the securities industry, except for federal government securities, municipal bonds, and bank securities.

The act prohibited payment of interest on demand deposits, and it restricted the level of interest rates that banks could pay on time and savings deposits. These restrictions were implemented by the Federal Reserve under its **Regulation Q**. By limiting the interest that banks pay to depositors, the act sought to increase the profitability, and thus the soundness, of the banking system.

The Glass-Steagall Act also established the Federal Deposit Insurance Corporation (FDIC). Before this act, bank deposits were not guaranteed by any governmental agency. If a bank failed, depositors had to stand in line with other creditors to gain a return of some portion of their deposits from the bank's remaining assets. Upon taking effect in 1934, the FDIC fully guaranteed the first $10,000 of deposits for any depositor in a commercial bank. The next $40,000 was insured for 75 percent, and the next $50,000 was insured for 50 percent. The system of deposit insurance remains in place today, although the insured amount has been increased over the years. Currently, deposits of $100,000 or less are fully insured by the FDIC. FDIC insurance became available to all depositors of national banks and to depositors of state banks that became members of the FDIC. The insurance feature was so popular that state banks flocked to become members of the FDIC. Member banks pay a small portion of their assets each year to the FDIC to insure their deposits, and the FDIC uses these fees to finance its governmental guarantee to the depositors.

Home Owners' Loan Act of 1933

The Home Owners' Loan Act of 1933 applied to the thrift industry many of the same ideas contained in Glass-Steagall. Before the passage of the Home Owners' Loan Act, all thrift institutions held state charters, but the act permitted the formation of federally-chartered savings and loan associations. In addition, the act provided for the voluntary conversion of state-chartered S&Ls to federal charters. The act authorized the Federal Home Loan Bank Board (FHLBB) to regulate the activities of federally-charted S&Ls. Thus, the FHLBB was to play a regulatory role for federal S&Ls that was similar to the regulatory role of the Office of the Comptroller of the Currency for national banks.

National Housing Act of 1934

The National Housing Act of 1934 followed swiftly on the heels of the Home Owners' Loan Act to complete the parallelism between federal regulation of national banks and federal regulation of federally-chartered S&Ls. Just as the Glass-Steagall Act had created the Federal Deposit Insurance Corporation to insure bank deposits, the National Housing Act established the Federal Savings and Loan Insurance Corporation (FSLIC), pronounced "fizz-lick," to guarantee deposits held in federal savings and loan associations. The National Housing Act placed FSLIC under the administration of the FHLBB. In addition to providing deposit insurance to all federal S&Ls, FSLIC also permitted state-chartered S&Ls to join FSLIC and to receive insurance for their deposits.

Bank Holding Company Act of 1956

A **bank holding company** (BHC) is a firm that owns or effectively controls one or more commercial banks. Bank holding companies may either be **one-bank holding companies** (OBHC) or **multibank holding companies** (MBHC). The 1956 act was aimed specifically at multibank holding companies and sought to bring the activity of MBHCs more firmly under federal regulation.[1]

---

[1] The Banking Act of 1933 imposed a variety of weak restrictions on BHCs.

BHCs arose largely to circumvent banking regulation. As we have seen, restrictions on branching impeded the growth of banks geographically, and the Banking Act of 1933 (Glass-Steagall) restricted the lines of business open to commercial banks. An MBHC could evade the geographical restrictions on banking by owning several banks. While the individual banks owned by the MBHC would technically meet the restrictions against opening branches, all of the banks owned by a single MBHC would be controlled by a single firm. An OBHC controls only a single bank, so it is not a vehicle for evading geographical restrictions. Instead, an OBHC provides a corporate form to engage in activities not open to commercial banks, such as activities in investment banking and financial services. Because the restrictions on lines of business in the Glass-Steagall Act apply only to banks, an OBHC can own a bank and, with other non-bank portions of the firm, engage in activities prohibited to commercial banks. As a result, the OBHC corporate form can bring banking and the prohibited activities under the umbrella of a single firm.

The Bank Holding Company Act of 1956 required existing MBHCs to register with the Federal Reserve and required prior approval for the formation of new MBHCs. The act empowered the Federal Reserve to examine the financial dealings of the BHC or any of its subsidiaries. Perhaps most importantly, the act required that MBHCs receive prior approval from the Federal Reserve before acquiring any additional banks or other non-bank firms. In addition, the law restricted the non-banking activities of MBHCs to finance-related lines of business and gave the Federal Reserve the authority to determine what kinds of non-banking activities were suitable for MBHCs. Finally, the law permitted non-banking subsidiaries of MBHCs to operate across state lines.

Bank Merger Acts of 1960 and 1966

Before 1960, bank mergers were not subject to general **antitrust laws** – laws that restrict the size and economic power that a single firm may hold in a geographic or economic market. Before the passage of the merger acts, banks could merely secure the approval of their direct regulator to merge. The Bank Merger Act of 1960 sought to extend general antitrust provisions to the banking sector. Under the act, bank mergers required the prior approval of the Comptroller of the Currency for national banks, of the Federal Reserve for state banks that were members of the Federal Reserve, or of the Federal Deposit Insurance Corporation for state banks that were not members of the Federal Reserve. The act further specified that proposed bank mergers were subject to the scrutiny of the Justice Department, the usual enforcement agency for antitrust laws. The act also instructed these regulatory agencies to consider the financial position of the merging banks before approving the merger. Perhaps most importantly, the law also specified that effects on competition in banking should be an important consideration in deciding merger cases.

The years immediately following the passage of the 1960 Act saw conflict between the Justice Department and the banking agencies over the importance of competition in deciding merger applications. The Bank Merger Act of 1966 clarified the importance of competitive effects by giving even greater weight to the effects of a merger on competition. Basically, the act insisted that any mergers likely to substantially reduce competition among banks should be rejected.

1970 Amendments to the Bank Holding Company Act

As noted earlier, the Bank Holding Company Act of 1956 pertained only to multibank holding companies (MBHCs) and was silent concerning the activities of one-bank holding companies (OBHCs). The 1970 amendments to the act brought OBHCs under the same regulatory umbrella with MBHCs. The amendments also specified that the activities of all BHCs must be "closely related to banking," and the amendments empowered the Federal Reserve to determine which activities were sufficiently similar to banking. In subsequent years the Federal Reserve ruled on a number of activities. Table 11.1 provides a sample of activities that have been permitted and forbidden to BHCs by Federal Reserve rulings.

Summary

From the Great Depression through 1970, Congress enacted a series of laws that helped to define the depository institution industry. The Glass-Steagall Act, the Home Owners' Loan Act of 1933, and the National Housing Act of 1934 created a system of depository institutions with federal guarantees for deposits and control of deposit rates by the Federal Reserve. For S&Ls, federal charters became possible for the first time, creating parallel systems for banking and savings and loan associations. Both types of banks and S&Ls could operate under either state or federal charters, with federally-insured deposits for all federally-chartered institutions, and the possibility of deposit insurance for state-chartered institutions as well. These laws sought to stabilize the deposit institution industry and to instill confidence among depositors. Thus, in addition to providing

Table 11.1
Activities Permitted and Forbidden to Bank Holding Companies

Permitted Activities
Making loans and extending credit (mortgages, finance companies, credit-card issuance and factoring)
Performing trust services
Servicing loans and other extensions of credit
Acting as an investment or financial adviser to a real estate investment trust (REIT)
Leasing personal property
Providing bookkeeping and data processing services
Appraising real estate
Providing insurance services related to an extension of credit
Issuing money orders, traveler's checks, and U.S. savings bonds
Forbidden Activities
Underwriting life insurance not related to the extension of credit
Land development or property management
Real estate brokerage
Management consulting
Travel agencies
Operating thrift institutions

Source: Regulation Y, Board of Governors of the Federal Reserve System.

guarantees to depositors, the federal government took more effective control of the operation of these institutions by providing for federal supervision.

In 1956, Congress passed the Bank Holding Company Act bringing multibank holding companies under the purview of the Federal Reserve. The 1970 amendments to the act also gave control of one-bank holding companies to the Federal Reserve System. These laws empowered the Federal Reserve to examine the finances of these BHCs and to control the lines of business in which they engaged, ensuring that their non-banking enterprises remained closely related to banking.

Further, the Bank Merger Acts of 1960 and 1966 defined the conditions under which bank mergers could occur. Most importantly, these acts established that a bank merger should be permitted only if such a merger would not adversely affect competition.

By 1970, the federal government had acquired a major role in depository institution regulation. The system appeared secure, with the ghosts of the Great Depression having long been banished. Few observers of the banking and S&L industries could foresee the storm that loomed on the horizon, a storm that would prove to have its origins in the elaborately crafted edifice of depository institution regulation that had just received its finishing touches.

Disintermediation

Throughout this text, we have stressed the benefits that a financial system confers on an economy. In Chapter 1, we saw that the presence of a financial system enriches the opportunity set of both surplus and deficit economic units. An important part of any such system is the existence of financial intermediaries, including depository institutions as a foremost example. In spite of these obvious benefits offered by financial intermediaries, the 1970s and early 1980s witnessed substantial disintermediation. **Disintermediation**, discussed in Chapter 10, is the process in which economic units sell and purchase financial claims directly without employing an intermediary such as a commercial bank or a savings and loan association.

Earlier in this chapter, we saw that the Federal Reserve's Regulation Q limited the interest that commercial banks and savings and loan associations could pay on deposits. Regulation Q prohibited the payment of interest by these institutions on demand deposits, and it limited the interest that banks and S&Ls could pay on time and savings deposits. In the 1970s, as market rates of interest crept above the permitted deposit rates at banks and S&Ls, many individuals withdrew their deposits and pursued higher interest rates by investing directly in securities.

Not only did these former depositors buy securities directly, but they withdrew their deposits from banks and S&Ls to invest in money market mutual funds. A **mutual fund** is a firm that collects investment from a wide range of investors and uses these funds to purchase a portfolio of securities. Each investor in the mutual fund then owns a fraction of the entire portfolio. (Chapter 17 explains the functioning of mutual funds in detail.) A **money market mutual fund** is a mutual fund that specializes in investing in money market instruments, and investing in a money market mutual funds is a close substitute for time or savings deposits that earn a specific rate of interest. Also, because many money market mutual funds allow investors to write checks against their investment, these money market funds offer a close substitute for demand deposits at banks or S&Ls.

A mutual fund is itself a type of financial intermediary. After all, it collects cash from investors and uses these monies to purchase a portfolio of securities. Thus, the decision to switch investment from an account at a bank or S&L to an investment in a money market mutual fund is not disintermediation in the strictest sense, because the investor still employs a financial intermediary. The investor has essentially switched from one intermediary (a depository institution) to another type of intermediary (a money market mutual fund). The process of eliminating one financial intermediary in favor of another is known as **gross disintermediation**.

In the 1970s, there was a tremendous surge in money market mutual fund investment. In 1973 there were essentially no money market mutual funds, but by 1983 money market mutual funds held more than 55 percent of all mutual fund assets. By 1980, there were 106 money market funds, constituting about 20 percent of all existing funds. Table 11.2 shows the phenomenal growth of money market mutual funds from 1974 to 1983, when assets invested in money market funds increased almost 100 times, from $1.7 billion to $162.5 billion, and the number of accounts rose from 208,000 to more than 12 million. While some of these funds originated from growth in the economy, the bulk of new investment in money market mutual funds came from other sources. In large part, the new investment in money market funds came from deposits held at banks and savings and loan associations. With Regulation Q restrictions keeping interest rates at depository institutions below competitive market rates for money market instruments, depositors responded to the strong incentive to close their bank and S&L accounts and pursue higher yields in money market funds.

The system established in the 1930s and elaborated over the following decades now faced a serious problem in the form of disintermediation. Depositors' pursuit of higher yields threatened the system of low and regulated deposit rates designed to ensure a stable financial system by providing depository institutions with low-cost funds. The disintermediation of the 1970s and early 1980s spurred the decision to deregulate the financial sector.

Table 11.2
The Growth of Money Market Mutual Funds, 1974–83

Year	Net Investment (billions of dollars)	Total Assets (billions of dollars)	Number of Funds	Number of Accounts (thousands)
1974	1.7	$1.7	15	N/A
1975	0.8	3.7	36	208.8
1976	−0.2	3.7	48	180.7
1977	0.0	3.9	50	177.5
1978	6.2	10.9	61	467.8
1979	33.5	45.2	76	2,307.9
1980	28.1	74.4	96	4,745.6
1981	105.2	181.9	159	10,282.1
1982	22.2	205.6	281	13,101.3
1983	−45.7	162.5	307	12,276.6

Source: *Mutual Fund Fact Book*, various issues.

Financial Deregulation

To fully understand the impact of financial deregulation, it is important to keep in mind the three essential features of the regulated system established in reaction to the Depression. First, regulations mandated low interest rates on deposits, thereby providing a cheap source of funds to banks and S&Ls. Second, the federal government closely regulated commercial activities of depository institutions. The restrictions on the activities of banks and S&Ls along with the cheap funding mandated by Regulation Q both contributed to the safety of the entire system. Third, the system of federal deposit insurance would be a promise of manageable risk given the cheap funds and restricted activities of depository institutions. At the same time, the insurance system would give depositors confidence that their deposits were secure. Thus, the entire system of depository institutions rested on the three legs of cheap funds, low-risk commercial activities, and deposit insurance.

The advent of high interest rates in the 1970s and early 1980s, along with the resulting disintermediation, threatened to amputate one of the three legs of the financial system. By 1980, legislators and regulators agreed that disintermediation could be stemmed only by financial deregulation. Just as the regulation of the 1930s and ensuing decade required laws, Congress moved to pass new laws to deregulate the financial system.

Depository Institutions Deregulation and Monetary Control Act of 1980 (DIDMCA)

The Depository Institutions Deregulation and Monetary Control Act of 1980 (DIDMCA) was the first major piece of legislation aimed at deregulating the financial system. DIDMCA abandoned Regulation Q by phasing out deposit rate ceilings by 1986. With money market rates in 1980 approaching 20 percent, banks and S&Ls were faced with the prospect of paying much more for funds than ever before.

To pay such competitive rates, these depository institutions would have to earn more. Accordingly, DIDMCA also granted new powers to depository institutions. The act permitted thrift institutions and credit unions to offer checking accounts.[2] The act permitted federally-chartered savings and loan associations new investment powers and granted the authority for S&Ls to enter new lines of commerce. Under the act, federally-chartered S&Ls could invest in corporate bonds and commercial paper. The traditional real estate activities of S&Ls were greatly extended. The size of permitted loans was increased from $75,000 per residence to 90 percent of the appraised value of the home. All geographical restrictions on real estate lending were removed, and the act abandoned the requirement that the S&L hold a first mortgage on any home it financed. The act also permitted S&Ls to make construction loans.

In addition to expanding the familiar real estate activities of thrift institutions, DIDMCA granted entirely new powers to thrift institutions. For the first time, thrift institutions were allowed to offer consumer loans and to issue credit cards. In addition, thrifts were allowed to make commercial loans up to 5 percent of their assets, and they began to accept commercial demand

---

[2] We have seen in Chapter 10 that these accounts are called negotiable order of withdrawal (NOW) accounts at thrifts and share draft accounts at credit unions. They function like regular checking accounts in all important respects.

deposits. In short, DIDMCA instituted a plan to phase out interest rate regulations for all depository institutions, and it greatly expanded the lines of business open to thrift institutions.[3]

The Garn-St. Germain Depository Institutions Act of 1982

The Garn-St. Germain Depository Institutions Act of 1982 followed quickly on the heels of the DIDMCA and freed depository institutions of much of the remaining restriction on their powers. First, the act empowered banks and S&Ls to offer money market deposit accounts (MMDA) similar in most respects to money market mutual funds, a provision aimed at stemming the flow of funds out of depository institutions. These MMDAs were to have no interest rate ceiling, a $2,500 minimum, no mandated maturity, and a restriction to three checks per month. Second, the law permitted mutual savings banks and S&Ls to make commercial loans of up to 10 percent of their assets. Third, the act allowed thrifts to make commercial loans of up to 30 percent of their assets. Fourth, thrifts were permitted to invest up to 40 percent of their assets in loans secured by commercial real estate. (Lending in these three categories could not exceed 60 percent of assets for a single institution.)

Summary

We have seen how the regulatory structure initiated in the 1930s and elaborated for 50 years created a depository institution industry that rested on the three legs of cheap deposit funds for the institutions, restricting banks and S&Ls to low-risk business activities, and federal guarantees of deposits. Faced with the serious problem of disintermediation, the DIDMCA and the Garn-St. Germain Act sawed off two of the three legs that supported the industry, by freeing deposit rates and allowing higher risk business activities. The two laws left intact the third leg, the federal deposit guarantees. Just as a stool cannot stand on one leg, depository institutions were left with a structure that invited disaster. Deposit guarantees had worked well for many years, so long as the operating environment of banks and S&Ls made funds cheap and profits stable. In the era of financial deregulation, funds were costly and banks and S&Ls were free to take higher risks to cover the higher costs of funds. This left a situation in which the government, and thus taxpayers, guaranteed the safety of deposits, but bank and S&L managers were free to take substantially higher risks with those deposited funds than ever before, a prescription for disaster that quickly led to a crisis in deposit insurance.

The Deposit Insurance Mess

This section begins by briefly explaining how banks and S&Ls found themselves losing money as the 1980s began and shows how these losses were instrumental in the passage of the 1980 and 1982 financial deregulation acts. We then consider the conceptual flaws in the design of the deposit insurance system and show how the regulators inadvertently contributed to the damage.

---

[3] DIDMCA also instituted uniform reserve requirements for all depository institutions and included other provisions to facilitate control over the money supply.

Setting the Stage for Disaster

Every depository institution relies on acquiring funds, usually deposits, at one rate and lending them at a higher rate to earn a positive spread – the difference between the rate earned on funds and the rate paid for the use of those funds. From this spread, the bank or S&L pays its operating costs (salaries, advertising, physical facilities, and so on) and a return to investors in the institution. (Chapter 12 explains the operation of banks in detail.) For example, before the late 1970s S&Ls were accustomed to paying 4–5 percent for deposits and lending those funds at 6–8 percent for home mortgages. From this comfortable 2–3 percent spread between the deposit rate and lending rate, the S&L could cover its operating costs with ease.

In 1979–80, interest rates reached record highs. Figure 11.1 shows 90-day T-bill yields over these two years. Constrained by Regulation Q, depository institutions were in the unpleasant position of seeing their deposits withdrawn to chase these higher rates. Yet banks and S&Ls were forced to replace the fleeing deposits with new funds at competitive market rates. Banks and S&Ls were accustomed to borrowing on a short-term basis from depositors and lending long-term for commercial loans or home mortgages. Even though deposits were withdrawn, the long-term loans remained in place, so banks and S&Ls had to find new funds to replace the vanishing deposits. In short, the institutions had to find these new deposits, no matter what the cost, because they had been using deposits to fund the various loans that they made to businesses, homeowners, and other borrowers.

Most of these long-term loans had originated in an era of lower interest rates, say 8 percent on average. With deposits leaving banks and S&Ls, these institutions now had to acquire funds at much higher rates, say 12 percent on average, leaving the institutions earning a negative spread of 4 percent. The problem of a negative spread would be worse the longer the maturity on the long-

Figure 11.1
90-Day T-Bill Yields, 1979–80

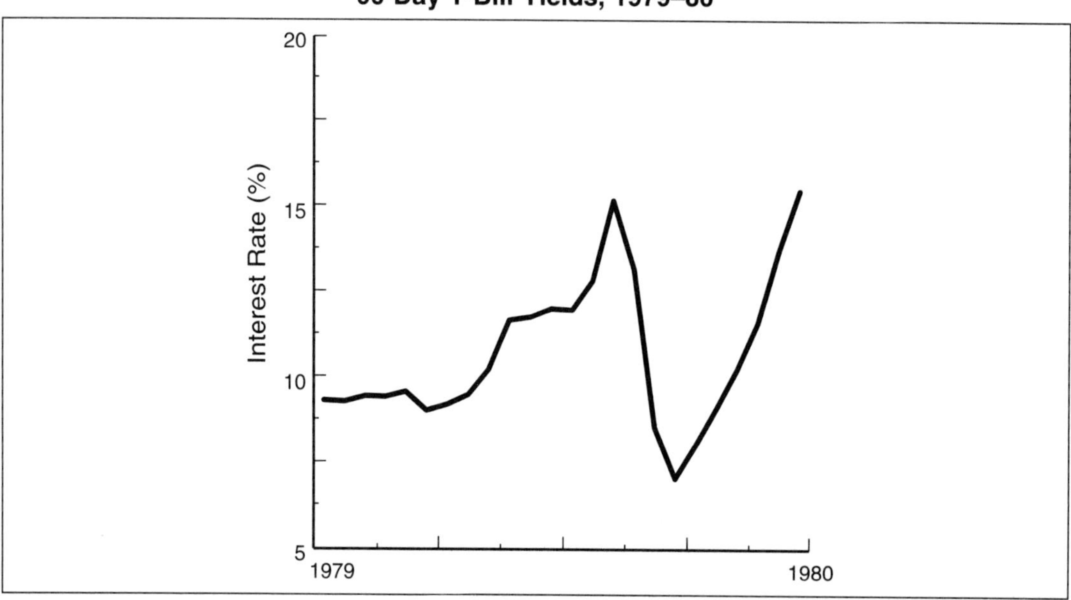

term loans. While banks tend to lend most heavily on commercial loans with a maturity of three to seven years, S&Ls made most of their loans as 30-year home mortgages. Consequently, the problem of negative spreads threatened S&Ls even more than commercial banks.

Besides suffering a negative spread on their loans, banks and S&Ls still had to pay their operating expenses, and many institutions started to lose money rapidly. A few years of heavy losses could erode an institution's capital and leave it bankrupt. For a bankrupt bank or S&L, the insured deposits would have to be honored by either the FDIC or the FSLIC.

Against the background of mounting losses, Congress passed DIDMCA and the Garn-St. Germain Act. By freeing deposit rates, banks and S&Ls could pay competitive rates and stem disintermediation. By entering newly permitted lines of business, banks and S&Ls could reap a higher return on their assets and earn their way out of the negative spreads on their existing long-term loans.

Consider an imaginary S&L manager in 1982 faced with a year of losses on lending due to a negative spread. Interest rates are still high, and the manager faces another year of losses, knowing that a few years of such losses will cause the S&L to fail and cause him to lose his job. The only bright stars on the horizon are the new powers just granted to S&Ls by DIDMCA and the Garn-St. Germain Act. It appears that the only hope for survival is to enter new businesses that can earn profits to offset losses on lending. With these new profits, the S&L might survive until interest rates fall. If so, the S&L will return to profitability, and the manager will keep his job. Many deposit institutions faced just such a prospect during the early 1980s.

Confronting eventual bankruptcy and unemployment, many banks and S&Ls decided to use their recently expanded powers to enter unfamiliar businesses. Even if the new operation appeared very risky relative to expected profits, it seemed to offer the only hope of survival.

Design Flaws in Deposit Insurance

There are at least four identifiable design flaws in the deposit insurance system created by the legislation of 1933–82. First, the design of the system encouraged managers of depository institutions to make inappropriate business and investment decisions (moral hazard). Second, the design flaws inherent in the deposit insurance system attracted managers likely to cause disasters (adverse selection). Third, the regulatory system adopted a policy of not allowing large banks to fail, intensifying the twin problems of moral hazard and adverse selection. Fourth, the pricing of deposit insurance failed to reflect the risk of the insured institutions. We consider each of these problems in turn.

Moral Hazard **Moral hazard** refers to the undesired incentives a contract gives to a contracting person or firm. For example, consider two students, John and Mary. John knows that Mary is a person of great intellectual ability and that she can certainly pass her course in financial institutions. Based on this knowledge, John bets Mary $10,000 that she will pass. In making this bet John unwittingly exposes himself to considerable moral hazard, because Mary now has a strong incentive to fail. Mary may find it worth her trouble to fail the course just to win the bet. Moral hazard is a typical feature of insurance contracts because the contract alters the incentives faced by the insured. For example, car insurance that covers stolen radios gives the insured an incentive to be careless in locking the car.

Moral hazard arises in deposit insurance because the insured depositors can afford to be careless in placing their deposits. No matter what bank or S&L the depositor chooses, the federal deposit insurance program guarantees her deposits. Therefore, the depositor has little incentive to investigate the soundness of the bank or S&L where she plans to place her deposits. These perverse incentives are unlike those faced by most investors. Investors normally are very concerned about the viability of the firm in which they plan to invest.

Deposit insurance also creates moral hazard for managers at insured banks and S&Ls. We can see the hazard that deposit insurance creates by considering how ordinary corporations raise funds. Corporations usually face a market discipline in raising funds to undertake a new business. If potential investors fear that the firm might fail, they will not invest. Similarly, if expected profits are not sufficient to justify the risk associated with the business, investors will not participate and the firm must abandon the project. (As discussed in Chapter 9, the trade-off between risk and return is exactly the problem considered by capital market theory.) Thus, corporate managers must weigh the risks and expected return carefully if they hope to attract investment funds.

The manager of an insured depository institution faces little market discipline in raising funds. The depositor knows that her funds are secure because of deposit insurance, and the depositor will receive a regulated rate of interest in any event (prior to the dismantling of Regulation Q). Therefore, the bank or S&L manager can raise new deposits without facing the market discipline of the investor inspecting the level of risk and return.

Adverse Selection **Adverse selection** is a feature of a contract that attracts undesirable partners. Adverse selection is a typical problem for insurance companies. For example, some firms offer insurance against the loss or theft of jewelry and cameras when vacationers travel abroad. Offering such a contract attracts dishonest travelers intent on committing fraud by pretending to suffer a loss on a non-existent watch or camera. The adverse selection arises because offering the contract attracts a disproportionate number of individuals anxious to exploit the insurance. While typical of many insurance contracts, the problem of adverse selection is not limited to insurance contracts. For example, a corporation with sloppy financial controls is likely to attract dishonest managers anxious to exploit the shoddy accounting.

The deposit insurance system is likely to attract bank and S&L managers who are likely to prefer excessively risky business strategies. Because the depositors lack any incentive to control management, the managers are free to operate the institution in a risky manner. In fact, the situation is even worse because the lack of monitoring by depositors is likely to attract dishonest managers as well.

The "Too Big to Fail" Policy Although not included in legislation, the deposit insurance system has operated under a policy that some banks are too big to be allowed to fail. Regulators of the financial system are most concerned with the overall viability of the entire system. The spectacular and highly visible failure of a very large bank could cause a loss of confidence in the banking system as a whole. In such a failure of confidence, depositors might rush to withdraw their deposits, generating more bank failures. This scenario envisions general financial panic and disruption stemming from the failure of a single large bank.

To prevent such a disaster, bank regulators have long operated under the policy that the very largest banks are too large to fail. In May 1984, Continental Illinois, one of the nation's ten largest banks, became insolvent. Not only did the FDIC guarantee all deposits up to $100,000, as the law requires, but it guaranteed all deposits, even those of the very largest depositors. In addition, the FDIC even guaranteed Continental Illinois's bondholders against the loss of their investment.

The "too big to fail" policy intensifies the problems of moral hazard and adverse selection already inherent in the deposit insurance system. Under the law, deposits are insured only for a maximum of $100,000. With this legal limitation, large depositors should have an incentive to monitor the soundness of their bank. These large depositors, such as corporations, are in a better position to monitor the soundness of their bank than are small depositors. If all deposits at the big banks are insured under the "too big to fail" policy, the large depositors have no incentive to monitor the soundness of their banks. Further, these large deposits are generally concentrated in the biggest banks, so the "too big to fail" policy actually helps to reduce the monitoring of the biggest and most important banks.

We have already seen that adverse selection attracts risk-oriented managers to depository institutions. Among depository institutions, these same risk-oriented managers will be attracted to the biggest banks, because these are the institutions that will not be allowed to fail no matter how disastrous the risky policies of the bank may be. As a result, the depository institution industry as a whole attracts risk-prone managers and concentrates them in the biggest banks where they can do the most harm.

In addition to the problems of moral hazard and adverse selection, the "too big to fail" policy stimulates unfair competition. For example, in late 1990 the Bank of New England was the 33rd largest bank in the U.S. with more than $20 billion in assets; it was also insolvent. Arguing that this bank was too big to fail, the FDIC guaranteed all its deposits. At about the same time, Freedom National Bank, a small bank in New York, became insolvent. Deposits in excess of $100,000 were not guaranteed by the FDIC, and depositors eventually received only about half of their deposits above $100,000. Such practices give a competitive advantage to large banks, in addition to providing perverse incentives to large depositors and bank managers.

Faulty Pricing Insurance firms typically price policies to reflect the risk of the insured. For example, young drivers face higher car insurance rates because young drivers as a group tend to have more frequent accidents. Under the deposit insurance system, all institutions pay the same rate to insure their deposits, without regard to the riskiness of the institution. Because all institutions pay the same price for deposit insurance, the pricing mechanism provides no incentive for managers to control the risk of failure. If deposit insurance fees were risk-based, managers would have to consider the trade-off between lower insurance rates and the riskiness of the strategies they would like to pursue.

Financial Deregulation and Deposit Insurance As we have seen, the deposit insurance system embodies significant design flaws by giving perverse incentives to managers due to moral hazard, adverse selection, the "too big to fail" policy, and a faulty pricing system. Nonetheless, the original legislation that established deposit insurance did contain important safeguards. In particular, banking legislation starting with Glass-Steagall in 1933 and continuing through 1970 constrained the kinds of activities that banks and S&Ls could undertake. By limiting banks and S&Ls to safer activities, these laws helped to offset the design weaknesses inherent in the deposit insurance system. Perhaps realizing the incentives for risky behavior that deposit insurance created, the design of these laws placed the riskiest activities out of bounds to managers at banks and S&Ls.

Financial deregulation in the early 1980s liberated depository institutions from the constraints of the old regulatory system but left the deposit insurance system intact. In the resulting deregulated environment, managers faced the desperate situation of negative spreads, and many turned to extremely high risk strategies in an attempt to "grow out of their problems." This approach called for banks and S&Ls to grow by accepting new deposits and using those funds to enter higher-risk businesses. One technique for accelerating deposit growth was to use brokered deposits. A brokered deposit is a deposit placed with a depository institution by a third party to the transaction, a deposit broker. For example, a deposit broker might find an investor with $1,000,000 to deposit. The broker would break the entire amount into ten $100,000 parts (to qualify for deposit insurance) and place each part with a different depository institution. By offering a premium on the generally prevailing deposit rate, an institution could readily attract new deposits to promote accelerated growth. If the risky ventures funded with these expanded deposits paid off, the institution would return to profitability and the manager's position would be saved. If these new ventures failed, the FDIC and FSLIC, and ultimately the U.S. taxpayer, would be left to pick up the pieces by paying the depositors.

As the 1980s progressed, many banks and S&Ls pursued highly aggressive expansion strategies by increasing deposits and entering new lines of business. Many of these ventures failed, with the most desperate problems being concentrated in the S&L industry, a concentration due to at least two factors. First, because S&Ls had more loans concentrated in long-maturity home mortgages, the negative spreads they faced with high interest rates would persist for a very long time. Thus, the high interest rates affected S&Ls more strongly than commercial banks. Second, because S&Ls are generally smaller than banks and because their activities had been concentrated in home mortgage lending for so long, S&L managers tended to be less sophisticated than their counterparts at commercial banks. Accordingly, they probably did a worse job of managing their new enterprises.

Hiding Worthless Institutions

By the mid-1980s, many depository institutions were really insolvent, although they continued to operate. Nor was this sad state of affairs a surprise, with many academics sounding a clear warning.[4] The continued operation of these thrifts was made possible in part by regulatory policies obscuring the insolvency of some institutions. In this section, we focus on the S&L industry, where the problems were more intense and more apparent.

---

[4] Problems were widely discussed at academic conferences and with regulators. One of the most active voices belonged to Edward J. Kane, now a professor at Boston College. Kane sounded a clear warning to the public in his book, *The Gathering Crisis in Federal Deposit Insurance*, Cambridge, MA: MIT Press, 1985. However, there was ample discussion of the pending problems before 1985.

Regulatory Forbearance In retrospect, federal regulators of the S&L industry contributed to the industry's problem by their practice of **regulatory forbearance** – permitting insolvent institutions to continue to operate. By practicing regulatory forbearance, the S&L regulators helped to sweep the growing problem of insolvency under the carpet. The regulators had three incentives of their own to behave in this fashion. First, the FSLIC lacked adequate insurance funds to close all insolvent thrifts and pay the depositors. Second, the Federal Home Loan Bank Board had a responsibility under the law to foster the development of the industry, a role that is incompatible with an extremely aggressive regulatory stance. Third, a regulatory agency is likely to be judged by the health of the institutions it regulates. By obscuring the miserable state of the thrift industry, the regulators hid their agency's failings. (Thus, the regulators suffered from moral hazard as well. The regulators had incentives that prevented them from regulating as forcefully as they should have.) Fourth, the Congress and executive branch were all too anxious to avoid any unpleasant reports about losses at depository institutions. After all, many of the most influential congressmen and senators on key banking committees received generous campaign donations from the industry.[5]

The regulatory agencies practiced forbearance in a variety of ways. Here we discuss the special accounting rules for the thrift industry and the use of mergers to avoid confronting the reality of a failed institution. Most businesses operate under accounting rules promulgated by the Financial Accounting Standards Board (FASB). These rules are known as Generally Accepted Accounting Principles (GAAP). Thrift regulators devised a more lenient system known as Regulatory Accounting Principles, or RAP accounting. Under RAP accounting, thrift institutions appeared to have considerably more capital than they would under GAAP accounting. Because GAAP rules more accurately reflect the economic worth of an institution, RAP accounting let insolvent S&Ls maintain the appearance of going concerns and provided a convenient excuse for regulators to allow actually insolvent institutions to continue in operation.

Merging Failed Institutions Faced with the need to close more thrifts than the available insurance funds would permit, regulators sometimes used mergers to dispose of ailing thrifts. To facilitate the merger, regulatory agencies might offer a payment to the acquirer or might extend some kind of regulatory forbearance to the acquirer. For example, branching for thrifts was subject to a variety of restrictions. In some merger cases, the regulators might allow an acquiring S&L to gain entry to a new market if the acquirer agreed to merge with a failing thrift. In such a merger, the acquirer received the valuable right of entry to a new market, but the regulators did not have to make a cash outlay to dispose of the failing thrift. Unfortunately, some acquirers accepted so many problem institutions that the acquirer itself became untenable and eventually failed as well.

Institutional Zombies In the movies, a zombie is a creature that is among the living dead. Already dead, but still moving among the living, these zombies wreak havoc by tricking the unsuspecting into thinking that the zombie is truly alive. Professor Ed Kane of Boston College has used

---

[5] See Edward J. Kane, *The S&L Insurance Mess: How Did it Happen?* Washington: The Urban Institute, 1989, p. 53.

the metaphor of zombies to describe thrifts that continued to operate even though they were insolvent.[6] By continuing to operate when insolvent, many zombie thrifts continued the same policies that had already resulted in their financial ruin. They accepted brokered deposits with high deposit rates, made loans outside their expertise, and bought securities they were unprepared to evaluate. Instead of being buried as a good zombie should, the twilight existence of these zombie thrifts made the thrift crisis even worse. Later in this chapter, we consider the extent of the S&L debacle and appraise the current condition of the thrift industry.

A New Round of Regulation

Faced with billions of dollars of losses in the thrift industry and a shaken banking industry as well, Congress realized that new remedies were required to return the financial system to stable ground. The first act that attempted to address the issues was the Competitive Equality in Banking Act of 1987 (CEBA). The CEBA was a feeble and partially self-defeating effort, and the administration and Congress soon realized that more realistic action would be required. The centerpiece of legislation designed to stabilize and reform the financial system was the Financial Institutions Reform, Recovery, and Enforcement Act of 1989 (FIRREA). Congress also enacted the Federal Deposit Insurance Corporation Improvement Act in November 1991.

Competitive Equality in Banking Act of 1987 (CEBA)

The CEBA explicitly recognized the problems with the FSLIC and the thrift industry by allowing the FSLIC to raise an additional $10.8 billion of new funds. The Act also restricted the FSLIC to spend no more than $3.75 billion per year to close failed thrifts. These amounts were completely inadequate to deal with the losses already incurred. The act also stressed the importance of letting failing banks and thrifts operate to provide services to local communities, a provision that failed to recognize that zombie thrifts had been the source of much of the losses in previous years. In short, this well-motivated act proved to be only a temporary measure at best.[7]

Financial Institutions Reform, Recovery, and Enforcement Act of 1989 (FIRREA)

By 1987, the FSLIC was essentially bankrupt and the FDIC was headed for serious difficulties as well. FIRREA reordered regulation of depository institutions and sought to put the deposit insurance fund on a sound footing. First, the act abolished the Federal Home Loan Bank Board and the FSLIC. Second, the act created the Office of Thrift Supervision (OTS) as a part of the Treasury Department. The OTS serves as a successor to the Federal Home Loan Bank Board,

---

[6] See Edward J. Kane, *The S&L Insurance Mess: How Did it Happen?* Washington: The Urban Institute, 1989. The first chapter is entitled "Zombie Thrifts and FSLIC: A Federal Ponzi Scheme?"

[7] Other provisions included limitations on the growth of nonbank banks, institutions that perform most of the functions of a bank but that do not both simultaneously make commercial loans and accept deposits. The act also changed the definition of a bank to include any FDIC-insured institution.

and it is intended to parallel the Office of the Comptroller of the Currency in its functions. Third, the functions of the FSLIC were assigned to the FDIC, making the FDIC the sole federal deposit insurance agency for banks and thrifts. Fourth, the act created two insurance funds to be managed by the FDIC. The Bank Insurance Fund (BIF) and the Savings and Loan Insurance Fund (SAIF) hold funds to guarantee deposits held in commercial banks and thrift institutions, respectively. Fifth, the act created the Resolution Trust Corporation (RTC) to manage the dissolution of failed thrifts and to liquidate the assets of failed institutions. For example, the RTC attempts to dispose of real estate investments owned by thrifts that have failed. Sixth, FIRREA permits any thrift to apply for a charter as a bank and, upon receiving a bank charter, to engage in all functions permitted to commercial banks. Seventh, for institutions that elected to remain thrifts, the act required that these institutions keep 70 percent of tangible assets in housing-related assets.[8] Eighth, FIRREA permitted BHCs to acquire thrifts. Ninth, the act instituted new definitions of capital and new capital requirements for both thrifts and banks. Tenth, the act gave regulators expanded powers to intervene in badly managed institutions to lessen losses.

Of these broad and sweeping changes, the reorganization of the insurance funds and the new approach to capital are probably the most important. Both BIF and SAIF offer the same protection to depositors, and FIRREA requires that both funds increase their funding to 1.25 percent of insured deposits, although both funds began their existence substantially below the target, with SAIF being more under-funded. Because of this greater shortfall, thrift payments for SAIF are higher than bank payments for BIF. For each $100 of deposits, SAIF-insured institutions must pay 20.8 cents and BIF-insured institutions must pay 12 cents. The differential in insurance rates will be phased out by 1998, and members of both funds will then pay 15 cents per $100 of deposits according to a schedule included in the act. Further, the FDIC is empowered to raise the insurance premium if the target of 1.25 percent of insured deposits is threatened. Currently, BIF appears to be adequately capitalized or nearly so, while SAIF will not achieve the required funding until after 2000.[9] Some observers believe that BIF and SAIF should be merged immediately, which would allow the combined BIF/SAIF fund to achieve full funding by 1998 and would give an assessment rate of $.60 to $.90 per $100 of deposits for all institutions, depending on their risk level.

FIRREA introduced three new capital requirements for thrifts. First, the law requires that core capital (common equity, noncumulative perpetual preferred stock, plus minority interest in consolidated subsidiaries, minus most intangibles, but including supervisory good will[10]) be at least 3 percent of total assets. Second, the law requires that thrifts' tangible assets be at least 1.5 percent of total assets. Finally, FIRREA imposed a risk-based capital condition, so that thrifts with riskier assets must have higher levels of capital.

---

[8] This provision has been amended to require only 65 percent.

[9] See Government Accounting Office, "Deposit Insurance Funds," March 1995.

[10] Supervisory good will is the premium above tangible net worth that an acquirer would pay for a troubled thrift. An acquirer might be willing to pay such a premium for the reputation of the thrift, the established customer base, or to obtain deposit insurance guarantees.

Table 11.3
Insured Deposits and the Bank Insurance Fund

Year	Value of Deposit Fund per Dollar of Insured Deposits
1984	$0.0119
1985	0.0119
1986	0.0112
1987	0.0110
1988	0.0080
1989	0.0070
1990	0.0021
1991	−0.0036
1992	−0.0001
1993	0.0069
1994	0.0080

Source: Federal Deposit Insurance Corporation, *Annual Report*, various issues. *FDIC Banking Review*, Winter 1995.

The Federal Deposit Insurance Corporation Improvement Act of 1991

Soon after being established, the BIF fell into difficulties. Table 11.3 shows the size of the BIF relative to insured deposits. In 1984, the fund held about 1.2 cents per dollar of insured deposits, which is close to the current goal of 1.25 cents. However, by the end of 1990, the fund fell to 2/10 of a cent per dollar of insured deposits, or about one-sixth of the target amount. The FDIC Improvement Act sought to recapitalize BIF by authorizing the FDIC to borrow up to $30 billion from the U.S. Treasury. These funds would be repaid by deposit insurance premiums that the FDIC would extract from its insured institutions. Nonetheless, as Table 11.3 shows, the BIF actually was insolvent by the end of 1991, and it remained insolvent until 1993, according to the report of the FDIC itself.

The act also instituted a requirement for prompt regulatory action to resolve problems with troubled institutions. Capital categories of institutions are well capitalized, adequately capitalized, undercapitalized, significantly undercapitalized, and critically undercapitalized. Table 11.4 shows the capital position of depository institutions insured by BIF and SAIF under this classification. More than 99 percent of all BIF-insured institutions are either well or adequately capitalized, and these institutions account for more than 99 percent of all assets. Approximately 99 percent of SAIF-insured depository institutions, with more than 99 percent of industry assets, are either well or adequately capitalized. Of all of these 12,774 institutions, only 18 are significantly or critically undercapitalized.

The act seeks to ensure that regulators take action appropriate to the degree of capital shortfall. The idea is to make regulators act and to limit the regulatory forbearance that intensified the losses in previous thrift failures. The act also requires regulators to prescribe accounting standards that will bring depository institution accounting into accordance with GAAP (generally accepted accounting principles). In addition, and perhaps of critical importance for the future, the act requires that the FDIC move to a risk-based assessment of deposit insurance fees by 1994. This has now been accomplished.

Table 11.4
Depository Institutions by Capitalization Category

	Number of Institutions	
Capital Category	BIF Insured	SAIF Insured
Well capitalized	10,721	1,774
Adequately capitalized	149	83
Undercapitalized	23	6
Significantly undercapitalized	11	5
Critically undercapitalized	1	1
	Assets of Institutions ($ millions)	
	BIF Insured	SAIF Insured
Well capitalized	$4,005,204	$679,921
Adequately capitalized	154,922	79,422
Undercapitalized	3,899	1,408
Significantly undercapitalized	1,292	3,335
Critically undercapitalized	3	44

Source: *FDIC Quarterly Banking Profile*, Third Quarter, 1994.

Capital Adequacy Measures and Requirements

Earlier we noted that FIRREA instituted new definitions of capital. The law also required the implementation of risk-based deposit insurance by 1994. The new law specified two kinds of capital: Tier I and Tier II. Tier I is the most basic type of core capital; Tier II capital is supplementary capital.

- Tier I capital
  - — Common stockholders' equity
  - — Non-cumulative perpetual preferred stock
  - — Minority equity interest in consolidated subsidiaries
    Less goodwill
- Tier II capital
  - — Allowance for loan and lease losses
  - — Additional perpetual preferred stock
  - — Hybrid capital instruments
  - — Subordinated debt
  - — Intermediate preferred stock
  - — Revaluation reserves

Tier I capital is the most solid capital that the bank possesses, while Tier II capital consists of additional capital that might not so easily be converted into cash to meet depositor demands. Thus, the new system distinguishes between the very different cash value of the capital in the two classes. In addition to the listing shown above, there are various restrictions on the role that each kind of instrument can play in the computation of the capital measure. Further, the computation of a bank's capital must take deductions for bank activities that impair the ready accessibility to the funds that the capital represents. For instance, the bank's capital computation will be reduced based on investments in subsidiary concerns and for cross holding of instruments with other banking organizations. These deductions ensure that the same capital is not counted for more than one organization. In the United States, regulators assess the capital adequacy by measuring the amount of capital that a bank possesses relative to its total assets. This measure is the Tier I leverage ratio (LR):

$$LR = \frac{Core\ Capital}{Assests}$$

Under the Basle Accord, the Bank for International Settlements (BIS) has also specified capital requirements that apply to the United States and to other member countries, including most industrialized nations. The BIS measures of capital adequacy use the same definitions of Tier I and Tier II capital, but these measures focus on the **risk-adjusted assets** of the institution. Risk-adjusted assets are found by applying risk adjustment factors to different asset categories on the balance sheet of the institution. For example, cash items have a risk adjustment factor of 0 percent, while residential mortgages have a risk adjustment factor of 50 percent, and consumer and credit loans have a risk adjustment factor of 100 percent. The intuition behind this risk adjustment is clear. Cash items do not require backing by capital because they represent solid, immediate, liquid assets. Residential mortgages are in a middle ground. There is a robust market for mortgages, so they can generally be sold in a short period of time, but they may not realize their full value if sold immediately, so they require substantial backing with capital. Credit card receivables and consumer loans cannot be converted to cash at the whim of the institution, so they embody a greater risk to the institution and require more substantial capital backing. Because the risk adjustment factors range from zero to 100 percent, the risk-adjusted assets of an institution will typically be smaller than the sum of assets shown on the firm's balance sheet. Table 11.5 shows the risk weights for items on the balance sheet.

In addition to regular balance sheet items (such as cash, securities, home mortgages, and loans), items off the balance sheet can also expose an institution to risk as well, and these off-balance-sheet items also should be backed by capital. As an example, consider a bank with a letter of credit commitment obligating the bank to provide a loan to a commercial customer upon demand. This letter of credit represents a potential demand for funds on the bank, and this commitment should be backed by capital. Therefore, various off-balance-sheet items have risk adjustment factors greater than zero.

When the bank's balance sheet is analyzed and these risk adjustment factors are applied, the calculation gives the institutions risk-adjusted assets, and the capital requirements specified by BIS use these risk-adjusted assets in computing capital requirements. BIS has two such requirements:

$$Tier\ I\ Capital\ Ratio = \frac{Tier\ I\ Capital}{Risk\text{-}adjusted\ Assets}$$

$$Total\ Risk\text{-}based\ Capital\ Ratio = \frac{Tier\ I\ plus\ Tier\ II\ Capital}{Risk\text{-}adjusted\ Assets}$$

The performance of a depository institution on these three measures (leverage ration, Tier I capital ratio, and total risk-based capital ratio) determines the category into which the institution falls as shown in Table 11.4. The criteria for capital adequacy are shown in Table 11.6. Notice that to be included as a "well-capitalized" institution, a bank must meet all three criteria of having a

Table 11.5
Risk Weights for Balance Sheet Items

Risk Weight	Risk-Asset
0%	Cash and balances due from Federal Reserve Banks and other OECD central banks
0%	Direct claims on, and portions of claim unconditionally guaranteed by, the U.S. Government and its agencies or other OECD central governments
0%	Direct local currency claims on, or guaranteed by, non-OECD central governments
0%	Gold bullion and Federal Reserve Bank stock
20%	Cash items in the process of collection
20%	All claims on U.S. depository institutions and other OECD depository institutions and short-term claims on non-OECD banks and non-OECD central banks
20%	Portions of loans and other claims conditionally guaranteed by the U.S. and other OECD countries' central governments
20%	Securities and other claims on U.S. Government-sponsored agencies (i.e., not explicitly U.S.-backed)
20%	Portions of loans and other claims collateralized by securities issued or guaranteed by the U.S. Government, or by U.S. Government agencies or Government-sponsored agencies or other OECD central governments
20%	Portions of loans and other claims collateralized by cash on deposit in the lending bank
20%	General obligations backed by the full faith and credit of U.S. state and local governments and political subdivisions of other OECD governments
20%	Claims on official multilateral lending institutions or development institutions
20%	Privately-issued mortgage-backed securities representing indirect ownership of a U.S. Government agency or U.S. Government-sponsored agency
20%	Investments in the shares of mutual funds whose portfolios contain assets qualifying for 0% or 20% risk weights
50%	Loans fully secured by first mortgages on 1–4 family residential properties (if made in accordance with prudent lending practices)
50%	Certain privately-issued mortgage-backed securities representing indirect ownership of a pool of residential mortgages which meet the criteria for the 50% risk weight
50%	Revenue bonds and similar obligations, including loans and leases, that are obligations of U.S. and other OECD municipal governments
50%	Credit-equivalent amounts of interest-rate swaps and foreign-exchange rate contracts
100%	All remaining assets or portions of assets not falling into above categories.

Source: John P. O'Keefe, "Risk-Based Capital Standards for Commercial Banks: Improved Capital-Adequacy Standards?," *FDIC Banking Review*, 6:1, Spring/Summer 1993, pp. 1–15.

Table 14.6
Criteria for Capital Adequacy Classification

	Total Risk-Based Capital Ratio	Tier I Risk-Based Capital Ratio	Leverage Ratio
Well-capitalized	≥ 10%, and	≥ 6%, and	≥ 5%
Adequately capitalized	≥ 8%, and	≥ 4%, and	≥ 4%
Undercapitalized	< 8%, or	< 4%, or	< 4%
Significantly undercapitalized	< 6%, or	< 3%, or	< 3%
Critically undercapitalized	Tangible equity is less than or equal to 2%.		

Source: *The FDIC Quarterly Banking Profile*, Third Quarter, 1994.

total risk-based capital ratio of 10 percent or better, a Tier I capital ratio of 6 percent or better, and a leverage ratio of 5 percent or better.

Measuring the Thrift Disaster

The crisis among depository institutions that began in the 1980s continues today, although many observers believe that the worst is over. Many more institutions remain to be closed, however, and the costs of closing these banks and thrifts will not be fully known for years. In this section, we consider the thrifts that have been closed by the Resolution Trust Corporation, a government entity established under FIRREA. It began closing thrifts in August 1989. We also consider the closing of commercial banks and savings banks under the control of the FDIC.

Thrifts Closed by the Resolution Trust Corporation

In 1989, FIRREA appropriated $50 billion for the Resolution Trust Corporation (RTC) and instructed the RTC to act as a receiver for bankrupt thrifts and as a conservator for failing thrifts. From congressional appropriations, borrowing, and asset recoveries, the RTC garnered a total of $227 billion in funds through 1994. Table 11.7 shows the sources and uses of funds for the RTC from its inception in August 1989 through December 1994. The $214 billion in outlays for failed thrifts has been distributed over many institutions. From inception through December 1994, the RTC resolved 744 failures with total deposits of $240 billion and almost 25 million deposit accounts.

Although the RTC had expended $214 billion by the end of 1994, this amount overstates the out-of-pocket cost incurred. The RTC holds an enormous portfolio of assets acquired in closing these institutions, including a gigantic portfolio of junk bonds, huge real estate holdings, and many other assets. For example, the RTC at one time owned a beach, a pullman railway car, and a collection of books and artifacts about magic. In 1995, best estimates of the total cost of the thrift crisis is about $90 billion.[11]

At the beginning of 1995, the RTC had only one institution in conservatorship and expected to resolve it in the near future. The RTC held $25 billion in assets at the beginning of 1995, and these were mostly assets of low marketability. Founded under a law that provides for automatic

[11] *RTC Review*, February 1995.

Table 14.7
Sources and Uses of Funds for the Resolution Trust Corporation, August 1989–December 1994

Sources	Billions of Dollars
Initial Treasury Appropriations	$18.8
FHLB Contribution	1.2
REFCORP Borrowings	30.1
Additional appropriations	40.7
Borrowings from Federal Financing Bank	22.9
Recoveries from receiverships	113.1
Total Sources	$226.8
Uses	
Resolution and receivership funding	$214.9
Advances for conservatorships	0.1
Federal Financing Bank interest	9.0
Other disbursements	–1.2
Total Uses	$222.8
Net cash available	**$4.0**

Source: Resolution Trust Corporation, *RTC Review*, various issues.

Table 14.8
The Rising Cost of Closing Thrifts

Period	Cumulative Thrifts Closed	RTC Estimated Cost to Date
August 1989–December 1990	352	$44 billion
August 1989–December 1991	584	$77.2 billion
August 1989–March 1992	640	$87.3 billion
August 1989 – December 1994	744	$88.2 billion

Source: Resolution Trust Corporation, *RTC Review*, various issues.

termination of the corporation, the RTC is scheduled to be disbanded at the end of 1995. Table 11.8 shows that early estimates of the cost of closing thrifts was quite optimistic, but recent estimates seems to be pointing toward a cost of about $90 billion.

Difficulties Among Commercial Banks

While insolvency has been concentrated among thrifts, commercial banks have not escaped their own difficulties. The late 1980s and early 1990s witnessed more bank failures than ever, even including the Great Depression. Before 1985, the largest number of banks to fail in a single year was 84 in 1937. As Table 11.9 shows, bank failures in recent years have been intense. In the last five years, more than 600 BIF-insured institutions have failed, with deposits exceeding $136 billion. While not all deposits are lost, these closed institutions have substantially drained the bank insurance fund. For example, the fund fell from $13.2 billion to $4 billion between 1989 and 1990. In 1991, banks with a total of $53.8 billion in insured deposits closed their doors, and the BIF finished the year with a negative value; it did not become positive until 1993.

Table 11.9
Recent Closing of Banks

Year	Number Closed	Insured Deposits at Closed Institutions
1984	79	$2.3 billion
1985	120	8.1
1986	138	6.5
1987	184	6.3
1988	200	24.9
1989	206	24.1
1990	169	14.5
1991	127	53.8
1992	122	41.2
1993	41	3.1

Source: FDIC *Annual Report*, 1993.

It seems to be clear now that the worst of the problems are over. The FDIC grades the financial soundness of the banks it supervises and maintains a "problem list" of weak institutions. The worst year for problem banks was 1987 with 1,575 banks on the list, holding assets of $359 billion. At year-end 1991, there were still 1,069 problem banks on the list, with assets of $611 billion. By 1995, the FDIC reported only 377 problem institutions, with total assets of $95 billion. Prospects suggest further strengthening of these institutions, and the end of the deposit institution crisis appears to be approaching. Thus, even if the number of problem banks has declined, the size of assets at risk has increased. Undoubtedly, some of those institutions will fail, adding to the total cost of bailing out the depository institution industry.

The Current Environment for Depository Institutions

From the Great Depression to the present, banking regulation has changed in response to a host of pressures. Starting with the creation of federal deposit insurance and the restriction of banking powers in the 1930s, a highly regulated deposit insurance evolved over the next 50 years. An evolving financial environment, largely the product of improved communication and transportation, led to substantial financial deregulation in the early 1980s. The experiment of deregulation quickly led to serious financial trauma, as failings in the system created perverse incentives for both the managers and regulators of deposit institutions. The exploitation of these design flaws cost more than $100 billion by the end of the 1980s and prompted new laws to recapitalize and strengthen the regulatory structure of the depository industry. These new laws have not yet been tested fully. They offer hope of an improved financial structure, but it remains apparent that the job is not yet complete.

The new structure provided by FIRREA and the FDIC Improvement Act certainly represents an improvement in form. Attempting to make regulatory intervention more objective by requiring regulatory action when capital reaches a certain level may help to reduce the incentive incompatibilities between the public good and regulators' desire. Similarly, the move to a risk-based deposit insurance system holds promise in reducing the moral hazard of bank and S&L managers. While the form of the regulatory structure may have improved, it remains to improve the substance. The new approach to capital standards and basing deposit insurance rates on the riskiness of individual institutions will succeed only if regulators possess the will to appraise the capital position and riskiness of institutions realistically.

The changes to the structure of regulation leave some old problems unaddressed. Because the basic promise of deposit insurance has not changed, the problem of moral hazard still remains – depositors have little or no incentive to monitor the soundness of the institutions in which they deposit money. None of the changes address the basic conflict between the interests of the depositors and the interests of the society at large. The policy that some institutions are "too big to fail" has not been altered in a convincing manner, if it has been addressed at all. As long as some institutions are too big to fail, competitive advantages will accrue to the largest institutions, and some depositors will receive better protection than others.

To some extent, recent changes in the law may repeat the mistakes of the past. By again requiring that thrifts keep a high percentage of their loans in real estate, the new laws push thrifts into the same situation that led to financial deregulation initially. If their assets are long-term and thrift liabilities (deposits) are short-term, thrifts will be highly susceptible to rising interest rates, just as they were in 1979–80. The restriction of thrift activity to real estate may also prevent institutions from achieving a level of diversification adequate for risk control. To some observers, the mandated concentration of thrift activity in real estate represents a march toward the past.

The Structure of the Depository Institution Industry

As we have seen in Chapter 10, commercial banks dominate the depository institution industry, with savings and loan associations holding second place, leaving only a minor role for savings banks and credit unions. Reflecting the importance of commercial banks, this section focuses on the structure of the banking industry.

This section goes on to consider major industry-wide trends in U.S. commercial banking. As we will see, the United States has thousands of banking firms, but there is a strong movement toward merger and consolidation among commercial banks. In spite of the bank merger movement, the number of available banking offices keeps growing, a growth that continues in the face of a number of bank failures in the 1980s.

In the United States, the basic regulatory structure of the banking industry has frustrated the emergence of truly nationwide banks. Only with the tide of financial deregulation are interstate banking operations beginning to emerge. The rapid technological innovation in computing and communications, coupled with relaxed banking regulations, suggest that the movement to interstate banking is likely to accelerate.

Banking Firms and Banking Offices

In 1934, there were 17,128 banking offices in the United States. Of these, 14,144 were main offices and 2,984 were branch offices. Total assets in the banking system stood at $46.4 billion in 1934, or $2.7 million of assets per office. At year-end 1993, the United States had 67,125 banking offices, with 10,957 main offices and 56,168 branch offices. For 1993, banking assets stood at $3.7 trillion, or about $55.2 million per office.

Figure 11.2
Banking Firms and Banking Offices

Number of U.S. Banking Offices

70,000
60,000
50,000
40,000
30,000
20,000
10,000
0

All U.S. Banking Offices (Main Offices plus Branches)

Branches

U.S. Banks (Main Offices only)

	1934	1937	1940	1943	1946	1949	1952	1955	1958	1961
Main offices	14,146	13,797	13,442	13,274	13,359	13,436	13,439	13,237	13,124	13,115
Branches	2,985	3,381	3,489	3,744	3,928	4,530	5,486	6,965	8,957	11,440
Total offices	17,131	17,178	16,931	17,018	17,287	17,966	18,925	20,202	22,081	24,555

	1964	1967	1970	1973	1976	1979	1982	1985	1988	1993
Main offices	13,493	13,517	13,511	13,976	14,411	14,364	14,451	14,417	13,137	10,957
Branches	14,703	18,053	21,810	26,643	31,322	36,792	39,784	43,347	46,619	56,168
Total offices	28,196	31,570	35,321	40,619	45,733	51,156	54,235	57,764	59,756	67,125

Source: *FDIC, Statistics on Banking, 1993.*

Figure 11.3
Grouth of Bank Assets

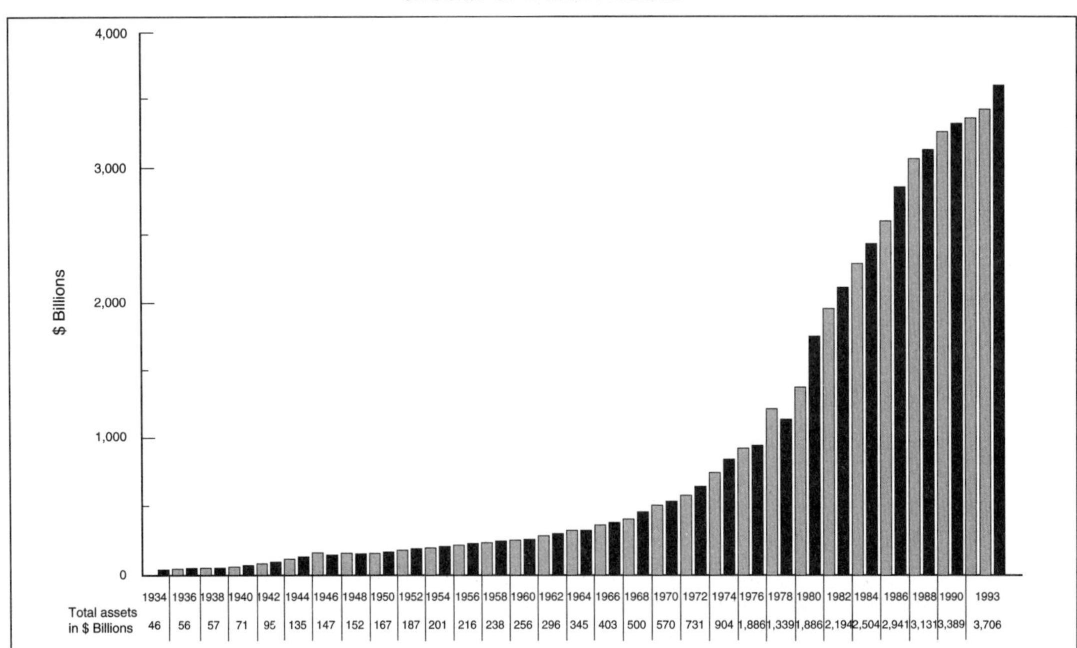

	1934	1936	1938	1940	1942	1944	1946	1948	1950	1952	1954	1956	1958	1960	1962	1964
Total assets in $ Billions	46	56	57	71	95	135	147	152	167	187	201	216	238	256	296	345

	1966	1968	1970	1972	1974	1976	1978	1980	1982	1984	1986	1988	1990	1993
Total assets in $ Billions	403	500	570	731	904	1,886	1,339	1,886	2,194	2,504	2,941	3,131	3,389	3,706

Source: *FDIC, Statistics on Banking, 1993.*

These statistics are quite startling, with the number of banks showing a decline and the number of branches increasing far more rapidly than the population. Figure 11.2 shows the change in branches over the last decades, while Figure 11.3 shows the growth of FDIC-insured assets for the same period. While inflation and population growth from 1934 to the 1990s surely account for much of the growth in the number of banking offices, other forces in the industry have also played major roles. As a point of comparison, we note that the United States has about one banking office to serve each 2,500 residents. This puts the United States in the middle of the pack compared with other industrialized countries. By comparison, Belgium has the highest density of offices by far with one office per 1,000 inhabitants. Switzerland and Germany have one office per 1,600 residents. Japan has one office per 2,700 people; Great Britain and Italy have one office per 3,000 citizens.[12]

Rules on Branching

Regulatory agencies control the privilege of banking firms to open additional offices or bank branches. For decades, some states have greatly restricted banks' abilities to open new branches. As examples, Texas, Colorado, and Illinois, in a practice known as unit banking, historically required that a bank could have only a single bank office. These restrictions are being dismantled gradually as part of a general movement toward financial deregulation. Now, Texas permits statewide branching, while Colorado and Illinois have moved to allow limited branching. **Statewide branching** is the practice of allowing a bank operating within a state to open branches anywhere in the state, while **limited branching** permits some branches to open but restricts either their location or the number of branches that banks may open. While restrictions on branching are easing, the effects of these laws persist.

In 1934, unit banking dominated the banking industry, implying that a bank could only grow as fast as it could raise deposits in a single geographical area. Unit banking, therefore, helped to ensure that banks remained small. Further, unit banking restrictions prevented banks from opening new offices to serve new customers. The only way customers in a newly developing geographical region could gain access to banking services was through the creation of a new bank.

Through the decades, restrictions on branching have eased. As recently as the 1970s, however, few states allowed banks to open new branches. In the great wave of financial deregulation in the 1980s, many states allowed banks to branch, although a number of states restricted branching. By 1993, 40 states and Washington, D.C. permitted statewide branching and 11 allowed limited branching. All states had abandoned the unit banking tradition. Table 11.10 shows the policies followed by the 50 states.

The Bank Holding Company Movement

Restrictions on branching helped to create a movement toward bank holding companies. As we have seen, Congress passed the Bank Holding Company Act in 1956 and amendments to the act in 1970 to bring multibank holding companies (MBHC) and one-bank holding companies (OBHC) more firmly under federal regulation. As we have also seen, creation of MBHCs was aimed squarely at evading the restrictions on bank branching by the various states. The OBHC was essentially a corporate form designed to allow entry to activities forbidden to banks *per se*. The mechanism employed by MBHCs was simple – a holding company would own many banks, and each bank would meet all

---

12 *The Economist*, February 25, 1995, p. 62.

Table 11.10
States by Status of Branching Regulations

Limited (11 states)		Statewide Branching (41 states and D.C.)
Arkansas	Minnesota	All other states and Washington, D.C.
Colorado	Montana	
Georgia	Nebraska	
Illinois	North Dakota	
Iowa	Wyoming	
Kentucky		

Source: FDIC, *Operating Banks and Branches*, June 1993.

branching restrictions. Through this means, the holding company could achieve a substantial portion of the economies of scale inherent in a large banking organization without breaking the law.

In 1957, immediately following the passage of the Bank Holding Company Act, there were only 50 holding companies controlling 417 banks and 851 branches. Together, the banks affiliated with these holding companies controlled only 7.5 percent of total bank deposits. There were about 13,000 banks and 22,000 bank offices in the United States in 1957, so banks affiliated with holding companies represented about 3.2 percent of banks and 3.9 percent of bank offices.

From 1957 through the 1980s, the role of bank holding companies grew tremendously. By 1986, holding companies controlled about 9,500 banks, 40,000 branches, and 90 percent of all U.S. bank deposits. Table 11.11 shows the ownership structure of commercial banks in the United States. Only 29 percent of commercial banks are independent today, and about 29 percent of all banks are part of an MBHC. Over 40 percent of all commercial banks operating in the United

Table 11.11
U.S. Commercial Banking Structure

		Assets		Deposits	
Organization	Number of Banks	$ Billions	Percent of U.S.	$ Billions	Percent of U.S.
Independent Banks	3,381	220	7.3%	183	7.8%
One-Bank Holding Companies	4,883	617	20.4	534	22.8
919 Multi-Bank Holding Companies	3,511	2,185	72.3	1,627	69.4
All Holding Companies	8,394	2,802	92.7	2,161	92.2
Total U.S. Commercial Banks	11,775	3,022		2,344	100.0

Source: Federal Reserve Board.

States are owned by an OBHC. In an environment with unrestricted branching, the OBHC form of organization appears to dominate MBHCs. A single bank with potentially many branches offers a more convenient and cost-effective corporate structure than an MBHC with numerous corporations, boards of directors, and individual bank identities. As barriers to branching continue to fall, OBHCs should prevail over MBHCs.

As we have seen, a BHC can enter businesses closed to banks. Thus, the prevalence of OBHCs argues that the need to avoid restrictions on bank activities remains a powerful motivation for the OBHC form of ownership. While restrictions on banking activities, such as those stemming from Glass-Steagall, remain potent, OBHCs will continue to be an attractive organizational form. MBHCs remain critically important today, testifying to the continuing restrictions on bank branching.

Regulation of Interstate Banking

The diversity of regulation by the states has had profound consequences on the structure of the banking industry, particularly on the existence of bank holding companies. Further, the dual regulatory structure has been largely responsible for the fact that there are no truly interstate banks operating throughout all states in the United States.

Origins of Interstate Banking Restrictions The U.S. system of preventing nationwide banks is unique in the industrialized world. Historically, interstate banking was associated with monopolist power and excessive political influence, at least in the popular imagination. The Federal Reserve long opposed interstate banking due to fears of an excessive concentration of financial power and possibly adverse effects on bank membership in the Federal Reserve System.[13] Legal restrictions continue to prevent interstate banking. First, because of dual regulation and the McFadden Act that allows national banks the same right to branch as state-chartered banks, interstate banking remains subject to the rules of the individual states. Second, the language of the McFadden Act gives national banks the same right to branch as state banks "within the State," thereby employing language that may itself prohibit interstate banking for national banks.[14] As with intra-state branching, interstate banking promises the benefits of a larger scale and better diversification. However, the benefits of interstate banking are most likely more significant.

In 1956, when Congress was considering the Bank Holding Company Act, Senator Douglas from Illinois (an historically unit-banking state) offered an amendment designed to frustrate interstate banking. The amendment, which became law, prohibited interstate acquisition of banking

---

[13] For a discussion of the history of interstate banking, see Robert T. Clair and Paula K. Tucker, "Interstate Banking and the Federal Reserve: A Historical Perspective," *Economic Review*, Federal Reserve Bank of Dallas, November 1989, pp. 1–20. Reprinted in Robert W. Kolb, *The Commercial Bank Management Reader*, Miami: Kolb Publishing Company, 1992. This discussion relies on the Clair and Tucker article.

[14] See David L. Mengle, "The Case for Interstate Branch Banking," *Economic Review*, Federal Reserve Bank of Richmond, 76:6, November/December 1990, pp. 3–17.

firms unless the state in which the acquisition was to take place specifically authorized such acquisitions by law. With the acceptance of the Douglas Amendment, interstate banking became impossible without action by an affected state, and each state had the power to block interstate banking within its borders. With acceptance of the Douglas Amendment, control over interstate banking passed to the individual states.

The Dawn of Interstate Banking From 1956 to 1978, there was no interstate banking, except by those organizations that were already operating across state lines in 1956 and had been "grandfathered" out of the 1956 restrictions. In 1978, Maine passed laws permitting interstate banking. New York and Alaska followed Maine's lead in 1982. Important differences existed among these three laws. The Maine law permitted out-of-state banks from any state in the nation to acquire a Maine bank – provided that the home state of the acquiring bank allowed Maine banks to acquire banks in the acquirer's state.

The Maine law, therefore, included a feature of **national reciprocity**. The acquirer's state had to reciprocate Maine's willingness to allow acquisitions. The Maine policy was one of national reciprocity because the acquirer could come from any state in the country, just so long as it was a reciprocating state. Maine's policy of national reciprocation differed from Alaska's, which permitted acquisitions in Alaska with no need for reciprocation. New York's law, like Maine's, permitted acquisitions based on national reciprocation.

After 1982, other states joined the movement to permit interstate banking. Some states joined to permit limited interstate banking under a policy of **regional reciprocity** – a policy in which each state in a group of states allows banks from other states in the group to acquire its banks, but all of the states in the group prohibit acquisitions from banks in states outside the group. For example, the Southeast states (including the District of Columbia, Florida, Georgia, Maryland, North Carolina, Tennessee, Virginia, South Carolina, Alabama, Louisiana, and West Virginia) formed a regional compact to permit interstate banking among banks from those states. Other compacts were formed in New England and among the Mid-Central states. Adopting regional compacts allowed limited interstate banking but helped to fend off competition from the large New York banks. By 1989, most states permitted some form of interstate banking, as Figure 11.4 shows. Only Montana, North Dakota, Nebraska, Iowa, Kansas, and New Mexico prohibited interstate banking entirely. As Figure 11.4 also reveals, few states permitted unrestricted acquisition of banks in 1989, so reciprocal arrangements dominated the interstate banking scheme.

Many of the laws permitting regional reciprocity included trigger dates for the liberalization of interstate banking. Based on laws already passed in 1992, the landscape of interstate banking will change remarkably in the very near future. Figure 11.5 shows the status of interstate banking in 1993, with almost all states permitting some kind of interstate banking.

Costs and Benefits of Interstate Banking

Most economists agree that interstate banking brings substantial benefits that would outweigh any likely costs. These benefits include enhanced competition, greater economies of scale and scope, improved organizational design, greater consumer convenience, improvements in payment processing, and a safer banking system.

Figure 11.4
The Status of Interstate Banking, 1989

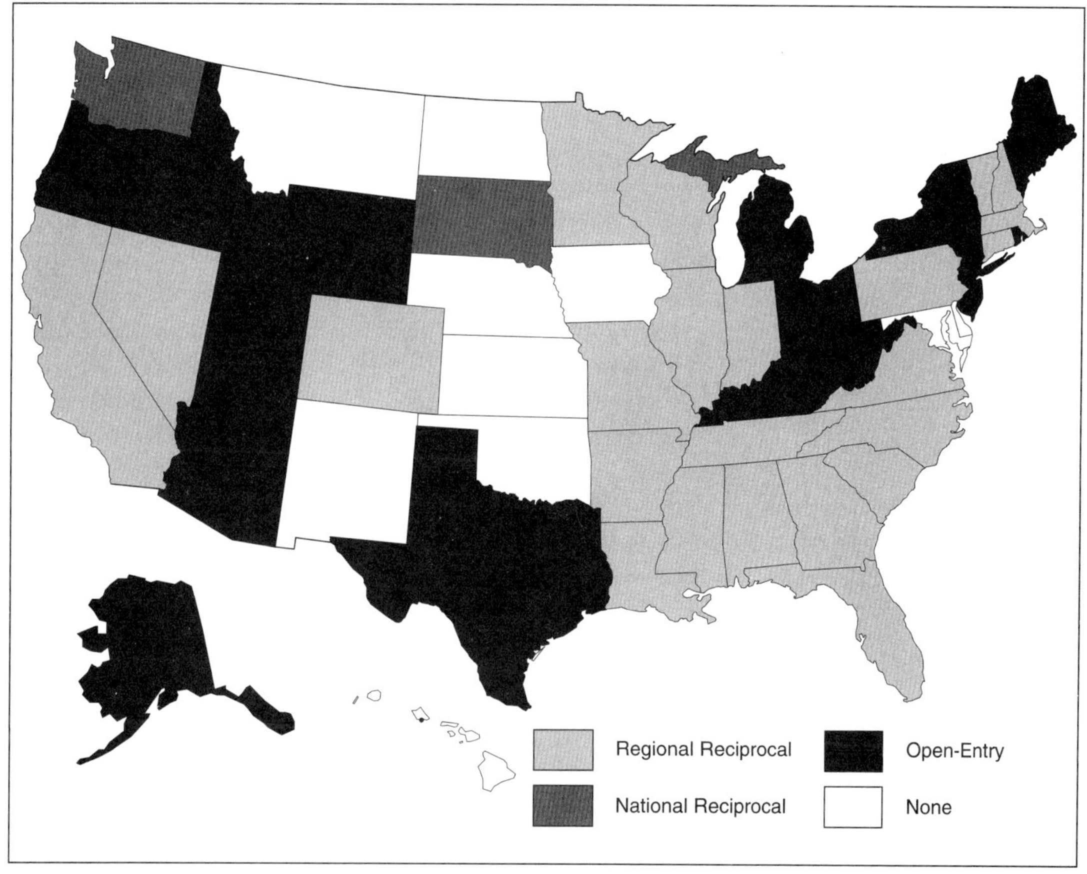

Source: Clair, Robert T., and Paula K. Tucker, "Interstate Banking and the Federal Reserve: A Historical Perspective," *Economic Review*, Federal Reserve Bank of Dallas, November 1989, pp 1–20. Reprinted in Robert W. Kolb, *The Commercial Bank Management Reader*, Miami: Kolb Publishing Company, 1992.

Interstate Banking and Competition One of the prime reasons for the historical resistance to interstate banking has been fear of competition. With unrestricted interstate banking, for example, small-town banks would face direct competition from their big-city cousins. These small banks have argued that the momentary benefits of heightened competition would soon be outweighed by a lack of competition when the small banks were driven out of business. While a system of aggressive interstate banking probably would cause some small banks to exit the market, it does not follow that there would be a lack of competition in small markets. Any number of large banks might compete in a small market that was previously the private preserve of a few small banks. (As we will see in Chapter 15 on international banking, many countries have only a few banks, all of which operate nationwide and offer adequate competition.)

Figure 11.5
The Status of Interstate Banking, 1993

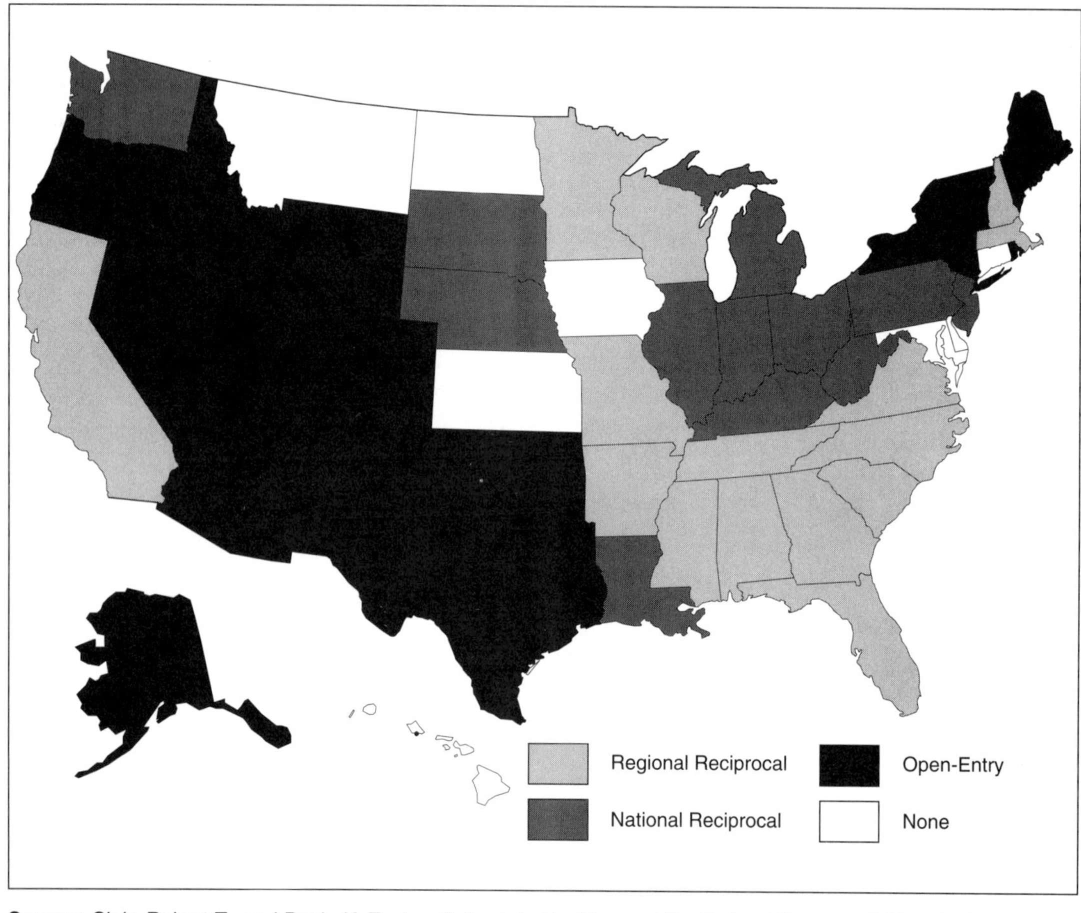

Source: Clair, Robert T., and Paula K. Tucker, "Interstate Banking and the Federal Reserve: A Historical Perspective," *Economic Review*, Federal Reserve Bank of Dallas, November 1989, pp 1–20. Reprinted in Robert W. Kolb, *The Commercial Bank Management Reader*, Miami: Kolb Publishing Company, 1992.

Economies of Scale and Scope Observers of the banking industry also tend to agree that nationwide banking would lead to greater economies of scale and scope. A firm captures **economies of scale** when it becomes large enough to improve the efficiency of its operations. In banking, for example, the most efficient computer systems require a high volume of transactions to justify their cost, so small banks may be too small to process transactions efficiently. If interstate banking allows banking firms to attain sufficient size, they may be able to capture economies of scale. A firm achieves **economies of scope** when a particular expertise it possesses can be applied to a larger market. For example, assume that a bank has superior abilities in appraising the risk of lending to high-technology firms. If the bank can operate across the country, it can apply that skill to a much broader scope than would be possible if it is forced to operate in a single state.[15]

While economies of scale and scope can be important, they can be overstated as well. There is good reason to believe that small banks (assets of $100 million or less) are too small to be truly efficient, but it also seems clear that almost all economies of scale are attained by medium-size banks (around $150 million in assets). Large banks ($250 million in assets and beyond) do not seem to be much more efficient than medium-size banks. Thus, while there are large economies of scale available to small banks, medium-size banks are unlikely to improve their efficiency by becoming larger.[16]

Improved Organizational Design Every bank must have a board of directors, a president, and other senior management; submit its own reports to regulators; face its own examination by bank examiners; have its own audit; and satisfy its own capital requirements. Even sister banks in an MBHC incur these parallel costs. If the MBHC were dissolved in favor of a single bank with many branches operating in different states, many of these costs could be reduced or eliminated. The potential savings from consolidating many banks into a single firm appear to be substantial.

While the benefits from combining banks probably outweigh the costs, a combined bank might face some additional costs. For example, some banks in MBHCs have their own identities with loyal customers. If the bank's identity is submerged in a larger banking corporation, the "brand name" of the submerged bank may be lost. Second, small banks have preferred reserve requirements. Up to $40.5 million, transaction account reserve requirements never exceed 3 percent. Beyond $40.5 million, the reserve requirement is 12 percent. Compared to many banks in an MBHC, a single combined bank would have substantially higher reserve requirements. Because reserves earn no interest, the combined firm would lose substantially more revenues to reserve requirements. In spite of these drawbacks, most observers believe that consolidating many separate banks into a single large bank would create an improved and more efficient organizational design.[17]

Consumer Convenience Imagine the convenience of being able to travel anywhere in the United States and cash a check at a branch office of your own bank. Today such convenience is

---

[15] This example is adapted from Elizabeth Laderman, "The Effects of Interstate Banking," *Weekly Letter*, Federal Reserve Bank of San Francisco, December 28, 1990, pp. 1–3. Reprinted in Robert W. Kolb, *The Commercial Bank Management Reader*, Miami: Kolb Publishing Company, 1992.

[16] For example, see Loretta J. Mester, "Efficient Production of Financial Services: Scale and Scope Economies," *Business Review*, Federal Reserve Bank of Philadelphia, January/February 1987, pp. 15–25.

[17] For a discussion of many of these issues see David L. Mengle, "The Case for Interstate Branch Banking," *Economic Review*, Federal Reserve Bank of Richmond, 76:6, November/December 1990, pp. 3–17. Reprinted in Robert W. Kolb, *The Commercial Bank Management Reader*, Miami: Kolb Publishing Company, 1992. The discussion of interstate banking in this text draws from Mengle's article.

only a dream because of limits on interstate banking. For travelers, a network of available banking services would be an important improvement. By the same token, when a family moves across the country, a system of interstate banking would dramatically ease the transition. By being able to maintain the same banking relationship, the family could draw on its established credit history and could more easily obtain financing for the many costs associated with a cross-country move. In addition, just as statewide branching has led to a greater availability of banking offices, interstate banking would be likely to have similar effects, thereby increasing consumer convenience.

Improved Payment Processing Check clearing is a costly banking function that is more expensive when one bank clears a check through another. With interstate banking, more checks would be cleared with the payer and payee having the same bank. Clearing checks internally is much cheaper than clearing through another bank, so interstate banking would improve the efficiency of the payment processing system.

Fewer Bank Failures Current banking regulation forces banks to concentrate their activities in a specified geographical area, limiting the bank's ability to diversify its lending and reduce its risk. For example, the steep recession in Texas during the mid-1980s had a drastic effect on real estate values and led to numerous defaults on mortgages. Many Texas banks held a large proportion of their assets in local real estate, and some of these banks failed simply because their lending was concentrated locally. Under a system of interstate banking, banking firms could diversify more fully to reduce their risks. This diversification benefit would accrue to the bank even if it did not change its operating policies. (See Chapter 9 for a discussion of portfolio theory.) The risk-reduction benefits of diversification would, therefore, improve the safety of individual banks and the entire banking system.

Concentration in Commercial Banking

We have already seen in Figure 11.2 that there are fewer banking firms today than at any time in the last few decades. Further, the number of banks and thrifts will likely continue to decline as more firms fail, and the movement toward interstate banking will further reduce the number of banks. Some observers believe that these trends may lead to an unhealthy concentration in the banking industry. This section considers the effects of a shrinking number of banks on the level of concentration and evaluates whether a lack of competition will result from the shrinking number of banks.

While the number of banking organizations in the United States has fallen in recent years, the shrinkage has not been shared equally by all segments of the industry. Table 11.12 shows how the number and relative importance of independent banks, OBHCs, and MBHCs have changed. In 1976, there were more than 10,608 independent banks, 1,495 OBHCs, and 301 MBHCs controlling 2,296 banks. As Table 11.12 shows, each kind of banking organization controlled about one-third of all assets. Since 1976, however, independent banks have become much less important, as they have fallen in number and the proportion of assets that they hold. OBHCs have increased in number but fallen in importance, and MBHCs have grown substantially, in number of banking firms, number of banks controlled, and assets in MBHC banks. By 1991, there were only 3,381 independent banks, and they controlled only 7.3 percent of banking assets. From 1976 to 1991, their numbers had decreased by about two-thirds, and their portion of assets had fallen

Table 11.12
Changes in the Banking Structure

Year	Independent Banks	OBHCs	MBHCs	Totals
1976				
Number of Organizations	10,608	1,495	301 firms; 2,296 banks	12,404 firms; 14,399 banks
Portion of total	73.7%	10.4%	15.9%	100%
Assets ($ billions)	303.7	341.5	358.5	1,003.7
Portion of total	30.3%	34.0%	35.7%	100%
1987				
Number of Organizations	4,375	4,919	985 firms; 4,465 banks	10,279 firms; 13,759 banks
Portion of total	31.7%	35.8%	32.5%	100%
Assets ($ billions)	233.7	537.0	1,826.7	2,597.3
Portion of total	9.0%	20.7%	70.3%	100%
1991				
Number of Organizations	3,381	4,883	919 firms; 3,511 banks	9,183 firms; 11,775 banks
Portion of total	28.7%	41.5%	29.8%	100%
Assets ($ billions)	220.2	616.5	2,185.3	3,021.9
Portion of total	7.3%	20.4%	72.3%	100%

Source: Dean Amel, "Trends in Banking Structure since the Mid-1970s," *Federal Reserve Bulletin*, February 1987; updated by Dean Amel.

by about 75 percent. OBHCs increased in number, but the proportion of assets controlled fell from 34 percent in 1976 to 20.4 percent in 1991. MBHCs tripled in number of firms and increased 50 percent in number of banks. Beyond growing in numbers, MBHCs doubled their share of assets from 35.7 percent in 1976 to 72.3 percent in 1991. During this same period, the number of banking firms fell by more than 3,000, and the number of banks fell by almost 3,000.

Table 11.12 shows that the number of banking organizations has fallen significantly, but that the average size of these firms has increased substantially. In 1976, for example, the average bank had $69.7 million in assets, but by 1991 average asset size was $256.6 million. By 1994, average asset size increased to $338 million. Table 11.13 demonstrates the change in the size distribution of banks. There are substantially fewer small banks now than a few years ago, so the banking industry in the United States is becoming more strongly dominated by larger banks. This trend will continue as banks struggle to gain sufficient scale to maximize their operating efficiencies. Although many U.S. banks may seem enormous, they are really quite small compared to banking institutions in other countries. Chapter 18 reviews the international banking scene, and there we will see that no U.S. bank is among the world's largest.

Table 11.13
Size Distribution of Banking Firms

Asset Size ($ millions)	January 1987		January 1994	
	Banks	Percent	Banks	Percent
Less than 25	4,868	33.1	2,221	20.3
25–50	3,729	25.4	2,791	25.5
51–100	2,985	20.3	2,776	25.3
101–500	2,454	16.7	2,543	23.2
501–1,000	263	1.8	244	2.2
1,001–3,000	244	1.7	198	1.8
3,000–10,000	111	*	129	1.2
More than 10,000	35	*	55	*

Source: FDIC, *Statistics on Banking*, various years.

"*" indicates less than 1 percent

Summary

This chapter reviewed the development of banking regulation in the United States, with a focus on the period from the Great Depression to the present. We have seen that laws stemming from the 1930s created a conservative industry with limited powers for banks and S&Ls. Advancing technology and communication, coupled with extremely high interest rates in the late 1970s, challenged this comfortable world and led to disintermediation. In response, the U.S. depository institution was liberalized, and depository institutions were permitted to enter new lines of business. Faced with a difficult economic environment, armed with perverse incentives, subject to moral hazard, and lacking expertise in many instances, bank and S&L managers quickly brought a large number of institutions to ruin. In response to the thrift crisis, Congress passed additional legislation aimed at restoring a credible depository institution industry. While final resolution of the thrift crisis has not yet been attained, observers continue to wonder whether a new financial stability has been achieved.

Eased restrictions on branch banking, the growing wave of interstate banking, and consolidation in the bank and thrift industries all point to a permanently changed environment. It seems unlikely that any set of laws can protect banks and thrifts from competition. As a result, the future probably holds the promise (or threat) of many fewer and much larger banks operating nationwide.

Questions and Problems

1. Which law established the Office of the Comptroller of the Currency (OCC)? What is the chief function of the OCC? Under what basic limits does it operate?

2. When, and by what law, did the federal government first impose reserve requirements on commercial banks? In brief, what is the purpose of those requirements?

3. Explain the meaning of "dual regulation." How did it originate? Does dual regulation continue today?

4. Which agency controls reserve requirements for commercial banks? What law gave this agency power over reserve requirements?
5. What is a banking panic? Explain how a banking panic may have systemic effects on the banking system?
6. What is a bank branch? Are national banks permitted to operate branches? Were they always permitted to have branches? Explain how the law on bank branches evolved from the 1860s through the 1920s.
7. Explain how deposit insurance for commercial banks works. Which agency of the federal government insures commercial bank deposits? When and by what act was this agency created?
8. Which act of the 1930s restricted the lines of business open to commercial banks? What were these restrictions, and why were they imposed?
9. Have banks always been able to pay interest on demand deposits as they can today? Explain the changes in banks' abilities to pay interest on demand deposits, tracing changes in the law and regulations from the 1920s to the present.
10. Explain the difference among the Federal Deposit Insurance Corporation (FDIC) and the Federal Home Loan Bank Board (FHLBB) and the Federal Savings and Loan Insurance Corporation (FSLIC). Which acts created these entities?
11. Explain the differences between a one-bank holding company and a multibank holding company.
12. Assume that bank holding companies are designed to circumvent banking regulation. Explain the rules that a one-bank holding company and a multibank holding company will try to avoid, and explain the origin and purpose of the rules they seek to evade.
13. Which laws restrict the activities of bank holding companies? (Be sure to distinguish one-bank and multibank holding companies.) Which agency regulates BHCs?
14. What is disintermediation and how does it differ from gross disintermediation?
15. What is a mutual fund? How is a money market mutual fund distinguished from mutual funds in general?
16. Why was disintermediation a problem for banks and S&Ls in the late 1970s and early 1980s? Explain.
17. Explain the important provisions of the Depository Institutions Deregulation and Monetary Control Act of 1980.
18. What new powers did the Garn-St. Germain Depository Institutions Act grant to thrift institutions? What already existing powers did it expand?
19. What three principles (the three legs referred to in the chapter) of depository institution management were imbedded in the legislation passed from the 1930s to 1970?

20. Explain the "too big to fail" policy. Comment on its effects on monitoring by depositors and its effects on competition.
21. Explain the difference between moral hazard and adverse selection. How does each principle interact with the deposit insurance system?
22. What is regulatory forbearance, and why did thrift regulators practice forbearance?
23. What moral hazards affected the behavior of thrift regulators?
24. After the passage of FIRREA, what is the status and function of the FHLBB, FSLIC, FDIC, RTC, SAIF, and BIF?
25. What fundamental change in the banking industry is revealed by the falling number of banking firms and the rising number of banking offices?
26. What is the relationship between the policy of unit banking and the idea of interstate banking? Do the two necessarily conflict? Do the two ideas conflict in spirit? Explain.
27. Explain the concepts of national reciprocity and regional reciprocity.
28. Explain the difference between economies of scale and economies of scope. How do these ideas relate to banking?

References

Calem, Paul S., "The Proconsumer Argument for Interstate Banking," *Business Review*, May–June 1993, pp. 15–29.

Clair, R. T. and P. K. Tucker, "Interstate Banking and the Federal Reserve: A Historical Perspective," *Economic Review*, Federal Reserve Bank of Dallas, November 1989, pp. 1–20. Reprinted in Robert W. Kolb, *The Commercial Bank Management Reader*, Miami: Kolb Publishing Company, 1992.

Clark, J. A., "Economies of Scale and Scope at Depository Financial Institutions: A Review of the Literature," *Economic Review*, Federal Reserve Bank of Kansas City, 73:8, September/October 1988, pp. 16–33. Reprinted in Robert W. Kolb, *The Commercial Bank Management Reader*, Miami: Kolb Publishing Company, 1992.

Corrigan, E. G., "The Banking-Commerce Controversy Revisited," *Quarterly Review*, Federal Reserve Bank of New York, 16:1, Spring 1991, pp. 1–13. Reprinted in Robert W. Kolb, *The Commercial Bank Management Reader*, Miami: Kolb Publishing Company, 1992.

Dale, B., "The Grass May Not Be Greener: Commercial Banks and Investment Banking," *Economic Perspectives*, Federal Reserve Bank of Chicago, 12:6, November/December 1988, pp. 3–13. Reprinted in Robert W. Kolb, *The Commercial Bank Management Reader*, Miami: Kolb Publishing Company, 1992.

Demirgüc-Kunt, A., "Deposit-Insurance Failures: A Review of the Empirical Literature," *Economic Review*, Federal Reserve Bank of Cleveland, 25:4, 1989, pp. 2–18. Reprinted in Robert W. Kolb, *The Commercial Bank Management Reader*, Miami: Kolb Publishing Company, 1992.

Government Accounting Office, "Deposit Insurance Funds: Analysis of Insurance Premium Disparity Between Banks and Thrifts," March 1995.

Kane, E. J., *The Gathering Crisis in Federal Deposit Insurance*, Cambridge, MA: MIT Press, 1985.

Kane, E. J., *The S&L Insurance Mess: How Did It Happen?* Washington: The Urban Institute, 1989.

Laderman, E., "The Effects of Interstate Banking," *Weekly Letter*, Federal Reserve Bank of San Francisco, December 28, 1990, pp. 1–3. Reprinted in Robert W. Kolb, *The Commercial Bank Management Reader*, Miami: Kolb Publishing Company, 1992.

Laderman, E., R. H. Schmidt, and G. C. Zimmerman, "Bank Branching and Portfolio Diversification," *Weekly Letter*, Federal Reserve Bank of San Francisco, Number 91-30, September 6, 1991, pp. 1–3. Reprinted in Robert W. Kolb, *The Commercial Bank Management Reader*, Miami: Kolb Publishing Company, 1992.

Levonian, M. E., "Risk-Adjusted Deposit-Insurance Premiums," *Weekly Letter*, Federal Reserve Bank of San Francisco, January 18, 1991, pp. 1–3. Reprinted in Robert W. Kolb, *The Commercial Bank Management Reader*, Miami: Kolb Publishing Company, 1992.

Mengle, D. L., "The Case for Interstate Branch Banking," *Economic Review*, Federal Reserve Bank of Richmond, 76:6, November/December 1990, pp. 3–17. Reprinted in Robert W. Kolb, *The Commercial Bank Management Reader*, Miami: Kolb Publishing Company, 1992.

Mester, L. J., "Curing Our Ailing Deposit–Insurance System," *Business Review*, Federal Reserve Bank of Philadelphia, pp. 13–24. Reprinted in Robert W. Kolb, *The Commercial Bank Management Reader*, Miami: Kolb Publishing Company, 1992.

Muckenfuss III, C. F., R. C. Eager, and C. H. Nielsen, "The Federal Deposit Insurance Corporation Improvement Act of 1991," *Bank Management*, 1992, pp. 37–44.

Nakamura, L. I., "Closing Troubled Financial Institutions: What Are the Issues?" *Business Review*, Federal Reserve Bank of Philadelphia, May/June 1990, pp. 15–24. Reprinted in Robert W. Kolb, *The Commercial Bank Management Reader*, Miami: Kolb Publishing Company, 1992.

Pozdena, R. J., "Bank Failures, Danish Style," *Weekly Letter*, Federal Reserve Bank of San Francisco, August 3, 1990, pp. 1–3. Reprinted in Robert W. Kolb, *The Commercial Bank Management Reader*, Miami: Kolb Publishing Company, 1992.

O'Keefe, John P., "Risk-Based Capital Standards for Commercial Banks: Improved Capital-Adequacy Standards?, *FDIC Banking Review*, 6:1, Spring/Summer 1993, pp. 1–15.

Randall, R. E., "The Need to Protect Depositors of Large Banks, and the Implications for Bank Powers and Ownership," *New England Economic Review*, Federal Reserve Bank of Boston, September/October 1990, pp. 63–75. Reprinted in Robert W. Kolb, *The Commercial Bank Management Reader*, Miami: Kolb Publishing Company, 1992.

Seballos, L. D. and J. B. Thomson, "Underlying Causes of Commercial Bank Failures in the 1980s," *Economic Commentary*, Federal Reserve Bank of Cleveland, September 1, 1990, pp. 1–4. Reprinted in Robert W. Kolb, *The Commercial Bank Management Reader*, Miami: Kolb Publishing Company, 1992.

Shaffer, S., "Challenges to Small Banks' Survival," *Business Review*, Federal Reserve Bank of Philadelphia, September/October 1989, pp. 15–27. Reprinted in Robert W. Kolb, *The Commercial Bank Management Reader*, Miami: Kolb Publishing Company, 1992.

Thomson, J. B., "Economic Principles and Deposit-Insurance Reform," *Economic Commentary*, Federal Reserve Bank of Cleveland, May 15, 1989, pp. 1–4. Reprinted in Robert W. Kolb, *The Commercial Bank Management Reader*, Miami: Kolb Publishing Company, 1992.

Operations of Commercial Banks 12

Overview

This chapter discusses some of the main operational areas of commercial banks. As described in Chapter 10, banks collect funds from many sources, including individuals and corporations, and use those funds mainly to make loans to other individuals and corporations. In the process, commercial banks provide benefits for society, such as risk reduction.

We start the chapter with a definition and discussion of bank liquidity. We then present a classical model of how commercial banks decide on the amount of vault cash they should hold. The chapter then shows how banks play an important role in helping businesses manage their own cash. In particular, commercial banks can help a firm speed its cash collections, as well as delay its cash disbursements.

The next major section of this chapter discusses the loan operations of commercial banks. We begin by describing the credit-granting operation at commercial banks. As we will see, one of the most important aspects of this operation is to determine the creditworthiness of potential borrowers, and we discuss several procedures that banks normally use. Because granting loans necessarily leads to eventual loan losses for commercial banks, we discuss this topic and its importance in recent years.

We also analyze the major types of bank loans. While the most common type is the amortized loan, in which the borrower makes equal periodic payments, there are other types of loans, such as add-on loans and discount interest loans.

Finally, the chapter presents a discussion of bank capital, starting with its formal definition for regulatory purposes. It is well known that the banking industry survives with much less capital than most other industries. We present a simple model that explains this unusual characteristic of the banking sector of the economy. As we will see, the reason commercial banks can comfortably use so much leverage is that they have the ability to diversify much more than most other types of businesses.

Liquidity Management

The concept of **liquidity** refers to the ease with which an asset can be converted into cash. Specifically, a liquid asset must meet the dual requirements of being easy to sell on short notice and of selling at a price that is very close to its market value; that is, there should not be undue transactions costs from selling liquid assets within a very short period of time. Thus, money market instruments are extremely liquid because they can be converted into cash very quickly, often within minutes, at a fair market price. By contrast, real estate investments are not normally very liquid since their convertibility into cash usually takes a fairly long period of time.[1]

[1] Theoretically, it is very easy to sell a real estate asset, or any other asset, almost immediately. With illiquid assets, however, this can usually only be done by offering a heavy discount relative to their fair market value.

For commercial banks, liquidity management is of utmost importance because many of the banks' liability owners can demand their convertibility into cash on very short notice, sometimes on demand. Thus, commercial banks must hold sufficient liquid assets to meet an uncertain demand for cash.

Modern commercial banks need not keep all their liquid assets in the form of cash. For example, if a bank is facing an unexpected liquidity crunch, it has access to the discount window at the Federal Reserve. Many banks, especially large ones, also have access to the money market, where they can quickly obtain the amount of funds needed to solve their liquidity crisis.

Of course, converting noncash assets into cash requires transaction costs. These transaction costs include clerical and managerial time and broker's fees. In addition, if an asset sold for cash is not very liquid, the transaction costs include the price discount from the asset's market value. In addition to transaction costs, holding liquid assets usually entails the opportunity cost of forgone interest, since liquid assets tend to pay lower rates than less liquid investments. The most obvious example is cash itself, which has a zero rate of return to the bank. Thus, banks must sacrifice some profitability in order to obtain liquidity.

In general, short-term assets are more liquid than long-term assets. Vault cash is the most liquid of assets. Reserves held at the Fed and deposits at correspondent banks are also extremely liquid. Somewhat less liquid are Treasury bills held by the bank, as well as other short-term securities in the bank's portfolio. Loans made by the bank are even less liquid but more profitable than the more liquid assets.

Cash Management

Vault cash is the most liquid of bank assets. Even though cash does not earn interest, all banks must keep some cash in their vaults since customers have the right to withdraw their demand deposits at will. Of course, in the normal operation of a bank, most customers will not retire their funds at the same time. Therefore, banks must hold sufficient cash to accommodate their customers' normal cash needs, without holding excessively high cash levels. In this section, we discuss two techniques for identifying the optimal amount of vault cash for banks to hold. Both models recognize that holding too much cash represents an opportunity cost to the bank, whereas holding too little cash requires too many transactions, and this, too, is costly. Consequently, there must be an optimal amount of vault cash to hold.

The Baumol model is presented first, and it assumes that the rate of cash demanded by the bank's customers is constant and known with certainty. The Miller-Orr model discussed later is a more sophisticated model that assumes that the bank's net daily cash demand follows a random path.

The Baumol Model

The Baumol model assumes that the bank uses cash at a known constant rate. The bank also incurs holding costs by keeping cash in its vault since it is forgoing interest income. Since these costs increase with the level of cash in the bank, focusing on this factor alone would lead the bank to hold the least amount of cash possible. However, as the bank depletes its cash, it must acquire new cash, perhaps by liquidating some of its marketable securities or by borrowing funds from depositors, the money market, the Fed, or other banks. Each time the bank transacts in this way, it bears transaction costs. Focusing on this factor alone, the bank would want to transact as few times as possible during the year to replenish its stock of cash. This could be done by having a very high cash level. The correct cash balance is found by combining the holding costs and transaction costs so as to minimize the total cost of holding cash for the bank.

Let us assume that a bank has a maximum cash balance of *C* dollars. If the bank's cash is depleted at a constant rate down to a level of zero cash, its average cash balance will be *C/2* dollars. This situation is shown in Figure 12.1. If the bank is able to earn a yearly rate of return of *r* from lending its funds, the annual opportunity cost of holding cash can be computed as the average amount of cash held *(C/2)* times the rate of interest lost because the funds were held in cash and not invested as loans *(r)*. Therefore, the bank's cost of holding cash over a one-year period is *(C/2)r.*

Suppose that over a year the bank will face a total demand for cash equal to *T* dollars. Since *C* dollars are acquired each time cash balances are restored, then cash balances will be restored *(T/C)* times per year. If the fixed cost of acquiring the cash is *F* dollars, the total transaction cost

Figure 12.1
Cash Level with a Constant Rate of Usage

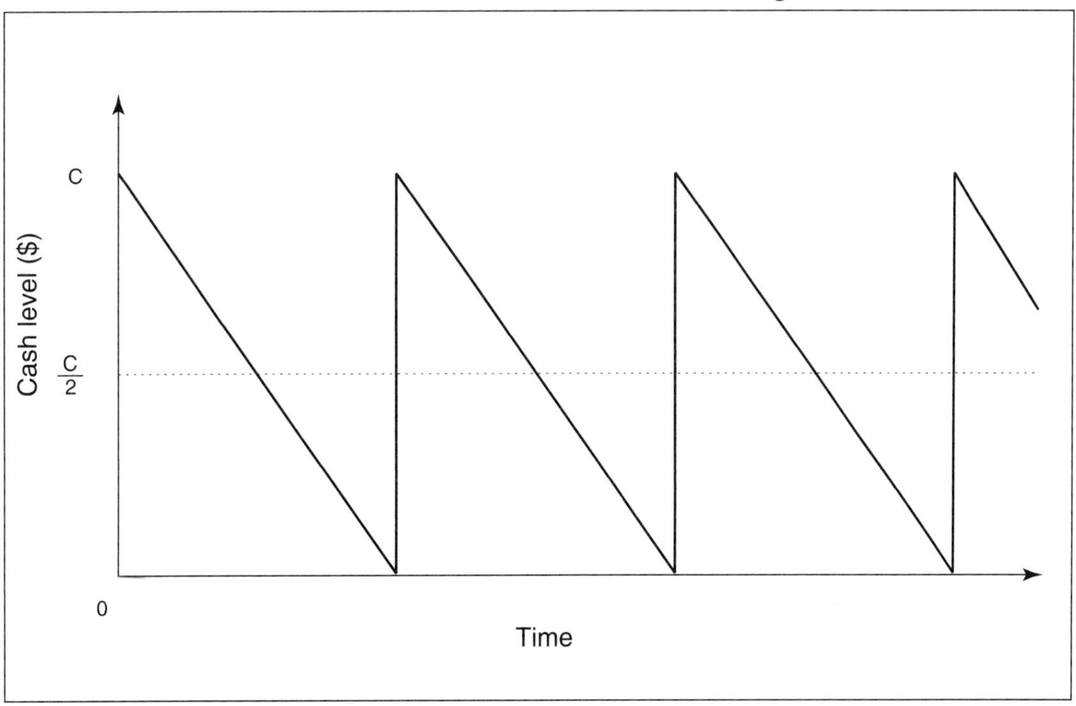

for the period will be $(T/C)F$. We can express the total cost (TC) of cash for a year as the sum of the holding costs and the transaction costs.

$$TC = \frac{C}{2} \times r + \frac{T}{C} \times F$$

With the help of calculus, it is possible to derive the optimal amount of cash to hold, C^*, which is given in Equation 12.1.

$$C^* = \sqrt{\frac{2\ FT}{r}} \qquad (12.1)$$

To illustrate the use of Equation 12.1, assume that the Sundance Bank has a total cash need of $50,000,000 for the coming year. The fixed cost of acquiring cash each time is $2,500, and the interest rate Sundance charges on its loans is 10 percent. Given these assumptions, what is the maximum amount of cash the bank should hold?

According to the Baumol model, the amount of cash to acquire each time, which is equal to the maximum cash level the bank will hold, is:

$$C^* = \sqrt{\frac{2 \times \$2{,}500 \times \%50{,}000{,}000}{0.1}} = \$1{,}581{,}139$$

Figure 12.2 graphs the transaction cost, holding cost, and total cost of holding cash. The figure shows that by acquiring more cash each time, the transaction cost decreases while the holding cost increases. Notice that the total cost reaches a minimum where the holding cost and transaction cost curves cross.

The Miller-Orr Model

The Baumol model relies upon a very simple view of the way the bank uses its vault cash. For example, it assumes that the bank uses cash at a constant rate, starting from some initial cash holding, C. In practice, the actual cash usage pattern of a bank may be much more erratic. The Miller-Orr model explicitly incorporates the randomness feature of actual cash flow usage.

The Miller-Orr technique is also known as the **control limit method**. The essential idea of the Miller-Orr model is that the cash level is allowed to fluctuate freely within an upper bound U and a lower bound L. Whenever the cash level reaches the upper bound U, the bank's management reduces the cash level down to a predetermined target level Z, by investing the excess cash, usually in short-term securities that are highly liquid. If, instead, the cash level reaches the lower bound L, then the bank increases the cash level back to the target level Z. Normally, this will be done by selling marketable securities. In this way, the cash flow will always fluctuate between the upper and lower bounds U and L, respectively. This situation is depicted in Figure 12.3.

The problem facing the bank manager using the Miller-Orr model is choosing the correct levels for the upper, target, and lower cash levels. While the mathematical derivation of these cash levels is complex, the basic idea is quite simple. Essentially, Miller and Orr assume that cash bal-

Figure 12.2
Cash Balance Costs

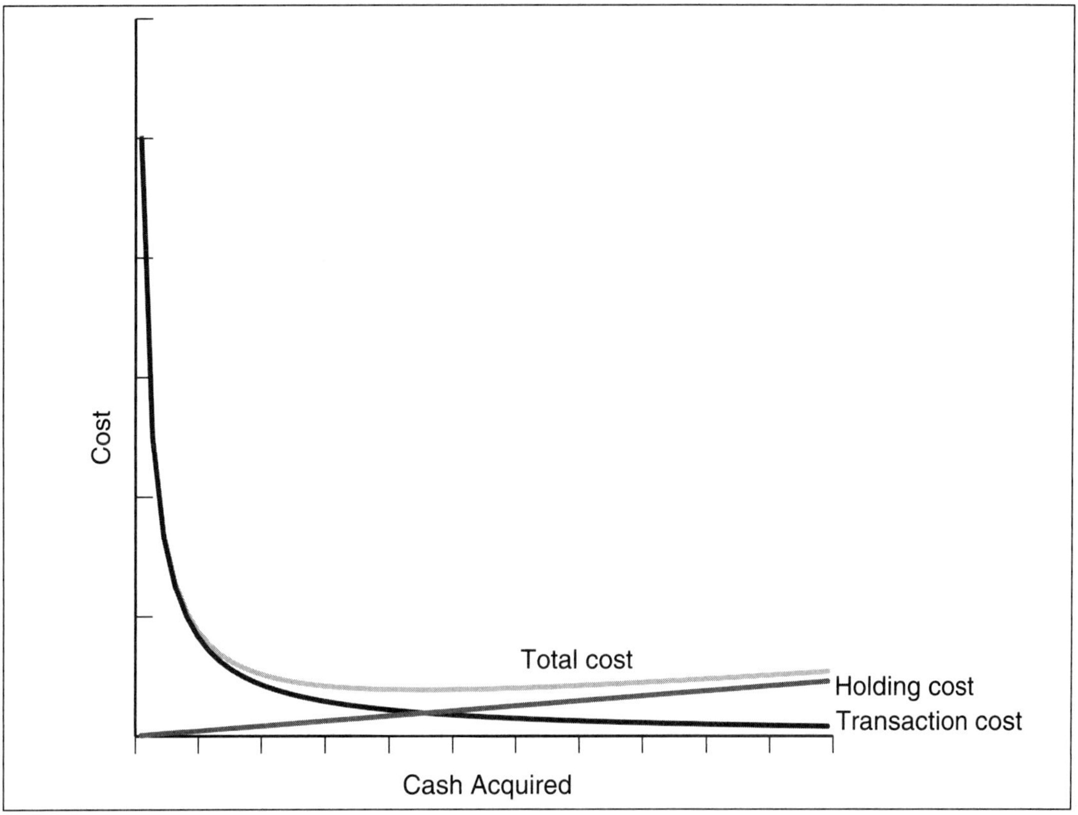

Figure 12.3
Cash Balances in the Miller-Orr Model

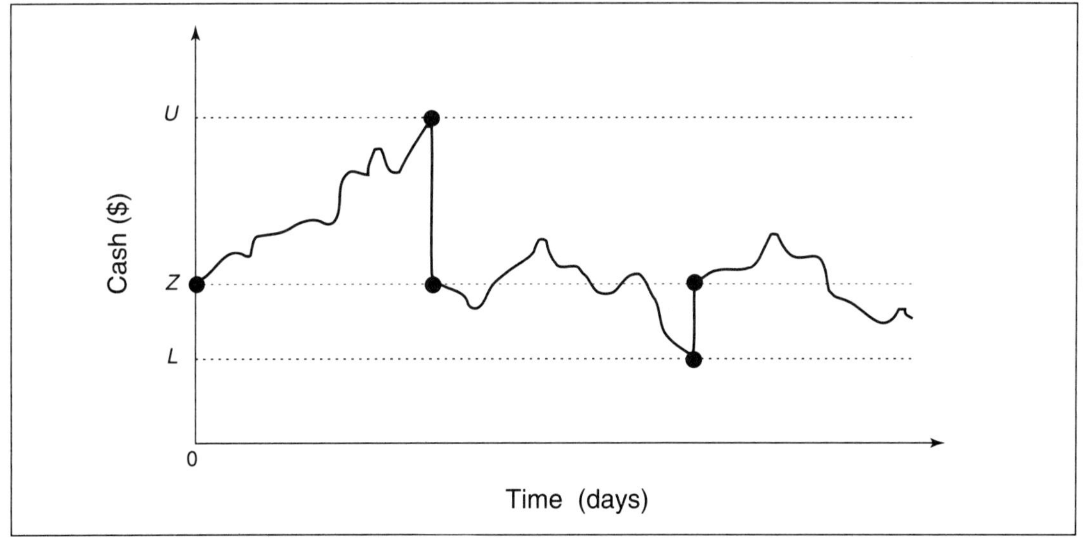

ance fluctuations are normally distributed, with a mean of zero. That is, the cash balance does not exhibit a tendency to increase or decrease over time. The lower limit, *L*, is set by management, based on their willingness to let the bank run out of cash. The next step is to estimate the variance of the bank's daily cash flows σ^2. Also, let *F* represent the fixed transaction cost, and $r_d = r/365$ be the appropriate daily interest rate. Based on this, the Miller-Orr model gives the target cash balance, the upper control limit, and the average cash balance.

The target cash balance formula is:

$$Z = \sqrt[3]{\frac{3F\sigma^2}{4\,r_d}} + L \tag{12.2}$$

The upper control limit formula is:

$$U = 3\,Z - 2\,L \tag{12.3}$$

The average cash balance formula is:

$$ACB = \frac{4\,Z - L}{3} \tag{12.4}$$

As an example, suppose that QuickSilver Bank knows that the cost of each cash transaction is $F = \$200$, that its opportunity cost of money is $r = 15$ percent per year, and that the standard deviation of daily cash flows is $\sigma = \$10{,}000$. Also, suppose that management has set the lower control limit, *L*, at \$100,000. Compute the target cash balance, *Z*; the upper control limit, *U*; and the average cash balance for the bank.

All we need to do is apply Equations 12.2 through 12.4.

$$Z = \sqrt[3]{\frac{3 \times \$200 \times (\$10{,}000)^2}{4 \times \left(\frac{0.15}{365}\right)}} + \$100{,}000 = \$133{,}170.34$$

$$U = 3 \times \$133{,}170{,}34 - 2 \times \$100{,}000 = \$199{,}511.02$$

$$ACB = \frac{4 \times \$133{,}170.34 - \$100{,}000}{3} = \$144{,}227.12$$

Notice that the target cash balance is not midway between the control limits. The same is true of the average cash balance. This is a curious feature of the Miller-Orr model.

Techniques of Cash Management There are techniques that nonbanking enterprises can use for speeding the collection of cash and for slowing the disbursement of cash. By using these techniques, these firms can conserve cash. Early collection of cash, or slow payment of cash, has important financial advantages that the cash managers of nonbanking firms must consider.

Banks play an important role in assisting many businesses in managing their cash better. This section discusses how banks help nonbanking firms better manage their cash. Since banks must price their cash management services so that they provide a net benefit to the nonbanking firm, it is important to understand the costs and benefits that cash management generates for nonbanking firms.

Effects of Conserving Cash

If a nonbanking firm pays \$1 one day later or if it collects \$1 one day earlier, the firm has the use of \$1 for an extra day in both cases. The essential advantage of conserving cash in these ways is that the firm may invest the extra cash to earn a return. For example, if the interest rate is 12 percent and the firm collects \$1,000,000 a day early, this gives the firm a financial benefit equal to the one day's interest on the million dollars. In this case, the interest earned by the firm is equal to:

$$\$1{,}000{,}000 \times \frac{0.12}{365} = \$329 \text{ per day}$$

There are many situations where the sums saved are large or where the firm collects or pays small sums regularly. In those cases, attention to cash management can pay large dividends.

Many firms face cash management problems that are much more complex than our example of a single payment of \$1 million. Consider, for example, a firm like Megastore with several million customers all over the country mailing in payments every month. Between the date the customer buys the goods in the store and the time Megastore actually receives payment, a long time passes. During this time, the credit customer benefits by having the good, without having made the payment. Megastore, on the other hand, has only an accounts receivable. The time between the sale and the collection of the funds is called the **float period**.

For Megastore, there is a strong incentive to reduce the period of the float by collecting the accounts receivable early. If Megastore can do this, it gains the use of the money that much earlier. For example, if Megastore's credit sales are \$10 million per day on average and the average collection period is 82 days, then Megastore will have an investment in accounts receivable of \$820 million.

$$\text{Accounts Receivable} = \$10{,}000{,}000 \times 82 \text{ days} = \$820{,}000{,}000$$

If Megastore could collect its funds tied up in accounts receivable faster, it would lower its investment in accounts receivable. For example, if the collection period were reduced by just three days, the new level of accounts receivable would be:

$$\text{Accounts Receivable} = \$10{,}000{,}000 \times 79 = \$790{,}000{,}000$$

This implies a \$30 million lower investment in accounts receivable, which could earn a return elsewhere. If the annual opportunity cost of money for Megastore is 10 percent, it could save \$3 million dollars each year by collecting faster.

Because the rewards of better cash management may be so great, there are well-developed techniques for improving the collection of cash and for slowing cash payments. In the implementation of these techniques, the role of commercial banks is crucial. The following section considers the costs and benefits of some major cash management techniques.

Concentration Banking and Lock Box Systems

In concentration banking, the firm instructs customers to mail their payments to a regional collection center rather than to the firm's home office. The firm receives funds in these regional collection centers sooner than they would reach the firm's home office. Therefore, the firm can begin processing the checks more quickly. Upon receipt, the firm deposits the check in a local bank. Periodically, the firm transfers funds from the local bank to the principal, or concentration, bank. The firm can transfer the funds electronically from one bank to another via a wire transfer, so the delay at this point of the process is negligible.

With a lock box system, the firm instructs customers to mail their payments to a post office box near the customers' homes. The firm then arranges with local commercial banks to collect the payments, to credit them to a local bank account as quickly as possible, and to report the transactions to the home office so it can use the funds right away.

Pricing Concentration Banking Services

To see how to evaluate concentration banking and lock box cash management systems, let us continue our example of Megastore. For Megastore, we assumed that sales average \$10 million per day, that the current collection period is 82 days, and that customers make all payments to the home office in Chicago.

Suppose Megastore can establish a lock box system with another nonbanking firm for an initial payment of \$4,000,000 and a yearly fee of \$1 million. The lock box system will decrease the collection period by 1.5 days. As another alternative, Megastore is considering a concentration banking arrangement. To this end, Megastore has asked the Sunshine Bank to give it a cost estimate. Sunshine Bank knows that it is customary on this type of deal to require an initial payment, I, and a yearly fee, Y. The bank also knows that it can offer to cut the collection period by 2.5 days. How must Sunshine price the concentration banking system in order to induce Megastore to choose the bank's proposal?

The solution to this pricing problem depends on a direct comparison of the costs and the benefits of the two options. In both cases, the benefits are the reduction in the collection period and the freeing of cash for other uses. The lock box system reduces the collection period by 1.5 days. Given sales of \$10 million per day, this means that the lock box system will free \$15 million for other uses. The concentration banking system reduces the collection period by 2.5 days, so this system frees \$25 million for investment elsewhere.

We need to evaluate the costs associated with the lock box system in present value terms. Assuming that the opportunity cost of money is 12 percent for Megastore, the lock box system costs \$4 million plus the present value of a perpetuity of \$1 million per year at 12 percent.

$$PV \text{ of Costs for Lock Box} = \$4{,}000{,}000 + \frac{\$1{,}000{,}000}{0.12}$$

$$= \$12{,}333{,}333$$

Table 12.1
Benefits and Costs of Lock Box and Concentration Banking Systems

	Benefit	Cost	Net Benefit
Lock Box	\$15,000,000	\$12,333,333	\$2,666,667
Concentration Banking	\$25,000,000	$I + Y / 0.12$	$\$25,000,000 - I - Y / 0.12$

For the concentration banking scheme, the costs are an initial fee of $\$I$ and a yearly expense of $\$Y$. Sunshine Bank knows that, for Megastore, the present value of all the costs for the concentration banking alternative is:

$$PV \text{ of Costs for Concentration Banking} = I + \frac{Y}{0.12}$$

Because the benefits and costs are all in present value terms, we can compare them directly, as shown in Table 12.1. As shown there, the lock box system gives a net benefit of \$2,666,667. If Sunshine bank wants to do business with Megastore, the concentration banking scheme must offer a higher net benefit. For the management of Megastore to favor concentration banking over the lock box system, the following relationship must hold:

$$\$25{,}000{,}000 - I - \frac{Y}{0.12} > \$2{,}666{,}667$$

Equivalently, to win this contract, Sunshine Bank must offer a combination of initial payment and yearly fee that meets the following condition:

$$I + \frac{Y}{0.12} < \$22{,}333{,}333$$

Figure 12.4 shows the locus of all possible initial payment/yearly fee combinations with which Sunshine Bank could obtain the concentration banking contract from Megastore. If Sunshine prices the offer so that it corresponds to a point inside the triangular shaded area in the figure, it will win the contract, assuming Megastore decides solely on financial considerations.

The Role of Banks in Delaying Payments

We have seen that collecting funds early has an advantage for a company. A reasonable delay in payments also provides benefits. Both strategies let the firm use cash longer to earn a return, and in both scenarios commercial banks play an important role.

A common technique for delaying payments is to use a distant bank for making payments. Because timely payment depends only on when the payee receives the check, not when the payee actually gets the use of the funds paid with the check, the payor tries to increase the time between when the check is received by the payee and the time when the funds are withdrawn from the payor's checking account.

Figure 12.4
Possible Initial Payment and Yearly Fee for a Concentration Banking System

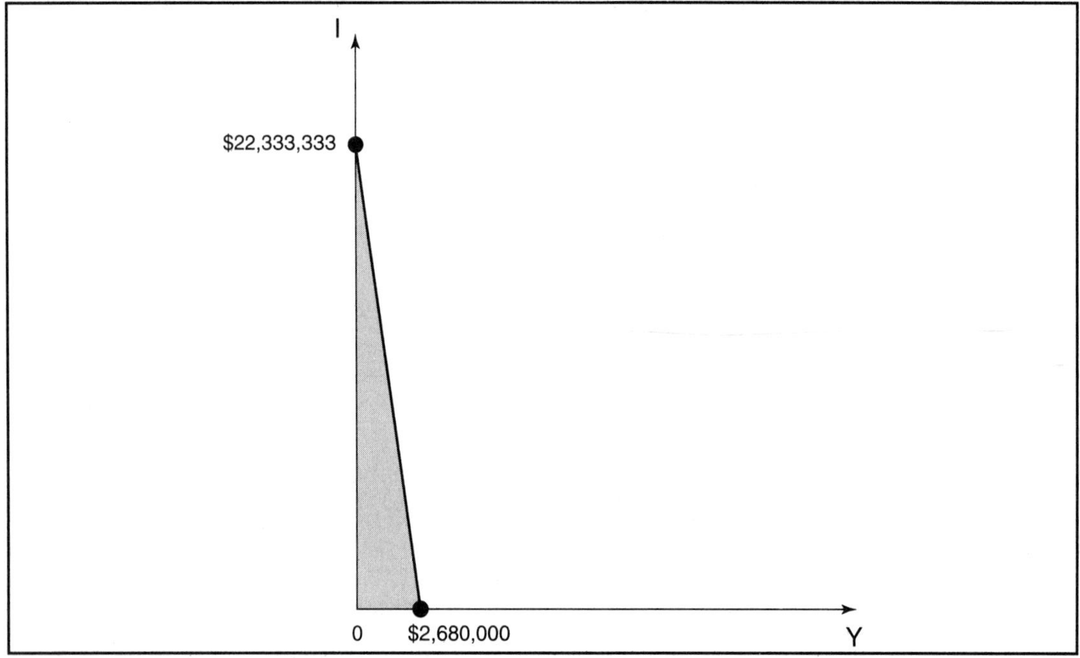

Many firms increase this time by using banks scattered over a wide location. Assume that a customer has bank accounts in both North Carolina and Oregon. With this strategy, the customer might pay a North Carolina supplier with a check drawn on an Oregon bank. Normally, it takes longer for a check sent to a distant bank to clear. This strategy also suggests that very small rural banks, which tend to be somewhat slower, might be best for increasing this portion of the float.

Loan Operations at Commercial Banks

As we saw in Chapter 10, by far the most important asset of commercial banks is the loan portfolio. Indeed, about 65 percent of all commercial bank assets are in the form of loans. This is not surprising since lending is the central activity of commercial banking. In this section we describe the credit-granting process and also discuss the mechanics of various types of loans.

The Credit-Granting Process When a bank grants credit, there is always some probability that the borrower will not pay. The problem faced by the bank is to grant credit to the right customers, even though the bank lacks complete information about them. There is an initial tendency to be very rigorous in the application of high credit standards. If the bank grants credit only to those customers that are of the highest quality, it will not grant credit to many potentially valuable customers. Such a strict credit policy results in lower profits. At the other extreme, if the bank sets its credit standards too loosely, it grants credit to many borrowers that will never pay, and the bank will incur losses for this reason. The task of the bank's loan manager is to strike a balance between these two undesirable extremes.

The problem, then, is one of balancing the benefit of additional interest income against the cost of increasing bad debts. In principle, the bank must choose the credit standards that maximize the difference between benefits and costs. While this principle is conceptually clear, the difficult managerial task for the bank is to actually find the right set of credit standards.

In making the credit-granting decision, the bank manager must somehow estimate the probability that the customer will pay. We have argued that it is not necessary, or even convenient, to be exceedingly strict in granting credit. To understand how the bank makes the credit-granting decision, consider a customer who requests a one-year loan for L dollars. The bank charges an annual interest rate of r_L. Also, the bank pays depositors an interest rate of r_B percent per year. If the borrower has a probability p of paying the $L(1 + r_L)$ dollars at the end of the year, and a probability $(1 - p)$ of not paying at all, then the expected revenue of the lending bank at the end of the year is:

$$E(\text{Revenue}) = L(1 + r_L) \times p + 0 \times (1 - \text{p}) = L(1 + r_L) \times p \qquad (12.5)$$

To obtain this expected revenue, the bank must invest L dollars today. As with any investment decision, the bank makes the one–year loan if it expects the credit-granting decision to have a positive NPV; that is:

$$E(NPV) = -L + \frac{L(1 + r_L)p}{1 + r_B} > 0 \qquad (12.6)$$

Equation 12.6 can be solved for the borrower's probability of payment, p, that is required to make the decision profitable for the bank.

$$p > \frac{L}{L(1 + r_L)}(1 + r_B) = \left(\frac{1 + r_B}{1 + r_L}\right) \qquad (12.7)$$

Inequality 12.7 provides insight into the main factors that determine the bank's credit-granting decision. For example, it expresses the intuitive fact that only borrowers with a sufficiently high probability of payment should be granted credit. Also, since the borrowing rate may vary somewhat from bank to bank, different banks may have slightly different credit-granting standards. As an example, Inequality 12.7 states that a bank with a high cost of borrowed funds, r_B, will be stricter in granting credit than a bank with a lower borrowing cost. More generally, a bank with a relatively small **spread** – the difference between the bank's borrowing and lending rates – will be stricter in its credit standards than a bank with a greater spread. The reason for this is that banks with slim spreads cannot afford to have too many of their borrowers default.

To illustrate, suppose Mr. Al Bondiga requests a personal loan at Great Union Bank to open a meatball sandwich shop. The loan amount is $800, and the bank will charge an annual interest rate of 15 percent. The principal and interest are to be repaid in one year. Great Union's cost of money is 10 percent. If Great Union believes that Mr. Bondiga has a 90 percent probability of paying, should he be granted the credit?

According to Inequality 12.7, Great Union should grant credit to any borrower with a minimum probability of payment of 95.65 percent:

$$p > \left(\frac{1 + 0.10}{1 + 0.15}\right) = 95.65\%$$

Since Al does not meet this minimum requirement, the credit should be denied.

Information and Credit Standards We have seen that banks grant credit based on the perceived probability that the borrower will pay. To estimate this probability and make better credit decisions, banks gather information on their prospective credit customers. Information gathering is costly, however, so all credit-granting institutions must also weigh the benefits of gathering information against the costs. For example, magazine publishers normally grant credit to subscribers without gathering much information on their creditworthiness. Because the magazine and the subscription bill are sent at about the same time, the magazine management can discover very quickly which customers will not pay. As a result, the risk exposure for magazine publishers is limited to the cost of a few magazines. Since gathering detailed credit information on potential subscribers costs more than the amount the firm is risking by granting the credit, it does not pay to gather the information.

In contrast to magazines, banks typically lend large amounts of money, and credit is likely to be extended repeatedly to the same customer, so it is generally advisable for banks to gather information about potential customers. Banks may decide to purchase information about potential customers from outside sources, and they also often ask for information directly from the customers. For instance, it is normal to ask a credit applicant to provide a financial statement or to complete a questionnaire.

In many cases, banks use a credit scoring model to evaluate the borrower's probability of payment. A **credit scoring model** is a statistically verified equation that predicts future payment performance. With this system, the bank asks the potential borrower to provide information about age, marital status, occupation, time at last residence, time at last job, income, home ownership, and so on. Such variables are presumed to have some predictive effect on the potential customer's probability of paying back the loan. Each answer contributes to a total credit score, and the bank grants credit only if the score is large enough.

The Five Cs A common way to analyze the key risk factors leading to an estimation of the probability of default is to group them into the five "Cs": capacity, capital, character, collateral, and conditions. **Capacity** refers to the ability of the borrower to repay the loan under normal circumstances. This ability is influenced by the borrower's management expertise, so the banker tries to assess the borrower's business acumen. In addition, the loan analyst makes a financial evaluation of the borrower's future cash flow to make sure it is sufficient to repay the interest and principal on the loan.

One of the functions of **capital** is to provide a cushion to absorb unforeseen financial downturns. Thus, a firm with sufficient capital can withstand one or more years of losses without losing its ability to service its debt. The lending bank must make sure that the borrower has the needed capital.

In analyzing **character**, the bank attempts to evaluate the borrower's honesty and integrity. Often, this is evaluated through a personal interview between the borrower and the bank's loan officers. Aspects such as the borrower's personality, demeanor, and way of dressing may influence the banker's perception of the borrower's character.

Collateral is an asset owned by the borrower that serves to guarantee repayment in case the borrower defaults on the loan. For example, if a bank grants a real estate loan to finance construction of a house, the collateral is usually the finished house itself.

The bank must also analyze the **conditions** of the economy and the outlook for the industry to which the borrowing firm belongs. For example, if a firm has a history of labor-management problems, the bank should consider the possibility that the loan may not be repaid should a prolonged strike occur, thus damaging the financial position of the firm.

The Loan Covenant Assuming that the borrower has already passed the test of the five Cs, the bank must still make sure that the funds will be used for their intended purpose. There is always moral hazard associated with granting a loan. For example, a borrower may receive a loan to expand her business but may decide to use the funds to place some bets on horse racing, instead. If all goes well at the race track, the business will be expanded, the loan will be repaid, and the borrower can keep the profits from betting. However, if her gambling skills are not up to par and she loses the money, there will be no expansion, and the loan may not be repaid.

The moral hazard temptation is a real problem for some borrowers. Since banks know about moral hazard, they almost always place certain restrictions on loans. These restrictions are set forth in the loan covenant. To ensure the borrower's compliance with the terms of the loan's covenant, banks engage in periodic monitoring of the loan. Covenants may include, among other things, requiring the borrower to maintain a minimum current ratio (current assets/current liabilities), as well as restrictions on cash dividends and the sale of major assets, and the subordination of future loans.

To further clarify the importance of loan covenants, consider the firm Wealth Transfer, Unlimited, operating under the slogan "We move wealth." In the absence of any prohibitions, Wealth Transfer might be true to its motto as follows. Sell 10,000 shares of common stock for $10 each, for a total of $100,000, and borrow $900,000 from Naive Bank. After these starting transactions, the balance sheet of Wealth Transfer would appear as shown in Table 12.2. In the top panel

Table 12.2
The Balance Sheet of Wealth Transfer

When the firm is founded:			
Assets		**Liabilities**	
Cash	$1,000,000	Debt	$900,000
		Equity	$100,000
Total Assets	$1,000,000	Total Liabilities and Owners' Equity	$1,000,000
After paying a large dividend:			
Assets		**Liabilities**	
Cash	$0	Debt	$900,000
		Equity	−$900,000
Total Assets	$0	Total Liabilities and Owners' Equity	$0

of the table, we see Wealth Transfer's balance sheet when the firm is founded and is flush with cash. The $1,000,000 in cash is offset by a large amount of debt and a small amount of equity.

Assume now that Wealth Transfer pays a dividend of $100 per share, paying out all of its cash. Each shareholder paid $10 per share and immediately gets $100 in dividends. This leaves the firm an empty shell, as shown in the bottom panel of Table 12.2. Now the firm has no assets and its equity is −$900,000. At that point Wealth Transfer declares bankruptcy. Because of the shareholders' limited liability, the missing $900,000 cannot be collected by the bank. Now you can see how brilliantly the firm is named, because Wealth Transfer achieves exactly what its name and slogan imply. It has transferred a considerable amount of wealth from the bank to the stockholders, and it is out of business.

While schematic, Wealth Transfer's behavior illustrates neatly an unscrupulous scheme that has happened all too often in the past. To curtail such wicked tactics, banks restrict dividend payments in the loan's covenant to avoid the **impairment of capital**. Capital is impaired when the firm strips itself of assets by paying an excessive dividend. This is exactly what Wealth Transfer did. Fortunately, bankers know the tricks that a firm's management might use to transfer their wealth to shareholders, and these cases are now relatively rare.

A Quantitative Approach to Granting Credit As mentioned earlier, some firms use a credit-scoring model to determine whether credit should be granted. Usually, the technique employed is a sophisticated statistical method called discriminant analysis. While the mathematical derivation of a discriminant score is fairly complicated, the idea is clear. The discriminant score should be used to discriminate between good payers and non-payers. Given enough data on past payment performance and the characteristics of the potential customer, it is possible to compute a statistical model of the following form:

$$\text{Score} = a_1 F_1 + a_2 F_2 + \ldots + a_n F_n \tag{12.8}$$

where:

a_i = a statistically determined weight
F_i = a financial variable

In Equation 12.8, the F_i terms are variables, such as the debtor firm's liquidity or the debt-equity ratio or any other variable deemed to be helpful in separating good payers from poor payers. The a_i terms are statistically estimated using the historical data on paying and non-paying borrowers. Figure 12.5 shows how discriminant scores might be distributed for both good and bad payers. In the figure, good payers tend to have higher scores than bad payers, although there are clearly some exceptions. The problem is to select the cutoff discriminant score upon which the credit-granting decision will be based.

In Figure 12.5 the two distributions overlap. This means it is impossible to use the discriminant score to separate the good from bad payers with complete accuracy. In other words, no matter how hard the firm tries to discriminate, it will always make some mistakes. For example, if a firm applying for a bank loan had a score falling in the range denoted by *X* in the figure, the bank would not be able to discern whether the firm is a good payer with a low score or a bad payer with

Figure 12.5
Discriminant Score Distributions for Good and Bad Payers

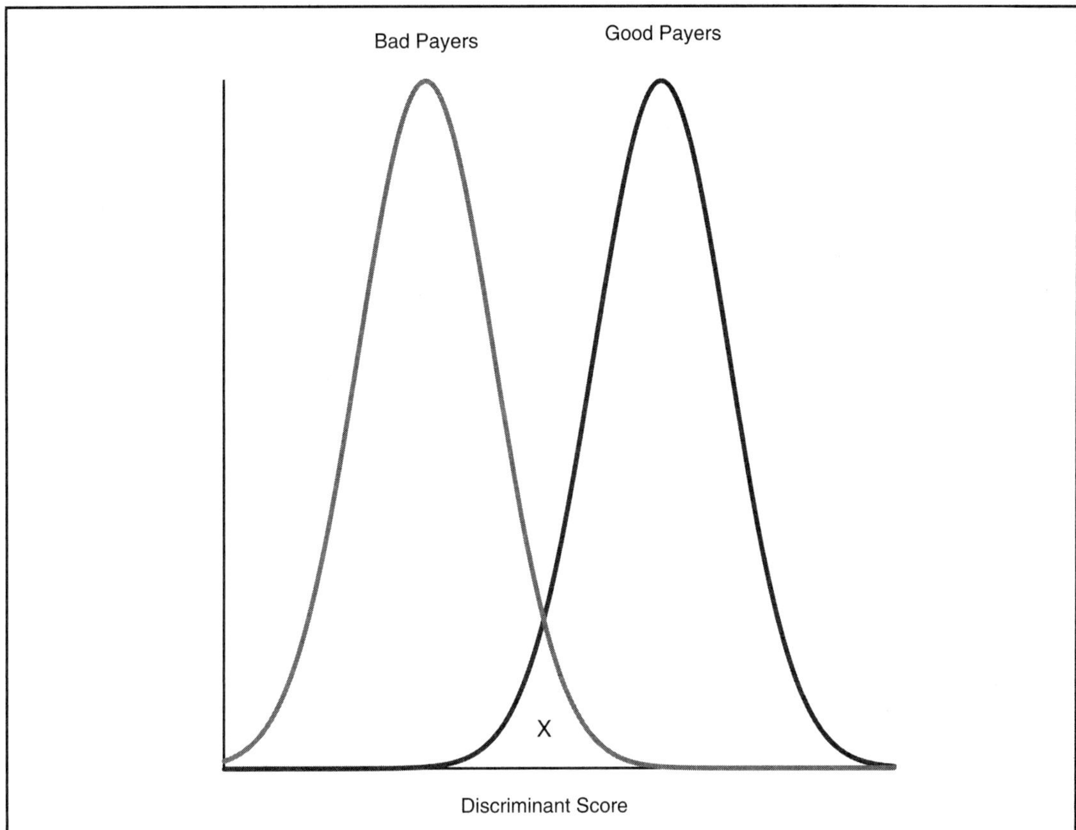

a high score. In this case, the bank must assess the costs of two types of mistakes: granting credit to a bad payer and denying credit to a good payer. If these costs can be quantified, they can enter the statistical model directly to compute the optimal cutoff score for the credit-granting decision. Otherwise, the bank's management must exercise subjective judgment in selecting a cutoff score. In general, the discriminant score approach has proven very useful in helping banks establish good credit standards.

Types of Bank Loans

There are various types of bank loans, according to the way in which the interest payments are calculated. In some types of bank loans, the quoted interest rate may differ significantly from the loan's effective rate. In this section we analyze the major types of loans.

Amortized Loans In this type of loan, the borrower is required to make equal periodic payments, so the loan takes the form of an annuity. Since each equal payment comprises both interest and principal, the interest portion of the payment decreases with each successive installment, whereas the principal component increases.

With amortized loans, the first step is to calculate the amount to be paid every period. If the loan amount is L dollars, the rate on the loan is r percent per period, and the number of payments is n, then the periodic payment is given by:

$$C = \frac{L}{PA(r, n)} \tag{12.9}$$

where $PA(r, n)$ is the annuity factor for r percent and n periods and is equal to:[2]

$$PA(r, n) = \frac{1 - (1 + r)^{-n}}{r} \tag{12.10}$$

Table 12.3 illustrates how each of the periodic payments is divided between interest and principal for a $1 million loan with an annual interest rate of 8 percent, and a maturity of 7 years, to be repaid in annual installments.

Add-On Loans The calculations required for an amortized loan are not simple, especially in the absence of a computer or financial calculator. To circumvent this computational difficulty, other types of loans have been favored in the past.

As its name implies, in an add-on loan the total interest for the loan is calculated and added on to the principal. The sum of the principal and interest is then divided over the number of periods to calculate the constant periodic payments.

To illustrate the mechanics of add-on loans, consider a $10,000 add–on loan with a 12 percent annual nominal rate, or 1 percent per month to be repaid in 36 equal installments. The first step is to calculate the total interest over the life of the loan:

$$\text{Interest} = \$10{,}000 \times 36 \times 0.01 = \$3{,}600$$

Table 12.3
How an Amortized Loan Is Paid
(r = 8%; n = 7 years)

Time	Payment	Interest	Principal	Balance
0				1,000,000.00
1	192,072.40	80,000.00	112,072.40	887,927.60
2	192,072.40	71,034.21	121,038.19	766,889.41
3	192,072.40	61,351.15	130,721.25	636,168.16
4	192,072.40	50,893.45	141,178.95	494,989.21
5	192,072.40	39,599.14	152,473.26	342,515.95
6	192,072.40	27,401.28	164,671.12	177,844.83
7	192,072.40	14,227.59	177,844.81	0.02

[2] In most cases, it is not necessary to calculate the annuity factor using the formula. The annuity factor can be calculated using a financial calculator, where it suffices to input the values for r and n to get the required answer, hence the use of the short-hand notation $PA(r, n)$.

The second step is to add this total interest to the principal to find the total debt:

$$\text{Total debt} = \$10,000 + \$3,600 = \$13,600$$

The final step is to divide this sum by the number of payments to obtain the periodic payment:

$$\text{Payment} = \frac{\$13,600}{36} = \$377.78$$

Thus, this add-on loan must be repaid in 36 payments of $377.78 each. The general expression used to find the periodic payment for an n-period add-on loan of L dollars, with a periodic loan rate of r_L, is:

$$\text{Payment} = \frac{L(1 + r_L n)}{n} \tag{12.11}$$

The effective rate of add-on loans is always greater than the nominal rate. If the stated periodic loan rate is r_L and the number of periods is n, then the effective rate, r_e, is found from the following expression:[3]

$$PA(r_e, n) = \frac{n}{1 + r_L n} \tag{12.12}$$

We can use this expression to find the effective rate in the example just discussed. We have:

$$PA(r_e, 36) = \frac{36}{1 + 0.01 \times 36} = 26.47$$

The solution to this equation is $r_e = 1.767$ percent per month, or an annual interest rate of 21.20 percent, which is substantially larger than the nominal annual rate of 12 percent. Such a large difference between the nominal and effective rates is not unusual for add-on loans, and the borrower should be aware of this fact.[4]

Discount Interest Loans With this type of loan, the lender receives payment of all the interest that will accrue on the loan at the time the loan is granted. Since the interest is prepaid, the borrower must only repay the principal, usually in equal payments.

As an example, consider a discount interest loan for $5,000 with a nominal annual rate of 18 percent, or 1.5 percent monthly, to be repaid in 24 equal monthly payments. The first step is to calculate the interest that will accrue over the life of the loan:

$$\text{Interest} = \$5,000 \times 24 \times 0.015 = \$1,800$$

---

[3] This expression has no general solution for the effective rate, r_e, so it must be solved using trial and error, a financial calculator, or an annuity table.

[4] In fact, the annual effective rate is even larger if we consider compounding over 12 months rather than simply multiplying the monthly rate by 12. Using compounding, the effective annual rate is $(1 + 0.01767)^{12} - 1 = 23.39$ percent.

The second step is to calculate the actual amount received by the borrower. This is equal to:

$$\text{Amount Received} = \$5{,}000 - \$1{,}800 = \$3{,}200$$

The final step is to calculate the monthly payments:

$$\text{Payments} = \frac{\$5{,}000}{24} = \$208.33$$

As with add-on loans, the effective rate for discount interest loans is usually higher than the nominal rate. We can calculate the effective rate on any discount interest loan by solving the following equation:

$$PA(r_e, n) = n(1 - r_L n)$$

For our example we have:

$$PA(r_e, 24) = 24(1 - 0.015 \times 24) = 15.36$$

The solution to this equation is $r_e = 3.928$ percent per month, or 47.14 percent per year. Note that the effective rate is more than 2.6 times the nominal rate in this example. Such outrageous effective rates are not uncommon in this type of loan.[5]

Notice that with a discount interest loan the borrower must request more funds than will actually be required. Thus, if a borrower actually needs N dollars to purchase, say, a new machine, then the discount interest loan requested from the bank, L, must be such that after the total interest is deducted, the borrower receives N dollars. In other words, the loan amount requested is given by:

$$L = \frac{N}{1 - r_L n} \tag{12.13}$$

In the example we saw that a borrower that requests $L = \$5{,}000$ receives only $N = \$3{,}200$, or $(1 - 0.015 \times 24) = 64$ percent of the funds requested. Thus, if \$3,200 is needed, the borrower must ask for $\$3{,}200/0.64 = \$5{,}000$ as the above equation indicates.

Truth-in-Lending

As can be seen from the previous section, the effective interest rate on some types of loans may differ dramatically from the stated or quoted rate, and many borrowers would have no way of knowing this fact. For this reason, Congress enacted the truth-in-lending legislation in 1968 so that borrowers could compare the true interest rate for the various types of loans. The legislation is intended to protect individuals borrowing relatively small amounts, because they are most likely to be unaware of the actual cost of loans.

---

[5] If an add-on loan and a discount interest loan have the same loan amount, L, the same nominal rate, r_L, and the same maturity, n, then the effective rate on the discount interest loan is always greater than the effective rate on the add-on loan. This relationship is illustrated in the example.

Some loans also contain noninterest costs that amount to an increase in the interest rate being charged. Under the truth-in-lending legislation, lenders must incorporate additional charges that are a part of the loan, including service charges and origination fees. The lender must include these costs in the calculation of the annual percentage rate (APR), and the borrower must be made aware of the APR of the loan.

Loan Losses

As we stated earlier, some loans will not be repaid, so the bank's management must be prepared to confront these losses. Borrowers may default on their loan obligations for many reasons, including a change in the economic environment, increased competition, managerial incompetence, or outright fraud. Banks make every effort to collect on delinquent loans, and in practice most delinquent loans are eventually repaid. However, when all recourse is exhausted, the bank must recognize the loss by charging it off.

The loan loss process is illustrated in Table 12.4 and described below. Suppose a borrower gets a $10,000 loan in cash from First Piggy Bank at time $t = 0$. By time $t = 1$, the borrower is delinquent on the loan and First Piggy believes it will be uncollectible. At that time, the bank accounts for the loss *before* it actually occurs by increasing its loan loss reserves, which are part of the bank's capital. This loan loss reserve increase comes from a $10,000 reduction in the bank's pre-tax income for $t = 1$.[6] By time $t = 2$, the bank's worst fears have come true, and the $10,000 loan will not be recovered. At that point, the bank charges off the loan by reducing both its loan account and its loan loss reserves by $10,000. Notice that at $t = 2$ the write-off does not affect the bank's earnings, since the loss was provisioned at $t = 1$.

Table 12.4
The Loan Loss Process

$t = 0$: The bank lends $10,000 in cash			
Cash	–$10,000		
Loans	+$10,000		
$t = 1$: The borrower is delinquent and the bank makes a loan loss provision			
		Loan loss reserves	+$10,000
		Pre-tax income	–$10,000
$t = 2$: The borrower defaults and the loan is written off			
Loans	–$10,000	Loan loss reserves	–$10,000

[6] Notice that this also reduces Piggy Bank's tax burden at $t = 1$. If the bank's marginal tax rate is 30 percent, then Piggy keeps an extra $3,000 in cash at $t = 1$ as a direct result of the loan loss provision.

Recent Loan Loss Experience at Commercial Banks

Table 12.5 presents recent loss expenses as a percentage of loans and leases for insured commercial banks of selected sizes. Losses have generally been much greater for the largest banks. For all banks considered together, the loss experience has been about 1.1 percent of loans and leases being charged off each year. Notice that the losses peaked in 1991.

Diversification and the Scarcity of Bank Capital

The banking industry is notorious for its heavy reliance on debt to finance its assets. We have seen, for example, that banks typically have capital levels in the range of 5–10 percent of their assets. As discussed in the previous section, regulators require banks to have only a very small proportion of their assets in the form of capital. Since debt adds financial risk to any firm, how can banks operate safely with such high levels of debt? Indeed, most manufacturing firms would soon become bankrupt if they used the levels of debt considered normal in the banking industry.

In essence, a bank can operate with so little capital because most of its funds are invested in a very well-diversified loan portfolio. Since most of the revenues of a bank are in the form of interest from this loan portfolio, the risk of a drastic reduction in revenue is very small. Thus, banks can count on a stable income stream to pay their fixed debt burden.

To formalize this argument we can use the concepts of risk and return introduced in Chapter 9 in the following stylized example. Suppose the only asset of the Markowitz Bank is its loan portfolio, with a total of L dollars. The portfolio is financed with deposits, D, and equity, E, so that $L = D + E$. The portfolio consists of n identical and independent loans, each of which earns an interest rate r_L. Thus, the interest income from each paying customer is equal to $(L/n)r_L$. Also, the bank pays an interest rate r_D on its deposits; this is the only expense the bank has. There is a probability p that each of the n loans will be repaid. If a loan is not repaid, all of the loan amount of L/n is lost and becomes a loan loss expense for the period. Given these assumptions, and after some simplification, the expected revenue from each of the loans is given by the following expression:

$$E(\text{Revenue/Loan}) = \left(\frac{L}{n}\right)[(1 + r_L)\,p - 1]$$

Table 12.5
Net Charge-Offs as a Percentage of Loans and Leases (insured commercial banks by consolidated assets)

Year	All Banks	Less than $100 million	$100 million to $1 billion	$1–$10 billion
1988	0.97	0.83	0.82	0.87
1989	0.96	0.71	0.75	1.04
1990	1.15	0.61	0.81	1.45
1991	1.64	0.64	0.93	1.68
1992	1.31	0.50	0.77	1.31
1993	0.75	0.30	0.51	0.88

Source: *The FDIC Quarterly Banking Profile*, various issues.

Since there are n such loans, the total expected revenue for Markowitz Bank is:

$$E(\text{Revenue}) = L[(1 + r_L)\, p - 1] \tag{12.14}$$

Since the bank takes a risk with each of its loans, at the end of the year it may not actually have the revenues it expects. To measure the loan portfolio's risk, we must calculate its standard deviation, σ_n. To do this, it is convenient to calculate the risk associated with putting all of the bank's assets into a single loan. After some algebra, the result is:

$$\sigma_1 = L(1 + r_L)\sqrt{p(1 - p)} \tag{12.15}$$

Since all of the bank's loans are independent of one another, we can use the techniques of Chapter 12 to calculate the standard deviation of the entire loan portfolio, σ_n, as follows:

$$\sigma_n = \frac{\sigma_1}{\sqrt{n}} = \frac{L(1 + r_L)}{\sqrt{n}}\sqrt{p(1 - p)} \tag{12.16}$$

It is interesting to note that the bank's total expected revenue is not affected by the number of loans outstanding, n. In contrast, the risk associated with those revenues depends critically on the number of loans. Indeed, the standard deviation of the total revenues diminishes quite rapidly as the number of the bank's loans increases.

To illustrate these concepts with a numerical example, assume that $L = \$100$ million, $r_L =$ 10 percent, $p = 0.99$, and $n = 1{,}000$. Thus, this bank has 1,000 identical loans of \$100,000, each of which has a 1 percent probability of default. The expected total revenue for the bank, using Equation 12.14, is equal to:

$$E(\text{Revenue}) = \$100{,}000{,}000\ [1.10 \times 0.99 - 1] = \$8{,}900{,}000$$

Thus, the bank expects an average revenue of \$8,900 from each loan: 99 percent of the loans are expected to generate \$10,000 in interest revenue, and 1 percent of the loans are expected to default. With each default, the bank expenses the entire loan amount of \$100,000.

We can now calculate the standard deviation for the bank under the assumption that it has a single loan of \$100 million. Using Equation 12.15, the standard deviation is over \$10 million:

$$\sigma_1 = \$100{,}000{,}000 \times 1.1\sqrt{0.99 \times 0.01} = \$10{,}944{,}861.81$$

Of course, no banker would even think of putting all of the bank's funds into a single loan because it is too risky, as the preceding calculation shows. By splitting its loanable funds into many independent loans, the bank can easily reduce the risk associated with its net revenues to a relatively small amount. If instead of having a single jumbo loan, the bank has 1,000 identical and independent loans, then from Equation 12.16 the standard deviation of the revenues from the portfolio can be reduced to about \$346 thousand:

$$\sigma_n = \frac{\$10{,}944{,}861.81}{\sqrt{1{,}000}} = \$346{,}106.92$$

These calculations show that Markowitz Bank can expect to have net revenues of \$8.9 million in the next year, with a standard deviation of about \$346 thousand. Thus, it faces relatively little risk. Indeed, assuming that the distribution of total revenues is essentially normal, there is only about 1 chance in 1,000 that revenues will be below the expected value by more than 3 standard deviations. In other words there is a 0.1 percent chance that revenues will not reach $\$8{,}900{,}000 - 3 \times \$346{,}106.92 = \$7{,}861{,}679.24$.

As long as the bank's interest expenses are lower than \$7.86 million, the bank will only have a 0.1 percent chance of losing money in a given year. If the bank considers this chance acceptable, and if it pays an interest rate of r_D = 8 percent to its depositors, the bank can support a level of deposits, D, equal to:

$$D = \frac{\$7{,}861{,}679.24}{0.08} = \$98{,}270{,}991$$

The above calculation shows that Markowitz Bank may have a debt-to-asset ratio of 98.27 percent without taking undue risk. Equivalently, the bank can operate with only 1.73 percent equity and face only 1 chance in 1,000 that its capital will be reduced in any given year.

Loan Correlation and Capital Requirements

Although the example just presented is highly stylized, it clearly shows why most banks can operate successfully with very little capital. The essential element of the model in the previous section is that the bank has a considerable number of independent loans.

In practice, loans are not totally independent of one another. For example, in a recession the default of one loan tends to be somewhat correlated with the default of other loans. Loan dependency may also come from the fact that some banks favor making loans to a particular industry, or within a particular geographical region. For example, during the 1980s many U.S. banks gave loans totaling several hundred billion dollars to Latin American countries. By the end of the decade many of those countries found themselves in a recession and unable or unwilling to repay the loans.

As loans become more interdependent, banks require more capital to operate successfully. However, some of the dependency can be compensated by having a greater number of loans in the portfolio. As long as the correlation between loans is not too great and the number of loans is very large, a bank can normally operate with a very small capital base.

Summary

In this chapter we discussed the main operational areas of commercial banks. The chapter began with a discussion of liquidity. The most liquid asset is vault cash, and we showed how commercial banks decide on the amount of vault cash they should hold. Two widely used models were presented. In the Baumol model, the bank is assumed to know with certainty its cash depletion pattern, whereas in the Miller-Orr model the daily cash flows are uncertain. Despite their essential differences, the two models give formulas that result in economies of scale.

We also showed how banks play a role in helping businesses manage their own cash. By engaging in concentration banking and in lock box systems, commercial banks help firms speed their cash collections and delay their cash disbursements.

The credit-granting decision is perhaps the most important operation at commercial banks. We discussed the procedures banks use to determine the creditworthiness of potential borrowers. Since granting loans eventually leads to loan losses, bank managers must attempt to minimize the losses.

After deciding to grant a loan, a bank must decide on what type of bank loan to give. While the most common type is the amortized loan, other types of loans were also presented, such as add-on loans and discount interest loans.

Finally, the chapter presented a discussion of bank capital and the new capital regulations that all internationally active banks must follow. We also gave a plausible explanation to the well-known fact that the banking industry survives with much less capital than most other industries. The essential reason for the industry's low capital is that commercial banks have the capacity to diversify much more than most other types of businesses.

Questions and Problems

1. What two properties must a liquid asset have?
2. Is buying a profitable office building a good way to invest a bank's excess short-term funds?
3. How can marketable securities act as a substitute for cash?
4. Does a Treasury bill have liquidity risk?
5. What is the cost of holding too much vault cash as an asset?
6. What is the cost of holding too little vault cash as an asset?
7. Your firm collects \$10,000,000 per year. If interest rates are 6 percent, what is the value of speeding up your collections by one day?
8. In the Baumol model, by what factor does the average cash balance change if the annual cash needs, T, increase by a factor of 3?
9. In the Miller-Orr model, why is there an upper control limit; in other words, why do firms not hold more cash than the amount indicated by the upper control limit?
10. In terms of the variables of the Baumol model, what is the average cash balance that a bank holds?
11. In terms of the variables of the Miller-Orr model, what is the average cash balance that a bank holds?
12. Would a firm be better off to collect \$100,000 in an accounts receivable one day earlier or to pay an account payable of \$100,000 one day later?
13. What is the difference between a concentration banking system and a lock box system?
14. The present value of all the costs of a lock box system is \$2 million for Modena & Company. The company is considering entering into a concentration banking agreement with LaSalle Bank. If the bank will charge an initial payment, I, and a yearly fee, Y, what combinations of I and Y will make the deal attractive for Modena? Assume an opportunity cost of money of 10 percent for Modena.

15. Assume that your firm collects $10,000,000 per year and that interest rates are 6 percent. A bank is trying to sell you a cash management system. A lock box system will cost $20,000 per year but should speed your accounts receivable by three days on average. What would be the savings (or extra cost) of adopting the lock box system?

16. With $10,000,000 in collections per year and interest rates of 6 percent, would your firm be interested in paying $100,000 per year for a concentration banking system that would speed your collection of accounts receivable by five days? What would be the extra savings or cost?

17. Compare the lock box and concentration banking alternatives of the previous two problems. Which is preferable? Why?

18. In the Baumol model, what is the value of the slope of the holding cost line?

19. A small bank uses the Baumol model to determine the optimal vault cash balance. The interest rate, r, is 10 percent, the fixed cost, F, of acquiring new cash is $30 per transaction, and the total annual cash needs are $2,000,000. Construct a table showing the holding costs, the transaction costs, and the total costs for $20,000, $25,000, . . . , $45,000. Based on these numbers, give a close estimate of the maximum cash the bank should hold. Compare this estimate to the actual value found from the Baumol formula.

20. A bank acquires $20,000 in cash each time it transacts, the holding costs are $2,000, and the transaction costs are $3,000. Find the average amount of vault cash, assuming the bank uses the Baumol model.

21. In the Miller-Orr model, show that the difference between the target cash level, Z, and the lower bound, L, is one-third of the difference between the upper and lower bounds.

22. A very conservative bank manager argues that the bank should extend loans only to those customers that are 100 percent sure to pay as promised. Is this reasonable? Explain.

23. In your bank's discussion about its new loan policy, you suggest that the bank should acquire complete information on the creditworthiness of customers. Is this reasonable? Explain what attacks might be made on this position.

24. What is a credit-scoring model? Explain how it might be used in making decisions about automobile financing by banks.

25. The Empty Nest Bank classifies customers according to the probability, p, that they will pay their loans. Empty Nest has an annual cost of borrowing money of 6 percent and provides loans at 10 percent. To which customers, in terms of their probability of payment, should the bank deny credit?

26. A customer comes to Lavoro Bank asking for a $10,000, 24-month amortized loan. If the current annual loan rate is 10 percent, how much must the customer pay each month?

27. Suppose the same customer of Problem 26 asks for a 6-month grace period on the 24-month loan. What is the new monthly payment?

28. If the customer of Problem 26 can only afford to pay $300 each month for the moment but will be able to make a "balloon" payment at the time of the final payment, find the balloon payment.

29. You just received a $1,000 add-on loan. The monthly interest rate is 1 percent, and you will repay it over 30 months. How much is the monthly payment?

30. In the previous problem, find the effective rate on the add-on loan.

31. Suppose the loan of Problem 29 is changed to a discount loan, with all the other variables remaining the same. What would the monthly payments be?

32. For the discount loan of the previous problem, what is the effective rate?

33. Explain how commercial banks can afford to use so little capital in comparison to the vast majority of manufacturing firms.

34. The loanable assets of Physical Bank are $10 million, and the current annual loan rate is 12 percent. The average customer of the bank has a probability of default of 2 percent. Find the expected revenue of the bank, assuming that it has (a) only one loan; (b) 1,000 loans.

35. If Physical Bank in the previous problem gives all its loanable funds to Engulf and Devour, Inc., what risk is Physical taking in terms of the standard deviation of its revenues?

36. Continuing with Physical Bank, what is its risk if it distributes the $10 million in loanable funds among 1,000 different independent and identical loans?

Suggested REALDATA Exercises

The following *REALDATA* exercises explore the concepts developed in this chapter:
Exercises 4, 10, 20

References

"Bank for International Settlements," fedpoints 22, Federal Reserve Bank of New York, Public Information Department, June 1988.

Brunner, A. D., D. Hancock, and M. M. McLaughlin, "Recent Developments Affecting the Profitability and Practices of Commercial Banks," *Federal Reserve Bulletin*, July 1992, pp. 459–83.

Hetzel, R. L., "Too Big to Fail: Origins, Consequences, and Outlook," *Economic Review*, November/December 1991, pp. 3–15.

Large, A., "Briefing [on the BIS capital adequacy rules]," *Euromoney*, August 1991, pp. 45, 48.

Llewellyn, D., "Bank Capital: The Strategic Issue of the 1990s," *Banking World*, January 1992, pp. 20–5.

Neuberger, J. A., "Risk and Return in Banking: Evidence from Bank Stock Returns," *Economic Review*, Federal Reserve Bank of San Francisco, Fall 1991, pp. 18–30.

Pozdena, R. J., "Recapitalizing the Banking System," *Weekly Letter*, Federal Reserve Bank of San Francisco, March 8, 1991.

Management of Commercial Banks 13

Overview

The primary goal of all investors is to obtain a rate of return on their investment that is in accord with the amount of risk taken. In this chapter we discuss the major ways in which commercial banks are managed in order to satisfy investors' goals.

We begin with a brief review of the main items in a commercial bank's financial statements, and we introduce concepts such as the adjusted net interest income and the depreciation tax shield. We also present the sources and uses of funds statement, which determines how the bank obtained its funds over a given period and how those funds were invested. Financial ratio analysis is also discussed at length because it is one of the most important tools available to commercial bank managers. To fully understand a bank's profitability, it is essential to understand the role played by leverage and asset turnover.

The profitability of a commercial bank can be measured in various ways. Our main focus is placed on understanding net interest margin, return on assets, and return on equity. In addition, bankers follow very closely the spread between the average rate on interest-earning assets and the average rate on interest-paying liabilities. If the spread becomes negative, as happened during part of the 1980s, many banks may suffer losses.

Another technique useful in bank management is the analysis of variations. With this technique, a commercial bank manager can pinpoint the cause of a change in the bank's profits between any two periods. For example, if profits have decreased from one year to the next, an analysis of variations can determine which portion of the change was due to lower interest rates, which to a smaller loan portfolio, and which to the interaction of the two variables.

We discuss how the composition of a commercial bank's liabilities can strongly influence both its profitability and its risk. In particular, we focus on how the bank's financial leverage affects risk and return. Consistent with our discussion of risk and return in Chapter 9, we conclude that a bank's expected profitability can be increased only at the expense of taking on greater risks. As an illustration of the concepts developed in this chapter, we present a plausible explanation for the collapse of much of the S&L industry in the 1980s.

Financial Statements as Managerial Tools

A commercial bank manager can obtain a great deal of information from the bank's main financial statements: the balance sheet, the income statement, and the sources and uses of funds. For the purposes of discussing the usefulness of a commercial bank's financial statements, we will use a simplified version of a commercial bank's balance sheet and income statement, shown in Tables 13.1 and 13.2. A detailed discussion of the accounts in each of these financial statements was presented in Chapter 10.

Table 13.1
Balance Sheet for Mirage Bank
(rounded to nearest thousand)

	Dec. 31, 1994	Dec. 31, 1995	Difference
Assets			
Cash	$200	$220	$20
Securities (6%)	600	580	–20
Loans (10%)	4,000	4,500	500
Fixed assets	1,000	1,200	200
Total Assets	5,800	6,500	700
Liabilities			
Demand deposits	$2,000	$1,700	–$300
Time deposits (6%)	2,500	2,900	400
Long-term debt (8%)	800	1,380	580
Total Liabilities	5,300	5,980	680
Common Stock	400	400	0
Retained Earnings	100	120	20
Net Worth	500	520	20
Total Liabilities and Net Worth	5,800	6,500	700

The Balance Sheet

As discussed in Chapter 10, the balance sheet of a commercial bank reflects its primary purpose of intermediating between lenders and borrowers in the economy. This is why loans are the main asset, and the various types of deposits constitute a commercial bank's main liability.

In the simplified balance sheet presented in Table 13.1 for Mirage Bank, a commercial bank's interest-earning assets are its securities portfolio and its loans. We assume that securities earn 6 percent interest and that the interest rate on loans is 10 percent. Similarly, its interest-paying liabilities consist only of time deposits and long-term debt, which, respectively, cost the bank 6 percent and 8 percent annually.[1] Demand deposits earn no interest in our model. While greatly simplified, these accounts capture the essence of a commercial bank's sources and uses of funds.

The Income Statement

A commercial bank's income statement also reflects its main activities: receiving interest from loans and paying interest to depositors. Not surprisingly, commercial banks generate most of their prof-

---

[1] We also assume that assets and liabilities change linearly throughout the year, so the arithmetic average should be used when calculating the interest income and expense of each type of account.

Table 13.2
Income Statement for Mirage Bank
(rounded to nearest thousand)

	1995
Interest income	$460
Interest expense	249
Net interest income (NII)	211
Loan loss provision	45
Adjusted NII	166
Other income	92
Administration expense	198
Depreciation	15
Earnings before taxes	45
Taxes	15
Net income	30

its by providing loans at a higher rate than the rate paid on deposits. In addition, in recent times banks have increasingly relied on noninterest income as a source of profits.

The simplified income statement presented in Table 13.2 defines several important financial relationships for commercial banks. First, net interest income (*NII*) is defined as:

$$NII = \text{Interest income} - \text{Interest expense} \tag{13.1}$$

For Mirage Bank, the net interest income is:

$$NII = \$460 - \$249 = \$211$$

Alternatively, if the average return on securities is r_S, the average return on loans is r_L, and the corresponding rates paid on time deposits and long-term debt are r_T and r_D, respectively, then net interest income can be written as:

$$NII = (r_S\, S + r_L\, L) - (r_T\, T + r_D\, D) \tag{13.2}$$

Using Table 13.1 and the interest rates given above, we can use Equation 13.2 to calculate the *NII* of Mirage Bank:

$$\begin{aligned} NII &= (0.06 \times \$590 + 0.10 \times \$4{,}250) - (0.06 \times \$2{,}700 + 0.08 \times \$1{,}090) \\ &= \$211.2 \end{aligned}$$

Next, adjusted net interest income is defined as net interest income minus loan loss provisions:

$$ANII = NII - LLP \tag{13.3}$$

For Mirage, we have:

$$ANII = \$211 - \$45 = \$166$$

After obtaining the adjusted net interest income, the bank's earnings before taxes are found by including its other income, other expenses, and depreciation:

$$EBT = ANII + OI - OE - Dep \tag{13.4}$$

In our example, we have:

$$EBT = \$166 + \$92 - \$198 - \$15 = \$45$$

Knowing the bank's earnings before taxes and its income tax rate, t, the bank's net income is equal to:

$$NI = EBT(1 - t) \tag{13.5}$$

Given an income tax rate of 34 percent for Mirage, its net income is:

$$NI = \$45\ (1 - 0.34) = \$29.7$$

Thus, the rounded net income of Mirage is $30.

Of course, the net income, NI, for the period is available to either reinvest in the company or to pay as a dividend to shareholders. Thus:

$$\text{Net Income} = \text{Retained Earnings} + \text{Dividends} \tag{13.6}$$

Notice that Mirage has decided to pay dividends equal to about $10 in 1995, since it earned $30 but retained only $20, as is clear by comparing the retained earnings for 1994 and 1995.

In reading an income statement, we must remember the difference between the earnings the income statement reports and the cash the firm receives. Cash flow is very important because only actual cash gives the bank the resources to meet its obligations. It is important to note that while depreciation is not a cash expense, it generates cash for the bank by reducing the firm's tax bill. This is known as the **depreciation tax shield**. To illustrate, notice that Mirage bank has earnings before taxes of $45 after deducting a depreciation expense of $15. Since the bank pays a 34 percent tax rate on any EBT, it pays $\$45 \times 0.34 = \$15.3$ in taxes. However, if the depreciation on its fixed assets were not a deductible expense, the bank's EBT would be $60, and the taxes paid in that case would be $\$60 \times 0.34 = \$20.4$. The fact that depreciation is allowed as an expense shielded the bank from paying $5.1 ($\$20.4 - \$15.3$) in taxes. In general, if t is the corporate tax rate, the depreciation tax shield can be calculated directly with the following formula:

$$\text{Tax Shield} = \text{Depreciation} \times t \tag{13.7}$$

Using the tax shield formula in our example, Mirage bank's depreciation tax shield is $15 × 0.34 = $5.1, just as we found before.

Sources and Uses of Funds Statement

The sources and uses of funds statement shows how the bank acquired its funds in a given period and how those funds were used. For example, if an individual makes a time deposit of $1,000 at the bank, and the bank uses the funds to make a $1,000 loan, then the time deposit is a source of funds for the bank, and those funds are used to increase the bank's loan portfolio.[2]

Clearly, banks obtain funds by incurring obligations to individuals and stockholders. Perhaps a less obvious example of a source of funds is a reduction of the bank's vault cash level. This is a source of funds because it generates cash for the bank. Similarly, a use of funds might be the cash purchase of an armored truck, or a reduction in the level of long-term debt of the bank.

For any bank, there are essentially three sources and three uses of funds that fall into pairs, as shown in Table 13.3. As a source of funds, a bank can increase a liability account. By issuing bonds, for example, a bank increases the funds available to it. Decreasing a liability account is a use of funds. For example, if a bank pays an existing debt, it uses funds to reduce that liability. Accordingly, an increase in a liability is a source of funds and a decrease in a liability is a use of funds.

If a bank increases an equity account, the increased obligation is a source of funds available to the bank. For example, if a bank issues new stock, the sale of stock brings in new funds to the bank. Likewise, if a bank decreases an equity account, perhaps by buying its own stock in the market or by paying dividends, it thereby uses funds.

Reducing an asset account provides a source of funds. As an example, a bank may reduce its fixed assets account by selling some of its buildings, thus generating cash.

Constructing a sources and uses statement for one year requires balance sheets for two years. Table 13.1 provides all the information necessary to construct the 1995 sources and uses statement for Mirage Bank. The right-most column of Table 13.1 presents the difference in each account from one period to the next. Using this column and the rules given in Table 13.3, we can build the sources and uses statement.

Table 13.3
Sources and Uses of Funds

Sources of Funds
Increase in a liability account
Increase in an equity account
Decrease in an asset account
Uses of Funds
Decrease in a liability account
Decrease in an equity account
Increase in an asset account

[2] As discussed in Chapter 3, a bank cannot actually use all of the new deposits to make loans since a portion must be kept in the form of required reserves.

Table 13.4 takes all the amounts from the difference column in Table 13.1 and classifies each as a source or a use of funds. Furthermore, the sources and uses of funds have been ranked by dollar amount in Table 13.4. For example, the two major sources of funds in 1995 for Mirage Bank were an increase in long-term debt ($580) and in time deposits ($400). Mirage Bank used nearly half the funds to expand its loan portfolio ($500) and to decrease its demand deposits ($300).

Note that all the information in Table 13.4 comes from the balance sheets of Table 13.1, with one exception. The sources and uses statement also reflects the cash dividend of $10 that Mirage Bank paid in 1995. We have seen that net income must go either to retained earnings or to pay dividends to the shareholders. On the balance sheets, the change in retained earnings for the year was $20. However, the income statement in Table 13.2 shows that Mirage Bank earned a net income of $30. The dividends paid to shareholders in 1995 do not appear on the balance sheet or the income statement, but they appear on the sources and uses statement. This allows a reconciliation of the three major financial statements.[3]

Management of Commercial Bank Profitability

This section explains how the combination of a bank's asset and liability structure, as well as its operations, determine the bank's ultimate profitability. One way to understand these interrelationships is through the use of the bank's financial ratios. We discuss the major financial ratios and show how to calculate them using the financial statements of Mirage Bank. The major commercial bank ratios can be divided into three groups: leverage ratios, turnover ratios, and profitability ratios.

Table 13.4
Sources and Uses of Funds Statement for Mirage Bank
December 31, 1994 to December 31, 1995
(rounded to nearest thousand)

Sources	
Increase in long-term debt	$580
Increase in time deposits	400
Net income from operations	30
Decrease in securities	20
Total Sources	1,030
Uses	
Increase in loans	$500
Decrease in demand deposits	300
Increase in fixed assets	200
Increase in cash	20
Dividends paid	10
Total Uses	1,030

[3] Many firms call the sources and uses statement the **Statement of Changes in Financial Position.**

Leverage Ratios

Leverage ratios calculate the extent to which a bank relies on debt. Other things being equal, a higher leverage ratio indicates a riskier bank because the interest payments on the debt are fixed even if the earnings of the bank fluctuate. As a result, should the bank's cash flow diminish excessively, the bank might miss its debt payments deadline, putting it in technical default.

Three important measures of leverage are the debt-to-assets ratio (D/A), the debt-to-equity ratio (D/E), and the equity multiplier (EM). These leverage measures focus on the structure of the firm's long-term financing. The debt-to-assets ratio (D/A) shows which portion of assets the bank finances with debt. The debt-to-equity ratio (D/E) shows the relationship between the firm's debt and equity financing. The debt-to-asset ratio is defined by:

$$\text{Debt/Asset} = \frac{\text{Total Debt}}{\text{Total Assets}} \tag{13.8}$$

For Mirage Bank, in 1995 we have $D/A = \$5{,}980 \ / \ \$6{,}500 = 0.92$.

The debt-to-equity ratio is defined similarly:

$$\text{Debt/Equity} = \frac{\text{Total Debt}}{\text{Equity}} \tag{13.9}$$

The D/E ratio for Mirage in 1995 is $D/E = \$5{,}980 \ / \ \$520 = 11.5$.

These two ratios convey essentially the same information. In fact, given one ratio we can calculate the other. For example, a debt/asset ratio of 92 percent implies that the firm must finance 8 percent of its assets with equity. The ratio of debt to equity then equals 92/8 or 11.5, which is exactly the debt/equity ratio calculated above. In general, the relationship between the debt/asset and debt/equity ratios is given by:

$$D/A = \frac{D/E}{1 + D/E} \tag{13.10}$$

The final leverage ratio we consider is the equity multiplier (EM), defined as the dollar amount of assets for each dollar of equity:

$$\text{Equity Multiplier} = \frac{\text{Total Assets}}{\text{Equity}} \tag{13.11}$$

For Mirage Bank, in 1995 this ratio equals $EM = \$6{,}500 \ / \ 520 = 12.5$. Thus, for each dollar of equity, the firm has 12.5 dollars of assets. The equity multiplier can also be expressed in terms of the debt/equity ratio. This is easily seen by noting that Total Assets = Debt + Equity. Thus:

$$EM = 1 + \frac{D}{E} \tag{13.12}$$

Turnover Ratios

Turnover ratios indicate the efficiency with which a bank uses its assets to generate profits. The most important turnover ratio for commercial banks is the Asset Turnover (*ATO*) ratio, defined by:

$$\text{Asset Turnover} = \frac{\text{Operating Income}}{\text{Assets}} \tag{13.13}$$

where the bank's operating income is defined as the sum of its interest income and noninterest income. The *ATO* for Mirage Bank in 1995 was (\$460 + \$92) / \$6,500 = 0.0849. This means that Mirage generated an income of \$8.49 for each \$100 of assets it held at the end of 1995.[4] The asset turnover therefore measures how productively Mirage utilizes all of its assets.

Profitability Ratios

Five widely used measures of profitability are the profit margin (*PM*), the net interest margin (*NIM*), the spread, the return on assets (*ROA*), and the return on equity (*ROE*). The profit margin is calculated as follows:

$$\text{Profit margin} = \frac{\text{Net Income}}{\text{Operating Income}} \tag{13.14}$$

From the 1995 income statement, the profit margin for Mirage Bank is *PM* = \$30 / (\$460 + \$92) = 0.0543, or 5.43 percent.

Banking firms often focus on the value of their net interest margin as a measure of profitability. The *NIM* is defined as follows:

$$\text{Net Interest margin} = \frac{\text{Net Interest Income}}{\text{Interest-Earning Assets}} \tag{13.15}$$

For Mirage Bank, the *NIM* for 1995 is *NIM* = \$211.2 / \$5,080 = 0.0416, or 4.16 percent. In recent years, the net interest margin for all banks has fluctuated, ranging from a low of 3.94 percent in 1990 to a high of 4.44 percent in 1993. In general, a *NIM* measure in the range of 4 percent is fairly typical.

The spread is also widely used as a profitability measure:

$$\text{Spread} = \frac{\text{Interest Income}}{\text{Earning Assets}} - \frac{\text{Interest Expense}}{\text{Interest-Paying Liabilities}} \tag{13.16}$$

Notice that the spread is just the difference between the average rate on interest-earning assets minus the average rate paid on interest-paying liabilities. In our model, the relevant assets are secu-

[4] Given that assets grew during 1995, it is more appropriate to find the asset turnover by using the average total assets rather than their ending value. For simplicity of illustration, we do not use this refinement.

rities and loans, and the corresponding liabilities are time deposits and long-term debt. Therefore, we can write the spread as:

$$\text{Spread} = \frac{r_S S + r_L L}{S + L} - \frac{r_T T + r_D D}{T + D} \tag{13.17}$$

The average rate on interest-earning assets for Mirage Bank is (6% × \$580 + 10% × \$4,500) / (\$580 + \$4,500) = 9.54 percent. Similarly, the average rate on interest-paying liabilities is (6% × \$2,900 + 8% × \$1,380) / (\$2,900 + \$1,380) = 6.64 percent. Therefore, the spread is 9.54% − 6.64% = 2.90 percent. Thus, Mirage Bank operates with a spread of 2.9 percent, or 290 basis points.

The return on assets ratio is given by:

$$\boxed{\text{Return on Asset} = \frac{\text{Net Income}}{\text{Total Assets}}} \tag{13.18}$$

Using our example, this ratio is ROA = \$30 / \$6,500 = 0.0046, or 0.46 percent. Thus, Mirage Bank generates less than 50 cents of profits for every \$100 in assets.

Table 13.5 shows the return on assets for insured commercial banks between 1988 and 1993. Notice that the return on assets is very small, particularly compared to typical manufacturing or industrial concerns. A typical ROA figure is about 1 percent. As the table shows, these figures have varied considerably by the size of bank, with large banks outperforming smaller banks in some years and underperforming smaller banks in other years.

Finally, the return on equity ratio is defined as follows:

$$\text{Return on Equity} = \frac{\text{Net Income}}{\text{Equity}} \tag{13.19}$$

For Mirage Bank we have ROE = \$30 / \$520 = 0.0577, or 5.77 percent. Typical ROE figures have been in the range of 12–15 percent, which is a marked increase compared to some recent

Table 13.5
Percentage Return on Assets
(insured commercial banks by consolidated assets)

Year	All Banks	Less than \$100 million	\$100 million–\$1 billion	\$1–10 billion
1988	0.82	0.64	0.74	0.77
1989	0.57	0.89	0.93	0.83
1990	0.48	0.70	0.76	0.35
1991	0.59	0.93	0.76	0.63
1992	0.93	1.04	1.01	1.02
1993	1.22	1.23	1.21	1.32

Source: *FDIC Quarterly Banking Profile*, various issues.

years. For example, in 1987 the ROE for all banks was only 1.49 percent, and as recently as 1991 the ROE was only 8.21 percent.

Each of these profitability measures provides a slightly different gauge of a firm's operating success. The profit margin reveals how much profit a bank earns on each dollar of operating income. The *ROA* and the *ROE* both determine the rate of return on some measure of investment. The *ROA* determines the return on all of the assets employed by the firm. By contrast, the *ROE* focuses only on the investment contributed by the shareholders.

The performance of Mirage Bank is dismal by all of these measures. Given the risk investors take, most will not be happy to find that their stock earns less than 6 percent per year. This poor performance also means that the bank will face great difficulties in attracting any new investment capital if potential investors regard these ratios as indicative of the future performance of Mirage Bank. Unless the two years of our data are unusual, Mirage may be a bank in serious financial distress.

Relationships Between Ratios

It is important to notice that several of these ratios are related to one another. We have already noted the relationship between the *D/A* and the *D/E* ratios, but the most important one is between the return on equity ratio and three of the other ratios. This is as follows:[5]

$$\boxed{ROE = PM \times ATO \times EM} \tag{13.20}$$

Equation 13.20 provides a connection among a profitability ratio (*PM*), a leverage ratio (*EM*), and a turnover ratio (*ATO*). It allows the bank manager to pinpoint the reasons that lead to a given return on equity. For Mirage Bank we have seen that in 1995 the *ROE* was 5.77 percent. This value can be broken down into its three components, using the values computed previously. For Mirage Bank we have 5.77% = 5.43% × 0.0849 × 12.5.[6] This clearly shows that the problem with the bank's low return on equity lies in its dismal asset turnover, indicating poor productivity of its assets. This recognition should lead the bank manager to concentrate on urgently improving the bank's asset turnover.

Another important relationship exists among the return on equity and the net interest margin ratios:

$$NIM = \frac{ROE}{1 - t} \times \frac{E}{IEA} + \frac{LLP - OI + OE + Dep}{IEA} \tag{13.21}$$

This relationship indicates that, to obtain a given return on equity, the bank must generate a certain net interest margin. In particular, the net interest margin required to produce a certain *ROE*

---

[5] This relationship is often referred to as the Du Pont equation. The student is asked to derive this relationship in an end-of-chapter problem.

[6] The product on the right actually gives 5.763 percent. The computational error is due to the rounding of each of the three ratios.

increases as the bank's tax rate, its equity level, its loan loss provisions (*LLP*), other expenses (*OE*), and depreciation increase. By contrast, the required *NIM* decreases as the bank's interest-earning assets (*IEA*), and its other income increase.

As an example, we use the 1995 figures for Mirage Bank to calculate the net interest margin required to produce a return on equity of 12 percent. The calculation is:

$$NIM = \frac{0.12}{1 - 0.34} \times \frac{\$520}{\$580 + \$4{,}500} + \frac{\$45 - \$92 + \$198 + 15}{\$580 + \$4{,}500}$$

$$= 0.0186 + 0.0327$$

$$= 0.0513$$

We have already seen that the *NIM* for 1995 was 4.16 percent, which produced a return on equity of 5.77 percent. The above calculation shows that in order to more than double the *ROE* to 12 percent, the bank must increase its *NIM* to 5.13, or about 23 percent more than the 1995 level. The challenge for the bank's management is to develop a detailed plan for obtaining this greater return on equity in the future.

Limitations of Ratio Analysis

All of these ratios are meaningful only in conjunction with a bank's past performance or in comparison with other banks. Also, none of these measures has a "correct" value. For example, it might seem that a higher debt-to-asset ratio is always better. After all, the higher the ratio, the greater the return on equity of the bank, according to the Du Pont equation. However, managing a firm to ensure a high debt-to-asset ratio may lead to an increased risk of default, as we show in a subsequent section. As always, it is important to recognize not only the benefits but also the costs of any financial decision.

When analyzing financial statements, we should always be on the look-out for "window dressing" tactics. For example, a simple way of "improving" any bank's liquidity is to take out a long-term loan right before the end of the fiscal year and repay it at the beginning of the next one. If the funds from the loan are kept in the form of vault cash, then the bank will appear to be very liquid. The moral is that ratios should be viewed as part of a whole, not just in isolation.

Analysis of Variations

Another managerial technique that is used to understand the origin of changes in the bank's net interest income is the analysis of variations. Banks continuously experience changes in the rates they receive on their assets, as well as those paid on liabilities. At the same time, the volume of assets and liabilities may also change. It is important for management to determine how much of the change in net interest income (*NII*) from one period to the next was due to changes in interest rates and how much to changes in volume.

The net interest income for a given period is equal to the difference between the interest income and interest expense. In the balance sheet depicted in Table 13.1 there are two interest-earning assets – securities (S) and loans (L) – earning rates of r_S and r_L, respectively. There are also two interest-paying liabilities – time deposits and long-term debt – paying rates of r_T and r_D, respectively. Given this simplified bank model, the net interest income for a given period, t, is equal to:

$$NII_t = (r_{St}\,S_t + r_{Lt}\,L_t) - (r_{Tt}\,T_t + r_{Dt}\,D_t) \tag{13.22}$$

Since banks are usually interested in understanding the reasons for a change in their NII from one period to the next, we must find an expression for the change in the net interest income between periods 0 and 1 ($\Delta NII = NII_1 - NII_0$) as a function of the changes in each of the rates and of the changes in the level or volume of each of the interest-earning and interest-paying accounts. Letting the symbol Δ represent the change in the variable immediately after it, we have, after some simplification:

$$\begin{aligned} \Delta NII = {} & [\Delta r_S\,S_0 + \Delta S\,r_{S0} + \Delta r_S\,\Delta S] \\ & + [\Delta r_L\,L_0 + \Delta L\,r_{L0} + \Delta r_L\,\Delta L] \\ & - [\Delta r_T\,T_0 + \Delta T\,r_{T0} + \Delta r_T\,\Delta T] \\ & - [\Delta r_D\,D_0 + \Delta D\,r_{D0} + \Delta r_D\,\Delta D] \end{aligned} \tag{13.23}$$

Although this expression seems cumbersome, it is only because there are four separate asset and liability accounts that contribute to the change in the net interest income. Each asset or liability contributes three terms to the expression. The intuition underlying this expression can be explained by referring to Figure 13.1, which depicts the interest income generated by the bank's loans through the interest rate and volume variables. The figure assumes that both the rate and the volume of the bank's loans have increased from one period to the next. Naturally, the income from loans will be greater in the second period, but the problem is to find how much of the change was caused by the rise in interest rates, how much was due to the increase in loan volume, and how much was a consequence of the simultaneous interaction of both variables.

If the loan volume had not changed, the interest income would have increased by an amount equal to $\Delta r_L L_0$. This change is shown as the area of the rectangle $r_{L0}ABr_{L1}$ in Figure 13.1. If the loan rates had remained the same, but the volume increased, then interest income would have increased by $\Delta L_0 r_{L0}$. This increase corresponds to the area L_0L_1DA in Figure 13.1. Each of these two areas account for the change in net interest income from loans if only one of the variables changes at a time. In fact, both the interest rate and the volume change simultaneously, and the portion of the change in the NII that is generated by the simultaneous change of the rate and the volume of loans is given by the "cross-product" term $\Delta r_L\,\Delta L$. This is represented in Figure 13.1 by the rectangle $ADCB$. By adding the three rectangles generated by the change in loan rates and volume, we obtain the total change in net interest income attributable to the loan component. By repeating the same analysis with the other three relevant accounts – securities, time deposits, and long-term debt – we obtain the bank's total change in net interest income.

To illustrate, consider the situation for Mirage Bank depicted in Table 13.6, showing only the interest-earning assets and interest-paying liabilities for 1994 and 1995, as well as the corresponding rates. For simplicity, assume that all the values in Table 13.6 were constant throughout each year. Then, we can find the net interest income for Mirage Bank in each of the years:

Figure 13.1
Analysis of Variations for Loans

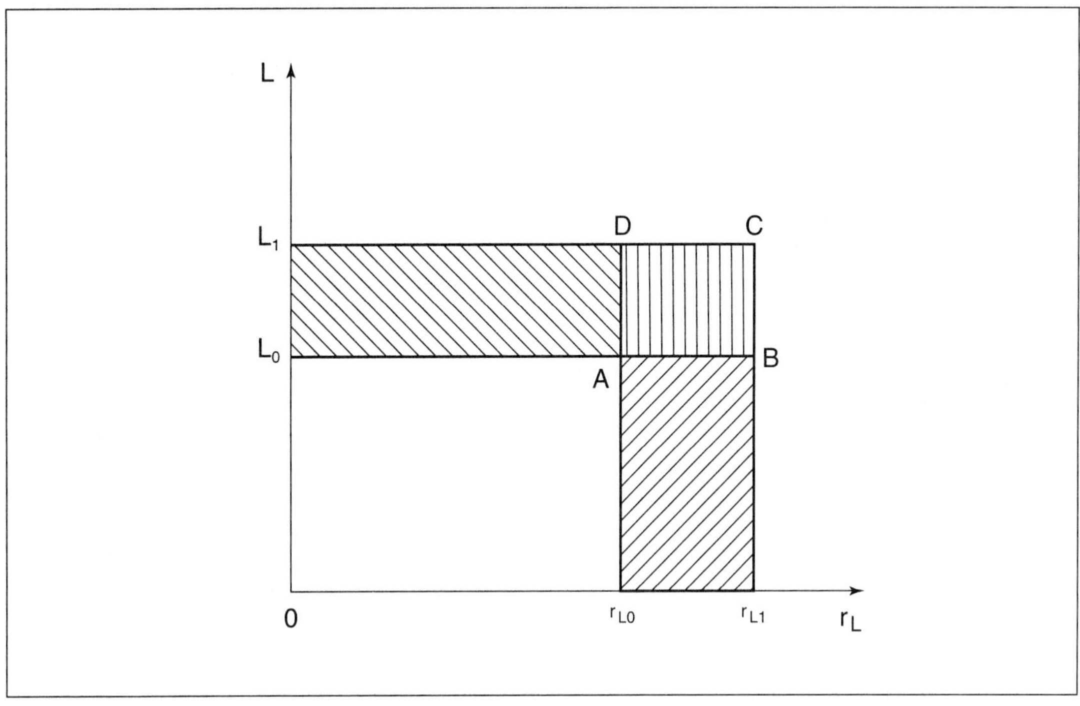

$$NII_{91} = \$600 \times 0.05 + \$4{,}000 \times 0.11 - \$2{,}500 \times 0.07 - \$800 \times 0.09$$
$$= \$223$$
$$NII_{92} = \$580 \times 0.06 + \$4{,}500 \times 0.10 - \$2{,}900 \times 0.06 - \$1{,}380 \times 0.08$$
$$= \$200.4$$

From the above calculations we can see that the net interest income for Mirage decreased by \$22.6 from 1994 to 1995. To understand how this change occurred, we perform an analysis of variations using the figures in Table 13.6. The numerical expression is:

$$\begin{aligned} -\$22.6 = {} & [0.01 \times \$600 + (-\$20) \times 0.05 + 0.01 \times (-\$20)] \\ & + [(-0.01) \times \$4{,}000 + \$500 \times 0.11 + (-0.01) \times 500] \\ & - [(-0.01) \times \$2{,}500 + \$400 \times 0.07 + (-0.01) \times \$400] \\ & - [(-0.01) \times \$800 + \$580 \times 0.09 + (-0.01) \times \$580] \end{aligned}$$

$$\begin{aligned} -22.6 = {} & [6 - 1 - 0.2] + [-40 + 55 - 5] \\ & - [-25 + 28 - 4] - [-8 + 52.2 - 5.8] \\ = {} & 4.8 + 10 + 1 - 38.4 \end{aligned}$$

Table 13.6
Analysis of Variations for Mirage Bank

	December 31, 1994		December 31, 1995	
	$	Rate	$	Rate
Interest Earning Assets				
Securities	$600	5%	$580	6%
Loans	4,000	11	4,500	10
Interest-Paying Liabilities				
Time deposits	$2,500	7%	$2,900	6%
Long-term debt	800	9	1,380	8

From these calculations we can see that the total net interest income decrease of $22.6 between 1994 and 1995 resulted from net increases of $4.8 from Mirage Bank's securities, $10 from the loans, and a $1 increase produced by time deposits. The only net decrease of $38.4 occurred in the long-term debt account. Unfortunately, this is the figure that dominated the overall change in the net interest income.[7]

Leverage, Profitability, and Risk

As we saw in Chapter 9, risk and expected return are inseparable. This means that one way to increase the bank's profitability is to increase its riskiness. Another way to increase risk is to use more leverage, or debt. This type of risk is known as **financial risk**. In this section we analyze how leverage simultaneously increases the bank's expected profitability and its financial risk.

Consider a very simple bank that generates only interest income and has all of its assets (A) in the form of loans earning an annual rate of r_L percent. The bank is financed solely with debt (D) paying r_D percent per year, and with equity (E). From the balance sheet identity, we have $A = D + E$. If we measure the profitability of the bank with the return on equity ratio, we have:

$$ROE = \frac{\text{Net Income}}{\text{Equity}}$$

$$= \frac{r_L A - r_D D}{E} \tag{13.24}$$

Recall that the equity multiplier ratio is defined as $EM = A/E = D/E + 1$. After simplifying we can write the return on equity for this simple bank as:

$$ROE = r_L + (r_L - r_D)\frac{D}{E} \tag{13.25}$$

[7] Notice that the cross-terms contribute relatively little to the change of each of the four accounts. This is a typical result.

This expression shows that the return on equity of our simple bank consists of two factors. The first portion of the bank's *ROE* is equal to its average lending rate r_L. Thus, other things equal, we can expect our bank to perform better when lending rates are high. Second, the bank's return on equity depends on its leverage. If the spread between lending and borrowing rates, $r_L - r_D$, is positive, then higher debt-to-equity ratios lead to a higher return on equity. Clearly, in this case high leverage is desirable. However, if the spread is negative, a high leverage is disastrous since, as the *D/E* ratio increases, the *ROE* decreases. In this case, a sufficiently high leverage will lead to a negative return on equity.

If commercial banks could control the spread so that it is always positive, banks would essentially have no financial risk, and it would be optimal to have leverage levels as high as possible. Unfortunately, banks have a hard time controlling the spread. The essence of the problem lies in the fact that interest rates are constantly changing. However, bank lending rates tend to change at a slower pace than the rates on interest-paying liabilities. The reason is that many loans have fixed interest rates and have relatively long-term maturities. For example, the typical mortgage loan is a 30-year fixed-rate loan. By contrast, most liabilities tend to have much shorter maturities. For example, savings accounts can be withdrawn on demand, and certificates of deposit typically mature in less than one year.

As a result of this pervasive mismatch in maturities between assets and liabilities, the market rates on liabilities, r_D, fluctuate much more than the rates on interest-earning assets, r_L. Consequently, especially when interest rates have an upward trend, it is possible to have a negative spread between the lending and borrowing rate. In other words, leverage provides banks with the opportunity to earn more when the spread is positive, but it also carries with it the risk of incurring losses when the spread turns negative.

Figure 13.2 shows the relationship between leverage, as measured by the debt-to-equity ratio, and profitability, as measured by the return on equity. The cases of positive, zero, and negative spreads are depicted there. As the figure shows, when the bank has a positive spread, it should use as much leverage as possible. When the spread is zero, leverage is irrelevant to the bank's profitability. Finally, the figure shows that when the spread is negative, leverage hurts a bank.[8] The existence of negative spreads should be only a temporary phenomenon; otherwise, banks could not survive. Nevertheless, when such a scenario occurs, it may be enough to lead a poorly capitalized bank into bankruptcy.[9]

An Explanation for the Demise of the S&L Industry

Although our model is simple, it can explain the essential reasons for the demise of many savings and loan institutions. Recall that the primary function of these institutions is to provide funds for mortgage loans. In fact, they have been a major force in the doubling of home ownership in the United States, from about one-third of American families in the 1930s, to about two-thirds in the 1980s.

---

[8] In our model, a negative return on equity will occur if $D/E > r_L / (r_D - r_L)$.

[9] This explains why government regulation requires a minimum capital for banks. It also explains the need to constantly monitor compliance with the capital requirement, since banks have a great incentive to break the rule whenever the spread is positive.

Figure 13.2
The Effect of Leverage on Bank Profitability

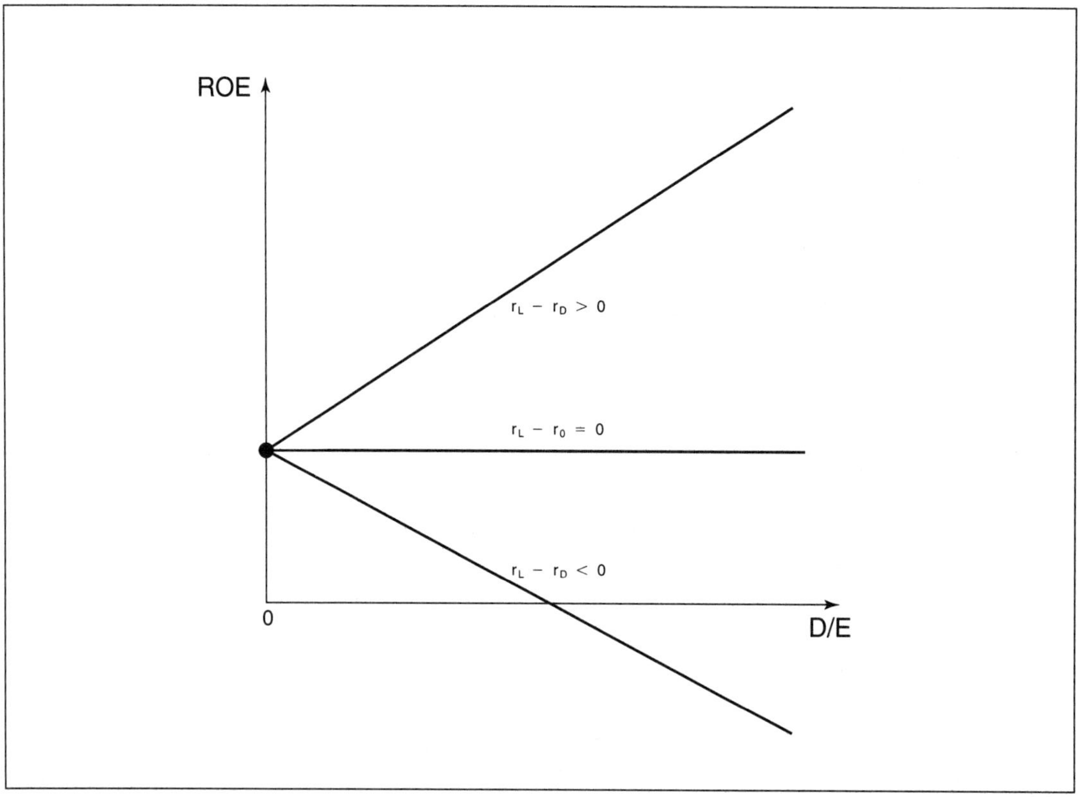

As long as interest rates on deposits were controlled (through Regulation Q), S&Ls were essentially assured of a positive spread and, therefore, were subject to very little financial risk. Their situation under regulation could essentially be described by the upward sloping line of Figure 13.2 where leverage has a positive effect on profitability, and risk is virtually nonexistent.

By the late 1970s and early 1980s the industry became increasingly deregulated and was forced to pay market rates to depositors. Since rates were at a historical high in the early eighties and rates on existing mortgage loans were fixed, S&Ls were suddenly faced with a negative spread. As losses mounted through the 1980s, many highly levered S&Ls succumbed as their small capital base eroded and, eventually, vanished. This S&L situation corresponds to the downward sloping line in Figure 13.2 where, given sufficient leverage, S&Ls would generate a negative return on stockholder's equity.

Given the tremendous maturity mismatch between the assets and liabilities of S&Ls, asset rates did not increase as fast as the rates on liabilities, so a negative spread occurred. A schematic representation of this phenomenon is shown in Figure 13.3, which depicts the evolution of the average loan rate and the average rate on time deposits for a typical S&L. The changes in the loan rates (r_L) and on short-term time deposits (r_T) are assumed to be of the same magnitude, but loan

Figure 13.3
Maturity Mismatch and Negative Spreads

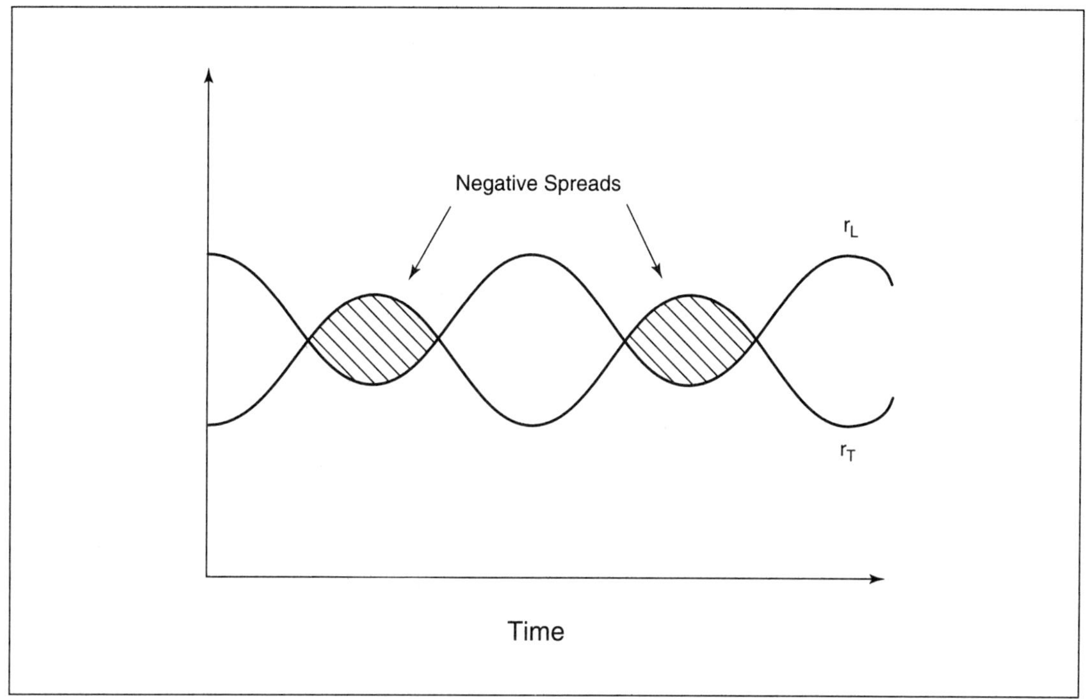

rates lag behind the time deposit rates. The lag occurs because loans have a much longer maturity than time deposits, so their average interest rate changes more slowly. As the figure shows, when interest rates on time deposits reach a peak, the spread is negative and, in that case, depository institutions with a maturity mismatch problem will suffer losses.

Currently, one of the major challenges for commercial banks and other depository institutions in a competitive marketplace is to manage their assets and liabilities in order to circumvent the widespread problem of mismatched maturities that may lead to negative spreads. This is the main focus of the next chapter.

Summary

This chapter discussed some of the most important concepts for managing commercial banks. We began with a discussion of how commercial banks use financial statements as managerial tools. Financial ratio analysis makes use of the bank's financial statements to gauge the financial health of the bank. Indeed, financial ratios are among the most important tools available to commercial bank managers.

The profitability of a commercial bank can be measured in various ways. We focused on the net interest margin, return on assets, and return on equity measures of profitability. In addition, we discussed the importance of the spread measure. In essence, if the spread becomes negative, banks may suffer losses.

We also discussed the technique of analysis of variations. This technique allows a commercial bank manager to pinpoint the cause of a change in the bank's profits between any two periods. In particular, an analysis of variations can determine the portion of the change that is due to lower interest rates, the portion that is due to a change in volume of the interest-earning and interest-paying accounts, and the portion that is due to the interaction of the two.

We then discussed how the composition of a commercial bank's liabilities can influence its profitability and risk. In particular, we focused on how the bank's financial leverage affects risk and return. To illustrate these concepts, we presented a feasible explanation for the collapse of the S&L industry in the 1980s.

Questions and Problems

1. How do the income statement and balance sheet differ in their summary of the events in an accounting period?
2. What are the three main financial statements?
3. Explain why the sources and uses of funds must be equal.
4. Define net interest income.
5. What is the difference between net interest income and adjusted net interest income?
6. If you know a commercial bank's earnings before taxes, *EBT*, and its tax rate, *t*, how can you determine the bank's net income?
7. React to the following statement: "Depreciation has no importance in managing a commercial bank because it is not a cash expense."
8. How is the equity multiplier related to the debt-to-asset ratio?
9. Define the spread.
10. How is the spread related to the return on equity?
11. What is the purpose of the analysis of variations?
12. How can a negative spread develop for a typical savings and loan institution?
13. The text provides an expression for the D/A ratio in terms of the D/E ratio. Find the expression relating the D/E in terms of the D/A ratio.
14. Show that if a firm has a positive net income and uses some debt, then its *ROE* will always be greater than its *ROA*.
15. Starting from the definition of *ROE*, show that $ROE = PM \times ATO \times EM$. (Hint: You can always multiply and divide any ratio by the same amount without affecting the result.)
16. A bank offers loans at an annual interest rate of 10 percent and pays 7 percent on its deposits. The amounts of each asset and liability are \$9,000 and \$6,000, respectively, and they are the

bank's only interest-earning and interest-paying accounts. What is the bank's net interest income?

17. If the bank in the previous problem makes a loan loss provision of $40, find the bank's adjusted net interest income.

18. A bank has $250 in earnings before taxes and is in the 30 percent ordinary income tax rate. Find the bank's net income.

19. The value of a bank's buildings totals $3 million, and they were built five years ago. The buildings are depreciated on a straight-line basis over their 20-year life, with no salvage value. What was the original value of the bank's buildings?

20. In the previous problem, what amount of cash does the depreciation expense generate for the bank? Assume a 35 percent tax rate.

21. What is the possible range of values for the debt-to-asset ratio?

22. What is the possible range of values for the debt-to-equity ratio?

23. A bank has a debt-to-equity ratio equal to 50 percent. What is the bank's debt-to-asset ratio?

24. If a bank's equity multiplier is equal to 15, what is its debt-to-equity ratio?

25. If a bank's equity multiplier is equal to 15, what is its debt-to-asset ratio?

26. A bank wishes to obtain a return on equity of 15 percent next year. Its interest-earning assets are $100 million, its equity is $12 million, and its tax rate is 30 percent. The bank has no loan losses, other income, or other expenses. However, next year it will have an annual depreciation of $3 million. What must the bank's net interest margin be in order to meet its goal?

27. The only assets of Simpleton Bank are its loans, *L*, and its only liabilities are time deposits, *T*. The loan portfolio of $10 million earns a 12 percent interest rate, and the bank pays 8 percent on its $9 million in time deposits. For next year, both assets and liabilities are expected to grow by 20 percent, loan rates are expected to be 11 percent, and time deposit rates are expected to be 6 percent. Perform an analysis of variations on Simpleton Bank.

References

Brewer, E. III and T. H. Mondschean, "Ex Ante Risk and Ex Post Collapse of S&Ls in the 1980s," *Economic Perspectives*, Federal Reserve Bank of Chicago, July/August 1992, pp. 2–12.

Goudreau, R. E., "Commercial Bank Profitability Rises as Interest Margins and Securities Sales Increase," *Economic Review*, Federal Reserve Bank of Atlanta, May/June 1992, pp. 33–52.

Hetzel, R. L., "Too Big to Fail: Origins, Consequences, and Outlook," *Economic Review*, Federal Reserve Bank of Richmond, November/December 1991, pp. 3–15.

Levonian, M. E., "Have Large Banks Become Riskier? Recent Evidence from Option Markets," *Economic Review*, Federal Reserve Bank of San Francisco, Fall 1991, pp. 3–17.

Mester, L. J., "Banking and Commerce: A Dangerous Liaison?" *Business Review*, Federal Reserve Bank of Philadelphia, May-June 1992, pp. 17–29.

Neuberger, J. A., "Risk and Return in Banking: Evidence from Bank Stock Returns," *Economic Review*, Federal Reserve Bank of San Francisco, Fall 1991, pp. 18–30.

Smith, S. D. and L. D. Wall, "Financial Panics, Bank Failures, and the Role of Regulatory Policy," *Economic Review*, Federal Reserve Bank of Atlanta, January/February 1992, pp. 1–11.

Asset and Liability Management of Commercial Banks

14

Overview

This chapter introduces the three fundamental principles of security price movement. Although the principles are relatively simple, they remain somewhat unwieldy by themselves because it is difficult to assess the different, but simultaneous, influences of cash flows, maturity, and changing interest rates on security price changes. However, it is possible to develop a single measure of a security's price sensitivity to changing interest rates. This measure is called **duration**, and this chapter extends the basic security pricing principles to include this summary measure of sensitivity.

When managing a portfolio, the investor often has a particular horizon in view and would like to work to maximize the value of the investment at some future date. To this end, one of the most basic questions facing a portfolio manager concerns the proper maturity characteristics of the securities to hold in a portfolio. As discussed in this chapter, longer maturity securities tend to be more sensitive to interest rate changes and are riskier than comparable short-maturity securities, in the sense that their prices may fluctuate more.

This chapter also discusses the two-sided nature of interest rate risk. While prices drop when interest rates increase, for example, it is also true that the investor will be able to reinvest the future cash flows received from a security at a higher rate. Thus, securities are subject to **price risk** as well as to **reinvestment rate risk**. An important characteristic of all securities is that these two types of risk always work in opposite directions.

In the face of difficulties with forecasting interest rates, portfolio managers have learned to focus on various kinds of immunization techniques. An **immunization strategy** seeks to make a certain financial variable immune, or insensitive, to changes in interest rates. Some of these immunization strategies rely on the concept of duration as a key element. Others rely on the concept of the funding GAP. The **funding GAP** is the difference between assets and liabilities that are sensitive to variations in interest rates. We discuss both types of strategies in this chapter.

Security Pricing Principles

In security pricing, it is essential to understand the ways in which the prices of securities with different characteristics respond to changes in the market rate of interest. The effect of a given change in interest rates on the price of a security depends on three key variables:

1. The maturity of the security
2. The cash flow stream promised by the security
3. The level of interest rates at the time of the change in interest rates

This section develops three well-recognized principles of security pricing that explain how the price of a given security changes in response to a sudden change in interest rates. These principles demonstrate the different effects of a change in interest rates as a function of the security's three key variables. Throughout this section, we assume interest rates change instantaneously from one level to another and then examine the resulting security price change.

The starting point is the basic valuation equation for any security, shown in Equation 14.1. This expression simply states that the current price of a security (P_0) equals the sum of the present values of all promised cash flows from the security (C_t), when those cash flows are discounted to the present at the security's risk-adjusted discount rate (r).

$$P_0 = \sum_{t=1}^{M} \frac{C_t}{(1+r)^t} \tag{14.1}$$

We will refer to this fundamental equation throughout the chapter to explain how security prices are affected by changes in the general level of interest rates.

Interest Rates and Security Prices

The most basic relationship involving interest rates and security prices is given in Principle 1 below.

Principle 1
Security prices move inversely with interest rates.

To understand this principle, note that in Equation 14.1 the present value of the payment at time t depends on the value of the denominator, which depends on both the amount of time until the payment is to be received and the rate of discount applied to the payment. The higher the rate of interest in Equation 14.1, the larger the denominator and the smaller the present value of the cash flow. Since this is true of each payment, the price of the security decreases with an increase in the discount rate.

Principle 1 can be illustrated using a 30-year, 10 percent coupon bond, which we call Bond *L*. If the face value of this bond is \$100 and interest rates are 10 percent, then its price would be \$100 over its whole life, assuming interest rates remained at 10 percent. This bond must sell at par because its coupon rate is equal to the discount rate applied to the bond. Alternatively, the price of this, and any other, coupon bond can be obtained from the general formula:

$$P_0 = C\,\frac{1-(1+r)^{-M}}{r} + F(1+r)^{-M} \tag{14.2}$$

where C is the periodic coupon payment, r is the periodic interest rate, F is the bond's face value, and M is its maturity.

If interest rates change suddenly from 10 percent to 8 percent, we can use Equation 14.2 to compute the new price of the bond. In this case the new price is \$122.52. Conversely, if interest rates suddenly rise from 10 to 12 percent, the bond will trade for \$83.89, as summarized as follows:

Bond *L*: 30-year, 10% coupon

r	P_0
12%	\$83.89
10%	\$100.00
8%	\$122.52

Figure 14.1 shows the price of Bond *L* for a variety of discount rates, or yields. We will refer to this kind of graph as a **price/yield curve** because it shows how the bond's price is related to its yield. Notice the negative slope of the graph and its degree of curvature.

For a zero discount rate, the price of an *M*-year bond with a coupon of *C* and a face value of *F* is equal to:[1]

$$P_0(r = 0) = M \times C + F \tag{14.3}$$

Figure 14.1
The Price/Yield Curve for Bond *L*
(n = 30; C = \$10; F = \$100)

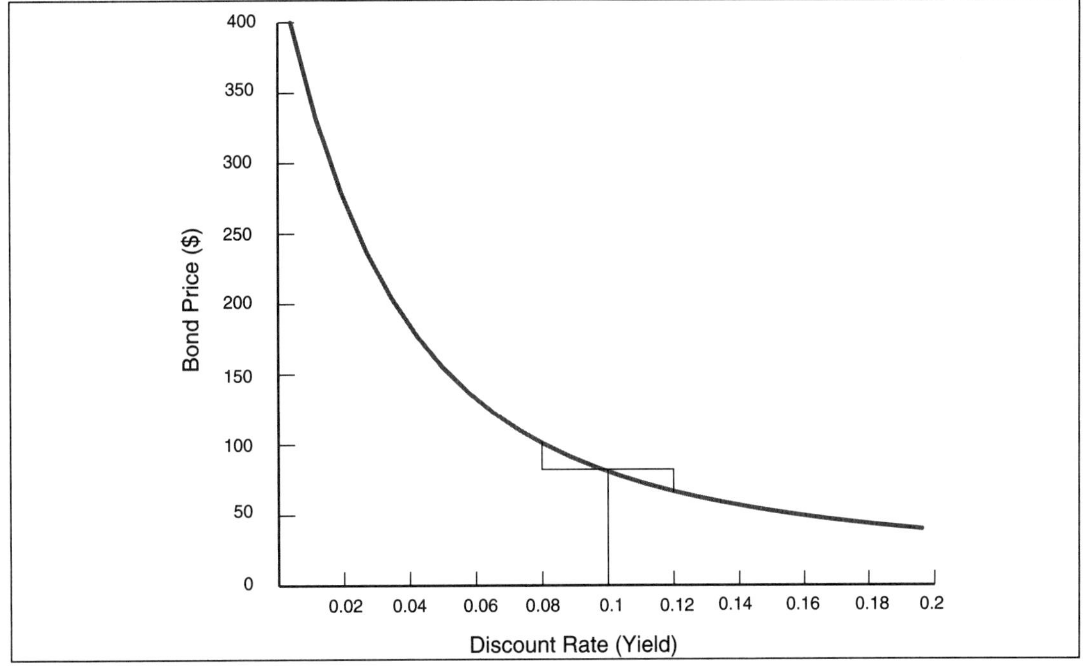

---

[1] If you try to obtain this expression from the general valuation formula for bonds, Equation 14.2, you will run into trouble because the operation involves dividing by zero, which is not permitted. Nevertheless, you can always use Equation 14.1 to value the bond, noting that all of the denominators are equal to $(1 + 0)^t = 1$.

For Bond L, the price for a zero discount rate is $30 \times \$10 + \$100 = \$400$.

At the other extreme, as yields become very high, the slope of the price/yield curve flattens and tends to become parallel with the discount rate axis. Thus, security prices tend to zero as yields increase.

As shown in Figure 14.1, the slope of the price/yield curve for Bond L is negative. This negative slope is a characteristic shared by all securities. The expression for the slope of the price/yield curve for any security is given by:[2]

$$\text{Slope} = -\frac{1}{1+r}\sum_{t=1}^{M} t\,\frac{C_t}{(1+r)^t} \tag{14.4}$$

Equation 14.4 confirms that the slope of any price/yield curve is negative, provided all of the cash flows are positive, a very mild requirement for securities. Notice that the slope of the price/yield curve measures how fast prices change as interest rates change. The slope expression in Equation 14.4 will be extremely useful in our discussion of duration later in the chapter.

Figure 14.1 also illustrates that price changes are asymmetric with respect to changes in interest rates. This fact is contained in Principle 2.

Principle 2
For a given security, the price increase caused by a yield decrease is greater than the price decrease caused by a yield increase of the same magnitude.

As noted in Principle 1, security prices vary inversely with yields. According to Principle 2, a given change in yield has a greater effect on the price of the bond when the yield drops than when the yield rises. We can illustrate this principle by considering Bond L again. Recall that Bond L is a 30-year, 10 percent coupon bond.

		Percentage Price	
Rate	**Price**	**Increase**	**Decrease**
8%	$122.52	22.52	
10%	$100.00		
12%	$83.89		16.11

For an initial rate of 10 percent, the price of Bond L is $100. If the interest rate decreases by 200 basis points to 8 percent, the price increases by 22.52 percent to $122.52. However, if the interest rate increases by 200 basis points, the price will decrease by 16.11 percent, from $100 to $83.89. We can see that for the same change in discount rates, a falling rate causes a price gain that is larger than the price drop caused by the same-size increase in rates. We can also see the same result in Figure 14.1. Graphically, Principle 2 is a direct consequence of the convex curvature of the price/yield curve.

---

[2] In terms of calculus, the slope of the price/yield curve is the derivative of the security's price with respect to its yield. Equation 14.4 can be obtained by differentiating Equation 14.1 with respect to r.

Maturity and Security Prices

While an increase in interest rates causes the price of any security to fall, according to Principle 1, the amount of the fall depends on the maturity of the security. Principle 3 states the relationship between maturity and the amount of change in the price of a security.

Principle 3
The longer the maturity of a security, the more sensitive is its price to a change in interest rates, holding other factors constant.

To understand why this principle holds for all securities, consider Equation 14.4, which indicates that the slope of the price/yield curve depends on the cash flows of the security C_t, on the level of interest rates, r, and on the maturity of the security, M. By increasing the maturity of a security, the summation in Equation 14.4 becomes greater because it has more terms. As a result, the negative slope of the price/yield curve becomes more negative as maturity increases, other things being equal. Principle 3 is verified by noting that price sensitivity is directly related to the slope of the price/yield curve: The greater the absolute value of the slope, the more sensitive is the price of the security to a change in the discount rate.

To illustrate the greater sensitivity of longer maturity securities to changes in interest rates, consider again Bond *L*, which has a maturity of 30 years and a coupon rate of 10 percent. For comparison, we introduce Bond *S*, which has a maturity of five years and a coupon rate of 10 percent. Thus, Bonds *L* and *S* have the same coupon rate, but Bond *L* has a longer maturity than Bond *S*. According to Principle 3, Bond *L* should be more sensitive to changes in interest rates than Bond *S*, because Bond *L* has the longer maturity. To illustrate this relationship, consider an initial position for both bonds in which they yield 10 percent and then observe the price change on each bond when the interest rate drops from 10 to 8 percent or rises from 10 to 12 percent.

Bond *L*: 30-year, 10% coupon
Bond *S*: 5-year, 10% coupon

	Interest Rates			Percentage Price Change	
	r = 8%	r = 10%	r = 12%	Yield Falls	Yield Rises
P_L	$122.52	$100.00	$83.89	+22.52	−16.11
P_S	$107.99	$100.00	$92.79	+7.99	−7.21

Bonds *L* and *S* differ only in their maturities, with their coupon rates and initial yields being the same. When interest rates fall from 10 to 8 percent, both bond prices increase, in accordance with Principle 1. However, the price of Bond *L* increases by 22.52 percent, while the price of Bond *S* increases by only 7.99 percent. Similarly, an interest rate increase from 10 to 12 percent decreases the price of Bond *L* by 16.11 percent, whereas the price of Bond *S* decreases by only 7.21 percent. These numbers show that Bond *L* (with a maturity of 30 years) is more sensitive than Bond *S* (with a five-year maturity) to interest rate changes.

Figure 14.2 shows the price/yield curves for Bonds L and S. The figure shows that both bonds are priced at \$100 for a yield of 10 percent. This is the point where the two curves cross. For lower yields, both bond prices are greater than \$100, and for higher yields, both bond prices are below \$100. The main difference between the curves for the two bonds is the relative steepness, or slope, of the curve for Bond L, which shows its greater sensitivity to changes in yields. This is exactly the point of Principle 3: the longer the maturity, the greater the sensitivity of the bond's price to a change in yields.

In general, security price changes, ΔP, are related to interest rate changes, Δr, through the slope of the price/yield curve. The approximate formula is:[3]

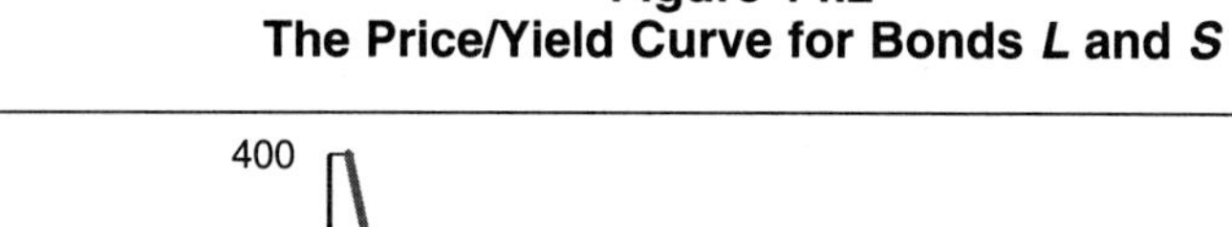

$$\Delta P \approx \text{Slope} \times \Delta r \qquad (14.5)$$

where the exact expression for the slope of the price/yield curve is given in Equation 14.4. Note that since the slope of the price/yield curve is negative for all securities, a positive change in interest rates produces a negative price change, in accordance with Principle 1. Since Equation 14.4 is rather cumbersome to evaluate, a very good approximation to the slope can be found from Equation 14.5 by computing the price change resulting from a change in interest rates and then dividing by the change in interest rates.

Figure 14.2
The Price/Yield Curve for Bonds *L* and *S*

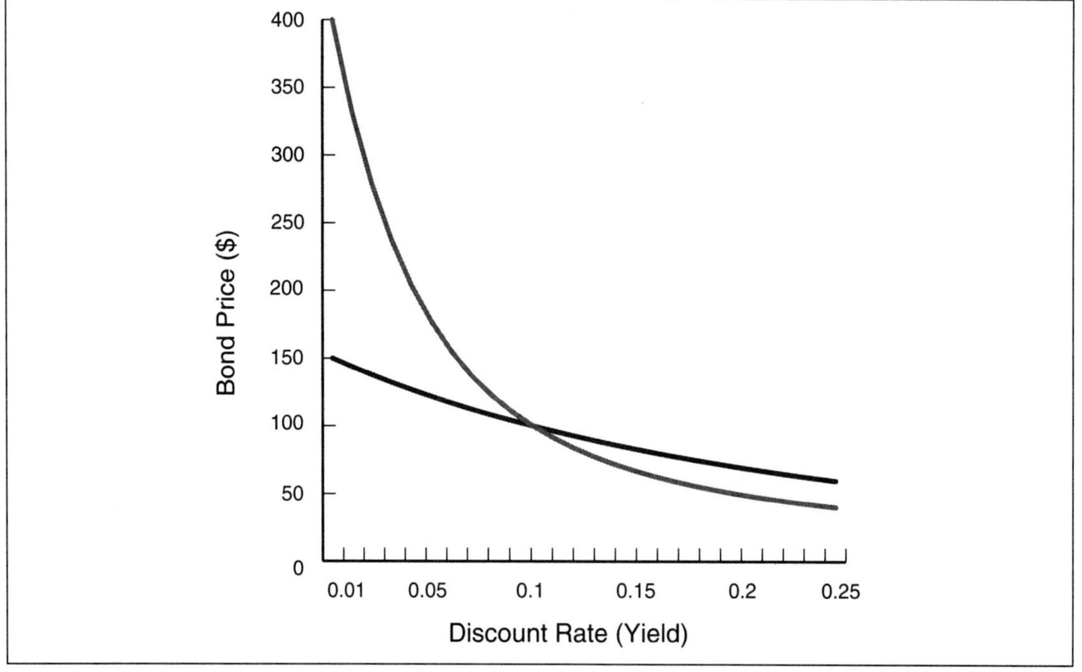

---

[3] Equation 14.5 is exact only for infinitesimal changes in interest rates. Of course, this is not possible in the real world. The accuracy of the equation decreases as the change in interest rates increases.

To calculate the approximate value of the slope for Bond L at an interest rate of 10 percent, consider an interest rate change of 2 percent. The approximate slope of Bond L is ($\$122.52 - \$100.00)/(0.08 - 0.10) = -1{,}126.0$ when interest rates drop from 10 to 8 percent, and it is $(\$83.89 - \$100.00)/(0.12 - 0.10) = -805.5$ when interest rates rise from 10 to 12 percent. Given the large assumed change of 2 percent, there is a substantial difference between the two slopes calculated. The average value of the slope is $-(1{,}126 + 805.5)/2 = -965.75$, and this figure provides a reasonably close approximation to the actual slope. In fact, the true value of the slope for an infinitesimal interest rate change away from 10 percent is equal to -942.69, calculated from Equation 14.4.

Principle 3 has immediate practical applications. Consider our two bonds; if interest rates rise, both bond prices will drop. Assume that interest rates rise by 2 percent on both bonds. The price of Bond L will drop more than the price of Bond S. If a bank carries both bonds in its investment portfolio and fears rising interest rates, it might consider selling Bond L because it is more sensitive than Bond S to the change in rates. Conversely, if the bank anticipates falling yields, the bank might consider selling Bond S and use the proceeds to increase its holdings of Bond L because its price would rise more than the price of Bond S.

The Need for a Summary Measure

The three principles of security pricing are all very important for a thorough understanding of how security prices are connected to interest rates. However, since each of the principles assumes that all other factors are held constant, except for the one under examination, it is still difficult to compare the price sensitivity of different securities. As an example, consider Bonds X and Y.

Bond X: 30-year, $C = \$14$, $F = \$100$, $r = 10\%$; $P = \$137.71$
Bond Y: 20-year, $C = \$7$, $F = \$100$, $r = 10\%$; $P = \$74.46$

Although both bonds have the same yield, their maturities and coupon rates differ. If we consider only the maturity, we would think that Bond X is more sensitive than Bond Y, in accordance with Principle 3. However, because the other variables are not equal for both bonds, Principle 3 does not apply, so our conclusion could be wrong. Merely by inspecting the features of these bonds, we cannot decide which is more sensitive to a change in interest rates. It would be very convenient to have an index of a security's price sensitivity to interest rate changes that allowed direct comparisons between various securities.

For Bonds X and Y, Table 14.1 shows that the two bonds have virtually identical price sensitivities to interest rate changes. For a drop in yields from 10 to 9 percent, the price of Bond X increases by 9.97 percent, while the price of Bond Y rises by 9.78 percent. Similarly, if yields rise from 10 to 11 percent, the price of Bond X falls by 8.45 percent and the price of Bond Y falls by 8.47 percent.

Here we find that two bonds of very different coupon and maturity can have a price sensitivity that is almost identical. Accordingly, it would be very useful to have a summary measurement of a security's price sensitivity that reflects all of the factors affecting its price sensitivity – the maturity, the cash flow stream, and the discount rate. Such a measure is called **duration**.

Table 14.1
Relative Price Changes of Bonds *X* and *Y*

Bond	Price at 9% (% Change)	Price at 10.0%	Price at 11% (% Change)
X	$151.37 (9.97%)	$137.71	$126.08 (−8.45%)
Y	$81.74 (9.78%)	$74.46	$68.15 (−8.47%)

Duration

A concept first developed in the late 1930s by Frederick Macaulay, **duration** is a single number for each security that summarizes the key factors that affect the sensitivity of a security's price to changes in interest rates.[4] In its original interpretation, duration was designed to measure the economic life of financial instruments, in contrast to their maturity, or legal life. Consider, for example, that the applicable interest rate is 10 percent for Securities *A* and *B*, and that they have the characteristics given in Table 14.2.

Both securities have a maturity of two years and pay the same cash flows of $10 and $100. However, the timing of the cash flows is inverted for the two securities: Security *A* pays the $100 in year 1, whereas Security *B* pays it in year 2. Because Security *A* pays the bulk of its cash flow earlier than Security *B*, it seems reasonable to argue that *A* has a shorter economic life than *B*, even though both have the same two-year maturity.

To measure the intuitive difference in economic lives just discussed, Macaulay introduced the concept of duration. In essence, the duration, *D*, of a security is the weighted average of the various times at which its cash flows occur. Thus, we have Equation 14.6 on the following page.

Table 14.2
The Cash Flows of Securities *A* and *B*

	Year 1	Year 2	Price
Security *A*:			
Cash flow	$100.00	$10.00	
Present value (r = 10%)	$90.91	$8.26	$99.17
Security *B*:			
Cash flow	$10.00	$100.00	
Present value (r = 10%)	$9.09	$82.64	$91.73

[4] See F. R. Macaulay, *Some Theoretical Problems Suggested by the Movements of Interest Rates, Bond Yields, and Stock Prices in the United States Since 1856*, New York: Columbia University Press, 1938.

$$\text{Duration} = \sum_{t=1}^{M} t \times w_t \tag{14.6}$$

In Equation 14.6, the weight, w_t, that applies to time period t is equal to the present value of the associated cash flow, C_t, divided by the current price, P_0, of the security. Thus, the weight that applies to time t is:[5]

$$w_t = \frac{\dfrac{C_t}{(1+r)^t}}{P_0} \tag{14.7}$$

Substituting Equation 14.7 into 14.6 and rearranging, we get the final expression for Macaulay's duration (D):

$$D = \frac{1}{P_0} \sum_{t=1}^{M} t \frac{C_t}{(1+r)^t} \tag{14.8}$$

Operationally, the duration equation takes the time periods when cash flows are received and multiplies each time period by the present value of the cash flow promised at that time. All of these products are summed, and the sum is divided by the current price of the bond. Since duration is a measure of the average life of a security, as shown in Equation 14.6, it is expressed in time units such as days, months, or years.

How to Calculate Duration

As an example of how to calculate Macaulay's duration, let us again consider Securities A and B, both with two-year maturities. Using the present values and prices calculated in Table 14.2, the duration of Security A is:

$$D_A = 1\frac{\$90.91}{\$99.17} + 2\frac{\$8.26}{\$99.17} = 1.08 \text{ years}$$

Similarly, the duration of Security B is:

$$D_B = 1\frac{\$9.09}{\$91.73} + 2\frac{\$82.64}{\$91.73} = 1.90 \text{ years}$$

Consistent with our discussion, we find that Security A has a much shorter duration, or economic life, than Security B. Not surprisingly, the duration of each security in our example tends to be much closer to the $100 cash flow than to the $10 cash flow. The time line in Figure 14.3 shows the relative position of the duration of Securities A and B.

---

[5] Since the price of a security is equal to the sum of the present values of all its cash flows, it follows that the sum of the weights is always equal to 1. This is a basic requirement when calculating any weighted average.

Figure 14.3
Time Lines for Securities A and B

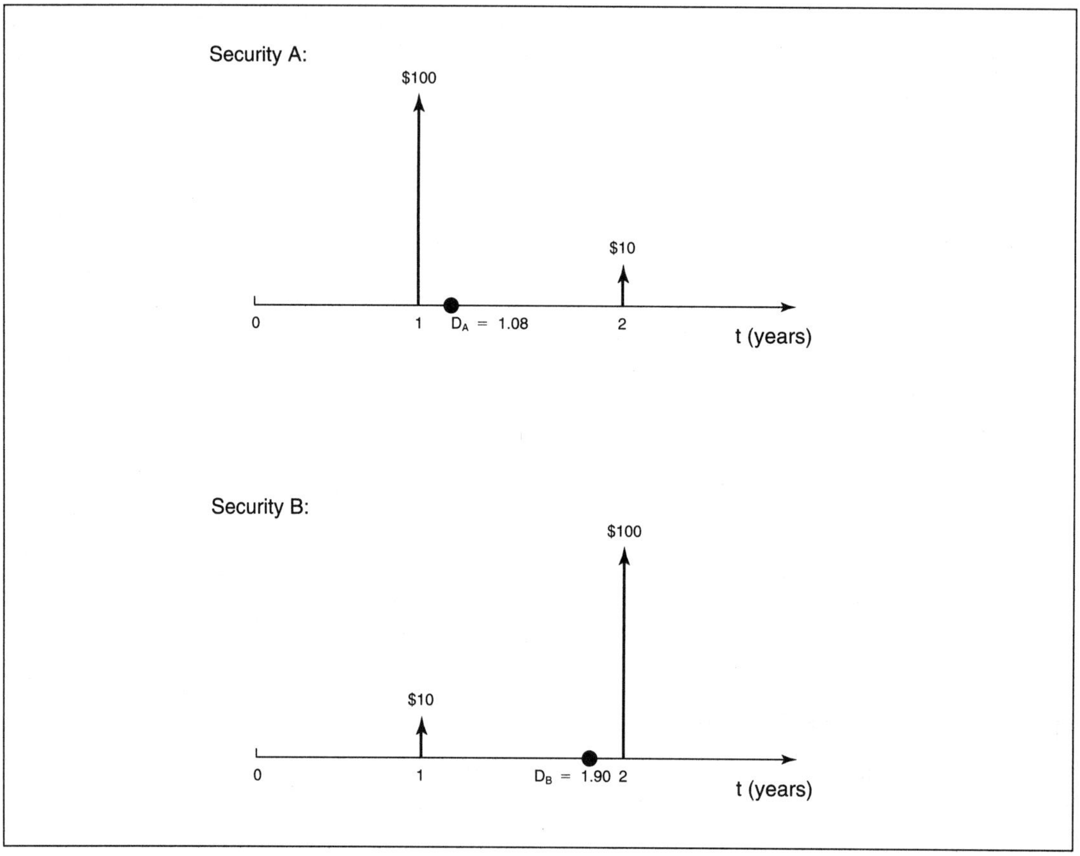

Security A:

t (years)	0	1	2
Cash flow		$100	$10

$D_A = 1.08$

Security B:

t (years)	0	1	2
Cash flow		$10	$100

$D_B = 1.90$

Duration and the Slope of the Price/Yield Curve

The power of the duration concept can only be unleashed by realizing that it is intimately connected to the slope of the price/yield curve. Indeed, by comparing the slope expression given in Equation 14.4 with the definition of duration in Equation 14.8, we have:

$$\text{Slope} = -D\frac{P_0}{1+r} \tag{14.9}$$

Since we have seen that the slope of the price/yield curve measures the sensitivity of a security's price to changes in interest rates, it follows from Equation 14.9 that the higher the duration of a security, the greater its sensitivity to interest rate changes, other things equal.

We can use the expression for the slope of the price/yield curve given in Equation 14.9, and substitute it in Equation 14.5, which measures the change in a security's price resulting from a change in the level of interest rates. This results in the following expression:

$$\Delta P \approx -D \frac{P_0}{1+r} \times \Delta r \tag{14.10}$$

A more elegant way to express Equation 14.10 is the following:[6]

$$\frac{\Delta P}{P_0} \approx -D \frac{\Delta(1+r)}{1+r} \tag{14.11}$$

Equation 14.11 indicates that, for any security, the percentage price change it suffers is directly proportional to the percentage change in the one-year discount factor, $(1 + r)$. For example, if interest rates change from 10 to 12 percent, the percentage change in the one-year discount factor is 1.82 percent $[(1.12 - 1.10)/1.1]$, so any security with a duration equal to five years will suffer a 9.1 percent drop in price $[-5 \times 1.82\%]$. Note, however, that the values given by Equations 14.10 and 14.11 are only approximations and that their accuracy diminishes as interest rate changes increase.[7]

We can now see why Bonds *X* and *Y* could be so different in maturity and coupon and still have the same percentage price changes – they have virtually the same duration. For Bond *X*, the duration is 10.043 years, and for Bond *Y*, the duration is 10.002 years. Thus, Bonds *X* and *Y* have essentially the same sensitivity to changes in interest rates. Because they have almost the same duration, the prices of Bonds *X* and *Y* will change by about the same percentage amount for a given percentage change in yields.

Duration as an Elasticity Measure

We can rearrange Equation 14.11 to express duration as the negative of the security's elasticity of price with respect to a change in the discount factor $(1 + r)$:

$$D \approx -\frac{\dfrac{\Delta P}{P_0}}{\dfrac{\Delta(1+r)}{(1+r)}} \tag{14.12}$$

Equation 14.12 shows that duration is essentially an elasticity measure. Macaulay's duration gives a single measure of the way in which a security's price changes for a change in the discount factor, $(1 + r)$. As before, this formula is only an approximation; it gives the exact value only for infinitesimal changes in interest rates.

---

[6] Notice that $\Delta r \equiv \Delta(1 + r)$. For example, if interest rates change from 10 to 12 percent, then $\Delta r = 0.12 - 0.10 = 0.02$, and $\Delta(1 + r) = 1.12 - 1.10 = 0.02$.

[7] The careful reader will note that Equation 14.10 appears to violate Principle 2 because it seems to indicate that price changes are symmetric. This apparent violation is a direct result of the approximate nature of the equation.

The Intrinsic Error in the Duration Measure

To see how discrepancies between actual prices and prices estimated by the price change formula involving duration arise, consider Figure 14.4. The figure shows a portion of the price/yield curve for an arbitrary security. The straight line is tangent to the curve at point *O*, which corresponds to a yield of r_0 percent and a price of P_0. The tangent line shows the estimated price of the security according to the duration formula. Thus, if interest rates change from r_0 to r_1, the formula in Equation 14.10 gives a new security price of P_1, corresponding to point *A* on the straight line. The price calculation using duration produces an error because the exact price after the change is actually equal to P_1*, corresponding to point *B* on the price/yield curve.

We can see that the essential problem is that the price change formula involving duration, Equation 14.10, does not take into account the curvature of the price/yield curve. By assuming that price and yields are linearly related around the point *O*, the formula produces an error. Figure 14.4 clearly shows that the error increases as the change in interest rate increases.[8]

Figure 17.4
Understanding the Error in the Duration Formula

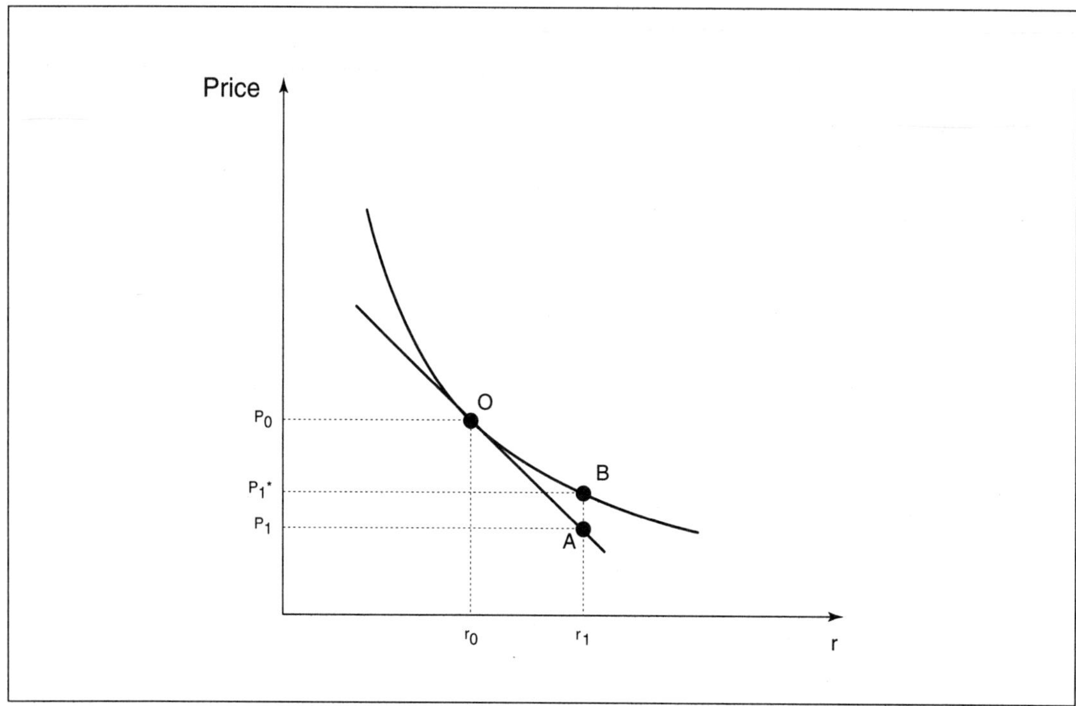

---

[8] In an attempt to correct for the intrinsic error caused by the use of duration, researchers have suggested adding a correction factor. The theory on which this correction factor is based is called **convexity**. For a thorough discussion of convexity, see Robert W. Kolb, *Investments*, 4th ed., Miami: Kolb Publishing Company, 1995.

Some Qualifications on Duration

The conclusions we have reached about duration are based on three assumptions. First, we assume that the yield curve is flat at the time the yield change occurs. Second, we assume that only parallel shifts in the yield curve occur. Therefore, the yield curve after the change in rates is still flat. Finally, the analysis holds for a single change in yields. We consider the practical implications of each assumption in turn.

Restriction to Flat Yield Curves

The analysis of this chapter has assumed that the yield curve is flat. As we saw in Chapter 7, the yield curve relates the yield on a security to the time remaining until the security matures. For example, in the bond pricing formula, Equation 14.2, all cash flows are discounted at a single common rate, no matter how far into the future a cash flow is actually received. This assumption was carried over into our duration measure. By considering only a common yield for all of the payments, we have implicitly assumed that the yield curve is flat. The practical implications of this assumption are not as limiting as they might at first appear.

Restriction to Parallel Shifts in Yield Curves

Our analysis has also focused on a parallel shift in yield curves. Because we are using the same yield to discount all cash flows without regard to the time that they are actually paid, we have seen that the yield curve is assumed to be flat. By the same token, if we consider a change in the one common yield applied to all of the security's cash flows, we are assuming that the yield curve shifts in a parallel fashion. For example, if yields are at 10 percent, we have assumed a flat yield curve at 10 percent. If we then consider a change in yields to 11 percent, our analysis assumes that the resulting yield curve is flat at 11 percent. Because the yield curves are flat before and after the yield change, they have shifted in a parallel fashion.

These two assumptions, of a flat yield curve and a parallel shift, are potentially very limiting to the practical application of our analysis. After all, yield curves are seldom flat, and changing yields typically result in a yield curve with a new shape. However, researchers have found that these concerns have only very small practical results.[9] As a consequence, it seems permissible to use Macaulay's duration measure with little concern for the effects of changing yield curve shapes.

Restriction to a Single Change in Yields

In our analysis, we have focused on a single change in yields, but in actual markets, yields change frequently. This can be important because duration changes as yields change. This occurs because the slope of the price/yield curve changes as the yield changes, and we have seen in Equation 14.9 that duration is proportional to the slope of the price/yield curve. Therefore, when interest rates change frequently, we have to recalculate the duration of the security at each new yield in order to have a reasonably close estimate of the price change that will occur in the next yield change. In

---

[9] G. O. Bierwag surveys the practical importance of yield curve shapes on duration models in his book, *Duration Analysis*, Cambridge, MA: Ballinger Publishing Company, 1987. See Chapters 11 and 12 particularly.

practical portfolio management, the need to rebalance a portfolio based on its changing duration is a problem that can be managed quite satisfactorily.

Thus, the assumptions that we have made turn out not to interfere too much with the practical application of duration to security investing. In fact, the last decade has seen its use become almost universal among portfolio managers, especially for fixed-income portfolios.

The Two Sides of Interest Rate Risk

Interest rate risk is the possibility that interest rates may vary unexpectedly. As we have already discussed at length, such changes will necessarily affect the price of all securities. Thus, it might appear that an increase in interest rates is something that security holders should avoid at all cost. Surprisingly, this is not necessarily true. For example, while prices decrease when interest rates increase, it is also true that investors will be able to reinvest the future cash proceeds from any security at a higher interest rate. Thus, there is a beneficial as well as a negative effect to interest rate changes.

There are two major risks resulting from a change in interest rates. First, there is **price risk**, as contained in the three universal principles already studied. Price risk is damaging when interest rates increase. Second, a security is also subject to **reinvestment rate risk**, which is detrimental to the security holder when interest rates decrease.[10]

To illustrate the two-sided nature of interest rate risk, consider a security that provides a four-year annuity of $100 per year plus a cash flow of $160 in year 5. If interest rates are 10 percent, the current value of this security is $416.33. You believe that interest rates may change by 2 percent immediately after you buy the security, but you are uncertain about the direction of the change. Given your doubts, you wish to know the possible values of your accumulated wealth by the time the security matures at time 5. Assume that you reinvest all the proceeds of the security at the prevailing rate.

Table 14.3 shows the accumulated value of each of the payments at maturity. For example, the payment of $100 received one year after you purchase the security will accumulate to $\$100(1 + 0.10)^4 = \$146.41$ when the security matures, if interest rates remain at their current level. However, if interest rates increase to 12 percent just after buying the security, then the same payment will accumulate to $157.35 when the security matures. The other values in the table are similarly calculated.

As Table 14.3 shows, if the five-year security is held to maturity, its owner faces a relatively large risk, since the resulting terminal wealth may be as low as $646.66 if interest rates fall to 8 percent, or as high as $695.28 if interest rates increase to 12 percent just after the security is bought. If interest rates remain unchanged, the security will provide a terminal wealth of $670.51. Thus, the investor may benefit or suffer from an interest rate change, depending on the direction of the change.

---

[10] Reinvestment rate risk has been painfully obvious for investors in the early 1990s. As medium- and long-term investments such as CDs matured, many investors found that the new rates at which they could roll over their money were as low as 3 percent – the lowest rates in more than 30 years.

Table 14.3
Terminal Wealth with a Five-Year Horizon

		Rate (%)		
Time	Cash Flow	8	10	12
0	−$416.33			
1	100.00	$136.05	$146.41	$157.35
2	100.00	125.97	133.10	140.49
3	100.00	116.61	121.00	125.44
4	100.00	108.00	110.00	112.00
5	160.00	160.00	160.00	160.00
Terminal Wealth		$646.66	$670.51	$695.28

Portfolio Immunization Techniques

If one holds the position that it is impossible to forecast interest rates, active portfolio management has little appeal. If the portfolio manager does not know how to alter a portfolio to take advantage of an expected shift in interest rates because he or she has no good reason to expect one shift rather than another, active portfolio management has no useful role.

As portfolio managers have accepted this perspective, passive strategies have become more popular, particularly a set of techniques known as **portfolio immunization**. For an immunized portfolio, the terminal wealth is not affected by a change in interest rates. In recognition of an inability to predict interest rates, many portfolio managers find it makes sense to immunize their portfolios against losses caused by changes in interest rates. Immunization techniques involving duration fall into two general categories: the Planning Period Case and the Bank Immunization Case. Even though they both rely on duration, they are conceptually very different.

The Planning Period Case

The first basic type of immunization for portfolios concerns managing a portfolio toward a horizon date. For many portfolios, especially bond portfolios, there is a definite planning period, with the goal being to achieve a target value for the portfolio at the end of the planning period. For example, a wealthy family might establish a trust fund for a child, with instructions that the child have access to the funds on his or her twenty-first birthday. In such a situation, the portfolio should be managed with that horizon or planning period in view. A similar problem occurs in pension fund management, with the portfolio manager managing the securities in the pension fund with a horizon date set in the future when pensions become payable.

To illustrate how a portfolio manager with a definite planning horizon can immunize a portfolio against unexpected interest rate changes, consider once again a security that pays $100 for each of the next four years, plus a final payment of $160 five years from now. As Table 14.3 shows, this security sells for $416.33 when interest rates are 10 percent. The table also shows that any investor planning to hold the security until maturity faces considerable uncertainty regarding the terminal wealth provided by the security.

Now assume that another investor has a planning period of three years and decides to hold the same security until just after the third payment of $100 is received, at which time it will be sold at its market price. Since interest rates may change, the market price at time 3 is determined by discounting the payments to be received at times 4 and 5 at the rate prevailing at time 3. The results are shown in Table 14.4. As shown there, the accumulated interest at time 3 increases and the price at time 3 decreases as the interest rate increases. In other words, reinvestment rate risk and price risk work in opposite directions.

As Table 14.4 shows, with a three-year investment horizon both types of risk counteract each other almost perfectly for our five-year security. Equivalently, the investor's terminal wealth at time 3 is essentially the same regardless of the level of interest rates. In fact, if interest rates move in either direction, the investor with a three-year horizon actually receives slightly more terminal wealth than if interest rates remain unchanged!

Although it is not immediately apparent, the virtual elimination of terminal wealth risk using the three-year holding period strategy for the security just analyzed is due to the fact that it has a duration of 3.006 years, as the reader can verify. This example illustrates the following general rule:

A portfolio is immunized when its duration matches the planning horizon.

Knowing this general rule, we can understand why holding the five-year security to maturity gives an uncertain terminal wealth. The problem arises from the fact that the duration of the security is less than the planning period. With a duration of 3.006 years, and a planning period of five years, this security is not immunized against interest rate changes.

Derivation of the Immunization Rule

An analysis of Table 14.4 reveals that immunization in the example of the five-year security whose owner has a three-year horizon occurs because the change in the accumulated interest at the investor's planning horizon is the same as the change in the price of the security at that same time, but of opposite sign, for any change in interest rates. It is also useful to note that the accumulated

Table 14.4
Terminal Wealth with a Three-Year Horizon

		Rate (%)		
Time	Cash Flow	8	10	12
0	–$416.33			
1	100.00	$116.64	$121.00	$125.44
2	100.00	108.00	110.00	112.00
3	100.00	100.00	100.00	100.00
Accumulated Interest		$324.64	$331.00	$337.44
Price at $t = 3$		$229.77	$223.14	$216.84
Terminal Wealth		$554.41	$554.14	$554.28

interest involves a process of compounding the cash flows received up to the horizon, whereas the calculation of the price at the horizon requires discounting all cash flows to be received from that date until the security matures.

If we denote the terminal wealth for a given level of interest rates, r, as $TW(r)$, the maturity as M, the planning horizon as H, and the cash flow provided by a security at time t as C_t, then we can write the terminal wealth at the horizon as:

$$TW(r) = \sum_{t=1}^{H} C_t(1 + r)^{H-t} + \sum_{t=H+1}^{M} \frac{C_t}{(1 + r)^{t-H}} \tag{14.13}$$

The first summation in Equation 14.13 calculates the accumulated interest from time 1 to the planning horizon, time H. For example, the very first payment received after purchasing the security, C_1, will compound at a rate r for $(H - 1)$ periods. Similarly, the second summation represents the present value of all cash flows from time $(H + 1)$ to time M, the security's maturity, evaluated at time H. This present value is the price of the security at time H. The terminal wealth is the sum of these two components. Also, as Equation 14.13 stresses, the terminal wealth received by the investor depends on the level of interest rates, r.

Since the term $(1 + r)^H$ inside each summation does not depend on the index t, it can be taken out of the summations. Thus, Equation 14.13 can be expressed as follows:

$$TW(r) = (1 + r)^H \left(\sum_{t=1}^{H} \frac{C_t}{(1 + r)^t} + \sum_{t=H+1}^{M} \frac{C_t}{(1 + r)^t} \right) \tag{14.14}$$

Now note that the terms inside the brackets in Equation 14.4 are nothing but the present value of all cash flows, discounted to time zero. In other words, the terms in brackets represent the price of the security at time zero, so we have:

$$TW(r) = (1 + r)^H \times P_0(r) \tag{14.15}$$

To illustrate the use of Equation 14.15, consider the situation shown in Table 14.4 for an interest rate of 10 percent. For the horizon of three years, Equation 14.15 indicates that the terminal wealth is $(1.10)^3 \times \$416.33 = \$554.14$, which is the same value calculated in the table.

Equation 14.15 is the fundamental expression needed to obtain the rule stating that the terminal wealth from a security or portfolio is immunized against interest rate changes when the planning horizon is equal to the duration of the security or portfolio. Using this equation, we can evaluate the change in terminal wealth resulting from a small change in interest rates. The resulting expression is:[11]

$$\Delta TW(r) = H(1 + r)^{H-1} \times P_0(r) \times \Delta r + (1 + r)^H \times \Delta P_0(r) \tag{14.16}$$

---

[11] Once again, this expression is only an approximation. It is only exact for infinitesimal changes in the level of interest rates. The reader with a knowledge of differential calculus can derive this expression as an exercise.

Since our objective is to eliminate any variation in terminal wealth caused by a change in interest rates, we wish to have $\Delta TW(r) = 0$. Applying this requirement to Equation 14.16, recalling that $\Delta r \equiv \Delta(1 + r)$, and rearranging, we obtain:

$$H = -\frac{\frac{\Delta P}{P_0}}{\Delta\frac{(1 + r)}{(1 + r)}} \tag{14.17}$$

Thus, Equation 14.17 shows that the planning horizon must be equal to the right-hand side in order to immunize a security or portfolio against variations in interest rates. All that remains is to recall that the right-hand side of this equation is approximately equal to the duration of the security or portfolio, as shown in Equation 14.12. Therefore, immunization requires satisfying the condition $H = D$, which proves the general rule stated above.

The Bank Immunization Case

This second form of immunization gets its name from the fact that it first came into prominence in commercial banking. In its simplest possible form, a commercial bank obtains its funds from two basic sources: equity (E) and the acceptance of deposits and other liabilities (L) from the public. The bank then uses those funds to make loans and purchase other assets (A). Given the balance sheet identity, we can write $E = A - L$.

One of the main concerns of commercial banks is to avoid a deterioration of their equity value, E. Since the value of equity, like the value of any other security, may vary as a result of changes in the level of interest rates, commercial bank managers are constantly monitoring the effect of interest rate changes on the value of the bank's equity. We already know that the change in the price of any security as a result of a change in interest rates is proportional to the duration of that security, as Equation 14.10 shows, so the objective of management is to minimize the duration of its equity. Ideally, commercial banks attempt to eliminate the duration of equity.

To understand how the duration of equity can be eliminated, at least in principle, we use the balance sheet identity and the fact that durations are additive.[12] In other words, given that $E = A - L$, we have:

$$D_E = D_A \times \frac{A}{E} - D_L \times \frac{L}{E} \tag{14.18}$$

Equation 14.18 expresses the fact that the duration of any portfolio is the weighted average of the duration of each of its components. In the case of our simple bank, its equity can be viewed as a portfolio consisting of buying assets and selling liabilities, with the weights being A/E and $-L/E$ for assets and liabilities, respectively.[13]

---

[12] The reader is asked to prove this basic fact about duration in an end-of-chapter problem.

[13] Notice that the sum of the weights add to 1.0, as they must.

Applying Equation 14.10 to the bank's equity, we obtain:

$$\Delta E \approx -D_E \frac{E}{1+r} \Delta r \qquad (14.19)$$

From Equation 14.19 it is clear that if the bank is to immunize the value of its equity against changes in interest rates, it must reduce the duration of its equity to zero. From Equation 14.18, this means that the following condition must hold for the bank to be immunized:

$$\frac{D_A}{D_L} = \frac{L}{A} \qquad (14.20)$$

According to Equation 14.20, equity value immunization is achieved by a commercial bank when the ratio of the average durations of its assets and liabilities is equal to the bank's leverage, as measured by the ratio of its liabilities to its assets. Since the ratio of liabilities to assets is less than 1.0, immunization requires that the average duration of the bank's assets be less than the average duration of the bank's liabilities. Unfortunately, one of the pervasive problems in commercial banking is the short duration of the liability portfolio, due to the fact that most deposits can be withdrawn on very short notice. By contrast, most of the asset portfolio consists of loans that have been provided for longer periods, since banks make commercial and consumer loans and also provide long-term mortgage financing of up to 30 years. As a result, in practice it is very hard for commercial banks to achieve the condition for immunization given in Equation 14.20.

To illustrate these results, consider Table 14.5, where Panel A shows the position of Simple National Bank, which holds a liability portfolio with a market value of $900 and an asset portfolio with a market value of $1,000. Given the balance sheet identity, this implies that the current value of the bank's equity is $100. The average duration of the liability portfolio is one year, and the average duration of the asset portfolio is five years. Assume, for the sake of simplicity, that the average interest rate earned or paid on each portfolio is 10 percent. With very different durations on the two portfolios, the bank has considerable interest rate risk. According to Principle 1, if

Table 17.5
The Balance Sheet of Simple National Bank

Assets		Liabilities	
Panel A: 10% Interest Rate			
Asset Portfolio (Duration = 5 years)	$1,000	Liability Portfolio (Duration = 1 year)	$900
		Owner's Equity	$100
Panel B: 12% Interest Rate			
Asset Portfolio	$909.09	Liability Portfolio	$883.64
		Owner's Equity	$25.45

interest rates fall, security values will rise, so the value of both portfolios rises as well. But according to Equations 14.10 and 14.11, the asset portfolio is five times as sensitive to a change in interest rates as the liability portfolio because its duration is five times as large. If interest rates rise, however, all security values fall, and the asset portfolio will fall in value much more than the liability portfolio.

To see the effect of an interest rate change on the bank, assume that interest rates rise from 10 percent to 12 percent on both the asset and liability portfolios. Then, from Equation 14.10 we can see that for Simple National Bank the change in the value of the liability portfolio will be:

$$\Delta L \approx -1\left(\frac{\$900}{1.10}\right) 0.02 = -\$16.36$$

For the asset portfolio, the same change in rates creates a much larger drop in the portfolio's value:

$$\Delta A \approx -5\left(\frac{\$1{,}000}{1.10}\right) 0.02 = -\$90.91$$

The effects on the bank are shown in Panel B of Table 14.5. Because the duration of the asset portfolio is so much greater, the effect of the rise in rates caused its value to drop much more than the value of the liability portfolio. Consequently, starting from a position of \$100 of owners' equity, the bank moved to an equity position of only \$25.45 after the rise in interest rates.

The same values can be calculated using Equations 14.18 and 14.19. From Equation 14.18 we find the duration of the bank's equity, which is equal to:

$$D_E = 5 \times \frac{\$1{,}000}{\$100} - 1 \times \frac{\$900}{\$100} = 41 \text{ years}$$

We can now substitute the duration of equity just calculated into Equation 14.19 to find the change in the bank's equity value caused by an interest rate increase of 2 percent.

$$\Delta E = -41\left(\frac{\$100}{1.10}\right) 0.02 = -\$74.55$$

This calculation shows that the equity value of Simple National Bank will plunge by \$74.55 if interest rates increase by 2 percent, leaving it with a final equity value of \$25.45. This is the same result we obtained before.

As the example illustrates, the equity of Simple National Bank is subject to considerable interest rate risk, a prospect that is not cherished by its shareholders. However, by careful management of its liabilities and assets, the bank might achieve the immunized balance sheet shown in Panel A of Table 14.6, where the asset and liability portfolios have average durations of 3.15 and 3.5 years, respectively. In this case, the duration of the bank's equity can be found using Equation 14.18 and is equal to:

Table 14.6
The Immunized Balance Sheet of Simple National Bank

Panel A: 10% Interest Rate			
Assets		**Liabilities**	
Asset Portfolio (Duration = 3.15 years)	$1,000	Liability Portfolio (Duration = 3.5 years)	$900
		Owner's Equity	$100
Panel B: 12% Interest Rate			
Assets		**Liabilities**	
Asset Portfolio	$942.73	Liability Portfolio	$842.73
		Owner's Equity	$100

$$D_E = 3.15 \times \frac{\$1{,}000}{\$100} - 3.5 \times \frac{\$900}{\$100} = 0 \text{ years}$$

Since the duration of the bank's equity has been eliminated, the value of equity is now insensitive to changes in interest rates. At this point, the bank's equity is essentially immunized because the change in rates leaves the equity value of the bank unchanged. This is shown in Panel B of Table 14.6. Note, however, that the values of the bank's asset and liability portfolios have changed and are now equal to $942.73 and $842.73, respectively. Since the value of both assets and liabilities drops by the same amount, the value of the equity remains unchanged.

It must be noted that perfect immunization is very difficult for many financial institutions to achieve. Due to the nature of commercial banking, which involves accepting short-term deposits and making long-term loans, meeting the immunization condition shown in Equation 14.20 is very difficult in practice. Nevertheless, commercial banks continually strive to approach the durations dictated by Equation 14.20 as much as possible, even if perfect immunization cannot be achieved. In fact, virtually every bank in the country has an asset/liability management committee. The committee plays a crucial role in the management of the bank, and the maturity and duration structure of the two sides of the bank's balance sheet are among the most important issues the committee addresses.

The Funding GAP

In addition to duration-based techniques for managing interest rate risk, commercial banks can also immunize other financial variables by using the funding GAP, or simply GAP, analysis. As we have seen, with duration techniques, the focus is on maintaining the value of a bank's equity. With the GAP technique, the objective is to immunize the bank's net interest income or net interest margin.

In any commercial bank some assets and liabilities are sensitive to changes in interest rates, while others are not. For example, an adjustable-rate mortgage is an example of a variable rate asset, since the rate on the mortgage will fluctuate periodically with the general level of interest rates. Similarly, a three-month CD is a variable rate liability when viewed over a one-year horizon, since when the CD matures the bank will probably issue another CD at the prevailing rate at that time. Thus, over a one year horizon, the bank faces interest rate risk on the proceeds of the CD.

We can classify all the assets and liabilities of a commercial bank into the following four categories according to their sensitivity to interest rate changes:

Variable rate asset	*VRA*
Variable rate liability	*VRL*
Fixed rate asset	*FRA*
Fixed rate liability	*FRL*

It is important to note that classifying an asset or liability as either variable rate or fixed rate depends critically on the time horizon chosen. For example, we have seen that a three-month certificate of deposit is a variable rate liability over a one-year horizon, but it is a fixed rate liability over a one-month horizon. Consequently, special care must be exercised to consider the appropriate horizon when classifying a bank's assets and liabilities.[14]

The **funding GAP** is defined as the difference between the bank's assets and liabilities that are sensitive to changes in interest rates over the planning horizon. Formally, we have:

$$GAP = VRA - VRL \tag{14.21}$$

The importance of the GAP concept lies in the fact that changes in the bank's net interest income and net interest margin are closely related to its funding GAP. This connection is shown in the next section.

Net Interest Income and the Funding GAP

Whenever a commercial bank wants to keep its net interest income, *NII*, immune from variations in interest rates, it must manage its funding GAP closely. To understand how the GAP affects the bank's net interest income, recall that a bank's *NII* is defined as the difference between interest income and interest expense. In terms of our classification of assets and liabilities, we have:

$$NII = VRA \times r_{VA} + FRA \times r_{FA} - VRL \times r_{VL} + FRL \times r_{FL} \tag{14.22}$$

In Equation 14.22, the subscripts for each interest rate variable identify the average rate corresponding to each type of asset or liability. For example, r_{VA} represents the average rate for all variable rate assets.

[14] Notice that, over a sufficiently long horizon, all assets and liabilities are classified as variable rate. Of course, to paraphrase the great economist John Maynard Keynes, over a sufficiently long horizon, we will all be dead.

By definition, an interest rate change will only affect variable rate assets and liabilities over the planning horizon. Thus, we have:

$$\Delta NII = VRA \times \Delta r_{VA} - VRL \times \Delta r_{VL}$$

If we also assume for the sake of simplicity that the change in interest rates is the same for assets and liabilities, so that $\Delta r_{VA} = \Delta r_{VL} \equiv \Delta r$, then the change in net interest income, ΔNII, can be expressed as:

$$\Delta NII = (VRA - VRL)\Delta r \qquad (14.23)$$

From Equations 14.21 and 14.23 we get the desired relationship between a change in interest rates and a change in the bank's net interest income:

$$\Delta NII = GAP \times \Delta r \qquad (14.24)$$

We can now see how a bank might immunize its net interest income against changes in interest rates. According to Equation 14.24, interest rate changes must be multiplied by the bank's funding GAP to obtain the change in net interest income. It follows that immunizing the net interest income requires that the bank eliminate its funding GAP. In other words, we have the following simple immunization rule:

A bank immunizes its net interest income over a given planning horizon whenever its variable rate assets are equal to its variable rate liabilities.

Notice from Equation 14.24 that the change in net interest income has the same sign as the change in interest rates. This means that if the bank's management strongly believes that interest rates will rise, it should try to maximize its funding GAP. Conversely, if interest rates are expected to decline, the funding GAP should be made as negative as possible. Unfortunately, the business of forecasting is very risky, and many banks prefer not to speculate on the future course of interest rates. In that case, the best strategy is to minimize the absolute value of the funding GAP. Ideally, when future interest rates are very uncertain, the funding GAP should be zero if the bank is to avoid a fluctuation in its net interest income.

Net Interest Margin and the Funding GAP

The funding GAP is also very important in managing the bank's net interest margin. Recall that the *NIM* is defined as the bank's net interest income for each dollar of earning asset it holds. Thus:

$$NIM = \frac{NII}{EA} \qquad (14.25)$$

From Equation 14.25 we can see that a change in net interest income will produce a change in net interest margin equal to:

$$\Delta NIM = \frac{\Delta NII}{EA}$$

or, using Equation 14.24:

$$\Delta NIM = \frac{GAP}{EA} \times \Delta r \qquad (14.26)$$

Equivalently, we can also write Equation 14.26 as follows:

$$GAP = EA \times \frac{\Delta NIM}{\Delta r} \qquad (14.27)$$

As was the case with the net interest income, changes in the bank's net interest margin as a result of interest rate changes depend critically on the funding GAP. Specifically, the *NIM* will not fluctuate when interest rates change if the funding GAP is equal to zero. Although this is extremely hard to achieve in practice, it is possible to manage the bank's assets and liabilities in order to keep the GAP within acceptable levels.

To illustrate these results, consider a bank with earning assets of $100 million. The bank's projections call for an *NIM* of 4 percent over the next year. Since the bank believes that interest rates may fluctuate by 200 basis points, the expected *NIM* may not be achieved. Nevertheless, the bank's management is willing to accept a variation of 50 basis points in the *NIM* as a result of the expected change in interest rates. This means that the bank can accept an *NIM* as low as 3.5 percent. To find the maximum range of the funding GAP that is consistent with the fluctuation in *NIM* that the bank can tolerate, we apply the values of this example to Equation 14.27. The calculation is:

$$GAP = \$100 \text{ million} \times \frac{50bp}{200bp} = \$25 \text{ million}$$

This means that if the bank has a funding GAP of $25 million, and interest rates change by 200 basis points in either direction, the *NIM* will change by 50 basis points in the same direction. Notice that the same 50 basis point fluctuation will occur if the bank has a funding GAP of −$25 million, but the change in *NIM* will be of opposite sign as the change in interest rates. Thus, if the bank maintains the absolute value of the GAP at less than $25 million (between −$25 million and +$25 million), it will experience a variation in *NIM* of less than 50 basis points whenever interest rates do not fluctuate more than 200 basis points.

Given the practical difficulty of maintaining a GAP of zero, this example illustrates how the GAP technique may be used to keep the variability of net interest income at levels that commercial banks find reasonable.

The Funding GAP and Equity Immunization

In the previous sections we have seen that duration techniques are most useful when immunizing the value of a bank's equity. In particular, the duration of equity must be set to zero to achieve immunization. We have also seen that the funding GAP technique is most appropriate when the objective is to immunize either the net interest income or the net interest margin of a bank. In this section we show how the funding GAP technique can also be used to immunize equity. Surprisingly, we will see that it is normally not possible to immunize *both* the bank's equity and its net interest income simultaneously.

We begin by modeling the equity value of the bank as the present value of all future dividends. This valuation model was described in Chapter 5. To simplify, we assume that the bank's net income is equal to its net interest income, *NII*, and that the bank follows a constant dividend payout policy. This means that if the annual earnings of the bank are equal to *NII*, the dividend payment for that year will be $d \times NII$, where d is a fractional number representing the percentage of the bank's earnings that are paid as dividends. Finally, we assume that the bank has the same net income every year, forever. The value of the bank's equity is just the present value of all future dividend payments. Thus, we have:[15]

$$E = \frac{d \times NII}{r} \tag{14.28}$$

Using Equation 14.28 and the methods of differential calculus, we find the expression for the change in the value of the bank's equity that results from a change in interest rates:

$$\Delta E = \frac{d \times \Delta NII}{r} - \frac{E}{r}\Delta r \tag{14.29}$$

We can now substitute Equation 14.24 into Equation 14.29 and simplify to get:

$$\Delta E = \frac{d \times GAP - E}{r}\Delta r \tag{14.30}$$

From Equation 14.30 we can see that a bank will immunize its equity against interest rate changes if it meets the following condition:

$$GAP = \frac{E}{d} \tag{14.31}$$

Several conclusions can be obtained from Equations 14.30 and 14.31. First, a bank must maintain a positive GAP if it is to have any hope of immunizing its equity. This is due to the fact

---

[15] Although these assumptions seem restrictive, they are actually very mild and do not substantially affect the conclusions of this section.

that both E and d are positive financial variables in Equation 14.31.[16] This has the immediate implication that if the bank's equity is immunized, its net interest income cannot be immunized because the GAP is positive. Conversely, when the GAP is zero, so that the net interest income is immunized, the bank's equity will fluctuate with interest rate changes. Indeed, from Equation 14.30, if GAP = 0, we have:

$$\Delta E_{(GAP=0)} = -\frac{E}{r}\Delta r \tag{14.32}$$

From Equation 14.32 we can see that the bank's equity will decrease when interest rates increase, even though its net interest income remains unchanged because the GAP is zero. Thus, when the net interest income is immunized, the bank's equity value will fluctuate in the opposite direction of the change in interest rates.[17]

To illustrate these results, consider a bank with \$100 million in variable rate assets earning an average interest rate of $r_{VA} = 10$ percent. The bank also has \$100 million in variable rate liabilities, on which it pays $r_{VL} = 9$ percent annual interest. There are no fixed rate assets or liabilities, or any other income or expense. Thus, the bank expects to have a net interest income of $\$100 \times 0.10 - \$100 \times 0.09 = \$1$ million for this year. If we assume that the bank will have the same earnings every year, that it pays half of its net earnings as dividends, and that the required rate of return on its equity is 20 percent, then the value of its equity will be equal to:

$$E = \frac{0.5 \times \$1 \text{ million}}{0.20} = \$2{,}500{,}000$$

Assume now that all interest rates experience a parallel shift of 1 percent. Thus, the interest rates on the bank's assets and liabilities increase to $r_{VA} = 11$ percent and $r_{VL} = 10$ percent. In this case, the bank's new net interest income will be $\$100 \times 0.11 - \$100 \times 0.10 = \$1$ million, the same as before the change. Since this bank has a GAP of zero, its net interest income is immunized. However, after the parallel interest rate shift, the required rate of return is 21 percent, rather than 20 percent, so the new value of the bank's equity is:

$$E = \frac{0.5 \times \$1 \text{ million}}{0.21} = \$2{,}380{,}952$$

In this example, an increase in the level of interest rates decreased the value of the bank's equity by over \$119,000, even though the net interest income remained at \$1 million before and after the change.

---

[16] Some might argue that equity can become negative. In fact, this actually happened to many banks during the 1980s. While this is true, no banker would want to immunize its bank's equity in such a dismal situation.

[17] Another simple way to see this result is to focus on Equation 14.28, noting that *NII* is constant when the GAP is zero, and that the interest rate is represented by r in the denominator. Under this scenario, E and r vary in opposite directions.

From the analysis presented in this section we conclude that banks cannot simultaneously immunize their net interest income or margin and the value of their equity. Given this conflict, which financial variable should be immunized? In times of uncertain interest rates, bank management should protect the value of the bank's equity as its primary concern. After all, obtaining a positive net interest income is really only an intermediate step in the bank's quest to maintain and increase the value of the shareholder's investment.

Summary

This chapter began by examining how security prices respond to changes in interest rates. The three universal principles discussed show that:

1. Security prices move inversely to interest rates.
2. Price changes are asymmetric. That is, a given drop in interest rates causes a larger price increase than the price decrease caused by the same size increase in rates.
3. Securities of longer maturity are more sensitive to interest rate changes than otherwise equal short-term securities.

While these three principles accurately summarize the response of security prices to interest rate changes, it would be very useful to have a single measure that summarizes these different effects. Macaulay's duration is a single number that allows direct comparison of the sensitivity of different bonds with changes in interest rates. Duration measures the economic life of a security, as opposed to its maturity. The higher the duration, the more sensitive is a security to changes in interest rates. We also considered the way in which duration can be used to estimate security price changes that result from changing yields. In addition, we showed that duration is connected to the slope of the price/yield curve of a security.

Since the best evidence available suggests that interest rates cannot be forecast accurately on a consistent basis, many portfolio managers have adopted a passive strategy of portfolio immunization. An immunized portfolio is established to meet a certain goal. When the goal is to make the market value of a commercial bank's equity insensitive to interest rate changes, bank managers use duration-based immunization techniques. If, instead, the goal is to maintain a certain level of net interest income or net interest margin, most banks use the funding GAP technique.

The GAP technique can also be useful to immunize the bank's equity. Interestingly, a positive GAP is required for equity immunization. This means that a bank cannot simultaneously immunize its net interest income, which requires a zero funding GAP, and the value of its equity, which requires a positive funding GAP.

Questions and Problems

1. What are the three key variables that influence security pricing?

2. Assume that you are a money manager with a large stock of cash that you will be investing in bonds. You anticipate a strong upward movement in interest rates in general. What do your beliefs imply about the kinds of bonds you will select for investment, particularly with respect to maturity and coupon?

3. Again, assume that you expect sharply rising interest rates, and you will buy one of the follow-

ing two bonds: a 20-year 8 percent coupon bond or a 15-year 9¾ percent coupon bond. Does this give you enough information to make a decision? What else might you need to know?

4. Consider three 8 percent coupon bonds with 10-, 15-, and 20-year maturities. Which is the most sensitive to a change in interest rates? What do we mean by saying that one bond is more "sensitive" than another to changes in interest rates? Is the difference in sensitivity between the 10- and 15-year bonds the same as the difference in sensitivity between the 15- and 20-year bonds?

5. Two bonds in your portfolio have durations of four and six years. If interest rates rise by 1 percent, how will the price changes of the two bonds compare? Can you say what the ratio of the price changes for the two bonds will be?

6. As an investor, you are trying to decide between two bonds as investments for a four-year investment horizon. The first has a 12 percent coupon and matures in three years. The other is a zero coupon bond maturing in five years. Compare and contrast the risks associated with each bond and their suitability for your investment horizon.

7. Consider a five-year pure discount bond with a face value of $1,000 that yields 10 percent compounded annually. What is its price? What will its price be if interest rates suddenly rise to 11 percent? What will its price be if interest rates suddenly fall to 9 percent? Are the capital gain and loss the same?

8. What is the price of a three-year, 8 percent annual coupon bond yielding 11 percent and having a face value of $1,000? Assuming annual compounding, what is the duration of the bond?

9. For the bond of the previous question, assume that interest rates suddenly rise to 13 percent. Compute the new price of the bond by discounting the cash flows at the new rate and by using the duration price change formula. Are the two answers the same? Why or why not?

10. What is the duration of a pure discount bond yielding 8 percent and maturing in three years and having a face value of $1,000?

11. What is the duration of a 12 percent annual coupon bond maturing in five years and yielding 11 percent? Assume a $1,000 face value. (Question: Do you really need to know the face value to make this computation?)

12. Compare the sensitivity of the bonds in the two preceding questions.

13. Show that durations are additive. In other words, show that, if the duration of Security *A* is D_A, the duration of Security *B* is D_B, and the proportion of your money invested in each security is w_A and w_B, respectively, then the duration of the two-security portfolio, *P*, is equal to $D_P = D_A\, w_A + D_B\, w_B$. The prices of Securities *A* and *B* are P_A and P_B, respectively.

14. Today you purchase a $1,000 face value bond paying an 8 percent annual coupon and maturing in five years, for a price of $930. Assuming that you are able to reinvest all coupons at 11 percent, what is your terminal wealth after five years? Make the computations assuming a reinvestment rate of 7 percent.

15. Assume you have an investment horizon of five years. You purchase a pure discount bond with a five-year maturity and a face value of $1,000 for a purchase price of $621. Your friend purchases a 10 percent annual coupon bond with a face value of $1,000 at par. What is the current interest rate on each bond? Assuming that rates do not change, what will be the terminal wealth for each bond, assuming that your friend reinvests all coupons? Assume that immediately after purchase, interest rates drop to 8 percent. What will be the terminal wealth for the two investments?

16. What is portfolio immunization and what role does duration play in an immunization attempt?

17. What is a "passive" portfolio management strategy?

18. What is the difference between the "bank immunization" and the "planning period" immunization cases? Which would be more appropriate for a portfolio manager managing a portfolio with a horizon date eight years from now?

19. Given two bonds with durations of 7.3 years and 2.2 years, you are asked to split investment funds between them so that the resulting portfolio will have a duration of five years. Assume that you have $1,000,000 to invest. How much would you commit to each bond?

20. A bank has hired you as a consultant to advise it on its interest rate exposure. The bank has an asset portfolio of $1,000,000 with a duration of five years, and the portfolio is currently yielding 12 percent. This asset portfolio is funded by a liability portfolio, also worth $1,000,000 with a duration of 1.5 years and which is yielding 10.5 percent. Your problem is to advise the bank on its risk exposure in case interest rates change by 1 percent in either direction. Analyze the resulting position of the bank for both of these cases.

21. Assume that you are asked to manage a $1,000,000 immunized portfolio with a horizon date of three years. Two bonds are available to you: a five-year pure discount bond yielding 10 percent and a two-year 12 percent annual coupon bond yielding 12 percent. How would you make up the immunized portfolio from these two bonds?

22. For the preceding problem, what will be the terminal wealth of the portfolio assuming that interest rates do not change for three years? Now assume that interest rates drop by 1 percent on both bonds. Calculate the terminal wealth at the end of three years. Do the same assuming a 2 percent rise in rates.

References

Bierwag, G. O., *Duration Analysis: Managing Interest Rate Risk*, Cambridge, MA: Ballinger Publishing Company, 1987.

Christensen, P. E., F. J. Fabozzi, and A. LoFaso, "Bond Immunization: An Asset Liability Optimization Strategy," *The Handbook of Fixed Income Securities*, 3rd ed., Homewood, IL: Business One Irwin, 1991.

Chua, J. H., "A Generalized Formula for Calculating Bond Duration," Financial Analysts Journal, September/October 1988, pp. 65–7.

Malkiel, B. G., "Expectations, Bond Prices, and the Term Structure of Interest Rates," *Quarterly Journal of Economics*, May 1962, pp. 197–218.

Morrissey, T. F. and C. Huang, "A Nomogram for Estimating Duration," *Financial Analysts Journal*, January/February 1987, pp. 65–7.

Taylor, R. W., "Bond Duration Analysis: A Pedagogical Note," *Financial Analysts Journal*, July/August 1987, pp. 71–2.

Winkelmann, K., "Uses and Abuses of Duration and Convexity," *Financial Analysts Journal*, September/October 1989, pp. 72–5.

International Banking

15

Overview

This chapter provides an overview of international banking. As an area of inquiry, international banking has several distinct facets. First, we may think of the foreign activities of domestic U.S. banks. Second, many foreign banks operate branches in the United States. Third, banks from the major industrial nations compete in many countries around the world. This chapter considers each of these dimensions of international banking.

The discussion begins by considering the foreign activities of commercial banks holding U.S. charters. Recent years have seen only modest expansion of U.S. banks in the international arena, largely due to the problems that have plagued U.S. depository institutions in general. The chapter considers the regulatory environment that governs the foreign activities of U.S. banks and shows that this legislation is intended to stimulate the international activities of U.S. banks, at least in part.

The analysis then turns to the role of foreign banks in the United States. The last decade has witnessed a tremendous increase in foreign bank activity in the United States, with some estimates indicating that 30 percent of commercial bank lending in the United States originates with foreign-owned or-controlled banks. Clearly, foreign banking in the United States is a major competitive force with which U.S. banks must contend. As the chapter also discusses, the U.S. banking regulations concerning international banking are largely intended to ensure that foreign and U.S. banks compete under the same set of rules.

Large banks from the industrialized countries compete in a worldwide arena. Thus, Japanese and U.S. banks compete both in Japan and the United States, but they also compete in many other countries as well. As the chapter indicates, the last decade has seen a dramatic emergence of Japanese banks. Whereas the largest banks of a decade ago were mostly British and American, Japanese banks now clearly dominate the lists of the world's largest banks. To a large extent, the tremendous growth of Japanese banks is due to the problems that have plagued British and U.S. banks. However, Japanese banks have also grown rapidly because of differences in industrial organization.

In many foreign countries, including Japan, commercial banks operate in a much freer regulatory environment than do U.S. banks. In particular, many foreign countries allow their commercial banks to engage in investment banking activities. In addition, Japanese banks have been very strongly capitalized, which allows them to be very aggressive in opening new markets. During the same time, U.S. and British banks have confronted a crisis in their own capital bases. The chapter also considers the Basle Accord, an international agreement that mandates new and higher levels of capital for the major banks of the world.

On the international level, as with the domestic market, the main business of commercial banks is lending. International lending involves special risks, largely because of a web of international regulation and governmental policies. In the 1970s and early 1980s, commercial banks loaned huge sums to governments of emerging nations. Many of these borrowers defaulted, leading to the international debt crisis of the mid-1980s. In considering the development of the debt crisis, the chapter analyzes some of the special risks involved in international lending.

Foreign Activities of U.S. Banks

U.S. banks seek entry to banking markets in other countries to serve the international needs of existing customers and to establish new business with foreign customers. Banks may participate in foreign markets by operating banks in the U.S. with foreign interests or by establishing banking offices outside the United States. Since the 1960s, foreign activities of U.S. banks have grown dramatically, and the large U.S. presence in foreign markets dates from that period. Table 15.1 shows the claims of U.S. banks on foreigners by area of the world. Most claims on foreigners are concentrated in Latin America and the Caribbean. Together, claims on Europeans and Asians are about the same as claims on Latin America and the Caribbean.

With many U.S. industrial corporations having extensive foreign investments, U.S. banks must establish foreign operations to serve the needs of their original U.S. customers in those foreign ventures. U.S. commercial banks, like all firms, seek new customers to expand business and increase profits. By opening offices in foreign countries, U.S. banks hope to attract new deposits and new loan customers. Table 15.2 presents a percentage balance sheet for foreign branches of U.S. banks and shows the main asset and liability categories for these institutions. As Table 15.2 indicates, a substantial portion of the foreign office's assets are claims on the parent or on other foreign branches of the same bank, and the same is true of the liability structure of these foreign branches.

While total foreign bank activity may be most concentrated in Latin America and the Caribbean, as Table 15.1 shows, foreign branches are concentrated in just a few countries. Table 15.3 shows the distribution of foreign branch assets and liabilities for several key countries. Of the total assets of foreign branches of U.S. banks, 60 percent are concentrated in the United Kingdom, the Bahamas, and the Cayman Islands. In briefest terms, banks have established branches in these countries because they offer a stable political climate and relaxed banking regulations.

Table 15.1
Banks' Foreign Assets by Area of World
(billions of dollars)

Area of the World	Assets
Europe	119.3
Canada	17.8
Latin America and Caribbean	217.1
Asia	103.3
Africa	3.1
Other	2.8
Total	464.5

Source: *Federal Reserve Bulletin*, March 1995, Table 3.18.

Table 15.2
Percentage Balance Sheet of Foreign Branches of U.S. Banks

Assets	
Claims on U.S. parent bank	25.54%
Claims on other U.S. banks	2.04
Claims on U.S. nonbanks	4.38
Claims on foreign branches of U.S. parent	20.33
Claims on foreign banks	15.06
Claims on foreign public borrowers	3.37
Claims on foreign nonbanks	16.49
Other assets	12.79
Total Assets	100.00
Liabilities	
Negotiable CDs	2.46
To U.S. parent bank	23.90
To other U.S. banks	2.44
To U.S. nonbanks	8.45
To foreign branches of parent bank	20.25
To foreign banks	12.02
To foreign official institutions	3.43
To foreign nonbanks	18.52
Other liabilities	8.53
Total Liabilities	100.00

Source: *Federal Reserve Bulletin*, March 1995, Adapted from Table 3.14.

Table 15.3
Distribution of Foreign Branch Assets and Liabilities by Country

	Percent of total
United Kingdom branches	31.6%
Bahamas and Cayman branches	29.2
All other branches	39.1
Total	100.0

Source: *Federal Reserve Bulletin*, March 1995, Table 3.14.

U.S. Regulation of International Banking Activities

Regulation of international banking activities by agencies of the U.S. government can be traced to the Edge Act of 1919, named for its sponsor, Senator Walter E. Edge of New Jersey. More recently, the international activities of U.S. banks are principally regulated by the International Banking Act of 1978 (IBA) and by Regulation K (Reg K) of the Federal Reserve Board, which went into effect in 1979. In 1981, the Federal Reserve Board provided for the establishment of International Banking Facilities (IBFs), and the International Banking Act of 1987 (IBA 1987) updated some of the rules for international operations. In many instances, these laws also regulate the behavior of foreign banks operating in the United States We consider each of these laws and regulations in chronological order.

The Edge Act and Edge Act Corporations Prior to 1920, virtually all international banking services available to U.S. interests were provided by British banks. During and immediately after World War I, the need for U.S. banks to stimulate U.S. trade by operating internationally became clear. The Edge Act, passed in 1919, provided for the establishment of Edge Act Corporations (EACs or Edges) to conduct foreign banking operations under the supervision of the Federal Reserve Board.

Under the Edge Act, national banks of sufficient size could seek the approval of the Federal Reserve Board to operate EACs. These corporations could operate in foreign countries or in the U.S. EACs engage in international banking operations and foreign financial transactions, while their permitted U.S. domestic activities are extremely limited. Many EACs hold foreign investments for their parent banks instead of providing banking services directly.[1] Under the Edge Act, foreign banks were not permitted to own or operate EACs. By 1978, there were 124 EACs holding total assets of $16.8 billion, concentrated most heavily in Miami and New York.

International Banking Act of 1978 The International Banking Act of 1978 (IBA) made important changes in the framework of regulation for international banking. The IBA eliminated the reserve requirement that had been imposed previously on EACs. Perhaps even more importantly, the IBA allowed foreign banks to own and operate EACs in the United States. The new law also permitted domestic branching of EACs, which was much cheaper than establishing a completely new EAC. In sum, these changes sought to strengthen the powers of EACs and to permit EACs to compete with foreign-owned banks on a more even footing.

The IBA contained a number of other provisions aimed at creating a level playing field for U.S. and foreign banks. The law required that U.S. offices of foreign banks that accept deposits of less than $100,000 participate in FDIC insurance, and it imposed reserve requirements on offices of foreign banks that matched those requirements for domestically chartered banks. The IBA prohibited foreign banks operating in the United States from branching to another state, unless the new branch was to be restricted to only the activities permitted to EACs. Finally, the IBA also subjected U.S. offices of foreign banks to examination and supervision by U.S. banking authorities.

Regulation K

Although in force before the passage of the IBA, Regulation K of the Federal Reserve Board received substantial modification in 1979. This basic regulation is the vehicle under which the Federal Reserve Board exercises its authority over international banking operations. Under Regulation K, bank activities abroad are restricted to operations of a financial nature. Regulation

---

[1] Originally, an EAC had to engage either in foreign banking or foreign investment activities, but not both. This restriction was later dropped.

Table 15.4
Major Permissible Overseas Activities of Commercial Banks

Commercial banking
Commercial, consumer, and mortgage lending
Mortgage banking
Factoring
Leasing
Acting as a fiduciary
Underwriting life insurance
Providing financial advisory services
Data processing
Investment banking outside the U.S.
Operating travel agencies

Source: Adapted from Charles W. Hultman, *The Environment of International Banking*, Englewood Cliffs, NJ: Prentice Hall, 1990.

K follows the spirit of the IBA by attempting to ensure that domestically chartered banks have the same privileges as those open to U.S. offices of foreign banks. Table 15.4 lists the most important of these permitted activities.

International Banking Facilities

In 1981, the Federal Reserve Board announced regulations that permitted the establishment of International Banking Facilities (IBFs). In essence, these rules permitted U.S. banks to establish a facility to receive deposits from foreigners and allowed these deposits to be free of reserve requirements and interest rate limitations. The purpose of these enabling regulations was to allow U.S. banks to attract funds from foreigners that were otherwise going to non-U.S. banks that operated in a freer regulatory environment. Today, IBFs hold deposits of about $300 billion, with 80 percent of IBFs being based in New York.

International Banking Act of 1987

The International Banking Act of 1987 (IBA 1987) brought U.S. offices of foreign banks under the control of the Federal Reserve Board. The act essentially put these offices of foreign banks on the same regulatory footing as U.S. national banks. As a result of this legislation, the Federal Reserve has the power to examine these banks, and their expansion in interstate commerce is restricted to the same rules that govern domestically chartered banks. For these foreign offices that accept retail deposits, the act required FDIC insurance.

Activities of Foreign Banks in the United States

Foreign banks have a dramatic and growing presence in the United States. By 1995, total assets were approaching $1 trillion, with more than $550 billion of these assets held in IBFs. The vast bulk, about 75 percent, of these assets of foreign banks are held in New York. New York, California, and Illinois branches account for 95 percent of all assets held by U.S. branches of foreign banks. Most of these foreign banks are based in Europe, but the Japanese have more U.S. bank branches than any other country. Many of these foreign branches are growing rapidly. A few years ago growth rates in assets for these foreign offices exceeded 100 percent, but that rapid growth is now slowing.

In large part, this extremely rapid growth has been due to the vacuum formed by U.S. banks as they attempt to weather the banking crisis. Because of their financial troubles, many of the larger U.S. banks suffered downgrading of their debt in the late 1980s and early 1990s. Further, the environment of restricted lending by U.S. domestic banks in 1991–92 offered good lending opportunities for well-capitalized foreign banks that operate in the United States.

Japanese branches in the United States have grown extremely quickly. For example, these Japanese branches increased their loans from less than $20 billion in 1984 to more than $100 billion in 1989. While about 40 percent of this U.S. lending was to U.S. affiliates of Japanese firms, the Japanese branches were very aggressive in lending to U.S. commercial and industrial firms. In 1989, commercial and industrial lending by Japanese branches in the United States exceeded $50 billion, and these branches lent approximately $15 billion for real estate loans.

Japanese banks have a much larger presence in the United States than do U.S. banks in Japan. Roughly 20 U.S. banks compete in Japan with about $30 billion in assets. This compares to about 36 Japanese banks in the United States holding about $370 billion. Foreign banks in total control about 25 percent of U.S. banking assets, with over half of that amount in Japanese banks. Measuring by bank assets, Japanese banks have about 14 percent of the U.S. banking market.[2] After this period of success, many Japanese banks suffered very serious problems of their own with bad investments and real estate loans in the mid-1990s.

International Commercial Banking

The last decade has witnessed a revolution in the international commercial banking scene. In brief, the story is one of tremendous growth by Japanese banks and a receding into the background of British and U.S. banks. This section reviews this phenomenon. In large part, these shifts are due to the tremendous economic successes of the Japanese in other fields of commerce. To a considerable extent, Japanese advances in commercial banking have also been made possible by the weak capital condition of many U.S. banks and by the restrictions on investment banking and ownership of equities in other corporations that face U.S. banks. For example, Japanese banks hold about 20 percent of corporate shares. As a result, the banks serve as a source of strength to the corporations, and the banks also draw more freely on funds generated by their related corporations.[3]

One of the most important topics in international banking today is the revision of capital standards for most of the world's banks. Central bankers of the leading industrial nations agreed

---

[2] For these statistics, see E. Gerald Corrigan, "Trends in International Banking in the United States and Japan," *Quarterly Review*, Federal Reserve Bank of New York, 14:3, Autumn 1989, pp. 1–6. Reprinted in Robert W. Kolb, *The Commercial Bank Management Reader*, Miami: Kolb Publishing Company, 1992.

[3] Sun Bae Kim, "Banking and Commerce: The Japanese Case," *Weekly Letter*, Federal Reserve Bank of San Francisco, March 29, 1991, pp. 1–3. Reprinted in Robert W. Kolb, *The Commercial Bank Management Reader*, Miami: Kolb Publishing Company, 1992.

to new and more stringent rules for bank capital that commercial banks were to meet by the end of 1992. This section discusses the rules of the Basle Accord that stipulate these new capital requirements.

The World's Largest Banks

Table 15.5 shows the dramatic change in international banking from 1980 to 1994. In 1980, four of the ten largest banks in the world were British and two were based in the United States; none was Japanese. In 1994, seven were Japanese, two were French, and the other was Chinese. No British, no U.S., no German, and no Swiss bank made the top ten. During the 1980s, U.S. banks continued to expand, but many failed as part of the general crisis among depository institutions. For example, between 1988 and 1991, almost 700 U.S. banks holding assets of about $150 billion failed. Many of the largest U.S. banks merged, while many others reduced capacity with massive layoffs and the closing of bank offices. Bad domestic loans, coupled with losses in international lending, left many U.S. banks in a weakened capital position. This weakened capital position led to the downgrading of debt issues for these institutions.

The dominance of Japanese banks goes far beyond merely having the largest banks. Table 15.6 shows the assets of the world's banks by nationality. Japanese banks account for more than 25 percent of all world banking assets. Assets of Japanese banks now approach $2 trillion, which is almost three times the size of all U.S. banks.

The ability of Japanese banks to become so large is due to the very different regulatory environment in which they operate. In Chapter 11, we noted that U.S. commercial banks cannot engage in investment banking. In Japan, as in most other countries, commercial banks face no such restrictions. Japanese banks, in particular, are often associated with enormous industrial firms in addition to conducting investment banking operations.

International Capital Standards

As discussed in Chapters 11 and 12, in 1988 bank supervisors from the Group of Ten countries (Belgium, Canada, France, Italy, Japan, the Netherlands, Sweden, Switzerland, the United

Table 15.5
The World's Largest Banks, 1980 and 1994

1980	1994
1. Credit Agricole	1. Fuji Bank
2. National Westminster	2. Dai-Ichi Kangyo Bank
3. Barclays	3. Sumitomo Bank
4. Bank America	4. Sakura Bank
5. Citicorp	5. Sanwa Bank
6. Banco do Brasil	6. Mitsubishi Bank
7. Lloyds	7. Credit Agricole
8. Midland	8. Industrial Bank of Japan
9. Paribas	9. Credit Lyonnais
10. Algemene Spaar-en Lijfrenteras	10. Industrial & Commercial Bank of China

Source: *The Economist*, May 2, 1992; *The Banker*, July 1994.

Table 15.6
Assets of the World's Banks by Nationality

Nation	Banks Assets ($ billions)
Japan	$1,683.4
Germany	786.6
United States	693.1
France	688.4
Switzerland	386.6
Italy	374.5
United Kingdom	332.2
Netherlands	212.9
Nordic countries	187.5
All other	914.4
Total	6,260.0

Source: Bank for International Settlements, *64th Annual Report*, 1994.

Kingdom, the United States, and Germany) met in Basle, Switzerland to develop new capital standards for the world's banks. The main goal of the agreement that came out of these meetings, known as the Basle Accord, was to provide for more coherent bank capital measurement and a strengthening of the capital position for weaker banks.

The Accord called for banks to achieve a level of capital equal to 8 percent of the bank's risk-weighted credit exposure by the end of 1992. This capital is to consist of two types of capital: Tier 1 or core capital and Tier 2 capital. Tier 1 capital consists of disclosed reserves, common stock, and non-cumulative preferred stock. At least half of the mandatory 8 percent capital is to be from Tier 1. Tier 2 capital consists of undisclosed reserves, asset revaluation reserves, hybrid capital instruments, and subordinated debt. Figure 15.1 shows the position of the ten largest banks in the key countries. All of these institutions now meet the capital requirements.

International Lending

For international commercial banking, lending beyond the bank's domestic market is the key act that fuels bank growth and promises the largest profits. As many banks have learned in the last 20 years, it is also one of the most hazardous lending enterprises in which a bank can engage. This section reviews sources of loans and terms of lending for international bank loans.

After considering the basic lending operations of banks, the section examines the origins of the international debt crisis that mainly resulted from the financial difficulties of less developed countries. It also considers the magnitude of the crisis and examines the slow resolution of the problem that now seems under way. The section also examines the evaluation of potential borrowers.

Sources and Terms of International Bank Lending

In 1980, lending by banks was the single largest source of international financing. Largely because of bank problems with loans to less developed countries (LDCs) and also due to bank difficulties

Figure 15.1
Capital Adequacy by Nation

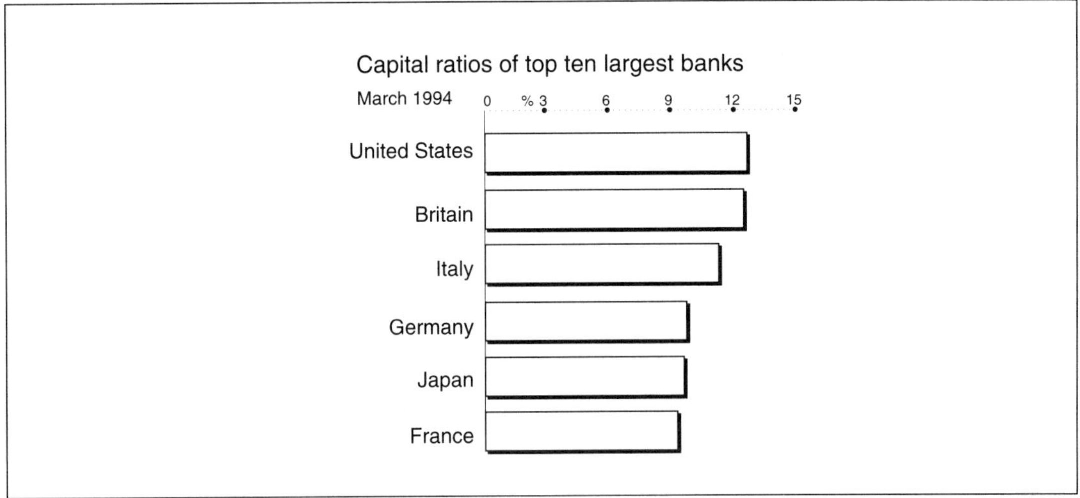

Source: *The Economist*, March 4, 1995.

with capital, bank lending now accounts for only about 20 percent of international borrowing. To a large extent, bank borrowing has been replaced by the issuance of bonds on the international market. Nonetheless, banks continue to lend more than $100 billion annually in the international market.

Most international bank lending is conducted by the largest banks from the industrialized countries. From the 1980s to the present, seven countries account for two-thirds of all international bank lending. They are Great Britain, Japan, United States, France, Switzerland, Germany, and Luxembourg. Figure 15.2 shows the level of external bank lending over recent years, which now exceeds $200 billion. As the figure indicates, the vast majority of this lending is in the form of **Euro-loans** – loans denominated in a convertible western currency. **Foreign loans** are loans made in some other currency. In 1994, foreign loans accounted for less than 1 percent of all international bank lending. The figure also shows new voluntary lending. Voluntary lending contrasts with loans that banks extend to debtors who renew their loans and excludes the loans that banks are effectively forced to grant because of defaults on the part of borrowers. As Figure 15.2 indicates, there was virtually no new voluntary lending. (This topic is discussed later in the section on the international debt crisis.)

Borrowers are principally concentrated among the wealthy industrial countries. About 75 percent of these loans went to these industrialized nations, while another 15 percent was loaned to OPEC nations. Less than 10 percent went to non-OPEC developing nations, and virtually nothing was lent to Eastern European nations. Thus, bank lending today is largely restricted to the best credit risks, and poorer nations are largely excluded from receiving bank loans.

As we have seen, banks make most of their loans in western currencies; of these loans, U.S. dollar loans dominate all other currencies. Table 15.7 shows the currency distribution of these loans for recent years. While the U.S. dollar has long been the currency of choice, it has captured

Figure 15.2
International Bank Lending, 1987–94

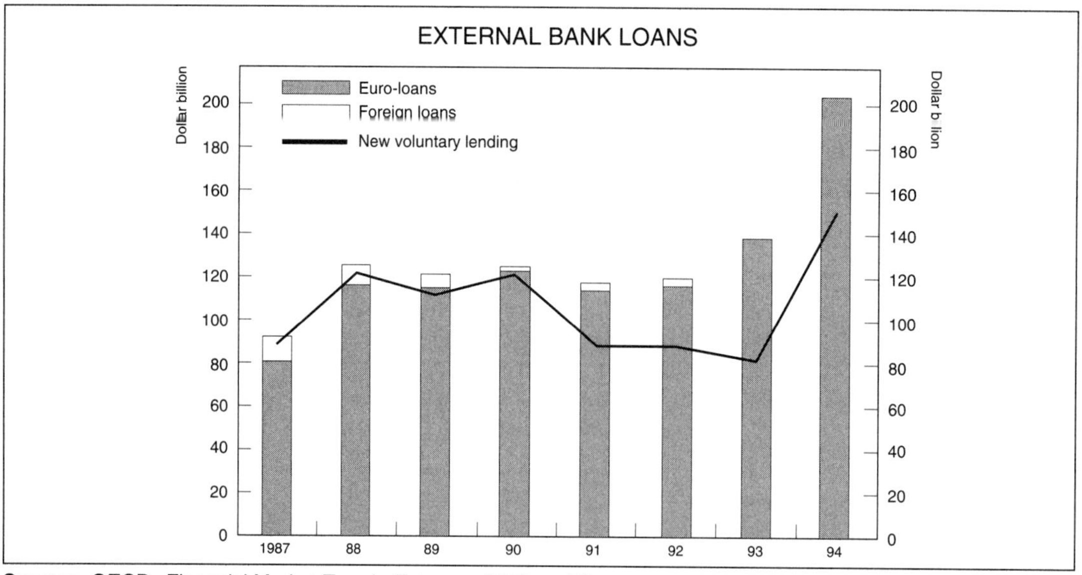

EXTERNAL BANK LOANS

Source: OECD, *Financial Market Trends*, February 1995, p. 73.

an even larger market share in the last five years, largely at the expense of the Deutschemark and the Japanese Yen.

In summary, international bank lending today is an approximately $100–120 billion annual market. British banks continue to lead, but Japanese banks have seized market share. Borrowing from banks is restricted primarily to wealthy countries, and most loans are granted in U.S. dollars.

The LDC Debt Crisis

The immediate origins of the debt crisis can be traced to the first oil embargo by the Organization of Petroleum Exporting Countries (OPEC) in 1973. During that year, oil prices quadrupled in a very short period. OPEC countries found themselves with huge inflows of U.S. dollars, the stan-

Table 15.7
Currency Distribution of International Bank Loans

	1990	1991	1992	1993	1994
U.S. dollar	58.9%	85.5%	75.4%	81.0%	78.6%
Pound sterling	17.5	3.2	1.9	2.2	9.3
ECU	8.7	4.2	15.0	6.4	4.4
Deutschemark	6.7	1.9	1.8	3.2	1.2
Japanese yen	1.7	0.1	1.4	0.7	0.3
Swiss Franc	0.1	0.6	0.3	0.6	0.2
Other	6.4	4.5	4.2	6.1	6.0

Source: OECD, *Financial Market Trends*, February 1995, p. 77.

dard currency of the international petroleum market. Many of these petrodollars flowed into the major banks of the industrial world.

These banks, now flush with OPEC deposits, faced the problem of recycling these funds to earn a return that would allow the payment of interest on the deposits. The result was a dramatic expansion in international lending, much of it directed toward governments of less developed countries. In the period from 1973 to 1979, banks loaned about $60 billion to communist countries and about $150 billion to less developed countries.

These loans were generally made in U.S. dollars, and many individual loans were enormous. As a result, banks formed lending syndicates to pool funds and thereby serve the needs of a large borrower. In many cases these borrowers were the governments of LDCs, so this kind of lending was known as **sovereign lending**. As a general rule, these loans were term loans with typical maturities in the range of five to seven years. Generally they were offered on a floating rate basis, with the interest rate being pegged to the London Interbank Offered Rate (LIBOR). For example, a loan might be offered for seven years at a rate 200 basis points above LIBOR, with the interest rate being reset every six months.

With the full benefit of hindsight, the extent and structure of the lending that occurred in the late 1970s set the stage for disaster. First, the amount of lending to many LDCs was (at least in retrospect) far beyond the ability of the borrowing countries to repay. Second, the interest rates on these loans were set as floating rates. This pricing policy placed all interest rate risk on the borrower. Third, because the loans were denominated in U.S. dollars as a general rule, the sovereign borrower received the burden of exchange risk. Thus, the lending arrangements that dominated the market for sovereign lending placed the interest rate and foreign exchange risk on the financially unsophisticated governments of LDCs, shifting those risks away from large banks. This is particularly ironic, because these large lending banks were exactly the parties that should have been most able to manage the interest rate and currency risk that they transferred to the borrowers.

Lenient lenders and overeager borrowers had now set the stage for serious financial trouble. In 1979, a second major effort by OPEC resulted in substantially higher oil prices and the demand by LDCs for additional loans to finance their energy consumption. The resulting pattern of lending to LDCs ran from $22 billion in 1978 to $35 billion in 1979 to $39 billion in 1980 and to $40 billion in 1981.[4]

As 1979 drew to a close, the Federal Reserve changed the conduct of monetary policy to focus on the money supply rather than the level of interest rates. This policy shift, coupled with the oil price increases of 1979, resulted in extremely high interest rates. As a result, the international loans priced as a floating rate above LIBOR were marked to a higher interest rate. This was not merely an increase in nominal rates because the industrial economies instituted a successful battle against inflation, with the result of higher real interest rates. These factors alone would have been sufficient to cause very serious difficulties for many LDC borrowers, but there was one additional factor that restricted the repayment ability of these borrowers as well.

Worldwide recession led to falling demand and prices for raw commodities, a trend that continued for most of the 1980s. Many LDC borrowers had agricultural products as virtually their

---

[4] See Alan C. Shapiro, *Multinational Financial Management*, 3rd ed., Boston: Allyn and Bacon, 1989.

sole means of earning dollars on the world market. These borrowers now faced a situation of a rising cost of borrowing (in the form of higher real interest rates) and a lowered ability to repay (due to reduced prices and lowered demand for their agricultural products).

In the second half of 1982, Mexico, Brazil, and Argentina all announced that they were unable to repay their international loans as scheduled. By mid-1983 about 25 LDCs had made similar announcements. Together these defaulting countries accounted for about 70 percent of all bank loans to LDCs. For many of these countries, exports of raw materials provided the only means of earning the western currencies that could be converted into dollars to repay their debt. (This excludes LDCs with significant oil production, such as Mexico, Venezuela, and Nigeria.)

In 1983, for example, Mexico's annual scheduled debt service reached 70 percent of annual exports, while Brazil and Chile's debt services exceeded 50 percent of annual exports. Most other LDCs had a ratio of 25 percent or higher. These ratios reflect the impossible position of the debtor countries. Taking Mexico as an example, merely meeting its debt servicing obligation would have required that 70 cents of every dollar (or other western currency) received for exports would have to flow to the lending banks. This would leave virtually nothing to buy needed western technology or other materials. Faced with an impossible repayment situation, it is not surprising that countries opted to default. As a result, the banks were forced to allow more lenient repayment terms, to reschedule the debt payments, and, in effect, to lend more money to these defaulting countries.

Much of this disaster might have been foreseen by alert bankers. Instead, banks rushed to loan, and granted loans that were quite large relative to bank capital. By 1982, for example, U.S. banks had loans outstanding to LDCs that exceeded bank capital by more than 50 percent. Figure 15.3 shows bank capital as a percentage of loans to LDCs for the years 1977 through 1990. Faced with this drastic situation, banks stopped lending to LDCs, leading to a restoration of their capital to LDC loan ratios in the late 1980s. However, this policy retarded development in LDCs, since these countries were largely denied access to capital markets.

The secondary market value of LDC loans provides one measure of the extent of the debt crisis. Figure 15.4 shows the market value of LDC debt as a percentage of the face value of the debt. For example, the market value of international debt for Chile, Mexico, and Venezuela dipped below 40 cents on the dollar in 1989 and 1990, as the figure shows. In market value terms, this meant that about 60 percent of the loaned funds were lost. Figure 15.4 also refers to the Baker 15. The Baker 15 are 15 heavily indebted countries (Argentina, Bolivia, Brazil, Chile, Colombia, Ivory Coast, Ecuador, Mexico, Morocco, Nigeria, Peru, Philippines, Uruguay, Venezuela, and Yugoslavia) named after Secretary of State James Baker, who worked on debt restructuring arrangements. As Figure 15.4 also shows, the debt of 12 of these countries, other than Chile, Mexico, and Venezuela, had a market value for their debt as low as 25 percent of face value.

As Figure 15.4 also indicates, the market value of the debt of all of these countries increased substantially in 1991. By 1994, the market value of debt issued by the Baker 15 had climbed to about 60 percent of par value, indicating that the debt crisis is moving toward a resolution. However, in early 1995, the Mexican peso collapsed, losing about half of its value relative to the dollar. Many other South American countries experienced less dramatic but still serious currency devaluations in this period, and market values for Baker 15 debt hovered around 50 percent of par.

Table 15.8 shows that debt servicing for LDCs is less onerous now than in the mid-1980s, but the proportion of export revenue that must be devoted to servicing debt in LDCs is still quite high. Further, exports have not increased over the last decade, while the total amount of debt continues to grow. As a result, it appears that the prospect of immediate crisis has been lessened, but serious difficulties remain for these borrowers and their lenders.

Summary

This chapter explored the world of international banking by considering the activities of U.S. banks in foreign countries. The discussion then turned to the role of foreign banks in the United States, and we noted that regulation was a key factor in determining the terms of competition

Figure 15.3
Bank Capital as a Percentage of Bank Loans to LDCs

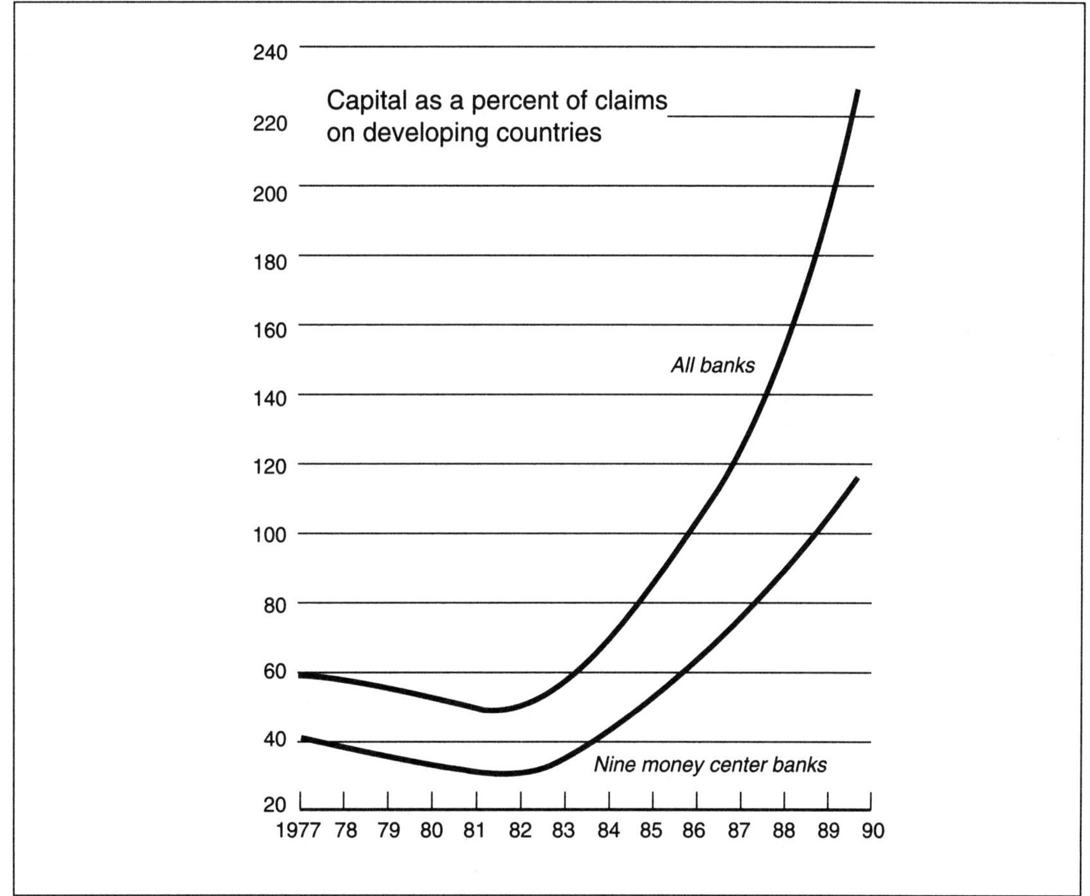

Source: International Monetary Fund, *Private Market Financing for Developing Countries*, December 1991, p. 9.

Figure 15.4
Secondary Market Prices for LDC Loans
(in percent of face value)

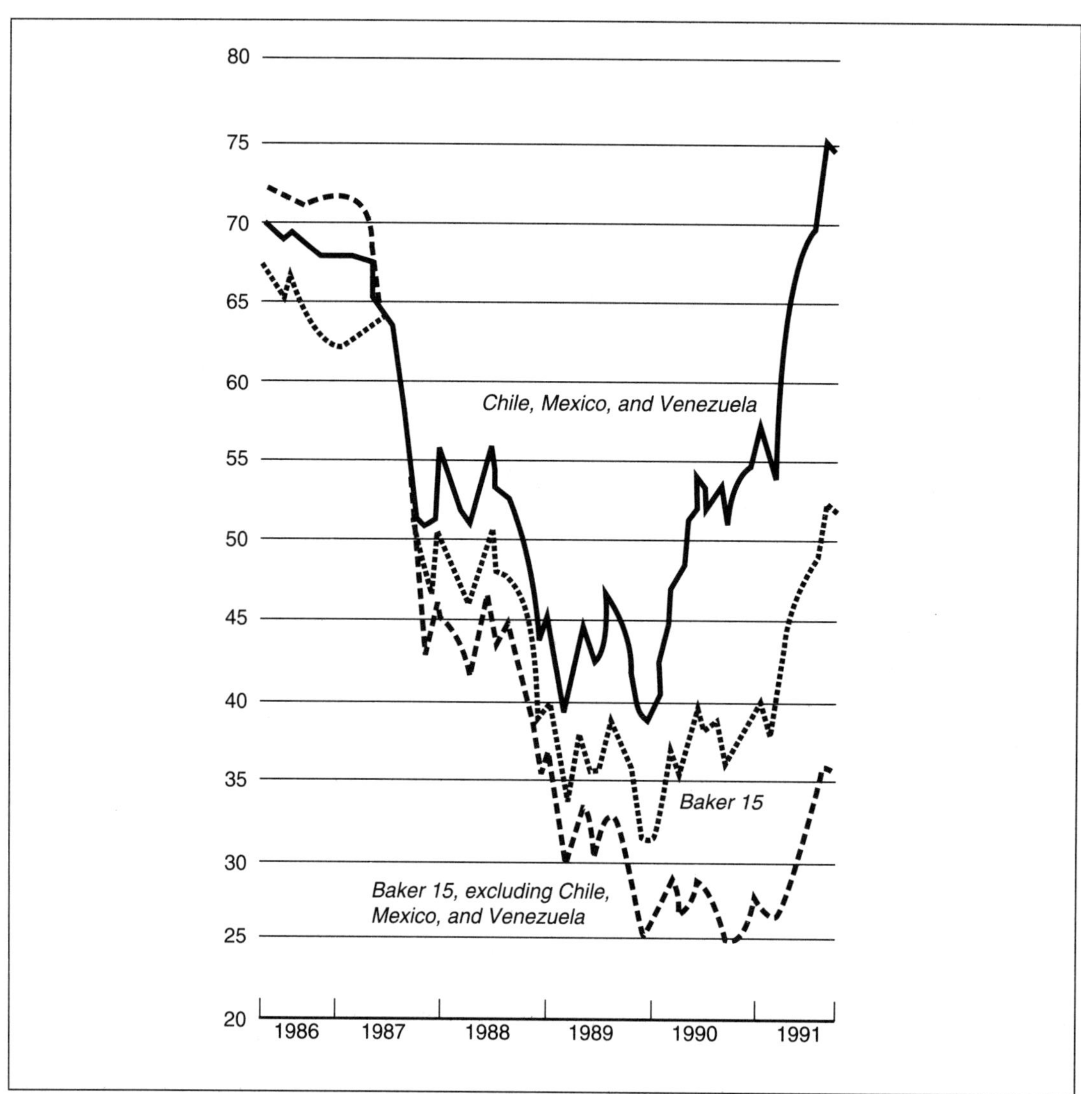

Source: International Monetary Fund, *Private Market Financing for Developing Countries*, December 1991, p. 14.

between domestic U.S. and foreign banks. The chapter also analyzed the role of large banks in international banking, and we noted the extremely rapid emergence of Japanese banks among the ranks of the world's largest commercial banks.

The chapter reviewed the enabling legislation and the economic role of entities such as Edge Act Corporations and International Banking Facilities. We discussed the Basle Accord, which now governs capital requirements for banks from key industrial countries.

Table 15.8
LDC External Debt and Debt Service

Year	External Debt as a Percentage of Gross Domestic Product	Annual Debt Service as a Percentage of Annual Exports
1986	39.8	22.5
1987	38.0	20.8
1988	34.9	19.2
1989	33.0	16.1
1990	31.4	15.2
1991	30.8	15.0
1992	34.1	14.5
1993	33.6	15.4
1994	33.1	15.3
1995	30.8	13.6

Source: International Monetary Fund, *World Economic Outlook*, May 1994.

We considered the typical terms of international lending by banks and saw that the market is principally open to wealthy nations seeking loans denominated in dollars. Finally, we considered the LDC debt crisis, saw how the lending practices of sovereign lending contributed to the crisis, and observed that conditions for many highly indebted LDCs appear to be easing.

Questions and Problems

1. Why do banks operate abroad?
2. In what countries or regions of the world are the foreign operations of U.S. banks most heavily concentrated?
3. Explain the basic operations of an Edge Act Corporation. Where are Edge Act Corporations principally concentrated?
4. Are Edge Act Corporations subject to reserve requirements on their deposits? Explain the legislation that controls this issue.
5. What kinds of foreign activities are permitted to U.S. chartered banks and what law or regulation governs those activities?
6. What is an International Banking Facility? Briefly explain its operations.
7. Among foreign banks operating in the United States, which country dominates?
8. Explain recent changes in the ranks of the ten largest banks in the world.
9. Explain the aims of the Basle Accord and briefly indicate the new rules it imposes on banks.
10. Explain the difference between Euro-loans and foreign loans.
11. Consider the typical borrower in the Euro-loan market. Explain what kind of borrower this would be and discuss the kind of loan that they might receive.

12. What is sovereign lending? What has happened to the role of sovereign lending in international finance?

13. Explain how the typical structure of sovereign lending helped to cause the LDC debt crisis.

References

Baer, H. L., "Foreign Competition in U.S. Banking Markets," *Economic Perspectives*, Federal Reserve Bank of Chicago, 14:3, May/June 1990, pp. 22–9. Reprinted in Robert W. Kolb, *The Commercial Bank Management Reader*, Miami: Kolb Publishing Company, 1992.

Baer, H. L. and D. D. Evanoff, "Payments System Issues in Financial Markets that Never Sleep," *Economic Perspectives*, Federal Reserve Bank of Chicago, 14:6, November/December 1990, pp. 2–15. Reprinted in Robert W. Kolb, *The Commercial Bank Management Reader*, Miami: Kolb Publishing Company, 1992.

Corrigan, E. G., "Trends in International Banking in the United States and Japan," *Quarterly Review*, Federal Reserve Bank of New York, 14:3, Autumn 1989, pp. 1–6. Reprinted in Robert W. Kolb, *The Commercial Bank Management Reader*, Miami: Kolb Publishing Company, 1992.

Corrigan, E. G., "Reforming the U.S. Financial System: An International Perspective," *Quarterly Review*, Federal Reserve Bank of New York, 15:1, Spring 1990, pp. 1–14. Reprinted in Robert W. Kolb, *The Commercial Bank Management Reader*, Miami: Kolb Publishing Company, 1992.

Hirtle, B., "Factors Affecting the Competitiveness of Internationally Active Financial Institutions," *Quarterly Review*, Federal Reserve Bank of New York, 16:1, Spring 1991, pp. 38–51. Reprinted in Robert W. Kolb, *The Commercial Bank Management Reader*, Miami: Kolb Publishing Company, 1992.

Kamata, S., "Managing Risk in Japanese Interbank Payment Systems," *Economic Review*, Federal Reserve Bank of San Francisco, Fall 1990, pp. 18–32. Reprinted in Robert W. Kolb, *The Commercial Bank Management Reader*, Miami: Kolb Publishing Company, 1992.

Kim, S. B., "Banking and Commerce: The Japanese Case," *Weekly Letter*, Federal Reserve Bank of San Francisco, March 29, 1991, pp. 1–3. Reprinted in Robert W. Kolb, *The Commercial Bank Management Reader*, Miami: Kolb Publishing Company, 1992.

Lamfalussy, A., "Globalization of Financial Markets: International Supervisory and Regulatory Issues," *Economic Review*, Federal Reserve Bank of Kansas City, January 1989, pp. 3–8. Reprinted in Robert W. Kolb, *The Commercial Bank Management Reader*, Miami: Kolb Publishing Company, 1992.

Pavel, C. and J. N. McElravey, "Globalization in the Financial Services Industry," *Economic Perspectives*, Federal Reserve Bank of Chicago, 14:3, May/June 1990, pp. 3–18. Reprinted in Robert W. Kolb, *The Commercial Bank Management Reader*, Miami: Kolb Publishing Company, 1992.

Shapiro, A. C., "International Banking and Country Risk Analysis," *Midland Corporate Finance Journal*, 4:3, Fall 1986, pp. 56–64. Reprinted in Robert W. Kolb, *The Commercial Bank Management Reader*, Miami: Kolb Publishing Company, 1992.

Strongin, S., "International Credit Market Connections," *Economic Perspectives*, Federal Reserve Bank of Chicago, 14:4, July/August 1990, pp. 2–10. Reprinted in Robert W. Kolb, *The Commercial Bank Management Reader*, Miami: Kolb Publishing Company, 1992.

Wang, C. N., "The Costs of Default and International Lending," *Economic Commentary*, Federal Reserve Bank of Cleveland, March 1, 1989, pp. 1–4. Reprinted in Robert W. Kolb, *The Commercial Bank Management Reader*, Miami: Kolb Publishing Company, 1992.

Zimmerman, G. C., "Slower Growth for Foreign Banks?" *Weekly Letter*, Federal Reserve Bank of San Francisco, January 25, 1991, pp. 1–2. Reprinted in Robert W. Kolb, *The Commercial Bank Management Reader*, Miami: Kolb Publishing Company, 1992.

Part 4

Non-Depository Financial Institutions

Part IV of the book analyzes the operation and performance of non-depository financial institutions. Chapter 16 concentrates on finance conglomerates and finance subsidiaries. These financial enterprises can be broadly classified as financial conglomerates or financial subsidiaries. A financial conglomerate offers a mix of financial services that may range from banking–related activities, to insurance, to real estate. A finance subsidiary is a firm that is owned by another firm and is principally engaged in providing financial services. A captive finance subsidiary principally assists its parent firm in conduct its business. Each of the big three U.S. auto manufacturers owns a captive financial subsidiary that provides financing for automobiles manufactured by its parent.

Chapter 17 discusses investment companies. These are firms that collect funds from a wide group of investors and invest them in a portfolio of securities. Investment companies can be closed–end investment companies and mutual funds. A closed–end company accepts funds only at its creation. A mutual fund, by contrast, is always willing to receive money from new investors at any time. This chapter also discusses performance evaluation for mutual funds. Performance evaluation is critical in light of the fact that many investors believe that mutual funds can outperform the market for the level of risk that they bear. This issue is also examined in the chapter to understand what investors can reasonably expect from their mutual fund portfolios.

Chapter 18 presents the principles that govern the insurance industry. In essence, insurance companies benefit society by offering risk-transferring services. A conceptual understanding of the insurance function relies heavily on the principles of Portfolio Theory presented in Chapter 9. The two major types of insurance companies are life and property/liability insurance companies. Life insurance companies concentrate on selling whole life, term, universal, annuities, and health insurance. Property/liability insurance companies accept the risks related to the effects of natural disasters – flood, fire, hurricane, earthquakes – on property.

Chapter 19 provides an overview of pension funds. One of the most important and obvious roles of pensions is to provide retirement income insurance. As such, pensions constitute an important element of the labor contract. Pension assets are divided among several different basic types of pension plans. The social security system administered by the federal government may be treated as a public pension plan. There are also several types of private pension plans. This chapter explains the essential operations of these different plans. From a managerial perspective, pension funds are best viewed as a type of financial intermediary. The fund collects monies from the

worker and the employer during a worker's life, invests these monies during the employee's working years, and eventually uses the proceeds to pay the worker a retirement income. The long–term nature of the pension fund's obligation creates special management problems, which this chapter explores. This chapter also briefly considers the regulation of pension funds in the United States.

Financial Conglomerates and Subsidiaries 16

Overview

We have seen that commercial banking constitutes a well-defined industry, due in large part to federal and state regulatory structures that oversee the industry. Every commercial bank is essentially in the business of taking deposits and making loans. By contrast, this chapter considers financial enterprises that are extremely diverse. The chapter begins with a broad overview of the role of finance companies in the economy. As we will see, these firms play a dominant role in some financial sectors, particularly in consumer financing and leasing.

The discussion then turns to a close examination of financial firms that can be classified as either financial conglomerates or financial subsidiaries. A **financial conglomerate** is a firm offering a mix of financial services that may range from banking-related activities, to insurance, to real estate. These varied financial services may be offered by independent corporate entities with their own brand-name identities. Such a firm becomes a conglomerate because all of the diverse firms share a common ownership. This chapter explores three very different financial conglomerates: GE Capital Corp., Merrill Lynch., and Sears, Roebuck and Co.

A **finance subsidiary** is a firm principally engaged in providing finance services that is owned by another firm. Under this definition, we will see that GE Capital and the financial business associated with Sears Roebuck are themselves subsidiaries. A **captive finance subsidiary** is a financial subsidiary principally engaged in assisting its parent firm conduct its business. The best examples of captive financial subsidiaries arise in the automobile industry. Each of the big three U.S. auto manufacturers owns a captive financial subsidiary that principally provides financing for automobiles manufactured by its parent. After considering the motivation for captive financial firms, we examine the operations of General Motors Acceptance Corporation and Ford Credit.

The chapter concludes with a discussion on asset securitization. **Asset securitization** is the process of packaging financial claims so that those claims may be traded in the financial market as a security, such as a debt instrument. This important trend in finance is critical to the operation of financial conglomerates and captive finance companies because it provides these firms with a way of recycling their loanable funds.

An Overview of Finance Companies

Table 16.1 presents selected features from the aggregated balance sheets of U.S. finance companies. Assets of finance companies consist principally of accounts receivable – the monies due on the loans made by the finance companies. About 80 percent of all finance company assets are receivables. The remainder consist principally of real estate and equipment. The lending of finance companies shown in Table 16.1 is concentrated in business lending, followed by consumer lending, with a minor role in real estate lending. Almost two-thirds of all finance company lending is lending to businesses.

Table 16.1
Balance Sheet of Domestic Finance Companies
($ billions)

Assets	
Accounts receivable	524.2
Consumer	130.3
Business	76.7
Real estate	63.2
Less reserves	460.9
Accounts receivable, net	177.2
All other	
Total Assets	638.1
Liabilities and Capital	
Bank loans	21.6
Commercial paper	171.0
Due to parent	50.0
Other loans	228.2
All other liabilities	95.0
Capital, surplus, and undivided profits	72.3
Total liabilities and capital	638.1

Source: *Federal Reserve Bulletin*, March 1995, Table 1.51.

Finance companies borrow heavily to secure their loanable funds, and Table 16.1 reflects this high leverage. About 90 percent of finance company liabilities are debt. This debt arises largely from the issuance of commercial paper, bank loans, borrowings from the finance company's parent, and other types of loans. Table 16.2 shows the capital-to-asset ratio for some leading finance companies. While these reveal considerable range, some are as low as 8 percent, with the median being about 14 percent.

Table 16.3 presents data for the ten largest finance companies in the United States. General Motors Acceptance Corporation, which we examine in more detail later in the chapter, is the largest with assets exceeding $100 billion. It is approximately ten times larger than the tenth largest firm in the industry. Table 16.3 also shows the type of relationship, if any, that each finance company has to its parent, along with information about the type of business pursued by each company. Firms with diversified lines of business are generally active in both consumer finance and commercial finance. Finally, Table 16.3 shows the debt ratings for these firms. For the most part, these have been fairly steady over recent years.

While Table 16.1 showed the concentration of finance company lending to businesses, Table 16.4 shows the purposes for which finance companies lend. By far, the largest single type of finance company lending activity is leasing. Compared to commercial banks, finance companies hold about four times as much in leasing receivables, and their share has been increasing steadily for the last ten years. As we will see later in this chapter, finance companies are a major force in heavy equipment leasing, including aircraft and railway rolling stock. The second category of lend-

Table 16.2
Capital to Asset Ratios for Selected Finance Companies

Company	Capital/Assets Ratio (in percent)
General Electric Capital Corp.	9.9
Ford Motor Credit	8.4
American Express Credit	11.5
ITT Financial Corp.	17.9
IBM Credit	8.2
Transamerica Finance	25.2
Toyota Motor Credit	12.3
General Motors Acceptance Corp.	7.8
Chrysler Financial	15.8
Sears, Roebuck Acceptance Corp.	18.7
John Deere Credit	27.7

Source: E. M. Remolona and Kurt C. Wulfekuhler, "Finance Companies, Bank Competition, and Niche Markets," *Quarterly Review*, Federal Reserve Bank of New York, Summer 1992.

ing activity is in the financing of installment sales. Many finance companies own private label credit cards. For example, a department store may have its own credit card, but the actual financing operation behind the credit card is often run by a finance company. In addition, some finance companies issue their own credit cards, with the Discover Card by Sears, Roebuck being a prime example. Finance companies are second only to commercial banks in providing consumer credit. However, banks dominate consumer installment credit, with more than twice as much in receivables as finance companies. Table 16.5 shows that finance companies hold 15 percent of all consumer borrowing, which is about one-third as much as that held by commercial banks but more than the consumer finance provided by all savings and loan associations.

Table 16.3
The Ten Largest Finance Companies by Assets

Company	Assets ($ billions)		Type of Business	Senior Debt Rating
General Motors Acceptance Corp.	105.1	Captive	Diversified	AA-
General Electric Capital Corp.	70.4	Nonfinancial	Diversified	AAA
Ford Motor Credit	59.0	Captive	Diversified	AA-
Chrysler Financial	24.7	Captive	Diversified	BBB-
Household Financial	16.9	Independent	Consumer	A+
Associates Corp. of North America	16.6	Nonfinancial	Diversified	AA-
Sears, Roebuck Acceptance Corp.	15.4	Captive	Consumer	N.A.
American Express Credit	14.2	Captive	Consumer	AA
ITT Financial Corp.	11.7	Nonfinancial	Diversified	A
CIT Group	11.4	Bank holding co.	Diversified	A+

Source: E. M. Remolona and Kurt C. Wulfekuhler, "Finance Companies, Bank Competition, and Niche Markets," *Quarterly Review*, Federal Reserve Bank of New York, Summer 1992.

Table 16.4
Loans Held by Domestic Finance Companies

Type of Loan	Millions of Dollars
Consumer	174,928
Real estate	77,907
Business	351,280
Motor vehicles	113,222
Equipment	154,312
Other business	59,893
Securitized business assets	23,853
Total	604,115

Source: *Federal Reserve Bulletin*, March 1995, adapted from Table 1.52.

Table 16.5
Role of Finance Companies in Consumer Credit

Holder	Millions of Dollars	Percent of Total
Commercial banks	421,634	46.52
Finance companies	133,684	14.75
Credit unions	118,050	13.03
Savings institutions	38,275	4.23
Nonfinancial business	58,591	6.47
Securitized assets	135,928	15.00
Total	906,162	100.00

Source: *Federal Reserve Bulletin*, March 1995, adapted from Table 1.55.

Financial Conglomerates

As the name implies, a financial conglomerate consists of many pieces, each of which is itself a business engaged in providing some type of financial service. Because different conglomerates select different businesses and combine them in unique ways, generalizations about the operations of financial conglomerates are very difficult. Due to this diversity, this section approaches financial conglomerates by considering three diverse firms in some detail. As we will see, these firms are quite different in the businesses they include and the way in which they combine the various elements.

General Electric Capital Corporation

General Electric Capital Corporation is owned by the General Electric Corporation. GE is a leading industrial firm making everything from light bulbs to commercial aircraft engines. GE Capital consists of many businesses. Prominent among these are several firms specialized in leasing airplanes, rail cars, computers, trucks, automobiles, semi-trailers, and ship cargo containers. Several other firms are in insurance-related businesses, including mortgage insurance, business insurance, and reinsurance. (Reinsurance is essentially insuring insurance companies, a process by which an insurance company insures a risk and then diversifies its risk by finding other firms to insure itself against large losses.) Table 16.6 shows the categories of businesses operated by GE Capital and the percentage of sales and income the company derives from each. As the table shows, specialty insurance and consumer services provide the bulk of profits.

We briefly consider several of these businesses to indicate the range of GE's financial activities. Polaris Aircraft Leasing is wholly owned by GE Capital. Most major airlines lease a substantial number of their aircraft, and many of them lease from Polaris. Polaris manages about 500 commercial airliners with an asset base around $2 billion, making it one of the world's largest aircraft leasing operations. Polaris leases to 37 airlines in 16 countries, including Xiamen Airlines, the state operated airline of China. (Even communists lease!)

In the corporate finance area, GE Capital finances acquisitions, recapitalizations, and restructurings of corporations. Recently GE Capital provided $100 million of credit for the recapitalization of Six Flags Theme Parks. It also provides working capital financing to large firms. GE Capital was active in the leveraged buyout (LBO) fad of the 1980s and experienced serious difficulties as some highly leveraged firms failed. As stated in GE Financial's Annual Report: "We must admit to having gone too far and to have harshly learned the lesson that the only way to avoid loss from a foolish loan is to refuse to make it."

GE acquired Kidder Peabody, a well-known full-line investment banking and securities brokerage firm, in the 1980s. Kidder has 50 offices worldwide and focuses on offering services to firms and wealthy individuals, as opposed to retail securities brokerage. At one time, Kidder was the fifth largest domestic underwriter. In addition, Kidder is active in financial derivatives (futures, options, swaps, and financial engineering). Kidder trades derivatives for its own account and helps firms use derivatives to manage their own financial risks. In the mid-1990s, trading scandals at Kidder led GE to sell the firm and exit the securities business.

Fleet Services is the largest automobile fleet management company in the United States with a fleet of more than 500,000 vehicles. Fleet serves corporations by providing them with an entire fleet of vehicles. For its vehicles, Fleet Services will finance, secure titles and licenses, maintain, and provide operational management. Fleet Services has more than $4 billion in assets. Recently, Fleet began to service about half of Federal Express's total fleet of 24,000 vehicles.

Because these diverse businesses are wholly owned by GE Capital, they do not provide financial statements to the public. Instead, GE Capital reports the consolidated results from all of its operations. Table 16.7 presents a percentage balance sheet for GE Capital. Total assets are about $120 billion. About 60 percent of these assets are in receivables, and about 20 percent are in cash

Table 16.6
Lines of Business for General Electric Capital Corporation

Type of Business	Percent of Sales	Percent of Operating Income
Specialty Insurance	22	26
Consumer Services	18	24
Equipment Management	16	13
Mid-Market Financing	8	15
Securities Broker-Dealer	22	15
Specialized Financing	14	7

Table 16.7
Percentage Balance Sheet
for General Electric Capital Corporation

Assets	
Cash	1%
Marketable Securities	17
Receivables	58
Net Property, Plant and Equipment	10
Deposits and Other Assets	14
Total Assets	100%
Liabilities and Equity	
Notes payable	45%
Accounts payable	3
Other current liabilities	2
Deferred charges	5
Long-term debt	22
Other Long-term liabilities	14
Common stock	1
Capital surplus	2
Retained earnings	6
Shareholder equity	10
Total Liabilities and Equity	100%

and marketable securities. About half of GE Capital's liabilities consist of notes and accounts payable, while long-term debt accounts for almost one-fourth of total resources. GE Capital has total revenues of more than $22 billion and recently earned about $1.5 billion after tax. The overwhelming bulk of both its income and expenses consisted of interest.

GE Capital is financed primarily with short-term debt. Each year GE Capital issues more than $1 trillion dollars of debt, most of it commercial paper. In most years, GE Capital is the largest issuer of commercial paper in the world, and it maintains triple-A ratings from Moody's and Standard & Poor's.

In summary, GE Capital is an enormous and extremely diversified financial powerhouse. Even though it is diversified throughout the financial sector, GE Capital leads in many of the markets in which it competes. Due to its size, GE Capital is one of the most important borrowers and lenders in the U.S. economy, and it is an extremely important portion of General Electric Corporation.

Merrill Lynch

The name of Merrill Lynch immediately conjures up an image of bulls in commercials for the Merrill Lynch brokerage firm. Most observers probably think the brokerage operations constitute the entirety of Merrill Lynch. In fact, the brokerage operation, Merrill, Lynch, Pierce, Fenner & Smith (MLPF&S) is only the most visible portion of the entire firm. Merrill Lynch & Co., Inc., is a holding company that consists of a number of subsidiaries. Together they provide investment, financing, insurance, and related services.

The company consists of five subsidiaries operating in the United States, with a number of other subsidiaries and affiliates operating abroad. In the United States, the principal subsidiary is MLPF&S, one of the largest securities firms in the world. MLPF&S is a broker for securities, options, futures, and some insurance products. It is also a dealer in options and securities. In addition, MLPF&S is one of the most prominent investment banking firms in the United States. Merrill Lynch concentrates its activity in financial derivatives (such as futures, options, and swaps) in Merrill Lynch Derivative Products, Inc. Merrill Lynch Asset Management (MLAM) manages mutual funds and provides investment advisory services. Merrill Lynch Government Securities, Inc., is a primary dealer in obligations issued by the U.S. government, such as Treasury bills, notes, and bonds. Merrill Lynch Insurance Group, Inc., is engaged in insurance underwriting and sells annuity products through its own subsidiaries. Merrill Lynch Life Insurance Company sells life insurance and annuities.

Merrill Lynch has about 40,000 employees and 200 million shares outstanding. Total revenues are in the range of $16–20 billion per year, with typical earnings in the range of $1–2 billion. Table 16.8 presents a percentage balance sheet for Merrill Lynch, reflecting the consolidation of all of its subsidiaries. As Table 16.8 shows, Merrill's assets are overwhelmingly concentrated in current assets. As most of its assets are either in money market instruments or marketable securi-

Table 16.8
Percentage Balance Sheet
for Merrill Lynch & Co., Inc.

Assets	
Cash	4%
Marketable Securities	26
Receivables	15
Inventories	34
Other Current Assets	12
Net Property, Plant, and Equipment	1
Investment in Subsidiaries	6
Other Non-current Assets	1
Deposits and Other Assets	1
Total Assets	100%
Liabilities and Equity	
Notes payable	51%
Accounts payable	16
Other current liabilities	18
Long-term debt	9
Common stock/capital surplus	1
Retained earnings	3
Shareholder equity	2
Total Liabilities and Equity	100%

ties, this is not surprising. The one-third of its assets held in inventories are essentially inventories of securities. These assets are financed mainly by short-term liabilities, included notes payable and accounts payable. As the balance sheet shows, Merrill Lynch, like almost all finance companies, is a very highly leveraged concern.

Merrill Lynch derives its income from five principal sources, as the percentage income statement of Table 16.9 shows. Merrill earns commission incomes for brokerage services as it executes orders for its clients, and this represents about 17 percent of its revenues. It earns interest and dividends from securities it owns and from its interest in its subsidiaries. Interest and dividends account for 43 percent of Merrill's gross revenues. Merrill Lynch also actively trades securities for its own account. On the income statement of Table 16.9, this trading income is shown as Merrill's revenues from its principal transactions. These contrast with its brokerage operations, in which Merrill acts as an agent for others. Merrill Lynch is also the largest investment banking firm in the world, at least according to most rankings in most years. From investment banking, Merrill earns about 11 percent of its revenues. Finally, Merrill manages mutual funds and provides other asset

Table 16.9
Merrill Lynch Consolidated Percentage Income Statement

Revenues	100%
Commissions	17
Interest and dividends	43
Principal transactions	18
Investment banking	11
Asset management and custodial fees	9
Other	2
Interest expense	36
Net Revenues	64
Non-Interest Expenses	32
Compensation and benefits	3
Occupancy	2
Communications and equipment rental	2
Depreciation and amortization	2
Brokerage, clearing, and exchange fees	2
Advertising and market development	2
Professional fees	4
Other	
Total Non-Interest Expenses	49
Earnings Before Income Taxes	15
Income tax expense	7
Net Earnings	8

management services to its clients and earns about 9 percent of revenues from this source. Together, these revenues are approaching $20 billion annually.

The expenses incurred to generate this revenue fall into two main categories. About one-third of all revenues are expended for interest on various borrowings. As we have seen from Merrill's balance sheet, these are mainly short-term borrowings. The other main expense is for personnel compensation and benefits, and this is also about one-third of all revenues. Other significant expenses are for buildings and rent, office expenses, communication equipment, and so on. Merrill earns about 8 percent of revenues for total net income of about $1–2 billion.

The distribution of revenues and expenses reflected in its income statement shows that the brokerage business is Merrill's core enterprise. MLPF&S operates more than 500 offices in 29 countries with more than 12,000 agents. Much of Merrill's business is built on individual clients. Today Merrill Lynch holds billions of dollars of clients' funds, much more than any other firm; assets under management continue to grow by more that $200 million per business day. In total, Merrill holds about 2.5 percent of all U.S. household financial assets. The Merrill Cash Management Account (CMA) is one of its most popular products. A CMA combines a checking, money market, and brokerage account, so a customer can write checks directly against the securities in her portfolio. Much of the funds held by Merrill are held by Merrill Lynch Asset Management (MLAM). MLAM manages both mutual funds and private accounts, with 120 different portfolios. In a single year, MLAM introduced 15 new mutual funds.

In the early 1970s, Merrill was almost exclusively a brokerage firm, but it has worked hard to enter other lines of business, particularly in the capital markets. However, Merrill is a significant, and sometimes dominant, force in its other endeavors as well. This is particularly true in investment banking, as Merrill is the leading underwriter of both U.S. and global debt and equity securities.

Financial derivatives have become extremely important in financial markets, as we saw in Chapter 6. These futures, options, swaps, and more exotic instruments typically involve extremely high leverage and can offer very complicated payoffs and conditions. Most investment banking and brokerage firms, including Merrill, are deeply involved in trading derivatives for their own account and in advising clients on their use. In recent years, Merrill has come to derive significant revenues from this source, although some think that derivatives are intrinsically dangerous. Perhaps it is accurate to say that active trading of derivatives by any firm may increase the volatility of its revenues and earnings.

Trading derivatives is one danger faced by many investment banking firms, but advising clients can also subject a firm to financial risk. Through the early 1990s, Merrill Lynch acted as broker and (perhaps) adviser to Orange County, California. Orange County managed a portfolio of government funds totaling about $7 billion. Under the management of the Orange County treasurer, Robert Citron, the county borrowed about $13 billion, to create a leveraged portfolio with a total value of about $20 billion. These funds were all short-term obligations, and they were mostly invested in long-term bonds and in some financial derivatives that effectively behaved like long-term bonds. Merrill Lynch acted as the principal broker for these transactions. When interest rates rose in 1993–94, the value of the Orange County portfolio fell dramatically. As a result, Orange County declared bankruptcy on December 6, 1994. Total losses are about $2–3 billion dollars. Orange County has filed suit against Merrill Lynch, asserting that Merrill acted inappropriately in selling extremely risky securities to Orange County and in giving Orange County poor advice. Other lawsuits from related parties are in the wings. This potential liability may cloud Merrill's future for years to come.

Sears, Roebuck and Co.

Sears, Roebuck has been a household word in retailing for more than 100 years. At one time the largest retailer in the world, Sears was recently passed by Wal-Mart and has had its share of difficulties with its core business of merchandising. In the years leading to the early 1990s, Sears built and acquired a substantial financial empire organized into four groups: Sears Merchandise, the retailer; Allstate, a major insurer; Dean Witter Financial Services, a securities dealer and lender; and Coldwell Banker Real Estate Group, a major real estate brokerage concern. Today, Sears is the world's third largest retailer and has largely dismantled its financial operations. This section explores the house that Sears built in the years leading to the end of 1991 and shows how it disposed of almost all financial operations to concentrate on retailing.

Taking the end of 1991 as a reference point, Table 16.10 shows the composition of revenues and expenses for these units. At that time, Allstate Insurance had assets of more than $45 billion and offered a wide range of insurance services to firms and individuals, including property/liability insurance, such as home owner's and automobile insurance, as well as life insurance. Total property/liability premiums now exceeded $15 billion annually, while life insurance premiums were above $4 billion annually. Allstate had an extremely substantial portfolio of securities to back its obligations to policy holders. Of its $45 billion in total assets, more than $38 billion was invested in securities and mortgage loans. About $32 billion of these investments was concentrated in debt instruments.

Dean Witter Financial Services consisted of two divisions: Securities and Credit Services, with Credit Services including the Discover Card, Sears Payment Systems, and Lending Services. Dean Witter's securities unit consisted of numerous securities brokerage firms, with many of them residing on the premises of Sears stores. In addition, Dean Witter managed a family of investment companies with about $50 billion in assets under management. Dean Witter traded securities for its own accounts and realized about $460 million in before-tax trading profits in 1991. Net income for the securities operations totaled $171 million, while credit services earned $174 mil-

Table 16.10
Selected Financial Statistics for Sears, Roebuck and Co., 1991
($ millions)

	Sears Merchandise	Allstate Insurance	Dean Witter	Coldwell Banker	Total
Total revenue	31,433	19,350	4,942	1,613	57,338
Net income	486	723	345	61	1,615
Total assets	24,829	45,776	23,379	9,925	103,909
Receivables	13,537				
Investments		38,861		8,839	
Capital			2,120		

Source: Sears, Roebuck and Co., *1991 Annual Report*.

lion. At the end of 1991, more that 1.4 million merchants accepted the Discover Card ("It pays to discover."), with more than 41 million cardholders.

Coldwell Banker Real Estate Group included three units: Homart Development Co., a developer of commercial real estate; the Coldwell Banker Residential Group, a real estate brokerage firm; and Sears Mortgage Corporation, an originator of home mortgages and the home of Sears Savings Bank. Homart Development specialized in developing regional malls and community centers. It also operated those properties, with 39 malls under management, while owning and operating 21 office buildings. Coldwell Banker had more than 1,900 real estate offices with more than 40,000 real estate agents. The Sears Mortgage Group originated mortgages, funding more than $8 billion of mortgages annually. In the process, the mortgage group worked closely with Coldwell Banker. Nearly one-third of the mortgages were originated by clients of Coldwell Banker real estate. More than 25 percent of home owners buying a home through Coldwell Banker secured their mortgage from the Sears Mortgage Group. The mortgage group held a portfolio worth more than $20 billion. The Coldwell Banker Group had total revenues exceeding $1.6 billion in 1991, with more than half coming from real estate commissions and interest. This left Coldwell Banker with a net after-tax income of more than $60 million, while assets approached $10 billion.

By the end of 1991, Sears was largely a financial services firm, with more than half of profits coming from its financial enterprises. By 1995, Sears was on the verge of becoming a pure retailing firm again. The financial businesses of Sears had been, or were being, divested to allow Sears to concentrate almost exclusively on retailing. The remainder of this section focuses on the dismantling of the Sears financial empire.

In September 1992, Sears announced that it would dispose of its financial businesses to concentrate on its core, but struggling, retail operations. This move followed Moody's downgrading of Sears bonds by just four days. Sears announced that it would sell 20 percent of Allstate and the entirety of Coldwell Banker. In addition, Sears announced that it would spin off Dean Witter Financial Services as a separate company by selling shares in a new and independent Dean Witter. The new Dean Witter was scheduled to include the profitable Discover Card. In 1993, Sears spun off Dean Witter (including the Discover Card) to its shareholders, and Dean Witter is now an independent company listed on the New York Stock Exchange. Total assets for Dean Witter are about $30 billion. In addition, Sears also divested Coldwell Banker and its mortgage businesses.

In 1993, Sears also distributed 20 percent of Allstate to Sears shareholders, while retaining an 80 percent interest. In 1995, Sears distributed the remaining 80 percent of Allstate to Sears shareholders. Now Allstate is an independent company, listed on the NYSE, that continues to grow, with total revenues above $20 billion annually, with assets of about $60 billion.

Summary

The companies we have examined, GE Capital, Merrill Lynch, and Sears, Roebuck and Co. reflect the tremendous diversity among financial service companies, and the different experiences that firms may have in this industry. GE Capital is owned by a predominantly industrial firm, while Sears is best known as a retailer. Of the three, Merrill Lynch is most truly a purely financially oriented firm. While all three may be, or may have been, finance companies, they take radically different approaches to their business and operate in different fields of finance. For example, of the three, only GE Capital is heavily committed to leasing. For its part, Sears tried to make use of its high level of name recognition by locating Dean Witter offices in its department stores and by launching the Discover Card.

In a sense, diversification and the desire to enter new businesses have driven all three firms. GE Capital represents an extension beyond manufacturing for GE; Merrill Lynch has extended its financial services far beyond its traditional role of a securities brokerage firm; and Sears migrated from a strictly retailing operation to a predominantly financial firm, and back again. Comparing these firms shows the tremendous diversity within the financial services industry. Clearly, there are many ways that firms can earn their keep (or have their lunches eaten) while still being regarded as finance companies.

Captive Finance Subsidiaries

We have noted that a captive finance subsidiary is a financial firm that is affiliated with, and generally wholly owned by, a non-financial firm. The captive firm issues debt, which the parent firm guarantees, and uses these funds to finance the sales of the parent firm. The financing takes two different principal forms. First, the parent can make the sales of its product and initiate the receivables. The parent would then sell the receivables to the subsidiary. Under this approach, the parent assesses the credit of its customers and makes the credit-granting decision. Second, the captive can assess the credit of potential customers and make the credit-granting extension itself. In either case, the parent receives cash, and the subsidiary holds the debt obligation of the customer.[1] This pattern of industrial firm and captive finance subsidiary is clearest among automobile manufacturers. General Motors, Ford Motors Company, and the Chrysler Corporation have General Motors Acceptance Corporation (GMAC), Ford Credit, and Chrysler Credit, respectively, as their associated finance subsidiaries.

By using a financial subsidiary, a firm has already decided to finance the purchases of its customers. Alternatively, the firm could have insisted that its customers secure financing elsewhere. A firm can have a cost advantage over other lenders if the good being financed has a higher value to the firm than to some other lender. Further, when it is difficult or expensive to arrange for financing and the exchange of merchandise, the firm has an incentive to facilitate the sale by ensuring that the financing is not a stumbling block. Both of these conditions appear to be met in the case of automobile manufacturers. If the customer defaults, the manufacturer is probably in a better position than a bank to dispose of the repossessed automobile. Also, because securing credit for a car purchase from a bank can take extra time and expense, auto companies can facilitate sales by providing credit immediately. Further, the auto company has more immediate information than a bank about the value of the item being financed.

Motives for Creating a Captive Finance Subsidiary

Mian and Smith suggest that finance captives can be used to implement price discrimination schemes because the firm can set two prices – the price of the good and the price of the financing. Monopolists or oligopolists are more likely to employ price discrimination schemes than firms in an

---

[1] This account follows Shehzad L. Mian and Clifford W. Smith, Jr., "Accounts Receivable Management Policy: Theory and Evidence," *Journal of Finance*, 47:1, March 1992, pp. 169–200.

environment of perfect competition. Thus, it is likely that firms in concentrated industries are more likely to form subsidiaries to advance their policy of price discrimination. For example, Mian and Smith use the automobile industry as an example of using captive finance subsidiaries for price discrimination. By being able to set both the price of the auto and the price of financing, the auto company has two instruments to control the final price to the consumer.

Because establishing a captive firm is potentially quite expensive, most captives are formed only by the largest firms (such as large manufacturers and large retail firms). These large firms also have the volume of business necessary to justify the investment in specialized credit-evaluation techniques and personnel.

Further, Mian and Smith argue that financing by a seller creates tax advantages because the firm can recognize the sale under an installment loan as the funds are received. This tax benefit is lost unless the seller finances. Mian and Smith maintain that the creation of a captive finance subsidiary creates the opportunity for specialized financial contracts that solve financial problems. For example, the optimal debt employed in financing automobile manufacturing might differ from that of the subsidiary. As debt covenants often restrict the ratio of debt to assets, creating a subsidiary allows two different ratios of debt to assets, one for the parent and one for the subsidiary. Thus, the combined manufacturer-subsidiary may be able to meet restrictions on its level of debt more easily if there are two distinct firms.

Some authors have suggested that firms with captive subsidiaries present an opportunity for shareholders to expropriate wealth from the bondholders of the firm.[2] As noted earlier, the parent usually guarantees the debt of the subsidiary, but the subsidiary offers no guarantees for the debt of the parent. By shifting assets from the parent to the subsidiary, the firm could reduce the collateral backing the debt of the parent. This could have the effect of transferring wealth from the bondholders by removing the collateral of the firm from their reach. The parent could transfer these assets by selling receivables to the subsidiary at prices below their market value. But others argue that firms would have little incentive for such maneuvers because such actions would adversely affect the reputation of the firm. Large firms that are likely to have captives should be reluctant to destroy their valuable reputations.[3]

In summary, Mian and Smith's empirical findings support several important conclusions about captive finance subsidiaries. First, captives are employed mainly by very large firms. These firms have the volume of sales to justify the expense of creating the subsidiary. Further, large firms in concentrated industries have more market power, and they are better able to employ a captive in implementing price discrimination. Second, the creation of captive finance companies may allow firms to capture tax benefits by providing financing for their own sales. Third, the existence of two firms, the parent and subsidiary, allows superior tailoring of financial contracts, particularly

---

[2] See E. Han Kim, J. J. McConnell, and P. Greenwood, "Capital Structure Rearrangements and Me-First Rules in an Efficient Capital Market," *Journal of Finance*, 32, 1977, pp. 789–810.

[3] For evidence that captives do not lead to wealth expropriation, see Ileen B. Malitz, "A Re-Examination of the Wealth Expropriation Hypothesis: The Case of Captive Financial Subsidiaries," *Journal of Finance*, 44:4, September 1989, pp. 1039–47 and Shehzad L. Mian and Clifford W. Smith, Jr., "Accounts Receivable Management Policy: Theory and Evidence," *Journal of Finance*, 47:1, March 1992, pp. 169–200.

in debt covenants. Fourth, the fears that captives may be useful in expropriating the wealth of bondholders does not appear to be justified by the empirical evidence.

Automobile Finance Captives

The clearest examples of captive financial subsidiaries arise in the automobile manufacturing industry. In this section we discuss Ford Credit and General Motors Acceptance Corporation (GMAC) as examples of this financing phenomenon.

General Motors Acceptance Corporation (GMAC) Founded in 1919, GMAC is a wholly owned subsidiary of General Motors Corporation (GM). The primary business of GMAC is to provide financing services through GM automobile dealers. By providing a ready source of financing, GMAC helps to stimulate sales of GM automobiles, which is GMAC's prime function. GMAC also does business in insurance, mortgage banking, marine financing, and investment services. By far, automobile financing is GMAC's main business.

GMAC finances automobiles on both the retail and wholesale level. Typical operations at the retail level begin when a customer purchases a new or used auto through a GM dealer. The GM dealer extends credit to the purchaser of the automobile, so GMAC is not the initial grantor of credit. GMAC purchases the retail installment obligation from the dealer, after the obligations are analyzed for their credit soundness. Thereafter, GMAC collects and administers the obligation. GMAC holds a lien on the automobiles that it finances and generally requires collision insurance on the vehicle to protect GMAC's financial interest in the car.

GMAC also has extensive wholesale automobile financing operations. GMAC offers financing to GM dealers to finance the dealer's acquisition of automobiles from GM. In essence, GMAC helps dealers finance the inventory of cars that they hold for sale. GMAC maintains a lien on the inventory in case the dealer fails to pay for the automobiles as promised. In addition to providing inventory financing, GMAC also makes term loans to dealers for their operations, such as for remodeling, purchasing real estate, or providing working capital.

GMAC is also active in leasing, insurance, mortgage banking, and marine financing. GMAC helps dealers finance the purchase of fleets of automobiles which the dealer then leases. GMAC

Table 16.11
Abbreviated Percentage Balance Sheet for GMAC

Assets		Liabilities and Stockholder's Equity	
Cash	5%	Notes payable	40%
Finance receivables	68	Accounts payable	2
Inventories	2	Accrued expenses	2
Net property and equipment	14	Other current liabilities	6
Investment in subsidiaries	5	Long-term debt	33
Other assets	6	Net common stock	2
		Retained earnings	6
		Stockholder's equity	9
Total Assets	100%	**Total Liabilities and Stockholder's Equity**	100%

retains a financial claim on the automobiles until the dealer has completely repaid the loan. In the insurance field, GMAC offers automobile, homeowners, and liability insurance. More closely related to its primary role of fostering sales of GM cars, GMAC offers insurance against mechanical breakdown of automobiles. Dealers can insure their automobile inventories through GMAC as well.

In the mortgage banking field, GMAC grants mortgages on residential real estate. Many mortgages in the United States are packaged and bought and sold as securities, a field in which GMAC is active also. In marine financing, GMAC plays a role similar to its role in automobile sales. It offers financing for purchasers of boats and also extends inventory financing to yacht dealers.

Of all of its varied activities, GMAC is principally involved in financing activities that support automobile sales. GMAC derives about 85 percent of revenues from its financing operations and finances about 35 percent of all GM autos sold. This gives a total of about 2 million cars financed per year.

GMAC holds about $80 billion in total assets, distributed as shown in Table 16.11. The vast bulk of these assets, almost 80 percent, are finance receivables. These are amounts due from the various loans that GMAC has made, with most stemming from automobile lending. In essence, almost all of GMAC's assets are financial claims or equipment on lease, with very little of its assets devoted to plant or equipment for operations. GMAC finances these assets with tremendous amounts of debt. As Table 16.11 indicates, just about half of all liabilities is due in short-term financing. Another 22 percent of assets is financed by longer-term debt. Equity and retained earnings amount to only about 16 percent of total assets. With such high levels of debt, GMAC is a major borrower in the U.S. economy. Most of its short-term financing is raised by selling commercial paper.

GMAC enjoys gross revenue exceeding $12 billion per year and has net income of about $1 billion per year. Therefore, GMAC is a critically important component of GM. GMAC has earned about $1 billion in each of the last five years, providing GM with much needed financial stability and desperately needed cash infusions through the dividends it pays to GM.

Ford Credit Like GMAC, Ford Credit is wholly owned by its parent, the Ford Motor Company. Ford Credit's primary line of business is providing financing related to the sales of Ford automobiles, but it also operates an insurance business and has a financing arm designed to finance automobiles manufactured by other firms. Each year, Ford Credit finances millions of automobiles and extends loans totaling about $100 billion.

Table 16.12 presents an abbreviated balance sheet for Ford Credit, with total assets of $70 billion. Thus, Ford Credit is almost as large as GMAC. Like GMAC, Ford Credit holds the overwhelming percentage of its assets as finance receivables or other financial investments. Besides equipment that is owned and leased, Ford Credit has very little invested in physical assets.

Also like GMAC, Ford Credit finances its assets with a very high percentage of debt, most of which is short-term debt. At the end of 1994, Ford Credit had more than $30 billion in commercial paper outstanding, with more than $33 billion in total debt payable within one year. As at GMAC, this amounts to about half of all assets. Ford Credit has total annual revenues of about $8 billion, with more than $6.7 billion coming from its financing activities. (The other portion came from investment income and insurance sales.)

Table 16.12
Abbreviated Percentage Balance Sheet for Ford Credit

Assets		**Liabilities and Stockholder's Equity**	
Cash	1%	Accounts payable	1%
Receivables	73	Notes payable	81
Other current assets	1	Other current liabilities	2
Net property and equipment	18	Capital surplus	1
Investment in subsidiaries	4	Retained earnings	7
Deposits	3	Shareholder equity	8
Total Assets	100%	**Total Liabilities and Stockholder's Equity**	100%

Summary Ford Credit and GMAC are very similar in their operations, although Ford Credit is about half the size of GMAC. As captive subsidiaries, both exist to support car sales by providing financing. Both finance retail sales of automobiles and both provide wholesale financing of dealer automobile inventories. Consistently profitable, Ford Credit and GMAC provide their parents with needed stability to offset the uncertain sales of automobiles.

Asset Securitization

As mentioned in the Overview, asset securitization is the process of converting financial claims into securities that can be traded in the financial markets. Asset securitization plays an increasingly important role in financial markets and is a critical tool for finance companies.

Mortgages and Asset Securitization

One of the earliest, and still the largest, economic sectors to exploit asset securitization is the market for residential mortgages. When a family purchases a home, it generally borrows funds from a financial institution such as a savings and loan association for a substantial portion of the value of the home. In addition to the profits from lending, the lender often earns a fee or closing costs for completing the transaction. The lender holds a mortgage on the home and receives payments from the borrower, typically for a period of 30 years. Before asset securitization, the lender would hold the mortgage until the debt was repaid. Under this system, the lender could only lend if it was willing to commit the funds for the entire duration of the loan.

Few lenders today hold mortgages until repayment. Instead, mortgages are bundled to create pools of individual family mortgages, and these pools are traded as securities. By committing a mortgage to a pool, the lender sells its claim to receive the mortgage payment and transfers its mortgage on the house that was financed.

The initial lender finds this opportunity attractive because it frees funds for new investment. In particular, a savings and loan can make a mortgage loan and earn a fee for closing the deal, sell the loan and regain its cash funds, and repeat the cycle. In essence, the savings and loan is in the business of initiating and packaging mortgage loans and has left the business of long-term lending.

Asset securitization in the mortgage market has been stimulated by a variety of key factors. First, home mortgages are fairly homogeneous with similar terms and similar collateral arrangements. Today the terms on mortgages are more standardized to make them more amenable to asset securitization. Second, the loan is backed by the physical collateral of the house. Most asset securitization is based on lending on underlying collateral, so the assets that are securitized are based on **asset-backed** or **asset-based loans**. Third, in the case of mortgage markets, various arms of the federal government guarantee the payments on the mortgages to the owner of the loans. The government programs offer these guarantees to stimulate a greater level of lending for homes and thus to provide more citizens with housing. Fourth, compared with holding the entirety of a loan oneself, an investor can achieve diversification by purchasing a security representing a fractional share of many mortgages. This protects the security holder from problems that can arise with a particular home – such as default or a fall in the value of the collateral.

Finance Companies and Asset Securitization

While many finance companies buy and sell securities based on home mortgages, we have seen that much of their business is concentrated in other areas of lending. In recent years, asset securitization has spread to automobile financing and credit card receivables, two bread-and-butter areas of finance company activities. Asset securitization of automobile loans or credit card debt operates very much like the pooling and securitization of mortgages described in the preceding section. For convenience, we will focus on automobile receivables, although the discussion applies to credit card receivables as well.

To create a security based on automobile loans, a financial firm creates a bundle of similar loans and offers investors the chance to purchase a security with this bundle of loans serving as the underlying asset. From the point of view of a potential investor, the main problem with such a security is the chance of default. Even though the security includes many car loans, default on any one will reduce the returns that the investor might anticipate. To offset this default risk, almost all such asset-backed securities include some kind of **credit enhancement** – a reduction in the default risk of a security. For example, GMAC might create a security and offer it to the public. In doing so, GMAC might include a guarantee that it will make good on any defaults beyond a certain percentage of the assets in the pool. In other situations, the creator of the security could seek a third-party guarantee of a similar nature. In general, these credit enhancements raise the quality of the security and make it a safer investment.

Securities based on automobile loans have the four features that helped the market for mortgage-backed securities develop. First, automobile loans are fairly homogeneous, with similar terms and a monthly payment. Second, the securities are backed by a claim on the financed automobiles themselves. Third, the credit-enhancing strategies discussed above play a similar role in the federal government guarantees provided for mortgage-backed securities. Fourth, investors in these asset-backed securities achieve diversification in their lending because the security represents claims on many different auto loans.

For a finance company like GMAC, asset securitization plays a key role. We have seen that the primary purpose of GMAC is to provide auto financing to stimulate sales of GM cars. GMAC's financing activity is clearly limited to the amount of available funds. If GMAC can originate auto loans, package those loans as securities, and sell them, GMAC turns its loans into cash. GMAC can then use this cash to make new loans. By actively participating in asset securitization of its car loans, GMAC moves from being an ultimate provider of credit to being principally an initiator of loans – exactly the role that helps GM sell cars.

Summary

This chapter has explored the diffuse world of finance companies and financial conglomerates. Finance companies are freer from regulation than many other types of financial institutions, such as banks, savings associations, or insurance companies. Largely because of this freedom from regulation, finance companies constitute an industry composed of vastly different kinds of companies. We noted that finance companies are extremely active in leasing, consumer lending, and asset-based lending. As a whole, these firms are extremely leveraged and have a strong preference for short-term debt.

In the United States, there are a number of extremely large finance companies with a wide range of businesses. We considered General Electric Capital Corporation, the financial arm of Sears, Roebuck, and Merrill Lynch as three examples of financial conglomerates. All offer varied financial services and operate on an international stage. While there are important similarities, we noted major differences in ownership structure and the types of finance operations that each finds attractive.

We considered the rationale for captive finance companies and noted that these would most likely be attractive to large firms. Financing installment sales through a captive finance company may offer tax benefits unavailable through other channels. We considered General Motors Acceptance Corporation and Ford Credit as two examples of captive financial subsidiaries.

The chapter concluded with a brief overview of asset securitization. We saw that this trend toward packaging debt into securities came to maturity in the mortgage market and that the same principles are now being applied to other forms of debt, such as automobile loans and credit card receivables.

Questions and Problems

1. Explain the difference between a financial conglomerate and a financial subsidiary.
2. Can a financial conglomerate be a financial subsidiary? Explain. Give an example of such a firm.
3. What is a captive finance subsidiary? Give an example.
4. Do finance companies as described in this chapter accept demand deposits? Can subsidiaries of finance companies accept demand deposits? Explain.
5. Many of the financial subsidiaries described in this chapter are separate corporations, distinct from their parents. Why are so many firms organized this way? Explain.
6. Explain why some manufacturing firms create captive finance subsidiaries.
7. How might automobile firms use their captive finance subsidiaries to promote price discrimination?
8. Explain how an unscrupulous firm with a captive subsidiary might transfer wealth from bondholders to stockholders.
9. Explain how lenders might use asset securitization to free more loanable funds.
10. Explain the role of credit enhancement in asset securitization.

References

Goldberg, C. J. and K. Rogers, "An Introduction to Asset-Backed Securities," *Journal of Applied Corporate Finance*, 1:3, Fall 1988, pp. 20–31.

Goldberg, H., "Asset Securitization and Corporate Financial Health," *Journal of Applied Corporate Finance*, 1:3, Fall 1988, pp. 45–51.

Kim, E. H., J. J. McConnell, and P. Greenwood, "Capital Structure Rearrangements and Me-First Rules in an Efficient Capital Market," *Journal of Finance*, Volume 32, 1977, pp. 789–810.

Malitz, I. B., "A Re-Examination of the Wealth Expropriation Hypothesis: The Case of Captive Financial Subsidiaries," *Journal of Finance*, 44:4, September 1989, pp. 1039–47.

Mian, S. L. and C. W. Smith, Jr., "Accounts Receivable Management Policy: Theory and Evidence," *Journal of Finance*, 47:1, March 1992, pp. 169–200.

Investment Companies and Performance Evaluation

17

Overview

The prospective investor, faced with thousands of stocks and bonds to choose from, may find the task bewildering. An individual investor cannot learn about all of the different firms and the investment prospects associated with their securities. If one also wishes to consider both international securities and government securities of various types, then the task becomes even more hopeless. How can one intelligently form a portfolio faced with such information overload?

One possible answer for many investors is to place funds with an **investment company**. An investment company is a firm that collects funds from a wide group of investors. These collected funds are then invested in a portfolio of securities, and each of the investors in the fund has title to a fractional share of all of the investments in the portfolio. The staff of the investment company manages the portfolio and tries to invest the funds where they will earn a high return for the level of risk.

These investment companies come in two forms, closed-end investment companies and mutual funds, each of which will be discussed in detail. Essentially, the difference between the two forms depends on how they accept funds for investment. A **closed-end company** accepts funds only at its creation, and the funds contributed at that point form the investment base that the company has to invest throughout its life. A **mutual fund**, by contrast, is always ready to receive money from new investors. The new funds are then used to expand the portfolio. These differences in the ways in which money flows into the investment companies have far-reaching implications, which are considered in detail later in this chapter.

After explaining the institutional features of investment companies and the ways in which they are regulated and taxed, this chapter discusses performance evaluation for mutual funds. As mentioned throughout this book, there are important advantages to investing in a diversified portfolio, rather than merely committing funds to one or two favorite stocks. We have also seen evidence that markets are quite efficient in the weak and semi-strong versions of the efficient markets hypothesis.

Because investment companies constitute well-diversified and professionally managed portfolios, might it be possible for them to outperform the market for the level of risk that they bear? This might be a reasonable hope for two reasons. First, mutual funds are well-diversified, so their level of unsystematic risk should be very low. Second, investment companies hire professional security analysts. If these analysts have genuine stock selecting skills, this should be revealed by the superior performance of the investment company. These issues are examined to complete the discussion of the CAPM, the EMH, and what investors can reasonably expect from their portfolios.

General Features of Investment Companies

Investment companies are essentially a phenomenon of the twentieth century. Overall, the growth of investment companies has been very strong. During the period from 1940 to 1993, investment companies grew at an annual rate of 14.9 percent, increasing the total size of assets 1,525 times. However, as Table 17.1 indicates, the strong growth has not been shared equally between closed-end companies and mutual funds. Mutual funds have increased their size more than 3,370 times during this period, while closed-end companies have had an asset increase of fewer than 180 times. As a result, the mutual fund asset pool is almost 14 times as large as that of closed-end companies. This vast difference in growth, coupled with the fact that the closed-end companies dominated in 1940, clearly shows a marked preference for mutual funds.

This preference for mutual funds must be due to the difference in the way the funds are invested. In fact, mutual funds have the natural advantage in growth, because they are open-ended. Their ability to continue to receive funds at any point makes growth substantially easier. Closed-end companies, once established, can grow in asset size only through successful investment of the originally contributed funds. The closed-end segment of the investment company industry can only grow through the creation of additional closed-end companies.

Investment companies, whether closed-end companies or mutual funds, share a number of common features in their organizational form. When soliciting funds, both closed-end and open-end companies must provide a prospectus to prospective investors. This is the same requirement faced by firms planning to issue stocks or bonds, and the investment company must face the same process described in Chapter 8. The closed-end company needs to circulate a prospectus only when it is being established. Once founded, the closed-end company will not receive any more funds from the public, so there is no further need for a prospectus. The mutual fund, by contrast, needs to revise and distribute a prospectus continually, since it is always prepared to accept new funds.

In mutual funds and closed-end companies, investors purchase shares. A share is simply a title to a fraction of the assets of the investment company. The total assets of the company, minus

Table 17.1
Investment Company Assets
($ millions)

Year	Mutual Funds	Closed-End Companies	Total
1940	448	614	1,062
1950	2,531	872	3,403
1960	17,383	2,084	19,467
1970	50,646	4,024	54,679
1980	138,333	8,053	146,386
1990	990,177	55,272	1,045,449
1993	1,510,047	110,000	1,620,047

Source: Wiesenberger Financial Services, *Investment Companies 1994*, New York: Warren, Gorham & Lamont, 1994.

the liabilities, constitute the **net asset value**. The **net asset value per share** is simply the total net asset value of the company, divided by the number of shares outstanding. In the case of the closed-end company, the number of shares is constant. For a mutual fund, the number of shares may increase or decrease.

Both kinds of investment companies perform the function of investment advisers and clerical staff. The investment company must keep accurate records of ownership of shares in the company and provide reports and payments to the shareholders. The reports may consist of monthly statements of the account, along with quarterly and annual reports of the fund's performance and financial standing. Investment companies also make payments to their shareholders. These may take the form of dividends or of capital gains distributions. The dividend is essentially like a cash dividend paid on the common stock of any corporation. The capital gains distribution is made for the purposes of taxation.

Essentially, the owners of a mutual fund are the indirect owners of the securities in the mutual fund's portfolio. If a shareholder were to manage his or her own portfolio and to trade securities, he or she would realize profits and losses on those transactions. These profits and losses would generate tax liabilities. Investment companies are typically organized so that they do not pay taxes themselves, but the shareholders pay the taxes. The capital gains distribution is a bookkeeping technique for keeping track of the tax liability of the share owners.

The management of an investment company takes on the function of the investment advisor by making all of the decisions about which securities will be held in the firm's portfolio. In committing funds to an investment company, the investor puts his faith in the investment capabilities of the firm's management. The company charges a fee for this service, which is stated as a percentage of the net asset value held by the company. Usually, this fee is ½ to 1 percent annually.

In addition to these common features, there are important differences between closed-end companies and mutual funds as two kinds of companies. Further, within each category, there is a wide variety of difference as well. This is particularly true among mutual funds. Given the vastly greater size of mutual funds, the following discussion of closed-end companies is rather brief, allowing more attention to the mutual funds.

Advantages of Investment Companies

The investment company industry is clearly quite large, with substantial fees being earned by company managers. To justify these fees, managers must offer something of value to attract investors.

Diversification One of the most important benefits of investment companies is the fact that they provide a ready-made portfolio for the investor. A small investor does not have enough funds to construct his own portfolio of 20 to 30 stocks without incurring very large transaction costs on a percentage basis. If the investor wants to hold 20 stocks, and the average stock price is $50 per share, the investor would need $100,000 to avoid trading in odd lots. For many investors, this is too large an amount to commit to the stock market. Providing a diversified portfolio to very small investors is probably the main benefit that investment companies provide.

Clerical Function The second clear benefit provided by investment companies is the clerical and management function. Managing a portfolio of 20 stocks is a time-consuming task, with much bookkeeping. The investment company achieves important economies of scale in this function that benefit the individual investor.

Professional Management A third possible benefit, and one that is often claimed by investment company managers, is providing professional investment advice. One of the key rationales for using a professional money manager is to capitalize on his or her greater knowledge of the market. However, it is not clear that investment companies really succeed in providing this benefit to their clients. As a group, on a risk-adjusted basis, investment company managers are not able to substantiate their claim to having expertise in picking winning securities. Even though the group may not be able to demonstrate such expertise, it is still possible that particular managers may really have expertise, nonetheless. This issue is examined in greater detail later in this chapter.

Closed-End Investment Companies

The most striking fact about closed-end investment companies is their refusal to accept new funds for investment. Once the original shares are issued, no more shares can ever come into existence. Further, the investment company itself will not redeem shares for their owners. Instead, shares of closed-end companies trade in a public market for whatever price the laws of supply and demand allow.

Intrinsic Value of Closed-End Funds

Since virtually 100 percent of the company's assets are in securities, it might seem that the closed-end shares would trade in the marketplace for an amount equal to the net asset value per share. This is not the case, however. Because the shareholders cannot redeem the shares for their net asset value, the price of the shares is free to wander away from the net asset value. In particular, the share price may be more or less than the net asset value. If the share price exceeds the net asset value, it is said to be at a **premium**, while a share price below the net asset value is at a **discount**.

Discounts and Premiums on Closed-End Funds

Figure 17.1 presents quotations for closed-end companies. The net asset value per share is reported for each company, followed by the stock price. The final column of figures shows the premium, or discount, on the stock price. Shares of closed-end funds often sell at a discount to their net asset value. These discounts tend to be persistent and frequently large. At times this average discount has been as large as 25 percent. At the end of 1993, the average discount was about 4 percent. While the factors that determine discounts are not perfectly understood, they do appear to be related to taxes and past performance.[1]

---

[1] See Morris Mendelson, "Closed-End Fund Discounts Revisited," *The Financial Review*, 1978, pp. 48–72, and Hans R. Stoll, "Discounts and Premiums on Shares of Diversified Closed-End Investment Funds," Working Paper No. 11–73, The Wharton School, University of Pennsylvania, 1978.

Figure 17.1
Quotations for Closed-End Investment Companies

CLOSED END FUNDS

Friday, November 17, 1995

Closed-end funds sell a limited number of shares and invest the proceeds in securities. Unlike open-end funds, closed-ends generally do not buy their shares back from investors who wish to cash in their holdings. Instead, fund shares trade on a stock exchange. The following list, provided by Lipper Analytical Services, shows the exchange where each fund trades (A: American; C: Chicago; N: NYSE; O: Nasdaq; T: Toronto; z: does not trade on an exchange). The data also include the fund's most recent net asset value, its closing share price on the day NAV was calculated, and the percentage difference between the market price and the NAV (often called the premium or discount). For equity funds, the final column provides 52-week returns based on market prices plus dividends. For bond funds, the final column shows the past 12 months' income distributions as a percentage of the current market price. Footnotes appear after a fund's name. a: the NAV and market price are ex dividend. b: the NAV is fully diluted. c: NAV, market price and premium or discount are as of Thursday's close. d: NAV, market price and premium or discount are as of Wednesday's close. e: NAV assumes rights offering is fully subscribed. v: NAV is converted at the commercial Rand rate. y: NAV and market price are in Canadian dollars. All other footnotes refer to unusual circumstances; explanations for those that appear can be found at the bottom of this list. N/A signifies that the information is not available or not applicable.

Fund Name	Stock Exch	NAV	Market Price	Prem /Disc	52 week Market Return
World Equity Funds					
ASA Limited -acv	N	36.30	38 1/4	+ 5.4	−14.8
All Seasons Glbl	O	5.15	4 1/4	−17.5	21.4
Anchor Gold&Curr	C	5.66	5 1/4	− 7.2	−12.5
Argentina	N	10.40	10 1/4	− 1.4	−17.9
Asia Pacific	N	13.22	12 1/4	− 7.3	−19.9
Asia Tigers	N	11.42	9 5/8	−15.7	−12.4
Austria	N	10.00	8	−20.0	−1.2
BGR Prec Metals -cy	T	17.03	13 3/8	−21.5	−10.8
Brazil -c	N	22.26	20 7/8	− 6.2	−28.8
Brazilian Equity -c	N	14.11	13 1/2	− 4.3	−30.6
Cdn Genl Inv -cy	T	41.69	31	−25.6	3.9
Cdn Wrld Fd Ltd -cy	T	4.77	3 1/2	−26.6	−10.3
Central Eur Eqty	N	20.98	16	−23.7	8.9
Chile	N	25.64	22 5/8	−11.8	−0.7
China	N	11.99	11 3/4	− 2.0	−22.1
Clemente Global -c	N	10.86	8 3/8	−22.9	−4.3
Czech Republic	N	13.47	12 3/4	− 5.3	−1.2
Economic Inv Tr -cy	T	90.50	63 1/2	−29.8	N/A
Emer Mkts Grow	z	48.45	N/A	0.0	N/A

Fund Name	Stock Exch	NAV	Market Price	Prem /Disc	12 Mo Yield 10/31/95
U.S. Gov't. Bond Funds					
ACM Govt Inc	N	9.35	9 5/8	+ 2.9	10.2
ACM Govt Oppty	N	N/A	7 3/8	0.0	9.6
ACM Govt Secs	N	8.94	8 5/8	− 3.5	11.2
ACM Govt Spec	N	7.22	6 7/8	− 4.8	11.9
Amer Govt Income -c	N	5.87	5 5/8	− 4.2	14.2
Amer Govt Port -c	N	7.00	6 7/8	− 1.8	15.5
Dean Witter Govt	N	9.21	8 1/4	−10.4	7.3
Excelsior Income -c	N	18.87	16 1/8	−14.5	6.8
Kemper Int Govt	N	8.25	7 1/8	−13.6	8.2
MFS Govt Mkts -a	N	7.55	6 1/2	−13.9	7.1
Putnam Int Govt -a	N	N/A	7 5/8	0.0	7.7
RCM Strat Glbl	N	11.36	10 1/8	−10.9	9.6
U.S. Mortgage Bond Funds					
2002 Target Term -ac	N	14.18	12 1/4	−13.6	6.7
Amer Govt Term -c	N	8.83	8 1/2	− 3.7	7.0
Amer Oppty Inc -c	N	6.65	6 1/8	− 7.9	16.3
Amer Sel Port -c	N	12.76	11 '	−13.8	10.2
Amer Str Inc II -c	N	13.01	11 3/8	−12.6	11.4
Amer Str Inc III -c	N	12.40	11	−11.3	11.3
Amer Str Income -c	N	13.08	12 3/8	− 5.4	12.5
BlckRk 1998 Term -ac	N	9.72	9	− 7.4	6.2
BlckRk 1999 Term -ac	N	9.18	8 1/4	−10.1	7.1
BlckRk 2001 Term -ac	N	8.86	7 5/8	−13.9	7.3
BlckRk Adv Term -ac	N	10.23	8 3/4	−14.5	7.9
BlckRk Income -ac	N	7.68	7 1/8	− 7.2	10.3
BlckRk Inv 09 -ac	A	13.49	11 1/2	−14.8	8.9
BlckRk Inv Q Tm -ac	N	9.27	8	−13.7	8.2
BlckRk Str Tm -ac	N	9.05	7 5/8	−15.7	7.8
BlckRk Tgt Tm -ac	N	9.85	9 1/8	− 7.4	7.2
Heritage US Govt -c	N	12.61	11 3/8	− 9.8	9.9
Hyperion 1997 Tm -ac	N	7.86	7 1/4	− 7.8	7.3
Hyperion 1999 Tm -ac	N	7.55	6 5/8	−12.3	8.1
Hyperion 2002 Tm -ac	N	8.57	7 1/4	−15.4	8.2
Hyperion 2005 -ac	N	9.10	7 5/8	−16.2	9.1
Hyperion Tot Rtn -ac	N	10.51	8 7/8	−15.6	10.4
Inc Opp 1999	N	9.45	8 1/4	−12.7	6.4
Inc Opp 2000	N	9.79	8 1/2	−13.2	6.7
Liberty 1999	N	8.50	7 3/8	−13.2	6.2
Mentor Income -ac	N	10.21	8 7/8	−13.1	10.1
Nations 2003 -a	N	8.51	7 5/8	−10.4	8.0
Nations 2004 -a	N	8.74	7 3/4	−11.3	8.0
PIMCO Comm Mtg -c	N	13.68	12 5/8	− 7.7	9.8
TCW/DW Term 2000	N	8.86	7 5/8	−13.9	6.2
TCW/DW Term 2002	N	9.32	8	−14.2	8.4
TCW/DW Term 2003	N	9.09	7 5/8	−16.1	7.6
Triple A&Govt 97 -ac	A	9.74	9 7/16	− 3.1	5.3

Fund Name	Stock Exch	NAV	Market Price	Prem /Disc	12 Mo Yield 10/31/95
U.S. Mortgage Bond Funds					
2002 Target Term -ac	N	14.18	12 1/4	−13.6	6.7
Amer Govt Term -c	N	8.83	8 1/2	− 3.7	7.0
Amer Oppty Inc -c	N	6.65	6 1/8	− 7.9	16.3
Amer Sel Port -c	N	12.76	11 '	−13.8	10.2
Amer Str Inc II -c	N	13.01	11 3/8	−12.6	11.4
Amer Str Inc III -c	N	12.40	11	−11.3	11.3
Amer Str Income -c	N	13.08	12 3/8	− 5.4	12.5
BlckRk 1998 Term -ac	N	9.72	9	− 7.4	6.2
BlckRk 1999 Term -ac	N	9.18	8 1/4	−10.1	7.1
BlckRk 2001 Term -ac	N	8.86	7 5/8	−13.9	7.3
BlckRk Adv Term -ac	N	10.23	8 3/4	−14.5	7.9
BlckRk Income -ac	N	7.68	7 1/8	− 7.2	10.3
BlckRk Inv 09 -ac	A	13.49	11 1/2	−14.8	8.9
BlckRk Inv Q Tm -ac	N	9.27	8	−13.7	8.2
BlckRk Str Tm -ac	N	9.05	7 5/8	−15.7	7.8
BlckRk Tgt Tm -ac	N	9.85	9 1/8	− 7.4	7.2
Heritage US Govt -c	N	12.61	11 3/8	− 9.8	9.9
Hyperion 1997 Tm -ac	N	7.86	7 1/4	− 7.8	7.3
Hyperion 1999 Tm -ac	N	7.55	6 5/8	−12.3	8.1
Hyperion 2002 Tm -ac	N	8.57	7 1/4	−15.4	8.2
Hyperion 2005 -ac	N	9.10	7 5/8	−16.2	9.1
Hyperion Tot Rtn -ac	N	10.51	8 7/8	−15.6	10.4
Inc Opp 1999	N	9.45	8 1/4	−12.7	6.4
Inc Opp 2000	N	9.79	8 1/2	−13.2	6.7
Liberty 1999	N	8.50	7 3/8	−13.2	6.2
Mentor Income -ac	N	10.21	8 7/8	−13.1	10.1
Nations 2003 -a	N	8.51	7 5/8	−10.4	8.0
Nations 2004 -a	N	8.74	7 3/4	−11.3	8.0
PIMCO Comm Mtg -c	N	13.68	12 5/8	− 7.7	9.8
TCW/DW Term 2000	N	8.86	7 5/8	−13.9	6.2
TCW/DW Term 2002	N	9.32	8	−14.2	8.4
TCW/DW Term 2003	N	9.09	7 5/8	−16.1	7.6
Triple A&Govt 97 -ac	A	9.74	9 7/16	− 3.1	5.3

Fund Name	Stock Exch	NAV	Market Price	Prem /Disc	12 Mo Yield 10/31/95
Investment Grade Bond Funds					
1838 Bd-Deb	N	21.85	21 5/8	− 1.0	7.9
All-American Tm -ac	N	14.30	12 1/4	−14.3	9.4
Amer Cap Bond -c	N	21.05	19 7/8	− 5.6	8.0
CNA Income -c	N	9.73	10 3/8	+ 6.6	10.5
Circle Income -ac	O	11.94	10 3/4	−10.0	8.5
Current Inc Shs	N	14.09	12 1/4	−13.1	7.6
Fortis Secs	N	9.25	8 1/2	− 8.1	10.0
Ft Dearborn Inc -a	N	16.67	15 1/8	− 9.3	7.5
Hatteras Income -a	N	N/A	16 3/8	0.0	8.6
INA Investments	N	19.37	17 1/8	−11.6	8.1
Independence Sq	O	18.60	17 1/2	− 5.9	7.6
InterCap Income	N	18.01	16 1/4	− 9.8	9.2

Source: *The Wall Street Journal*, April 3, 1995.

Recently, new research on discounts and premiums has adopted the noise trader approach to explaining this phenomenon. Charles Lee, Andrei Shleifer, and Richard Thaler cite four disturbing facts about discounts and premiums on closed-end funds:[2]

1. New funds appear on the market at a premium and move rapidly to a discount.
2. Closed-end funds usually trade at substantial discounts relative to their net asset values.

---

[2] C. M. C. Lee, A. Shleifer, and R. H. Thaler, "Anomalies: Closed-End Mutual Funds," *Journal of Economic Perspectives*, 4:4, Fall 1990, pp. 153–64. See also their related paper, C. M. C. Lee, A. Shleifer, and R. H. Thaler, "Investor Sentiment and the Close-End Fund Puzzle," *Journal of Finance*, 46:1, March 1991, pp. 75–109. Finally, for an accessible treatment of these issues, see J. Bradford De Long and Andrei Shleifer, "Closed-End Fund Discounts," *The Journal of Portfolio Management*, 18:2, Winter 1992, pp. 46–53.

3. Discounts (and premiums) are subject to wide variation, both over time and across funds.
4. When closed-end funds are terminated, either through merger, liquidation, or conversion to an open-end fund, prices converge to net asset values.

Lee, Shleifer, and Thaler suggest that smart money traders have limited opportunities to trade to exploit departures from net asset value. First, there is little way to arbitrage the differential. Second, the supply of investors willing to make long-term bets against prices that depart from net asset values is quite limited. These factors allow persistent and wide divergences between net asset values and the prices of closed-end fund shares.

Mutual Funds: Growth and Diversity

Since 1940, the total asset size of mutual funds has grown very rapidly. In addition to this growth in assets, the industry has grown in two other important dimensions. First, the number of mutual funds has increased dramatically, and second, there are now many more types of mutual funds. From only 68 mutual funds in 1940, the industry has grown to more than 3,100 now.

There are also different types of mutual funds. In 1940, there were principally only stock, bond, and income mutual funds. By the 1980s, mutual funds specializing in money market instruments and municipal bonds had also emerged. These differences are important, since each mutual fund must specify the kind of investment strategy that it intends to follow. Table 17.2 gives a basic classification of some of the major types of mutual funds.

In its prospectus, each mutual fund is required to state its investment objectives and to follow that plan in the management of its investment strategy. For example, the T. Rowe Price Growth and Income Fund recently stated its investment objective in the following terms:

> *The fund seeks to provide investors with long-term growth of their capital, a reasonable amount of current income, and a growing level of income. To achieve these objectives, the Fund will invest primarily in income-producing equity securities which have prospects for growth of both capital and dividend income. Up to 30 percent of the assets may be invested in convertible and corporate debt securities, preferred stocks, and securities of foreign issuers when consistent with the Fund's objectives. The Fund may also, to a limited extent, lend portfolio securities. While the Fund will ordinarily remain substantially invested in equity securities, it may, for defensive purposes, establish and maintain reserves in money market instruments including repurchase agreements with banks and broker-dealers.*

In addition, there are a number of other kinds of specialized mutual funds. Some focus on international securities, while others focus on stocks of emerging companies, securities in the energy field, and other specialties. The break-up of AT&T has even led to a mutual fund that holds all of the new telephone companies in the same proportions as they were valued before the break-up. This gives investors who liked the old way of holding telephone securities an easy way of doing so. Not surprisingly, this new mutual fund has been dubbed the "Humpty Dumpty Fund."

Without doubt, one of the most important features in the development of mutual funds in the recent past has been the emergence of the money market mutual fund – a mutual fund that

Table 17.2
Types of Mutual Funds

Aggressive Growth
A mutual fund that seeks maximum capital appreciation through the use of investment techniques involving greater than ordinary risk, such as borrowing money in order to provide leverage, short selling, hedging, options, and warrants.

Growth
A mutual fund whose primary investment objective is long-term growth of capital. It invests principally in common stocks with growth potential.

Growth and Income
A mutual fund whose aim is to provide for a degree of both income and long-term growth.

Balanced
A mutual fund that has an investment policy of "balancing" its portfolio, generally by including bonds, preferred stocks, and common stocks.

Option/Income
The investment objective of these funds is to seek a high current return by investing primarily in dividend-paying common stocks on which call options are traded on national securities exchanges. Current return generally consists of dividends, premiums from expired call options, net short-term gains from sales of portfolio securities on exercises of options or otherwise, and any profits from closing purchase transactions.

Income
A mutual fund whose primary investment objective is current income rather than growth of capital. It usually invests in stocks and bonds that normally pay higher dividends and interest.

Corporate Bond
A mutual fund whose portfolio consists primarily of bonds. The emphasis of such funds is normally on income rather than growth.

Municipal Bond
A mutual fund that invests in a broad range of tax-exempt bonds issued by states, cities, and other local governments. The interest obtained from these bonds is passed through to shareholders free of federal tax. The funds's primary objective is current tax-free income.

Short-Term Municipal Bond
These funds invest in municipal securities with relatively short maturities. They are also known as Tax-Exempt Money Market Funds.

Money Market
Also called a liquid asset or cash fund, it is a mutual fund whose primary objective is to make higher interest securities available to investors who want immediate income and high investment safety. This is accomplished through the purchase of high-yield money market instruments, such as U.S. government securities, bank certificates of deposit, and commercial paper.

Source: Investment Company Institute, *1991 Mutual Fund Fact Book*, Washington, DC: Investment Company Institute, 1991, pp. 12–13.

holds money market securities. From their inception in 1974, money market mutual funds have come to dominate the market. Correspondingly, money market mutual funds have come to dominate in asset size as well, even though that dominance is currently not as strong as it was in recent years. Table 17.3 shows the distribution of funds by different types of mutual funds in 1980, 1990, and 1993.

Ownership of Mutual Fund Shares

Along with the growth in money market mutual funds, the ownership mix of mutual funds has been changing dramatically as well. Mutual funds have traditionally been regarded as investment vehicles particularly well suited to small investors, usually individuals. About 50 percent of all accounts have a value less than $10,000. However, institutional investors have become very active in money market funds, even spurring the creation of money market funds designed specifically for institutional investors.

Load versus No-Load Mutual Funds

Compared with closed-end investment companies, two of the main reasons for the rapid growth of mutual funds are their open-ended character, or readiness to accept new funds, and the ease of redemption. The owner of shares in a mutual fund may withdraw the money invested in the fund at any time by returning the shares to the mutual fund and receiving the net asset value of those shares, or at least an amount very close to the net asset value. This makes a mutual fund a very liquid form of investment.

In handling investments and redemptions, mutual funds themselves fall into two main categories, however. These are called load and no-load funds. A **load fund** imposes a sales charge to invest in the fund. Usually, this load charge is a percentage of the invested assets and is charged when the investment is made. Some load funds charge a redemption fee as well. For example, $10,000 invested in a load mutual fund with a 7 percent sales charge would yield a net asset value of only $9,300 for the investor. The $700 load charge would go to pay for the salesperson's commission and other expenses involved in making the sale. Although the stated load is 7 percent, the effective load is really higher. In this example, one pays $700 as a sales charge and receives shares with a net asset value of $9,300. From this perspective, the load is 7.53 percent of the net asset value actually received.

By contrast, a **no-load fund** imposes no sales charge. A $10,000 investment in a no-load fund yields $10,000 worth of net asset value. Load funds charge their fee to provide compensa-

Table 17.3
Percentage of Funds Invested by Type of Mutual Fund

Type of Fund	1980	1990	1993
Money Market	55.3	38.8	22.2
Short-Term Municipal Bonds	1.4	7.8	5.0
Equity Funds	30.4	23.0	36.1
Bond and Income Funds	12.9	30.4	36.7

Source: Investment Company Institute, *1994 Mutual Fund Fact Book*, Washington, DC: Investment Company Institute, 1994.

tion for salespersons, essentially. No-load funds operate only by mail and have no sales force. Since there is no persuasive evidence of a difference in performance, no-load funds seem to have a clear advantage for the investor. In spite of this fact, load funds are purchased about as frequently, due to the phenomenon cited in the adage: "Mutual funds are sold and not bought." Presumably, this applies to load mutual funds.

Costs of Investing in Mutual Funds

In addition to a load, mutual funds also charge other fees for the services they offer. The management of a mutual fund performs many tasks in the arena of record keeping and managing the portfolio. Expenses for these services must be borne ultimately by the investors in the fund. To finance these fees, each account is subject to an annual charge, which is a percentage of assets. As Table 17.4 shows, these expenses differ in size by the type and size of the mutual fund. Usually they fall in the range of ½ to 1 percent of the assets per year. By far, the largest percentage of these fees goes to the managers of the portfolio. This management service is often provided by a company external to the mutual fund; however, the management company is also often related to the mutual fund. In addition to these expenses, which are delineated in the reports of the fund, there are other expenses, such as commissions, which are not so apparent. While these commissions may be reported in the annual report, they are not normally part of the percentage levied against each account for expenses.

Mutual Fund Quotations

Figure 17.2 presents mutual funds quotations from *The Wall Street Journal*. The quotations give the name of the mutual fund, the net asset value per share, and the offering price. If the offering price differs from the net asset value, the difference is the load charge. For no-load funds, the col-

Table 17.4
Expense Ratios by Type of Mutual Fund

	Average Expense Ratios		
	Highest 10%	Lowest 10%	All Funds
Fund Objective			
Stock Funds	1.65%	0.47%	1.02%
Bond Funds	1.60	0.52	0.96
Municipal Bond Funds	1.37	0.44	0.79
Money Market Funds	1.08	0.39	0.68
Size of Fund			
Less than $50 million	1.71%	0.54%	1.13%
$50–250 million*	1.24	0.50	0.83
More than $250 million	0.97	0.36	0.63

*Sample excludes funds with expense ratios of 2 percent or more.

Source: "Mutual Funds," in *Encyclopedia of Investments*, Marshall E. Blume and Jack P. Friedman (eds.), Boston: Warren, Gorham, and Lamont, 1982, p. 516.

Figure 17.2
Quotations for Mutual Funds

MUTUAL FUND QUOTATIONS

Tuesday, March 28, 1995

Ranges for investment companies, with daily price data supplied by the National Association of Securities Dealers and performance and cost calculations by Lipper Analytical Services Inc. The NASD requires a mutual fund to have at least 1,000 shareholders or net assets of $25 million before being listed. Detailed explanatory notes appear elsewhere on this page.

	Inv. Obj.	NAV	Offer Price	NAV Chg.	– Total Return – YTD	13 wks	3 yrs	R
AAL Mutual:								
Bond p	BIN	9.57	10.05	−0.03	+4.7	+4.9	+5.7	D
CaGr p	GRO	15.28	16.04	−0.02	+9.1	+9.0	+7.4	C
MuBd p	GLM	10.67	11.20	−0.02	+6.7	+7.1	+6.7	C
SmCoStk p	MID	11.28	11.84	+0.09	+9.1	+12.8	NS	..
Util p	SEC	9.35	9.82	−0.03	+3.3	+2.4	NS	..
AARP Invst:								
BalS&B	S&B	15.08	NL	−0.03	+5.3	+5.5	NS	..
CaGr	GRO	32.37	NL	+0.01	+7.4	+7.6	+5.7	D
GiniM	MTG	14.85	NL	−0.05	+3.6	+3.7	+5.3	D
GthInc	G&I	33.86	NL	−0.04	+6.7	+6.7	+11.1	A
HQ Bd	BND	15.34	NL	−0.06	+4.3	+4.3	+6.5	D
TxFBd	ISM	17.48	NL	−0.03	+7.0	+7.5	+7.4	B
ABT Funds:								
Emrg p	CAP	14.20	14.91	+0.09	+5.7	+7.9	+8.8	C
FL HI	MFL	10.17	10.68	−0.01	+7.1	+7.6	NS	..
FL TF	MFL	10.94	11.49	−0.02	+7.0	+7.7	+7.7	A
GthIn p	G&I	10.91	11.45	+0.01	+6.5	+7.0	+4.5	E
UtilIn p	SEC	11.01	11.56	−0.02	+5.1	+5.0	+5.5	E
AHA Funds:								
Balan	S&B	11.79	NL	...	+5.0	+5.4	+7.4	C
DivrEq	GRO	13.70	NL	...	+8.2	+8.7	+10.6	B
Full	BND	9.49	NL	−0.04	+4.1	+4.3	+6.8	C
Lim	BST	10.08	NL	−0.02	+3.3	+3.5	+4.8	C
AIM Funds:								
Agrsv p	SML	31.91	33.77	+0.27	+11.4	+15.6	+25.3	A
BalB t	S&B	15.55	15.55	+0.01	+6.9	+7.3	NS	..
Chart p	G&I	8.97	9.49	+0.03	+10.7	+11.3	+6.5	E
Const p	MID	19.02	20.13	+0.12	+10.6	+13.2	+13.9	A
BalA p	S&B	15.55	16.33	+0.01	+7.1	+7.6	+8.6	B
GlAgGrA	WOR	10.53	11.06	+0.07	+4.6	+7.0	NS	..
GlAgGrB	WOR	10.51	10.51	+0.07	+4.5	+6.8	NS	..
GoScA p	MTG	9.17	9.63	−0.05	+3.3	+3.4	+4.6	E
GovSecB	MTG	9.17	9.17	−0.04	+3.2	+3.4	NS	..
GrthA p	GRO	11.47	12.14	+0.06	+11.1	+12.9	+4.1	E
GrthB t	GRO	11.31	11.31	+0.05	+10.8	+12.6	NS	..
HYldA p	BHI	9.16	9.62	...	+4.4	+4.5	+9.7	B
HYldB t	BHI	9.16	9.16	...	+4.3	+4.4	NS	..
IncoA p	BND	7.44	7.81	−0.02	+4.8	+5.0	+6.9	C
IncoB	BND	7.42	7.42	−0.02	+4.6	+4.8	NS	..
IntlEqA p	ITL	11.98	12.68	+0.08	−1.2	−0.3	NS	..
IntlEqB	ITL	11.94	11.94	+0.08	−1.4	−0.5	NS	..
LimM p	BST	9.93	10.03	−0.02	+2.9	+3.2	+4.6	C
MuniA p	GLM	8.04	8.44	−0.01	+4.4	+4.8	+7.2	B
Sumit	GRO	9.85	NA	+0.05	+10.3	+12.2	+8.6	C
TeCt p	SSM	10.71	11.24	−0.01	+4.5	+5.0	+7.1	B

Source: *The Wall Street Journal*, March 29, 1995.

umn showing the offering price begins with "N. L." The final column shows the change in the net asset value since the close of the preceding day's trading.

Mutual Fund Families

Another feature of the mutual fund industry shown by the quotations is the existence of families of mutual funds. These families are companies that offer a number of different types of mutual funds to span the range of possible investor needs. These families generally allow an investor in one fund to switch investment from one fund in the family to another with just a phone call. This gives investors considerable flexibility to take advantage of whatever beliefs they have about the direction of the market.

The basic idea behind this strategy is to switch funds based on beliefs about market conditions. An investor anticipating substantially higher interest rates might decide to keep money in a money market mutual fund until the higher rates develop. By contrast, an investor expecting a major surge in the stock market might switch funds to an aggressive growth or growth mutual fund.

Regulation and Taxation of Investment Companies

The tendency to bring more and more dimensions of the securities business under regulation, which characterized the 1930s, continued into the 1940s. The Investment Company Act of 1940 gave the SEC control over investment companies, both closed-end companies and mutual funds.

The act has two main purposes. First, it aims at disclosure of information to prospective investors, and second, it attempts to curb some potential abuses by managers of investment companies. The investment company must provide a prospectus to any new investor, and the terms governing the prospectus are similar to those for stocks or bonds.

Many potential abuses by management are specifically restricted by the act. For example, changing the goals of the investment company without the consent of the investors is prohibited by the act. The act also stipulates the care that must be taken to protect the securities themselves. One potential area of abuse, which is controlled by the act, stems from collusion between managers of the company and brokers and underwriters. Because of this possibility, brokers and underwriters are allowed to hold only a minority interest in these companies.

Taxation of Investment Company Returns

Many investment companies, both closed-end companies and mutual funds, are exempt from federal income taxation. The rationale for this policy is that the investment company holds the securities as an agent of the investor. If investment companies were taxed, and the individual investors in the fund were also taxed, then this would amount to double taxation. The law avoids double taxation of investment companies but not of dividends. To qualify for this treatment, the investment company must distribute at least 90 percent of its investment company taxable income to its shareholders each year. Individuals are then taxed on the proceeds they receive from the mutual fund.

Mutual Fund Performance

Having discussed the different components of mutual fund returns, now consider how those returns compare to their risk-adjusted market return. In other words, are mutual funds able to outperform the market by earning a return that is higher than the market rate of return for the fund's level of risk? In the long run, one would expect the riskier funds to pay a higher return commensurate with their greater risk. In general, this seems to be what happens. Since 1958, growth funds, the most aggressive strategy represented, have outperformed the others. Normally, one would expect these kinds of funds to rank in the following order of decreasing performance: growth funds, growth/income funds, income funds, and balanced funds. As just observed, growth funds have succeeded in providing the highest return, and they are followed by growth/income funds, as we would expect. However, growth/income funds are followed by balanced funds, with income funds bringing up the rear.

Ultimately, however, one invests in a particular mutual fund. So the principal issue is to find the mutual fund with the best performance prospects having the kind of portfolio appropriate to the investor. Unfortunately, this is not so easy. Most research shows that there is very little consistency between rankings for one year and the next.[3] This variability in performance makes it difficult to evaluate the performance of mutual funds. One technique that seems quite reasonable is to compare the performance of mutual funds to various market indexes.

Mutual funds are managed portfolios, so if they have talented management, it would seem reasonable to expect them to outperform stock market indexes, which are essentially unmanaged portfolios. In general, mutual funds do not outperform stock market indexes of comparable risk. Risk adjustment is a necessary part of correct performance comparison, especially in those cases where performance is not consistent. Even when funds are classified by type, some high-risk types do not necessarily outperform the market indexes in each period. Table 17.5 shows the performance of a number of different types of stock mutual funds for three-, five-, and ten-year periods ending in 1994. The table also shows how mutual fund performance compares with the S&P 500. As Table 17.5 shows, mutual funds certainly do not outperform the S&P 500 in general.

As we have seen in the preceding chapters, the Capital Asset Pricing Model has achieved a wide degree of acceptance among academics over the years since its introduction. Perhaps more importantly, it has also received considerable acceptance from market practitioners. One of the most important practical uses of the CAPM has been in the area of performance evaluation. Probably the clearest example of this application of the CAPM is in the appraisal of mutual fund performance. The performance question is this: How well does a mutual fund perform in achieving a level of returns – *given its level of risk*? The idea that performance can only be evaluated accurately when the risk level is taken into account is a central tenet of the CAPM, so this application of the theory is extremely important.

Table 17.5
Mutual Fund Performance

	% Annualized Total Returns for Period Ending 3/31/94		
	3 Years	5 Years	10 Years
Maximum Capital Gains	12.5	12.9	12.0
Small Company Growth	15.2	14.7	13.4
Long-Term Growth	10.7	12.1	13.0
Growth & Current Income	9.8	11.0	12.9
Balanced	9.5	10.1	12.2
Equity Income	10.7	10.1	12.2
Flexible Income	12.9	11.2	12.2
S&P 500 Index	9.1	12.1	14.7

Source: *CDA/Wiesenberger Mutual Funds Update*, March 31, 1994.

[3] See, for example, M. C. Jensen, "Risk, the Pricing of Capital Assets, and the Evaluation of Investment Portfolios," *The Journal of Business*, April 1969, 42:2, pp. 167–247.

Methods of Performance Evaluation

There are three well-accepted methods for evaluating the performance of mutual funds or other managed portfolios, and all stem directly from capital market theory. Each attempts to measure the fund's performance relative to a specification of the risk-adjusted return appropriate to a portfolio of the same risk. A successful performance occurs when a portfolio earns a return greater than the market equilibrium return it should have achieved.

The Sharpe Index

Consider our familiar equation for the capital market line:

$$E(R_p) = R_f + \sigma_p/\sigma_m\,[E(R_m) - R_f] \tag{17.1}$$

This equation essentially looks to the future, expressing a relationship between the expected future return of a portfolio and other parameters. In performance measurement, we want to consider how well a portfolio did in the past. Accordingly, let us transform Equation 17.1 into a historical, or *ex post*, version by simply removing the expectation operators.

$$R_p = R_f + \sigma_p/\sigma_m\,[R_m - R_f] \tag{17.2}$$

Subtracting R_f, dividing by σ_p, and rearranging gives Equation 17.3.

$$[R_p - R_f]/\sigma_p = [R_m - R_f]/\sigma_m \tag{17.3}$$

The terms in brackets are the excess returns for the portfolio and for the market. If the Capital Market Line holds historically, actual data will be in exact accordance with Equation 17.3. Therefore, the Sharpe Index (SI) is given by the left side of Equation 17.3.

$$\mathrm{SI_p} = \frac{R_p - R_f}{\sigma_p} \tag{17.4}$$

To apply this measure, consider the following data for a given period's performance, shown in the following table. These data show returns, standard deviations, and the value of the Sharpe Index for the market portfolio and for several portfolios.

Asset	Return	Standard Deviation	Sharpe Index
R_f	.0700	.00	–
Market	.1977	.31	.4119
Portfolio *P*	.1400	.17	.4118
Portfolio *Q*	.1600	.17	.5294
Portfolio *R*	.1800	.28	.3929

These data show the individual variation we always find in portfolio performance, so we cannot expect Equation 17.3 to hold exactly for every portfolio's historical performance. If Equation 17.3

holds for a particular portfolio, then the portfolio falls exactly on the CML as shown for Portfolio *P* in Figure 17.3, which is consistent with our data.

The market and any portfolio lying exactly on the CML will have an SI of .4119. If a portfolio lies above the CML, such as *Q*, it has an SI value greater than the market's. If a portfolio lies below the CML, such as *R*, its SI value is less than the market's. In Figure 17.3, it is easy to see that Portfolio *Q* beats *R*, because *Q*'s Sharpe Index exceeds that of Portfolio *R*. In general, a portfolio with a higher Sharpe Index is desirable. If the Sharpe Index for a portfolio exceeds the Sharpe Index value for the market, then the portfolio has beaten the market.

The Treynor Index

Just as the Sharpe Index is drawn from the CML, the Treynor Index is the exact equivalent drawn from the *ex post* SML. By exactly the same line of reasoning, we have the Treynor Index (TI).

$$TI_p = \frac{R_p - R_f}{\beta_p} \tag{17.5}$$

For the market, the Treynor Index value always equals the market risk premium ($R_m - R_f$) because the market's beta is always 1.0. Therefore, with the Treynor Index, a portfolio beats the market if it has a TI value in excess of the market risk premium. Having a TI greater than the market risk premium also means that such a portfolio will lie above the security market line. In general, the greater the Treynor Index, the better the risk-adjusted performance of the portfolio.

Figure 17.3
The *Ex-Post* CML

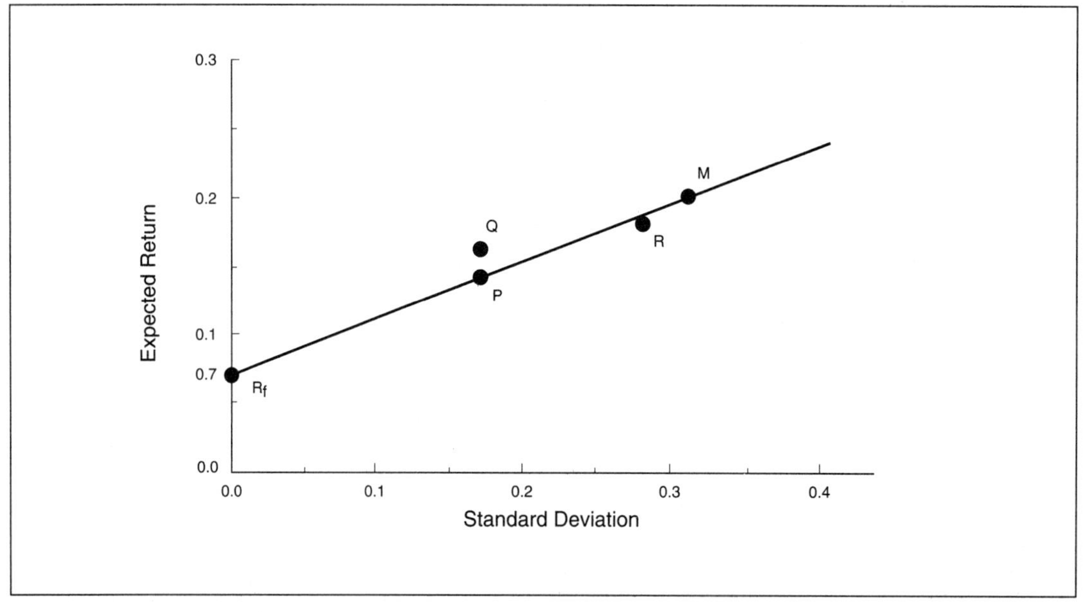

Jensen's Alpha

According to the *ex post* SML, we have the following relationship:

$$R_j - R_f = \beta_j(R_m - R_f) \tag{17.6}$$

Equation 17.6 says that the excess return on Security or Portfolio j should equal the excess return on the market times the beta of j. We can recast this relationship in the form of the following regression equation:

$$(R_j - R_f)_t = \alpha_j + \beta_j(R_m - R_f)_t + \epsilon_{jt} \tag{17.7}$$

Expressing this relationship as shown in Equation 17.7 should not have any effect on the estimated β_j. If the relationship in Equation 17.6 holds for Security or Portfolio j and we estimate Equation 17.7, we would expect to find the constant term $\alpha_j = 0$. This α_j is the constant return on Security j, after taking the beta of Security j into account.

If α_j equals zero, then Equation 17.6 holds and j's performance equals that of the market. By contrast, if α_j is significantly greater than zero, then j is outperforming the market. Likewise, if α_j is significantly less than zero, j underperforms the market. To apply Jensen's alpha, we estimate Equation 17.7 and then look for alphas significantly greater than zero to find the investment vehicles that have outperformed the market. Most studies of mutual fund performance apply one of these three methods.

Risk-Adjusted Mutual Fund Performance

Mutual funds normally employ professional security analysts to help make decisions about which stocks are worthy of investment. In addition, many large mutual funds have an enormous amount of funds under management. With a great deal of capital under management, mutual funds should be able to hold well-diversified portfolios. Further, if their professional security analysts have useful stock selection ability, they should be able to pick stocks that have a higher risk-adjusted return than the market portfolio.

Alternatively, if mutual funds underperform a portfolio made up of the risk-free asset and the market portfolio, then this would be a strong piece of evidence consistent with the semi-strong version of the Efficient Market Hypothesis. If well-capitalized and well-diversified mutual funds, with the services of their professional security analysts reviewing public information, cannot outperform the equivalent risk portfolio comprised of the market portfolio and the risk-free asset, then what other group of investors could hope to?

In his classic study, Jensen reviewed the performance of 115 mutual funds over the period from 1945 to 1964.[4] In doing so, he compared the return of each mutual fund relative to a benchmark portfolio that was made up of the market portfolio and the risk-free asset in proportions that made the risk of the mutual fund and the constructed portfolio equal. In a semi-strong and efficient market, the mutual funds should not be able to beat the benchmark portfolio. If the market

---

[4] See Michael C. Jensen, "The Performance of Mutual Funds in the Period 1945–64," *Journal of Finance*, May 1968, pp. 389–416.

were not semi-strong and efficient and the analysts had real ability, then the mutual funds might beat the market.

Ignoring the management fees and any sales fees that the mutual funds might have, the benchmark portfolio slightly outperformed the mutual funds by .4 percent. The results are shown graphically in Figure 17.4, in which the zero point on the *x* axis indicates a tie between the mutual fund and the benchmark portfolio. As the figure indicates, most of the funds were beaten by the benchmark portfolio, although some mutual funds did beat the benchmark portfolio over this period. Because every mutual fund also has management fees, which go in part to pay its analysts, it is also important to evaluate mutual fund performance taking those fees into account, as shown in Figure 17.5. When management fees are considered, the benchmark portfolio beat the mutual funds by an average of 1.1 percent. This still does not include any sales fees that are charged by some mutual funds.

One possible response to these results is to acknowledge that mutual funds as a group cannot beat the benchmark portfolio. However, some funds do, in fact, beat the benchmark, and this might be due to skill rather than luck. Some market analysts may have real skill that allows them

Figure 17.4
Performance of 115 Mutual Funds Relative to an Equal Risk Benchmark Portfolio, Not Including Management Fees

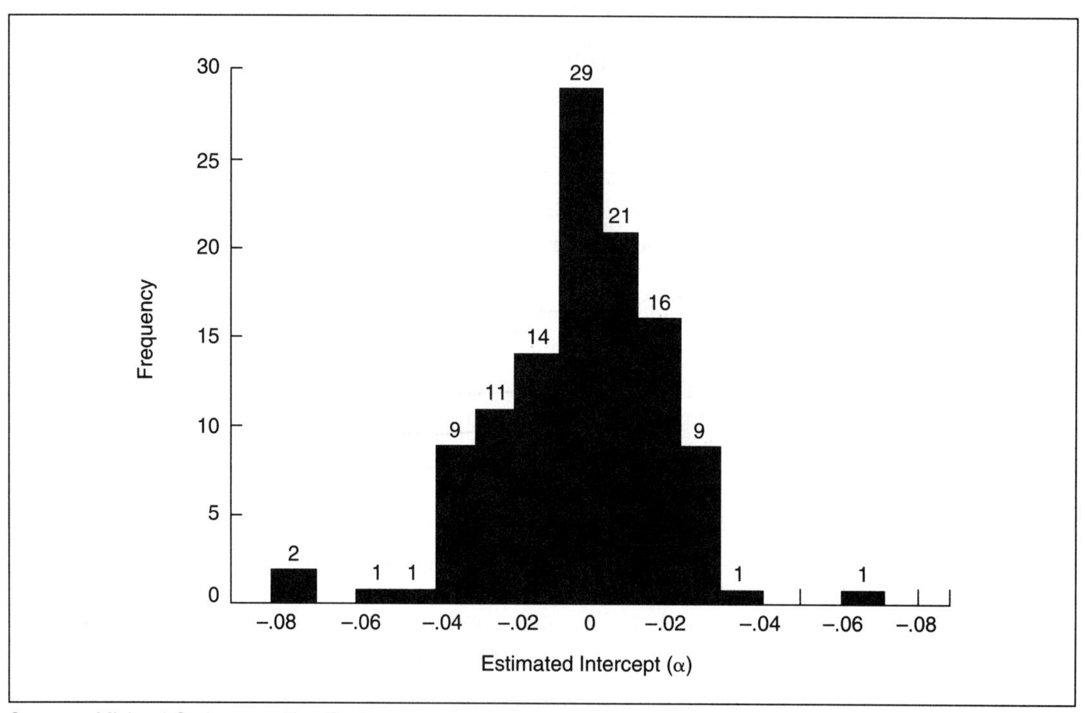

Source: Michael C. Jensen, "The Performance of Mutual Funds in the Period 1945–64," *Journal of Finance*, May 1968, pp. 389–416.

to beat the market, and it would be very difficult to be sure using statistical tests. However, Jensen's results are consistent with the view that those mutual funds that do beat the market do so by chance. In other words, the number of mutual funds that beat the market is about what one would expect to happen by chance, with no real skill being involved.

The long-term performance record of individual mutual funds also supports the view that even those mutual funds that beat the market do so by chance. True ability should lead to consistently good performance, but there appears to be very little correlation between good performance in one year by a mutual fund and its performance in the next year. While the performance of mutual funds appears to be fully consistent with the semi-strong EMH, it does not follow that mutual funds provide no useful benefit to society or that they should be avoided as an investment vehicle. Although mutual funds apparently do not have the ability to beat the market, they may provide useful diversification services to many investors in a cost-effective way.

International Investment Companies

There are two essentially different ways for the U.S. investor to invest in international markets via investment companies. First, some U.S.-based investment companies specialize in foreign securities. Second, there is a growing mutual fund industry based outside the United States. This section considers each in turn, along with an evaluation of foreign mutual fund performance.

Figure 17.5
Performance of 115 Mutual Funds Relative to an Equal Risk Benchmark Portfolio, Including Management Fees

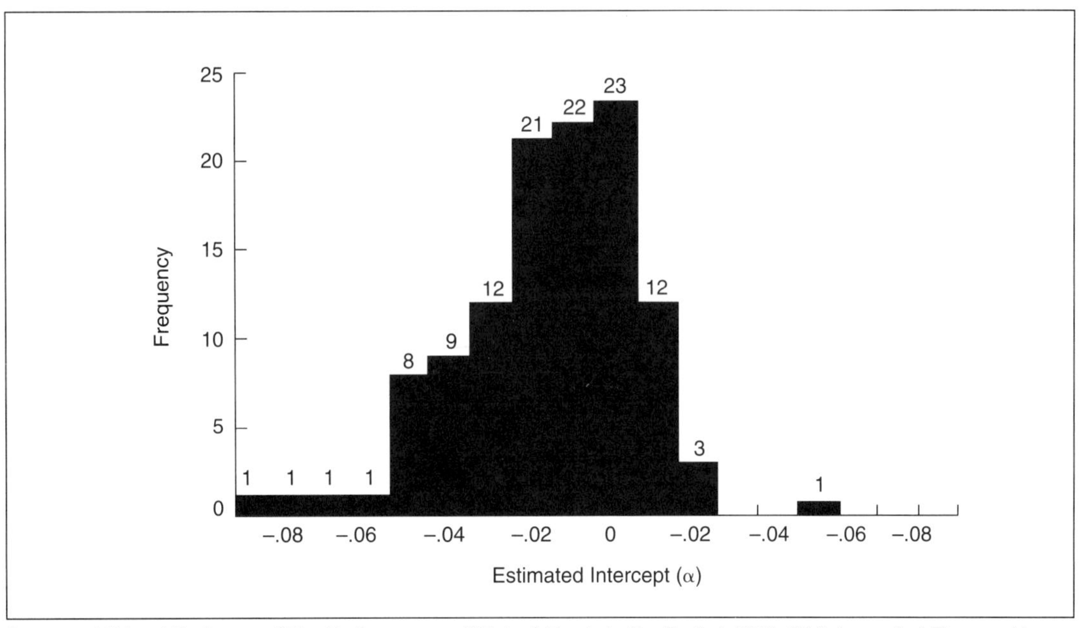

Source: Michael C. Jensen, "The Performance of Mutual Funds in the Period 1945–64," *Journal of Finance*, May 1968, pp. 389–416.

U.S.-Based Investment Companies

In the United States, there is a wide variety of both investment companies and mutual funds specializing in non-U.S. securities. Some closed-end funds specialize in the securities of a particular country, such as the Mexico Fund and the Korea Fund, which invest strictly in the securities of Mexico and Korea. A number of international mutual funds hold balanced portfolios of the securities from many countries.

We have seen the advantage of international diversification in Chapter 9. These international mutual funds provide a form of ready-made international diversification. Mutual fund families, such as T. Rowe Price and Fidelity, offer international funds, but there are many other funds specializing in international securities. As an example of the portfolio held by international mutual funds, we consider the portfolio composition of the T. Rowe Price International Stock Fund in mid-1994. The net asset value of the fund was $5.1 billion at market value. Of this amount, 92.5 percent was invested in common stock. Virtually all of the rest of the funds were invested in short-term investments, presumably to meet withdrawals and to provide liquidity. The three industries with the largest concentration of investment were banking (7.4 percent), building materials and components (6.3 percent), and merchandising (6.1 percent). Table 17.6 shows the distribution of the fund's investment across countries.

Foreign Mutual Funds

In addition to U.S.-based investment companies that specialize in investment abroad, foreign countries have their own mutual funds. These funds may either specialize in their own domestic markets or they can be international. Table 17.7 shows the assets held in foreign-based mutual

Table 17.6
Distribution of Assets for
T. Rowe Price International Stock Fund,
April 30, 1994

Country	Percentage of Assets	Country	Percentage of Assets
Argentina	0.7	Malaysia	6.3
Australia	2.8	Mexico	4.6
Austria	0.1	Netherlands	6.7
Belgium	1.7	New Zealand	2.4
Brazil	0.9	Norway	1.1
Canada	0.3	Portugal	0.3
Chile	0.6	Singapore	2.3
Denmark	0.2	South Korea	0.7
Finland	0.2	Spain	1.9
France	6.2	Sweden	1.3
Germany	4.2	Switzerland	4.3
Hong Kong	4.9	Thailand	1.6
Italy	3.4	United Kingdom	13.3
Japan	20.4	Short-Term Investments	8.2

Source: T. Rowe Price, *Semi-Annual Report T. Rowe Price International Stock Fund*, April 30, 1994.

funds among prominent countries. The largest amounts are in Japan and France. Together, all non-U.S. countries hold just over $2 trillion, and this almost exactly matches the $2.01 trillion held in U.S. mutual funds.

The distribution of funds in foreign countries can differ markedly from that in the United States. For example, nearly 90 percent of German holdings are concentrated in debt instruments. In France, about 75 percent are invested in debt. In the United Kingdom, the industry is organized more on the U.S. model, with equity investment being a larger portion of the whole.

Investment Performance of International Mutual Funds

We have seen that studies of U.S. mutual funds find that they are generally unable to beat the market averages. More formally, mutual funds appear unable to earn an excess risk-adjusted rate of return.

Robert Cumby and Jack Glen explored the performance of 15 international mutual funds based in the United States.[5] One of their tests utilized Jensen's alpha, which we discussed earlier

Table 17.7
Assets of Foreign Mutual Funds

Country	Assets ($ billions)
Australia	$20.7
Austria	17.8
Belgium	11.5
Canada	86.7
France	483.8
Germany	205.2
Hong Kong	24.8
Italy	56.5
Japan	448.7
Korea	67.9
Luxembourg	229.7
Mexico	16.0
Netherlands	33.6
Spain	65.5
Sweden	21.2
Switzerland	28.2
United Kingdom	141.3
Total (All Non-U.S.)	2,003.3
Total (USA)	2,011.3
Total (World)	4,014.6

Source: Investment Company Institute, *1994 Mutual Fund Fact Book*, Washington, DC: Investment Company Institute, 1994.

[5] R. E. Cumby and J. D. Glen, "Evaluating the Performance of International Mutual Funds," *Journal of Finance*, 45:2, June 1990, pp. 497–521.

in this chapter. To conduct Jensen's test requires using a proxy for the market portfolio, and Cumby and Glen used both a U.S. index and a world index of stock market performance as proxies for the market portfolio. In each case, they found that mutual funds were not able to achieve positive alphas with any regularity. That is, international mutual funds did not earn a superior risk-adjusted return. Therefore, these results are broadly consistent with Jensen's classic study for domestic U.S. mutual funds.

Summary

This chapter explored the features of investment companies. Investment companies are either closed-end companies or mutual funds. Both are essentially managed portfolios in which investors own fractional shares of the entire portfolio. Closed-end companies accept funds for investment only at creation, while mutual funds accept new funds at any time. In recent years, U.S. investors have shown a preference for mutual funds. Investment companies are regulated by the SEC under the Investment Company Act of 1940. Most investment companies are not taxed directly at all, but they pass their profits to shareholders, who pay personal taxes directly.

In finance theory, diversified portfolios are especially important because only by diversifying can an investor escape from unsystematic risk. Preceding chapters showed that investors should hold a well-diversified portfolio as their portfolio of risky assets. Investment companies fulfill this condition. Because investment companies hold professionally managed portfolios, it is also important to determine whether they beat the market by earning a supernormal risk-adjusted return. If they did so consistently, their performance would constitute evidence against semi-strong market efficiency. Based on considerable research, it appears that investment companies as a group cannot beat the market. A particular investment company might beat the market, but such a claim is not supported by the evidence.

Questions and Problems

1. What is the difference between a closed-end investment company and a mutual fund?
2. What is the "net asset value" of a share in an investment company?
3. How do mutual funds charge for their services?
4. What are some of the different kinds of investment strategies that can be observed among different mutual funds?
5. What is a "money market mutual fund"?
6. Why are there families of mutual funds?
7. For the most part, mutual funds are free of federal taxation. Why is this?
8. Respond to the following claim: "Mutual funds appear to have underperformed the market because of the necessary costs that mutual fund investment involves. However, if we consider transaction costs for both the market index and for mutual funds, then mutual funds tend to outperform the market index."

9. "To measure the performance of a mutual fund, calculate the long-term (10-year) average return earned by the mutual fund and subtract the average return earned by the S&P 500 over the same period. If the result is greater than zero, the mutual fund beat the market." Comment on this way of measuring mutual fund performance.

10. "Just as in industry, some firms perform well and others perform badly. Even if mutual funds as a group cannot outperform the market, there are some firms that can. For any five-year period, there will be some mutual funds that underperform the market and some that outperform the market. This is true even on a risk-adjusted basis. Therefore, some funds do, in fact, outperform the market." Comment on the validity of this claim.

Suggested REALDATA Exercises

The following *REALDATA* exercises explore the concepts developed in this chapter:
Exercises 21–23

References

Bonser-Neal, C., G. Brauer, F. Neal, and S. Wheatley, "International Investment Restrictions and Closed-End Country Fund Prices," *Journal of Finance*, 45:2, June 1990, pp. 523–47.

Brauer, G. A., "Closed-End Fund Shares' Abnormal Returns and the Information Content of Discounts and Premiums," *Journal of Finance*, 43:1, March 1988, pp. 113–27.

Cumby, R. E. and J. D. Glen, "Evaluating the Performance of International Mutual Funds," *Journal of Finance*, 45:2, June 1990, pp. 497–521.

Eun, C. S., R. Kolodny, and B. G. Resnick, "U.S.-Based International Mutual Funds: A Performance Evaluation," *The Journal of Portfolio Management*, 17:3, Spring 1991, pp. 88–94.

Ferris, S. P. and D. M. Chance, "The Effect of 12b-1 Plans on Mutual Fund Expense Ratios: A Note," *Journal of Finance*, 42:4, September 1987, pp. 1077–82.

Fong, H. and O. A. Vasicek, "Forecast-Free International Asset Allocation," *Financial Analysts Journal*, 45:2, March/April 1989, pp. 29–33.

Fong, H. G., "Forecast-Free International Asset Allocation," *Quantitative International Investing: A Handbook of Analytical and Modeling Techniques and Strategies*, Chicago: Probus Publishing, 1990, pp. 203–9.

Fredman, A. J. and G. Scott, "An Investor's Guide to Closed-End Fund Discounts," *American Association of Individual Investors*, 13:5, May 1991, pp. 12–16.

Fredman, A. J. and G. Scott, "Fixed-Income Investing: A Look at Closed–End Bond Funds," *American Association of Individual Investors*, 13:3, March 1991, pp. 8–13.

Gibson, R. C., *Asset Allocation: Balancing Financial Risk*, Homewood, IL: Dow Jones-Irwin, 1990.

Golec, J. H., "Do Mutual Fund Managers Who Use Incentive Compensation Outperform Those Who Don't?" *Financial Analysts Journal*, 44:6, November/December 1988, pp. 75–8.

Lee, C. M. C., A. Shleifer, and R. H. Thaler, "Anomalies: Closed-End Mutual Funds," *Journal of Economic Perspectives*, 4:4, Fall 1990, pp. 153–64.

Lehmann, B. N. and D. M. Modest, "Mutual Fund Performance Evaluation: A Comparison of Benchmarks and Benchmark Comparisons," *Journal of Finance*, 42:2, June 1987, pp. 233–65.

Lynn, S. M., "Combining Active Management with Indexing," *Quantitative International Investing: A Handbook of Analytical and Modeling Techniques and Strategies*, Chicago: Probus Publishing, 1990, pp. 55–60.

Perold, A. F. and R. S. Salomon, Jr., "The Right Amount of Assets under Management," *Financial Analysts Journal*, 47:3, May/June 1991, pp. 31–9.

Samuelson, P. A., "Asset Allocation Could Be Dangerous to Your Health," *The Journal of Portfolio Management*, 16:3, Spring 1990, pp. 5–8.

Samuelson, P. A., "The Judgment of Economic Science on Rational Portfolio Management: Indexing, Timing, and Long-Horizon Effects," *The Journal of Portfolio Management*, 16:1, Fall 1989, pp. 4–12.

Sharpe, W. F., "Integrated Asset Allocation," *Financial Analysts Journal*, 43:5, September/October 1987, pp. 25–32.

Tallman, E. W., "Financial Asset Pricing Theory: A Review of Recent Developments," *Economic Review*, Federal Reserve Bank of Atlanta, 70:6, November/December 1989, pp. 26–41.

Wainscott, C. B., "The Stock-Bond Correlation and Its Implications for Asset Allocation," *Financial Analysts Journal*, 46:4, July/August 1990, pp. 55–60.

Insurance Companies

18

Overview

In this chapter we present the fundamental principles that govern the insurance industry. Insurance companies benefit society by offering risk-transferring services. By pooling many independent risks, insurance companies can significantly reduce the risk they bear, so they are better equipped to manage risk than individuals or corporations. We present a detailed, yet simple, model of how the risk-reduction mechanism is achieved. The analysis relies heavily on the principles of Portfolio Theory given in Chapter 9.

We also discuss the two major types of insurance companies: life and property/liability insurance companies. Life insurance companies concentrate on selling various types of policies: whole life, term, universal, annuities, and health insurance. We explain the basic financial reasoning required to determine the premium to be paid for each of these policies.

Property/liability (P/L) insurance companies accept risks related to the effect of natural disasters – flood, fire, hurricane, earthquakes – on property. They also insure against other unpredictable events such as auto accidents. In addition, P/L insurance companies sell policies to cover the risk that corporations, professionals, and individuals in general may be legally liable for negligence. For instance, they sell medical and legal liability insurance to protect physicians and lawyers, respectively, against lawsuits brought by disgruntled clients.

Although both life and P/L insurance companies are in the business of accepting and pooling risks, they differ in significant ways. For example, estimating the probability of incurring a loss on a given policy is much more difficult in many cases for P/L insurance companies than it is for life insurance companies. Factors such as this have been responsible for recent losses in the P/L insurance area.

How Insurance Companies Benefit Society

The purchase of an insurance contract cannot be enjoyed in the same sense that a new automobile or a new house is enjoyed by its purchaser. Nevertheless, Americans spend about 2 percent of their disposable income each year on life insurance, and they spend additional amounts on health, homeowner's, and other types of insurance. Surely having insurance is perceived by most individuals as a net benefit, at least in the long term.

The fact that insurance companies benefit society is also supported by their existence for many centuries. In the United States, the first life insurance company was established in 1759.[1]

[1] Its original name was "The Corporation for Relief of Poor and Distressed Presbyterian Ministers and of the Poor and Distressed Widows and Children of Presbyterian Ministers." This company is the oldest life insurance company in continued existence in the world, although it is now known by the somewhat less descriptive name of Presbyterian Ministers' Fund.

Although most life insurance companies are relatively new, 34 have been in existence for more than a century, and more than 750 have been in business for at least 25 years.

Insurance companies benefit society by accepting certain risks that individuals are not willing to bear. In most cases, the risk transferred cannot be easily diversified by the individual. For instance, many people buy life insurance to protect the livelihood of their families in case they die unexpectedly. Thus, for a person earning $40,000 per year, it might seem reasonable to purchase, say, $400,000 of life insurance by paying a $2,000 annual premium. If the insured survives the year, the premium is a net expense, but if the individual dies, the rest of the family can continue to enjoy the life style to which they are accustomed. Since life is not diversifiable, many are willing to pay to protect their family against a financial disaster in the event of their death.

Just as people transfer the financial risk associated with dying to insurance companies, they also transfer other non-diversifiable risks. Among the most important are the risk of a major health problem (health insurance) and the risk of fire or flood in the home (homeowner's insurance). But why are insurance companies willing to take other people's risks in exchange for what seems like relatively small premiums? To answer this question, we must invoke the concepts of Portfolio Theory discussed in Chapter 9. As we will see in the following section, by pooling many different and unrelated policies, insurance companies are able to generate profits while retaining their overall risk at very reasonable levels.

Risk and Return for Insurance Companies

As discussed earlier, insurance companies are willing to accept the risk associated with individual policyholders. In exchange, they receive an annual premium. The essential feature of the risk-transfer process is that, while individuals may not be able to diversify a risk, insurance companies do have that diversification ability.

From the perspective of an insurance company, any individual risk is only a small element of a very large portfolio consisting of many insurance policies. Thus, if an auto insurance policyholder has a car accident, the company must pay the damages. As a result, the company probably incurs a loss on that particular policy. However, by selling many thousands of similar policies, which are essentially independent of one another, the insurance company can be assured that only a small fraction of the policyholders will suffer an accident. This allows the insurance company to pay for damages using the premiums paid by the majority who did not suffer an accident. Thus, insurance not only transfers risk between policyholders and the insurance company, but it is also a way of sharing risk among policyholders.

In essence, the set of policies held by an insurance company constitutes a well-diversified portfolio. Consequently, while individual policies may be very risky in isolation, the risk of the portfolio is significantly lower. Thus, insurance companies can count on their premium income to pay for the expenses arising from policies that claim benefits.

To formalize these ideas, we use the concepts of risk and return introduced in Chapter 9. Suppose that the only asset of the Marcus Life Insurance Company is its life insurance portfolio. The portfolio consists of n identical and independent one-year life insurance policies with a value of L dollars each. Marcus Life charges each policyholder an annual premium of R dollars. Thus, the firm's total annual premium income is $n \times R$ dollars.

There is a probability p that a given policyholder will live the entire year. In that case, Marcus Life has a net revenue equal to the entire premium income, R. Naturally, there is also a probability $(1 - p)$ that a policyholder will die during the year, in which case the insurance company must pay the beneficiaries the promised L dollars. In this case, the company's net revenue would be $(R - L)$.[2] Given these assumptions, the expected net revenue from each of the policies is given by the following expression:

$$E(\text{Net revenue/policy}) = R - L(1 - p)$$

Since there are n such policies, the total expected net revenue for Marcus is:

$$E(\text{Net revenue}) = n[R - L(1 - p)] \tag{18.1}$$

Because the insurance company is taking a risk with each of its policies, at the end of the year it may not actually have the net revenues it expects. To measure the life insurance portfolio's risk, we calculate its standard deviation, σ_n. To do this, it is first convenient to calculate the risk associated with assuming that all of the firm's assets are pooled into a single insurance policy. In this case, the large single policy of $n \times L$ dollars would produce a net revenue of $n \times R$ dollars with probability p, or result in a net loss of $n(R - L)$ dollars with probability $(1 - p)$. Using the definitions of variance and standard deviation given in Chapter 9, and after some algebra, the standard deviation for this single life insurance policy can be written as:

$$\sigma_1 = nL\sqrt{p(1 - p)} \tag{18.2}$$

Since we are assuming that all of the insurance company's policies are independent of one another, we can use the techniques of Chapter 9 to calculate the standard deviation of the entire life insurance portfolio, σ_n, as follows:

$$\sigma_n = \frac{\sigma_1}{\sqrt{n}} = L\sqrt{np(1 - p)} \tag{18.3}$$

It is interesting to note from Equation 18.1 that the insurance company's total expected net revenue is directly proportional to the number of policies outstanding, n. In contrast, the risk associated with those revenues depends only on the square root of the number of policies. This means that expected revenues grow faster than risk as the company increases the number of policies it holds. As a result, the probability that the firm will sustain a net loss during the year diminishes as the company's size increases, holding other factors constant. In other words, there are economies of scale in the insurance industry, as the following example shows.[3]

We can illustrate these important concepts with a numerical example. Assume that each life insurance policy at Marcus Life has a value of $L = \$100{,}000$, that the one-year survival probabil-

---

[2] We are disregarding the time value of money here. We incorporate this variable in a later section.

[3] This result explains why the most successful insurance companies tend to be huge conglomerates. They are simply exposed to less risk of incurring losses than smaller companies.

ity for each policyholder is $p = 0.99$, and that there are $n = 1{,}000$ policies. Thus, this life insurance company has 1,000 independent and identical policies, each with a 1 percent probability of paying $100,000. Assume, for simplicity, that Marcus has no other income or expenses. If each policy pays a premium of $R = \$1{,}600$, we can use Equation 18.1 to find the company's expected net revenue.

$$E(\text{Net revenue}) = 1{,}000\,[\$1{,}600 - \$100{,}000 \times 0.01] = \$600{,}000$$

Thus, Marcus expects an average net revenue of $600 from each policy. This occurs because each of the policies generates $1,600 in premium revenue, but only 1 percent of the policies are expected to pay the $100,000 benefit during the year.

We can now calculate the standard deviation for the insurance company under the assumption that it has a single jumbo policy of $100 million. Using Equation 18.2, the standard deviation is nearly $10 million.

$$\sigma_1 = 1{,}000 \times \$100{,}000\,\sqrt{0.99 \times 0.01} = \$9{,}949{,}874.37$$

A comparison of the expected net revenue of $600,000 and the standard deviation of almost $10 million immediately indicates that holding a single jumbo life insurance policy is exceedingly risky for Marcus, since the actual net income at the end of the year could be significantly less than expected, and could easily be negative.[4] Fortunately, by holding many independent policies rather than a single policy, Marcus Life can easily reduce the risk associated with its net income to a very small amount. If instead of having a single jumbo policy of $100 million, the company has 1,000 identical and independent policies of $100,000 each, then the expected net revenue remains at $600,000 but the standard deviation of the revenues from the portfolio can be reduced to less than $315,000. Using Equation 18.3 we have:

$$\sigma_n = \$100{,}000\,\sqrt{1{,}000 \times 0.99 \times 0.01} = \$314{,}642.65$$

These calculations show that Marcus Life can expect to have a net income of $600,000 at the end of the year, with a standard deviation of about $315,000. Marcus now faces much less risk than before. To quantify the probability that Marcus will actually have a loss during the year, we can assume that the distribution of net income is essentially normal and evaluate the probability that net revenue will be less than or equal to zero. Using the standard normal distribution table, we find that zero revenue is 1.907 standard deviations to the left of the mean of $600,000, so there is a 2.83 percent chance that net revenue will be negative.[5] Figure 18.1 is a graphical depiction of this situation, where the shaded area to the left of the vertical axis represents the probability of net losses for Marcus.

---

[4] Of course, net income could also be much greater than expected. Recall, however, that one of the basic assumptions in finance is that investors are risk averse, so they dislike unexpected losses more than they value unexpected profits of the same magnitude.

[5] With a single jumbo policy, the probability of losses is 47.61 percent.

Figure 18.1
The Distribution of Net Revenues for Marcus Life
(n = 1,000; R = $1,600; p = 0.99; L = $100,000)

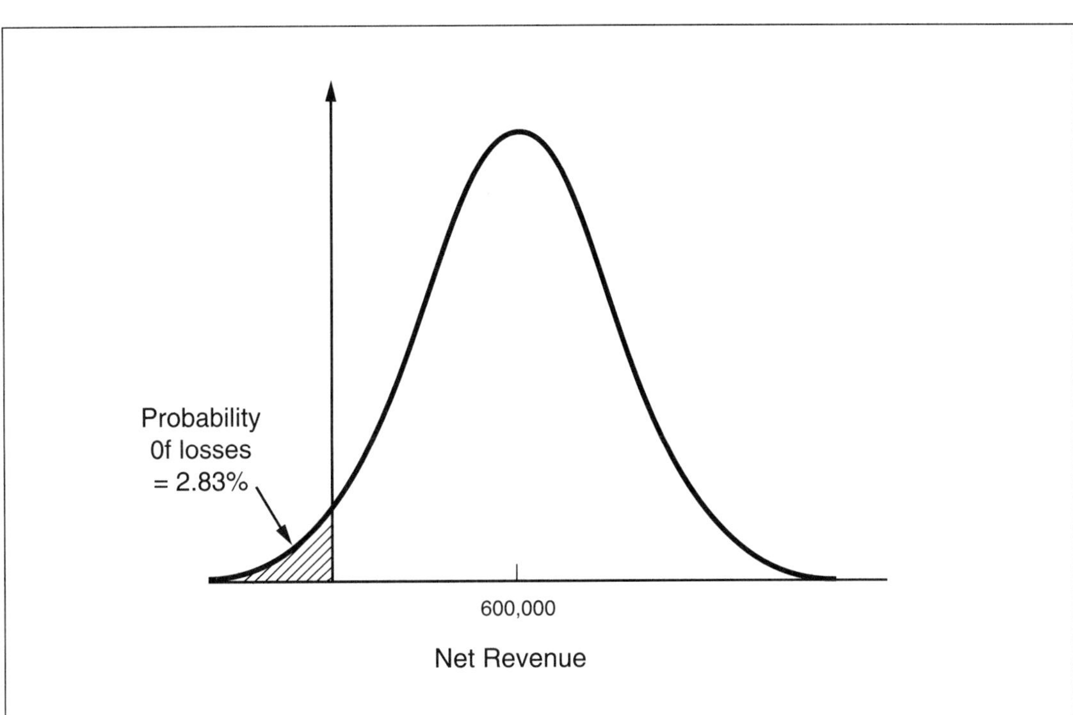

Notice that the example of Marcus Life Insurance assumes that the company has only 1,000 policies. This is a very small number of policies for an insurance company. Yet the chances of incurring losses in any given year are relatively small. To improve its odds of surviving in the long run, Marcus might try to sell more policies. Table 18.1 shows the expected net earnings, the standard deviation of earnings, the Z score, and the probability that earnings will be negative when the number of policies, n, varies between 500 and 3,000, assuming all other variables do not change. As shown in the table, if Marcus sells 3,000 policies, it faces only a 0.05 percent probability of suffering a loss from an unexpectedly high number of claims. In other words, with 3,000 policies, the company would only have 5 chances in 10,000 of suffering losses in any given year.

Types of Insurance Companies

Insurance companies come in two major varieties, according to their ownership: stock and mutual. A stock insurance company is very similar to other corporations. For example, its main goal is to maximize the value of its stock, and it is controlled by the stockholders. By contrast, a mutual insurance company is owned by its policyholders and is a non-profit organization. In practice, however, the management of a mutual insurance company makes most of the decisions with little or no opposition from its policyholders/owners. We can also classify insurance companies according to the types of policies they sell. The two major types are life and property/liability (P/L) insurance companies, which we consider in turn.

Table 18.1
Risk and Return for Marcus Life Insurance Company as a Function of the Number of Insurance Policies (L = \$100,000; R = \$1,600; p = 0.99)

n	Expected Net Revenue	σ_n	z-score	Probability that Net Revenue < 0
500	\$300,000	\$222,486	−1.3484	8.88%
1,000	600,000	314,643	−1.90693	2.83%
1,500	900,000	385,357	−2.3355	0.98%
2,000	1,200,000	444,972	−2.6968	0.35%
2,500	1,500,000	497,494	−3.01511	0.13%
3,000	1,800,000	544,977	−3.30289	0.05%

The z-score measures the distance between a revenue of zero and the expected revenue. The unit of distance measurement is one standard deviation.

Life Insurance Companies

Today life insurance companies hold about 400 million policies with a total insured value of almost \$11 trillion. As a comparison, in 1980 the total insured value was about \$3.5 trillion. This represents an average annual compound growth rate of almost 10 percent. While a portion of this growth was induced by inflation, much of it was real growth. Therefore, the importance of the life insurance industry in the United States has grown over the last decade. Table 18.2 shows the ten largest life insurance companies in the United States, along with information on their size and recent performance. Together, U.S. life insurance companies have assets approaching \$2 trillion.

The Consolidated Balance Sheet

Table 18.3 shows the consolidated balance sheet for financial assets and liabilities for all life insurance companies in the United States. The table shows that most of the assets have been used to purchase corporate bonds and stocks, as well as mortgages and government securities. Most of the funds came from pension funds and policy reserves. Of these, reserves for annuities are by far the most important. Notice that the cumulative net worth of life insurance companies is a very small fraction of their financing sources. Only about 7 percent of assets are financed with equity.

The Consolidated Income Statement

Table 18.4 presents the consolidated percentage income statement for life insurance companies in the United States. Notice that while premium receipts represent nearly 70 percent of total income, investments generate a sizable 27.81 percent of total income. Nevertheless, the greatest individual source of income is annuities.

Not surprisingly, the majority of the life insurance companies' income is used to pay benefits to policyholders. Eighty-three percent of all income was used to pay benefits or to make additions to reserve funds. Reserve funds are set aside in anticipation of future benefit payments. In addition, insurance companies as a group generated a profit margin (net income/total income) of 3.6 percent, of which 2 percent was retained and 1.6 percent was paid out as dividends to stockholders.

Table 18.2
The Ten Largest Life Insurance Companies

Rank/Name	Assets ($ billions)	Net Worth ($ millions)	Net Worth/ Total Liabilities
1. Prudential Insurance	121.3	8,004	7%
2. Metropolitan Life Insurance	102.9	6,406	7
3. Teachers' Insurance and Annuity Association	67.5	3,170	5
4. New York Life Insurance	50.7	3,449	7
5. Northwestern Mutual Life Insurance	40.6	2,030	5
6. Aetna Life Insurance	33.9	1,706	5
7. John Hancock Mutual Life Insurance	33.7	1,815	6
8. Connecticut General Life Insurance	33.4	2,031	6
9. Principal Mutual Life Insurance	32.3	1,641	5
10. Equitable Life Insurance Society	31.5	1,832	6

Source: *Financial World*, September 13, 1994.

Table 18.3
Consolidated Balance Sheet of Life Insurance Companies
(billions of dollars)

Assets	
Checkable deposits and currency	5.3
Money market fund shares	42.6
Mutual fund shares	118.4
Corporate equities	156.7
Treasury securities	344.7
U.S. Government agency securities	117.6
Tax-exempt securities	227.2
Corporate and foreign bonds	750.4
Mortgages	215.5
Open market paper	9.4
Policy loans	83.3
Miscellaneous assets	116.1
Total Assets	1,854.9
Liabilities	
Life insurance reserves	470.4
Pension fund reserves	1,092.6
Federal Home Loan Bank loans	0.3
Taxes payable	1.3
Miscellaneous liabilities	184.0
Total liabilities	1,748.6
Net Worth	106.3

Source: Federal Reserve Board, "Flow of Funds Accounts," Third Quarter 1994.

Major Types of Life Insurance Policies

Life insurance companies offer many traditional products. The main ones are whole life, term life, universal life, annuities, and health insurance policies. We focus on each of these products in turn.

Whole Life In this type of policy, the purchaser pays fixed annual premiums, which entitle the policyholder's beneficiaries to the value of the policy in case of death. As the name implies, the policy is active over the owner's whole life. These policies accumulate a so-called cash value that may be retired by the policyholder in exchange for a reduction in the amount of the policy. If it is kept in the company, the policyholder earns a rate of return on the cash value that is determined at the time the policy is written.

The Premium on Whole Life Insurance Policies Suppose a life insurance company issues 1 million whole life policies, each one for $100,000, to individuals with a current age of 25 years. Given the mortality rate tables, how much should the actuarially fair premium be?[6]

Table18.4
Consolidated Percentage Income Statement of Life Insurance Companies (millions of dollars)

	Percent of Total Income
Premium Receipts	
Life insurance	19.07
Annuities	32.09
Health	14.48
Investment Income	27.81
Other Income	6.55
Total Income	100.00
Benefit Payments	54.70
Additions to Policy	
Reserve funds	28.30
Operating Expenses	
Agent commissions	4.60
Office expenses	6.80
Taxes	2.00
Dividends	1.60
Additions to Special	
Reserves and Surplus Funds	2.00

Source: American Council of Life Insurance, "Life Insurance Fact Book Update," various issues.

[6] An actuarially fair premium is one in which the company neither loses money nor earns a profit. Technically, it requires the present value of all benefits paid to equal the present value of the premiums received. In practice, of course, insurance companies charge more than the fair value, that is, they apply "load factors" in order to earn a profit.

For this example we will assume that during the first 52 years of the policies' existence the probability of dying is directly proportional to the number of years, t, since the policies began. The mortality rate increases linearly, and by year 52 the probability of dying is 2.667 percent. From then on, the probability of dying on any given year decreases linearly, and by year 75 it is zero again.[7] This stylized mortality rate schedule is depicted in Figure 18.2.[8]

The basic principle in fair pricing is that the present value of all the benefits paid by the insurance company over the entire life of the policies must equal the present value of all the premiums the insurance company receives over the same period. Thus, if the amount of each policy is L, the age of the policyholders is a years, the mortality rate t years after the policies start is m_t percent, no one lives beyond age 100, and the annual cost of money is r percent, then the present value of all the benefits paid by the insurance company is:

$$PV_{\text{benefits}} = L \sum_{t=1}^{100-a} m_t(1 + r)^{-t} \tag{18.4}$$

Figure 18.2
Hypothetical Mortality Rate Schedule for the Whole Life Example

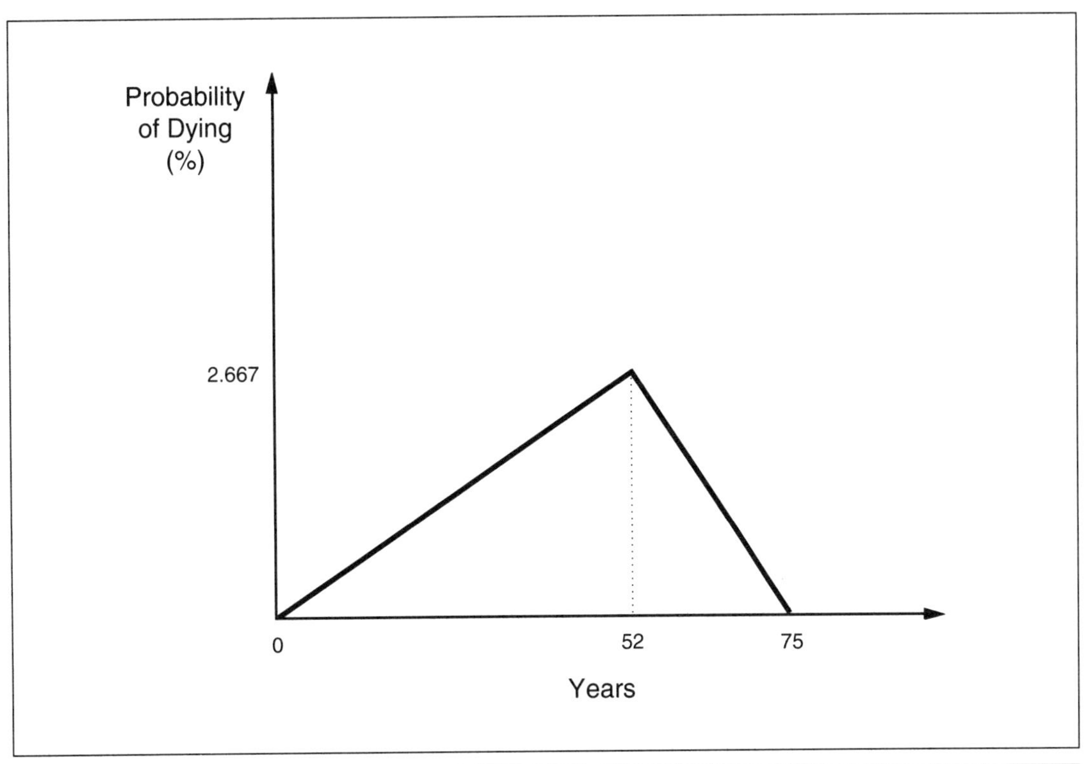

[7] The rate of 2.667 percent in year 52 is required to assure that the mortality rates add to 1.0.

[8] While clearly very simplified, this mortality rate schedule reflects the main characteristics of actual mortality tables. For instance, actual mortality rates increase at first, then decrease. Also, actual mortality tables assume that everyone is dead by age 100.

For example, if a 34-year-old individual has had a \$100,000 policy for nine years, and the mortality rate for the tenth year is m_{10} = 3 percent, then the insurance company expects to pay \$100,000 × 0.03 = \$3,000 on that policy at the end of the tenth year.[9] This expected amount at time 10 is then discounted to time 0 to find its present value. The calculation is repeated for each year until the individual reaches 100 years of age. In this example there are 75 calculations to make. The present value of the benefits is the sum of these 75 yearly benefits.

Similarly, if the premium, R, is the same every year, and the percentage of policyholders who have survived t years after the policies start is s_t, then the present value of all premiums received by the insurance company is:[10]

$$PV_{\text{premiums}} = R \sum_{t=0}^{99-a} s_t (1+r)^{-t} \tag{18.5}$$

By making Equations 18.4 and 18.5 equal, and solving for the whole life policy premium, R, we obtain:

$$R = L \frac{\sum_{t=1}^{100-a} m_t (1+r)^{-t}}{\sum_{t=0}^{99-a} s_t (1+r)^{-t}} \tag{18.6}$$

For our example we use the hypothetical mortality rates shown in Figure 18.2 to compute the values of m_t and s_t for $t = 1, 2, \ldots, 75$ and $t = 1, 2, \ldots, 74$, respectively. Notice that the survival rate at time 0 is 1.00, at time 1 it is $1.00 - m_1$, at time 2 it is $1.00 - m_1 - m_2$, and so on. The sum in the numerator of Equation 18.6 is 0.0552155, and the sum in the denominator is 10.39263. The premium is:

$$R = \$100{,}000 \frac{0.0552155}{10.39263} = \$531.29$$

Thus, the annual fixed fair premium payment for the class of 25-year-old individuals buying whole life insurance policies is \$531.29. Notice that we have disregarded the contribution that operating and other costs might have on the premium. The cash value feature has also been disregarded in the example. Similarly, in practice, insurance companies apply a "load" factor that increases the premium. Despite these shortcomings, the process just described contains the essential elements of whole life insurance pricing.

---

[9] Of course, the company either pays the full \$100,000 or pays nothing at time 10. The \$3,000 should be interpreted as the average amount paid per policy. In other words, if there are 100 identical policies, the company expects to pay \$300,000, or \$3,000 per policy at the end of the period.

[10] Notice that the two summations have limits that are shifted by one year. The reason is that we assume the benefits are paid at the end of each year, whereas the premium payments are made at the beginning of the year.

Term Life While whole life policies offer protection over the insured's entire life, term life policies only offer protection for a limited period, usually one year. For a given policy amount, *L*, the premium increases each year. This is due to the fact that the probability of dying over the next year increases with the policyholder's age at the beginning of the year.[11]

The Premium on Term Life Insurance Policies Suppose the probability of dying over the next year for an individual of age a is p_a. Assume that all benefits are paid at the end of the year. Then, for a policy amount of *L*, and an annual cost of money of *r*, the fair premium, *R*, paid at the beginning of the year is equal to:

$$R = \frac{L \times p_a}{1 + r} \tag{18.7}$$

For example, if the insurance company has a cost of money of 10 percent, the fair premium on a one-year $100,000 term life insurance policy for a 30-year-old individual, whose probability of dying over the next year is 0.133 percent, is equal to:

$$R = \frac{\$100{,}000 \times 0.00133}{1 + 0.10} = \$120.91$$

In this example, an individual can buy a relatively large amount of term insurance for a small premium. This illustrates the risk-sharing characteristic of insurance: Those that survive after one year are subsidizing the few that die. Of course, this "altruistic" mass behavior is due to the fact that at the beginning of the year each policyholder is uncertain about being alive at the end of the year.

Universal Life This is a type of policy that was introduced in 1979 and has gained tremendous popularity over the years. In essence, it is a very flexible type of policy that allows the insured to pay in excess of the pure premium each year. The excess funds can then be used to invest in money market instruments or other investments that the policyholder chooses. This means that the insurance company does not guarantee a fixed rate of return on the funds. Rather, the policyholder bears interest rate risk and default risk on the investments.

This type of policy is so flexible that the policyholder may choose not to pay a premium on any given year. In that case, the insurance company simply takes the premium payment from the policyholder's investment funds. Not only is the premium payment flexible with universal life policies, but the amount of death benefits can also be changed at the policyholder's option. In addition, the policyholder can withdraw money from the accumulated investment funds.

---

[11] Do not confuse the mortality rate schedule for a given class of individuals with the probability of dying in a given year. The mortality rate schedule takes a group of individuals, say 1,000 individuals of age 25, and predicts how many of them will die this year, how many the next year, and so on, until age 100, by which time all 1,000 are presumed dead. The probability of dying is the proportion of individuals of a given age that are expected to die over the next year. For example, if after five years 100 individuals have died, and 90 more are expected to die during the sixth year, the mortality rate for year 6 is 90/1,000 = 9 percent. However, for the 900 survivors that reached age 30, the probability of dying next year is 90/900 = 10 percent.

Clearly, insurance companies are providing two separate services with universal life policies: pure life insurance, and investment services. To emphasize that this type of policy is a hybrid, it is said that the policyholder makes *contributions* or *considerations*, rather than premium payments.

Annuities As we saw in Chapter 5, an annuity is a finite series of equal payments that occur at periodic intervals. Insurance companies also offer annuities, and there are several variations to the annuity theme. The most important are fixed-period annuities and life annuities.

Fixed-Period Annuities In this type of annuity, the equal payments occur over a fixed period of time, usually ten years. With the fixed-period annuity, the insurance company continues to pay benefits to the annuitant's heirs in case death occurs prior to the annuity's expiration. Because of this, there is no risk of losing benefits because of early death.

The fixed-period annuity is the easiest to price because there is very little randomness in the payments. For example, suppose that you purchase an annuity that will make n yearly payments of C dollars each, starting T years from now. To receive the benefits, you have agreed to make M yearly payments of R dollars each (M is less than T), with the first payment due today. The cash flow stream for this contract is depicted in Figure 18.3. To find the fair premium for this annuity, assume that the insurance company's annual cost of money is r percent. As before, in fair pricing the present value of the benefits paid by the insurance company must equal the present value of the premiums it receives. From Figure 18.3 we see that both the premiums and the benefits constitute annuities, as defined in Chapter 5. Thus, the following relationship must hold:[12]

$$R = \frac{C \times PA(r, n)}{PA(r, M) \times (1+r)^T} \tag{18.8}$$

where the short-hand notation $PA(r, x)$ is the present value of an annuity factor for a discount rate of r percent and x cash flows of \$1 each. From this expression, it is seen that the premium increases with the amount of the annuity (C) and with the amount of time the insurance company will pay

Figure 18.3
Cash Flow Stream for a Fixed-Period Annuity

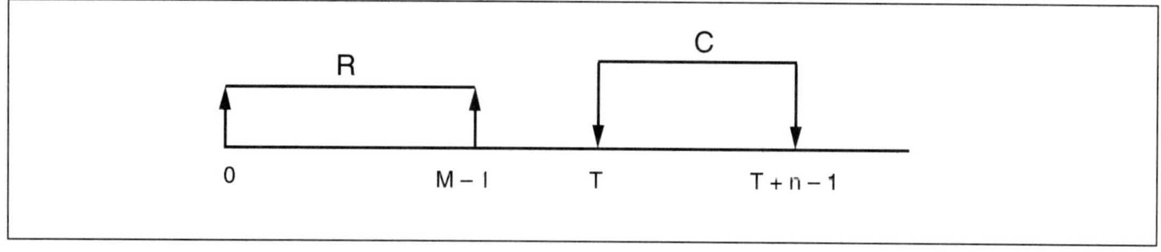

[12] This expression follows from equating the present values of benefits and premiums at time −1. We are disregarding interest rate risk, as well as the possibility that the annuitant dies before making all M premium payments.

benefits (n). Similarly, the periodic premium decreases with the number of premium payments and with the length of time before the annuitant begins to receive the annuity benefits.

To illustrate, assume that $C = \$10,000$, $r = 10$ percent, $n = 10$ payments, $M = 7$ payments, and $T = 20$ years. Then, the annual premium the annuitant must pay is:

$$R = \frac{\$10,000 \times PA(10\%, 10)}{PA(10\%, 7) \times (1 + 0.10)^{20}} = \$1,876.07$$

In this example, the annuitant is required to make seven annual payments of \$1,876.07 in the near future in order to receive \$10,000 per year for 10 years, starting 20 years from now.

Life Annuities This is a type of annuity that pays equal periodic amounts until the annuitant dies. A common version is the joint life annuity, in which the annuity pays benefits until the last member of a predetermined group has died. It is commonly used by retired couples to guarantee the financial security of the last survivor. Since life annuities pay benefits until the annuitant dies, they contain an element of randomness, so their pricing relies on actuarial methods based on mortality tables. Aside from this added element of complexity, pricing life annuities follows essentially the same principles used to value fixed-period annuities.

Health Insurance Many people carry health insurance to protect themselves against unexpected financial distress resulting from a catastrophic illness. A large share of private health insurance is provided by life insurance companies. Health insurance consists of three basic types of coverage: medical expenses, loss of income, and dental. Medical insurance includes medical, hospital, and surgical expenses. Loss of income insurance includes accidental death, disability, and dismemberment coverage. Dental coverage includes regular check-ups and oral surgery.

In addition to life insurance companies, there are other important health care providers. The Blue Cross/Blue Shield group of companies are nonprofit organizations that were created in the 1930s with the purpose of providing health insurance to anyone who requested it. The "Blues," as the group of 73 independent companies is known, cover hospital and medical expenses for over 90 million Americans. Given their huge size, they have great negotiating power with hospitals and doctors, and they help to keep health costs under some control.

Although the Blues are perceived by many to be a monolithic organization, in fact they are essentially independent companies. In the early 1990s some observers believed that some of them were in dire financial straits. Although they are not for profit, many of the Blues have bought for-profit companies in recent years, perhaps in an effort to improve their financial position.

Another important group of health care insurers are Health Maintenance Organizations, or simply HMOs. They act also as health providers by having a physical location where the insured receive medical treatment from doctors, many of whom are full-time employees of the HMO. The popularity of HMOs has expanded, as they are perceived to provide reasonable medical care at a relatively low cost.

Medicare and Medicaid are the federal government's health programs. Medicare can be used by all Americans over the age of 65, regardless of income. Medicare receives funds from all workers, who must contribute 1.45 percent of their salary. Medicare is part of the Social Security organization. While entrance to Medicare is age-determined, participation in Medicaid is open only to lower-income individuals.

Property and Liability Insurance Companies

As the name implies, property and liability (P/L) insurance companies sell policies that protect personal property against flood, fire, theft, and other unexpected occurrences. Property insurance includes auto insurance and homeowner's insurance. The wisdom of carrying these types of property insurance was made evident for many policyholders after recent Florida hurricanes and California earthquakes and storms.

Liability insurance provides protection against lawsuits brought against the policyholder for negligence. The greatest demand for liability insurance is by companies trying to shield themselves against damaging product liability lawsuits and by physicians and other professionals protecting themselves against malpractice suits.

Perhaps the most famous case of a liability lawsuit against a corporation is the Bhopal (India) disaster of December 3, 1984, that occurred in a pesticide plant owned by Union Carbide. This remains the worst industrial accident on record. As a result of a toxic gas leak, more than 3,500 people died, leaving an estimated 200,000 others with a variety of injuries and ailments. As a result of the Bhopal accident, Union Carbide lost about $1 billion in value, literally overnight. After years of litigation, on February 14, 1989, the Indian government ordered Union Carbide to pay survivors $470 million in damages.

Financial Performance of P/L Insurance Companies

The largest firms in the industry are household names, as Table 18.5 shows. Table 18.5 ranks these ten firms by net premiums written and shows the policyholders' surplus for each firm as well. Property and liability insurance companies derive their income from two main sources: premium payments and investment income. Typically, premiums comprise about 85 percent of total income. The difference between the premiums received and the sum of benefits paid and operating expenses give the **underwriting gain** or **loss**. P/L companies have lost money about as often as they have made money on underwriting over the last 25 years. Therefore, the investment income that these firms earn helps to offset the uncertainty of underwriting income.

Although the basic principles outlined for life insurance companies also apply to P/L insurance companies, we can see that their financial performance is very different. This can be explained by the very different lines of business that each type of company insures. For example, while mortality tables exist that determine with great statistical precision the percentage of people that will die at any given age, the probability estimates for P/L companies are much more rudimentary. Indeed, disasters such as the one at Bhopal are very rare (fortunately!) and, therefore, hard to predict. Only a handful of similar accidents have occurred: The near-meltdown at Three Mile Island in 1979 and the real meltdown at Chernobyl in 1986 come to mind. Such a dearth of major industrial accidents makes the work of P/L actuaries very difficult.

A second cause for the losses incurred by P/L insurance companies in the 1980s is the fact that many of the benefits require replacing property that has appreciated in value. For example, if a hurricane destroys a house built 15 years ago, it must be rebuilt at today's cost. Given the high

Table 18.5
The Ten Largest Property/Casualty Insurance Companies

Rank/Name	Net Premiums Written ($ millions)	Policyholders' Surplus ($ millions)
1. State Farm Mutual Automobile Insurance	22,226	21,270
2. Allstate Insurance	15,802	7,145
3. State Farm Fire and Casualty	7,081	3,825
4. Liberty Mutual Insurance	4,801	2,670
5. Farmers Insurance Exchange	4,674	1,894
6. Continental Casualty	4,624	3,598
7. Nationwide Mutual Insurance	4,457	3,323
8. United Services Automobile Association	3,018	3,511
9. St. Paul Fire & Marine Insurance	2,551	1,814
10. Lumbermens Mutual Casualty	2,419	1,718

Source: *Financial World,* September 13, 1994.

inflation levels of the late 1970s and early 1980s, rebuilding the house could easily cost twice its original cost. While P/L insurance companies make provisions to account for inflation when setting their premiums, inflation is essentially unpredictable. Since the late 1980s, inflation has been low and stable, averaging about 3.5 percent per year. Consequently, in the 1990s many P/L insurance companies have been able to recuperate from the disastrous 1980s.

Finally, low market interest rates have hurt the investment portfolios of P/L insurance companies. Although interest rates peaked in the early 1980s, they have been steadily declining since then. By the end of 1992, interest rates were at their lowest level in 30 years. Since then, however, interest rates have risen considerably. Table 18.6 shows the financial investments held by P/L insurers.

Naturally, P/L insurance companies tried to eliminate their underwriting losses by increasing the premiums on their policies. Many policyholders responded by complaining of unfair pricing practices. The problem has acquired a strong political flavor. Indeed, the outcry against premium increases is so great that in 1988 California voters passed Proposition 103. This piece of legislation requires P/L insurers (among other things) to reduce substantially the premiums on all auto insurance and to avoid giving any consideration to the place of residence of the policyholder.

In light of the passage of Proposition 103, it is perhaps not surprising that several insurance companies announced they would no longer operate in California. If the P/L companies actually expect to lose money in California after the mandated reduction in premium rates, then it is optimal for them to stop selling P/L insurance policies in California. It is also obvious that if all drivers pay the same rate, regardless of their geographical location, then drivers in small towns, where car accident rates are low, will unwillingly subsidize drivers in Los Angeles, San Francisco, and other large cities, where car accident rates are much higher. It is not yet clear whether the California revolt against insurance companies will have a net benefit for society or whether it will create more problems than it solves.

Table 18.6
Financial Assets and Liabilities of Property and Liability Insurers
($ billions)

Assets	
Checkable deposits and currency	5.1
Security repurchase agreements	33.6
Corporate equities	105.3
Treasury securities	133.3
U.S. government agency securities	45.4
Tax-exempt securities	151.6
Corporate and foreign bonds	104.7
Commercial mortgages	3.9
Trade credit	51.6
Miscellaneous assets	27.8
Total assets	662.3
Liabilities	
Taxes payable	1.3
Miscellaneous liabilities (includes reserves for underwriting losses)	472.7
Total liabilities	474.0
Net Worth	188.3

Source: Federal Reserve Board, "Flow of Funds Accounts," Third Quarter 1994.

Summary

The fundamental principles underlying the insurance industry are the same as those of portfolio theory. By pooling many independent risks, insurance companies significantly reduce the risk they bear. As a result, they are well equipped to manage risk. Thus, insurance companies provide a valuable service to society.

We presented a simple model of how the risk-reduction mechanism is achieved. If risky insurance policies are independent of one another, then the risk, measured by the standard deviation of net income, decreases with the number of policies the insurance company sells.

The insurance industry is divided into two major types of companies: life and property/liability insurance companies. Life insurance companies sell mainly whole life, term, and universal life insurance, as well as annuities and health insurance. Whole life policies are valid over the insured's entire life, and the annual premium is usually constant. Term policies are valid for a limited amount of time, usually one year, and require higher premium payments every year for a given coverage amount. In universal life policies, the policyholder's contribution includes the premium and an excess that is used by the insurance company to invest according to the policyholder's instructions. Annuities are contracts that promise a periodic fixed payment over a certain period of time. Health insurance protects against illnesses.

Property/liability insurance is designed to transfer the risk associated with natural disasters, such as flood and fire, as well as accidents affecting property. In addition, P/L insurance covers risks associated with negligence. The Bhopal disaster of 1984 remains the largest case thus far.

While both life and P/L insurance companies accept and pool risks, they differ in significant ways. For example, estimating the probability of a loss is relatively easy for a life insurance policy, given the wealth of information that mortality tables applicable to millions of individuals provide. Assessing probabilities is much more difficult for many P/L insurance policies. For example, the probability that another nuclear accident like the ones at Three Mile Island or Chernobyl will occur within the next year is very difficult to ascertain, simply because these are the only two significant nuclear accidents in history. This difficulty in appraising probabilities has contributed to recent losses for the P/L insurance industry.

Questions and Problems

1. Describe the essential function of insurance companies.
2. What is a fair insurance premium?
3. Why do most people seek to have insurance, even though actual premiums are not fair but contain a load factor?
4. What are the major types of insurance companies?
5. Suppose an insurance company can either issue a single policy for $1 million, or it can diversify by having 100 policies of $10,000 each. If the policies are independent of each other, by what factor will the company reduce its risk when it diversifies?
6. An insurance company has 1,000 identical, one-year, $100,000 life insurance policies. The probability that the company will have to pay benefits on a policy is 5 percent. Policyholders must pay a premium of $6,500. Find the expected net revenue and the standard deviation of net revenue for this company.
7. In Problem 6, what is the probability that the insurance company will suffer net losses at the end of the year?
8. In Problem 6, what is the probability that the insurance company will have a net revenue greater than $2 million?
9. Describe the essential features of a whole life insurance policy.
10. Describe the essential features of a term life insurance policy.
11. Suppose a group of 40-year-old individuals purchase whole life insurance policies for $100,000 each. Also assume that the annual mortality rate is constant at 2.5 percent. Find the present value of the benefits the insurance company is expected to pay over the next 40 years if the annual cost of money is 10 percent.
12. In Problem 11, find the fair constant annual premium payment.
13. Suppose that a group of individuals of the same age purchase whole life insurance. For each dollar of life insurance, the present value of the benefits over the life of this group is 0.10. Similarly, the present value of the constant premiums is 20. Find the relationship between the fair premium and the amount of insurance for this group of policyholders.

14. If you purchase $50,000 of one-year term life insurance, and your premium is $2,000, what is the implicit probability that you will die during the next year? Assume that the cost of money for the insurance company is 10 percent and that the company applies a 20 percent load factor to the premium.

15. You purchase a 10-year annuity, which will pay you $20,000 per year, starting 30 years from today. The policy states that you will pay five equal annual premiums, the first one due immediately. The insurance company's annual cost of money is 12 percent. Find the premium payments, assuming they are fair.

16. You purchase a 20-year annuity, which will pay you $10,000 per year, starting 30 years from today. The policy states that you will pay five equal annual premiums, the first one due immediately. The insurance company's annual cost of money is 12 percent. Find the premium payments, assuming they are fair.

17. Why do the answers in Problems 15 and 16 differ, even though the total annuity payment is $200,000 in both cases?

References

American Council of Life Insurance, "Life Insurance Fact Book," various issues.

American Council of Life Insurance, "Life Insurance Fact Book Update," various issues.

Brewer III, Elijah, Thomas H. Mondschean, and Philip E. Strahan, "Why the Life Insurance Industry Did Not Face an 'S&L-Type' Crisis," Federal Reserve Bank of Chicago, *Economic Perspectives*, September/October 1993, pp. 12–24.

Geer, C. T., "What Every Investor Should Know About Life Insurance," *Forbes*, June 22, 1992, pp. 206–7.

Insurance Information Institute, "Property/Casualty Insurance Facts," various issues.

Kopcke, R. W., "The Capitalization and Portfolio Risk of Insurance Companies," *New England Economic Review*, Federal Reserve Bank of Boston, July/August 1992, pp. 43–57.

McGee, R. T., "The Cycle in Property/Casualty Insurance," *Quarterly Review*, Federal Reserve Bank of New York, Autumn 1986, pp. 22–30.

Nye, D. J. and R. W. Kolb, "Inflation, Interest Rates, and Property-Liability Insurer Risk," *Journal of Risk and Insurance*, March 1986, pp. 144–54.

Randall, R. E. and R. W. Kopcke, "The Financial Condition and Regulation of Insurance Companies: An Overview," *New England Economic Review*, Federal Reserve Bank of Boston, May/June 1992, pp. 32–43.

Willoughby, J. and M. K. Ozanian, "Ranking Insurance Companies," *Financial World*, October 1, 1991, pp. 24–5.

Pension Funds 19

Overview

This chapter provides a broad overview of pension funds, beginning with a discussion of the purposes of pensions. One of the most important and obvious roles of pensions is to provide retirement income. However, we will see that pensions also help to determine the relationship between employer and employee and constitute an important element of the labor contract. To stimulate saving for retirement, many forms of pensions receive favorable tax treatment from the U.S. government. These tax factors are very significant economically, and they play a major role in shaping pension habits among U.S. workers.

Pension assets today approach $3 trillion in the United States, and they are divided among several different basic types of pension plans. In a certain respect, the social security system administered by the federal government may be treated as a public pension plan. There are also several types of private pension plans. This chapter explains the essential operations of these different plans.

From the management perspective, pension funds are best viewed as a type of financial intermediary. The fund collects monies during a worker's life from contributions made by the worker and the employer. The pension fund invests these monies during the employee's working years and uses the proceeds to pay the worker a retirement income. The long-term nature of the pension fund's obligation creates special management problems, which this chapter explores. Finally, this chapter also briefly considers the regulation of pension funds in the United States.

The Role of Pensions

This section considers three different roles that pension funds serve. First and foremost, pension assets provide retirement income for workers. This perspective is fundamental, and workers are usually most interested in this aspect of their pension plans. Second, the contracts implicit or explicit in pension arrangements also are a means by which employers offer guarantees to their employees and provide employees with incentives to perform as the employer desires. Finally, pensions in the United States are an important means of deferring taxes for many individuals. This section considers each of these three roles of pensions.

Retirement Income and Its Risks

Pensions may be viewed as a form of deferred compensation. During their work life, employees earn wages, which they receive immediately. They also accrue pension benefits, which generate retirement income. In the United States, approximately 11.5 million people receive pensions, with an average annual payment of about $7,000. For elderly Americans, these pension payments represent about 30 percent of their total income.

Most large firms and governmental entities provide some kind of pension plan for their employees. Why do so many employers and employees make the deferred compensation arrangement of a pension plan a part of the labor contract? After all, employees could receive all of their compensation as wages and create their own retirement savings. The widespread existence of pension plans suggests that pension plans provide benefits that would not be available to employees who sought to create their own retirement savings plans.

Zvi Bodie argues that employers operate pension plans because the employer can provide retirement income insurance more economically than the employees themselves.[1] First, employees desire the same standard of living after retirement that they enjoyed during their working lives. Ensuring a continuing retirement income requires the ability to project the financial resources necessary to continue a given lifestyle and the discipline to follow the saving plan that will create the pool of wealth necessary to fund retirement income. For most workers, firms are better able to make the necessary financial projections, and they are more adept at managing the invested assets during the worker's income-earning years. In addition, by providing part of the total compensation as pension contributions, the employer acts as a substitute for saving discipline on the part of the employee. By enforcing savings and astute management of the investments, the employer can help provide the employees with a continuing standard of living in retirement.

Many employees expect to receive social security payments in retirement as well as their pensions, but the government can change social security payments. As a result, citizens face the risk of a shortfall in retirement income resulting from a change in social security policy. Some pension plans provide a way of allowing individuals to avoid that risk, by promising to increase pension plan payments if social security payments fall. These plans are called **integrated plans**. (As we will see, not all types of pension plans provide insurance against social security shortfalls.)

No one knows the date of his or her own death in advance. If retirement income is funded by a fixed pool of assets at the date of retirement, there is some probability that those funds will be exhausted before death. Some (but not all) pension plans transfer this longevity risk from the employee to the pension plan. Accurate mortality predictions for the population at large are much easier than they are for a specific individual. Because many individuals are covered in a pension plan, the pension plan can accurately predict the level of funds necessary to provide a given standard of living for the entire group. By contrast, the life span of a particular individual is quite difficult to predict. By transferring the risk of a long life from the individual to the pension plan, the individual avoids considerable risk without imposing undue risks on the pension plan.

Retirement income planning faces other risks besides those considered here. In addition to standard of living risk, social security risk, and longevity risk, retirement income depends also on the success of the investment policy followed during the employee's working life, and it depends on inflation during and after the working years. The employee acting alone would face these last two risks, and the pension plan must face them as well.

In summary, the employer has advantages over the typical employee in providing guarantees for retirement income. The employer has economies of scale because it operates the pension plan for many participants. As a result, the pension fund can gather more investment information than

---

[1] See Zvi Bodie, "Pensions as Retirement Income Insurance," *The Journal of Economic Literature*, March 1990, 28:1, pp. 28–49. This section draws liberally from Bodie's article.

the individual. Because of its larger size and presumably greater financial sophistication, the employer may have preferential investment opportunities and should be able to economize on transaction costs involved in investing the pension fund assets. Acting on his or her own initiative, the employee has difficulty in avoiding longevity risk. The employer, by pooling many employees in the pension plan, can avoid the longevity risk of individuals.

Pensions as Tax Shelters

While a detailed treatment of the tax aspects of pensions is beyond the scope of this text, the basic tax advantages of pension contributions are quite clear. Contributions to pension funds, whether made by the employer or the employee, are tax-deferred. The amounts contributed to the plan are free of federal income taxation in the year the contribution is made, and no tax is paid on these funds until the employee starts to withdraw pension benefits. As these benefits are withdrawn, the recipient pays income tax on them as though they are regular income. Thus, a contribution made for a 30-year-old worker that is eventually withdrawn by a 70-year-old pensioner avoids taxation for 40 years, during which time the funds earn a compounded return.

We have seen that employer pension contributions may be regarded as part of the employee's total compensation package. Pension taxation rules permit employers to deliver a portion of the compensation as tax-deferred income by making pension contributions. In many instances, employees can also make contributions to their own pensions, and these are also tax-deferred contributions. By contrast, individual savings not directed to a pension plan must usually be paid from after-tax income, so the tax deferral inherent in pension contributions is extremely advantageous.

Types of Pension Plans

There are many types of retirement income plans. This section considers the main ways of providing retirement income, starting with the social security system, which is not a true pension plan at all. We then consider a variety of types of pension plans and other specialized forms of saving and investing for retirement.

The Social Security System

The U.S. federal government operates the **Old Age and Survivors Insurance Fund**, better known as Social Security, which was established in 1935 among the wave of New Deal legislation. Virtually every worker in the United States participates in this compulsory plan, with wages being withheld under FICA (Federal Insurance Contribution Act). While originally planned to operate like a private pension plan, social security has been expanded and modified successively, generally to extend and expand benefits. FICA withholding can be substantial. Beginning in 1990, 7.65 percent of each worker's pay is withheld to a maximum of $3,856 per year. The employer pays an equal matching amount on behalf of the employee.

Upon qualifying, individuals receive payments from the fund that continue as long as they live. While the system is complex and there are many exceptions, basic eligibility begins at age 62. Payments to recipients exceeded $400 billion in 1995. For most retired Americans, social security is an important component of retirement income. By itself, however, social security payments alone do not provide most recipients adequate income to maintain the life style they enjoyed during the working years. Therefore, other forms of retirement income are critically important.

Public versus Private Plans

All pension plans may be classified as public or private. A **public pension plan** is a plan sponsored by a governmental agency. For example, employees of state governments generally receive pension payments under a state pension plan. By contrast, a **private pension plan** is a plan sponsored by a non-governmental entity, such as a corporation.

Table 19.1 shows the ten largest states by population and provides information about public pension payments in those states. As the table shows, California is the largest state by population and currently has about 358,000 individuals receiving pensions from public pension plans in the state. Each recipient receives an average of almost $11,000 per year. Compared with public pension plans, there are many more private pension plans, and many more individuals participate in private plans. About 45 million U.S. workers contribute to private plans and more than 9 million people receive payments from private pension plans. The average annual benefit for these recipients is $6,359. The average payment from private plans is substantially lower than the average amounts shown in Table 19.1. This may be due to the tendency of government workers to have longer careers with the same employer or to the generous nature of some public pension plans.

Defined-Benefit and Defined-Contribution Plans

In addition to being public or private plans, standard pension plans may also be classified as defined-benefit or defined-contribution plans. This section considers the basic features of each kind of plan and contrasts the advantages of each.

Defined-Benefit Plans In a **defined-benefit plan**, the plan sponsor promises to pay a certain benefit to retirees. This promise is often stated as a percentage of a worker's salary in the last few

Table 19.1
Public Pension Recipients and Benefits for 10 Most Populous States

State	Number of Pension Recipients (thousands)	Mean Annual Benefit
California	358	$10,981
New York	245	11,084
Texas	150	8,119
Florida	200	7,323
Pennsylvania	192	7,534
Illinois	92	8,938
Ohio	149	10,587
Michigan	98	11,384
New Jersey	74	10,309
North Carolina	89	9,242

Source: U.S. Department of Labor, *Trends in Pension 1992*, p. 362. Data are for year-end 1989.

years before retirement. Making the pension benefit depend upon the last year, or last few years, of a worker's career is called **back-end loading**. The plan often aims to provide a specified **replacement rate** – the percentage of the employee's salary that will be replaced by the pension benefit. A typical replacement rate is 30 percent, meaning that the annual pension benefit is 30 percent of the salary used to compute the benefit. Many defined-benefit plans are integrated with social security. In an **integrated plan**, the pension fund aims to provide a total replacement of salary from a combination of pension payments and social security. A typical replacement rate for an integrated plan might be 50–60 percent. In an integrated plan, the pension fund decreases its own payments if social security payments rise, but it may also increase its payments if social security payments are cut.

The defined-benefit plan insulates the worker from the uncertainties of the market place. An integrated plan also affords some protection from changes in social security payments. The plan sponsor promises a given benefit and must earmark enough assets to generate the defined benefit. If investments in the pension fund fail to earn a sufficient return, the plan sponsor should compensate for the shortfall. If the investments perform particularly well, the sponsoring firm keeps the excess return beyond that needed to provide the defined benefit.

Merely accepting employment at a firm with a defined-benefit plan does not qualify a worker to start accruing pension benefits. Many defined-benefit plans require a waiting period before the worker is guaranteed to receive the specified pension benefits. The process of qualifying for the pension benefit is called **vesting**, and a worker who has qualified is said to be **vested**. Rules for vesting differ from plan to plan, but they often require some minimum period of service. As a typical example, a worker might become vested after working for the firm for five years. Upon becoming vested, the worker would qualify to receive benefits based on the previous service. However, if a worker leaves an employer before vesting, all pension benefits may be sacrificed.

In the typical defined-benefit plan, all of the pension fund assets are managed by a trustee. Usually the trustee will hire money managers to invest the funds in specific securities following the guidelines established by the trustee. Throughout the investment process, the trustee dictates the investment strategy for the entire pool of assets.

Defined-Contribution Plan In a **defined-contribution plan**, the plan sponsor promises to make a given contribution to the pension funds of each employee each pay period. Once the sponsor makes the specified contribution, it completes its financial obligation. In many defined-contribution plans, workers are immediately vested upon employment. In addition, defined-contribution plans have little or no back-end loading. For example, a defined-contribution plan might pay a constant percentage of a worker's salary as a pension benefit.

In operating a defined-contribution plan, the employer typically specifies a range of possible investment alternatives under the plan. The pension assets contributed by the employer are held in individual accounts for the benefit of each employee, and the individual usually has considerable discretion in allocating those funds among the alternatives approved by the pension plan. For example, an employer might approve a variety of mutual funds, savings plans, and insurance company investment products. The employer might make monthly contributions for a given employee, and the contributed funds would be allocated among the investment vehicles as the employee specified.

A Comparison of Defined-Benefit and Defined-Contribution Plans Table 19.2 contrasts defined-benefit and defined-contribution private pension plans in the United States. Of the approximately 730,000 plans in existence, about 20 percent are defined-benefit plans. However, many more workers are covered under defined-benefit plans rather than defined-contribution plans. Of the 42 million workers covered by a plan, 28 million participate in defined-benefit plans. As Table 19.2 shows, about half of all full-time workers in the U.S. are covered by some type of plan, and about two-thirds of workers are fully vested.

Private pension plans have assets of $1.5 trillion, with 60 percent being held in defined-benefit plans. Table 19.2 shows that defined-contribution plans are growing very rapidly. Today substantially more new funds are being directed toward defined-contribution plans. Of the $91 million contributed annually, $65 million, or 71 percent, is going to defined-benefit plans. Similarly, defined-benefit and defined-contribution plans are approximately equal in the total size of payments.

Retirement saving is necessarily one of the longest range financial endeavors that an individual faces. Because the planning horizon between saving for retirement and spending the funds

Table 19.2
Defined Contribution and Defined Benefit Pension Plans

Number of plans	
Total	729,922
Defined-benefit	145,952
Defined-contribution	583,971
Number of covered workers (thousands)	
Total	42,283
Defined-benefit	28,010
Defined-contribution	14,273
Percentage of private workers with coverage	
All workers	45
Full-time workers	51
Percent of covered workers fully vested	66
Pension plan assets ($ millions)	
Total	$1,503,534
Defined-benefit	911,982
Defined-contribution	591,653
Pension plan contributions ($ millions annually)	
Total	$91,248
Defined-benefit	26,300
Defined-contribution	64,948
Pension plan benefit payments ($ millions annually)	
Total	$118,645
Defined-benefit	60,450
Defined-contribution	58,195

Source: U.S. Department of Labor, *Trends in Pension 1992*, p. 10.

for retirement income is so long, there are greater uncertainties and special risks. Defined-benefit and defined-contribution plans differ markedly in the kinds of risk that they involve and the parties that bear the risk.

Earlier in this chapter, we saw that employers often manage pension plans for their employees because of the employer's presumably greater financial sophistication and the economies of scale involved in managing a large pool of funds. These features are available with a defined-benefit plan, but they are largely missing in a defined-contribution plan. In a defined-contribution plan, ultimate responsibility for investment decisions usually rests with the employee, although the employer establishes the broad parameters by determining what investment choices will be available.

Pension plans, we noted earlier, also provide employees with the discipline to save. For both defined-benefit and defined-contribution plans, the employer makes contributions and the savings are equally forced. Thus, neither type of plan performs better in enforcing saving discipline.

In a defined-contribution plan, the employee bears social security risk and longevity risk. When the employer makes the specified contribution to an employee's individual account, the employer has completed its financial responsibility. The employee's standard of living will be subject to changes in social security because defined-contribution plans cannot be integrated with social security. Further, the employee bears the longevity risk, because the pool of funds available at retirement must suffice for the rest of the employee's life. However, the employee may easily avoid the longevity risk by purchasing a lifetime annuity through an insurance company, as explained in Chapter 18.

In a defined-benefit plan, the plan sponsor promises a certain payment to the pensioner, so the plan sponsor bears the investment risk. If investment returns are poor, the sponsor must make good the shortfall. Conversely, if returns exceed the return necessary to pay the pension benefits, the employer reaps the gain. In a defined-contribution plan, the employee bears the investment risk.

While the allocation of investment risk appears to give a strong advantage to defined-benefit plans, there are risks beyond mere investment returns. In a defined-benefit plan, the plan sponsor keeps control of all of the pension monies. If these funds are invested in losing enterprises, there is a danger that the entire amount might be lost. For example, Pan Am airlines invested much of its pension monies in Pan Am stock. When the airline failed, the stock became worthless, and many Pan Am employees both lost their jobs and were left with pitifully small pension benefits. Further, as we discuss later in this chapter, the sponsor of a defined-benefit plan must compute the funding level necessary to generate the promised benefits. In some cases, the employer has underfunded the pension plan, leaving the employees in the lurch. By contrast, in defined-contribution plans, the contributions are often removed from the control of the employer as they are made, and this gives the employee considerably greater comfort in knowing that the funds will not be diverted to aims other than the interest of the pensioner.

Individual Retirement Accounts and Keogh Plans

In this section, we consider two retirement savings plans, both recognized by special provisions in the federal income tax code. We begin by considering the common features of these plans and then discuss the special provisions of each. Individual Retirement Plans (IRAs) and Keogh plans allow individuals to save for retirement on a tax-deferred basis. All contributions to these plans escape federal income taxation in the year the contribution is made. Funds in these special accounts earn a compound return over the years before retirement, and the monies in these accounts are not taxed during this investment period. As the retiree withdraws money from the accounts, the withdrawals are taxed as ordinary income. Thus, the tax shelter provision of these plans parallels the tax benefits of other pension plans.

In some circumstances, individuals covered by other pension plans, such as an employer's defined-benefit plan, can create a second or even third plan to save for retirement. For example, an auto worker covered by her firm's plan might also run a car repair business. A portion of the income from the car repair business could be placed in one or more of the pension plans discussed in this section.

Both plans restrict the amount and timing of contributions and the terms and conditions of withdrawal. In general, the plans limit the contributions individuals can make and include tax penalties for withdrawing funds before retirement.

Individual Retirement Account When they were first created in 1976, rules for Individual Retirement Accounts (IRAs) were quite simple and fairly generous in permitting contributions. The original rules allowed an individual to contribute the lesser of $2,000 or 100 percent of taxable income to an IRA on a tax-deferred basis each year. Contributions to IRAs were available to everyone, even if covered by an employer's pension plan. Thus, IRAs provided a convenient tax-sheltered retirement savings plan available to everyone. IRAs were wildly popular under the original rules, and by 1995 there were 22 million IRA accounts with more than $350 billion in assets.

The Tax Reform Act of 1986 placed important new restrictions on contributions to IRAs. Under this law, individuals covered by an employer's retirement plan cannot make tax-deductible contributions to IRAs. In addition to restricting IRA tax-deductible contributions to those not covered by an employer's plan, the new law also imposed income tests. Individuals with adjusted gross income (AGI) of $25,000 or less, and married couples with an AGI of $40,000 or less, are allowed to make a $2,000 tax-deductible contribution. The new law still permits individuals and married couples to contribute up to $2,000 or $2,250 to IRAs even if they do not qualify under the rules stated above, but the contribution is not tax-deductible. Earnings in the principal remain tax-deferred until withdrawal, however. These new restrictions mean that many individuals cannot make tax-deductible contributions, so IRAs have grown very slowly under the new law.

Because they are intended as a vehicle for retirement savings, IRAs are subject to restrictions on withdrawals. Any withdrawals made before the age of 59.5 years are subject to an immediate tax penalty of 10 percent. The remaining 90 percent of the withdrawal is taxed as ordinary income in the year of the withdrawal. Withdrawals after age 59.5 are taxed as ordinary income, and rules require individuals to begin making withdrawals after age 70.5. Recently, Congress has been considering a new liberalization of IRA rules to stimulate retirement savings once again.

Keogh Plan A Keogh plan, named after a sponsoring legislator, is a pension plan designed for self-employed persons. Keogh plans are also permitted for a person covered by a company plan who runs a separate business, such as the auto worker with a sideline car repair business. It is also possible to cover employees under a Keogh plan as well, and Keogh plans may be created as defined-benefit or defined-contribution plans.

While the complete rules governing Keogh plans are quite complex, a typical Keogh might be established as a defined-contribution plan based on profits from a sole-proprietorship with no employees. The maximum percentage of profits that can be contributed is 20 percent, up to an annual maximum contribution of $30,000.

Under the current tax law, withdrawals from the plan are discouraged until age 59.5 years. Any amounts withdrawn before this time are subject to a special penalty tax of 10 percent of the amount withdrawn, and the remaining 90 percent of the funds are taxed as regular income. Further, at age 70.5, the worker has to begin to make withdrawals from the plan.

Keogh plans are subject to many rules and require registration with the IRS. In addition, there are several different kinds of Keogh plans, so establishing a Keogh plan may require the services of an attorney specializing in such matters.

Employee Stock Ownership Plans (ESOPs)

An Employee Stock Ownership Plan (ESOP) is a special kind of private defined-contribution plan. In an ESOP, employees receive shares in the corporation for which they work. In some cases, employees use ESOPs to acquire an entire company so that the company becomes completely worker-owned. ESOPs must hold at least 51 percent of their assets as an investment in the parent corporation. Currently, there are more than 8,000 ESOP plans in the United States and more than 8 million employees participate in an ESOP. Total assets committed to ESOP plans exceed $60 billion.

ESOPs offer important tax advantages and may afford companies with significant improvements in worker morale and productivity. Foremost among the tax advantages is the deductibility of contributions made by the corporation to the ESOP, and lenders to firms controlled by their ESOPs receive special tax incentives. ESOPS benefit from other special tax provisions, but Congress tends to change some of these often. Through an ESOP, employees own part or all of the corporation, and some observers believe that this ownership interest improves the motivation of employees. Under an ESOP, the covered employees own some or all of the corporation, so they are working for themselves in some sense.

From the point of view of personal portfolio management, there is one substantial drawback to ESOPs, however. Under an ESOP, an employee's job and savings are concentrated in a single enterprise. This feature of ESOPs violates the first principle of portfolio management – that assets should be diversified. If the business fails, the employee not only loses her job, but also loses her pension.

Firms often establish ESOPs in times of crisis, particularly to extract wage concessions from employees or to defend against a takeover attempt. A firm faced with grim economic prospects might agree to create an ESOP and give employees stock in the corporation in return for accepting lower wages. Similarly, a firm faced with a takeover attempt might place shares in the hands of its employees in the belief that the employees, fearing the loss of their jobs if the takeover is successful, would be more likely to support current management in resisting the takeover attempt.

Management of Pension Funds

This section considers the financial management of pension funds. Whether a defined-benefit or defined-contribution plan, the pension fund represents a major commitment of funds by the plan sponsor. In a defined-contribution plan, the investment decisions are typically given to the employee. By contrast, in a defined-benefit plan, the employer usually manages the entire pool of funds.

In this section, we adopt the point of view of a corporation that manages a defined-benefit plan. Such a firm faces a pension liability that is largely concentrated in the future upon the retirement of its current employees. To meet this liability, the corporation must fund the pension plan with assets today and manage those assets until employees retire. Of course, the firm wants to meet its obligation with the least expenditure. As a result, the manager of the pension fund must strive to earn a high return while controlling risk.

The Pension Liability

Workers covered by a pension plan realize that a portion of their compensation is being deferred and collected in the pension plan. By accepting less than their full pay in the present period, employees are implicitly helping to finance the firm in exchange for the expectation of a suitable return in their retirement years. The employee must trust the employer to deliver the deferred compensation at retirement. Thus, the pension arrangement in a typical defined-benefit plan rests on an implicit contract between employer and employee. Because the pension contract is only implicit, it depends on trust.

Because of this implicit obligation, and because the employee effectively lends to the employer by deferring compensation, the employee runs the risk of the employer failing to fulfill its obligation. Richard A. Ippolito and William H. James observe:

> *A problem can arise for pension-covered workers because much of the economic value of the pension promise is implicit. While the pension typically promises a benefit proportional to wages at retirement, the firm virtually always retains the right to terminate the plan. This flexibility is presumably included to help the firm meet business exigencies. If, however, the firm were to take advantage of the implicit nature of the promise, that is, to terminate the contract midstream solely for the purpose of cheating workers, a large transfer would be effected from workers to stockholders.*[2]

Even though employees face large potential damages from pension plan terminations, firms have strong incentives to treat their employees fairly. Most firms require the good will and best efforts of their employees to succeed. A firm that violates the employees' trust by terminating a pension plan might reap a substantial one-time windfall profit, but its ability to succeed in the marketplace would be adversely affected. Therefore, we focus on the case of responsible employer behavior in managing a defined-benefit plan.

Following the discussion by Dennis Logue,[3] we identify four factors that influence the size of the pension liability in a defined-benefit plan for a particular worker:

---

[2] Richard A. Ippolito and William H. James, "LBOs, Reversions and Implicit Contracts," *Journal of Finance*, 47:1, March 1992, p. 141.

[3] Dennis E. Logue, *Managing Corporate Pension Plans*, New York: Harper-Collins Publishers, Inc., 1991. See Chapter 3.

1. The rate of growth in the worker's wages
2. The number of years the worker will continue in employment
3. The number of years the worker will live in retirement
4. The rate of discount to be used to compute the present value of the payments implied by the first three points

As an example, consider a 50-year-old worker who earns $50,000 per year. She has worked for ten years already, and expects to work for 20 more years, with raises of 5 percent per year. Based on actuarial tables, her life expectancy at retirement will be 15 years. The company expects to offer a pension equal to 2 percent of final salary multiplied by the years of service. The appropriate discount rate is 10 percent. To compute the current value of the pension obligation associated with this worker, the pension manager needs to estimate her final annual salary, compute the annual pension amount, find the present value (at her retirement date) of the annuity that she will receive, and discount the present value of the annuity to the present.

Based on the information given here, the firm can calculate its pension liability associated with her career to date. (Of course, if she continues with the firm, her salary and the firm's pension obligation will continue to grow.) Were she to retire today, her annual pension payment would be her final annual salary of $50,000 times 2 percent times her 10 years of service to date, for a total of $10,000. That pension payment would begin at the normal retirement of age 65 and continue until her expected death at 80. The present value of this stream of payments is the present value of an annuity that begins in 20 years, pays $10,000 for 15 years and is discounted at 10 percent:

$$PV = \left(\frac{1}{1.1}\right)^{20} \sum_{t=1}^{15} \frac{\$10{,}000}{1.10^t}$$

$$= \frac{\$76{,}061}{1.1^{20}}$$

$$= \$11{,}333$$

Thus, for her service to date, the firm has a pension liability for this worker of $11,333 in today's dollars. The firm would compute its liability over all of its workers to determine its total pension liability. Because it is dealing with many workers, uncertainty about the life expectancy, length of career, or future salary would tend to average out, making a close estimate possible.

Under federal regulation, firms are not allowed to operate their pension plans on a "pay as you go" method, meeting current pension expenses from current pension contributions. Instead, the firm must establish a pool of assets that will fund the pension plan. A pension plan with an asset pool exceeding the present value of its pension obligations is **overfunded**. If the value of the assets is not as great as the present value of the future pension payments, the plan is **underfunded**.

Computing the degree of overfunding or underfunding is not a simple matter. For example, the degree of funding necessary for a plan depends on the rate of return the pension plan assumes it will earn over the future. The estimated adequacy of the funding also depends on the discount rate applied to the future pension payment that the fund anticipates. This discount rate is not necessarily the same as the rate at which the assets are projected to grow in value. The higher the estimated investment rate and the higher the discount rate applied to the future liabilities, the lower the present value of the obligation. By assuming a high rate of return on assets and a high discount rate, firms can reduce the amount of pension contributions necessary to achieve a given level of funding for the plan. Actually achieving the target rate of return depends on skillful management of the plan's assets.

Managing Pension Assets

The typical firm that establishes a pension plan most likely has no special expertise in managing a large investment portfolio, such as the pool of assets that would fund the pension plan. As a result, many firms hire external management to manage their portfolio. With external management, the plan sponsor must still monitor and evaluate the investment management that the plan assets receive. If a firm decides to manage plan assets with personnel internal to the firm, it must develop the special expertise of money managers and incur the cost of establishing the necessary controls. Whether management of plan assets is internal or external, the plan sponsor must determine the overall investment policy that will guide fund assets.

Investment policy must balance competing risk and return preferences of the plan sponsors and the workers who hope to receive pensions. In a defined-benefit plan, the workers tend to prefer conservative management to ensure against loss of principal. From the workers' point of view, their pension income is fixed by the promise of a defined benefit. If the fund is managed conservatively and there is a shortfall, the plan sponsor will have to contribute new funds to provide the defined benefit. Therefore, if the sponsor is financially strong and fully committed to paying the defined benefit, workers will prefer conservative management.[4]

From the sponsor's point of view, there is an incentive to accept riskier management. More aggressive management raises the expected return on the portfolio while increasing risk. If expected returns are realized, then the shareholders will receive the benefit of the aggressive management. Similarly, in a public defined-benefit plan, the taxpayers have a role analogous to that of the shareholders in a private defined-benefit plan. By contrast, a defined-contribution plan involves no potential disagreement in the appropriate risk level between the plan sponsor and the plan's beneficiaries. In a defined-contribution plan, the participants are the owners of the plan assets, and they bear all risks associated with the plan. If the investment policy is too conservative, pension income will be reduced. If the investment policy is too aggressive, the participants bear the risk of capital loss. In general, for a defined-contribution plan, the management of the plan's assets should be tailored to reflect the risk and expected return preferences of the participants. This can be achieved by allowing the individual participant to select from a wide range of investment vehicles of varying levels of risk.

Table 19.3 shows the different asset allocation that different types of pension funds make. For example, the table shows that all types of funds place some of their monies in money market

---

[4] Note that workers may prefer a somewhat riskier policy in certain circumstances. If plan assets are weak, excessively conservative management might guarantee a shortfall in benefits. If the plan sponsor is also financially weak, the sponsor may not make up the shortfall. In this circumstance, a reasonable worker might prefer that assets be managed more aggressively.

investments. This makes sense because all types of funds require liquidity. In other asset categories, there are some striking differences. Only 4 percent of union-sponsored funds invest in international stocks, compared to 44 percent of corporate funds and 37 percent of public funds. Union funds are quite willing to hold real estate mortgages, with 59 percent of such funds holding such instruments. This compares with only 16 percent of corporate funds and 39 percent of public funds. On the whole, Table 19.3 shows that corporate funds tend to be somewhat more aggressive in managing pension assets. This makes sense, given our observation that corporation stockholders capture the benefits of investment performance beyond that necessary to pay the defined benefits of the plan.

Table 19.4 shows the allocation of pension funds across broad asset categories. About 40 percent of all private pension assets in the United States are invested in either common stocks or bonds. Fully 26 percent of these assets do not fall in any of the specified categories. However, most of these unspecified funds are invested with insurance companies.

Regulation of Pension Funds

Pension plans have been regulated by state and federal law for many decades. However, in 1974 Congress passed the Employee Retirement Income Security Act (ERISA). This act revolutionized the regulation of pension funds. Because it is so comprehensive, ERISA provides a fresh starting point for understanding the basic structure of pension regulation. This section reviews the most important portions of ERISA. The discussion also highlights the Pension Benefit Guaranty Corporation (PBGC) that was created by ERISA.

Table 19.3
Choice of Assets by Fund Types
(percent of funds holding assets of a given type)

Type of Asset	Corporate Funds	Public Funds	Union-Sponsored Funds
Money market	100	100	100
Conservative stocks	91	90	84
Growth stocks	77	78	75
International stocks	44	37	4
Equity index funds	40	38	43
Actively managed bond funds	76	90	88
Junk bonds	9	9	4
International bonds	35	28	4
Bond index funds	24	24	41
Dedicated bond portfolios	27	13	27
International index funds	9	14	0
Real estate ownership	53	56	73
Real estate mortgages	16	39	59
Venture capital	21	23	8
Leveraged-buy-out funds	8	8	0

Source: Adapted from Dennis E. Logue, *Managing Corporate Pension Plans*, New York: Harper-Collins Publishers, Inc., 1991, Table 4.1, p. 127.

Table 19.4
Asset Allocation of Private U.S. Pension Fund Assets

Type of Asset	Percentage of Assets Invested in Asset Category
Common stocks (foreign and domestic)	26
Bonds (foreign and domestic)	15
Real estate	–
Mortgages	–
Loans and private placements	–
Investment companies (mutual funds, etc.)	19
Cash and short-term assets	14
Other assets	26

Source: Lorna M. Dailey and John A. Turner, "U.S. Private Pensions in World Perspective: 1979–1980," in U.S. Department of Labor, *Trends in Pensions 1992*, pp. 11–34.

Employee Retirement Income Security Act (ERISA)

The Employee Retirement Income Security Act (ERISA) applies to private pension plans, so the plans of state and local government are beyond its scope. The act includes four main titles. Title I aims at protecting employees' pensions and is administered by the Department of Labor. Titles II and III, regulated by the Internal Revenue Service, deal with participation, vesting, and funding. Title IV primarily concerns plan terminations and is the responsibility of the Pension Benefit Guaranty Corporation (PBGC), a new governmental entity created by the act.

Pension Protection Under ERISA Prior to the enactment of ERISA, the employer and the pension fund operated for a firm were legally distinct. The employer had no liability for the pension obligation, so the employer could be quite profitable while the pension fund failed. ERISA made the employer ultimately responsible for the pensions.

ERISA also revolutionized the investment activities of pension funds. At the heart of ERISA's investment rules lies the **prudent man rule**. Under the prudent man rule, pension funds must be managed as a prudent, knowledgeable, and disinterested professional would do. For example, a prudent man would hold a well-diversified portfolio, so failing to diversify would provide evidence of imprudence. Similarly, a corporation might transfer a building to its pension fund at an inflated cost. A prudent man, acting in the best interest of the pension fund, would never willingly accept such a transaction. While the prudent man rule is certainly imprecise, it at least gives a conceptual standard for the reasonable management of pension fund investments.

ERISA imposed new funding requirements on pension plans. Before the passage of ERISA, there were no rules for the funding of pension plans, so employers could leave the plan underfunded or even operate the plan on a pay-as-you-go basis. While ERISA's rules on funding are complex, they are intended to increase the amount of funds backing the pension and to reduce the risk that the pension plan will be unable to deliver on its pension promise. In essence, the ERISA funding rules require pension plans to correct deficiencies on a fixed schedule of 5–18 years, depending on the nature of the deficiency.

ERISA's Rules on Participation and Vesting Prior to ERISA, the employer was free to set the rules for participation in pension plans. Under ERISA, any adult worker qualifies to participate in the pension plan after one year of service. (If the plan offers immediate vesting, the qualification period is two years.) These rules were intended to prevent firms from delaying pension participation to younger workers.

Vesting was entirely a matter of employer discretion before the passage of ERISA. In the pre-ERISA era, it was common for vesting to occur at the date of retirement. If an employee quit just before retirement, he or she could be excluded from receiving a pension. Similarly, an unscrupulous employer could fire an employee approaching retirement to avoid paying a pension.

There were two primary motives for such late vesting arrangements. First, employers could use late vesting to bind workers to the firm. For example, an employee with 25 years of service and 5 years to retirement might be unwilling to quit and lose the pension benefits that were accruing. Second, some firms had unscrupulous intentions to defraud the workers of their anticipated pensions as they approached retirement.

ERISA stipulated minimum standards for vesting and currently permits firms to adopt one of two vesting schedules. First, the employee may become 100 percent vested after five years. Employees who quit before five years receive zero from the pension plan, while those who remain for at least five years retain full rights to their accrued benefits. Second, the pension plan may allow gradual vesting between the third and seventh years of employment. Of course, firms may also offer more liberal vesting schedules.

The Pension Benefit Guaranty Corporation (PBGC)

Created by ERISA, the Pension Benefit Guaranty Corporation is a government corporation that insures pension benefits for participants in private pension plans. About 85,000 plans and 40 million participants are covered by the PBGC. The PBGC charges plan sponsors an insurance fee each year to cover the risk that a plan will fail and be unable to pay its pension benefits. Based on the revenues from these premiums, the PBGC promises to pay pensions for workers who were covered by terminated plans. In 1993, the PBGC paid $722 million to 158,400 individuals. Another 188,000 will receive payments from PBGC when they reach retirement age. For example, the bankruptcies of Eastern and Pan Am airlines left the PBGC holding the bag on plans that were underfunded by $700 million and $900 million, respectively.

Congress determines the level of insurance premiums that pension plans must pay to the PBGC. When the law was passed in 1974, the level was set at $1 per covered participant per year. The annual premium has risen to $19 per participant, plus a surcharge of as much as $53 per participant for a severely underfunded plan. Premium income now exceeds $900 million annually.

In recent years, the PBGC has been losing money – its premium income is less than it has been required to pay for pensions in plans that were terminated. The problem in the funding of PBGC has at least two sources. First, Congress sets the funding and has been unwilling to set a rate high enough for the PBGC to meet its obligations while remaining financially healthy. Second, the form of the premium gives pension plan managers adverse incentives. Because the insurance premium has a cap of $72 per participant and because the risk-based surcharge depends only on the degree of underfunding and not the quality of the portfolio of pension fund assets, pension managers have incentives to leave plans underfunded and to hold risky assets in their pension fund. From the point of view of the PBGC, the true risk of an insured pension plan depends on both the level of funding and the quality of assets in the plan. A rational insurance premium would have no upper bound and would reflect both underfunding and asset quality. By 1995, the negative equity of the PBGC was about $3 billion.

The continuing deficits of the PBGC are reminiscent of the savings and loan crisis discussed in Chapter 11. Legislation requires both the PBGC and savings and loan insurers (FSLIC) to provide specified payments under certain circumstances. Both organizations were forced to charge insurance premiums that failed to reflect the entire risk that was being insured. The federal promise and the structure of both organizations also gave S&L and pension fund managers incentives to take unwise risks. Based on these parallels, some observers believe that the PBGC may someday require a federal bailout similar to that in the thrift industry.[5]

Summary

This chapter began by introducing the social rationale for pension plans. As we saw, pensions serve to provide retirement income, but they also provide an important part of the labor contract for motivating employees and building employee loyalty to the firm. In this connection, we saw that pensions are essentially deferred compensation that the employer may be able to manage better than the employee. There are many kinds of pension plans. We distinguished public and private pension plans, and defined-benefit and defined-contribution plans. In addition, we considered the role of social security, and we analyzed Employee Stock Ownership Plans (ESOPs).

The chapter considered the basic precepts of pension fund management. We noted that a defined-benefit pension plan consists of extensive obligations to pay a series of payments extending from an employee's retirement to death. A crucial part of pension plan management is the correct assessment of the magnitude and timing of the pension liability. With many participants, the law of large numbers helps the pension manager arrive at accurate estimates of the pension fund's obligation. To meet these obligations, a pension plan has a pool of assets. The pension manager must invest these assets to generate income so that the company can pay its pensions as promised.

The chapter concluded with a review of pension fund regulation. The keystone piece of legislation for pension funds is the Employee Retirement Income Security Act (ERISA). We considered the different rules imposed by ERISA and noted how the Act revolutionized the management of pension funds. Finally, we considered the role of the Pension Benefit Guaranty Corporation (PBGC), which is itself a creation of ERISA. The PBGC acts as an insurance fund, charging insurance premiums to pension funds and promising to make pension payments to workers participating in pension plans that fail.

Questions and Problems

1. Explain the three main roles of pension plans.
2. How do employers use pension arrangements to motivate their workers? Why don't firms merely pay higher wages instead?

---

[5] See, for example, Peter A. Abken, "Corporate Pensions and Government Insurance: Deja Vu All Over Again?" *Economic Review*, Federal Reserve Bank of Atlanta, 77:2, March/April 1992, pp. 1–16, and Dennis E. Logue, *Managing Corporate Pension Plans*, New York: Harper-Collins, 1991.

3. What kinds of advantages might the employer have in operating a retirement savings plan?
4. How do pensions act as tax shelters? Explain the basics of the taxation of pension contributions and withdrawals.
5. Explain the difference between a public and private pension plan.
6. What is an integrated pension plan?
7. What is the basic difference between a defined-benefit and a defined-contribution pension plan?
8. What is back-end loading? In what kinds of plans might it occur? Explain.
9. Who bears the investment risk and the longevity risk in a defined-contribution pension plan? Explain.
10. Explain the aspect of Employee Stock Ownership Plans that flies in the face of standard finance theory.
11. Explain the potentially catastrophic risks inherent in defined-benefit pension plans.
12. Explain the degree of precision with which pension managers can measure the present value of the pension liability for a single worker. How do pension managers solve this problem in liability measurement?
13. Consider the employee and pension fund participants in a defined-benefit plan. Explain the different preferences for investment risk of the pension assets that these two parties might have.
14. Explain how the Pension Benefit Guaranty Company insurance plan gives pension managers inappropriate incentives.
15. If employers use pensions in developing labor contracts, explain how the Employee Retirement Income Security Act affects the usefulness of pensions as a tool for aligning employer and employee incentives.

References

Abken, P. A., "Corporate Pensions and Government Insurance: Deja Vu All Over Again?" *Economic Review*, Federal Reserve Bank of Atlanta, 77:2, March/April 1992, pp. 1–16.

Ambachtsheer, Keith P., "The Economics of Pension Fund Management," *Financial Analysts Journal*, 50:6, November/December 1994, pp. 21–31.

Bodie, Z., "Pensions as Retirement Income Insurance," *Journal of Economic Literature*, 28:1, March 1990, pp. 28–49.

Deutschman, A., "The Great Pension Robbery," *Fortune*, January 13, 1992, pp. 76–8.

Fabozzi, F. J. (ed.), *Pension Fund Investment Management*, Chicago: Probus Publishing Company, 1990.

Haugen, R. A., "Pension Management in the Context of Corporate Risk Management," *Journal of Portfolio Management*, Fall 1989, pp. 72–8.

Hinz, Richard P., John A. Turner, and Phyllis A. Fernandez (ed.), *Pension Coverage Issues for the '90s*, U.S. Department of Labor, 1994.

Ippolito, R. A. and W. H. James, "LBOs, Reversions and Implicit Contracts," *Journal of Finance*, 47:1, March 1992, p. 141.

Logue, D. E., *Managing Corporate Pension Plans*, New York: Harper Collins, 1991.

Pension Benefit Guaranty Corporation, *Annual Report*, 1991.

Appendix

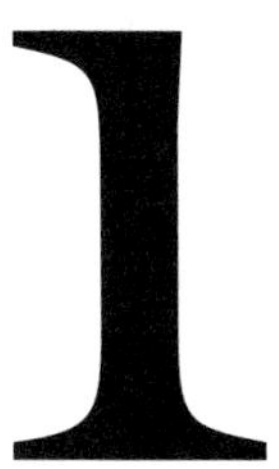

Cumulative Distribution Function for the Standard Normal Random Variable

	.00	.01	.02	.03	.04	.05	.06	.07	.08	.09
0.0	.5000	.5040	.5080	.5120	.5160	.5199	.5239	.5279	.5319	.5359
0.1	.5398	.5438	.5478	.5517	.5557	.5596	.5636	.5675	.5714	.5753
0.2	.5793	.5832	.5871	.5910	.5948	.5987	.6026	.6064	.6103	.6141
0.3	.6179	.6217	.6255	.6293	.6331	.6368	.6406	.6443	.6480	.6517
0.4	.6554	.6591	.6628	.6664	.6700	.6736	.6772	.6808	.6844	.6879
0.5	.6915	.6950	.6985	.7019	.7054	.7088	.7123	.7157	.7190	.7224
0.6	.7257	.7291	.7324	.7357	.7389	.7422	.7454	.7486	.7517	.7549
0.7	.7580	.7611	.7642	.7673	.7704	.7734	.7764	.7794	.7823	.7852
0.8	.7881	.7910	.7939	.7967	.7995	.8023	.8051	.8078	.8106	.8133
0.9	.8159	.8186	.8212	.8238	.8264	.8289	.8315	.8340	.8365	.8389
1.0	.8413	.8438	.8461	.8485	.8508	.8531	.8554	.8577	.8599	.8621
1.1	8643	.8665	.8686	.8708	.8729	.8749	.8770	.8790	.8810	.8830
1.2	.8849	.8869	.8888	.8907	.8925	.8944	.8962	.8980	.8997	.9015
1.3	.9032	.9049	.9066	.9082	.9099	.9115	.9131	.9147	.9162	.9177
1.4	.9192	.9207	.9222	.9236	.9251	.9265	.9279	.9292	.9306	.9319
1.5	.9332	.9345	.9357	.9370	.9382	.9394	.9406	.9418	.9429	.9441
1.6	.9452	.9463	.9474	.9484	.9495	.9505	.9515	.9525	.9535	.9545
1.7	.9554	.9564	.9573	.9582	.9591	.9599	.9608	.9616	.9625	.9633
1.8	.9641	.9649	.9656	.9664	.9671	.9678	.9686	.9693	.9699	.9706
1.9	.9713	.9719	.9726	.9732	.9738	.9744	.9750	.9756	.9761	.9767
2.0	.9772	.9778	.9783	.9788	.9793	.9798	.9803	.9808	.9812	.9817
2.1	.9821	.9826	.9830	.9834	.9838	.9842	.9846	.9850	.9854	.9857
2.2	.9861	.9864	.9868	.9871	.9875	.9878	.9881	.9884	.9887	.9890
2.3	.9893	.9896	.9898	.9901	.9904	.9906	.9909	.9911	.9913	.9916
2.4	.9918	.9920	.9922	.9925	.9927	.9929	.9931	.9932	.9934	.9936
2.5	.9938	.9940	.9941	.9943	.9945	.9946	.9948	.9949	.9951	.9952
2.6	.9953	.9955	.9956	.9957	.9959	.9960	.9961	.9962	.9963	.9964
2.7	.9965	.9966	.9967	.9968	.9969	.9970	.9971	.9972	.9973	.9974
2.8	.9974	.9975	.9976	.9977	.9977	.9978	.9979	.9979	.9980	.9981
2.9	.9981	.9982	.9982	.9983	.9984	.9984	.9985	.9985	.9986	.9986
3.0	.9987	.9987	.9987	.9988	.9988	.9989	.9989	.9989	.9990	.9990
3.1	.9990	.9991	.9991	.9991	.9992	.9992	.9992	.9992	.9993	.9993
3.2	.9993	.9993	.9994	.9994	.9994	.9994	.9994	.9995	.9995	.9995
3.3	.9995	.9995	.9995	.9996	.9996	.9996	.9996	.9996	.9996	.9997
3.4	.9997	.9997	.9997	.9997	.9997	.9997	.9997	.9997	.9997	.9998

Index

C

G

H

I

R